EASTERN CHRISTIANITY AND POLITICS IN THE TWENTIETH CENTURY

Edited by Pedro Ramet

CHRISTIANITY UNDER STRESS
Volume I

Duke University Press   Durham and London

©1988 Duke University Press

All rights reserved

Printed in the United States of America

on acid-free paper ∞

Library of Congress Cataloging-in-Publication Data

Eastern Christianity and politics in the twentieth century

edited by Pedro Ramet.

p. cm. — (Christianity under stress ; 1)

Bibliography: p.

Includes index.

ISBN 0-8223-0827-4

1. Church and state—Orthodox Eastern Church—History—20th

century.   2. Church and state—Oriental Orthodox churches—

History—20th century.   3. Communism and Christianity—

History—20th century.   4. Orthodox Eastern Church—Doctrines—

History—20th century.   5. Oriental Orthodox churches—Doctrines—

History—20th century.   6. Christianity and politics—History—20th

century.   I. Ramet, Pedro, 1949–   .   II. Series.

BX335.E27   1988   87-27029

281.9—dc 19   CIP

To

DONALD W. TREADGOLD,

friend and colleague,

who stood by me in times of stress

Contents

Preface

This is the first book in a multivolume work, *Christianity under Stress*, which will deal with contemporary issues in church-state relations, focusing on the communist world. A second volume, *Catholicism and Politics under Communism*, is already in preparation. A third volume, *Protestantism and Politics in Eastern Europe and the Soviet Union*, is currently in the planning stage.

This volume could not have been put together without the assistance of the following scholars, who generously took time to read certain of the chapters herein and to offer suggestions for their improvement: Stella Alexander, Alex Alexiev, Zachary T. Irwin, Andrzej Korbonski, George P. Majeska, Stevan K. Pavlowitch, Dimitry Pospielovsky, Gjon Sinishta, Peter F. Sugar, Frank Sysyn, Donald W. Treadgold, Larry Watts, and the anonymous readers for Duke University Press.

I also wish to thank the Graduate School of the University of Washington for its generosity in providing a publication subsidy for this book; also the Zoryan Institute, of which Gerard J. Libaridian is the director, for preparing the translation of Claire Mouradian's chapter on the Armenian Apostolic church; and both Dennis J. Dunn and Westview Press for permission to reprint an adapted version of Bohdan Bociurkiw's chapter, originally published in *Religion and Modernization in the Soviet Union*, edited by Dennis J. Dunn (Westview Press, 1977). Jane Ellis's chapter was also included in her *Russian Orthodox Church: A Contemporary History* (Croom Helm, 1986; Indiana University Press, 1986).

Pedro Ramet

I

INTRODUCTION

1

Autocephaly and National Identity in Church-State Relations in Eastern Christianity: An Introduction

Pedro Ramet

Christianity, as Georges Florovsky once noted, is essentially a social religion whose reference point is society. The social character of the Christian faith underlies the concept of religious services and infuses the social commitment of Christian organizations. Christianity affirms the existence of a divine plan and a divine law, against which society's deviations from the divine plan may be judged. Hence, Christianity, as much as (if not more than) other religions, has had from the beginning a social and political concern.

The early Christians believed quite literally that Christ would soon return, to establish a thousand-year kingdom on earth, and that it was their task to prepare for his "second coming" by rebuilding society on new foundations. In other words, "the early church was not just a voluntary association for 'religious' purposes. It was rather the New Society, even the New Humanity, a *polis* or *politeuma*, the true City of God, in the process of construction. And each local community was fully aware of its membership in an inclusive and universal whole. The church was conceived as an independent and self-supporting social order, as a new social dimension, a peculiar *systema patridos*, as Origen put it. Early Christians felt themselves, in the last resort, quite outside of the existing social order, simply because for them the church itself was an 'order,' an extraterrestrial 'colony of Heaven' on earth."[1] The church, often identified as the "Body of Christ," was coextensive with the Kingdom of God on earth. Hence, as late as the high Middle Ages, ecclesiastical unity and political unity were seen as dimensions of the same goal, and the "Prince of Peace" was expected to usher in *political* peace—the millennium. Even when the sense of expectancy of the Second Coming faded, medieval monarchs and prelates retained their enthusiasm for the creation of a unified Christian monarchy, even theocracy, in the civilized world.[2]

Ecclesiastical unity did not survive the fifth century, however, when a controversy sprang up between certain churches of the East (the Armenian, Egyptian, Syrian-Jacobite, and Ethiopian churches) and the rest of Christendom. The controversy took the form of a dispute as to whether Christ had two natures (divine and human) or only one (being divine and human at the same time), but more broadly involved the more fundamental question of whether individual churches were to interpret their own traditions or to submit to external, albeit collective, authority. The turning point came in A.D. 451, when Christendom convened a church council in the city of Chalcedon. This council declared the one-nature (monophysite) doctrine to be heretical. Those churches that were in the minority were henceforth known as "Monophysite" churches, while those accepting the council were henceforth known as "Chalcedonian" churches, the latter term now being applied only to churches in communion with the patriarchate of Constantinople.

A new rift developed subsequently between the churches of the western and eastern Mediterranean basin, which began to drift apart at least as early as the seventh century.[3] The seeds of disunity lay in divergent customs, Eastern refusal to honor papal claims to supremacy, political division, geographic distance, differences of language, and minor doctrinal uncertainties, poignantly epitomized in the seven-hundred-year controversy over whether the Holy Spirit proceeds only from the Father or from both the Father and the Son (the *Filioque* controversy). As the two factions went their separate ways, Latin Christianity took up the Aristotelian classics, building up a scholastic tradition that was rational and legal in orientation, emphasizing man's fallen state and outlining the steps to be taken to win "redemption." Greek Christianity, by contrast, proved more inclined to contemplation and preserved more clearly the early Christian tradition of *sobornost* (conciliarity or togetherness). The Orthodox tradition also spoke of the "divinization" of man by God—a concept entirely foreign to Western Christianity.[4]

The equation of religious unity with political unity and later with national identity became the raison d'être for autocephaly in the Orthodox world. Especially with the growth of nationalism in the nineteenth century, to be a nation meant to have a church of one's own, and to be entitled to one's own state. By contrast, subject peoples, such as Macedonians, Belorussians, and Ukrainians, were described as "lacking a true history";

they were said to speak the "dialects" of other "historical" nations and were denied the right to have their own autocephalous churches.

The term *autocephalous* comes from the ancient Greek and means that the body in question has its own head and is therefore independent or self-governing. Autocephaly has usually been granted by one of the ancient patriarchates, most often by the Ecumenical Patriarchate of Constantinople, although the Moscow patriarchate has also made the grant of autocephaly at times—for example, in 1970, to the Orthodox church in America. Historically, autocephaly has been the surest guarantee that the local clergy would be natives and that the language of the pulpit and of liturgy would be the local language.

There are currently some twenty autocephalous Eastern churches, plus an additional two that claim autocephaly but whose claims do not enjoy universal recognition (the Macedonian Orthodox church and the Orthodox Church in America). To this number one may add the Russian Orthodox Church Abroad, which makes no claim to autocephaly but also does not accept the authority of either the Moscow patriarchate or the Orthodox Church in America, and hence functions independently. Attempts were made earlier in this century to launch autocephalous Orthodox churches for Croatia, Belorussia, Ukraine, and Turkey, but, for diverse reasons, none of these survived.

The majority of the churches are Chalcedonian Orthodox, which means that they base their legitimacy on their claim to fidelity to the Council of Chalcedon. This group includes the ancient patriarchates of Constantinople (which has jurisdiction over Turkey, Crete, other islands in the Aegean, Mount Athos, and all Greeks in diaspora), Alexandria (which has authority over some ten thousand believers in Egypt and 150,000 to 200,000 throughout the rest of Africa), Antioch (which has adherents in Syria, Lebanon, Iraq, and the United States), and Jerusalem.[5] The largest Chalcedonian churches are the Russian Orthodox church with perhaps as many as 50 million adherents, and the Romanian Orthodox church, with some 15 to 17 million adherents. The smallest church is the Church of Sinai, which consists of a single monastery, Saint Catherine's, located at the foot of the Mountain of Moses; this church has fewer than twenty monks and fewer than one hundred faithful.[6] Other Chalcedonian churches are the Albanian Orthodox church (now surviving only in emigration), the Bulgarian Orthodox church, the Church of Cyprus, the Czechoslovak Orthodox church, the Georgian Orthodox church, the Greek Orthodox church, the Polish Autocephalous Orthodox church, the Serbian Orthodox church, and, as already mentioned, the Macedonian Orthodox church and the Orthodox Church in America. (In addition, the Finnish and Japanese Orthodox churches enjoy autonomous status—the former under the Ecumenical Patriarchate of Constantinople and the latter under the Moscow patriarchate.)

Besides these, there are also five important non-Chalcedonian Orthodox churches. These churches are, except for the Armenian church, Monophysite and hence are distinguished by their insistence on the unity of Christ's nature. This category embraces the Armenian Apostolic church, the Coptic church in Egypt, the Ethiopian Orthodox church, the Malabar Jacobite church (along the southwest coast of India), and the Syrian Jacobite church. Finally, in a category by itself is the Nestorian church, which has adherents in Iraq and eastern Syria.

This book is concerned with the social and political roles of the Eastern churches and therefore embraces churches of both the Chalcedonian and Monophysite traditions. It includes all of the nationally affiliated Chalcedonian churches, including the Macedonian and the suppressed Ukrainian church, and two non-Chalcedonian churches. Because of the particular interest associated with Russian Orthodoxy, I decided to devote an entire section to this subject, bringing together essays on four distinct aspects of the religious life of Orthodox Russians. The Finnish church is included as an example of an autonomous (as opposed to autocephalous) church. Omitted from separate treatment here are the ancient patriarchates (which are discussed within the context of certain chapters), the Malabar church (which emerged as an extension of the Syrian-Jacobite church), the Church of the Sinai (concerning which there is little to say, given its small size), and the Egyptian, Syrian, Cypriot, and Nestorian churches. The book is organized around three central themes: nationalism, co-optation, and opposition.

The term *nationalism* is here used to mean devotion to a cultural-linguistic collectivity, manifested in "respect for the national history, culture, traditions, and . . . national religion"[7] and in the aspiration to promote the specific culture and way of life identified as that of the nation. Whether through their nurturing of indigenous literary and artistic developments or through their defense of national culture and independence against foreign penetration or domination, Orthodox churches have frequently assumed importance as nationalist institutions. Church nationalism has sometimes been supportive of regime aims (e.g., in Russia, Romania, Bulgaria), and sometimes in conflict with them (e.g., in Yugoslavia and Albania). The nationalism of Eastern churches involves them in the politics of their respective societies and enters into the calculus of church-state relations.[8]

By *co-optation* is meant the drawing of the church into a stable cooperative relationship with the state, in which, in exchange for certain benefits
(such as subsidies and perhaps state salaries and pensions for the clergy,
or perhaps bare toleration), the church agrees (or is forced) to be a "loyal"
church and to advance regime goals in specific areas. A co-opted church
is a dependent church, and such dependence can be achieved through a
variety of means, including financial, administrative, legal, and extralegal
means. Precedents for current co-optive arrangements can be found in
Byzantine Caesaropapism, in the Ottoman *millet* system in the Balkans,
and in the subordination of the Russian Orthodox church to the Petrine
and post-Petrine state apparatus in Russia. Depending on the degree of
control the state is able to assert over the co-opted church, the latter may
assume the guise of either a pliant tool or a cooperative partner.

Finally, the church may be characterized by *opposition*. This may take
the form of nationalist opposition to a hostile occupier, or of critical opposition to a non-Christian or non-Orthodox state, or of internal opposition
within the church itself, in which alternative views of society become reflected in a struggle for dominance within the church (as happened, for
instance, in the case of the Russian "Living Church" movement).

Nationalism

There are several issues subsumed under the rubric of *nationalism*. On
one level the autocephalous church figures as an authentication of national identity. The establishment of national patriarchates in Bulgaria
and Serbia, in particular, figured as part of the state-building process and
was closely associated with the assertion of national identity. On another
level the church has often been itself a nationalist institution. The Russian church, for example, has long identified Russian nationality with
Orthodox religion, and most Soviet citizens assumed this linkage through
the end of the 1920s. Moreover, even today some dissident voices in the
Russian Orthodox church seek to rehabilitate church saints as authentic
Russian heroes,[9] harkening back to the belief of the early-nineteenth-
century Russian playwright Griboedov that "a Russian feels fully Russian
only in his Orthodox church."[10] Closely linked with the Ukrainianization
drive of the 1920s, the Ukrainian Autocephalous Orthodox church was
likewise a nationalist church, as are the Balkan Orthodox churches. In the
early years of this century the Bulgarian and Greek churches competed
actively for jurisdiction in Macedonia, with the Bulgarians appointing parallel bishoprics to rival the Greek ones, and the Greeks responding by
backing Turkish repressions of the Bulgarians.[11] The Bulgarian church

has preserved its nationalism to this day, celebrating with pomp the one-hundredth anniversary of the liberation of Bulgaria from Ottoman rule (in 1978)[12] and continuing to insist that the Macedonians of Yugoslavia are ethnic Bulgarians who should be stripped of their autocephalous church and placed under the Sofia patriarchate. In neighboring Romania the Iron Guard and its associated organization the Legion of the Archangel Michael (established in 1927) placed great stress on Christian religion, and the legion opened every meeting with an Orthodox service. Some Orthodox clergymen viewed the Iron Guard, which briefly held power during World War II, with approval, believing that it would strengthen the Orthodox church.[13] Even today the Romanian church preserves its nationalist demeanor—as can be clearly seen on those occasions when it speaks out on the subject of Soviet-occupied Bessarabia. The Serbian church, likewise, is infused with nationalism and sees itself as the bastion of the Serbian people against threats from Croats, the Albanians of Kosovo, and the antinationalist communist regime in Belgrade.[14] Like the nationalism of the Serbian church, that of the Egyptian Coptic church is fueled by fears of cultural threat. The short-lived Coptic National Movement (1952–54), which had its own flag and uniform, was most likely formed in response to Islamic assertiveness on the part of the Muslim Brotherhood in Egypt. The movement promoted the learning of the Coptic language and tried to obtain a separate radio station for Copts. Even after the movement's suppression, it has remained commonplace for Egyptians to refer to "the Coptic people," as if the Coptic religion were a badge of separate ethnicity.[15]

Ecclesiastical nationalism is often underpinned by a conviction that if the church is deeply rooted in the national ethos, then the national ethos, the national culture, cannot survive without the church. This conviction is exemplified in Bishop Andrei Ukhtomsky's comment to Alexander Kerensky in 1917: "It is not the Church which should fear separation from the state, but the state [which] should fear its separation from the Church. . . . To separate the Russian state from the Church would mean the separation of the nation from its conscience, its deprivation of moral foundations."[16] Or again, if the nation is identified with the religion, then the nation becomes infused with transcendent value and conversion becomes tantamount to assimilation. The Ethiopian example is apropos. As Adrian Hastings has noted, traditional Ethiopia closely identified religious affiliation and national identity, equating Ethiopianness with Christianity, even though many Ethiopians, even in the northern highlands, were never Christians.[17] Carrying Judaic themes into its symbology and myth, the Ethiopian Orthodox church promoted the notion that the Ethiopian nation was not merely *a* "chosen people" but *the* "chosen people." This equation of Ethiopian Orthodoxy with Ethiopian identity was sensed also by people conquered in the course of the nineteenth century, who often resisted conversion precisely because they perceived in Christianization a form of assimilation.[18]

On yet a third level Orthodox churches have often buttressed state objectives by figuring as engines of linguistic, and therefore ethnic, assimilation. The language of liturgy, of the sermons, and of instruction in Orthodox schools has therefore been a politically charged issue. In pre-Bolshevik Russia the Orthodox church was one weapon in the tsarist effort to Russify Poland, Belorussia, and Ukraine. The Bulgarian church similarly set up schools in Macedonia and parts of Albania in the hope of "Bulgarianizing" these regions, while the Greek Orthodox church fostered Greek language and Greek national identity among Albanians in what Greek nationalists preferred to call "northern Epirus." Indeed, up until Albanian independence in 1912, Orthodox services in Albania were conducted in Greek and the Orthodox were called "Greeks"; Islamic services were conducted in Arabic and Muslims were called "Turks"; Catholic services were conducted in Latin and Catholics were called "Latins."

Not surprisingly, language has been a salient issue in Orthodox church politics. Albanian Orthodox priest Papa Kristo Negovani was killed by Greek fanatics in 1905 when he tried to promote the Albanian language in schools and introduce it into the liturgy. Later, one of the first decisions taken by the Albanian Orthodox clergy at the "founding" Congress of Berat (in 1922) was to declare that Albanian would be the liturgical language in Orthodox churches in that country.[19]

The language issue was also important in the history of the Orthodox church in Czechoslovakia, where the Ruthenian clergy struggled during the nineteenth century to maintain the Old Slavonic liturgy in the face of Magyarization pressures. Due to ecumenical currents in the first quarter of this century, the Orthodox church in Czechoslovakia was also influenced by the national impetus of the Catholic *Jednota* movement, which sought, without success, to gain papal approval for liturgy in the Czech language and for other modernizing reforms.[20]

In Poland, on the other hand, linguistic controversy set the lower clergy against the hierarchy of the Orthodox church in the interwar years. The lower clergy, who were younger and mostly of Belorussian and Ukrainian ethnicity, wanted to introduce Belorussian and Ukrainian in the pulpit, with the Ukrainian clergy also championing the use of "Ukrainian Church Slavonic" for the liturgy. They also sought to decentralize the church and obtain more autonomy for the local parishes. The hierarchy, which consisted of Russians, Ukrainians, and Belorussians, resisted both derussification and decentralization. Meanwhile, by 1937, the Warsaw government had decided on a program of confessional homogenization. Orthodox priests were ordered to preach in Polish (even though their congregations were almost entirely Ukrainian and Belorussian), Orthodox believers were pressured to join the Catholic church and to send their children to Catholic schools, and between 1937 and 1939 some 150 Orthodox churches were either closed or destroyed.[21]

Ecclesiastical nationalism consists in several distinct aspects of church activity: in the church's preservation and development of the cultural heritage, in the church's use of a specific language for liturgy and instruction, in the advancement of specific territorial claims on putative ethnic grounds, and in the cultivation of the social idea itself, that is, the idea that a given people, united by faith and culture, constitute a nation.

Co-optation

The strong interest that states are apt to have in ecclesiastical matters can be seen quite clearly in the active interest displayed by political authorities in the question of autocephaly. Often, as in the case of Finland and Poland in the 1920s, political authorities have favored autocephaly both in the interest of excluding foreign ecclesiastical authority and in order to minimize conflicts of loyalty. The Greek Orthodox church was separated from the Ecumenical Patriarchate in 1833, just four years after the achievement of national independence, specifically to free the church of any Turkish influence. It is interesting to note that this move was taken in the face of strong resistance on the part of the Greek patriarch of Constantinople, who refused to reconcile himself to Greek Orthodox autocephaly until 1850.[22] Similarly, in the Romanian case church autocephaly was granted (in 1885) on appeal from the Romanian king, while in Albania King Zog pushed through autocephaly in 1929 both for reasons of national authentication and to free the Albanian clergy of foreign influence.

One of the least-known cases of this kind involves a project to create an autocephalous Turkish Orthodox church. This idea was first proposed in the summer of 1917, and by June 1921 a draft law setting up a Turkish Orthodox church had been submitted to the Great National Assembly in Ankara. Proautocephalist currents were given a further boost in February 1922 when the Turkish Ministry of Justice forbade, as "treason," any contacts between Orthodox communities in Turkey and the Ecumenical Patriarchate. After compulsory population exchanges with Bulgaria and Greece, conducted between 1923 and 1925, however, the number of "Karamanlis" (the Turkish-speaking Orthodox group that formed the nucleus of the church's support) dropped from some fifty thousand to around two thousand. And though the Turkish government continued to make use of this rump "Turkish Orthodox church" as a tool in its relations with the Ecumenical Patriarchate, and seemed to endorse it insofar as it smacked of Turkish nationalism, the church gradually atrophied and by 1969 may have numbered no more than three hundred persons.[23]

Co-optation per se can take diverse forms, but in every case it is characterized by a tendency of the government to view the church as an agency of state. The most thoroughly documented effort to achieve ecclesiastical co-optation involves the Russian Orthodox church, whose hierarchy is closely supervised by the state's Council for Religious Affairs. According to a secret report originally submitted to the Central Committee of the CPSU by Council Deputy Chairman V. Furov,

> the Council [for Religious Affairs] controls the Synod. The question of selection and appointment of its permanent members used to be, and still is, completely in the hands of the Council; candidacy of special members is also determined upon previous agreement by appropriate officials of the Council. All topics to be presented for discussion at the Synod are first submitted by Patriarch Pimen and the permanent members of the Synod to the executive committee of the Council and its departments. Furthermore, the Council approves the final "Decision of the Holy Synod."
>
> Exercising its constant and unrelenting control over the activities of the Synod, appropriate officials of the Council conduct systematic work to educate and enlighten the members of the Synod, maintain confidential contacts with them, shape their patriotic views and attitudes, and exert necessary influence on the entire episcopate through the members of the Synod and with their help. . . .
>
> The Council and its commissioners in various locations are paying constant and unrelenting attention to the study of the system and activity not only of the members of the Synod but also of the episcopate in general. There is no consecration of a bishop, no transfer without thorough investigation of the candidate by appropriate officials of the Council in close cooperation with the commissioner, local organs and corresponding interested organizations.[24]

Furov's report, which probably was written in 1978,[25] illustrates the regime ideal of a docile and submissive hierarchy—though even this report concedes that some Orthodox clergy disregard the harsh Soviet legal strictures governing religious organizations. In fact, as Dimitry Pospielovsky points out, CRA reports and official descriptions of the church-state relationship must be taken with "a grain of salt." Some defiant bishops are able, for instance, to assure themselves of good report cards with the authorities by maintaining cordial relations with the local CRA functionaries and by extending discreet and generous bribes. In this case the functionaries would typically lull Moscow with reassuring reports about the progress being made in combating religion in the districts concerned, while turning a blind eye to the construction of new churches and so forth. On the other hand, a fully cooperative bishop might be given a bad report if he should fail to extend appropriate bribes. Moreover, church cooperation notwithstanding, there have been "serious frictions" between the hierarchy and the regime in recent years. And in cases when the authorities have placed bishops in concentration camps—as occurred at least twice during Khrushchev's rule—the Russian church hierarchy has tried, albeit cautiously, to disassociate itself from the regime's verdict. Yet in other ways the Russian Orthodox church displays unmistakable symptoms of the co-optive syndrome: its leading organ, *Journal of the Moscow Patriarchate*, is subjected to strict censorship; admissions to its seminaries are closely controlled by the KGB, and some of those who enter the seminary and are subsequently ordained as priests are said to be KGB plants; and Patriarch Pimen, for his part, has been known to make speeches "full of civic loyalty to the Soviet social system."[26]

The Russian Orthodox church has also figured as an instrument in Moscow's peace propaganda against the West and has lent its support to Soviet foreign policy in diverse ways, even acting as intermediaries for the state in 1975 by conducting political talks with Israeli ministers.[27] The Russian church was also used to extend Moscow's supervision of East European societies into the religious sphere, in the late 1940s, when the Orthodox churches of the newly satellized states were placed under the jurisdiction and authority of the Moscow patriarchate. Between 1945 and 1948 the Kremlin also tried to bring the Orthodox churches of Western Europe and the United States of America under the control of the Moscow patriarchate and, through various means, to assert the primacy of the Moscow patriarchate in the Orthodox world, even over the Ecumenical Patriarch.[28]

The Bulgarian regime's view of the churches is betrayed in the fact that their supervision is entrusted to the Ministry of Foreign Affairs.[29] The Bulgarian Orthodox church's role in foreign policy is, not surprisingly, a carbon copy of that of the Russian Orthodox church and includes solid support for Warsaw Pact peace propaganda, criticism of American foreign policy, endorsement of all major moves of Soviet foreign policy, and a role in the reception of and contact with foreign diplomats.[30] The Bulgarian

Orthodox patriarch rendered a special service to the regime in March 1984 when he wrote to Pope John Paul II to ask him to intervene to obtain the release from prison of Sergei Antonov.[31] Antonov, a Bulgarian government official, had been implicated in the plot to kill the pope (in May 1981).

For the Russian and Bulgarian churches co-optation, the price of survival, has meant legal impotence and institutional weakness. Indeed, it was not until 1983 that the Bulgarian Orthodox church was able to print additional Bulgarian-language Bibles—the first since the war.[32] In Romania, by contrast, co-optation has given the Orthodox church not merely fiscal security but even the basis for a flourishing theological life. The Romanian Orthodox church has, of course, repaid this debt. Patriarch Justin knows full well what is expected of him and told the Second Congress of the Front for Democracy and Socialist Unity (in 1980):

> A warm word, coming from the heart, is also owed to the first citizen of the country, our highly esteemed President Nicolae Ceauşescu; as a brother of the holy soil of our Fatherland, he carries the torch of love for the nation, which warms the hearts of millions upon millions of people, in robust arms which fashion the image of a new Romania, the image of a free, independent . . . Romania. . . . Highly esteemed President of the Republic, that is why we all treasure you, why we all honor you, why we all love you.[33]

Nor is co-optation unique to communist systems, as the example of Greece shows. In that country the government established a tradition of frequent intervention in church matters at an early stage, beginning with Ioannis Capodistrias, the first head of state. A few years later Georg von Maurer, a German Protestant appointed to the Greek regency in 1832, drew up a constitution for the Orthodox church, viewing it as a department of the state. The church constitution was modeled on the Russian example; it banned correspondence between the clergy and any religious authorities outside Greece and placed church administration in the hands of a synod, held responsible to the king. This constitution empowered the state to "transfer, suspend, or entirely depose" the bishops, and between 1917 and 1935 archbishops and bishops were repeatedly being elevated and deposed according to how they suited the rival Greek governments taking power in alternation.[34]

Co-optation may at times be inverted, with the result that the church exercises disproportionate influence in matters of government and policy. Prerevolutionary Ethiopia presents an example of this pattern, with the church in the western parts deriving its power from its immense landholdings and from traditional law.[35] Although the church's power began to

wane in the later years of Emperor Haile Selassie's reign, it was still powerful enough to compel circumspection on the emperor's part, not merely
in strictly religious spheres, but in secular matters as well.[36] Haile Selassie,
in fact, owed his succession in 1917 to the church's excommunication of
his predecessor, Emperor Iyassu, and church anointing—the ceremonial
conferral of kingship—signified that church consent was a prerequisite to
governance. The church created the Eritrean Unionist party, which pushed
for annexation to Ethiopia and constituted an important underpinning of
Amhara-Tigre ethnic identity. By 1955 Emperor Haile Selassie was able
to assert some control over the church, and after the Derg Revolution in
1974 the church was formally disestablished and shorn of its privileged
position.[37]

Opposition

Opposition is analytically a more complex phenomenon because one is
dealing with two distinct species of opposition. On the one hand, the
church may itself engage in activities or espouse views that are in opposition to the policies of the regime. On the other hand, church-state
relations may be affected by opposition within the church itself. Given
the atheistic nature of communism, any religious organization constitutes,
at some level, an "opposition" body, and it may win adherents among
non-believers precisely insofar as it offers an alternative worldview to that
propounded by the regime, i.e., insofar as it represents at least a symbolic
or even perhaps an "ideological" opposition. Naturally, under conditions
of political monopoly the politically disaffected may be apt to exaggerate
the independence of the church and thus its potential for resolute self-
defense—as is the case in the Soviet Union, where "few people are aware
of the degree of [church] dependence on local authorities and of the degree
of [church] weakness."[38] Opposition may be "soft," as in the case of the
Serbian Orthodox church's "loyal opposition," or it may be "hard," as in
Egypt, where President Anwar Sadat imprisoned Pope Shenouda III, spiritual head of Egypt's 6 million Copts, for what proved to be a three-year
term.[39]

Already in the interwar Kingdom of Yugoslavia the Serbian Orthodox
church showed itself prepared to cross swords with the regime. Most of
their differences concerned legislation, specifically in the early period the
church's refusal to accept laws governing its activity, which it considered
unfavorable. Later, the Serbian Orthodox church created an uproar over
the government's proposal to sign a concordat with the Vatican. The Bel-

grade patriarchate published a series of booklets condemning the draft document and on March 21, 1937, established the newspaper *Pastirski glas*, under the editorship of Vlastimir Tomić and Milan Sretenović. Created to defeat the concordat, the paper came into open conflict with state authorities; but its articles carried great weight among Orthodox clergy and laity.[40] Ultimately, the Serbian patriarchate succeeded in defeating the concordat.

Since the war the Serbian Orthodox church finds itself in political "opposition" principally where Serbian national interests are concerned. As the self-appointed guardian of the Serbian people, the Serbian Orthodox church became embroiled in Serb-Croat antagonisms during the Croatian nationalist euphoria of 1971 and spoke out volubly after Albanian nationalist riots in Kosovo in 1981 and 1982 when local Albanians attacked local Serbs, including Serbian clergy, and set fire to Serbian church buildings. For the Serbian church, the riots were not merely a problem for the Yugoslav federation, but placed the Serbian nation, in particular, under siege.[41]

Likewise in Egypt, the church was drawn into an opposition role through its desire to defend the interests of what it came to view as a "beleaguered minority." This understanding of the situation has not been shared by all the Coptic clergy, to be sure, and Father Matta al-Miskeen, described by one observer as the Coptic patriarch's "most serious clerical critic," has repeatedly urged Patriarch Shenouda to abandon this opposition mentality and to shift focus to the spiritual role of the church.[42]

In the late 1970s Egyptian Copts became concerned over moves to remodel civil law dealing with libel, theft, and apostasy, to conform to Islamic religious law. In late summer of 1977 the Coptic patriarch ordered Copts to observe a fast in protest of the draft legislation, and by early 1978 there were violent scenes between Muslims and Christians in the provinces of Assiut and Minya.[43]

Intersectarian violence sharpened in 1981, and in response Egyptian President Sadat arrested large numbers of Islamic fundamentalists, balancing those arrests with the arrest of the Coptic patriarch, Shenouda III, as well as of eight Coptic bishops, thirty priests, and 130 lay Copts.[44] This action only incensed the Coptic community, however, and in reply the "Coptic Boards in the Near East" issued a statement on September 7, 1981, asking Sadat to release Shenouda and demanding an end to religious discrimination in Egypt. The statement declared that Sadat, as the holder of secular power, did not have the right to banish the Coptic patriarch; it further demanded constitutional guarantees to the Copts, recognition of "the Coptic ethnic group," the right to form a Coptic political party and establish a Coptic university, an end to censorship of Coptic publications, and revelation of the "real" population of Egyptian Copts.[45]

The Coptic church's Egyptian nationalism also became a problem in the 1980s. As long as Egypt and Israel were legally at war, the church's intransigent refusal to take part in any Christian ceremonies in Jerusalem or to allow any Egyptian Christians to make pilgrimages to Israel coincided well with Egyptian foreign policy. But even after Sadat signed the Camp David accords with Israel, the Egyptian Coptic church refused to alter its policy in this area and thus came into conflict with the government's policy line.[46]

Eventually the Coptic patriarch was allowed by Sadat's successor, Hosni Mubarak, to reemerge from banishment to a monastery. But even then, some residue of earlier frictions still soured the atmosphere. As a result, certain sectors circulated rumors that Shenouda had been involved (prior to his 1981 banishment) in organizing sectarian sedition—charges that, had they been founded in fact, would have meant the death penalty for Shenouda.[47]

The second species of opposition with which we are concerned is opposition within the church itself, where one segment of the clergy is at variance with another segment. Such opposition may have its roots in the natural divergence of interests between lower clergy and hierarchy, in the exploitation of manipulable priests by regimes in "patriotic priests' organizations," in episcopal rivalries, or in religious ferment from below.

Communist regimes have been particularly prone to use intraecclesiastical fissures as openings and have often backed suitable lower clergy against their hierarchy. In Bulgaria, for instance, the Fatherland Front set up a group of nine lower clergymen to produce guidelines for reforms of the church, to weaken the exarch, and to increase the participation of lower clergy, laity, and women in the administration of the church and in church elections. To the party's satisfaction, the group also suggested the conversion of monasterial holdings into collective farms and the "active participation" of priests in the agricultural collectivization drive.[48] The party hoped that this bridgehead would ultimately enable them to convert the Bulgarian Orthodox church into a subservient tool of party policy.

In Russia communist sponsorship of the modernizing "Living Church" movement in the early 1920s was designed to serve both this purpose and the splintering of the church into conflicting factions. The Living Church movement enjoyed genuine support among a number of clergy and for a while had control of most parish churches and the support of a large number of bishops; its radical proposals and its obvious affiliation with the regime made it suspect in the eyes of the faithful, and the movement lost steam after 1923.[49] The authorities' view of the Living Church is seen in the fact that their "Renovationist strategy" was developed and promoted by a department of the GPU, the Soviet secret police.[50] Moreover, a secret party document of 1929 notes explicitly that party support of the Living Church was designed to cause the church to disintegrate from within and thereby to produce a steady erosion of religiosity.[51] Not surprisingly, the Living Church's opposition to the hierarchy went in tandem with a co-optive relationship with the party. As Dimitry Pospielovsky observes, an important distinction between the Renovationists of the Living Church and the patriarchate was the former's "unquestioning loyalty to the Soviet government and its socialist ideals. They attempted to collaborate with it, and this left them open to OGPU infiltration and manipulation. Ironically, by the second half of the 1920s, the 'revolutionary' Renovationists came much more closely to resemble the prerevolutionary 'reactionary' synodal church, in the form of its organization as well as in its spirit of subordination to the state, than did the Patriarchal Church, which [now] insisted on separation and independence from the state."[52] More recently, the co-optation of the Russian Orthodox church has itself inspired free-thinking clergymen and laymen to speak out, to organize various committees, and to publish critical materials in samizdat. Among these persons are Aleksandr Ogorodnikov (imprisoned in 1978) and Fr. Gleb Yakunin (imprisoned by 1981).[53]

In Romania, by contrast, the leading opposition movement within the Orthodox church dates back to precommunist days. Founded in 1923 by a Romanian Orthodox priest from Transylvania named Iosif Trifa, the "Lord's Army" movement involved millions of Orthodox believers, including priests, in evangelization and open-air meetings in its heyday in the mid-1930s to early 1940s. Even after Fr. Trifa was defrocked in 1935 by a hierarchy resentful of the movement's independence, the Lord's Army continued its activity. The communist regime barred the organization in 1947 and imprisoned its leaders, but the movement still claimed some 400,000 members as of 1978. The raison d'être for its continuation is precisely the co-optation of the Bucharest patriarchate. A document released by a Christian Committee for the Defense of Religious Freedom and Freedom of Conscience in August 1978, on behalf of the Lord's Army, makes this point quite clearly:

> The fairly widespread impression that the Orthodox Church enjoys a privileged position in Romania is only partially correct. It is only one section of Orthodox church members who are safe from per-

secution: these are the conformists, who are willing to compromise
with the atheists, or to resign themselves in the face of certain violent measures. . . . [By contrast,] the Lord's Army has continued
its intense activity without interruption, and on an increasing scale.
The movement's ability to resist, its ingenuity and boldness, and the
determination and perseverance of its members will provide a totally
unique chapter in the history of the Orthodox Church.[54]

Opposition is no less than conflict, and in conflict lies politics. The
reality of or potential for opposition is what makes the church a political body. Just as any state has a policy or posture toward the religious
organizations functioning within its territory, so too do the religious organizations have policies or postures vis-à-vis the state. Where interests
diverge, there is already latent opposition.

Patterns in Church-State Relations

The three variables described here may be combined in different ways,
and these different combinations give rise to different patterns in church-
state relations. For example, nationalism may be a source of opposition
(as in the Serbian case today) or a buttress of co-optation (as in Bulgaria).
Or again, opposition of the lower clergy to the hierarchy may figure as
an opportunity for alliance between regime and lower clergy (as in the
postwar East European states), may arise in reaction to the co-optation
of the hierarchy (as has been the case in the Russian Orthodox church in
recent years), or may be irrelevant to the course of church-state relations
(as in the case of the Coptic church in Egypt).

Using the expression "simple co-optation" to mean the co-optation of
the hierarchy and perhaps of the church apparatus as a whole, and "complex co-optation" to mean the co-optation of only certain sections of the
lower clergy, one may identify the following patterns in church-state relations in the Orthodox world: (1) *simple co-optive-nationalist*, in which
the hierarchy is co-opted and espouses a nationalist line endorsed by
the regime (examples: contemporary Bulgaria, Greece, Macedonia, Romania); (2) *nonnationalist dependent*, in which the church is too weak to
offer any resistance to the policy of the state (examples: contemporary
Czechoslovakia, postrevolutionary Ethiopia, Poland); (3) *nationalist defiant* (independent-oppositionist), in which a church's opposition is organ-
ically related to its nationalism; this configuration may involve complex-
co-optive features (examples: contemporary Serbia, interwar Bulgaria);
(4) *simple co-optive-antinationalist*, in which an otherwise nationalist

church is sapped of its nationalist strength by the slow strangulation of being "quarantined" from the public and is penetrated and co-opted by the regime (example: Russia).

Naturally, any church-state relationship is subject to change, and probably no sensibly parsimonious listing, let alone a listing of merely four configurations using three variables, would exhaust all the possibilities for church-state relations. Indeed, the weight and significance of these variables themselves (nationalism, co-optation, opposition) may change over time: a church relatively faction-free at one juncture may be riven by internal opposition at the next; a state interested in promoting nationalism may be supplanted by a state positively hostile to nationalism.

Church autocephaly has usually been valued both as an authentication of Christian culture/national identity and as an assurance of the exclusion of foreign clerical or even political influence. It is something more as well, namely, a definition of the arena in which church-state issues will be resolved and of the status and prerogatives to be enjoyed by the ecclesiastical organization in this relationship.

2

The Doctrinal Foundation of Orthodoxy

Michael A. Meerson

The first impression that the Orthodox church creates is one of overwhelming cult; the main manifestation of Orthodoxy is liturgical worship. Man in the Orthodox perspective is above all a liturgical creature who finds his fulfillment in glorifying God. Even the church's doctrine is understood in the concept of divine worship, as based on the liturgical approach that characterizes much of the Bible. The liturgical emphasis in such bedrock portions of the New Testament as the Gospel of John[1] and the book of Revelation[2] perfectly corresponds with the findings of modern Orthodox theologians, from Fr. Pavel Florensky, who argued that man is a cultic creature,[3] to Fr. Georges Florovsky, who stated that "Christianity is a liturgical religion and the Church is first of all a worshiping community."[4]

The Orthodox church believes itself to be the Temple, the same Temple that was revealed to Moses and was built and consecrated by King Solomon[5] and was twice physically destroyed, but was restored spiritually by the Son of God for spiritual sacrifice to be continued always and everywhere until the last day of the world (John 2:18–21; 4:21–24). Thus Orthodox worship has inherited the Old Testament liturgical structure, but since the new Temple is "the Body of Christ," the cult becomes henceforward a Christocentric one.

This biblical background is well manifested in the Orthodox office, which is composed of readings from the Old Testament—the Psalms (a permanent part of all services), the Pentateuch, the prophets, and the historical books—and from all the books of the New Testament (Revelation excepted). Furthermore, the text of every Orthodox service is permeated with biblical language and imagery. Thus the Orthodox office is sometimes called a meditation on Scripture by means of worship.

The daily cycle of the office includes eucharistic celebration, called the Divine Liturgy, and other services such as vespers, compline, vigil, matins, "the hours." The origin of this office is monastic. Its rules are determined by the special rubrics of the "typicon," which is an amalgamation of two ancient rituals: the ritual of the Monastery of St. Sava of Jerusalem and that of St. Theodore the Studite of Byzantium. But as a whole the Orthodox office is an extremely complex historical conglomerate.[6] Its fundamental feature is Christocentrism. As the Temple of the Old Testament was the heart of the very existence of ancient Israel, and her priesthood, prophetism, and kingship were centered upon it, so the God-man Jesus Christ, as the ultimate priest, prophet, and king, is at the heart of Orthodox worship, theology, and ecclesiastical structure.

One enters the Orthodox faith through the sacrament of baptism, which is understood as spiritual birth. In putting on Christ in this sacrament the natural man dies, together with the original sin innate in him. A new man is engendered, as it had been stated by Jesus in His conversation with Nicodemus in the Gospel of John (3:3-8). The Orthodox church accepts any baptism performed by a Christian in the name of the Holy Trinity, the Father, the Son, and the Holy Spirit. It can be performed by a layman in absence of a priest. The Orthodox baptize by threefold immersion into blessed water in the name of the Holy Trinity.

The Orthodox church believes in a Triune God—Father, Son, and Holy Spirit—who possesses one essence in three persons. The Holy Trinity is a mystery of unity in diversity: each of the persons is distinct. The Father is the origin, source, and cause of Godhead, born from none and proceeding from none. In the language of the Eastern Fathers, He is the principle of unity. The Son is born of the Father from all eternity; the Spirit proceeds from the Father from all eternity. The knowledge of God in three persons and the way to Him was revealed by the incarnate Son, Jesus Christ, who thus remains "the apostle and the high priest of our religion" (Heb. 3:1).[7]

According to the Epistle to the Hebrews, the center of the Christian cult is Jesus Christ, who is the sacrifice and the sacrificer. Thus at every Divine Liturgy an Orthodox priest, before bringing the offering to the altar, during the Cherubic hymn for the consecration, invokes the name of Jesus Christ as "our High Priest who did commit to us the ministry of this liturgical and bloodless sacrifice. . . , [as] the Offerer and the Offered, the Receiver and the Received."[8]

The importance of the theology of the Epistle to the Hebrews for Or-

thodox doctrine is further illustrated by the fact that the Epistle is read in
church twice during the liturgical year: during the Great Lent, while the
church prepares the faithful for the celebration of Pascha, the feast of the
Resurrection of the Lord; and during Advent, while the church meditates
on the mystery of the Incarnation of the Son of God.

According to the Orthodox understanding of the Epistle, Jesus Christ,
the Son of God, being "the radiant light of God's glory and the perfect
copy of His nature," who "took to Himself descent from Abraham . . . and
became completely like His brothers" (2:16–17), and who "experienced
death for all mankind" (2:9), "was raised from death by God" (13:20) and
"entered into the very heaven" (9:24) as "a forerunner for us" (Hebrews,
6:20), so that He could "intercede for us in the actual presence of God"
(Hebrews 9:24). Thus He "has opened for us a living opening through
the curtain, that is to say, His body" (Hebrews 10:19), a new way "to
approach the throne of grace" (Hebrews 4:16), in order that we "through
the blood of Jesus have the right to enter the sanctuary" (Hebrews 10:19).
For Christ, "who offers Himself only once to take the faults of many
on Himself" (Hebrews 9:28), "by virtue of that one single offering has
achieved the eternal perfection of all whom He is sanctifying" (Hebrews
10:1).

Through His sacrifice the Son of God "became a high priest for ever"
(Hebrews 6:20), "an ideal high priest, holy, innocent and uncontami-
nated, beyond the influence of sinners, raised above the heavens" (Hebrews 7:26), and He became "the mediator of the new and better covenant
founded on better promises" (Hebrews 8:6;9:15), "the Leader of our salvation" (Hebrews 2:10), "the one who sanctifies His brothers" (Hebrews
2:11), "the apostle and the high priest of our religion" (Hebrews 3:1),
"the great Shepherd of the sheep by the blood that sealed an eternal
covenant" (Hebrews 13:20).

According to the Epistle, the cult of the Old Covenant knew innumerable sacrifices; the cult of the New Covenant knows only one: the sacrifice
of Jesus Christ. That is the scriptural theological ground for the Orthodox liturgy, at the very heart of which stands the Eucharist. The church
teaches that in the Eucharist the bread and wine are changed into the Body
and Blood of Christ. The Eucharist, or the reception by the faithful of
heavenly food in the Communion of the Body and Blood of Christ, as it
was instituted by the Lord Himself, is also called the Lord's Supper. As
one Orthodox theologian put it, "all the holy suppers of the Church are
nothing else than one eternal and unique Supper, that of Christ in the
Upper Room. The same divine act both takes place at a specific moment in
history and is offered always in the sacrament."[9]

This sacrament of the breaking of bread held from the outset the most important place in the church; its central significance is attested by the New Testament and by Christian writers of the first and second centuries. Believing that in the Holy Communion the faithful receive the true Body and Blood of Christ, the Orthodox church does not accept the Latin doctrine of transubstantiation, which distinguishes the substance, which changes, from the accidents, which do not change. Orthodoxy understands the Eucharist in the light of the high priesthood of Jesus, who brought His humanity into heavenly sanctuary, introduced it into eternity. The glorified humanity of Jesus henceforward does not belong to this world with its laws and limitations, though it has preserved its connection with this world and the ability to manifest itself through the matter of this world. This power of eternal sacrifice is manifested in the visible world as the freedom from the limitations of time and space. The Lord risen and glorified can manifest Himself through matter, but not in matter. Such is the mode of His new presence in the world, according to the modern Orthodox theologian Fr. Sergei Bulgakov, who maintained that the Eucharist could be understood only on christological grounds.[10] By virtue of His divinity Jesus is able to expand his corporeality by transforming bread and wine into His Body without consuming them.[11] Being changed spiritually (by the power of the Holy Spirit, as invoked by the priest at the consecration of the Holy Gifts) into the Body and Blood of Christ, they remain bread and wine in this world, where they do not undergo any "transubstantiation." The mystery is that they belong now to both levels of existence: as bread and wine on earth and Body and Blood in the heavenly sanctuary. Such is the traditional Orthodox view of the Eucharist, expressed by Eastern Fathers from St. Gregory of Nyssa and St. John of Damascus to the Eastern Orthodox patriarchs of the nineteenth century.[12]

The sanctification of the Holy Gifts occurs throughout the Divine Liturgy, whose essential part consists in the invocation of the Holy Spirit and the blessing of the elements. All the faithful, laity and clergy alike, communicate under two species. Unlike Catholics, the Orthodox do not practice the adoration of the Holy Gifts outside the liturgy; they are used only for Communion.

The Eucharist constitutes the Body of Christ. Through communion with the Body and Blood of Christ, the faithful become members of His Body. The Orthodox church embodies all three New Testament images of the church: that of St. Matthew as congregation; that of St. Paul as Body of Christ; and that of St. John as vine and branches.

The communal character of the Eucharist reflects the image of St. Matthew, that of gathering in Christ's name: "Where two or three meet in my name, I shall be there with them" (Matt. 18:20). Unlike the Roman Catholic mass where a priest can celebrate Eucharist alone, the Orthodox liturgy is always a deed of the congregation, at least of two or three members of it. Hence the name for the Orthodox eucharistic service is "liturgy," which means "common work" in Greek.

Orthodoxy understands St. Paul's analogy of the body, given in 1 Corinthians (12:12–27), in a eucharistic sense. Since the faithful partake of the Body and Blood of Christ, they become members of His Body. And finally, for the Orthodox, St. John's image of vine and branches reflects the same eucharistic dependence of the faithful on Christ: "I am the vine, you are the branches. Whoever remains in me, with me in him, bears fruit in plenty; for cut off from me you can do nothing" (John 15:5).

In terms of the Epistle to the Hebrews, Christ "shared in flesh and blood" (2:14) in order that we may "share in Christ" (3:1) and thus may "share in the heavenly call" (3:1) of Jesus, who "entered into heaven itself" (9:25). Jesus calls "brothers" those who believe in His name (2:12). He "delivers them from the power of death, that is the devil, from the lifelong bondage of the fear of death" (2:14–15) because He Himself "tasted death" (2:9) but overcame it by His "power of an indestructible life" (7:16). Thus He delivers His people from death and brings them into "His rest," that is "the unshakeable kingdom" (12:28). By following Jesus, who is "the firstborn of this kingdom" (1:6), through His sanctifying blood (9:12,14), His people enter His kingdom and become "the church of first-born who are enrolled in heaven" (12:23).

That is the foundation of the Orthodox teaching on salvation. In the Eucharist the matter of the world is sanctified by becoming the Body and Blood of Christ, which are given to the faithful to be in communion with Him. By partaking of a holy substance they become sanctified themselves. Through the humanity of the incarnate Son of God, divine nature reclothes human nature without destroying it. The Orthodox church understands the salvation of all men as the deification of human nature. But it is not a physical or magical act; it is the appropriation of the holy gift by human effort with the help of divine grace. Man is called to become god by grace. Although the divine essence is inaccessible for creatures, man can find unity with God through divine energies. In order to express this notion of salvation through deification, Russian theologians of modern times introduced the term "God-manship." The humanity of Christ after His resurrection is the state of deification all humans are called to.

The example of deified humanity is given in the person of the Mother of God, the Virgin Mary. In adoring the humanity of Christ the church venerates His mother, from whom He received that humanity. As many

Orthodox theologians have pointed out, Mariology is simply an extension of Christology. The Virgin Mary is the supreme example of cooperation between the will of God and will of man. In our age with its emphasis on the right of woman to decide if she does or does not wish to give birth, one can easily understand to what extent the power of God to send a new human being into the world depends on the cooperation and willingness of man. Hence Mary is not merely the instrument but the very condition of the Incarnation. Christ could not have been incarnated without her consent, violating human nature. Therefore she represents the human aspect of the Incarnation. Since all the holiness accessible to humanity is attained in the Virgin Mary, she represents the whole of humanity. The Orthodox believe that, after dying a natural death, she was not subject to corruption but ascended into heaven in the flesh and entered the realm of divinity remaining totally human. She lives in her glorified body at the right hand of Christ.

The Epistle to the Hebrews says also that "we are surrounded by a great cloud of witnesses" (12:1)—the saints of former times. For the Orthodox, the high-priesthood of Christ helps in understanding the nature of the church. The church is comprehensible only in the light of and in communion with the transfigured and risen humanity of Jesus. "The human race, first in the person of the Holy Virgin and then as the whole church, follows the God-man after His ascension," Fr. Sergei Bulgakov writes.[13]

The cult of the saints is an important part of Orthodox faith. The saints are our intercessors and our protectors in heaven, just as the Virgin Mary remains the mother of the human race and intercedes for it. The church addresses its supplications to the Mother of God and to the saints, invoking their help. This "cloud of witnesses" neither separates us from Christ nor mediates between God and man. The saints are members of the same Body of Christ, who have already ascended into His heavenly sanctuary. Without this concept of deified humanity, the Incarnation becomes simply a voluntary self-humiliation of God devoid of power to confer on us the means of sanctification. But the members of the Body of Christ become deified in Him. Since the saints become "gods by virtue of grace,"[14] the church venerates them.

Icons in the Orthodox church are the expression of this veneration of sanctified, deified humanity. They are not images of God, who remains indescribable; they are images of God-manhood, of the humanity that entered heaven.[15] As Timothy Ware puts it, "the icons which fill the church serve as a point of meeting between heaven and earth. As each local congregation prays at the liturgy, surrounded by figures of Christ,

Mother of God, saints, angels, these visible images remind the faithful unceasingly of the invisible presence of the whole company of heaven at the liturgy. The faithful can feel that the walls of the church open out upon eternity, and they are helped to realize that their Liturgy on earth is one and the same with the great Liturgy of heaven. The multitudinous icons express visibly the sense of 'heaven on earth.' "[16]

The church inwardly possesses the power of sanctification. It is holy because it has the perfect high priest. Holiness is the end to which everyone in the church is called by Jesus, who is "the apostle of our religion" (Heb. 3:1). Orthodox theology speaks of the deification of man by means of acquisition of the Holy Spirit as the aim of Christian life. Before the outpouring of the Holy Spirit, the community of faithful established by Jesus was barren. The Holy Spirit, which was poured unto them at Pentecost, created from them the church, and He lives forever in it.

The presence of the Holy Spirit in the church is explained by another supreme ministry of Jesus—that of the prophet. Jesus, "the high priest of our religion" (Heb. 3:1), fulfills His ministry to the church by sending the Holy Spirit, which is the fulfillment of the church. In the Nicene-Constantinopolitan Creed, which is sung at every celebration of the Eucharist, the Orthodox also profess their faith in the Holy Spirit, who spoke through the prophets. If in the past God spoke by the Holy Spirit "through the prophets," as the Epistle to the Hebrews states, "in our own time . . . he has spoken to us through his Son" (Heb. 1:2). The Holy Spirit ultimately descends on the Son to the extent that the Son becomes the source of the Holy Spirit for the church. "The Counselor, the Holy Spirit, whom the Father will send in my name . . . will teach you all things, and bring to your remembrance all that I have said to you" (John 14:26). "I will send him to you. . . . When the Spirit of truth comes he will guide you into all truth . . . he will declare to you the things that are to come . . . for he will take what is mine and declare it to you" (John 16:7, 13–14). So Jesus promised His apostles.

Since the Holy Spirit abides in the Son in fullness and through Him is given to the church, the latter possesses the inalienable gift of prophecy. This is reflected in the Orthodox teaching on the prophetism of all the faithful. The prophecy of Joel: "Their sons and daughters shall prophesy" (Joel 2:23–32), which is read at the Orthodox celebration of Pentecost, was interpreted by the apostle Peter as the gift of the Holy Spirit to the church (Acts 2:14–21).

The tongues of fire that descended upon the apostles formed the treasure of the gifts of the Holy Spirit which resides in the church. The apostles conferred this gift of the Holy Spirit on believers after baptism (Acts 19:1–7). Likewise the corresponding gift, "the seal of the gift of the Holy Spirit," is accorded in the sacrament of Chrismation, which the Orthodox church administers immediately after baptism. Since in the primitive church only the apostles or their appointees conferred the gift of the Holy Spirit on the faithful through the laying on of hands, Chrismation is an episcopal sacrament. The holy chrism used for it is blessed by the assembly of bishops of a local church. It can be administered only by a bishop or by a priest as his delegate. Therefore all converts to Orthodoxy from confessions deprived of the apostolic succession of priesthood are received into the church through the sacrament of Chrismation. Only after that can they participate in the Holy Eucharist and other sacraments. Chrismation is an individual Pentecost in the life of each Orthodox Christian. The church believes that St. John referred to this personal Pentecost in his First Epistle, by saying: "But you have been anointed by the Holy One, and have all received the knowledge. It is not because you do not know the truth that I am writing to you, but rather because you know it already" (1 John 2:20–21).

Through Chrismation every member of the church becomes a prophet and is called to act as a conscientious witness to the truth. Jesus calls everyone to bear witness to His name (Matt. 10:32–33; Luke 18:9). From the beginning not only the apostles but all believers preached the word. At the feast of the Myrrh-bearing Women the church glorifies the faithful women as apostles to the apostles themselves. The church canonized several women as equal to the apostles because of their missionary activity.

As the word of the Gospel is entrusted to the whole church, so the fullness of faith, the truth, belongs to the church as a whole. When the apostle Paul said, "We have the mind of Christ" (1 Cor. 2:16), he meant the church. The conscience of the church is super-personal. The fullness of faith is too vast to be held in the mind of an isolated believer; it is guarded by the whole church and transmitted from generation to generation as tradition. The unity and continuity of tradition follow from the fact that the church is always identical with itself, is headed by the same high priest Christ Jesus, and is guided by the same Holy Spirit. The historical forms of the church's existence change, but the unity of its life remains unchanged. This tradition binds together the communities of Paul and the local churches of today.

Many Orthodox writers point to loyalty to tradition and the awareness of living continuity with the church of the apostles as the distinctive characteristic of the Orthodox church. Orthodox tradition includes the faith that Jesus imparted to the apostles, the Bible, the creed, the decrees of the ecumenical councils, the theology developed by the church fathers, the liturgy, and also such liturgical arts as choral music and iconography. However, since tradition is not a static deposit but the life of the Holy Spirit in the church, it constantly assumes new forms, "which supplement the old without superseding them."[17]

"Thus," Fr. Bulgakov maintains, "Church tradition is the life of the Church in the past which is also the present. It is a divine truth revealed in human words, deeds, and decisions. It is the divine-human body of the Church, living in space and time. Least of all is it an eternal obligatory law, which is only a small part of tradition. It is rather an inner law of the Church, arising from its unity."[18]

To ensure the continuity of the tradition of faith, the Lord established the structure of apostolic succession in the church. The assembly of the apostles was the hieratic receptacle of the Holy Spirit. For the transmission of the gifts of the Holy Spirit along the line of faithfulness to the teaching of Christ, the charismatic succession of the apostles became necessary. The Book of Acts tells that the first believers "remained faithful to the teaching of the apostles, to the breaking of bread and to the prayers" (Acts 2:42). We can find nowhere in the New Testament any evidence of a spontaneous, unorganized administration of the sacraments. This function belonged either to the apostles or to their appointees. The Orthodox church maintains that at first the Eucharist was celebrated by the apostles and charismatics instituted by them, later by bishops and presbyters whom bishops appointed. According to the testimony of such Apostolic Fathers as St. Ignatius the Theophore, who belonged to the generation that still remembered the apostles, the bishop is one who celebrates the Eucharist, and only the Eucharist celebrated by a bishop is valid. Also for such early Christian writers as St. Ireneus of Lyon, Tertullian, and St. Cyprian, the church centers on the bishop legitimated by the apostolic succession established by the Lord.

Since in the memory of the church the celebration of the Eucharist was always the prerogative of the bishop, or a presbyter who acted as the bishop's deputy, it is logical to admit that after the apostles the authority for administering the sacraments came to the hierarchy in episcopal form, with presbyters and deacons dependent on it. Thus the hierarchy bears in itself the mysterious power received by direct and uninterrupted succession from the apostles.

But this power is not mysterious in itself. It derives from the Eucharist, because the Orthodox theology of the church and of the ecclesiastical hierarchy is above all else a theology of communion of the faithful with the eternal Hierarch—Christ Jesus. Orthodox ecclesiology is Christocentric and anthropocentric at the same time. The sacraments do not exist by themselves; they are meaningless outside of man. "The most general definition of sacrament is the action of the church manifested in man. Man is a temple, an altar, a priest who brings forth an offering and who receives it,"[19] like Christ who is sacrificer and sacrifice. Thus the church, a divine race born into the human race through the Eucharist, is the "invisible" which exists in the visible. Being a mysterious reality expressed in concrete forms of human and earthly life, the church is knowable by faith alone.[20] We profess this faith in the following words of the creed: "I believe . . . in one Holy Catholic, and Apostolic Church." Thus the reality of the church is revealed only to the eyes of faith, that is, "the assurance of things hoped for, the conviction of things not seen" (Heb. 11:1). But as such, the Orthodox church can be knowable only through the Orthodox experience of the church life.[21] The invisible life of the church is indefinable because life is indefinable.[22] Therefore the church itself is an overall sacrament and for this reason can be further developed in sacraments.[23]

Besides the sacraments of baptism, Chrismation, and Eucharist, the Orthodox church practices the sacrament of penitence, or forgiveness of sins; the sacrament of holy orders, or ordination to the three hieratic degrees: the bishopric, the priesthood, and the deaconate—always performed by bishops; the sacrament of marriage; and the sacrament of unction of the sick.

The church also performs numerous acts of sanctification and rites that possess sacramental power. By their means the church blesses all aspects of human life, confers the Holy Spirit through material things, and thus transfigures all creation, paving the way for "the new heaven and the new earth."

To be sure, the supreme high priest Jesus confers the Holy Spirit in the sacraments of the church always and invariably by means of the hierarchy. But the church is not an institution that simply preserves what Jesus left to it before His ascension, but is His Body, of which He remains the head (Col. 1:18). Therefore the church has authority to produce sacraments from itself and to set up its own hierarchy for the celebration of these sacraments. For the Orthodox, the church is first, the hierarchy second. The church as the Body of Christ, the Temple of the Holy Spirit, is the fullness from which the hierarchical ministry radiates.

In Roman ecclesiology Christ begins the line of succession of priests just as God in the Old Testament instituted the successive line of priests "after the order of Aaron" (Heb. 7:11). Before Jesus ascended to heaven, He appointed the apostle Peter as His locum tenens on earth. Thus through Peter as *vicarium Christi* Jesus initiated the hierarchical line of pontiffs. Such was the official statement of the Roman church.[24]

Orthodox ecclesiology remained faithful to the New Testament point of the Epistle to the Hebrews, according to which Christ as "the high priest for ever after the order of Melchisedec" (6:20) can have no substitute or vicar on earth. He is not the first priest in the line of successive priests.[25] He is ever present "in the midst of the congregation of the children God has given Him" (Heb. 2:12–13). By virtue of His eternal eucharistic sacrifice, celebrated on all altars, Christ fashions His church which has power to produce all other sacraments and to raise hierarchy for their celebration.[26]

In spite of the fact that the priesthood of the New Covenant was established by Christ in the form of apostolic succession, the hierarchy is not successive from Christ as its first high priest "according to the order of Aaron" (Heb. 7:11). The eternal high priest abolishes that order once and for all. On the contrary, the priesthood of the New Covenant exists through an identification with Christ by virtue of His divine humanity;[27] it proceeds from His eternal priesthood. Thus the hierarchical-sacramental scheme of the Roman church—Christ-hierarchy-sacraments-church—is subject in Orthodox theology to the following inversion: Christ-Eucharist-church-sacraments-hierarchy.[28]

These two ecclesiologies express themselves differently in their respective understanding of the "catholicity" of the church. The Roman church understands catholicity extraterritorially as a universal expansion among all peoples. In Orthodox perception catholicity means that the church is identical with itself in its every part.[29] The church is "catholic" because the sacrifice of its high priest is one, indivisible and identical; it transcends time and space and embraces eternity. Thus in the Orthodox liturgy the priest prepares the Holy Bread for communion with the prayer: "Divided and distributed is the Lamb of God: who is divided, yet not disunited; who is ever eaten, yet never consumed; but sanctifying those who partake thereof."

Orthodoxy understands the catholicity of the church in terms of the Epistle to the Hebrews: "But what you have come to is Mount Zion and the city of the living God, the heavenly Jerusalem where the millions of angels have gathered for the festival, with the whole Church in which everyone is a 'first-born son' and a citizen of heaven. You have come to God himself, the supreme Judge, and been placed with the spirits of the saints who have been made perfect, and to Jesus, the mediator who brings a new covenant and a blood for purification" (12:22–25). The universal church embraces the human race together with the whole assembly of angels. Thus *catholicity* means that every Orthodox is united with the wholeness of this invisible church that is the foundation and the substance of the church visible. Every Orthodox is "catholic" as long as he is in communion with this invisible church in truth.[30]

The belief that all faithful irrespective of their position in the church body receive the gift of the same Holy Spirit and are in communion with the same Christ is the foundation of the Orthodox teaching on "sobornost." "Sobornost," the Russian translation of the notion of catholicity, renders the substance of the church (the Greek word *ecclesia* means "gathering," "assembly," *sobor* in Slavonic) as a unity expressed in plurality, as the plenitude that is manifested in its every part. *Sobornost* means the unity of all church members within the organic fellowship of the church as the Body of Christ, each person maintaining his full freedom and personal responsibility for the life of the church and the purity of its teaching. It also means the unity of all members of the church in time and space, the unity which embraces every Orthodox communicant of the past and present. Thus where the faithful are gathered together for the eucharistic celebration, which is a participation in the one sacrifice of Christ, there the church is given in its "catholicity" or in its "sobornost." That is why each communicant belongs to this "chosen race, a royal priesthood" according to the expression of St. Peter (1 Peter 2:9).

But this "royal priesthood" of all faithful in no way contradicts the existence of a specially ordained hierarchy. On the contrary, the priesthood of the people of God is the very condition for the functioning of the hierarchy. For the latter cannot come into being and function in a society deprived of grace, or one that refuses to accept it. Under such circumstances the hierarchy loses its power, as is the case with heretical or schismatic groups, or as it happened at one time in Soviet Russia, when the government refused to recognize the hierarchy of the Orthodox church, making its legal functioning close to impossible. Therefore in the Orthodox church the priesthood of the faithful and the functional ordained hierarchy are conditions for each other.

The fullness of truth and fullness of the magisterium are present in every local community having a bishop at its head, "the successor of Peter and the other apostles."[31] The consecration of a bishop-elect by an assembly of bishops (two or three at least) in the Orthodox church expresses the Orthodox belief that the bishop is not a successor of any particular apostle but of all of them. For the Orthodox, it is Christ Himself, the supreme high priest, who ordains His new hierarch through the hands of other bishops.[32]

The consecration of a new bishop by the assembly of other bishops at the liturgy also manifests the unity of local churches, of which the bishops are the heads. These local churches are not separate as if they were provinces of a state. They are united by one faith, and this unity is expressed by the concelebration of their bishops. Therefore, in practical ecclesiastical terms, *sobornost* or *catholicity* means also *conciliarity*, expressed in the regular convening of church councils (or bishops' synod at least) where the whole church is represented, its officers are elected and give accounts of their activity, and where the truth is spoken from the floor.

Here we come to the third ministry of Jesus as the supreme king, which is the basis of the government of the Orthodox church. In the prayer during the cherubic hymn the priest invokes Jesus as the "King of Israel, who rulest over those in heaven and on earth." Jesus is universal king, but His kingship is limited to the society of those who accept it, to the church. He is the invisible head of the church, who governs it through the Holy Spirit. The Orthodox teaching on the royal priesthood of all believers and on sobornost or conciliarity is founded on this firm belief in the kingship of Christ.

As members of the body of Christ, all believers belong to this "royal priesthood"; but as every body needs a skeleton, the church hierarchy performs this function in the church. Also the flock groups naturally around the shepherds, who assume the leadership in the church. Thus the hierarchy, without losing its charisma, becomes an institution. Institutionalism being introduced, the church is composed of hieratically organized congregations. The church canon law governs their relations. The numerous canons that regulate church organization and discipline form the corpus of Orthodox canon law, which outlines the structure of the church as institution. These canons, formulated by ecumenical and local councils, reflect Orthodox ecclesiology.

As pointed out, each local church is constituted by the community of the faithful, gathered around their bishop for eucharistic celebration. Therefore no power can exist by divine right outside and above the local eucharistic community. Throughout the history of the Orthodox church, this local community has corresponded to the diocese, the smallest of the institutional units of which the church is composed.

The bishop being first of all the one who presides at the eucharistic celebration, the episcopal authority is a spiritual one. Being a servant of the church (Luke 22:26), the bishop governs the church in agreement with it. He is not above the church. Sobornost on the diocesan level is ensured in two ways: by apostolic succession (which is the expression of the dependence of a bishop on his fellow bishops), and election by the people. In the early church the bishop was elected by the people of the diocese, clergy and laity together. This tradition is preserved in the office of the ordination of a bishop when the people at a certain moment must announce their agreement by saying the word "worthy" (aksios in Greek) referring to the elect.

The Moscow local council of the Russian Orthodox church in 1917–1918 restored the procedure of the election of bishops by the clergy and laity. This ruling of the Moscow council, which became void under the communist regime in the Soviet Union, is followed by the Orthodox Church in America.[33]

As Fr. Bulgakov has pointed out, election by communal choice, while a preliminary condition, is perfectly compatible with the decisive value of ordination through the laying on of hands. Human choice cannot replace the divine act of imposition of hands, but together they constitute the condition of Orthodox catholicity.[34]

Bishops being elected and duly ordained, canon law defines the rights of the bishops and the relations among them. All bishops, notwithstanding canonical differences due to historical or political circumstances, are entirely equal from the charismatic viewpoint: there is no superior bishop among them.

If there is no superior bishop, or pope, in the Orthodox church, what then holds it together? Attachment to the heavenly king, the act of communion in sacraments. The universal Orthodox church is constituted by the communion of the heads of the local churches. Unity is created by the concelebration of the Eucharist by bishops, representing their churches. "The church is not monarchical in structure, centered round a single hierarch; it is collegial, formed by the communion of many hierarchs with one another, and of each hierarch with the members of his flock. The act of communion therefore forms the criterion for membership of the church. An individual ceases to be a member of the church if he severs communion with his bishop; a bishop ceases to be a member of the church if he severs communion with his fellow bishops."[35]

Thus Orthodox unity is realized not as unity under a single authority but as unity of faith and tradition, ensured by the apostolic succession of the hierarchy. Orthodox communities around the world recognize reciprocally their hierarchy and their sacraments. We find the same form of unity in the primitive church, even in apostolic times. In the course of history local churches headed by bishops formed parts of a composite canonical unity with the council of bishops and a primate at the head. Thus archbishoprics, metropolitanates, and patriarchates came into being. Their primates, often heads of autocephalous churches, sometimes enjoyed substantial administrative authority but were never considered chief guardians of Orthodox faith, or possessors of special charisma that elevated them over other bishops.

The local autocephalous churches that developed in the course of history are branches of Orthodox communion. As it has been observed, "while the hierarchy of each autocephalous church is entirely independent in the exercise of its ministry, it is joined by this mutual recognition with, and finds itself under the silent observation of, the hierarchy of the entire Orthodox world. This does not often appear when ecclesiastical life is normal, but becomes evident in the case of any violation. Then the hierarchy of an autocephalous church lifts its voice to defend Orthodoxy which has been transgressed by another church. Different churches intervene."[36]

Orthodox theology nevertheless acknowledges the need for a special hieratic agency that expresses the unity of the church. Before the separation of Eastern and Western churches in the eleventh century, the bishop of Rome filled the function of such an agency. After the separation, the primacy devolved upon the patriarchate of Constantinople. But nowadays this primacy is purely symbolic. As Fr. John Meyendorff puts it,

> the relations of autocephalous churches with each other are determined by a kind of hierarchy of honor headed by the "ecumenical" patriarch of Constantinople as *primus inter pares*. The order of precedence among the three other Oriental patriarchates (Alexandria, Antioch, Jerusalem) was fixed in the fifth century. . . . The patriarchate of Moscow, established in 1589, is accorded . . . fifth place in this hierarchy. Other autocephalous churches are assigned a place in accordance with the date when they became ecclesiastically independent. This system, which is theoretically nothing more than an adaptation of ancient canon law to modern conditions, undoubtedly has the great advantage of being very elastic. It permits autocephalous churches to be founded, abolished, then re-established again in the course of history without affecting the entire organization of the Church.[37]

It also left intact the cultural pluralism which corresponded to the ethnic diversity of the autocephalous churches.

But the Orthodox also are well aware of the disadvantages of the church's decentralization, particularly during the long period in which the church has failed to convene ecumenical councils. From the first church council of Jerusalem described in the Book of Acts (ch. 15), the church was governed by councils, local as well as ecumenical. Diocesan bishops as representatives of their dioceses regularly assembled to discuss matters of doctrine and discipline. For resolving problems of universal ecclesiastical importance, ecumenical councils were convened. After the seventh ecumenical council in the eighth century, the practice of assembling for ecumenical councils fell into oblivion. Besides that, the fall of ancient patriarchates and of some of the younger Orthodox churches under Turkish captivity led to the alienation of local churches from each other and to inevitable provincialism. Fr. Meyendorff indicates that as a consequence of this development, "independent by right and in fact, the autocephalous churches are too inclined to live in isolation from each other, they are unable to take any common action effectively, and they lack a common system for training of the clergy. The effect of nationalism, the disease that ravaged Eastern Europe in the nineteenth and twentieth centuries, can be overcome in the ecclesiastical sphere only with great difficulty. The church often comes to be regarded as nothing more than a mere adjunct of the nation, a mere instrument useful in helping to preserve the language and customs of the people."[38]

But nowadays with our civilization tending toward unification, the Orthodox churches are becoming more aware of the principles of universal ecumenicity. The general democratization of life, being a late product of Christian civilization, has influenced retroactively the domain of religion. Liberty becomes a necessary condition for advancement of the Gospel. And the decentralized organization of Orthodoxy, autonomous but united, perfectly suits the religious needs of the modern world accustomed to freedom but weary of its spiritual rootlessness. Also, as Fr. Meyendorff points out, "the absence of any binding centralized authority permits the various hierarchies of the church today to adopt different political attitudes without rupturing the doctrinal and sacramental bonds of unity."[39]

Now the question arises as to the Orthodox attitude toward temporal power, the state. This attitude from the outset was colored by the general eschatological orientation of the church, expressed in the Epistle to the Hebrews: "There is no eternal city for us in this life, but we look for one in the life to come" (Heb. 13:14). Therefore Orthodoxy failed to develop its own political philosophy. For the primitive church, the pagan state was "the beast who mouthed its blasphemies against God . . . and made war against the saints" (Rev. 13:1–8).

When the Roman Empire converted to Christian ideology, the church entered into very close relations with it, which both parties called "symphony." This pattern of relationship remained intact for many centuries, until the Russian Empire introduced in the eighteenth century the Lutheran notion of the supremacy of the monarch in the church and eventually reduced the Russian Orthodox church to the status of "the department of the Orthodox confession." As far as Greek and other oriental Orthodox churches are concerned, they developed after the fall of Byzantium and under Turkish rule a rather strong inner autonomy, but paid a heavy price in their attachment to nationalistic movements.

The fall of the Byzantine Empire for Greek-speaking churches and the fall of the Russian Empire for Slavic churches put an end to the established political order and to a pattern of relationship between church and state that was considered immovable. But as Fr. Bulgakov has stated, the connection of Orthodoxy with the monarchical system "was never of exclusive importance":

> The Orthodox church has existed in various countries under different political regimes: in the republics of Novgorod and Pskov, as well as under the despotism of Ivan the Terrible, and under heterodox governments; and never has it lost its fullness and its power. Today the church exists under the yoke of Communism, and abroad in the emigré communities, and in the entire world, independent of political conditions. There is no interior and immovable connection between Orthodoxy and this or that system of government; the Orthodox may have different opinions and different political sympathies. This is a matter of their conscience as citizens and of their intelligence.[40]

As Fr. Bulgakov rightly observed, the separation of church and state, at first imposed by force, has finally been accepted with gratitude by the Orthodox churches. Liberty better corresponds to the church's dignity and vocation than alliance with the political regime. But delivered from the temptations of clericalism, the church retains its ambition to influence the society in a democratic way.[41] In democratic society the Orthodox church is becoming more itself. It is regaining its inner liberty and mobility, is restoring its catholic, conciliatory character. The Orthodox church does not change inwardly, for it believes that it always possesses the same "unshakable kingdom" (Heb. 12:28) and always depends on its eternal King, "Jesus Christ, who is the same today as He was yesterday and as He will be for ever" (Heb. 13:8).

3

The Historical Tradition of Church-State Relations under Orthodoxy

Aristeides Papadakis

The conversion of the Roman emperor Constantine early in the fourth century and the legal establishment of Christianity as the official religion of the empire by the end of the century were altogether momentous changes. They created a radically new situation, which rapidly set the tone for the church's understanding of itself in relation to the secular world and the new Christian empire of Byzantium for the next thousand years. There was, in general, little in Orthodoxy's ideological vision of the world and the state in the following centuries that did not stretch back in a direct line of descent to these critical decades. The vision even survived the breakup of the empire itself, as the sixteenth-century concept of "Moscow, the Third Rome," indicates. Although this was also a form of Russian religious nationalism, and a distortion of the Byzantine Christian universalism established in the fourth century, its roots were nevertheless ultimately Byzantine.[1] This being so, any historical reconstruction of church-state relations under Orthodoxy must necessarily begin with the fourth century of the Christian era.

The Byzantine Theocracy

The fourth century forms a bridge between two fundamentally distinct periods in the history of the church. Constantine not only brought the age of the persecutions to a close, he also inaugurated a new and unprecedented era of toleration and imperial patronage.[2] Public responsibility, influence, wealth, and authority, which would have been inconceivable for the church fifty years before, were now there for the asking. Nor was this all. The government soon began to take the lead in ecclesiastical matters, to intervene personally in theological controversy, to convoke councils, and even to legislate on heresy and schism. At the same time it began a sustained if unsystematic suppression of paganism so that by the 390s its association with the ancient cults came to an abrupt end.[3] Under Theodosius I (379–395) Christianity became binding on the whole empire. The state as such had become Christian. As a result, Christianity was gradually transformed by a previously hostile government into the official religion of the empire. The church henceforth was to serve the empire, just as Roman religion had done in the past; the empire, on the other hand, was to act as its protector and guardian. Recognition and patronage had been translated into partnership with the state.

The new orientation certainly took many by surprise. Still, the emperors took their patronage seriously, and the church was understandably grateful for their protection. Thus it was easy to assume the hand of providence at the turn of events. As a matter of plain fact, before the fourth century Christian writers had often acknowledged the providential role of the pax romana in the spread and expansion of Christianity. Not surprisingly, the views of Eusebius of Caesarea, Constantine's personal publicist, biographer, and bishop, were not very different. In his influential *Life of Constantine*, for example, the emperor is conceived as the culminating point of human history, the man charged to inaugurate a new world empire—the universal duplicate or complement of the universal church. As God's chosen instrument, the first Christian emperor (and by extension all his successors) was to be God's heir to universal rule, his only divinely ordained representative on earth. As there was one God in heaven, so there could be only one emperor on earth. Moreover, the emperor, to paraphrase another of the same panegyrist's tracts, was to fashion his government after the original divine model, so as to conform with the monarchy of God.[4] His power was to be a terrestrial copy of the heavenly prototype, a replica of God's own sovereign rule in heaven.

As we should expect, Constantine's conversion was crucial to this theology of empire, inasmuch as he had been called and converted directly by God, rather than by ordinary men. Quite simply, Christ himself had converted the emperor, thereby implicitly sanctioning his power and position both in the church and the empire. On the whole, the durability and longevity of the emperor's privileged position in the church during the long Byzantine millennium lies in this simple fact.[5] The unique nature of his calling is the reason why it was never questioned or criticized.

Similarly, the Roman government with all its pre-Christian traditions also did not find the transition envisioned by Eusebius to be an obstacle. The concept that the empire was a reflection of the divine ideal had precedents in Hellenistic theories of kingship.[6] The emperor, it is true, was no longer a godlike figure; in the new Christian context he was forced to renounce his divine attributes as well as any claims to divinity. All the same, he was still divinely appointed and his absolutism remained intact, even if it was now obscured by a "Hellenistic ideology in Christian garb."[7] In summary, neither the church nor the empire found the newly Christianized political ideology hampering. On the contrary, both viewed it as part of God's providential plan for humanity.

But the vision of a unitary Christian society also haunted, mutatis mutandi, the medieval West. For it too had once been part of the homogeneous Roman world of the fourth century. In Latin Christendom, however, the collapse of political authority and the subsequent feudalization of the social order made possible the development of a different tradition, a different political cosmology from that of Eastern Christendom.[8] In contrast with the East, Western ecclesiastical policy sought an absolute separation of the two spheres and even the subjection of the state to the unifying authority of the pope. The fear that the church might become an instrument of the state if a division were not maintained propelled the popes on a course of papal hegemony, rather than partnership with the feudal world. Hence the medieval papacy's extreme claims to temporal rule and its fierce struggle to dominate society during the Investiture controversy. Hence, too, the juridical terminology and context in which church-state relations were defined in the West. That the West continues to think of the church and papal primacy in exclusively legal terms is not surprising. Suffice it to say, the modern debate of separation of church and state is ultimately rooted in this same juridical understanding of the problem.

But how did the contrasting Byzantine theory of society—conceived as a permanent organic unity, as a single political and ecclesiastical whole—evolve in the East? As we have said, the initial vision, canonized in the fourth century, was never altered. Be this as it may, elaboration was not totally lacking, as Justinian's sixth *Novella* indicates. The preamble of this edict was issued on April 17, 535.

The greatest blessings of mankind are the gifts of God which have been granted us by the mercy on high: the priesthood and the imperial authority. The priesthood ministers to things divine; the imperial authority is set over, and shows diligence in, things human; but both proceed from one and the same source, and both adorn the life of man. Nothing, therefore, will be a greater matter of concern to the emperor than the dignity and honor of the clergy; the more as they offer prayers to God without ceasing on his behalf. For if the priesthood be in all respects without blame, and full of faith before God, and if the imperial authority rightly and duly adorn the commonwealth committed to its charge, there will ensue a happy concord which will bring forth all good things for mankind.[9]

The most striking element of this famous document is the recognition that a clear distinction does indeed exist between the empire and the church. Justinian, in fact, is the first to acknowledge this polarity since the time of Constantine. The fact that the *sacerdotium* ministers to "things divine" and the *imperium* to "things human" does not however efface or cancel their connection or complementarity; the two, proceeding as they do from the same origin, are interdependent agencies or allies. There can be no rivalry, nor is a sharp dichotomy between them possible or admissible. Emperor and patriarch, however distinct and separate, together constitute, as the later ninth-century *Epanagoge* put it, the greatest and most necessary parts of a single organism.[10] Ideally, the two were to work in harmony, the one as spiritual guide, the other as secular administrator, in order to bring about the desired accord within a single theocratic structure.

But Justinian's edict is important for yet another reason: it failed to explain just how the joint responsibility and mutual dependence of church and state, spiritual and temporal, were to be maintained. Their powers or spheres of competence were never legally defined in this or any other Byzantine text. Nor were the relations between the two ever linked by any formal treaty or juridical agreement. Strictly speaking, the only tie binding them together was their common Orthodox faith. The Byzantines, it seems, believed that the cooperative partnership between them would never break down and that the inherent tension between the sacramental and eschatological aspirations of Orthodox Christianity could be reconciled with the values and culture of secular society. There was as such no need for any juridical limitations. In effect, as one scholar reminds us, Byzantine political thought "assumed that the state, as such, could become intrinsically Christian."[11]

Le mal byzantin

The assumption of course was unrealistic, if not unrealizable. As the history of the Byzantine state indicates, the delicately balanced dualism did occasionally break down, usually to the church's disadvantage. Historians, as a consequence, have often asserted that the church was forced to surrender its freedom, to function as a department of the state. By gaining control over the temporal and the spiritual, the emperor became in fact both pope and caesar. The result, understandably, was the enslavement of the church. Anyone familiar with Byzantine historiography will of course recognize the term *Caesaropapism*, the label used to describe this Byzantine pattern. Characteristically, the term has sometimes been applied to contemporary Orthodoxy's alleged ability to adjust to the changed circumstances of the modern totalitarian state.[12] Church-state relations in Muscovy, imperial Russia, and the modern Soviet regime have often been described as "Byzantine" and "Caesaropapist" in essence.

Beyond any doubt, the emperor's sacrosanct status in Eastern Christendom had no parallel in contemporary medieval Europe. His right to interfere in the church's institutional structure was unlimited. He not only published and confirmed its disciplinary canons; he also enforced them. His influence in ecclesiastical appointments, moreover, was recognized and, indeed, never questioned. It was he who selected the patriarch and confirmed his dignity; and of course he could dismiss him or compel him to resign. Statistically speaking, nearly a third of the patriarchs of Constantinople were forced to relinquish their office under imperial pressure. Equally, the emperor had the power to rearrange dioceses, to promote bishops, and even to transfer them from one diocese to another. In addition, some emperors attempted to overturn the equilibrium by claiming as their own the right to define doctrine. Such was the case with Leo III and his son Constantine V in the eighth century. Typical, too, was the monarch's prerogative to convene and preside over councils and to sign their proceedings. In sum, the emperor's control of the ecclesiastical administration was considerable and at times all-embracing. In keeping with his divine election and charismatic position in society, the emperor was also given extraordinary liturgical privileges. Like the clergy, he could enter the sanctuary and partake of the sacrament, whereas the laity received the sacrament from a priest. He thus enjoyed privileges normally restricted to the bishop or the priesthood. These included the permission to bless the faithful with the three-candled episcopal candelabra, to cense the icons, congregation, and altar, and even to deliver sermons.

Such, in the main, is the evidence used to explain Byzantine Caesaropapism, the Orthodox church's alleged submission to the secular state. All the same, the argument has left many modern scholars increasingly uncomfortable; most, if not all, have vigorously criticized it as being nothing less than a massive oversimplification of the Byzantine experience. The evidence, it is argued, is far too manifold and complex to be subsumed under any one pattern such as Caesaropapism.[13] Besides, the theory is in reality a thinly disguised expression of Western hostility toward Eastern Orthodoxy: if fierce independence identified the Latin, Western church, passive submission typified the East. But the allegation will also not stand up to any serious, scrupulous criticism. In fact, it is both inaccurate and misleading in its interpretation of the practical politics of the Byzantine world. On purely historical grounds, the label (which, significantly, is of Western origin) best reflects the political pretensions of the papacy. For it was the popes, rather than the Byzantine emperors, who repeatedly put forth their own claims to imperial rule; it was they, and not the emperors of the East, who attempted to combine in their single office the powers of both *regnum* and *sacerdotium*. Excepting the case of the iconoclast emperor Leo III, such pretensions to kingship and priesthood were never made in Byzantium.

By and large, the emperor's extraordinary liturgical and administrative privileges are well documented. Still, these concessions do not constitute irrefutable proof of Caesaropapism. In the first place the primary concern of the church was never with the externals of its administrative structure, but with its faith and doctrinal integrity, responsibility for which was reserved exclusively to the clergy. The definition of dogma remained the inviolable right of the episcopate and the church at large. It was never (nor could it ever be) transferred to the emperor, however exaggerated or extensive his prerogatives. Ultimately, his task was to preserve and defend the faith; he could neither define nor alter it. True, individual emperors often tried. Arianism, monophysitism, monothelitism, iconoclasm, and union with the West, to name only the more famous Byzantine church-state crises, make this luminously clear. And yet, in none of these cases, in which the defiance of the church was unmistakable and unyielding, did the emperor ever succeed in imposing his views on the church. As Maximus the Confessor put it in the seventh century, "None of the emperors was able, through modifying measures, to persuade the holy Fathers to conform to the heretical teachings of their day."[14]

The church, then, could and did resist the emperor. A list of those opposing the government—patriarchs, bishops, clergy, and individual monks and laymen—would be a long and impressive one. In short, organized opposition was not uncommon. Theodore of Studios, the famous monastic reformer and abbot of the largest monastery in Constantinople, supplies a typical illustration from the ninth century. His fierce resistance to the government's controversial ban on images exasperated more than one iconoclast emperor. Significantly, his conviction that the sovereign's only task was to attest to the church's faith ("nothing else has ever been given them by God in the matter of divine doctrines; nothing else, should it come to pass, will endure")[15] ultimately prevailed, as the restoration of images in 843 testifies. But the emperor also had to be cautious when removing a patriarch. In 1262 patriarch Arsenius excommunicated Michael VIII for deposing and blinding the child-emperor John IV. As we should expect, Arsenius was in turn asked to step down. The end result, however, was the Arsenite schism. This lasted nearly fifty years and was in its consequences far more damaging to the dynasty than if Arsenius had been retained. Undeniably, the emperors were quite successful in dealing with individual patriarchs and recalcitrant ecclesiastics. (Theodore himself was banished three times.) Nevertheless, the fact remains that the Byzantine emperor was virtually helpless "whenever [he] had to cope with the Church as an institution."[16]

In summary, although the church surrendered the discipline and management of its external affairs and administration to the state, that surrender was always contingent on the emperor's own submission to the divine law, the spiritual and moral authority of the church and its doctrine. His right of appointment, promotion, and supervision did not automatically render him the church's ultimate leader. The crucial condition was always his faith, his good standing in the church. Plainly put, perfect Caesaropapism involving total control never existed in Byzantium.[17] The church never acknowledged or recognized, officially or unofficially, the supremacy of the temporal in spiritual matters. The theory over which the West has often been scandalized was never acceptable practice. The emperor may have been an absolute Caesar but he was never pope—ultimate custodian of the Christian faith. His lay, nonpriestly character was never in question. His liturgical privileges, it is worth emphasizing, did not confer actual sacramental authority.

The disadvantages and defects of the Byzantine "symphony" cannot, of course, be minimized. The government's protective tutelage was often ponderous and even harmful. It was naive to believe that the gulf separating the two spheres could be fully bridged. Still, our eagerness to criticize the Byzantines should be tempered by the knowledge that their "politico-ecclesiastical experiment was an earnest attempt to solve a real problem."[18] It should not obscure the fact that their task—to create a genuine Christian society, a single Christian commonwealth—was a lofty if unattainable undertaking.

The Centuries of Captivity

For Orthodox Christendom the fall of Constantinople in 1453 was a decisive turning point—a major break in its long history. The unitary Christian society of Byzantium with its delicate balance between church and
state was no more. The Orthodox sovereign, whom the imperial Byzantine
church had recognized as God's representative on earth for over a millennium, had simply vanished, and was replaced by a non-Christian in-
fidel sultan. The end of the empire was a calamity, as any cursory survey
of the history of Orthodoxy in the Balkans and the Greek peninsula under the Ottomans will reveal. All political freedom was lost. In addition,
spiritual stagnation quickly set in. The corrupt and incompetent Ottoman
system brought in its wake dislocation, demoralization, and venality, and
these progressively permeated the ecclesiastical structure. Still, the church
survived, despite the widespread bewilderment and radical readjustment
that had to be made. Contemporaries themselves saw its physical preservation as the proof that the gates of Hell could not prevail against it.

The Byzantine legacy contributed to this resilience. The church's traditional unwillingness to enter into competition with Caesar and its indifference to the possession of power made bearable and acceptable the difficult
and unusual political situation with which it was now faced. However,
survival was also made possible by the Ottomans themselves.[19] The rapprochement achieved between the church and the sultan, less than a year
after the fall of the city, would have been inconceivable otherwise. Understandably, Mehmed II realized that the vast majority of his subjects were
Orthodox, and that their industry and numbers, particularly in southeastern Europe, were indispensable to the general economic prosperity of the
empire and the repopulation and rebuilding of Constantinople. Besides, he
feared Latin Christendom and the fact that the church might again turn
to the West for assistance as it had done in the past. A more favorable
settlement could conceivably neutralize this problem; the patriarchate, as
a result, might not be tempted to continue its pre-1453 unionist activities
with the West. Hence the preference given the antipapal faction in the
church by the sultan. The first patriarch under the Turkocracy, favored by
Mehmed himself, was none other than the antiunionist scholar and monk
Gennadius II Scholarius.[20]

Besides these immediate practical considerations, however, the Ottoman
sultan was also motivated by Islam's long tradition of tolerance of Christianity. The idea was enshrined in the Koran, notably in its explicit recognition of the monotheistic tie existing between Islam, Christianity, and
Judaism. "Verily, whether it be of those who believe, or those who are

Jews or Christians or Sabaeans, whosoever believe in God and the last day and act aright, they have their reward at their Lord's hand, and there is no fear for them, nor shall they grieve."[21] This common bond explains the tolerant treatment that Christians had received earlier at the hands of their Arab conquerors. In Arabic lands, as a rule, Christians had to remain loyal and obedient and were undoubtedly restricted and discriminated against, but they were seldom systematically proselytized or persecuted. Conversion or total integration into the Islamic state, at any rate, was not compulsory.

Mehmed's minority home rule policy, imposed on his new polyethnic and multireligious empire, was thus rooted in Islamic law and tradition.[22] The Turkish sultan was merely institutionalizing the protection Christians had previously enjoyed in earlier Islamic states. As long as minority groups were monotheistic, they were viewed as people protected by Islam, free to enjoy a certain degree of self-government under their own administrators. True, the Ottoman Empire was founded on holy war and, therefore, on the championship and extension of Islam. All the same, Islamic law was not changed. In comparison with Reformation Europe, with its well-known religious wars and excesses, the Ottoman state was one of the most tolerant.

This special protection under which the church functioned during the Turkocracy is traditionally known as the *millet* or ethnarchic system.[23] The arrangement remained unaltered until the nineteenth century. All non-Muslim minorities, such as Jews, Copts, Armenians, and Orthodox, were divided into individual communities (millets) under the leadership of their own highest ecclesiastical authority. The community alone determined an individual's status and position in Turkish society. Orthodoxy, accordingly, was recognized as a separate faith, as an independent millet under the personal jurisdiction of the patriarch of Constantinople. (The Orthodox millet was, in fact, the first to be organized with the election of Gennadius II and, as such, set the standard for the subsequent establishment of the other religious minorities.) More specifically, the patriarch of Constantinople became the head or *millet bashi* of all Orthodox Christians within the Ottoman realm, regardless of their individual race or nationality; Greeks and Slavs were treated alike, their common profession of faith being the sole factor determining their millet membership. The entire Orthodox population, in other words, was viewed as one autonomous religious unit arranged along confessional lines. It did not, as such, correspond to any ethnic, national, or linguistic reality. The idea of differentiating along such divisions was altogether alien and unknown to Muslim tradition. The system had to be non-national. For Muslim law did not recognize any distinction between church and state, religion and secular society. Rather, it identified the two.

The Millet at Work

It was by means of this confessional compartmentalization that the Turks hoped to solve their minority problem. Practically, this arrangement, in which every minority had its own communal autonomy based on religious affiliation, did not provide full citizenship or full equality. Millions of Orthodox were protected people (*zimmis*) only and paid extra taxes. They remained second-class citizens even if they were guaranteed their lives and properties, freedom of worship, and the use of most of their churches and monasteries. Thus, discrimination was a basic and inseparable element of the system. Still, the arrangement was not unwelcome. Its advantages were well expressed (from the church's perspective, at least) by a patriarch of Jerusalem in the late eighteenth century.

> See how clearly our Lord, boundless in mercy and all-wise, had undertaken to guard once more the unsullied Holy and Orthodox faith. . . . He raised out of nothing this powerful empire of the Ottomans, in place of our Roman [Byzantine] Empire which had begun, in a certain way, to cause to deviate from the beliefs of the Orthodox faith, and he raised up the empire of the Ottomans higher than any other kingdom so as to show without doubt that it came about by divine will, and not by the power of man. . . . The all-mighty Lord, then, has placed over us this kingdom, "for there is no power but of God," so as to be to the people of the West a bridle, to us the people of the East a means of salvation. For this reason he puts into the heart of the Sultan of these Ottomans an inclination to keep free the religious beliefs of our Orthodox faith and, as a work of supererogation, to protect them, even to the point of occasionally chastising Christians who deviate from their faith, that they have always before their eyes the fear of God.[24]

In short, the arrangement was viewed as providential, as "a means of salvation," insofar as it did not threaten the purity of the Orthodox faith, the integrity of the church's canonical structure, or the physical existence of the patriarchate. Indeed, the privileges of the patriarchate included the inviolability of the patriarch's person. If in 1453 systematic liquidation was the fate of the dynasties and rulers of the Balkan states, and of the Byzantine aristocracy and emperor, the same was not true of the ecclesiastical hierarchy. Its independence and corporate identity, as a rule, were left undisturbed.

But if Constantinople was now the seat of ecclesiastical authority for the entire Orthodox population, it was also the civil and administrative center of the Orthodox community, of the largest and most important millet in the Ottoman state. The patriarch, as such, was vested with both ecclesiastical and civil jurisdiction, with administrative and legal functions. If church discipline, control of the clergy, episcopal elections, management of church property, and questions of doctrine were all under his jurisdiction, so were all civil cases. Matters such as divorce, marriage, inheritance, guardianship of minors, and taxation were all handled by the patriarchal courts or by the extensive administrative structure created for this purpose. Commercial cases, theft, and even murder involving Christians only were likewise handled by independent church courts. The patriarch, in short, was invested with considerable jurisdiction and power, with new, heavier secular duties, all of which went well beyond those he had enjoyed in the Byzantine state. Besides, his authority now extended over a wider area, as more and more independent Orthodox states and patriarchates were submerged under the Turkish tide. With the subsequent conquest of Crete, Cyprus, and the Arab world (which included the ancient patriarchates of Jerusalem, Antioch, and Alexandria), the patriarch's authority became even greater. For he did not represent (to repeat) the dominant Greek ethnic group of the millet only, but all Orthodox Christians in general.

Clearly, church-state relations in the Turkish period were far more complex. The patriarch, by virtue of his new civil authority, was transformed into a recognized Ottoman official. He had as such become an instrument and auxiliary of the Turkish bureaucracy, the sole intermediary between the Ottoman state and his large Orthodox flock.[25] Indeed, the sultan seldom dealt directly with the millet. This meant that the patriarch was under the close scrutiny and control of the state at all times and had to bear the responsibility for anything that went wrong. He alone was responsible for the fidelity and obedience of all Orthodox Christians; for maintaining public order within the millet; and for seeing that its obligations to the state were met. These were his basic duties. As the numerous executions and banishments of this bleak period demonstrate, this was seldom an easy task. When the Greek Revolution broke out in 1821, for example, St. Gregory V was hanged from the patriarchal gate, presumably because he had failed to secure the good behavior of his restless flock. The degree of control and responsibility was thus considerable.

Another equally debilitating result of this close association with the state was the control that accompanied all patriarchal and episcopal elections. Every election—done according to canon law by a governing resident synod—had to be confirmed by the sultan. The process was likewise the same with all newly elected patriarchal officials; even dismissals had to have the government's approval. Furthermore, the sultan could intervene frequently and decisively in any election if he so desired. The process therefore soon came to be accompanied by corruption, which was rampant in the Turkish bureaucracy. Shortly after the conquest, Symeon of Trebizond inaugurated a custom by offering the sultan one thousand gold pieces for the patriarchal throne.[26] Not surprisingly, every subsequent patriarch was required to make similar payments. What was initially an occasional practice soon became the rule, as Turkish officials refused to abandon the custom. As a result, the "gift" to the sultan one hundred years later had risen to three thousand gold pieces. Patriarchal elections had become, before long, a lucrative business, as more patriarchs meant more ready cash. Thus, although theoretically and canonically the patriarch was elected to office for life, his tenure was, in fact, never secure. The threat of deposition was always present. Between 1595 and 1695, for example, there were sixty-one changes on the patriarchal throne, with the average tenure being twenty months. It was not uncommon for a patriarch to hold office several times.

Needless to say, this disreputable struggle for office, with its factions, rivalries, and intrigues, was demoralizing. But it was also costly for the patriarchate and the millet in general, since successful candidates normally recouped their losses by taxing the dioceses.[27] The cost of purchasing the office was, in effect, added to the patriarchate's budget. But there were other disadvantages: the permanent necessity of purchasing every office resulted in dependence on the Phanariots. This wealthy class of Greek bureaucrats living in the Phanar district of Constantinople, to which the patriarchate itself had moved in 1601, provided the loans needed to bribe the Turkish authorities. Their infiltration and progressive domination of the patriarchate is explained by their wealth and influence at the Sublime Porte. Their involvement in the patriarchate's affairs, particularly in the eighteenth century, is well known.

Clearly, the checkered relationship between church and state during the Turkish period was far from ideal. Under their Turkish masters only the very saintly among the clergy could retain their sanity or constancy to their calling. The real achievements of the church during this period of instability were, nevertheless, considerable. Its fundamental accomplishment, no doubt, was the preservation of the Orthodox Christian identity of the peoples of the Balkan peninsula. Turkish misrule, it is true, did little to suppress or discourage religious and cultural continuity among the Orthodox. Still, it was the church that sustained this continuity with its doctrinal fidelity and unconditional loyalty to tradition. True, continuity with its Byzantine past, in terms of theological and spiritual creativity, was understandably weakened. Education, learning, and theology had to be sacrificed. And yet, the one common faith derived ultimately from Byzantium and, shared by Slav and Greek alike, continued to be kept alive. It is, perhaps, the principal legacy of the Turkocracy to contemporary Orthodoxy.

The Nineteenth Century

The nineteenth century marks a new chapter in church-state relations for the Orthodox world of the Near East and the Balkans. By then the fragile Ottoman state was in decline, whereas the growing forces of nationalism and secularism were in full swing. The age of national independence had dawned. True, the patriarchate continued to be under Turkish rule and was not abolished, nor was its primacy, as the first see of Orthodoxy, ever challenged. However, by the end of the century its vast jurisdiction and authority, its legal and financial powers, had in large part vanished as a result of the fragmentation and decentralization of the Ottoman state. Besides, much of its once large flock had been absorbed by the newly formed Orthodox nation-states. In effect, new loyalties were emerging for Orthodox Christians, even for those still within Ottoman territories.

But changes for the church were also to be seen within the new independent Orthodox states. Needless to say, an exhaustive examination of this development is beyond the scope of this survey. Only a few general observations can be made here. In the first place, the early protagonists in the struggle for independence were in general anticlerical. Their ideals were those of the Enlightenment and the French Revolution, currents that, as is well known, had little sympathy for religion. Hence the indifference, hostility, and even bitter opposition of many of these patriots toward the patriarchate and the whole Phanariot establishment in Constantinople. Equally, these nationalists were familiar with the way in which the triumphant secular state in the West had handled its relationship with the church. As a result, they too saw the relationship in almost exclusively subservient terms. Separation of church and state, therefore, was neither a plausible nor a desirable alternative. Nor did they want any suggestion of a "symphony of powers" in the tradition of Justinian's sixth *Novella*. On the contrary, their aim was the subordination of religion to the secular power. Significantly, one of the first steps taken by these independent states was to separate the church within their frontiers from the authority of Constantinople. By declaring it autocephalous, by "nationalizing" it, they hoped to control it.

The millet system, no doubt, contributed to this growth of ecclesiastical autocephaly. The Turkish solution to the minority problem, as we have seen, had emphasized the universality of the Orthodox faith rather than national or linguistic differences. In any event, antagonism between different ethnic groups within the Orthodox millet was, as a rule, rare before the nineteenth century.[28] All the same, the seeds of nationalism were also being nurtured by the same general Turkish indifference to ethnic divisions. Nineteenth-century secular nationalism, as a result, had no problem in reviving these dormant sentiments among the population. Another factor, less decisive perhaps, was the example set earlier by Russia.[29] Its autonomy was already several centuries old, as it had won the right from Constantinople to appoint a Russian as its primate shortly before the breakup of the Byzantine state. This was an important step in its independence, because the metropolitan of Moscow had till then been a Greek, appointed exclusively by Constantinople. But Russia's autonomous nationalist image was further enhanced in 1589 when its metropolitan was elevated to patriarchal status by Jeremias II of Constantinople. The emancipation occurred some two hundred years before the dawn of modern nationalism. To summarize, both the millet and the Russian example were important contributing causes in the formation of the autonomous national church.

Nonetheless, the primary factor determining the institutional and organizational structure of nineteenth-century autocephaly was the Western, and at times explicitly Protestant, orientation of its architects.[30] Thus, in the kingdom of Greece the new ecclesiastical constitution of July 1833 provided for a state church organized around a holy synod and its presiding archbishop; the entire body was subject to the king, who was not even an Orthodox. The church, in effect, was politicized as its clergy were transformed into civil servants. The civil authority, moreover, could interfere in the church's affairs just as freely as it could with its state-appointed hierarchy. The church, in sum, was stripped of its authority and became—in imitation of the Western model—an agency of the state. A recent authoritative guide in these matters has arrived at the startling conclusion that the constitution of 1833 was not a significant improvement over Ottoman times. In both cases the hierarchy had been transformed into part of the state machinery. The same scholar further notes that "the tragedy of this is that the position of the Church, which should have been bright in independent Greece, was, in fact, not substantially improved under later Christian rulers."[31]

Significantly, the author of this government-supervised Orthodox Church of Greece was none other than the German Protestant Georg von Maurer. That he had modeled his creation on the situation in Bavaria, his homeland, where both Protestantism and Catholicism were dominated by the secular power, is reasonably certain. Exact parallels between certain articles of the Greek text of 1833 and those of the 1818 Constitution of the Bavarian Protestant church, have in fact been found.[32] Plainly put, the settlement was fundamentally Protestant and Western, alien to the Byzantine tradition of church-state relations. It was, at best, an "honored captivity"[33] inspired largely by the modern secularized state, rather than by any Byzantine pattern. In some respects this vulgar imitation of Western models did not differ from the one introduced into Russia by Peter the Great in the eighteenth century. The Petrine system, it is worth pointing out, was also inspired by the state-controlled synods and churches in the Protestant West.

In any event, the results of nineteenth-century national autocephaly were often disastrous. Ultimately, this metamorphosis of Orthodoxy into an extension of the state, as the religious expression of the nation, weakened the church. It was, quite simply, often unable to resist or defend itself against the state and its inroads. Since ecclesiastic structure and organization were identified with the nation, it could only conform or accommodate itself to the existing political order. Understandably, the phenomenon is widely recognized by Orthodox theologians and historians as little more than a bastard, even heretical, ecclesiological disorder, an abnormal growth of Orthodox ideas about the true nature of the church. For the church as the Body of Christ, as a community beyond nationality, can never become the nation. It knows in fact neither Greek nor Jew, neither male nor female, since all are one in Christ Jesus. Moreover, the ancient principle of autocephaly, which simply gives a group of dioceses the right to elect their own primate, becomes an ecclesiological absolute in which the diocese's territorial boundaries become coterminous with a nation's frontiers. Autocephaly itself is not so much in question as is its nationalization or transformation into something other than what canon law envisions by the principle.

Kiev and Orthodox Messianism

The establishment of Orthodox Christianity in Kiev in 988 is without doubt one of the most important events in the making of Russia. St.

Vladimir's conversion determined not only Russia's religious consciousness and culture, but her very destiny. We have already noted her spiritual
and canonical dependence on Byzantium during most of the medieval
period: even after his move to Moscow (1328) the metropolitan of Kiev
continued to be appointed by the mother church of Constantinople. But
medieval Russia inherited from Christian Byzantium its collaboration with
the church as well as its theocratic concept of empire. For Russia alone
among the Orthodox family of nations had managed to retain its political freedom. The free and independent Muscovite princes consciously and
deliberately saw themselves as the legitimate heirs of Byzantium and its
Christian universality. With the fall of the second Rome, Constantinople,
Moscow had become the third and last Rome. As the monk Philotheus
put it in his letter to Tsar Basil III early in the sixteenth century: "If thou
rulest thine empire rightly, thou wilt be the son of light and a citizen of
the heavenly Jerusalem, as I have written thee. And now, I say unto thee:
take care and take heed, pious tsar; all the empires of Christendom are
united in thine, for two Romes have fallen and the third exists and there
will not be a fourth."[34] In sum, Moscow, the "Third Rome," was now
the center of Orthodox Christendom, the final stronghold of Orthodoxy;
it alone was destined to continue the mission that the first and second
Romes had abandoned, either because of heresy, the Turks, or the union
of Florence, which the Greeks had signed with the heretical West in 1439.

And yet, the theory of the Third Rome was not identical in all respects with Byzantine universalism. The messianic and nationalistic element with which it was tainted had little to do with Byzantine tradition.
Quite simply, the idea that the Russians were somehow a chosen people—
the sole guardians of the true faith—was interpreted nationalistically.
Muscovite messianism, in short, was often used by ambitious tsars for
exclusively secular or imperialistic ends. After all, these rulers were concerned with creating a strong centralized monarchy, as were indeed most
of Europe's secular-minded sovereigns. This being the case, the church
was increasingly viewed by the tsars as an inseparable yet subordinate
part of the Russian autocracy. As a matter of plain fact, the centuries
following the fall of Constantinople form a historical whole in Russian
church history, culminating in the total abasement of the church under
Peter the Great. By and large, then, the Russian union of church and state
(in the person of the Orthodox tsar) had different goals and results from
the Byzantine pattern on which it was partially modeled.

But it was not the Orthodox tsars alone who promoted this integration
between church and state. Powerful circles in the Russian church (including members of its monastic wing) were also strong advocates of the Third

Rome ideology and the collaboration between the secular and spiritual that the theory implied. In the early sixteenth century they were led by Abbot Joseph of Volokolamsk. Their views were in some ways traditional. Dedicated though they were to theocratic monarchy, they nevertheless believed that the church had to be free and supreme in its own sphere. The church's alliance with the state was, as such, conceived in terms of a harmony of equal powers, rather than in secular tsarist terms of subordination or subjugation. But its advocates were also a pro-property clerical party, in that they wished to retain (with the state's help) the vast monastic and ecclesiastical domains used by the church and the monasteries for various charitable and religious purposes. No less striking were the views of the opposition. This party, known as the Non-Possessors, since they were against the enormous landholdings of the monasteries, was led by the monk Nilus Sorsky. These outspoken advocates of monastic poverty were generally convinced that the church would lose its independence if it took an active part in politics, or if it refused to keep its distance from the state autocracy. They were thus unconvinced by the enthusiasm and nationalism of the Josephites. A "Holy Russia" centered in Moscow was not part of their vision of things.

Obviously, the quarrel between these two opposing schools of thought dealt with more than one issue. Different conceptions of monastic life and asceticism, divergent attitudes on landholding, as well as irreconcilable views on the treatment of heretics (the pro-property party believed this to be a matter of both the spiritual and the secular arm) were all major areas of disagreement. In the final analysis, however, at the center of the debate were two very different conceptions of the church's relationship to the state. To be sure, both Nilus and Joseph were canonized—an implicit recognition that certain elements of their visions of Russia's religious future were reconcilable. All the same, this made no difference, since the followers of St. Joseph eventually won the debate. However, this was a limited triumph. For it was not the Josephites' grandiose vision or the church as a whole that benefited from the victory, but Russia's new monarchy with its own secular theocratic plan. The development was decidedly one-sided. As one scholar rightly notes, "the Byzantine Middle Ages were well over by the sixteenth century and the further development of the Russian Empire along the lines of a secularized modern state, which in the eighteenth century was destined completely to subject the Church to its will and confiscate its property, justified the misgivings of Nil and his party a posteriori."[35]

The church of course did not immediately lose its freedom. The power wielded by certain seventeenth-century patriarchs makes this quite clear.

And yet by the middle of the century the stage was being set for the secularization of the Russian church. This is particularly evident with the brief but turbulent reign of Patriarch Nikon (1652–58). Nikon's own controversial reforms, along with his attempts to gain greater freedom for the church, are indeed some of the reasons why Peter the Great proceeded to his own radical reorganization some sixty years later. The patriarch's domination of Alexis Romanov (Peter's less-determined father) may have been momentary, but the lesson was not lost; it was bound to provoke sharp opposition, especially from someone as autocratic as Peter. The events of Nikon's pontificate were a clear portent of what was to come. The ultimate blow to "Holy Russia"—the suppression of the patriarchate—was only decades away.

The patriarch's unconventional views were, to be sure, unprecedented. He had sought to break with the Byzantine past by setting the church above the state, by reversing the dualism of powers implicit in both Muscovite and Byzantine traditions. He believed, in brief, in the supremacy of the spiritual power and in its ultimate right to supervise the secular. Thus, the tsar was viewed as subordinate to the patriarch and to ecclesiastical authority in general.[36] Hence Nikon's assumption of the epithet "Great Lord," a title reserved exclusively for the tsars. The patriarch was thus a Russian Hildebrand whose very pronounced ideas on authority were threatening to revolutionize relations between church and state. Significantly, though not surprisingly, the new ideology was founded on a Latin forgery, the so-called Donation of Constantine, the famous text used by the medieval papacy to buttress its ingenious claim to temporal power.[37] As we should expect, Nikon's deposition, which followed his retirement to a monastery, had the tsar's total approval. The synod of 1666, which condemned him, found his ideas totally alien to the Byzantine mentality. That it should have pronounced in favor of the Byzantine ideology of Justinian's sixth *Novella* was to be expected. "Let this be the conclusion and result of the discussion, that the king or emperor has the preeminence in political matters, and the patriarch in ecclesiastical; that so the harmony of the ecclesiastical constitution may be the better preserved in its integrity and unfringed upon, and may so abide for ever and ever."[38] Moreover, Nikon's zeal as a reformer was disastrous in the extreme. The separation of millions of Old Believers who refused to accept his new liturgical changes was unfortunately permanent. Besides, it weakened the ecclesiastical organization and, as such, contributed to the church's subsequent inability to resist Peter's reforms. Whatever the case, the precarious foundations of the old Muscovite ideology suffered irreparable damage under Nikon's all too arbitrary and aggressive leadership. The threat to the state was not forgotten.

The Synodal Period (1721–1917)

Peter (1682–1725), however, waited for some time before formally depriving the church of its leadership.[39] When Patriarch Hadrian died in 1700 the young tsar simply allowed the throne to remain vacant for twenty-one years. Only then did he issue the *Dukhovnyi reglament*, his famous *Ecclesiastical Regulation*, unilaterally abolishing the office of patriarch altogether (1721). The supreme authority in the church was no longer the patriarch but a collegiate body, the Most Holy All-Ruling Synod, composed of twelve ecclesiastics (three of whom were bishops), and a government official (a layman appointed by the tsar) known as the chief procurator. The latter, although not formally a member of the college, gradually became in fact the principal ecclesiastical administrator in the Russian state, its minister for religious affairs. In the nineteenth century he was given cabinet status and, as such, was the only spokesman or intermediary between the synod and the tsar. All in all, Peter had achieved his purpose: the quasitheocracy of old Muscovy with most of its Josephite assumptions was gone. In the future ecclesiastical authority would have no voice in Russia's national destiny.[40] Nor would there be any impetuous or aggressive Nikons, any second sovereigns to question the tsar's power. Indeed, "the fatherland need have no fear of revolts and disturbances from a conciliar administration such as proceed from a single, independent ecclesiastical administrator. For the common people do not understand how the spiritual authority is distinguishable from the autocratic; but marveling at the dignity and glory of the Highest Pastor, they imagine that such an administrator is a second Sovereign, a power equal to that of the Autocrat, or even greater than he, and that the pastoral office is another, and a better, sovereign authority."[41] The threat posed by the patriarch—the need to eliminate him as a potentially dangerous source of competition—could not have been expressed more candidly or explicitly.

As a matter of plain fact, the head of the Russian church (the tsar was acknowledged "supreme judge" of the synod but not head of the church) was no longer an individual, but an uncanonical body with no precedent in Orthodox canon law.[42] Neither its ideology nor authority was in fact derived from Orthodox tradition. As noted earlier, the synod was modeled on Protestant synodal bodies, thereby foreshadowing the later constitution of the Orthodox Church of Greece. So un-Orthodox in inspiration was the

Ecclesiastical Regulation that its chief author, Theophanes Prokopovich, equated the Orthodox practice of an independent and autonomous church headed by a patriarch with "popery."[43] This being so, it is not surprising to learn that at the dawn of the twentieth century virtually all the Russian bishops opted for a restored patriarchate. When pressed to name the reforms most needed by the church in 1905, the majority expressed the view that the synodal system was not an organic expression of the church's consciousness but an abnormal and indeed uncanonical phenomenon.[44] It simply had no institutional precedent in the entire history of the Orthodox church.

Peter, of course, was not concerned with either church history or canon law. On the contrary, his system was entirely and deliberately politically inspired. It had indeed come into being solely by an act of state legislation. His new creation accordingly was not viewed as a divine institution with historical or canonical precedents, but simply as a department of the state. Institutionally speaking, it was not part of the church but a state agency, part and parcel of Russia's secularized autocratic regime. A provision added to the lengthy *Regulation* in 1722 illustrates all too clearly Peter's view of the matter. According to this clause, a priest discovering from a confessing person any plot or seditious intent against the state had to disclose the information and the person's name to the secret police. That is to say, the priest was obliged to break the secrecy of the confessional. "And the sanctity of the confessional is not infringed by this disclosure, for the admission of an intended lawlessness which the confessing person is not ready to renounce and does not include in his sins is not a confession or a part of a confession, but a cunning trick to seduce the conscience."[45] Even the church's spiritual forces and powers were to be put to secular uses.

As is well enough known, it was not until November 4, 1917, that the church finally succeeded in throwing off its bondage to the state. Only then was the patriarchate again restored—with the election of Tikhon, metropolitan of Moscow—days before the overthrow of Kerensky's Provisional Government by the Bolsheviks. Doubtless Russia's past might have been different, as Aleksandr Solzhenitsyn argued recently in his eloquent testimony on the agony of the church under Soviet rule: "The study of Russian history during the last few centuries convinces one that the whole of our history would have taken a far more humane and harmonious course if the Church had not renounced her independence and if the people had heeded her voice in a way comparable, for instance, to Poland."[46] To be sure, the submission was real enough. Had the church not become an agent of the Romanov dynasty, things might have been quite different. And yet this should not obscure the fact that the Russian church in 1721 was divided, leaderless, and weak. Its endorsement of Peter's unilateral action was given under duress. The protests of Russian churchmen, not to mention the equally helpless objections of the Orthodox patriarchates of the East, were simply in vain. Clearly, the physically stronger tsar had the advantage. It is worth pointing out, moreover, that the surrender was neither total nor fatal. The Russian church did not lose either its identity or its spiritual vitality; nor did it deny its social and pastoral responsibility.[47] Its devout elders, pastors, and conscientious bishops continued their mission despite their disapproval of the new regime. It is not our task here to examine Russia's religious life in the last two centuries. Still, we need only point to the church's remarkable vitality and achievement in the areas of missionary work, spirituality, and education to realize that any sweeping condemnation of the synodal period would be historically misleading and inaccurate.

This, then, has been the historical tradition of church-state relations under Orthodoxy. As our synoptic account has shown, the historical experience of the Orthodox church has been very different from the history of the West. The East has never known anything like the powerful institution of the medieval papacy, or the legal and juridical categories of the West, with which Western Christianity has usually interpreted its relationship to the state. On the contrary, a utopian vision uniting church and state in a universal Christian society has frequently played the dominant role in the East. There were seldom, if ever, any juridical agreements separating secular from spiritual, state from church. All the same, neither in Russia nor in Byzantium was this vision ever fully realized. The state's eagerness to abuse its power would not permit it. What is Caesar's and what is God's will always be basically incompatible. The antinomy and the tension between them cannot be eliminated. Indeed, the fact that Caesar was seldom godly has often had a paralyzing effect on the church. True, this was not always the pattern in Byzantium or early Muscovy where the lay power was still Christian. However, in more modern times, as in Ottoman Turkey or imperial Russia, the inability of the church to resist the encroachments of the secular power has usually meant total domination by the state.

To be sure, the Eastern vision has often scandalized the West. Critics have frequently charged that as a result of its too close identification with the "establishment," the Orthodox church has had to abandon its social commitment and, indeed, to become indifferent to the world and its problems. As with most historical generalizations, however, this too is an oversimplification. We have noted in passing that the charge would not be entirely accurate for the synodal period of the Russian church. Nor is it a true reflection of the situation in Byzantium.[48] More seriously, the generalization is, to an unusual degree, a gross misunderstanding of the church's self-awareness. The church, it is true, is in the world, but it simultaneously must be totally not of this world. Thus, what critics have usually interpreted as escapism or quietism or a lack of responsibility is essentially an affirmative stand corresponding to Orthodoxy's understanding of itself as a sign of the Kingdom, as a sacramental and eschatological reality. The Eastern experience, in sum, cannot be viewed solely as a "withdrawal" or as a failure to involve the church in the world and its problems. To do so is to fail to recognize that the church cannot divorce itself from its eschatological source, from that which stands at the very center of primitive Christianity. To sunder itself from this reality, to transform itself primarily into a social agency is to relinquish its essential nature and vocation. Ultimately, "that which to a western 'activist' appears to be the cause of eastern 'otherworldliness' . . . is, in fact, the very condition of any true discovery of the world and the source of any genuine theology of Christian action and involvement in it."[49]

II

THE RUSSIANS AND ORTHODOXY

4

The Russian Orthodox Church

Philip Walters

When after 1917 the tsarist autocracy in Russia was replaced by a Marxist-Leninist dictatorship, the situation for the Russian Orthodox church as an institution in society altered radically. Government protection gave way to government persecution. The latter was to some extent a reaction against the former state of affairs: Lenin himself, in common with a large proportion of the intelligentsia in late-nineteenth-century Russia, was deeply hostile to religious institutions, which he saw as a tool used by the exploiting classes to keep the workers in subservience. For two centuries before 1917 the church's own creativity had been stifled by the tsarist government's protective hand, and while the mass of the peasantry remained deeply loyal to the traditional faith of the church, the educated classes were growing more and more frustrated with the church's apparent inability to respond creatively to the need for political and social change in Russia. By the beginning of the twentieth century, however, just such a creative response within the church was beginning to be formulated, and although the movement for reform of the church and of society itself along Christian lines was abruptly ended in 1917 and the church entered a period when it was forced to struggle for its very existence, the seeds sown in the twenty years before the Revolution were able to take root and to grow again in the twenty years since the early 1960s. By this time the Soviet government was practicing a new policy toward the church: toleration of a limited institutional existence for the church in the interest of the state's own pragmatic ends, coupled with a systematic discouragement of independent thought and action within the church. It has been the tension between these logically incompatible policies that has provided the context for the contemporary religious dissent movement in the USSR.

The Situation of the Orthodox Church in the Late Nineteenth Century

In the Russian Empire of the late nineteenth century the Russian Orthodox church at once enjoyed extensive privileges and suffered from serious restrictions, both consequent on its status as the established religion of the empire. Since 1721, when Peter the Great had abolished the patriarchate, the church had been part of the state's administrative machinery. It was run by the Holy Synod, a body of bishops which was supposed to be directly answerable to the tsar, but which was chaired by the chief procurator, a government-appointed layman who was the tsar's representative. His role, originally conceived as that of the tsar's watchdog to ensure that the synod's decisions did not violate the law of the land, had evolved in such a way that all effective power over the church was in his hands. From 1880 to 1905 the procurator was K. P. Pobedonostsev, a conservative who understood the church's primary function to be to promote the stability of the tsarist autocracy.[1]

The Russian Orthodox church was established by law as the state church, supported financially by the government and defended against its religious rivals by the laws of the empire. It alone had the right to proselytize, and until 1905 defection from the church by an Orthodox Christian was a punishable offense.

One area in which the Orthodox church and its clergy could obviously be of most use to the authorities was in combating the influence of non-Orthodox denominations over the population of the Russian Empire. In the late nineteenth century the church's efforts were directed primarily toward the Old Believers, the Eastern Rite Catholics, and sectarians of both indigenous Russian and foreign origin.[2]

Meanwhile, however, the Russian Orthodox church suffered from all manner of irksome restrictions. By the end of the nineteenth century the church was one of the few organizations in imperial Russia that could not acquire property freely. Every acquisition had to be authorized by the tsar. In theory these restrictions were designed to prevent the church from becoming responsible for unprofitable property, but it was felt that the real reason was that the civil authorities wanted to minimize the amount of property that would become tax-exempt on passing into the church's hands. The whole administrative structure of the church was hampered by inefficient bureaucracy. Bishops found it extremely difficult to govern their dioceses properly. Their activities at diocesan level were controlled by a consistory of which the chairman was appointed by Pobedonostsev himself; and in any case they were moved about too frequently to become really effective in any locality. Priests at the parish level—the "white" or married clergy as opposed to the "black" or monastic clergy from whose ranks the bishops were appointed—suffered from lack of contact with their spiritual superiors, financial poverty, and a large number of purely administrative duties laid on them by the secular authorities. They were for example required by law to report to the police on the activities and political views of their parishioners, and even on antistate attitudes gleaned during confession, although this was forbidden by church canons. There was widespread anticlericalism among the faithful, to whom priests appeared all too often as instruments of oppressive government policies rather than as protectors or spiritual advisers. The parish was moribund as a center for spiritual or even social life. Nevertheless, there is evidence to show that many priests were dissatisfied with this state of affairs, and in the early twentieth century there was agitation by priests for a more autonomous existence for the parishes. This was resisted by the authorities, who feared loss of local control and the emergence of priests as champions of popular grievances. Barred from higher church appointments and beset by contradictory claims that made their jobs extremely difficult, the "white" clergy were building up resentment against the administrative structure of both church and state, and their grievances were to feature prominently in the church reform movement of the coming years.

At times of natural disaster or civil disturbance, the clergy were expected to exhort their flocks to obedience and the quiet acceptance of suffering. Another vehicle for the promotion of civil obedience and the combating of revolutionary ideas was the system of parish schools. These schools certainly made a significant contribution to general education, particularly in the provinces, but their development after 1884 was a consequence of a decision by Tsar Alexander III, who agreed with Pobedonostsev that the best way to prevent the recurrence of the type of civil disorder that had characterized the 1860s and 1870s was to revive popular loyalty to the imperial system through religious education. The same policy applied to the theological academies and seminaries of the church. Discipline was harsh, and courses concentrated on spiritual and liturgical matters while condemning all forms of socialist or progressive thinking. These institutions became ever more notorious as hotbeds of student protest and rebellion, producing as well as priests a fair proportion of committed revolutionaries, of whom the most famous was Stalin himself.

The Intellectual Climate in the Late Nineteenth Century

Among that small section of the population of the Russian Empire in the late nineteenth century with higher or university education, and particularly among those belonging to the "intelligentsia" who were preoccupied with analyzing what was wrong with Russian society both socially and politically and with suggesting ways to put it right, there was almost universal antipathy toward the Orthodox church as an institution and toward religious faith in general. Atheism or positivism were characteristic of all sections of the progressive intelligentsia for decades before Marxism took hold in the later 1890s.

Throughout the nineteenth century, however, a certain proportion of the intelligentsia had remained committed to the development of social and political ideas derived from what they believed to be the true doctrines of Russian Orthodoxy. Called the "Slavophiles," as opposed to that group of the intelligentsia known as the "Westernizers," they believed that social and political institutions in Russia should be modeled on the Orthodox understanding of the community rather than on inappropriate enlightenment ideas from the West.[3] A central concept in classical Slavophilism is that of "sobornost," which may be defined as "individual diversity in free unity." The concept found concrete expression in such Slavophile proposals as the following: that the old Russian local community (*obshchina*) should be revived as the most important social unit; that the community should be run according to the Orthodox principle of unanimity rather than according to the divisive principle of majority rule, derived from Western Enlightenment models; and that the head of the Russian state, the tsar, should be the sacrificial beast of burden for the cares of the whole community rather than the autocratic ruler of both the bodies and minds of his people. No real attempt was ever made by the secular authorities to adopt any of the Slavophiles' suggestions, however. By the end of the century the relative optimism of earlier years about effecting change in Russia had faded, and Slavophiles tended to find themselves pushed either into overt reformist political action or else into explicitly supporting the autocracy in its unreformed state. However, Slavophile ideas underwent a revival in the late nineteenth and early twentieth centuries when they were adapted in the light of contemporary social and political requirements by Vladimir S. Solovev (1853–1900), the most influential Russian Orthodox religious philosopher of his time; in turn they influenced such thinkers as Nikolai A. Berdyaev (1874–1948) and Sergei N. Bulgakov (1871–1944). The ideas of all these representatives of the "Silver Age" of Russian culture, as well as of the "classical" Slavophiles, are of central importance in the development of "unofficial" Orthodox thought in the contemporary Soviet Union.[4]

When hopes for the introduction of liberal Western-inspired reforms in Russia began to fade after 1825, the imperial government for its part adopted a program that bore some external resemblance to certain aspects of the Slavophile program, but that in fact proved most appropriate to the preservation and further development of an autocratic and nationalist system in which the church would play a supportive rather than a critical role. The doctrine of "Orthodoxy, autocracy, and nationality" was first enunciated in 1832 by Count S. S. Uvarov,[5] and it guided the policies of the last two Russian tsars, Alexander III (1881–94) and Nicholas II (1894–1917), and also of Pobedonostsev. The latter had friends among the Slavophiles but found himself quite out of sympathy with any of the reformist aspects of their programs.[6]

The Church Reform Movement of the Early Twentieth Century

With its role thus determined for it, it is hardly surprising that by the end of the nineteenth century the church had completely failed to develop any practical program for social or political involvement within society with the aim of improving the lot of the peasant or industrial worker through such channels as charitable activity at parish level, trade union organization, or political education; nor indeed had it had the opportunity or stimulus to develop the theological equipment to justify this kind of involvement. In the face of growing political polarization in Russian society at the beginning of the twentieth century, however, a growing movement for reform in these directions was beginning to make itself felt within the church. It involved priests, bishops, and laymen, and the ideas being raised were to have led to the emancipation of the church from its close identification with the state and to its responsible involvement in social and political reform. Discussion groups and even Christian political parties were formed, activity coming to a head in the year of political liberalization 1905–6.[7]

While this struggle for political and social reform went on, the movement for ecclesiastical reform was enthusiastically endorsed by a significant proportion of clergy of all ranks, including bishops.[8] The basic point on which all were agreed was that the church should return to canonical self-government and that a national council (*Pomestny Sobor*) should be convoked as the instrument for effecting this. Most wanted a patriarch restored, but nobody was proposing that the Orthodox church should lose its primacy in the imperial system, nor that the autocracy should end;

and while many bishops of conservative tendency, like Antoni Khrapovit-sky, confined their reformist aspirations to the restoration of the patriarch, other conservatives were suspicious even of this step, which they sus-pected could lead to conflict between church and state. Representatives of the "white" clergy opposed the idea too, though for different reasons—they favored a thorough democratization of the church, with priests and bishops elected at the local level.

During 1903 the tsar was persuaded by the growing pressure for re-form in church circles and the press to take action. At the same time he was preparing to grant a measure of toleration to non-Orthodox faiths in the empire. Both moves were opposed by conservative members of the government, and by Pobedonostsev, but the latter began to lose control of the situation in 1903. The Toleration Manifesto of April 17, 1905, meant that reform of the Orthodox church was now urgent: it needed the insti-tutional strength to join the other newly legalized denominations in equal competition; the Orthodox church was now in the paradoxical position of having to watch impotently while newly legalized non-Orthodox churches began to hold conferences and revitalize their corporate life.

The Pre-Council Commission

Pobedonostsev tried to defuse the situation in 1905 by calling for a poll of the views of all the bishops, expecting that they would back his own view that as little reform as possible was necessary. He was disappointed: most called for radical reforms. Pobedonostsev retired as procurator after the October Manifesto of 1905, in which the tsar promised elections for a duma in 1906. A pre-council commission was then established by the new procurator. It was presided over by Metropolitan Antonii of St. Peters-burg and addressed itself, in various subcommissions, to identifying and debating the needed areas of reform before the council should actually assemble.

In May 1906 the relevant subcommission decided that the office of pa-triarch should be restored. Another subcommission discussed the desirable relationship between church and state. Some felt that, now that Russia was altering its political structure, the church ought to be wary of con-tinuing its close identification with the imperial system: the Duma was a secular body, potentially hostile to the church; and the church, in effect disestablished by the Toleration Manifesto, might soon have to fend for itself as one interest group among many in a pluralist society. In the end it was decided that the tsar personally, as Orthodox emperor, should remain as protector of the church, but that the church should have full internal

freedom and that the procurator should once again act simply as intermediary between tsar and church. The question of the relationship between
the church and the Duma was ignored. One subcommission considered
the internal organization of the church at diocesan and parish level, rec-
ommending greater autonomy for bishops and a revivified parish life: the
parish should become a real *obshchina*, with the rights of a legal person,
which would coordinate worship, religious education, and the social and
financial well-being of the community through self-help financial management and the promotion of local agriculture, industry, and charitable
works. Reform of the church court system was discussed. The need for securing greater independence for the church in managing church properties
was raised, as well as the question of whether subsidies on the traditional
scale would continue to come from the government. It was agreed that the
harsh discipline and narrow curriculum of the seminaries and academies
must be reformed.

The New Period of Reaction and the Events of 1917

Widespread civil unrest and the outspoken radicalism of the Duma during 1906 meant the end of the period of political liberalization. The tsar
suspended the pre-council commission at the end of 1906, no doubt fearing the development of another center for opposition beside the Duma.
Years of political reaction then set in, and the council was never summoned during the rest of the life of the empire (although a comparable
body was convened in 1912). Right-wing organizations such as the Black
Hundreds and the Union of Russian People flourished. The new prime
minister, Stolypin, was firmly opposed to the idea of a church council and
a patriarch, and planned (though without success) to set up a ministry of
denominations that would control the activities of all religious groups in
the Russian Empire, treating them all, including the Orthodox church, as
of equal status. Meanwhile, the court and the procurator, V. K. Sabler,
were falling more under the influence of Grigori Rasputin, whose scandalous life and dominant influence over the tsar's church policies combined
to frustrate church reformers and clear-sighted conservatives alike. Sabler,
who had been Pobedonostsev's deputy at the turn of the century, was
procurator from 1911 to 1915 and reassumed firm control of the church.
The church under his direction campaigned for right-wing parties in the
Third and Fourth Dumas, despite the continuing protests of large numbers
of the "white clergy." The reforming Metropolitan Antonii of St. Petersburg died in 1912. During the last years of the empire, the government
attempted to have docile reactionary men who supported Rasputin placed

in the leading sees of St. Petersburg, Moscow, and Kiev, but succeeded chiefly in keeping the most able men out of these positions. War and revolution soon engulfed the imperial system; the church, institutionally paralyzed, could only look on. When the tsar abdicated in February 1917, the synod welcomed the fall of the monarchy and hailed the February revolution as "the hour of general freedom for Russia."[9] It was during the period of the Provisional Government under Prime Minister Kerensky that the National Council was finally convened (August 1917).[10]

The conducting of elections to the council, its convening in Moscow, and its deliberations were a feat of organization at a time when civil society was disintegrating into chaos. The council was a landmark in the history of the Russian Orthodox church in another sense: it was the first council that represented the church as a whole. Of the 564 church members who gathered in Moscow, about three hundred—the majority—were laymen, and each member had one vote. The councils convoked in the sixteenth and seventeenth centuries had been composed of clergy only. In this way the 1917 council made substantial progress toward embodying the concept of sobornost.

It was clear that the council had no intention of abandoning the concept of the "ruling" role of the Orthodox church in the new Russian state. It also declared for obligatory religious instruction and for continuing financial support from the state. The first decision of the council was, however, to elect a patriarch, in order to ensure the autonomy of church rule in a time of chaos, despite opposition from a considerable minority of the "white" clergy who feared a perpetuation of the rule of the "black" clergy. The successful candidate was Tikhon (Belavin), who had recently been elected presiding bishop of the Moscow diocese.

The Bolsheviks were by now in the center of Moscow. Although the council continued its sessions until September 1918, none of its decisions except that of restoring the patriarchate was ever put into effect; but the fact that the church now had its own leader helped it to weather the storms to come, as did the fact that it had passed legislation reestablishing its pre-Petrine canonical conciliar structure and had delegated new responsibility to the parishes, which were therefore able to continue to function even when the central church administration was paralyzed.[11]

The Bolsheviks Confront the Church

The decisions taken by the council affecting the inner life of the church (which the church has never been able to put properly into effect) were of a wise and enlightened nature reflecting the best goals of the church reform movement. The council also passed a number of decrees on church-state relations which were based on the assumption that Bolshevik power would be temporary and which therefore turned out to be entirely unrealistic. It was these that the Bolsheviks were happy to seize on as proving the essentially reactionary nature of the church. At this stage, Bolshevik hostility was directed chiefly against the Orthodox church rather than at religion in general. Until the later 1920s, in fact, sects and churches that had been disadvantaged under the empire enjoyed greater freedom than they had ever known.

On January 23, 1918, the authorities issued the Decree on Separation of Church from State, which had the effect of disestablishing the Orthodox church: the state would not interfere in the affairs of the church, but the church would be deprived of rights within the state; the church would be separated from the educational system and religious bodies would no longer be allowed to own property. Throughout Russia church property was seized and violence and murder perpetrated against clergy and believers. The church lost all its educational and welfare facilities.

A few days before the decree, Patriarch Tikhon reacted in the name of the church to the authorities' hostile policies. He denounced their bloody deeds and the seizure of church property, called on the faithful to rise in defense of the church, and anathematized the Bolsheviks. It is clear that this denunciation was a political statement and that the church was now officially in opposition to the new regime. This policy continued for about a year. As it became obvious that that the new government was likely to stay in power, however, Tikhon tried to move to a position of political neutrality, but the regime was now on the offensive. In December 1921 a group of émigré clergy in Yugoslavia, the "Karlovci," condemned the Bolsheviks and called for armed intervention to unseat them. Tikhon's dissociation of himself and the church from these sentiments was ignored by the government, which chose to interpret the Karlovci message as representing the true attitude of the church within Russia. In 1922, during the widespread and serious famines that followed the Civil War, the authorities came upon an ideal excuse for a showdown. Tikhon had organized a church initiative to provide aid to the starving, but the government had rejected the church's help and now turned the tables. In February 1922 the state ordered that church valuables be sold to buy food for the famine victims, and Tikhon agreed that unconsecrated items could so be used. However, the authorities persisted in requiring valuables of any kind; the patriarch was bound to protest; he called on his flock to offer nonviolent resistance, but there were widespread riots. The whole incident was a strategic victory for the state, which succeeded in creating the impression that the church was resisting a humanitarian initiative out of respect for outmoded traditions and even for counterrevolutionary motives: the Karlovci clergy had voiced the hope that the famine might be used by the church to unseat the Bolshevik regime.

Many clergy were put on trial for resisting the seizure of church valuables. The most notable victim was Metropolitan Veniamin of Petrograd, who was executed. At many of these trials the government recruited certain churchmen to testify against their fellow believers. These men belonged to the "Living Church" or "Renovationist" movement, which by this time formed a kind of opposition party within the church dedicated to the support of Soviet power.[12]

The Ideology of the Living Church

It is possible to discover many lines of continuity between parts of the church reform movement before the Revolution and the Living Church. Some members of the prerevolutionary politically reformist "Group of 32" priests, which had had to cease its activities during the years of reaction after 1906, continued to promote Christian socialist ideas of an increasingly radical nature. After the February Revolution of 1917 a "League of Democratic Clergy and Laymen" was formed in Petrograd, including some former members of the "Group of 32" and advocating a socialist revolution. Aleksandr I. Vvedensky and B. V. Titlinov, later prominent figures in the Living Church, were members of this league. It is Titlinov who provides one of the most all-embracing pedigrees for the Living Church movement, enlisting somewhat indiscriminately the nineteenth-century Slavophiles, Dostoyevsky, Solovev, Tolstoy, participants in the Religio-Philosophical Meetings of 1901–3 that brought together church representatives and members of the secular intelligentsia, and the reformist priests of the First and Second Dumas.[13] The very breadth of this field should lead one to the correct conclusion that not all of these figures shared the later views of the Renovationists to the same or indeed any extent. Many early-twentieth-century progressive religious figures were later opposed to the Living Church and its aims: Bulgakov, who called himself a Christian Socialist, differentiated his own views from those of the revolutionary socialists of his own day, pointing out that his own socialism was a question of the pragmatic application of practical ethics, not the construction of a comprehensive worldview.[14]

As we have seen, the promotion of socialist political ideas before the Revolution lay particularly with the "white" clergy, and in its most positive manifestation the Living Church movement can been seen as continuing the aspirations of these radicalized clergy for social justice. Bishop Antonin Granovsky, by far the most attractive of the Living Church leaders, continued to champion these aspirations in their purest Christian-inspired form, as he had done before the Revolution, and to work toward purifying the liturgy itself and making it more accessible to the ordinary believer, by, for example, replacing Old Church Slavonic with Russian as the language of the liturgy.

There were other more equivocal aspects to the Living Church movement present from the very beginning, however. Certain of its leaders, notably Vladimir D. Krasnitsky, took up the interests of the "white" clergy as a distinct social class, and his own activities on their behalf came to be characterized as the aggressive pursuit of a set of narrowly defined objectives in which a predominant element was Krasnitsky's own self-aggrandizement. There is also an element of simple triumphalism in the Living Church. An examination of the background of many of the prominent Renovationists reveals the startling fact that they had been involved before the Revolution in such reactionary organizations as the Black Hundreds and the League of Russian People. The motive of such people seems to have been to stay on the winning side, and they have been compared with those former Marxists in Italy or Germany who when the time was right became fascists or Nazis.[15] As Vvedensky commented, "It is good to be someone who triumphs."

It is therefore impossible to speak of the Living Church movement as a united whole, or to characterize it simply as a "left-wing" movement within the church. Faced with a regime which called itself democratic and socialist but was proving ever more clearly its essentially authoritarian and centralist nature, men of diverse types could be attracted to the Living Church movement for widely differing reasons. It is a paradox, but perhaps an inevitable one in a political and social system built on a logical discontinuity between claims and reality, that by the second half of the 1920s the Living Church, with its close organizational identification with the security organs of the state and its theoretical advocacy of the official state ideology (socialism defined in terms of class interest), came to resemble the prerevolutionary "reactionary" patriarchal church that it claimed to have supplanted much more closely than did the traditional patriarchal church, which insisted on separation from the state and the preservation of its own autonomous worldview.[16] Incidentally, it is in the light of the experiences of the church in attempting to operate under Soviet power that we should understand the tendency for those contemporary Orthodox Christians in the Soviet Union who are seeking the freedom to develop the social, political, and artistic consequences of their faith nevertheless to hold tenaciously to what they perceive as the "traditional" doctrines of their church and to be suspicious of those who attempt to "update" the faith itself.[17]

The Fate of the Living Church

Patriarch Tikhon was indicted in May 1922, and Living Church leaders, with the support of the government, visited him in prison. They then announced that he had given them full executive powers, and they set up a "Higher Church Administration" with Bishop Antonin at its head. They began publishing a journal and extending their control over the dioceses, to which noncelibate bishops from the ranks of the "white" clergy were appointed. Several prominent patriarchal bishops went over to the Living Church, including the future patriarch of the Orthodox church, Metropolitan Sergii (Stragorodsky). The Renovationists soon controlled 80 percent of all church buildings in the USSR.

The Living Church then suffered from internal schism. After being censured by Krasnitsky, Bishop Antonin founded the "League for Regeneration of the Church," concerned with reforming the church's spiritual life, making services more accessible to the masses, and social and moral reform. He expressed the hope that the whole Living Church movement was motivated "not by clerical, caste or mercenary motives, but by elevated Christian socialist ideals." Krasnitsky was left to lead the rest of the Living Church, which he had declared to be working in the interests of the "white" clergy and to be for the church what the Communist party was for the state, controlling and guiding it in the interests of political goals.

Despite internal splits within the Living Church, early 1923 saw it in a stronger institutional position than the patriarchal church. It held a council in April and May of that year, expressing loyalty to the Soviet state and denouncing capitalism as a sin. It passed resolutions against the monastic orders and declared that married "white" clergy could become bishops.

It was not clear how far the Soviet authorities themselves were wholeheartedly behind the Living Church even at this stage. Some commentators see the Living Church in its 1923 council as trying to gain popularity both with the Soviet authorities and with the mass of believers by undoing some of its earlier reforms of church life and liturgy and thereby attempting to resemble the patriarchal church, which still commanded the allegiance of the mass of the believers. Certainly the Soviet authorities now seemed strangely reluctant to pursue the patriarchal church to extinction. Patriarch Tikhon's trial was postponed again and again; and then on June 25 he was released and began expressing his loyalty to the Soviet

regime and his determination never again to interfere in political questions. His release was marked by a mass return of the faithful to the
patriarchal church. The Soviet leaders may have decided that they had
better leave Tikhon as head of the church since he alone commanded this
kind of mass support. To the average believer the preoccupations of the
Living Church seemed both obscure and of minor importance. From now
on, both Tikhon and the Soviet government were hostile to the Living
Church, whose numbers and influence gradually declined, although the
last Living Church liturgy in the USSR was not celebrated until 1946.

Metropolitan Sergii's Declaration of 1927

On his release from prison Tikhon signed a *Confession* admitting the anti-
Soviet nature of his behavior hitherto. From the point of view of the state,
this was a powerful document: it left them the option of putting Tikhon
on trial for his self-confessed crimes at any future date if he showed
signs again of disloyalty to the state. However, there was a qualitative
difference between Tikhon's attitude and that of the Living Church, and
one that the Russian Orthodox church always sought to maintain. In his
Confession Tikhon made it clear that his crimes were his personally and
that the church did not share in his guilt. More significantly, Tikhon did
not promise to collaborate actively with the state, but limited himself
to the statement that he was "henceforth not an enemy of the Soviet
government." Certainly his confession did not cause any diminution of
Tikhon's popularity in the eyes of the faithful.

   Tikhon died in April 1925, leaving a *Testament* confirming his unwaver-
ing loyalty to the Soviet state. This did not prevent the Soviet authorities from imprisoning his three nominated successors. Leadership of the
church finally devolved on Metropolitan Sergii (Stragorodsky), who had
by now returned from the Living Church, [18] and had been designated as the
third successor to the third of Tikhon's original nominees. He was released
in 1927, and in July of that year he issued a *Declaration of Loyalty* to the
Soviet Union, "whose joys and successes are our successes, and whose setbacks are our setbacks." [19] Tikhon had moved from a position of implacable
opposition to the Bolsheviks to one of loyalty to the secular government
but political neutrality; by the time of Sergii's *Declaration* it was clear that
the Soviet authorities would be content with nothing less than the positive
endorsement by the churches of all aspects of Soviet domestic and foreign
policy. From 1927 to the present day this has been the position of the
hierarchy of the Russian Orthodox church. For his part, Sergii presumably hoped that he would now be allowed to run the internal affairs of the

church without interference from the state, and that the state would allow
the church to continue to exist within Soviet society without having to
compromise its spiritual integrity, as the Living Church had been logically
compelled, and indeed prepared, to do. This was to be a far from easy task.
Anatolii Levitin, a Russian scholar living in Switzerland, who has written
a massive volume on the subject, criticizes the Living Church for its voluntary self-subordination to the prevailing political regime, re-creating a
subservient role for the church similar to that which it had been forced
to play in the Pobedonostsev era. Russian émigré scholar Regelson agrees
with this assessment, and goes on to say that Sergii, in espousing the same
policy, did the patriarchal church a grave disservice.[20] It is difficult to assess
accurately the scale of reaction within the church to Sergii's *Declaration*.
Many clergy criticized Sergii; others commended him for making a wise
decision. A number of communities of believers went into schism, and
reports suggest that consternation and disorientation among the faithful
was very widespread, with a large consequent influx of believers into the
"underground" Orthodox church. But any such assessment must remain
largely academic because the events of the 1930s were soon to force all
believers into a more or less underground existence.[21]

The Holocaust of the 1930s

The Soviet attack on religion had concentrated in the first instance on the
Orthodox church. After about 1928, however, the antireligious campaign
became comprehensive and all denominations suffered equally. Although
according to the Soviet constitution the church is separate from the state
and any citizen may confess any religious faith, the practice of the state,
faithfully reflecting the policy of the Communist party as the only permitted political party, has been to encourage religious faith to die out by
means of education, propaganda, and simple persecution. All these methods have varied in intensity but remain constant features of Soviet life.
The 1930s saw the last of these methods applied with savage ferocity.

The basic law on religion, which remains fundamentally in force to this
day, is the 1929 Law on Religious Associations. While the 1918 law had
concentrated on demolishing the external edifice of the Orthodox church,
the 1929 law starts at the very bottom, making no distinction among
religions and defining the only religious unit for legal purposes as the
"dvadtsatka," a group of at least twenty people who are allowed to apply
to the authorities in their locality for registration as a congregation and
to use a registered building for the performance of their cult. It is important to realize that no other religious activity or institution has any

legal status: evangelizing, educating young people in religion, producing and distributing religious literature, organizing any kind of religious activity outside a registered building, or using donations to finance such things as libraries or medical and social aid are all either illegal or actively discouraged; hierarchies, central church administrative offices, theological academies and seminaries, official church publications, and monastic institutions exist only as long as the authorities deem it expedient to allow them to do so.

Despite Sergii's *Declaration*, he was never given the opportunity until the Second World War to give any practical demonstration of his loyalty. All religions suffered savage and comprehensive persecution during the late 1920s and 1930s, with particularly intense periods in 1928–32 and 1937–38. The context was the social engineering that accompanied the Soviet decision to undertake rapid industrialization and enforced collectivization of agriculture. The traditional way of life of the peasantry was brought to a violent end. There was widespread resistance to collectivization and fierce rioting on a massive scale. Millions were uprooted and moved to different parts of the country in mass population transfers; millions were executed, allowed to starve, or put into the spreading "archipelago" of forced labor camps.

During the first years of collectivization there was a savage antireligious campaign in the countryside. Church leaders and believers were arrested en masse and church buildings closed, destroyed, or converted to other uses. In 1932 the initial onslaught on the church came to an end, and although arrests and church closures continued, there were some hints of religious revival over the next four years. In 1936–38 the Great Purges marked another period of antireligious violence. The Communist party itself was purged and leading figures condemned in the course of show trials. Most of the surviving hierarchs of the churches were arrested, imprisoned, or executed as saboteurs, spies, or traitors.

By 1939 the Orthodox church had virtually ceased to exist as an institution: in the territory that was under Soviet control from 1919 to 1939 it is probable that no more than one or two hundred churches remained open out of a prerevolutionary total of some 46,000; clergy and laymen were in labor camps; and only four bishops remained at liberty. Contact between the hierarchy and their dioceses had all but ceased.

At the same time it must have been becoming obvious to the Soviet leaders that they had by no means succeeded in killing the faith among the population. They knew that an underground church existed, and no doubt suspected that when legally existing churches were closed the believers simply continued their religious activities in secret. In the mid-1930s the head of the League of Militant Godless made remarks indicating that some 57 percent of the Soviet population remained believers. The results of the 1937 census, which contained a question on religious affiliation, were suppressed, and the question did not reappear in the census of 1939.

The Second World War and Stalin's Volte Face

The situation of the church changed dramatically on the outbreak of the Second World War. The partition of Poland between Hitler and Stalin in 1939 doubled the number of Orthodox bishops in Soviet territory and increased the number of open churches by 40 percent. Stalin now for the first time made use of the church by allowing it to organize church life in the annexed territories. In 1941 a further dramatic development took place: Hitler violated the Nazi-Soviet pact and invaded the USSR. The first to react to this crisis was not Stalin but Metropolitan Sergii, who called on the Orthodox faithful to resist the aggressor and defend the motherland: he took full advantage of this opportunity to act in the spirit of his *Declaration* of 1927, although strictly speaking his action contradicted the law of 1929 that in effect forbids religious believers to involve themselves *as believers* in any social or political activity.

Meanwhile, a remarkable revival of church life was taking place in those areas of the Soviet Union passing under Nazi control.[22] The Nazis had not yet formulated a policy for the churches on formerly Soviet territory, so in practice there was tolerance for religious activity in occupied areas. The evidence of continuing mass adherence to religion that was available in the 1930s was now confirmed in concrete terms. In some western dioceses the number of churches reopened under the Nazis totaled up to half the prerevolutionary figure. In the Kiev diocese a handful of churches remained open in 1941; after the Nazi invasion about seven hundred were opened, as compared with a prerevolutionary total of 1,410. According to German estimates in October 1941, 95 percent of Ukrainians were believers.

The situation for the church in the areas of the USSR that remained under Soviet rule did not alter immediately. Nevertheless, Metropolitan Sergii sought to continue to demonstrate the church's willingness to help the nation at this time of crisis. In January 1943 he sent a telegram to Stalin asking that the church be allowed to open a bank account for the donations of the faithful toward the defense of the motherland. In granting this request, Stalin granted de facto recognition to the church as a legal person, again in discord with the 1929 legislation. Within ten days over 3 million rubles had been raised in Leningrad alone, together with another half million specifically designated for the building of a tank column named after the Russian hero and Orthodox saint Dimitri Donskoy.

The fundamental change in church-state relations came in September 1943. In that month Stalin summoned Sergii to the Kremlin; and four days later he was elected patriarch of the Russian Orthodox church at a specially convened council. The government then set up a Council for the Affairs of the Russian Orthodox Church, under the layman G. G. Karpov, to deal directly with the church hierarchy—a move which amounted to de facto legal recognition of the church as an institution. Patriarch Sergii died the following year: his successor Aleksii was enthroned at a magnificent council in 1945 attended by foreign Orthodox dignitaries. The 1945 council also introduced new directives on the administration of the church, centralizing administrative power at the expense of the dioceses and parishes, whose powers in this respect had theoretically been extended by the council of 1917–18.

Churches continued to be reopened,[23] the number of clergy and bishops grew, theological schools[24] and monasteries began to function again, and the church was allowed to publish an official journal. It is important to remember, however, that there was no change in the legislation governing religion: Stalin's policy was purely pragmatic and depended on a liberal interpretation of the law of 1929.

There were compelling reasons why the Soviet state needed to make some concessions at this time. Some steps had to be taken at a time of national crisis to avoid alienating the high proportion of the Soviet population who remained religious believers. It was also necessary to keep these people out of the underground and members of a church under centralized control. Most importantly, perhaps, Stalin had seen that the church could now be of positive help to the state in its diplomatic relations with the outside world. The first task for the church was enthusiastically to endorse the war effort. After the end of the war various other fields of activity for the church opened up, and the new policy of relative toleration of religion was to continue until the end of the 1950s.

Church-State Relations as Established in the 1950s

The two leading personalities in the church during the second half of the 1940s and the 1950s were Patriarch Aleksii and Metropolitan Nikolai,[25] who was in charge of foreign relations. They have been criticized for their alleged subservience to the demands of the state, but both men were genuine patriots who were able to serve most of the interests of the state with a clear conscience.[26] At the same time both men were astute politicians as well as individuals of considerable spiritual integrity.

Between 1945 and 1948 the USSR was extending its control over what are now the Soviet satellites in Eastern Europe. The church's commission was simultaneously to extend its own control over the Orthodox churches of Europe and the Near East, a task it accomplished with considerable success. Aleksii planned, as the culmination of his policy, to take over the traditional prerogative of the ecumenical patriarch in Constantinople (Istanbul) and hold a pan-Orthodox conference in Moscow, demonstrating Moscow's supremacy. This initiative was thwarted and replaced by a conference in 1948 to celebrate five hundred years of Russian autocephaly; but the pro-Soviet tone of the proceedings undermined their universal acceptability.[27]

After 1948 a new field opened up in which the church could be of use to the state: in promoting the concept of "peace" as a peculiarly Soviet aim in the postwar world, at the same time branding the capitalist countries as warmongers. Most important in this operation from the point of view of the Soviet authorities is that the church should appear to be an autonomous body in Soviet society giving an independent endorsement of Soviet policies. The World Peace Council, founded after 1948, supported the Soviet initiative. The peace movement came into its own with the outbreak of the Korean War, which the church, echoing the state, condemned as an example of blatant American aggression.

After the death of Stalin in 1953, Soviet foreign policy became more subtle but pursued the same ends. The Christian Peace Conference was founded in Czechoslovakia in 1958 and was a forum for genuine debate until the Soviet invasion of Czechoslovakia in 1968. Although the Russian churches were represented on the CPC, it was presided over by Czech churchmen. The Soviet Union was however able to use the forum of the CPC to promote many of its own aims and concepts, including the notion of "peaceful coexistence." This notion, especially beloved of Khrushchev, implied the avoidance of major war between the superpowers but did not exclude the use or encouragement of armed force in countries deemed to be struggling to free themselves from colonial oppression by the capitalist imperialist powers.

The Orthodox church has hosted peace conferences at home, the most important having taken place in Moscow in 1982. These conferences obviously could not be held if the government disapproved of them; and there are in fact clear advantages for the government in allowing and promoting them. Conferences of this kind give foreign delegates the impression that the churches of the USSR are autonomous bodies spontaneously endorsing the current policies of the Soviet government. Moreover, uninformed observers are left with the impression that the churches are acting freely in organizing these events and draw ill-founded conclusions about the general level of religious freedom in the USSR and even speculate about the influence the church may be able to exert on Soviet policy-making. One Western reporter wrote that the 1982 conference "highlights . . . the extent to which the Church has managed, in recent years, to reestablish its influence in an atheistic society."[28] To set this misleading statement in its context we need simply to quote the patriarchate itself, which notes that Orthodox church involvement in the global peace movement is "in accordance with the foreign policy of the USSR."[29]

Another international forum in which the Soviet Union achieved influence through the services of the church was the World Council of Churches, of which the Russian Orthodox church became a member in 1961. The wcc has come to be dominated by the voices of the churches of the Third World, and radical solutions to the social and political problems of these countries have been proposed more and more regularly over the years. The Russian Orthodox church naturally welcomes such proposals, which tend to coincide with the foreign policy aims of the Soviet state for Third World countries.

One other important area in which the Soviet church can be of service to the state is in building up a favorable image abroad of conditions within the Soviet Union. At the same time as endorsing the alleged Soviet desire for world peace, the church has systematically helped in concealing from Western audiences the extent of the restrictions on religious liberty that operate within the Soviet Union.[30] Thus in 1961, when the Orthodox church entered the wcc, it was able to conceal the fact that a massive and unexpected antireligious campaign had been under way in the Soviet Union since 1959, and no mention was made of the absence from the delegation of Metropolitan Nikolai, who had in fact just been removed from office and was to die, some claim murdered, a week after the conclusion of the assembly. His successor, Metropolitan Nikodim, was in Geneva; he was to be in charge of the church's foreign relations until 1972 (and continued to be very influential in this field up to the time of his death in 1978).[31] Similarly, in the late 1960s the Soviet churches were active in minimizing the impact in the West of the news of the schism in the Baptist church, a consequence of increased state pressure. In general, Soviet church delegations always stress that religious believers in the Soviet Union enjoy complete freedom to practice their faith.

The Orthodox church, then, was assigned in the 1950s an important auxiliary role in the promotion of the Soviet image in the world at large.

Possibilities for the church within the Soviet Union, however, remained extremely restricted. As we have seen, all religious activities beyond worship in a registered building are systematically discouraged. Punishment by the state of religious dissenters never ceased, even during the 1950s, nor did antireligious propaganda, though its intensity fluctuated. The discontinuity that many of the faithful began to perceive in the postwar period between the image of a strong and flourishing church for foreign consumption and the reality of a deeply deprived church at home was one of the factors that gave birth to the religious dissent movement of the 1960s and 1970s. The image of what the church could perhaps become if its leaders stood up more vigorously for their rights impelled dissenters to start urging their hierarchs to be much more vigorous in resisting state pressure.

Khrushchev's Antireligious Campaign (1959–64) and Its Effects

According to some observers, the accommodation between state and church during the 1950s allowed a certain amount of complacency, not to say triumphalism, to creep into the church establishment.[32] Although the church was now enlisted as an active proponent of Soviet political aims, the state was by no means reconciled to the existence within the USSR of Christianity as an alternative worldview. Antireligious activity varied in intensity during the 1940s and 1950s but was never allowed to subside entirely.[33] Atheist propaganda was resumed as early as 1944. It was now based on the notion not that religion was "reactionary"—the church had after all proved its patriotism during the war—but that it was "antiscientific." In 1950 the Soviet press called for more serious antireligious work, but at the same time warned against offending individual believers. In 1954 there was a brief but violent burst of antireligious activity, later known as the "Hundred Days Campaign." After this there were five years of relative toleration, until in 1959 Khrushchev suddenly launched a vigorous antireligious campaign that was a traumatic shock to religious believers throughout the Soviet Union.

The immediate reasons for this campaign have never been fully elucidated. Some have theorized that Khrushchev was coming under criticism in the Politburo for failures in certain fields and needed success in some self-contained venture to restore his reputation. The underlying reason, however, is undoubtedly the increase in overt religiosity since the death of Stalin.[34] Khrushchev's liberation of prisoners from the labor camps in the mid-1950s was a symptom of his intention to introduce reforms into the Soviet system, but one effect was to reintroduce into society a large number of priests, believers, and new converts to Christianity. By the time of his secret speech in 1956 denouncing Stalin's excesses, a religious revival was well under way in the Soviet Union, and it was given extra impetus by the general disorientation following this very denunciation: Stalin was demoted from his godlike status, and something had to take his place.

In the course of the antireligious campaign from 1959 to 1964 two-thirds of the 20,000 Orthodox churches then legally operating were closed, and many were pulled down. Priests and believers were arrested and put on trial. Again, no change in the 1929 law was involved.[35] The fact that this campaign could take place at all demonstrated to believers that their activities were supported by no legal guarantee and that the continued existence of the churches was as precarious as it had ever been. The Khrushchev antireligious campaign was the shock that gave birth to the contemporary religious dissent movement.

During the campaign the Baptist church was impelled by state pressure to introduce a number of measures to curtail its own evangelistic and educational activity. A group of Baptists who were not prepared to accept these restrictions broke away to form the *Initsiativniki* or "Unregistered Baptists" in 1961. They decided not to seek registration for their congregations and thus achieved the freedom of the outlaw. Similar pressure was brought to bear by the state on the Orthodox church. In 1961 an irregularly convened synod of bishops—the first comparable gathering since the council of 1945—was persuaded to accept a framework for a new relationship with the state.[36] In particular, the priest was deprived of all authority at the parish level, and executive power handed over to the *dvadtsatka*, which, as was well known, usually contained nonbelievers with a watching brief. A comparable schism to that in the Baptist church did not take place in the Orthodox church, but dissenting voices were raised appealing to the church hierarchy to be more steadfast in resisting state pressure. In 1965 the Orthodox priests Fr. Gleb Yakunin and Fr. Nikolai Eshliman wrote to the patriarch and the Soviet authorities[37] protesting excessive interference in church matters by the Council for Religious Affairs[38] and urging the patriarch to take action; unsuccessful attempts to have the 1961 regulations rescinded were a central feature of dissent within the Orthodox church during the 1960s. The only fully canonical council of the Russian Orthodox church since 1945, held in 1971 to elect Pimen patriarch as successor to Aleksii, did not tackle any of these issues. The fact that discontent was still alive within the church was however brought dramatically into focus by the intervention of Solzhenitsyn, for the first time publicly identifying himself as an Orthodox Christian, with his *Lenten Letter* to the patriarch in 1972,[39] again exhorting the church hierarchs to stand up to the state. In

1979 Fr. Gleb Yakunin put forward proposals to the effect that the Russian Orthodox church ought indeed to produce an "unofficial" wing, similar to the unregistered Baptists, which would grow in size as centralized Soviet control of the pressure on the "official" church grew.[40]

Achievements of the Church in Its Internal Life

As we have seen, the state's definition of the church's permissible activity is extremely narrow, confined as it is in legal terms to the practice of the cult within the four walls of a registered building. A certain latitude has at times been allowed to the church, however, most notably during the period 1943–59, and it is interesting to see that the church leadership has tried to take initiatives to improve the quality of its internal life within the bounds of what seems feasible at any given time in pursuance of the aim of Metropolitan Sergii to win at the price of political loyalty a certain internal freedom for the church.

When theological educational establishments were set up in the mid-1940s the church made efforts to improve the quality of the students presenting themselves for courses. A stricter selection procedure was soon introduced, together with entrance examinations and examinations at the end of each year.[41] At that time the church also took advantage of the opportunity provided by the state to enhance its prestige among the believing Soviet population, not only building new churches but introducing improvements into the liturgy and church singing.[42] The new generation of priests produced in the postwar seminaries and operating in the churches were generally of a higher caliber than those previously available.

In the post-Khrushchev period the hierarchy has continued its efforts. The seminaries have more than doubled their intake over the last decade and a half. When it is difficult to build new churches, the church has adopted the policy of "repairing" old church buildings, after which they often emerge considerably expanded in size. The church has tried, with varying success, to resist state pressure on at least two monasteries, the Zhirovitsy Monastery in Belorussia and the Pochaev Lavra. To some extent the church hierarchy has also attempted to defend a number of prominent religious dissidents who have incurred the state's anger. Fr. Dimitri Dudko was at first moved from church to church rather than suspended from his priestly functions; Fr. Gleb Yakunin, although suspended as a priest in 1965 by the patriarch, was later given the post of reader, and it seems that in 1978 or 1979 an offer may have been made to him by the church to reinstate him as a priest; by 1987 Fr. Gleb had in fact been reinstated.[43] Fr. Vasili Fonchenkov, a member of Fr. Gleb's "Christian Committee for the Defense of Believers' Rights," was removed from his position as a professor at the Moscow Theological Academy but still functions as a parish priest.

Some idea of the degree of confidence that the state has in the bishops of the Orthodox church to refrain from any activities that would be unwelcome to the state can be gleaned from the so-called *Furov Report*. This document principally comprises extracts from three reports, dated 1968, 1970, and 1974, signed by V. Furov, a deputy chairman of the Council for Religious Affairs, on the contemporary state of the Orthodox church.[44] Most interesting in the present context is a comprehensive categorization of all the functioning bishops of the church into three groups. The first includes seventeen bishops who "confirm in word and deed not only their loyalty but also a patriotic devotion to socialist society"; the second includes twenty-three bishops who are loyal to the state but also aim to bring as much life into the church as possible through their administrative and preaching activities; and the third includes seventeen bishops who "try to evade the laws on religious cults." Patriarch Pimen, who is generally known for an excessively supine attitude in the face of state pressure, comes into the first category; but it is interesting that, for example, the late Metropolitan Nikodim is placed in the second category. The metropolitan demonstrated, evidently in common with a good proportion of the episcopate, an ability to combine wordly cunning in relations with the state and the outside world with the zeal of true dedication to the Christian ideal in his pastoral manifestation.

The Movement for Religious Rights in the Orthodox Church

As we have seen, many Orthodox Christians were dismayed by the inability of their hierarchy to withstand in any effective way the pressure of the state when this was applied with renewed force under Khrushchev from 1959 to 1964. The initial concern for the Orthodox dissent movement was to try to awaken the hierarchy to what the dissenters saw as their simple Christian duty in this respect. By the early 1970s, however, the field was widening. Orthodox dissenters were involved in a general renaissance of religious awareness (which will be dealt with in the next section) and also in the growing movement within the USSR for civil and religious rights.

The aspirations of religious activists in this latter field were given a considerable boost by the ratification of the Helsinki Final Act in 1975, in which the Soviet Union participated. The Soviet Union had hoped that the Helsinki Conference would confirm the post–World War II frontiers of the European countries; but the conference was designed to debate both "security *and cooperation*" in Europe, and it was the presence of clauses relating to the latter concept that caused long and difficult discussions between East and West. The Final Act does indeed contain a number of clauses specifically relating to human and religious rights; the Eastern bloc countries evidently agreed to these as the price for their main objective. It is impossible to say how far the Soviet Union ever envisaged acting on these particular undertakings; but the fact that the Final Act was ratified at a time of "détente" certainly led religious activists in the Soviet Union to hope that some kind of breakthrough in securing their rights might indeed be in the offing.

In November 1975 Fr. Gleb Yakunin and the Orthodox layman Lev Regelson sent a report on the infringement of the rights of religious believers in the USSR to the general assembly of the World Council of Churches in Nairobi. This initiative sparked off the first public debate on this topic ever held by the wcc.[45] Encouraged by this response, Fr. Gleb went on in December 1976 to found the "Christian Committee for the Defense of Believers' Rights in the USSR," which began sending regular and plentiful supplies of documents to the West detailing the difficulties facing religious believers of all faiths and denominations.[46]

Fr. Gleb was to be disappointed in his hope that responsible individuals and organizations in the West would take up the challenge of his committee and bring pressure on the Soviet authorities to improve religious conditions within the USSR. Ignoring the spirit of Helsinki, the Soviet government soon moved decisively against all the unofficial Helsinki monitoring groups in the USSR, including Fr. Gleb's specifically Christian version. Fr. Gleb was arrested in 1979 and sentenced to ten years' deprivation of liberty for "anti-Soviet agitation and propaganda."

Orthodox Dissent: The Return to Prerevolutionary Roots

Russian nationalism, which had been thoroughly rejected by Lenin and the Bolsheviks, was revived by Stalin as part of the apparatus of his autocracy. However, his concern was with the outward form alone; and his sponsorship of Russian nationalist symbols did not accompany any promotion of intellectual or theological inquiry into the historical content of nationalism. Stalin's accommodation with the Orthodox church was just one aspect of his policy in this respect; as we have seen, however, the marriage was purely one of convenience from the point of view of the Marxist state.

Stalin died in 1953, and in 1956 Khrushchev initiated his de-Stalinization campaign, which exploded the myth of Stalin's doctrinal and moral infallibility in which a whole generation of Russians had been taught to believe. The ideological vacuum that followed provoked considerable interest among the population in reestablishing contact with their pre-revolutionary roots and history.[47]

The first searching came in the form of an interest in ancient Russian art and architecture. For example, in 1965 the All-Russian Society for the Preservation of Historical and Cultural Monuments was founded by a decree of the council of ministers of the RSFSR to halt the destruction of historical buildings, including churches. It seems that concern with the Russian cultural heritage must have had its champions at the highest level of government.

In this climate, Orthodox Christians began to rediscover the heritage of the nineteenth-century Slavophiles, of Solovev, and of those such as Berdyaev and Bulgakov who had attempted to relate Solovev's ideas to twentieth-century society. In 1964 the "All-Russian Social-Christian Union for the Liberation of the People" (VSKHSON) was founded in Leningrad by a small group of Orthodox Christians under the leadership of Igor Ogurtsov.[48] The union did not preclude the armed overthrow of the communist dictatorship, but its program for the new Russian state included elements derived from a liberal Christian interpretation of Russian nationalist themes. The union was broken up in 1967 and Ogurtsov sentenced to twenty years' deprivation of liberty.

The samizdat journal *Veche*, of which nine issues appeared in 1971–74 under the editorship of Vladimir Osipov, acted as a forum for neo-Slavophile ideas from all parts of the spectrum.[49] Osipov's aim was to provide a platform for "loyal opposition" not only to the policies of the state but to those of the state church as well. Osipov's aim reflected that of Eshliman and Yakunin in writing their 1965 letter—to persuade the Soviet authorities to obey their own constitution.

The priest Fr. Dimitri Dudko, of peasant origin, boldly held question-and-answer sessions in the various churches he occupied between 1973 and 1976, inviting his ever-growing flock to bring him their problems as Christians in an atheist society. His teachings are thoroughly imbued with traditional Orthodoxy. Fr. Dimitri in turn influenced a number of young people who in Moscow in 1974 founded a "Christian Seminar on Problems of the Religious Renaissance" and subsequently a journal, *Obshchina* (*Community*);[50] parallel groups arose in Leningrad. Aleksandr Solzhenitsyn is himself a fine example of a religious thinker who has discovered his spiritual roots in the Orthodox thinkers of the nineteenth and early twentieth centuries.

The social programs of those influenced by Slavophile ideas range from the liberal internationalism and ecumenism, derived directly from Solovev, of the Christian Seminar and the authors of the symposium *Iz-pod glyb* (*From under the Rubble*),[51] through the more purely nationalist preoccupations of such as Osipov and Solzhenitsyn (based on the perception that Russia is in a state of moral decay caused by the loss of a national religious consciousness), to the extreme Great-Russian chauvinism, xenophobia, and anti-Semitism that characterize the document *Slovo natsii* (*The Nation Speaks*).[52] As far as political ideas are concerned, three similar divisions can be observed: a "liberal" group (including Solzhenitsyn), a "centrist" group (including Osipov), and a "rightist" group (including Shimanov and the authors of *Slovo natsii*). The centrists and liberals want a government (for many of them, a monarchy) limited by certain built-in safeguards. It is not clear what form these safeguards should take, since all Slavophiles are wary of placing reliance on Western-type democracy, which they see as divisive and contrary to the spirit of sobornost, or on written constitutions. They prefer social and political relationships to be guided by the principle of Christian love. Solzhenitsyn, for example, wants a system of laws as a check on autocratic arbitrariness, but firmly denies that a Western-style democratic system is practicable for Russia at the present time. At the other end of the spectrum the Orthodox layman Gennadi Shimanov has advocated that in order to survive now that Marxism-Leninism has lost credibility with the Soviet public, the Communist party of the Soviet Union should simply transform itself into the Orthodox party of the Soviet Union, retaining all its trappings such as the secret police and using the same methods as at present to remain in power.[53] What he proposes might produce something very akin to the system prevailing under the last two tsars, or, more likely, a blending of Russian nationalist ideology with a Bolshevik power structure, with the loss of any distinctive Marxist-Leninist or Christian elements. This is a revival of the aim of the National Bolsheviks of the 1920s.[54] Many commentators have asserted that this kind of idea has adherents in the higher ranks of the party, [55] and while there is no sign of an initiative in the direction of a rapprochement with Russian nationalism from the party itself, many of the prominent dissenters of the 1970s were released from prison within the first year and a half of Gorbachev's tenure.

The Present Situation

The practice of religious faith is not illegal, but the authorities have a wide range of sanctions available to use against religious believers whose activities are unacceptable. Two articles of the penal code punish those who infringe the law on separation of church from state and who perform religious rituals that are deemed harmful to the health of citizens or encroach on the person or rights of individuals (Articles 142 and 227 of the Criminal Code of the RSFSR). The wording of these articles is so vague as to make them applicable to almost any kind of religious activity. Articles that do not relate to religious activity but that are regularly used against religious believers include Article 206, "hooliganism" (often in connection with alleged resistance offered to those carrying out searches of believers' homes), and Article 209, "parasitism" (useful in the case of believers who cannot find anyone to employ them); and for the most active believers, particularly those producing or distributing unofficial religious literature, Article 190–91 ("slandering the Soviet system," maximum penalty three years in prison or labor camp) and Article 70 ("anti-Soviet agitation and propaganda," maximum penalty ten years in prison or labor camp plus five years' exile).

An analysis of the penal code is of limited value only, however, since the activities of believers are known to be subject to secret laws. The Council for Religious Affairs communicates these to its local representatives, and it is not deemed expedient to inform believers about their content and existence. Some secret laws that were suspected by believers to exist were introduced into the first comprehensively revised religious legislation since 1929, published in 1975, and so became public for the first time. The most substantial innovation introduced in the 1975 legislation concerns the role of the Council for Religious Affairs at the local level: its powers in making decisions about the fate of local churches, whether to close them or open new ones in response to the petitions of believers, are greatly extended.[56]

There is also a wide range of administrative sanctions and simple extralegal pressures that can be used against believers. Atheist education is compulsory from kindergarten, and antireligious propaganda is endemic throughout public life.[57] A religious believer who falls afoul of the authorities is liable to defamation in the press without the right of reply. He may find it difficult to obtain adequate housing or permission to live in a particular city. His life and property may be threatened by antireligious activists in his locality. He will find it difficult to obtain more than the most menial job. If he has a responsible job or is receiving higher education and is discovered to be a believer, he will probably be dismissed.

Since 1979 the Soviet authorities have adopted a policy of comprehensive repression of all forms of dissent, including the religious variety. The church itself has had a hand in this. Fr. Dimitri Dudko, for example, was arrested in 1979 and kept in solitary confinement for six months, at the end of which time he appeared on Soviet television to recant his anti-Soviet activities. It seems likely that he was visited by at least one leading hierarch of his church who persuaded him that self-restraint is required if the church is to survive as an institution in Soviet society. Contemporary Soviet policy toward the church has not reverted to the modus vivendi established during the 1940s and 1950s. The state has continued to make use of the church for various purposes of its own both abroad (as an apparently autonomous body independently endorsing Soviet domestic and foreign policies) and at home (to help in discouraging dissent). In return, the state makes occasional concessions to the church that do not, however, involve substantial changes in the basic structure of church-state relations.

In general, the activities of the church continue to be scrutinized and controlled most closely by the government's Council for Religious Affairs; and at local level, especially since the Brezhnev era with its weakening of centralized control, the actual experience of individual believers and of religious communities depends to a large extent on the relative antireligious zeal or apathy of the local secular authorities, as well as on the degree to which the local dvadtsatka has been infiltrated by unbelievers.[58]

Conclusion

By the last decades of imperial Russia the church as an institution had been thoroughly co-opted by the state to serve the latter's political and social aims. During the 1920s and 1930s the Bolshevik regime rejected all notion of cooperation with the church despite the readiness first of Patriarch Tikhon to adopt a position of political neutrality and then of Metropolitan Sergi after 1927 to give active support to all aspects of Soviet reality. Only since the Second World War has the Soviet government begun to make use of the services of the church hierarchy, and the thoroughly pragmatic technique of allowing the church a very limited area of freedom in exchange for its active support of the regime remains state policy to the present day.

One theme that has always had ambiguous implications for church and state from the point of view of cooperation or conflict has been that of Russian nationalism. Throughout the later tsarist period the Russian Orthodox church became ever more closely identified with the Russian nation. The concept of the Russian people as a "God-fearing nation" has always been a fertile theme in Russian Orthodox thinking; but of course there have always been practical political consequences of the doctrine of a "national church" that have been exploited by the secular power. In the early Soviet period nationalist sentiment of any sort was energetically discouraged; but since the early 1940s the question of the role and even the survival of the Russian nation within the multinational Soviet Union has excited recurrent interest not only among Orthodox believers but also in certain circles of the party and the government. We have seen how at various times during the postwar period, particularly since Marxism-Leninism has been losing its creative impetus, the Russian nationalist theme has attracted the champions of a wide variety of views from, at one extreme, those Russian Orthodox reformers who are deeply concerned about halting the moral decay and promoting the spiritual regeneration of their nation to, at the other, those with an interest in preserving Soviet power by any means available, including the adoption of a secularized Great Russian chauvinism.

Opposition within the church to the policies of the state has varied in nature according to the kinds of tension arising out of varying relationships at different times between church and state. In the late tsarist period the main aim of the "dissenters," and later of the majority of the clergy and a significant proportion of the bishops, was to free the church from state sponsorship with all its ambiguous implications. During the persecutions of the 1920s and 1930s resistance among the Orthodox population took the form of rejection of the Living Church and later of continuing mass loyalty to the patriarchal church, even though the latter had been virtually annihilated as an institution. Under the present policy of limited accommodation, operative since the Second World War, opposition within the church both to the policies of the church leadership and to the policies of the state toward the church has crystallized most obviously in the dissent movement.

There is, however, another sense in which the church, by the very fact of its continuing existence within Soviet society, represents a form of opposition—a form that though largely potential is more permanent than any "dissent" movement and more difficult for the authorities to deal with, arising as it does out of the very paradox of the continuing legalized survival of religion in an atheist totalitarian state. The Orthodox church in the USSR (and, of course, the other religious bodies that enjoy a legal existence) constitute a unique anomaly: they are the only public bodies allowed to exist that are not under the direct leadership and control of the party apparatus and for which adherence to Marxism-Leninism is not a condition of membership. The leaders of the patriarchal church, as opposed to those of the Living Church for example, have always been conscious of the need to preserve the inner freedom of the church as far as possible. One effect of Soviet persecution of the church at all levels has been to purify it. Even to become a leader of the church demands readiness for self-sacrifice and is no easy road to choose. While a proportion of the hierarchy have certainly chosen to cooperate beyond the minimum level necessary with the security organs of the state, they are evidently in the minority and are generally identifiable to believers. The point is that there is no room in the church for men interested simply in a profitable career, and there is ultimately little danger in the present circumstances that the fact that a tension exists between the claims of the state and the aspirations of the church will be lost or obscured. Men such as Krasnitsky of the Living Church, who sought a career out of manipulating slogans relating to the rights of a particular "class," or such as Vvedensky, who found personal gratification in the triumphalist stance of his church, would not nowadays look to the Orthodox church as a forum in which to pursue these aims. The motivation of Patriarchs Tikhon, Sergii, and Aleksii in seeking an accommodation with the state was precisely in order to preserve true Orthodoxy, and, while giving total political loyalty to the state, to create an area, limited though it might be, in which they could have real freedom to organize the inner life of the church. That this area of freedom is in fact so extremely small is the consequence of almost intolerable and systematic pressure exerted by the state against the church rather than of any loss of perception of the essential distinction between church and state on the part of the Orthodox church.

The Russian Orthodox church has never been able to realize its full potential as an autonomous contributor to Russian or Soviet social or political life. The church has traditionally concentrated on the celebration of the liturgy as the central pillar of its religious activity, and inasmuch as each believer makes his own life a liturgy, he enters into unity with the body of the faithful, both living and dead, this entire relationship being described in terms of "sobornost." During the nineteenth and early twentieth centuries it proved possible for Orthodox philosophers and theologians to construct social and political doctrines on the basis of the concept of sobornost. The church as an institution made no attempt to assimilate these until 1905, however, and after 1917 it has been unable to do so, prevented as it is by law from involving itself in any kind of social or political activity. There are however ample grounds for believing, on the basis of the self-examination to which the church subjected itself between the end of the nineteenth century and 1917 and the witness of numerous Orthodox dissenters during the 1960s and 1970s who were looking back for inspiration to the earlier period, that the church would be quite capable of playing a responsible auxiliary role within Soviet society, helping to relieve social evils such as alcoholism and the breakup of the family and to run all kinds of charitable and medical institutions, if the Soviet authorities ever saw fit to allow it to do so.

FACT SHEET

Russian Orthodox Church in the USSR

Year of autocephaly
  Moscow Patriarchate 1589

Current strength of the church (1986)
  50 million faithful, approx.
  6,000 priests, approx.
  67 bishops
  1,300 monks and nuns, approx. (1970)

Chief news organs
  Zhurnal Moskovskoi Patriarkhii (monthly; approx. 20,000 copies)
  Journal of the Moscow Patriarchate (in English) (monthly; approx.
    2,500 copies)
  Bogoslovskie trudy (roughly twice a year; approx. 3,000 copies)

Number of churches and church facilities in operation (1986)
  6,500 churches, approx.
  3 theological seminaries
  2 theological academies
  6 monasteries, approx.
  10 convents, approx.
  1 publishing house

Patriarchs since 1900
  Patriarchate vacant (1721)–1917
  Tikhon (Belavin), 1917–1925
  Locum tenentes, 1925–1943
  Sergii (Stragorodsky), 1943-1944
  Aleksii (Simansky), 1945–1970
  Pimen (Izvekov), 1971–present

5

Publications of the Russian Orthodox Church in the USSR

Jane Ellis

The publishing department of the Moscow patriarchate chaired by Archbishop (now Metropolitan) Pitirim of Volokolamsk produces religious publications whose frequency and print runs are very restricted. The regular publications are the monthly *Journal of the Moscow Patriarchate*, the Ukrainian-language *Orthodox Herald* (*Pravoslavny visnyk*), and the *Bulletin of the Moscow Patriarchate*. The occasional publication *Theological Works* (*Bogoslovskye trudy*) is issued roughly twice a year; there is an annual church calendar; occasional small editions of the Bible and New Testament are printed; and there are occasional editions of liturgical and prayer books. The limiting factor in the department's production is that the state controls all paper supplies in the Soviet Union and makes only limited amounts available to the church. The state also controls all printing facilities, and the church's publications are all produced on state printing presses. The church was allocated three hundred tons of paper for all its publications during 1980. Archbishop Pitirim explained to a Western journalist: "This year, I published 50,000 copies of the Bible and the same number of the New Testament. We would have liked to produce more, but I have to reserve paper for the monthly journal. . . . Every year I have to balance my production like this, in order at one and the same time to serve the faithful and pursue theological education, to educate the people . . . and to deepen the knowledge of the servants of the cult."[1]

The limited paper allocation made to the church is clearly a means by which the state restricts the publication of religious literature. It is difficult to see how there can be a shortage of paper in the Soviet Union, which, with all the forests of northern Russia at its disposal, produced over 5.5 million tons of paper in 1978; this had increased to 5.7 million tons by 1983. Paper is one of the USSR's chief exports.[2] Furthermore, visitors to the Soviet Union are told that the USSR produces more books annually than any other country in the world. This means that the very low production of Scriptures and other religious literature (as well as some of the world-famous classics of Russian literature) is a matter of state policy.

Further evidence of this is provided by the fact that the churches are restricted in the amount of religious literature they are able to import. If shortage of paper were really the problem, importation would be the obvious way to remedy the dearth of religious literature, although it is true that this might be an embarrassment to the Soviet government, as constituting an admission of their inability to provide for their citizens' needs.

Sources of Information

Before proceeding to discuss the publications of the Russian Orthodox church in detail, a word should be said about the sources that have been used. Most of these fall into two categories: first, the official publications of the Moscow Patriarchate itself, principally *The Journal of the Moscow Patriarchate* (JMP), which will be discussed in detail later in this essay; and second, samizdat, the unofficially produced (usually typed or handwritten) documents that circulate clandestinely in the USSR and often find their way abroad. Of particular importance in the latter category are two samizdat documents that, for the purposes of the present essay, we have termed the Yakunin Report and the Rusak Report.

The Yakunin Report was written by Father Gleb Yakunin, an Orthodox priest who was imprisoned from November 1, 1979 to March 10, 1987. His report, dated August 15, 1979, is an analytical survey of the various aspects of the official existence of the Moscow Patriarchate. As such, it includes some observations on the church's publications.[3] Yakunin became known in the West as the coauthor (with layman Lev Regelson) of an open letter to delegates to the 1975 assembly of the World Council of Churches (WCC) in Nairobi, which received extensive publicity.

The Rusak Report, which at first appeared in the West under the pseudonym of Vladimir Stepanov, was written by Deacon Vladimir Rusak, who for many years worked in the editorial offices of the *Journal of the Moscow Patriarchate*. He was dismissed from this post, and suffered other hardships, after completing work in 1980 on a history of the Russian Orthodox church since 1917. Rusak recounted his experiences in an appeal to the 1983 assembly of the wcc in Vancouver.[4]

Another very important source is, strictly speaking, neither official nor unofficial: it is an official report that has been made available unofficially—or "leaked." This consists of extracts from reports of the Council for Religious Affairs under the Council of Ministers of the USSR dated 1968–74, apparently from a series of annual reports made to the Central Committee of the Communist Party of the Soviet Union (cpsu). The Council for Religious Affairs (cra) is responsible for seeing that Soviet legislation on religion is obeyed and for overseeing the life of the various religious bodies in the Soviet Union. The cra reports, as we shall call them, are an extremely revealing source for studying aspects of the church's life that are normally hidden, and one that provides firsthand evidence of the attitude of government officials to the church. The fact that they have reached the West through unofficial channels naturally raises questions as to their authenticity, but these are dispelled upon a careful study of the text. What is said there conforms both to what is already known of the functions of the cra and to what is said by the samizdat documents written by Russian Orthodox believers. In fact, it is largely true to say that the cra reports do not so much provide new information for students of the Russian Orthodox church as confirm what had already been pieced together from other sources, or what had been strongly suspected but could not be proved.[5]

Publication of the Scriptures

Bibles are not officially on sale anywhere in the Soviet Union. They are published, with official permission, only by recognized churches, and may be obtained only through local churches. (Apart from the Russian Orthodox publications, the Baptist church, the Georgian Orthodox church, and the Armenian Apostolic church have produced small editions of Scriptures in recent years.)

In addition to the 1979 editions of the Scriptures, the Moscow patriarchate published editions of the Bible in 1956, 1968, and 1976, the New Testament with Psalter in 1956, and the New Testament in 1976.[6] The 1976 edition marked the one hundreth anniversary of the publication of the first Russian Bible. Various figures and estimates have been given at different times for the sizes of these various editions. They quite often conflict, and so it is impossible to provide any reliable estimate of the numbers of Scriptures printed by the church. In particular, the figures provided by Rusak, who must be assumed to have more inside knowledge than the other sources quoted, often differ considerably from figures previously quoted. The 1956 edition was thought to number 25,000 New Testaments and either 50,000 or 25,000 Bibles.[7] The 1968 edition of the Bible, shared with the Baptists, was estimated to number up to 30,000 or 40,000 copies.[8] The 1976 centenary edition was quoted as numbering 100,000 Bibles and 75,000 or 50,000 New Testaments.[9]

In addition to these editions, Archbishop Pitirim announced in November 1983 (while on a visit to Finland) that the church had published 70,000 Bibles that year.[10] This has been widely reported, but there has not been any independent corroboration, so far as is known at present. When the figures are totaled, they show that since 1956 the Moscow patriarchate has published between 275,000 and 340,000 Bibles, plus 150,000 New Testaments. This is clearly woefully inadequate for a church widely believed to number around 50 million members. Foreigners have often remarked on the shortage of Bibles, both in the Orthodox church and among other denominations where study of the Scriptures is much more central to worship and personal devotional life. More than once foreign visitors to the theological schools have met young men studying for the priesthood who have no Bible of their own.

All the Bibles published by the Russian Orthodox church since 1917 have been in Russian. This means that many members of the church whose native language is not Russian must either read the Scriptures in a foreign language or make do with such prerevolutionary copies as have survived. This particularly affects Ukrainians, in whose republic there is the greatest concentration of Orthodox churches in the Soviet Union.

The Russian Orthodox church has not been permitted to import any Scriptures from abroad (although the Baptist church was allowed to import 25,000 Bibles at the end of 1978). Orthodox church leaders do accept gifts of small numbers of Bibles from church delegations visiting the Soviet Union. However, it appears that they are not distributed to believers, according to an experienced, Russian-speaking churchman who visited Moscow a few years ago. While this person was being shown around a church, a caretaker, taking advantage of the visitor's being left on his own for a few minutes, showed him into a very large storeroom packed from floor to ceiling with Scriptures that had been given as gifts by various foreign delegations, all carefully labeled with the date and name of the donor. When the room became full, the caretaker said, they would take a few Bibles out and burn them to make room for more.

Importation of Bibles has become a sensitive issue, particularly after an incident that occurred in 1978. A commentator on Moscow Radio, in reply to an American listener who wanted to know if he could bring a Bible into the USSR, stated: "The answer I was looking for [at the office of the Moscow patriarch] was not long coming. And to be completely frank with you, it was also unexpected. It seems that several years ago the Russian Orthodox Church officially applied to the Soviet authorities requesting that measures be taken to ban the import of Bibles not corresponding to the canonical text accepted by the Russian Orthodox Church. This request was agreed to."[11] This was an astonishing statement, implying as it did that the Russian Orthodox church preferred its members to have no Bibles at all rather than to read unauthorized translations. It was widely reported, in tones of indignation and incredulity, in the Western press. At that time Bishop Makari of Uman was representing the Russian Orthodox church in Geneva, and, evidently unaware of the source of the statement, he reacted strongly to reports of it in the Western press, which he described as "pure invention, typical of the western press," adding that the allegation "was quite idiotic."[12] Within a very short time Makari was recalled to the Soviet Union.[13] He has not returned overseas since (except on visits), although he had spent the entire eight years of his episcopal career up to 1978 representing his church abroad.

The sensitivity of the Soviet authorities concerning the importation of Bibles and New Testaments is also shown by the difficulties tourists have experienced in bringing even quite small numbers of Bibles into the USSR. It is hard to see the justification for this, since there is no law against bringing Bibles into the country. Although there are regulations prohibiting the import of "anti-Soviet" literature, it is not easy to see how Bibles can come into this category, as they have been officially published in the USSR. However, in practice tourists who have more than one Bible in Russian or another language of the USSR will have the extra copies confiscated, if they are discovered. That it is possible to bring in one Bible is confirmed by the Moscow Radio commentator quoted above: "You cannot bring in a large number of Bibles, more than one, in fact. But—and this is an important but—no customs official will take away your personal Bible."[14]

At present there is no sign that the shortage of Bibles in the Russian Orthodox church is likely to be remedied. Even the extent of the shortage is hard to estimate. No doubt many Orthodox believers have Bibles surviving from before the Revolution (in which case they will be in the old orthography), or, in the case of the Western republics, before the Second World War. It is true that reading and study of the Bible does not play the vital, irreplaceable role in the personal devotional life of Orthodox Christians that it does in the Evangelical churches in the USSR. Nonetheless, there is little doubt that most Orthodox believers would wish to have their own personal Bibles if it were possible. In addition, there must be many people on the fringes of church life who would be glad to have a Bible of their own. This adds up to a deficit of many millions of Bibles, and it is clear that the small occasional editions that are being authorized at present cannot meet a need on this scale. However, the church is evidently using to the full such opportunities as it has. Printings of the Scriptures have become more frequent and larger in recent years. A new translation of the Bible into modern Russian has been undertaken by members of the Leningrad Theological Academy in cooperation with the London-based United Bible Societies, who have been working on it for some years. The Gospel of John has been completed, but recent reports suggest that the translation is proceeding only very slowly, if at all.[15]

Liturgical Books

The situation is much the same as regards prayer books and liturgical books: although these have been published more frequently in recent years, there is still a great need for more. The appendix to this essay lists publications since publishing activity was resumed in 1946. In the first ten years, only a few small service books were produced. From 1956 (the same year as an edition of the Bible was published) the situation improved: a prayer book was published, and in the following years a number of liturgical books were produced. These were chiefly for the use of priests and were clearly intended to provide them with all the many Orthodox orders of service and instructions on using them: liturgies, sacraments, the many special rites, the daily services—the hours, matins, vespers—and the special services for saints' days and other commemorative occasions, of which there are many. If the church's activities are confined to worship, it is logical that its publishing program should concentrate first and foremost on providing the books needed for worship. For some unknown reason, no service books were published between 1965 and 1970, when the prayer book was published again, but in a longer form than the 1956 edition. More service books were printed during the 1970s. One of them, according to the CRA, was in an edition of 10,000 copies, which means there would have been enough for every active (as opposed to retired) priest to have a copy. In 1974, according to the CRA report, there were 5,994 priests. In 1979, after some delay, the first two volumes of a projected twelve-volume series of a *Manual for Priests (Nastolnaya kniga svyashchennosluzhitelei)* were published. If the CRA's figure of 20,000 copies of the first volume is correct, there are more than enough for all the active priests in the Soviet Union, and it is likely that copies are being sent to priests in the

overseas dioceses too. The year 1981 saw a burst of publishing activity:
the 1970 prayer book and the 1973 psalter were republished in a joint
edition numbering 150,000; the third volume of the *Manual for Priests*
was issued; 20,000 copies of the *Book of Hours* were published; and 20,000
copies of the second part of the *Psalter with the Order of Services* appeared
(the first part having been published in 1962).[16] Clearly the scope of the
publishing is increasing significantly, with the emphasis on literature for
public worship rather than private devotions, as is natural in a church
where corporate worship is so central.

Other Publications

The journal *Bogoslovskye trudy* commenced publication in 1960. Only
five issues had been published by 1970, but since then it has been issued
roughly twice a year. Issues No. 23 and No. 24 were published in 1983.
The CRA reports, the Yakunin Report, the Rusak Report, and other observers all agree that its circulation is 3,000 copies. The periodical has an
impressive editorial board that includes professors from both theological
academies and a few bishops, under the chairmanship of Metropolitan Antonii of Leningrad. However, its contents are rather dull. The majority of
the articles so far published have been on liturgical and historical subjects.
There is good reason for this: it is clearly important to use the church's
only theological publication to transmit basic knowledge about liturgical
practice to the clergy, since this is the major part of their ministry. Furthermore, Orthodox liturgics is so deeply traditional and so resistant to
change that it would be next to impossible to introduce any new ideological content into it. The state does not appear to have made any attempt to
do so, no doubt regarding the subject as an arcane and obsolete one best
left to the church. It is therefore in the interests of both church and state
to publish articles on a subject in which the church need fear no ideological
subversion and which the state regards as irrelevant. The preponderance
of historical articles may be explained by the fact that in Orthodoxy, with
its great emphasis on tradition, it is customary to treat current issues and
problems in the light of what the church fathers and the great luminaries
of the past have said about them. However, it is also true that in Soviet
literature and scholarly writing in general authors frequently retreat to
historical subjects because of the great ideological difficulties involved in
expressing any views on contemporary issues. Not infrequently they use
Aesopian language when discussing historical subjects to express views on
contemporary issues in a way that an experienced Soviet reader knows
how to interpret. This factor has no doubt compelled *Bogoslovskye trudy*

to concentrate more on the church's past than on its present. The emphasis on liturgics and history, useful though it may be, has meant that there is almost no evidence of original creative thinking in the church's only theological publication. The other subjects covered have included a series of papers presented at talks with the German Evangelical church and the Finnish Lutheran church, which cover the doctrines of both sides on such basic issues as baptism, salvation, and the Eucharist; a few articles on Orthodox teaching on the Incarnation, the Resurrection, and the Dormition of the Mother of God; and articles on the problems of translating the Bible into Russian. The periodical has also published some articles by widely respected Orthodox writers of the recent past, such as Father Pavel Florensky, V. N. Lossky, and Bishop Ignati (Bryanchaninov). While opportunities for publishing remain limited, the church is no doubt right to restrict itself to such basic matter, but there is no question that the livelier minds in the church would welcome something more stimulating if only the CRA and the censor would permit it.

Among other publications, the annual church calendar deserves mention. The calendar is a large-format eighty-page illustrated book giving information about feasts and saints' days, the organization and history of the church, and some facts about other Orthodox churches. According to the Rusak Report, this desk calendar and a wall calendar were published in editions of 50,000 copies up to 1964, and 40,000 copies thereafter.[17] The CRA report for 1974 states that 50,000 copies were printed annually, along with 40,000 copies of the wall calendar.[18] In 1979 Archbishop Pitirim stated that a total of 100,000 copies were to be printed the next year,[19] indicating a 10 percent increase over six years. However, bearing in mind that the calendars supply the overseas dioceses[20] as well as the Soviet ones, this is sufficient for only six or seven calendars per parish in the USSR. In fact, many are not distributed to the parishes, especially those most distant from Moscow, and one reliable source in 1982 said that even Moscow parishes receive only three to six copies each, depending on the size of the parish. The London diocese had great difficulty in acquiring copies of the 1982 calendar. Rusak noted that in 1979, one thousand calendars were sent to the CRA, plus others to district executive committees. He also gives several examples of shortfalls in the number of calendars received from the printers, the largest of which was 3,050 in 1970.[21]

The overseas publications of the Moscow patriarchate are *Messager de l'exarchat du Patriarche Russe en Europe Occidentale*, published in Paris in French and Russian; *Stimme der Orthodoxie* (The Voice of Orthodoxy), published in East Berlin in German; *Egyhazi Kronika* (Church Chronicle), published in Budapest in Hungarian; *One Church*, published in New York in English; and *Kanadski Pravoslavni Visnyk* (Canadian Orthodox Herald), published in Emonton partly in English and partly in Ukrainian.[22] The CRA reports also mention a bulletin published in Japanese in Tokyo with which the Moscow patriarchate has some connection. It seems that the publishing department does not exercise direct editorial control over the Paris, New York, and Edmonton publications, but that they restrict themselves to materials provided by the publishing department. The ties with *Stimme der Orthodoxie* in East Berlin are much closer, according to a CRA report, which states that the *JMP* editors "offer their literary and photographic materials every month and pay honoraria for articles published in the bulletin by authors (living in the Soviet Union)." This section of the CRA report refers to publications in the Soviet Union not noted elsewhere. It states that the publishing department "maintains relations" with "an annual church calendar and archpastoral festive and other messages in the Estonian language" and with "messages for Christmas and Easter and other periodic archpastoral addresses" issued by "Riga, Ufa and a few other dioceses."[23] It is not clear what "maintaining relations" means, but the inference is that these diocesan messages are not subject to direct editorial control by Moscow and are therefore probably issued after consultation with the local CRA commissioner.

The Journal of the Moscow Patriarchate

The *Journal of the Moscow Patriarchate* commenced publication in 1931, but after a few issues it was forced to close down in 1935, and it did not resume publication until 1943.[24] Since that time it has been published continually every month. Its editorial offices were located in the Novodevichi Monastery in Moscow until the opening of a well-equipped, purpose-built office close by in 1981. An English-language edition of the journal has been published since 1971; it consists entirely of translations from the Russian edition, though the items are sometimes shortened slightly, and some are omitted. The translations, according to the CRA, are done by highly qualified people outside the publishing department;[25] these appear not to be native English-speakers, and, considering this, the translations are generally of a high quality. Both the Russian and English editions have twelve issues a year. An additional special issue was published in 1978 describing the celebrations of the sixtieth anniversary of the restoration of the Moscow patriarchate in 1977.

In common with other religious publications in the Soviet Union, the print run (*tirazh*) of the *JMP* is not indicated, although this information is included in all other books and periodicals published in the USSR. This

is further evidence of Soviet sensitivity over the amount of officially published religious literature. According to a CRA report, the print run in both
1970 and 1974 was 15,000 copies.[26] The Yakunin Report in 1979 estimated
the print run at about 20,000 copies, though without supporting evidence.
However, in an interview with a foreign journalist in 1979 Archbishop
Pitirim gave the figure as 25,000 copies.[27] It is strange that Pitirim should
suddenly reveal a figure that had been kept secret for so many years, and it
seems probable that his figure is exaggerated. This is so because the most
recently available figures, those in the Rusak Report, are much closer to
the CRA's 1974 figures. Rusak gives a general figure of just under 14,000
copies a year, and a specific figure of 15,100 copies in 1977. (He notes that
the special 1978 jubilee edition was published in 25,000 copies, plus 5,000
copies in English.) Rusak reports that the Moscow churches each receive
ten copies of the journal, and that "in a village parish no more than ten
people know of the existence of the *Journal of the Moscow Patriarchate*,
and apart from the priest, who receives at very best only one copy either
for himself or for the church, even fewer read it."[28]

The print run of the English edition of *JMP* is given by the CRA and the
Yakunin Report as 3,000, but Pitirim, in the above-mentioned interview,
reduces it to 2,500. The English edition suffers a financial loss, since copies
of it are distributed abroad free of charge. A CRA report, which points
this out, states that copies of the Russian edition are also given away free
and that this adds up to a "significant deficit."[29] Rusak, more specifically,
says that one-third of the print run, 4,622 copies, is distributed free of
charge: this includes 3,930 abroad and forty-four to the CRA and other
state institutions. He also states that every edition of the English version
costs eight to ten thousand rubles.[30] The fact that an English edition of
JMP is published at all, given the shortage of religious literature in the
USSR, may seem surprising, since the amount of work involved in translating, editing, and printing must be considerable. However, expense is
evidently not a limiting factor; it is only the restriction on paper supply
that has to be taken into consideration. The fact that the Moscow patriarchate (with, as always, the approval of the CRA) is willing to expend
some of its precious paper on an English edition of its journal is a strong
indication of its wish to improve its contacts with churches overseas, and
of the state's backing for this. However, it may be going too far in this direction by publishing occasional English-language editions of books about
the church. The book about the church's life published on the sixtieth
anniversary of the restoration of the Moscow patriarchate (*The Moscow
Patriarchate, 1917–1977*) is well produced and has photographs on every
page, both black and white and color. The purpose of this and other books

is clearly to convey the impression that church life is continuing normally and that no real problems are being encountered. Though the book has the merit of bringing the Russian Orthodox church to the awareness of foreign churchmen, it is simultaneously promoting a one-sided view of the church that is indistinguishable from Soviet propaganda. It is clearly not in the church's interests to foster such a misconception. An English-language book entitled *The Local Council of 1971* was printed in 3,000 copies.[31] The Yakunin Report, mentioning the great need for religious literature, is probably right to refer to this book as literature "of an official (*offitsiozny*) type, needed by no one." It seems that the CRA is leading the church into a misordering of priorities in publishing literature of this kind when, as the Yakunin Report reminds us, "religious literature for the general reader [in the Soviet Union] is not published at all."[32]

Like Bibles, the *Journal of the Moscow Patriarchate* and other religious publications cannot be purchased at bookshops or any other public place in the Soviet Union. They are distributed only through the churches, although the method of allocating and distributing copies is not known. The CRA reports state that the journal is distributed through two channels, but at that point the text breaks off and there is a gap, so we do not know what the channels are.[33] The *JMP* is not listed in Soviet catalogs of periodicals, and it is not possible for individual believers to subscribe to the journal by mail.

The material in *JMP* is divided into sections that, as a CRA report notes, "have already become traditional."[34] The description of them given by the CRA in 1974 could be applied almost in its entirety to the 1984 issues. There is an official section giving the texts of messages from the patriarch and decisions of the Holy Synod; a section on church life that includes biographies of new bishops, accounts of important festivals, reports from the theological schools, news from the dioceses, and obituaries; a section entitled "In Defense of Peace" that reports on the church's activities within the Soviet Peace Fund and with several international organizations; a section describing the life and history of other Orthodox churches; a section on "Ecumenical Contacts"; a theological section, which, in the skeptical words of the CRA report, "contains reports on different aspects of the study and propaganda of the Bible, interpretation of its legends, explanations of some church festivals, materials on the life and activity of many 'Holy fathers' of Russian Orthodoxy."[35] There is also a section explaining aspects of divine services, such as the Creed, and a short bibliographical section describing recent publications of the church or of other Orthodox churches in socialist countries.

The CRA report makes one or two interesting comments about the con-

tent of *JMP*. It states that its "distinguishing characteristic" is "the op-
timistic character of the overwhelming majority of its material." This is
due to the fact that "in the opinion of many theologians, believers in the
USSR have found their place in life among non-Christians (atheists), and
that the experience of the last thirty years of the ROC [Russian Orthodox
church] inspires hope and has an exceptional significance for the whole
of Christianity and the whole world."[36] The CRA's own attitude to this
is not altogether clear. Presumably they approve of the positive attitude
to the situation of the church that they see reflected in the pages of its
journal, but one senses that they may be uneasy at such a wholehearted,
even hopeful, embracing of the given situation. However, elsewhere in the
report the CRA indicates that it views the church's optimism as misguided:

> The journal is the transmitter of the whole policy of the ROC, its
> most important platform by use of which the ideologues of Russian
> Orthodoxy try to preserve and strengthen the positions of religion
> and the church, to conceal from the reader the hidden manifestations
> of crisis which are actually taking place in the ROC, to create for
> religion the reputation of a socially progressive force, and to raise its
> prestige in the eyes of believing citizens in our state and abroad.[37]

This is a curious and rather ambiguous comment, since as we have seen
it is primarily the CRA that is responsible for ensuring that the church's
problems are not aired publicly and that it presents itself in a good light
to the world. Why then should it complain if the church does just that
in the pages of *JMP*? Implicit in this comment by the CRA is an admission that it does in fact regard the church's oft-proclaimed well-being as
illusory. However, its attribution of the church's eventual demise to "hidden manifestations of crisis" (*skrytye krizisnye yavleniya*), rather than to
its own efforts, is less than convincing, since it makes no attempt to explain how "manifestations" can simultaneously be "hidden." The tortuous
bureaucratic phraseology reveals the basic ambiguity of the comment.

The CRA remarks that with regard to the peace movement the journal
"maintains a realistic position" but is less approbatory of the journal's attitude to the Christian's role in society. It states that the attempt to reconcile
Christian and communist ideas in believers' minds "obliges churchmen to
impart a sciencelike [*naukoobrazny*] form to theology." It quotes a *JMP*
article by an East German theologian as saying: "The Gospel contains
within itself a tendency to socialism, to a rupture with the class society, to
confrontation with the feudal and bourgeois-capitalist form of life." One
might expect that the CRA would approve these words, but in fact it does
not, because the passage goes on to claim that the Gospel "explains the

world and simultaneously changes it." The CRA considers this to be claiming too much for religion: "Here there is an obvious glimpse of a desire to
idealize Christianity, to place it above all other theories, including above
the theory and practice of Marxism."[38] This is surely precisely what one
would expect to find in the journal of a Christian church. There is a hint
here that the CRA would prefer the journal to give at least equal importance
to Marxism, which does not augur well for the Christian integrity of the
journal. The CRA evidently does not wish *JMP* to say anything that would
lead its readers to think the church has any role to play in society: in the
Soviet Union any beneficial influence in society is the prerogative of the
Communist party. The CRA report quotes a paragraph from *JMP* which
explains that Christians must be involved in social life, helping to change,
renew, and transform it; but it is introduced with the comment that the
"ideologues of Orthodoxy" are "mystifying the role of the church" in this
way because they are attempting to "establish themselves in our conditions, and in doing so guarantee themselves a right to the future."[39] In
this statement the CRA reveals that it sees the church only as an institution attempting to prolong its own existence, not as an organism with
any intrinsic merit. The question of whether the church *has* in fact any
contribution to make to society is not even raised; it is simply assumed
that any influence it could have would inevitably be pernicious, and must
be opposed. As in other areas of church life, we see that the CRA's chief
concern is to cut the church off from society, to isolate it altogether. This
is strikingly shown, perhaps unconsciously, in the phrase quoted above,
"establish themselves in *our* conditions." This assumes that the whole of
Soviet life belongs to "us"—the party and the state—and that, though
religious believers are recognized to be citizens, they have no part in "our
conditions," but form a kind of unwanted excrescence.

The CRA report concludes by remarking that there are many articles
about saints and holy places in the journal, which aim to give believers
examples worthy of imitation in the Christian life and are intended "to
promote the preservation or the revival among believers of the old conceptions, customs, and traditions of 'holy places.'" The fact that these could
inspire believers in their daily lives is a matter for the CRA's disapproval,
and it promises to be more vigilant in future: "Control over them must be
strengthened in future, by having a more exacting attitude to manuscripts,
and removing from them propaganda about 'holy places' and other materials which could activate the church." The CRA's ideal, evidently, is a
journal that would not cause a believer to be in any way inspired or motivated to any kind of action by what he reads there. The church is to
be made to remain exactly as it is, not changing or influencing anyone

or anything. However, the CRA realizes that it would be hard for *JMP* to do anything of the sort, since: "in practice the journal does not reach ordinary believers because of its small print run."[40]

Censorship of *JMP*

The content of the *Journal of the Moscow Patriarchate* comes under close scrutiny from both the CRA and the Soviet censor, to whom all published matter in the Soviet Union is submitted before publication. Anatoli Levitin, a well-known samizdat author who emigrated in 1974, worked on *JMP* between 1956 and 1960 and has described how censorship was carried out:

From the very first days of my work at the journal I was convinced that an unbelievably harsh censorship prevailed over it. Immediately after an article had been written and accepted by the editors, it went to the Council for Religious Affairs.[41] The Council for Religious Affairs has an unlimited power of veto over any article. If it makes use of this right and forbids the article, the conversation is over, the article won't be published. If it makes corrections, the article may appear in a shortened form. However, the matter does not end here. When an issue of the journal is made up into pages, it must still be checked by Glavlit, which for its part may insert any corrections, and this again is an institution against which there is no appeal; there's nowhere to complain to.[42]

Levitin discovered that the censor did not permit articles to contain references to foreign sources: an article he wrote in defense of peace was rejected because, to describe the horrors of war, he quoted from Remarque's *All Quiet on the Western Front*. However, there was more to come: "The most surprising thing was that it was not allowed to make reference to Soviet sources either. 'What is this? It turns out that we're working for you?' said a representative of the Council. In general, the old principle of 'it will come to no good' lay at the basis of all the censor's work." The restrictions on subject matter and its treatment were also strict, as Levitin discovered the hard way:

In an article on Saint Nikolai I named several churches of St. Nikolai which had existed in Moscow. It was not allowed; those churches didn't exist any more! In a reportage from Peter, my home city, on the Monastery of St. Alexander Nevsky, occurred the lines: "Once again, as in years past, the people make their way through the cor-

ridors of the Lavra to the Cathedral." Not allowed—Glavlit canceled
the whole issue! "As in years past" meant that there had been a break
when the monastery had been closed.

At the end of an article about the Princess Olga, I spoke of the
great role which women had played in the history of the church. Not
allowed: Christianity stifled women.

Levitin soon concluded that the effect of the censorship was that "the
journal was deadly boring and no use to anyone."[43] He turned to writing
in samizdat instead.

Deacon Rusak's experience of working for *JMP* led him to conclusions
just as outspoken as Levitin's. He calls the censorship of the journal
"draconian." Every issue, according to Rusak, is sent to the CRA on the
twentieth day of the month, and they spend five days reading it. He notes
wryly that the CRA officials "are the most attentive and the most zealous
readers of the church journal." And this despite the fact that every em-
ployee of the publishing department already has his instructions regarding
the content of the journal and the preferred vocabulary. Among many examples he gives, Rusak mentions that the usual Russian word for "clergy,"
dukhovenstvo (the root of which means "spirit" or "spiritual") should be
abandoned in favor of the more neutral, less "churchly" words *pricht* or
klir.[44] After giving several examples of items before and after censorship
by the CRA, Rusak proceeds to a more central issue:

> The Council [CRA] does not merely make certain "editorial" recom-
> mendations. The entire structure of the journal has gradually been
> defined by the Council, and at best only one-third of the space has
> been made available to purely church historical events. The remain-
> der is peacemaking and ecumenism. The space which is useful to the
> church is bought at the price of that which is useful to the govern-
> ment. . . . The state is simply speculating on the functional duties of
> the church. The state is attempting to reduce the spiritual and salvific
> activity of the church . . . in the mind of the general public to a nar-
> rowly social and public phenomenon . . . and by this, as it were, to
> justify the very existence of the church in an atheistic [antireligious]
> state.[45]

Levitin's observations date from before 1960, Rusak's from a later date,
but they are both borne out by the CRA report for 1974, indicating that
little or nothing has changed over the years. The CRA states that it censors
every issue of *JMP* carefully because, although it has a small circulation,
it has a wide variety of readers, from ordinary believers and parish priests

to "official services and departments of foreign countries." This statement makes explicit the fact that the CRA regards it as part of its duties to influence foreigners' perceptions of the Russian Orthodox church. The report continues:

> The editorial department of the journal and the authors' collective in general correctly understand the tasks standing before the journal, but at the same time there are frequently found among the manuscripts prepared for printing texts whose content does not serve the interests of the state and the believer, does not promote the formation in the reader of lofty civil and patriotic qualities, and is in contradiction to the norms of Soviet legislation on cults. . . . A preparatory examination of texts takes place in the Council, notes and corrections are added.[46]

Attempts to Meet the Need for Literature

It is clear that the church is prevented from producing even a fraction of the religious literature needed by its members. Many, perhaps most, of its millions of members must pass much of their lives with little or no access to written materials relating to their faith. It is true that the reading of devotional and other materials is not a great feature of the Orthodox way of life, due no doubt to the high rate of illiteracy, until recent times, in Russia. Rather than read a book, a Russian Orthodox believer would be more likely to visit a church, pray before icons, talk to a priest, or journey to see a *starets* (elder) in a monastery. However, these traditional activities are becoming more and more difficult to perform due to the great shortage of priests, churches, and monasteries. Reading matter, were it available in sufficient quantities, might provide a substitute for those unable to visit churches or priests. However, the fact that religious literature is distributed only through churches means that only those able to attend church can obtain it—and so those who live far from any open church are doubly deprived.

The Rusak Report indicates very clearly that ordinary Orthodox believers do in fact want Christian reading matter. Rusak writes: "Hundreds and thousands of letters are addressed to the patriarch and the chairman of the publishing department of the Moscow patriarchate, in which people beg tearfully to be sent a Bible, or a church calendar, at their personal expense." Among several letters he quotes is one that states: "I would like to read the Bible. I have to confess that I have absolutely no idea of its content. I do not know where I can find one to read. . . . I would like to own a Bible. I will read it attentively again and again." Rusak says that the editorial staff of the publishing department includes a person whose duties consist solely of replying to such letters—always with a refusal.

Personal visitors to the offices of the publishing department, according to Rusak, even if they come from the far east of the Soviet Union, several days' journey from Moscow, or from the distant north, are told that the editorial staff cannot make sales.[47]

The publishing department appears to be doing its best in a very difficult situation, and is using to the utmost the very limited opportunities available to it. It has recently produced some films about the life of the church, in color and of quite good quality, which Archbishop Pitirim has shown on his travels to various countries. In 1979 he showed them in Stockholm at a biennial international Christian television festival, the first time that a representative from the Soviet Union had taken part in the festival.[48] Like all the products of the publishing department, the films portrayed the life of the church in a purely positive light, making no mention of any problems, but nonetheless they give a most interesting view of aspects of the church's life.

However, we have to conclude that the need for religious literature of all types—the Scriptures, liturgical and prayer books, the lives of the saints, church history, devotional works, commentaries, dictionaries, teaching materials, to name only those most urgently needed—is very great indeed. It is against this background that samizdat has grown up. Anatolii Levitin was not the only person, though he was one of the very first, to realize that the church was unable to provide religious literature and that believers would have to find ways of remedying the deficiency themselves. Samizdat does not consist only of the letters of protest that have been widely quoted in the West, but also of devotional and spiritual materials, sometimes book-length. The fact that people are willing to type out such lengthy texts, knowing that the penalty if they are discovered is at least confiscation and possibly imprisonment, is evidence of a deeply felt need for spiritual literature. Samizdat texts sometimes reach the West and are published there: such books are designated as *tamizdat* or "publishing over there" (from the words *tam*, "there," and *izdat*, "publish"). If tamizdat texts can be conveyed back to the Soviet Union by secret means, they help to supplement the believers' meager literary diet. In 1977 a periodical called *Nadezhda*, subtitled "Christian Readings," began to be published in this way. Thirteen issues have been published in the West (by 1986), and many more prepared for publication in the USSR. *Nadezhda* ("Hope") includes extracts from the church fathers, articles and letters by priests and pastors from both present and past, poetry and Christian contemporary literature, and works giving a Christian view of the current state of Russia and the Orthodox church.

Russian Orthodox literature is published in Russian abroad by the YMCA Press in Paris, the Catholic publisher "La Vie avec Dieu" in Brussels, the Orthodox Monastery of the Holy Trinity at Jordanville in New York state, and by other small centers in the United States and Canada. Like other religious literature, these works cannot be officially imported into the USSR, and they are sent by clandestine means. These publications are highly valued by Orthodox in the Soviet Union. A letter sent to "La Vie avec Dieu" is typical of many that have reached these Western publishers:

> Dear brothers! Above all I want to thank you with all my heart for the wonderful work that you have taken upon yourselves—the publishing of religious literature in the Russian language. . . . These books fill in the almost total absence of modern Russian literature on biblical studies. . . . This is a slender little stream, but it will not allow living faith to dry up, and it is not poisoned by compromises and self-deception.[49]

Appreciative though this letter is, it is undoubtedly right to describe the Orthodox literature coming from the West as no more than a "slender little stream." Despite their purely religious, nonpolitical content, such books are liable to be confiscated from tourists and other travelers if discovered at borders. Furthermore, it is common for large quantities of religious literature belonging to private individuals to be confiscated during lengthy searches of homes conducted by the militia or the KGB. Both these practices intensified during the early 1980s. Although the fate of such confiscated literature cannot be established with certainty, the ready availability of Christian books on the black market is highly suggestive. This means that believers can obtain books, but at a price. New Testaments were said to fetch thirty rubles and Bibles sixty rubles, or roughly half a month's average salary. However, in 1982 these prices had dropped to sixteen and forty rubles, respectively, indicating that black market Bibles and New Testaments were more widely available. Copies of the *Dobrotolyubiye* (Philokalia) were said in 1982 to cost five hundred rubles each, or about four months' salary. The fact that Christians are prepared to pay such large sums is ample evidence both of the scarcity of Christian literature and of the great hunger for it. And, of course, even books acquired on the black market are liable to reconfiscation in a subsequent house search.

The great demand for religious literature means that, almost inevitably, abuses creep into the informal distribution system. It is clear that some people must be profiting handsomely from the black market sales. Moreover, it has been reported that some bishops stockpile religious literature received from the West and use it as an "alternative currency." For example, an artist who had restored an entire church was offered as payment either two hundred rubles or a copy of the *Philokalia* (worth five hundred rubles); being a believer, he chose the latter and was delighted with the bargain, and the church profited by two hundred rubles. Another example of possible profiteering came to light when a number of Orthodox believers were arrested in Moscow on April 6, 1982, after lengthy house searches during which large quantities of religious literature were confiscated. Six thousand prayer books were taken from one address alone. It transpired that these believers had somehow been able to photocopy prayer books and other religious literature, have them bound, and sell them. The profiteering motive was fully represented in the Soviet press.

The newspaper *Sovetskaya Rossiya* devoted articles on two successive days, July 8 and 9, 1982, to criticism of the group of Orthodox Christians who organized this production of large quantities of religious books. They were arrested in April and tried and sentenced in December 1982 to terms of three to four years in labor camps. The article begins by quoting BBC broadcasts which assert that they were trying to help fellow believers by providing literature and that such activity was by no means criminal. The article attempts to correct this view by stating unequivocally that the men's sole purpose in producing the religious books was to make money. They are denounced as "speculators," as being "ready for crime for the sake of easy money," and as having deliberately set out to "think, how, without giving themselves too much trouble, they could make a thousand or two." No other possible motive is even considered. In addition, Rozanov is accused of being involved in foreign currency transactions (a serious offense: if true, it is surprising that his sentence was not longer); and Burdyug, who is regarded as the ringleader, of trying to send "anti-Soviet" writings abroad for publication. These accusations are, however, subsidiary to the main theme of the articles and seem to have been brought in to blacken the characters of those involved.

The articles give a fair amount of detail about the way the printing operations were carried out. Originally, the "firm" paid workers in state printing presses to produce religious literature for them, but then they decided to increase their profits by doing the printing themselves. They stole state equipment—a Xerox machine, an offset litho machine, binding equipment, etc.—and installed it in flats and dachas outside Moscow. The article states that the "firm" produced 61,500 pieces of literature in two years. It seems that the enterprise was very successful. This is an astonishingly large amount of literature to produce when working clandestinely under difficult conditions.

The question of what happened to the large profits that were allegedly the aim of the whole enterprise is left unclear. The article simply states that the illegally acquired funds were ordered to be returned to the state. It does not say whether they were in fact returned, what they amounted to, or what the "entrepreneurs" had done or tried to do with their ill-gotten gains. There are none of the references one might have expected to a luxurious way of life, ostentatious spending, or newly acquired possessions. All this strongly suggests that receipts from the sale of books were plowed back into producing more books: it is clear that the whole operation was quite costly and would have had to be self-financing.[50]

Whatever the motives of the people concerned, the arrests and large-scale confiscations in April made it clear that the KGB was still determined to remove religious literature from circulation. Another instance of this was the arrest on August 4, 1982, of Zoya Krakhmalnikova, the compiler of Nadezhda. Although her name had appeared on every issue of Nadezhda during the six or seven years of its publication, it had never been suggested to her officially that she was doing anything illegal. She was tried on March 31, 1983, and sentenced under article 70 ("anti-Soviet agitation and propaganda") to one year in labor camp plus five years' internal exile.[51] Her arrest, as well as the other actions mentioned above, make it clear that the Soviet authorities fear the spreading of the production and distribution of religious literature to channels that they cannot observe and control. They are determined to confine all literature production and distribution to the officially recognized channels of the Moscow patriarchate, where they can regulate it.

It is clear that the amount of religious literature published by the Moscow patriarchate has been increasing in recent years, and the signs are that this is likely to continue. In September 1981 the publishing department moved from its cramped quarters in the Novodevichi Monastery to rooms in a spacious new building close by. Before this, according to Rusak, the publishing department had been housed in cramped and inadequate quarters. At first the editorial staff had a small room in the patriarchate offices in Chisty Pereulok, then a room in the Dormition Church in the Novodevichi Convent. The premises then "expanded," still within Novodevichi, to a room measuring forty square meters for seven editorial and five administrative staff members. The other departments (photographic, tape recording, production, bookkeeping, dispatch, library, archive, storeroom, copying and typewriting, proofreading) were all accommodated underground, with no daylight during working hours. The photo laboratory was in a cellar where there was no ventilation to draw off chemical fumes.[52] The new building, said to be lavishly decorated, was built at the expense of the Moscow patriarchate at a reported cost of 2 million rubles. The publishing department's facilities include a darkroom, color laboratories, and a film editing studio, but not printing presses; its publications will continue to be printed on state presses.[53] Rusak gives further details about the new building, and different costs. He quotes a resolution of the Supreme Soviet dated July 18, 1977, to rent the Moscow patriarchate a 400-square-meter, two-story building in Pogodinskaya ulitsa because it was "insufficiently suitable for the further residence of citizens" (nine families). The publishing department had to rehouse the families, knock down the building, and then construct a new building for its own needs on the site. This cost 350,000 rubles, but only 70,000 rubles were provided by state funds for the construction of residential accommodations. The publishing department provided 138,000 rubles, and the remainder came from the economic department of the Moscow patriarchate. However, the building remains state property.[54]

Archbishop Pitirim has been quoted as saying that 116 people were employed in the publishing department in 1980 and that the number was expected to rise soon to 140.[55] Half the employees were women. By 1983 Pitirim said their numbers had risen to 150.[56]

Although the publishing department has new premises, there is no indication that the church's paper allocation will be increased to enable it to publish more literature. Private sources suggest that the improved facilities have been accompanied by greater state control over the department's work and more publications destined for overseas use and for foreign visitors than for the use of believers in the USSR.

The improvement in the publication department's premises and facilities, plus the slow increase in the number of publications, is in line with what the church is being permitted to do in other areas of its institutional life. Soviet policy toward the Russian Orthodox church is evidently to allow it increasing (but still inadequate) scope for meeting the various purely internal needs of the church, while continuing to monitor and control its internal affairs very closely indeed. Concessions to the church, such as the opening of the new publishing department premises, are given publicity abroad as part of the Soviet propaganda effort in support of the claim that there is freedom of religion in the Soviet Union. Such concessions, which are entirely at the discretion of the state, are a reward for the compliant and subservient attitude adopted by the church leadership. They should not be taken to indicate that the church has gained in either influence or freedom.

Service Books Published by the Moscow Patriarchate

Dates on the title pages of books are not always the same as dates of publication, due to delays.

Publications before 1976 are as listed in *The Moscow Patriarchate, 1917–1977*, p. 26; additional information, and information on subsequent publications, is to be found in the issues of *JMP* indicated.

Numbers of copies printed are taken from the CRA report for 1974, *Vestnik RKhD* No. 130, p. 328, and *Episkepsis* No. 252, 20.5.81, p. 6.

1946	Service to all the Saints who Shone Forth in the Land of Russia
1947	Service for the Nativity of Christ
1948	Service for the Epiphany
1950	Service for the Presentation of Our Lord
	Service for the Dormition of the Mother of God
	Service for St. Ioann, Metropolitan of Tobolsk
1956	Short Orthodox Prayer Book (*Kratky pravoslavny Molitvoslov*), 114 pp. (*JMP* 9/56, pp. 78–79)
1957	Typicon (*Tipikon*), 154 pp. Liturgical manual for priests on orders of service throughout the ecclesiastical year. (*JMP* 11/58, pp. 71–72)
1958	Book of Needs, or small Euchologion (*Trebnik*), 2 vols., 960 pp. Contains orders of service for sacraments (except the Eucharist) and many rites. (*JMP* 11/58, pp. 72–74)
1960 (dated 1958)	Service Book or Euchologion (*Sluzhebnik*). Liturgies of St. John Chrysostom, St. Basil the Great, and of the Presanctified Gifts, also litanies and prayers for vespers and matins and other prayers. (*JMP* 3/60, pp. 75–76)
1961	Menaion, or Menologion (*Mineya*). Orders of service for all the fixed days in the year commemorating a historical event or a saint or saints.
1962	Psalter with the Order of Services (*Psaltyr Sledovannaya*), 507 pp. Psalter, Book of Hours, calendar, and various prayers and hymns. (*JMP* 12/62, p. 71)
1964	Book of Hours or Horologion (*Chasoslov*), 322 pp. Contains fixed portions of the ecclesiastical office for the whole year, excluding the Liturgy. (*JMP* 12/63, p. 70)
1964	The Book of Eight Tones, or Octoechos (*Oktoikh*), Part 1, tones 1–4. Canons and hymns that form the variable part

of the daily services from the first Sunday after Pentecost
to the fourth Sunday before Lent (Septuagesima). (*JMP*
6/64, p. 79)

1965   The Book of Eight Tones, Part 2, tones 5–8.

1970   Orthodox Prayer Book (*Pravoslavny Molitvoslov*), 192
pp. (*JMP* 1/71, p. 73)

1970   Festal Menaion (*Mineya prazdnichnaya*). Orders of
service for the twelve great feasts of the ecclesiastical
year. (*JMP* 4/76, p. 77)

1972   Lenten Triodion (*Triod postnaya*). Orders of service from
Septuagesima to Easter Saturday. (*JMP* 4/76, pp. 77–78)

1973   Psalter (*Psaltyr*), 256 pp. In addition to the Psalter itself,
contains many services which include psalms. (*JMP* 1/75,
p. 79)

1977   Festal Triodion, or Pentecostarian (*Triod tsvetnaya*).
(dated 1975)   Orders of service from Easter Day to Pentecost. 10,000
copies printed (CRA).

1976   Collected Divine Services (*Bogosluzhebni sbornik*), 352
pp. Orders of the main services, including music; for
psalm-reader and choir. (*JMP* 9/76, p. 78)

1978   Service Book (*Sluzhebnik*), re-edition of the 1958 (1960)
(dated 1977)   Service Book, but in two parts, Part I, pp. 1–352, Part II,
pp. 353–608. Photographic reproduction of the 1903
synodal edition, with supplementary material. (*JMP*
1/79, p. 80)

1979   Manual for Priests (*Nastolnaya kniga svyashchenno-*
(dated 1977)   *sluzhitelei*) Vol. 1, 768 pp. Orders of chief services and
guidance on role of priest. 20,000 copies printed (CRA).
(*JMP* 1/79, pp. 79–80)

1979   Manual for Priests Vol. 2. Calendar from September to
(dated 1978)   February with the lives of the saints. (*JMP* 6/79, p. 79)

1981   Psalter and Prayer Book reissued jointly. 150,000 copies
printed (*Episkepsis*) (*JMP* 4/81, p. 78) *Manual for Priests,*
Vol. 3. (*JMP* 9/81, p. 79)

(dated 1980)   *Book of Hours.* 20,000 copies printed (*Episkepsis*). (*JMP*
5/81, p. 80)

(dated 1980)   *Psalter with the Order of Services,* 2 vols. Vol. 1 includes
the Psalter and offices for private use; Vol. 2 includes
the Menaion, Horologion, and Typicon, as well as other
chants and prayers. 20,000 copies printed (*Episkepsis*).
(*JMP* 5/81, p. 80)

1981   *The Book of Eight Tones (Oktoikh)* Part 1, 707 pp.; Part
        2, 672 pp. (reproductions of an earlier edition); Part 3,
        appendix with music. (*JMP* 10/82, p. 79)

1982   *All-night Vigil.* Liturgy (*Vsenoshchnoye bdeniye.*
        Liturgiya). 2 vols. Vol. 1, orders of main services,
        reprinted from 1976 and 1977 editions. Vol. 2 gives
        practical help in performing services. (*JMP* 12/82, p. 160)

1982   *Archieraticon* (*Chinovnik arkhiereiskogo svyashchen-*
        nosluzheniya). Vol. 1. 252 pp. Two books with music
        scores. Includes prayers said secretly and out loud by
        hierarchs at major services, and orders for various ordina-
        tion services. (*JMP* 2/83, p. 80)

6

The Orthodox Church in America

Michael A. Meerson

The Orthodox Church in America (OCA), which developed and grew on the North American continent, is the youngest autocephalous church in the family of Orthodox churches. It is unique among Orthodox churches insofar as it is unhampered by either political pressures or specific ethnic customs, and preaches the gospel in one of the most open societies existing today.

Orthodox missionary work was started in Alaska even before the American colonies began to fight for independence. The territory, once discovered, was inundated with Russian traders and developers. The arrival of the Russians also meant the propagation of their faith.[1] John Ledyard, a member of an expedition to Alaska, led by the famous seafarer Captain James Cook, wrote in his journal in 1776 that the expedition had come across a Russian colony of about five hundred people in Unalaska. They heard the Russians, Aleuts, and natives of Kamchatka sing evening prayers in the tradition of the Orthodox church.[2]

The government of Empress Catherine the Great, famous for its colonizing ambitions, responded to the appeal of developers for cultural and religious colonization of Alaska, and, in 1793, sanctioned the dispatch to Alaska of a group of eight missionaries. The group's work was short-lived, however,[3] and only one of them—the monk, Herman—survived. Herman remained among the natives, and much later, in 1970, the OCA canonized him as its patron saint.[4]

Yet the propagation of Orthodoxy among the Aleuts and the organization of the church's life in Alaska owe much more to the Siberian priest Innocent Veniaminov. He lived in Alaska from 1824 to 1858, serving for fifteen years as a missionary priest and for twenty-two years as a missionary bishop.[5] A man of many gifts, Innocent built a church with his own hands, founded a school, and set up a meteorological station. He learned the local dialect, and, as the people had no written language, he created an alphabet by adapting Cyrillic letters, compiling a dictionary, and developing a grammar for this language. Innocent subsequently translated the Gospel of St. Matthew and the Divine Liturgy into the written Aleutian language that he himself had created and wrote a catechism in Aleutian. He traveled all over Alaska, by dogsled and by canoe, and, as the first educated explorer in Alaska, he was elected to the Russian Academy of Sciences for his work on the ethnography of the region.[6]

The apostolic work of Innocent brought him to the attention of the Holy Synod and he was unanimously elected metropolitan of Moscow, the highest position in the Russian Orthodox church before the reestablishment of the patriarchate in 1917. Metropolitan Innocent welcomed the purchase of Alaska by the United States, seeing in this an opportunity for Orthodoxy to penetrate into the United States. With this in mind, he proposed to transfer the bishop's residence from Alaska to San Francisco, to appoint a bishop who spoke English, to replace all the Russian clergy with English-speaking priests, and to permit the Orthodox Church in America to conduct the liturgy and other services in English.[7] Although he drafted a plan for the gradual conversion of the Russian diocese into a local church in America, it took more than a century for this plan to be realized. Metropolitan Innocent died in 1879, and was canonized by the Moscow patriarchate, in 1977, on the recommendation of the OCA.

The Beginnings of Orthodoxy in the United States

Like other immigrants to America, Orthodox immigrants brought their faith with them. Starting in the late nineteenth century, they discovered the organizational beginnings established by the Russian Orthodox mission in the United States. In 1868 a multilingual parish, comprising Greeks, Russians, and Serbs, was founded in San Francisco and began to publish a newspaper under the title *The Slavonian*. In 1870 a separate diocese of Alaska and the Aleutian Islands was created, and soon the residence of the bishop was transferred to San Francisco.[8]

By 1870 Orthodoxy had also arrived on the East Coast, where Fr. Nicholas Bjerring preached in New York. Bjerring was a former Catholic professor who had converted to Orthodoxy after the First Vatican Council in protest of its endorsement of the doctrine of papal infallibility. Bjerring was ordained to the priesthood in St. Petersburg and sent to New

York as an Orthodox missionary. There he established a church in his
residence and began to publish the *Journal of the Eastern Church*. With
many friends in American social circles, among them the U.S. president,
Ulysses Grant, he contributed a great deal to introducing Orthodoxy to
American intellectuals. In 1884 he collected all the English translations of
services that had appeared in his journal and published them as a separate
book.[9]

However, Bjerring's work was an exception. By and large the Russian
church was not ready at that time for missionary work in the United
States, where it found itself in unfamiliar political, cultural, and religious
surroundings. The United States, with its unlimited personal liberty and
initiative, freedom of faith, and absence of any governmental pressure on
the church, was a legend even in Western Europe, not to speak of Russia. The difference in psychology and political awareness was intensified
by the peculiar position held by the Russian Orthodox mission outside
Russia. The church mission was regarded by the clergy, and even more
so by the imperial apparatus, as a religious emissary of the Russian Empire. It was no coincidence that upon returning to Russia the clergy and
bishops who had served abroad received their pensions from the Ministry
of Foreign Affairs.[10] This left a specific imprint on the consciousness of
the clergy, who looked upon their work abroad as a temporary mission,
of a diplomatic nature, that was to terminate upon their return to Russia
and be rewarded accordingly. With regard to the bishops, their term of
service was determined by the Holy Synod. The appointment of a bishop,
as a high-ranking church official, was authorized by the tsar himself. The
bishop was not his own master. He could not refuse his post and neither
could he extend the duration of his service.[11] Such a state of affairs could
hardly help the clergy penetrate American life. By the time a bishop had
become accustomed to American ways, he was usually recalled to Russia.
Moreover, by virtue of American democracy, a relationship between the
laity and the hierarchy was developing that was radically different from
that to which the Orthodox hierarchy was accustomed.

First of all, American religious life was free of the concept of "sacred
property"—property that belonged to the church, was managed by the
bishops, and could not be sold or transferred into secular hands—which
was characteristic of the Russian Empire, as well as of Byzantium, from
whom Russia inherited her religious-political structure. Although Peter
the Great's reforms in Russia created opportunities for violating this principle of "sacred property,"[12] they made no attempt to ban it. Only the
Bolshevik Revolution did this, along with doing away with ownership of
all private property.

Another feature of the life of the church in Russia was the almost complete exclusion of the laity from all aspects of church life. The people had
neither their own elected officers nor any control over finances and church
property. Priests and bishops were appointed and transferred by the Holy
Synod, without any participation on the part of parishes. The social network in the Russian Empire was dominated by a principle of hierarchical
structure, whether civil or ecclesiastical. Each official was appointed by
higher authorities. This entire hierarchical structure of authority extended
up to the emperor, who was the "autocrat by God's Will." A radically
different state of affairs existed in the United States. Church buildings
were bought and sold, and any community of the faithful was free to form
a religious corporation and purchase property without asking anyone for
permission to do so. Moreover, Orthodox immigrants found themselves
in a situation where open discussion of problems, free elections, constant
control over their elected officials, and the responsibility for their actions
were part of the way of life.

This new way of life influenced the creation of aspects of church life
unknown to countries where Orthodoxy was the state religion. Orthodox
immigrants followed a natural inclination in this respect and organized
their ecclesiastical life on their own initiative, purchasing church property
in the name of religious corporations they had formed themselves. The
Russian Orthodox hierarchy was not particularly sympathetic toward this
new development, which reduced their own role in church administration,
but they were not able to prevent it. In fact, the constant flow of clergy and
the frequent turnover among bishops only nurtured this new situation.[13]

In spite of this qualitatively new state of affairs, the Russian diocese
was able to assist those groups of Orthodox immigrants who turned to
it for help. While the Greeks kept to themselves, enjoying independent
church structures of their own, Slavs, Arabs, Romanians, and others established congregations and turned to the Russian bishop to obtain anti-
minsions[14] and to have priests appointed who could serve either in their
native language or in English. Since no other Orthodox church aspired to
patronage over these disparate parishes, they found themselves, de facto,
under the jurisdiction of the Russian Orthodox church. In fact, attempts
by Greeks and Arabs in America to obtain priests from the patriarchs of
Constantinople or Antioch, or from the Athos Synod, were unsuccessful.
These prelates were either uninterested in the fate of their countrymen
who had gone to America or did not want to tangle with a Russian church
that enjoyed the backing of the Russian Empire.[15]

Thus, due to circumstances involved in undertaking the patronage of
various ethnic groups, the Russian diocese was becoming the germ of a

multiethnic American church. To make matters more complicated, many Uniate[16] parishes transferred their affiliation to Orthodoxy through this diocese. If the Russian hierarchy was receptive to this state of affairs, in which church property was owned by lay people, then this very situation displeased the Catholic hierarchy in America, who continued to maintain control of church property. This gave rise to a conflict with immigrants from Eastern Europe, who belonged to the Uniate church. At the end of the nineteenth and the beginning of the twentieth century Carpatho-Russians, who had for several centuries belonged to the Uniate church, immigrated to America in increasing numbers from the eastern regions of the Austro-Hungarian Empire.

Before the arrival of these newcomers in America, the American Catholic diocese, consisting primarily of Irish, Italian, and Polish émigrés, had not been acquainted with Uniates. Treating their different customs, such as allowing married priests and the use of the Byzantine rite, with disdain, the American Catholic hierarchy alienated the Uniate communities and their priests. Upset and discouraged by the attitude of the Catholic hierarchy, the Uniate parishes began to turn to the Russian bishop, requesting to be received into the Russian Orthodox diocese so that they could safeguard their church property and preserve the self-administration of their parishes. The initiator of this movement was a Uniate priest named Alexis Toth, who convened the first conference of Hungarian priests in 1890 to discuss Uniate problems in America. The following year he and his parish joined the Russian Orthodox diocese. This laid the groundwork for the return of Uniate parishes to Orthodoxy. Eighty of them joined the Russian diocese eventually.[17] One historian of the OCA thinks that the main reason for the conversion of the Uniates to Orthodoxy was their fear of absolute control of their property by Catholic bishops. This would imply that it was not questions of theology and faith that impelled them to convert, but rather their resentment of the Catholic bishops.[18] At any rate, the Uniates brought with them a tradition of self-administration and communal organization to which, in great measure, the OCA owes its very existence.

The Revival of Sobornost

Archbishop Tikhon (Vasili Ivanovich Belavin, 1865–1925) began organizing various ethnic groups within the territory of his diocese. Following his recommendation to the Holy Synod, the diocese was made into an archdiocese, with vicar bishops for both the regional territories and the ethnic groups. Three dioceses were created: one for Alaska, with the bishop's seat in Sitka; another for the Syrian-Arab mission in Brooklyn; and a third for Canada. A group of Serbian parishes and a group of Greek parishes were established, for whom he also began to search for episcopal candidates. Tikhon's plan was that, in time, all these groups would evolve into dioceses within the structure of one American church. Another sphere of his work was the organization of theological education in the United States. He upgraded the existing missionary school in Minnesota, converting it into a seminary, and eventually the graduates of this seminary made it unnecessary to import further clergy from Russia. It was also during Tikhon's administration that a translation of the basic Orthodox services into English was published.

The third and possibly most significant achievement to his credit was Tikhon's attempt to bring the spirit of American democracy into Orthodox life. Just prior to leaving the United States for a new assignment, Archbishop Tikhon convened a sobor of Orthodox clergy in Mayfield. This sobor launched the conciliar history of the OCA. Starting with this sobor, the American archdiocese of the Russian Orthodox church began gradually to revive an authentic tradition of Orthodoxy, which had completely disappeared from practice in other Orthodox churches.

Tikhon thus laid the foundation for a multinational Orthodox federation in America and was planning an autonomous Orthodox church that would be directed by a synod of bishops, chaired by an actually independent hierarch, who would be a member of the ruling synod of bishops of the Russian Orthodox church. According to one observer, "had this plan been effected before the war, so that there would already have existed such an autonomous Orthodox Church in America, then the political events in Europe would have had little or no impact on the life of this Church, with the exception of strengthening its independence and unity. The sad disorganization and the disruptive division of the Church in America, resulting from European political events, would have been impossible."[19] However, the prerevolutionary synodical structure of the church and its imperial consciousness did nothing to help. Nor was the American diocese itself ready, whether financially or psychologically, to be autonomous or autocephalous.

Archbishop Tikhon's successors in the New York diocese did not understand the situation in the United States as well as he did. Not one of them nurtured the growth of the seeds of sobornost planted by Tikhon. The next sobor was convened only after the Russian Revolution, in 1919, and it was rather an extraordinary event, necessitated by the vital need of saving the very organizational structure of the archdiocese.

It was during the early years of the twentieth century that the ethnic Orthodox federation, which Tikhon had built into the framework of the

Russian diocese, began to fall apart. Russian imperial psychology was accustomed to dealing condescendingly with other ethnic Orthodox groups. It was not interested in them and did not understand their specific ethnic problems. Nor did it evince any concern for the organization of their life in the church. All this contributed to the birth of ethnic separatism within the church. This separatism produced a splintering into different ethnic Orthodox jurisdictions in America only after the collapse of the Russian Empire, when the Russian Orthodox church, suddenly subjected to severe repression by the Bolsheviks, was able neither to defend its jurisdictional rights nor to concern itself with other Orthodox churches.

It is true that Tikhon's direct successor, Archbishop Platon Rozhdestvensky (1907–14), launched a campaign among the Uniates, to bring them into Orthodoxy. It was during his administration that the majority of Carpatho-Russian Uniate parishes joined the Russian diocese. It was also under his administration that the Russian Immigrant Society was founded in New York. Two newspapers also made their appearance now, the *Russian Immigrant* (a daily) and the *American Orthodox Messenger*.[20]

At the beginning of the Russian Revolution the diocese of North America was one of sixty-four dioceses in the Russian Orthodox church and numbered eighteenth in size. It consisted of five bishops, seven hundred parishes, and more than four hundred priests from all the Orthodox nationalities. It also had five monasteries, one convent, and a seminary with seventy students. The diocese even planned to establish its own representative office in St. Petersburg. This plan, among many others, was thwarted by the Revolution.[21]

The Russian Revolution and the Autonomy of the American Diocese

The fall of Russian autocracy launched a new era in the life of the church, forcing it to reexamine the ecclesiastical and political premises of its activity. If the basic canonical structure of the church had been formed before the Roman Empire converted to Christianity, then all later development in the Orthodox church went hand in hand with the empire—at first the Byzantine Empire and later the Russian. Beginning with Bishop Eusebius of Caesaria, who introduced the monarchist concept that "the power of the emperor in the world is a reflection of God's power in Heaven" into the church's thinking, all the way to the last great ideologist and practitioner of the subjection of church to state, the oberprocurator of the Holy Synod in St. Petersburg, Konstantin Pobedonostsev, who asserted that the autocratic rule of the emperor is the highest form of authority, by virtue of its totality and indivisibility,[22] the Orthodox church not only lived in the grips of the empire—whether the Byzantine or the Russian—but also in an indissoluble spiritual bond with it. Thus, at the turn of the twentieth century, when Russian society was demanding radical political reforms, the Russian Orthodox church was proclaiming its loyalty to the Byzantine concept of a sacred kingdom and to the imperial autocracy.[23]

In its preliminary stages the Revolution greatly benefited the Russian church in that an all-Russian church sobor was finally convened. Although preparations for the sobor had been under way for some time (since the time of the Revolution of 1905–7 and the retirement of Pobedonostsev) and church officials were growing more adamant in their demands to convene a sobor, the tsarist government kept putting it off under various pretexts. Only the Provisional Government granted permission to convene a sobor. The sobor, consisting of Orthodox bishops, clergy, and lay people, convened in the Kremlin in August 1917 under the Kerensky government. It elected a patriarch and outlined a new framework for administration of the church that was in accordance with church canons and the principles of Orthodox ecclesiology. This reform was based on the most ancient canonical principle: the election of pastors by the entire church, and it reinstated the organic place of lay people in the body of the church.[24]

The North American diocese played a large role at the sobor, having sent two of its representatives Fr. Alexander Kukulevsky and Fr. Leonid Turkevich. The former was a member of the committee for developing parish statutes. On his recommendation the committee adopted the 1909 Standard Statutes for Parishes of the North American Diocese as the basis for its draft. As candidate for patriarch, Fr. Turkevich nominated Metropolitan Tikhon Belavin, his collaborator and superior in the American diocese. The latter was elected patriarch of Moscow and all Russia.[25] Both delegates brought back to the United States the resolutions and spirit of the sobor. Kukulevsky then chaired the all-American sobor, held in Cleveland in 1919, which was convened in a very difficult period for the diocese. Turkevich was at the head of the metropolia from 1950 to 1965.

The Bolshevik Revolution had catastrophic repercussions on the American diocese. All normal communications with the central church authorities were severed. The Moscow patriarchate was deprived of any access to international mail and telegraph communications, which were now monopolized by the new regime, and was cut off from its overseas dioceses and missions. Financial support ceased. Having survived on finances provided by the Holy Synod, the American diocese now found itself in a hopeless situation. Under these conditions one of the administering bishops, Evdokim, attempted to correct the situation by requesting that Serbian churches, joining the Russian diocese, transfer the management of their church property to the diocese. Another bishop—Evdokim's successor, Bishop Alexander—began to mortgage parish property that did not belong to the diocese. This could not but result in antihierarchical revolt. Observing a decline in authority, a schismatic Renovationist[26] faction sprang up. It was formed in New York in 1917 under the leadership of a priest, John Kedrovsky. He engineered an attack on the leadership of the Russian diocese in an attempt to appropriate its administration for himself. An all-American sobor was convened in 1919 for the purpose of asserting diocesan authority. Shortly after that, Metropolitan Platon Rozhdestvensky returned to the United States. He had been appointed head of the American archdiocese by Patriarch Tikhon, who made this appointment verbally, in the presence of Fr. Theodore Pashkovsky (later Metropolitan Theophilus, head of the American metropolia from 1935 to 1950) and Mr. Colton, chairman of the YMCA, who happened to be in Moscow at the time. Taking advantage of that period of unrest and the absence of an official letter from the patriarch, Kedrovsky (who had become the pro-Soviet "Living Church's" emissary to America and was passing himself off as the canonical archbishop of New York) commenced legal proceedings to appropriate diocesan church property.[27] As a result, the St. Nicholas Cathedral in New York passed into the hands of the Living Church. These attempts by the Renovationists to destroy the American archdiocese and appropriate its church property, on the one hand, and the disorder and lack of authority, on the other hand, forced the hierarchy to convene the third all-American sobor in Detroit in 1924. The sobor affirmed Metropolitan Platon, renamed the archdiocese a metropolia, and proclaimed a provisional autonomy for the American metropolia until an all-Russian sobor could be convened by the ROC. The sobor also defined the structure of ecclesiastical authority: the metropolitan was head of the metropolia and administrator of the church, together with the synod of bishops and representatives from the clergy and lay people, who were to be elected from periodically convened all-American sobors.

This resolution made by the Detroit sobor, to proclaim autonomy and reestablish conciliar administration of the metropolia, was ratified in accordance with a decree from Patriarch Tikhon,[28] which contained a mandate to diocesan archbishops stating that in the case of a breach in communications with the higher church authorities, they were to take full charge of their dioceses and administer them with the help of the clergy. In accordance with this same patriarchal decree, a diocesan bishop was to divide his diocese into several dioceses, grant full rights to vicar bishops, and ordain new bishops, bearing in mind that at a later date, when central church authority would be reinstated, these measures would be subject to ratification.

The sobor of Detroit obeyed the patriarchal decree, while obviously not aware of the historical significance of such an act. The proclamation of autonomy was made at a time when the body of the American Orthodox church was beginning to break up into isolated, even hostile, ethnic and political jurisdictional factions.

The disorder in the church that followed the revolution in Russia, the absence of uncontested authority, financial problems, and the level of political catastrophe—all this distracted the Russian hierarchy of the American metropolia from attending to a pressing concern for other ethnic groups that remained under its jurisdiction. The previously existing authority of the Russian Empire, which had backed the Russian hierarchy, had kept the various ethnic groups together, but with the fall of the Orthodox Russian Empire, all leanings toward ethnic separatism came to the surface, spawning the creation of a number of Orthodox jurisdictions.

As the famous church leader and Orthodox theologian Fr. Alexander Schmemann pointed out, during the centuries of the church's existence it had experienced a disintegration of universal consciousness. The autocephaly of the church was beginning to be understood in the sense of national consciousness or as an appurtenance of statehood. Although the principle of territorialism remained in force and in theory continued to be the canonical norm, in practice it acquired over time a nationalist dimension.[29] While the Orthodox lived in their own countries, they belonged to their own respective national churches. But with the beginning of mass emigration and the creation of ethnic enclaves in other countries, the national-political principle came into conflict with the principle of territorialism under the conditions of diaspora.

The diaspora showed, in accordance with Fr. Schmemann's statement, that the national churches, in effect, became "religious projections of a given people or, even a given state." And if "the Orthodox church degenerated into a federation of national churches, whose interrelationships were built similarly to relationships between sovereign states"[30] (i.e., on the principle of "noninvolvement" in each other's affairs and protection of one's own rights), then the Orthodox diaspora was also being built on the concept of independent ethnic jurisdictions, each representing a small member of that church community, the head and body of which are located on other continents. Along with communist regimes, the last fifty years have brought a division of Orthodoxy on political grounds and led to a separation of already existing ethnic churches into hostile juris-

dictions. By the time the Orthodox church in America was formed in
1970, Orthodoxy in America existed in the following divided condition:
"one Greek jurisdiction, three Russian, two Serbian, two Antiochian, two
Romanian, two Albanian, two Bulgarian, three Ukrainian, one Carpatho-
Russian, and several smaller jurisdictions."[31] The history of other Orthodox ethnic jurisdictions is not the subject of this chapter, since they
detached themselves from the Russian diocese and continued to live their
own independent lives.[32]

The Struggle of the Metropolia in Defense of Its Autonomy

After the sobor in Detroit proclaimed a provisional autonomy, and with
the growing immigrant population, as well as the simultaneous appearance
of other Russian jurisdictions and an increasing number of ethnic Orthodox jurisdictions, the American metropolia was faced with discovering its
own self-awareness as a church. In this period, historical surveys and research were undertaken. Church officials were struggling to preserve the
independence of the metropolia—that is, its very self—from the shock and
divisions that were tearing the church apart, both in Russia and abroad.

I shall be concerned here with only two foreign branches of the Russian
Orthodox church: the American exarchate of the Moscow patriarchate,
which came into being in the 1930s, and the Russian Orthodox Church
Abroad. Both of these churches, for several decades, encroached on the
metropolia, attempting to deprive it of its independence or, at least, to
impose their own conditions.

The Russian Orthodox Church Abroad was created at a meeting of emi-
grant Russian bishops in Yugoslavia in 1923. The meeting took place in
the small town of Sremski Karlovci (from which the church's other name,
the "Karlovci church," is derived) and was held under the patronage of
the Serbian patriarch. Having been created as a temporary ecclesiastical
administration for Russian emigrants, the Karlovci synod proclaimed itself
the national Russian church in diaspora.[33] The synod took a restorationist
stand on political matters, calling for the reinstatement of the house of Romanov, and placed the patriarch of Moscow in a difficult position. In May
1922, even before the Karlovci meeting took place, Patriarch Tikhon had
officially decreed that hierarchs who had emigrated for political reasons
had no right to speak on behalf of the Russian Orthodox church, that their
statements did not represent the "official voice of the Russian Orthodox
Church, due to their political nature," and did "not have ecclesiastical-
canonical significance."[34] After the meeting at Sremski Karlovci, the patriarch issued a decree that categorically and explicitly dismissed the ec-

clesiastical administration established there. He simultaneously passed on the administration of all Russian Orthodox churches in Western Europe to Metropolitan Evlogii, who was residing in Paris.[35]

However, the Synod of Bishops outside Russia declared that the patriarch and the ecclesiastical hierarchy in Soviet Russia were paralyzed, at best, and, at worst, actively cooperating with the government. The Karlovci synod demanded subordination from Metropolitan Evlogii, the head of the exarchate in Western Europe, and from Metropolitan Platon, the head of the American metropolia, both of whom had been appointed by Patriarch Tikhon. The synod also demanded that Platon nullify the autonomy, ratified by the Detroit sobor. These demands forced both Platon and Evlogii to leave the synod and break all relations with it. To this action the synod responded by creating parallel jurisdictions in Europe and America. In the United States the Synodal church grew into a more or less sizable jurisdiction only after the war, beginning with the end of the 1940s. Before this time it was the Moscow patriarchate that presented the greatest threat to the metropolia.

After the death of Patriarch Tikhon in obscure circumstances in 1925 and the arrest of the three interim administrators designated by the patriarch in his will, the Soviet authorities selected Metropolitan Sergii Stragorodsky, who was the substitute for the third locum tenens. After spending some time in a Soviet jail, under obvious pressure from the GPU (secret police), he agreed to what may have been an unavoidable compromise with the regime and slowly but surely surrendered the independence of the church.[36] Shortly after ecclesiastical authority was consolidated in Metropolitan Sergii's hands, he succumbed to the pressure of the regime and began attempting to spread Moscow's ecclesiastical authority over the centers of Russian Orthodoxy abroad: the Western European exarchate and the American metropolia. The obvious reason for this action was the Soviet government's desire to gain influence over the masses of political refugees living in Europe and America.

Already in 1928 Metropolitan Sergii demanded that Metropolitan Platon sign documents of nonparticipation in political activities that were directed against the Soviet regime. This demand was repeated in 1933. After receiving a rejection from the American metropolia, the Moscow ecclesiastical administration sent a bishop to America. Their intent was to create an exarchate in the United States that would be subject to Moscow. They also issued an interdiction against Metropolitan Platon.

It is true that in the 1930s the influence exerted by this exarchate in America was minor. However, pressure from the Moscow patriarchate continued even during the administration of Platon's successor, Metropolitan Theophilus. The latter was elected in 1934 at the Cleveland sobor, which ratified the total administrative independence of the metropolia and gave it the right to independently elect its own leader. In response to this decision of the sobor, the Moscow patriarchate issued in 1935 an interdiction against Metropolitan Theophilus as well—barring his repentance.[37]

Theophilus attempted to consolidate the various Russian Orthodox groups in America. He succeeded in concluding an alliance with the Karlovci jurisdiction and the independent Carpatho-Russian diocese. The bishops, clergy, and parishes from these groups joined the metropolia, headed by Theophilus, under the condition that the latter preserved her autonomy. The sixth all-American sobor of 1937 ratified this status of reunification.

The union of Russian Orthodox churches in the United States continued until World War II. At the beginning of the war there were 400,000 faithful and 330 parishes, divided into eight dioceses, in the American metropolia.[38]

The war period proved to be a new phase in the growth of the metropolia's self-awareness as a territorial church. In 1943 the first Orthodox chaplain was appointed from among the clergy of the metropolia to the armed forces. In 1944 the metropolia celebrated 150 years of Orthodoxy in America, which was brought here by Russian missionaries and had put down strong roots.

In the war the United States and the USSR were allied against a common enemy. After two decades of bloody terror, the Soviet government acknowledged the church, reinstated the patriarchy, permitted the election of a patriarch, and allowed a certain semblance of religious freedom. The election of Metropolitan Sergii as patriarch in September 1943 radically changed the relationship between the USSR and its allies.

Taking advantage of the rise in pro-Soviet feelings and the great deal of publicity they were getting, Metropolitan Veniamin, the exarch of the Moscow patriarchate, began a campaign of active propaganda among the American Orthodox to get the metropolia to subordinate itself to the Moscow patriarchate, especially since the primary reason for the separation—the persecution of the church—had now "ceased to exist." On the other hand, the Russian Orthodox Church Abroad, which had met in October 1943 in Nazi-occupied Vienna, condemned the election of the patriarch.

Sergii's successor, Patriarch Aleksii, elected in 1945, again demanded subordination from the metropolia and again received a refusal from her synod of bishops. The seventh all-American sobor ratified the autonomy of the metropolia. As a result of his failure to obtain the subordination of the metropolia, Patriarch Aleksii in 1947 repeated the old interdiction and extended it against all the bishops of the metropolia. As with all the previous interdictions, this last one had no noticeable effect on the life of the metropolia. The end of the 1940s was generally marked by a radical decline in influence of the patriarchal exarchate among the American Orthodox. The resurgence of Stalin's repressions in 1948, together with the launching of a massive anti-Semitic campaign in the USSR and the beginning of the cold war brought a natural end to this influence.

Yet this period saw the growth of a dividing influence from the Karlovci jurisdiction, which proved to be far more harmful and of more lasting duration. After the fall of Nazi Germany, the Russian Orthodox Church Abroad (ROCA) moved its headquarters from Munich to New York, without obtaining any approval from the administration of the American metropolia.

With the second immigration from the USSR—war prisoners, participants of the Vlasov movement, all those who managed to escape from the Soviet Union—the ROCA, which had been stressing its anti-Soviet politics and its Russian nationalism, began to grow rapidly and soon spread across the United States and Canada.[39] To this day the ROCA holds its own. As before, it still claims total ecclesiastical authority over all the Russian Orthodox in the world. After the granting of autocephaly to the OCA, the ROCA accused the OCA of being subordinate to the "false church," on the one hand, and of betraying herself to Western reformation, on the other hand. It forbade its members any church contact with the OCA.[40]

It is interesting to note here that despite the apparently vast irreconcilability of their ecclesiastical positions, the Moscow patriarchate and the ROCA have much in common. From the synodical epoch they both inherited a feeling of cringing before state rule and were both imbued with the spirit of imperial power. They both conceive the life of the church only under patronage of the state. The ROCA lives in a prison of daydreams about the prerevolutionary Orthodox autocratic monarchy and has thus canonized the last tsar; the patriarchate lives imprisoned by the totalitarian Soviet empire and follows its external and internal politics. Both are characterized by an extreme ecclesiastical nationalism,[41] both are conservative in their theology and liturgical life; both fear any reforms or renewal.

It is also no coincidence that in 1936 both churches independently condemned one of the most productive and broad-minded Orthodox theologians of our century: Fr. Sergei Bulgakov. He was a professor at the St. Sergius Orthodox Institute in Paris. In their condemnation the ROCA and the Moscow patriarchate (which passed judgment on hearsay, since Bulgakov's books, published in the West, could not be obtained in the

Soviet Union) attempted to deal a blow to the institute itself, which had
been so rightly called "the first truly free Russian theological seminary in
history."[42] The very spirit of novelty and theological creativity frightened
both the synod and the patriarchate. And yet, owing more to creative efforts in theological and ecclesiastical awareness than to church diplomacy,
the American metropolia was able to become a territorial autocephalous
church. Something should be said about the development of this awareness.

The Theological Basis for the American Territorial Church

From the middle of the last century an awakening began among Russian
Orthodox intellectuals, focused on discovering the role of Orthodoxy in
Christian history and in the contemporary world. It was also focused on a
reflection about the nature of the church in reaction to the grievous condition of the ROC under the rule of an imperial autocracy. Started by the
Slavophiles Kireevsky and Khomyakov and continued, first, by Vladimir
Solovev and, later, by a pleiad of twentieth-century religious thinkers,
this theological revival gradually attracted wide circles of church officials
and laid the groundwork for ecclesiastical reforms and revival. But Orthodox ideas were not fated to bear fruit in Russia. Together with normal
ecclesiastical life, the Revolution disrupted the natural development of
Orthodox ideas.

This development, however, was able to continue in exile. Its center
became the St. Sergius Institute in Paris, where the luminaries of Russian
theological thought gathered. Among its many theological subjects, the
institute was innovative in the field of ecclesiology. Fr. Nicholas Afanasiev,
a professor at the institute, reacting against Roman "universal" ecclesiology, developed the "eucharistic" teaching on the church.[43] According
to his research, the concept of "catholicity" did not signify for the early
Christians a geographical expansion of the church, but rather her onto-
logical omnipresence, which is realized in each liturgy, in each eucharistic
celebration presided over by a bishop, surrounded by the clergy and the
faithful people of God. Where the Eucharist is celebrated, there is Christ
and the church of the saints, in which the fullness of the "ecumenical"
or "catholic" church is given. A bishop's blessing is first and foremost a
blessing to celebrate the Eucharist. It is from this blessing that the right
stems to sanctify, to ordain priests as eucharistic delegates of the bishop,
and deacons as ministers of the territorial church. For this reason the fullness of apostolic charisma is present in each bishop, and, in this sense, all
bishops are equal. The names "metropolia" or "patriarchate" do not refer

to the catholic nature of the church, but to her geopolitical and demographic features. Thus the patriarch or metropolitan of each territorial church is not so much placed over the church, as he is considered first among equals in the hierarchy of the episcopacy.

This concept, rooted in the liturgical and canonical practice and theory of Orthodoxy, laid the groundwork for overcoming the jurisdictional approach, by which the bishop of a geographically larger diocese, or of a more important administrative center (metropolitan or patriarch), has power over bishops of smaller dioceses. Thus eucharistic ecclesiology replaced the jurisdictional concept of the church as an institution headed by hierarchs.

The ecclesiological teachings of Fr. Afanasiev, however, did not immediately bear fruit in reality. It took many years of inculcating this ecclesiastical awareness in the hierarchy and the people before it began to shape the life of the church. One of the theologians who developed and spread this teaching in America was Fr. Alexander Schmemann, dean of St. Vladimir's Seminary in New York. He himself was a student of Afanasiev at the St. Sergius Institute.

Such luminaries of Russian theology as Fr. Georges Florovsky, George Fedotov, Nicholas Lossky, Nicholas Arseniev, and Alexander Bogolepov (the last elected rector of the free Petersburg University) came to America and started teaching at St. Vladimir's Seminary. *Toward an American Orthodox Church*, written by Bogolepov, professor of canon law, became the practical application of eucharistic ecclesiology.[44] Its thesis was as follows: inasmuch as the fullness of the church is where the bishop, as head of a church community, celebrates the Eucharist, and three bishops of a given region must be present at the ordination of another bishop (since according to Orthodox canons, it is necessary to have three bishops to ordain a fourth), it follows that any church district that has three dioceses, with a minimum of three bishops and a theological seminary for educating the clergy, could be considered ecclesiastically self-sufficient and in this sense ready for autocephaly or self-administration. The problem of autocephaly does not lie in ecclesiastical authority but in ecclesiastical self-sufficiency.

In the American metropolia the presence of six bishops who could ordain new bishops, as well as the existence of theological seminaries to educate the clergy, meant that the American church had the practical prerequisites for autocephaly. The practical application of the principles of eucharistic theology has given the metropolia its ecclesiastical-canonical basis for demanding legal recognition of its independence, which it was constrained to proclaim in 1924, and then to defend. The request for autocephaly was finally presented in a discussion with representatives of the Moscow patriarchate.

The Proclamation of Autocephaly by the Orthodox Church in America

As a result of several years of negotiations, the Moscow patriarchate arrived at the conclusion that granting autocephaly to the American metropolia was only a matter of time and that the American metropolia was already independent, i.e., de facto autocephalous, making its return to the Moscow patriarchate impossible. That the Kremlin did not obstruct the metropolia's secession from the jurisdiction of the Moscow patriarchate may be attributable to the relative political uncertainty that prevailed in Moscow in the early years of the Brezhnev regime.

Hence, the Moscow patriarchate granted autocephaly to the American metropolia in April 1970. The document for autocephaly was signed by Patriarch Aleksii, six days before his death. A delegation led by Theodosius, bishop of Alaska and primate of the OCA since 1978, went to Moscow to accept the document, after the death of Patriarch Aleksii. That same year the fourteenth all-American sobor of the metropolia convened and officially proclaimed its autocephaly, taking the name Orthodox Church in America. This sobor thus became the first council convened by the territorial American Orthodox church. The birth of the OCA caused a great furor in the American Orthodox diaspora, with its ethnic jurisdictions, and in the entire Orthodox world.[45] However, several church groups in America, such as certain parishes of Albanian, Bulgarian, and Romanian Orthodox believers, chose to join the OCA, while preserving their ethnic character. Their bishops became members of the synod of the OCA. The OCA enjoys acceptance and equality in the family of Orthodox churches today. Only the Greek patriarchates of Constantinople, Jerusalem, and Alexandria still refuse to acknowledge its autocephalous status.

The Orthodox Church in America Today

From the middle of the 1950s the metropolia began to lose its ethnic character. English became the official language of all its publications, academic endeavors, and liturgy. The awareness of the new generation of the faithful and the clergy was turned, above all, toward missionary work. Since the mid-1950s there has also been an increasing flow of Americans converting to Orthodox Christianity. This flow has increased significantly since 1970 and the grant of autocephaly, which opened the doors of Orthodoxy not only to individual people but also to ecclesiastical communities: parishes and monasteries. Thus, for example, an entire Old Catholic diocese in Mexico converted to Orthodoxy and joined the OCA. On the basis of this diocese, a Mexican exarchate of the OCA was created. A survey of five hundred OCA members who had converted to Orthodoxy in the last thirty years showed that about 60 percent of these members converted to Orthodoxy according to the degree that the OCA, as a territorial church, became known to American society.[46] Thus the creation of a territorial church opened the doors of Orthodoxy to Western people, who converted from other religious and cultural traditions.

There are presently fourteen dioceses in the OCA, of which eleven are territorial and three are ethnic: the Albanian, the Romanian, and the Bulgarian; one is a foreign exarchate—the Mexican diocese; the others are individual parishes in Australia and Latin America.[47] The leader of the church is the metropolitan, who is the archbishop of Washington, D.C., and metropolitan of all America and Canada. He is elected by the council of the OCA and administers the church, between councils, together with a synod of bishops and the metropolitan council, comprising both clergy and lay people. According to an ancient rule, the synod of bishops meets twice a year in the spring and autumn.

The present primate of the OCA—Metropolitan Theodosius—is a native-born American. The OCA is the fifteenth autocephalous Orthodox church in the world. It enjoys complete freedom, which the American democratic system of religious organization offers it, and is administered, according to Orthodox norms, by regularly convening councils (which now meet every three years), attended by bishops, clergy, and lay delegates.

FACT SHEET

The Orthodox Church in America

Year of autocephaly
  Metropolitanate of All America and Canada of the Russian-Orthodox Greek-Catholic Church: established in 1924 by the fourth all-American sobor. The sobor proclaimed temporary autonomy of the metropolitanate.
  The canonical status of autocephaly was granted in 1970 by the Russian Orthodox church.
  The fourteenth all-American church sobor officially proclaimed autocephaly, 1970.

Current strength of church (1985)
  1 million faithful
  10 ruling bishops
  681 priests and monks

19 nuns
123 seminarians

Chief news organ
The Orthodox Church (20,000 copies)

Number of churches and church facilities in operation (1985)
558 churches
3 theological seminaries
1 theological faculty (academy)
6 sketes
7 monasteries

Metropolitans since 1924
Platon (Rozhdestvensky), 1924–34
Theophilus (Pashkovsky), 1934–50
Leonti (Turkevich), 1950–65
Irinei (Bekish), 1965–78
Theodosius (Lasor), 1978–present

7

The Russian Orthodox Church Abroad

Oxana Antić

The October Revolution of 1917 radically changed the sociopolitical order in Russia and with it the position of the Russian Orthodox church. At the end of the Civil War, which followed the Revolution, part of the clergy, together with remnants of the defeated White forces, fled Russia. The émigré clergy, cut off from contact with the church in Russia, carried on church life autonomously, and in 1921 convened the first council representing the Russian church in exile, in Sremski Karlovci, Yugoslavia. A few years later, in 1926, a split occurred in the ranks of the church which accounts for the fact that there are today three ecclesiastical organizations of Russian origin in the West: the Russian Orthodox Church Abroad,[1] the Orthodox Church of America,[2] and the "Paris Jurisdiction."[3]

The Russian Orthodox Church Abroad sees itself as a branch of the one Russian Orthodox church, together with the mother church in Russia and the Catacomb church.[4] The Russian Orthodox Church Abroad (or, more briefly, the Synodal church) considers itself rather the embodiment of the aspirations of Russian believers not only in the emigration, but also in Russia, and the guarantor of the preservation of historical consciousness. Continuing the traditions of the Russian Orthodox church, the Synodal church conducted several canonizations of Russian saints.[5] Religious, philosophical, and historical works, books for children and students, and other materials are being published at the church's publishing houses in the United States, Canada, and Federal Republic of Germany—some of which find their way into the USSR.[6] In addition, Archbishop Antonii of Geneva and Western Europe set up a broadcasting service to broadcast religious programs to the USSR.

The Synodal church has some impact, albeit indirectly, on the Russian religious scene, insofar as some active Orthodox believers appealed on various occasions to the hierarchs of this church, and members of the so-called Catacomb church have also declared that they consider themselves in canonical unity with the Synodal church.[7]

The Early Years

When the Bolsheviks took over in Russia in 1917 the Russian Orthodox church lost its privileged position and was targeted instead for repression. Church and state had already been separated by the short-lived Provisional Government. Now, on January 23/February 5, 1918, a decree of the Council of People's Commissars, personally signed by Lenin, ruled that religious instruction would not be permitted in either public or private schools and that "religious associations" (a term which refers to local churches as well as to the rights and duties of individual believers) did not enjoy the rights of juridical persons, which meant that they could not own property.[8]

Within a matter of weeks after the Revolution, the new regime started arresting and harassing clergymen and believers. Thousands were shot or sent to Siberia. The repression even intensified in the 1930s, resulting in the decimation of the clergy and the termination of all religious publications. By 1939 the majority of the country's churches would be closed down or destroyed.[9]

The Civil War (1917–23) divided the country into two political camps, broadly speaking, each hostile to the other. This created problems in maintaining normal communication lines between the sundry hierarchs of the Russian Orthodox church. In these circumstances, those hierarchs who were in the south of Russia under the administration of the White forces decided to call a south Russian council in Stavropol in May 1919 to discuss appropriate measures to be taken. Meeting on May 6, this council established a Provisional Supreme Administration of the Church for South Russia (or henceforth, Provisional Administration). Archbishop Mitrofan (Krasnopol'skii) of the Don province was appointed president of the new institution.

Patriarch Tikhon approved this new body, by issuing, together with the Holy Synod, Decree No. 362 (November 7/20, 1920), which accorded canonical recognition to the Provisional Administration. In specific, this decree noted: "If an eparchy loses all contact with its chief ecclesiastical administration, then the diocesan bishop must contact the bishops of the neighboring eparchies immediately in order to create a chief court of ecclesiastical administration (be it in the form of a provisional chief church administration, a metropolitan area, or in some other way."[10] Ironically, this decree was issued the very day that the Provisional Administration was leaving the country with the remnants of the White Army. But the administrative life of this new body continued, and the first meeting of the Orthodox bishops who left Russia was held on the ship while en route to Constantinople.

Shortly after arriving in Constantinople, Metropolitan Antonii (Khrapovitsky), senior among the bishops who had left Russia, convened an organizational meeting. The following month this Provisional Administration was recognized by the ecumenical patriarch in Constantinople,[11] and the Provisional Administration enjoyed at that time broad support among other Orthodox churches as well as among the leaders of Russian Orthodox parishes that had existed abroad long before the October Revolution. The Provisional Administration remained in Constantinople only until May 1921 when the Serbian patriarch invited the Russian bishops to move to Yugoslavia. This invitation was accepted, and the Provisional Administration moved to the town of Sremski Karlovci, where it remained until 1944.

The first council of the Russian Orthodox Church Abroad was convened in Sremski Karlovci in November 1921.[12] This council brought together thirteen bishops, twenty-three priests, and sixty-seven laymen, representing dioceses and parishes from all over the world. The council, taking into account the fact that those in emigration were cut off from the Moscow patriarchate, authorized the bishops, in assembly, to serve as the central church authority in emigration. All bishops possessed a vote in this synod, and the decisions required a simple majority.

The council of Sremski Karlovci also declared itself in favor of a restoration of the monarchy in Russia, though there was some difference of opinion as to whether a future tsar must be a Romanov or could belong to a collateral line. The church has not discussed this decision officially since then.

In October 1920 the Provisional Administration appointed Archbishop Evlogii administrator of the Russian parishes in Western Europe; the patriarch of Moscow recognized this appointment on March 21, 1921. Meanwhile, Patriarch Tikhon was facing difficult circumstances at home.[13] He was, without question, subjected to psychological and physical pressure by the regime, and one may surmise that his termination of the Provisional Administration in May 1922 came as a concession to the Soviet authorities.[14] When the bishops in emigration met again on September 13, 1922, they agreed to obey the patriarchal decree and dissolved the Provisional Administration. However, in its place the council formed a Provisional Sacred Synod of Bishops of the Russian Orthodox Church Abroad. Through this measure, the executive organ of the episcopal council came into being in its own right. Patriarch Tikhon died on April 7, 1925, before he could issue any further instructions to the Russian prelates abroad.

With Tikhon's death, Metropolitan Petr (Polyanskii) became locum tenens to the patriarchal throne, but no new patriarch was elected for the time. Metropolitan Petr did not cooperate with the Soviet government, however, and was therefore arrested in 1925 and sent to Siberia, where he died in 1936. Until his death, he was considered by the church in Russia, the Church Abroad, and the Catacomb church to be the head of the Russian Orthodox church as a whole.

The Break

Metropolitan Sergii (Stragorodsky), who administered the throne of the patriarch as vice locum tenens after 1925, also refused at first to cooperate with the Soviet government. But in 1927 he signed a declaration of loyalty, in which he said that the Soviet government's successes and setbacks are likewise the successes and setbacks of the church. Metropolitan Sergii also required clergy abroad to submit written declarations of loyalty to the Soviet government and threatened to excommunicate those who refused.[15] The bishops' council rejected this demand and declared it uncanonical, since it was signed by Metropolitan Sergii alone and not by other members of the Holy Synod in Moscow. This decision was a watershed for the émigré clergy and set the direction of the Russian Orthodox Church Abroad, not only ecclesiastically but politically.

Meanwhile, internal differences presented the Russian Orthodox Church Abroad with a threat to its unity. In 1926 Platon, metropolitan of the American diocese, and Evlogii, metropolitan of Western Europe, had demanded greater autonomy in the administration of their dioceses. Evlogii also insisted on remaining in canonical unity with the Moscow patriarchate. The differences between these two hierarchs and the rest of the synod proved insuperable. The two metropolitans left the Synodal church with large groups of believers.

The bishopric of Berlin and Germany, a part of the West European diocese of the Russian Orthodox Church Abroad before World War II, was confronted with a number of new and serious problems after Hitler's takeover in 1933. Atheist and anti-Slav by its philosophy and racist policies, the National Socialist party could not openly attack the church, since they proclaimed themselves anticommunists and the church had been one of the first victims of communist persecution in Russia. Therefore, stick-and-carrot tactics were applied to this weak, foreign community. The Russian Orthodox church, engaged in pastoral work among Russian émigrés, had to seek for ways of accommodation with the regime that could secure the church's survival. When, following the Nazi invasion of the USSR in 1941, hundred of thousands of prisoners of war and forced labor workers arrived in Germany, the clergy of the Russian Orthodox Church Abroad took pastoral care of the workers and even, in some cases, among the Russian POWs. The Russian Orthodox Church Abroad also rendered support to Orthodox communities that spontaneously appeared in those parts of the Soviet Union that were under German occupation.[16]

After the war Soviet press and also some circles in the West started a campaign against the Russian Orthodox Church Abroad, accusing its leadership of cooperation with the National Socialist regime. Several church hierarchs made public statements in defense of the Russian Orthodox Church Abroad, i.e., the patriarch of the Serbian Orthodox church, who had spent three years in a German concentration camp. Patriarch Gavrilo stated: "Metropolitan Anastasii has demonstrated the greatest wisdom and tactical skill in relations with the Germans, has always been loyal to the Serbs, was subject several times to house searches, and did not enjoy German confidence."[17]

In 1944 Soviet troops entered northern Yugoslavia, approaching Sremski Karlovci. Fearful of what might develop if they were captured by the Soviets, the bishops of the Church Abroad left Sremski Karlovci and moved to Munich, which was occupied by U.S. troops a few months later in May 1945. In 1949 the synod left Munich and found a new home in Mahopac, near New York City. Mahopac is today the Hermitage of Our Lady of Kursk and the summer residence of the head of the church. In 1958 the synod moved to New York City. However, the spiritual and religious center of the church is located in Jordanville, New York, where the church has a monastery, a seminary (with about forty seminarians enrolled at present), and the publishing house of the Pochaev Press.

The Synod's Relations with Other Churches

The relationship of the Russian Orthodox Church Abroad with other Orthodox as well as non-Orthodox churches, which had been unproblematic before 1927, became more clouded with each passing year. The political situation in general and the relations of the churches with the Moscow patriarchate in particular underwent a radical change after World War II, and the Russian Orthodox Church Abroad was inevitably affected.

The Synodal church's contacts with other Orthodox churches started to change drastically after 1945 when the Moscow patriarchate began an energetic campaign to establish contacts with Orthodox and non-Orthodox churches, buttressing the general Soviet foreign policy line and organizing large religious conferences.[18] As a rule, in making such contacts, the Moscow patriarchate expected that the other church would break off relations with the synod. In this way the synod lost official ties to all Orthodox churches except the Serbian, these ties being "frozen" rather than formally severed. The Roman Catholic and Protestant churches did not freeze their relations with the synod until the early 1960s, after the Moscow patriarchate gained admission, in 1961, to the World Council of Churches. Unofficial contacts, however, continue between the synod and several Orthodox churches as well as with other Christian churches. There are no official contacts, on the other hand, between the synod and either the Orthodox Church in America or the Paris Jurisdiction.

Moreover, all official ties to the Moscow patriarchate had been broken off in 1927 when the Russian Orthodox Church Abroad rejected Metropolitan Sergii's demand for declarations of loyalty to the regime. The bishops broke off relations with the Moscow patriarchate, stating that no normal contacts were possible any longer since—in the synod's view—the church authorities in the Soviet Union had come under the control of the government.

Some years later the Moscow patriarchate made an effort to draw the synod back under its wing. Shortly before the end of World War II Patriarch Aleksii sent an appeal for reconciliation to Metropolitan Anastasii (Gribanovskii). Since in Anastasii's view the situation had not changed in any significant way, he rejected the overture. Some thirty years later—in 1974—Patriarch Pimen would issue an open "Message to those who are in a state of schism and call themselves 'The Russian Orthodox Church Outside Russia,' who went out from the bosom of the Russian Orthodox Church." In this message the Moscow patriarch acknowledged that "in its relationship with society and the state, in the manner in which civic duties are carried out and in the manifestation of patriotic feelings, the views of Orthodox Christians at home and of those in the diaspora could never fully coincide."[19] No declaration of loyalty was expected from the believers at this point. On the contrary, the patriarch stressed his full comprehension of the fact that political convictions can form insurmountable problems. He continued, "Without any intention of exalting herself, the Russian Orthodox church nevertheless feels bound to warn those of her children who are alienated from her of the spiritual danger to which they are exposing themselves by neglecting the rightful canonical organization of their ecclesiastical life and the elimination of the spirit of hatred and enmity." The patriarch closed the message by expressing hope that, in spite of these difficulties, "the spirit of Christian love could melt the ice of hostility between brothers."[20] Metropolitan Filaret, primate of the Russian Orthodox Church Abroad, replied to this message, repudiating the accusation that his church nurtured "hatred and enmity" and underlining that "nothing can change our attitude toward godless communism."[21]

Though the bitterness sparked by the break between the Paris Jurisdiction and the synod has faded, the two organizations have not resumed normal relations, though some believers are active in both.

These divisions troubled Russia's deeply religious writer Aleksandr Solzhenitsyn, who in an appeal published in August 1974 expressed his distress at the disunity in Russian Orthodoxy in exile. In his view the split had shaken "not only the unity of our Orthodoxy, our common heredity of Patriarch Tikhon, but even our Christianity itself."[22] His appeal set off an intense exchange of opinions among the hierarchs of the three ecclesiastical organizations of Russian origin in the West. Metropolitan Filaret wrote to Metropolitan Irinei of the Orthodox Church in America and also sent an open letter to the clergy and laity of the Paris Jurisdiction. The heads of both organizations answered, and several noted theologians and religious writers also entered into the discussion, which spread into various émigré newspapers and magazines. But nothing came of it in the end, since all of the parties used the opportunity only to stress their particular points of view.[23]

The Present Situation of the Russian Orthodox Church Abroad

Some of the serious problems that the Russian Orthodox Church Abroad currently faces are very much the same as those with which other Christian churches are having to cope, namely, growing secularization, the strains of exposure of the congregation to confessional diversity and the consequent relativization of values, and the sundry social changes associated with urbanization and modernization. The old age of many of its priests and its strained financial situation add to the church's concerns. But in general a surprising number of parishioners, not only elderly people but also the young, view the church in national (or nationalist) terms, seeing in it an important link with their own culture and national Christian heritage.

As a result of World War II, the synod suffered heavy losses. Church property was lost in China and Eastern and Central Europe. Most of the parishes in North America followed Metropolitan Platon. These setbacks were aggravated by the postwar initiatives of the Moscow patriarchate. At the same time the Russian Orthodox Church Abroad was replenished with new blood. Eleven of the thirteen bishops who fled the Soviet Union at the end of World War II joined the synod, as did 90 percent of the lower clergy (including monks and nuns). Moreover, the "third emigration" (lasting from the mid-1960s to the beginning of the 1980s) brought new members to the church.

Today the Russian Orthodox Church Abroad is administered by one metropolitan, eight archbishops, seven bishops, thirty-eight archimandrites and igumen, eighty-one archpriests, 120 priests, thirty-three archdeacons, and thirty-one deacons. Not all of them are Russians; about half of the three hundred nuns are Arabs, while many of the priests are Greeks. The Russian Orthodox Church Abroad maintains parish schools, two parochial high schools in the United States, a boarding school with six hundred students, homes for the aged, an orphan house, parish centers, and libraries.[24]

Church services are conducted in Old Church Slavonic, in their original unabbreviated versions. In some countries national parishes have been formed where the liturgy is conducted instead in the language of the given country. In West Germany, when the liturgy is conducted in Old Church Slavonic, the sermon, in Russian, is simultaneously translated into German.

Conclusion

The Russian Orthodox Church Abroad is certainly one of the most conservative Christian churches in present times. Its clergy conducts a struggle for the preservation of the pure Orthodox faith, as it views it, and defends it against contemporary currents, such as modernism, reformism, and especially ecumenism. Its ecclesiastical views are very close to those of the Russian Orthodox church in the prerevolutionary period and of the present Serbian patriarchate, the patriarchate of Jerusalem, and the monkhood on the holy mountain of Áthos.

The spiritual ties between the Russian Orthodox Church Abroad and some active Orthodox believers in the Soviet Union have been manifested on several occasions. Members of the Committee for the Defense of Believers' Rights in the Soviet Union, headed by the Orthodox priest Gleb Yakunin, addressed an open letter, in 1979, "to the Russian Orthodox Christians in the homeland and the diaspora." In this letter four members of the committee expressed their deep satisfaction with the plan of the Russian Orthodox Church Abroad to canonize the "new martyrs"

(30,000 in all). Calling upon all of Russian Orthodoxy to participate in the preparations for the canonization, which they called "a matter of utmost importance," the authors of the appeal expressed their "deep perturbance" over the fact that "even as far as this great all-church and all-nation matter is concerned, the Synodal church remains, as it had been before, in solitude." The authors of the appeal also stressed their approval to canonize the last tsar and his family (among the "new martyrs"), explaining that the tragedy of the tsar and his family has become "a symbol-prologue to Russia's long road to Calvary."[25] After the canonization, Bishop Gregoriy (Grabbe) of Washington, D.C., and Florida told the press that the church had waited for sixty-six years before bestowing sainthood on the "new martyrs," but then it has been made possible because "suddenly and unexpectedly, we were able to contact reliable persons in the Soviet Union who provided us with ample information and lists of martyrs."[26] Not surprisingly, the Soviet press denounced the canonization as "a religious ceremony with political overtones," assailing the "split of Karlovci."[27]

The fact that some mental bonds and occasional contacts do exist between the Russian Orthodox Church Abroad and some believers in the Soviet Union is very remarkable, considering the difficulties that have to be overcome. This can serve as an explanation for the permanent attacks on the Russian Orthodox Church Abroad in the Soviet press.

The Russian Orthodox Church Abroad presents a fascinating case study in rivalry over legitimacy. Having been created in 1920 for purely religious reasons, the church defied the Moscow patriarch in 1927 over a political issue (though it may be granted that the regime's official atheism made this political issue simultaneously a religious issue). From that point on, neither organization has recognized the legitimacy of the other. The subsequent emergence of the autocephalous Orthodox Church in America only further complicated the situation from the synod's point of view, and the two churches coexist, somewhat uneasily, side by side in many cities in America.

Because neither the synod nor the Moscow patriarchate recognizes the other's legitimacy any longer, each has tried to delegitimize the other in the eyes of third parties. The Moscow patriarchate portrays the synod as reactionary and politicized. The synod portrays the Moscow patriarchate as the puppet of the Soviet regime. Their competition has even been extended into the World Council of Churches, where observers from the Synodal church were once welcome, but which, since the admission of the Moscow patriarchate in 1961, has ceased inviting observers from the Russian Orthodox Church Abroad.[28]

It is against this backdrop that the Soviet reaction to the canonization of

Nicholas II may be seen. The canonization represented, on the one hand, a symbolic challenge to the legitimacy of the Soviet state, by tying its foundation to the primal murder of Orthodox "saints." At the same time the Soviet regime's response, mocking the new saint as "bloody Nicholas"[29] and suggesting that the synod's next move should be to canonize Hitler,[30] reflects its desire to exploit the canonization for propaganda purposes and turn it against the church. The canonization, in short, should become an instrument for delegitimizing the synod, i.e., serve the very opposite purpose from what it was intended to serve.

Because the dispute ultimately derives from political grounds, it is not apt to be resolved short of the overthrow of the Soviet state or the dissolution of the Russian Orthodox Church Abroad. Dialogue becomes irrelevant and notions of reconciliation remain utterly fanciful. What gradually becomes clear is that the political and the religious are too closely meshed to be disentangled; the spiritual vision of the Russian Orthodox Church Abroad has in fact an unmistakable political dimension, and its politics, at the same time, are rooted in its spirituality.

FACT SHEET

The Russian Orthodox Church Abroad

Year of autocephaly
  1448: Russian Orthodox Church
  The Russian Orthodox Church Abroad does not claim to be autocephalous, but it broke relations with the Moscow patriarchate in 1927 and does not recognize any other ecclesiastical jurisdiction.

Current strength of the church (1984)
  150,000 believers
  180 monks
  239 archmandrites and priests
  300 nuns
  16 archbishops and bishops

Chief news organs
  Pravoslavnaya Rus (circulation 3,000 copies in 1984)
  Pravoslavnaya zhizn (circulation 2,196 copies in 1984)
  Pravoslavnoe obozrenie (circulation not known)
  Russkoye vozrozhdenie (circulation not known)

Vestnik Germanskoi Eparkhii (1,000 copies in Russian, 500 copies in German)

Pravoslavnyi put (circulation not known)

Number of churches and church facilities in operation (1984)
360 churches (estimate)
20 monasteries and convents
1 theological seminary
2 parochial high schools (in the United States)

Metropolitans since 1920
Antonii (Khrapovitskii), 1920–36
Anastasii (Gribanovskii), 1936–64
Filaret (Voznessenskii), 1964–85
Vitali (Ustinov), 1985–present

III
ORTHODOXY IN THE BALKANS

8

The Albanian Orthodox Church

Pedro Ramet

Albania's communists are fond of justifying their forcible extirpation of all religious organizations by describing them as foreign implants and denying them any link with Albanian nationalism. In fact, however, Christianity spread among the Albanian people in the first century, albeit in the face of resistance from the adherents of pagan faiths, and by the time of the Emperor Justinian had established its dominance in that area.

Yet for a number of reasons the linkage of the Orthodox faith with Albanian national identity *has* been weaker. Indeed, it is often pointed out that it was the Roman Catholic church, in the northern Gheg regions, which among Albania's three religions was most strongly animated by the nationalist impetus.[1]

Albanian Christianity lay within the orbit of the bishop of Rome from the first century to the eighth. But in the eighth century Albanian Christians were transferred to the jurisdiction of the patriarch of Constantinople.[2] With the schism of 1054, however, Albania was divided between a Catholic north and an Orthodox south. At the end of the eleventh century Rome established an archbishopric at Bar, and this archbishopric was gradually able to bring the bishoprics of Shkodër, Ulcinj, Drivast, and others under its jurisdiction. As a result, Catholicism spread in northern Albania, and in the second half of the twelfth century the Catholic church even made inroads in southern Albania.[3] In spite of this, Roman Catholicism remained a minority religion among Albanians, and the Orthodox faith was clearly dominant among the Tosks of southern Albania up until the beginning of the nineteenth century.[4] Yet doctrinal differences between Rome and Constantinople were slow to evolve, and the sense of true separation between Catholic Albanians and Orthodox Albanians dates only from the mid-eighteenth century.[5]

After the arrival of Ottoman power in the fourteenth century, Islam gradually spread, and the number of Christian churches and monasteries declined. Before the end of the nineteenth century, less than half of the Albanian population was still Christian.[6] Albania thus became a confessionally mixed society, in which there were no stable boundaries between the faiths. In fact, over the centuries Albanians often abandoned one faith or another for purely opportunistic reasons, such as the desire to obtain protection from a given power or the desire to escape the special tax levied on non-Muslims by the Sublime Porte. This would already incline one to expect the Orthodox faith to be weaker in Albania than elsewhere. To this one may add the fact that the Orthodox church was long the champion of Greek liturgy and Greek-language instruction, so that when the Albanian national movement appeared, nationalists of the Orthodox faith considered that their first task was to capture the Orthodox church and adapt it to the national task. This meant, in effect, that Albania's Orthodox church had to be autocephalous.

Albanian Orthodoxy Prior to the Communist Takeover

Albania's Christian population was largely unaware of the gathering rivalry between Rome and Constantinople until the early thirteenth century, when the East-West ecclesiastical schism came to be reflected in local politics. The Ottoman conquest between the end of the fourteenth century and the mid-fifteenth century introduced a third religion—Islam—but the Turks did not at first use force to spread Islam, and it was only in the 1600s that large-scale conversion to Islam began.[7]

The Orthodox community enjoyed broad toleration at the hands of the Sublime Porte until the late eighteenth century. Under the millet system the Orthodox church regulated the social life of its adherents, and in the absence of an autocephalous church, Albania's Orthodox population came under the jurisdiction of the patriarch of Constantinople. Orthodox learning and culture was thus Greek, and the schools opened by the Orthodox church in Ottoman times used Greek as the language of instruction. A Greek school operated in the monastery of St. Nahum on Lake Ohrid from the sixteenth century on. Additional Greek schools were opened in Zagorie and Himarë by the seventeenth century and in Vlorë by the mideighteenth century. After 1750, the number of Orthodox schools rose sharply, to a considerable extent as a result of the efforts of Kosmas Aitolos, who is said to have founded more than two hundred Greek schools in Albania.

The towns of Voskopojë (Moskhopolis) and Janina emerged as important centers of Greek culture, and by 1744 Voskopojë boasted a "New Academy" that rivaled the best Greek high schools of that age. A large number of religious and ecclesiastical works were also published in Voskopojë for distribution among Orthodox Christians in Albania and elsewhere. The clergy was itself active in this, and Archpriest Theodore Kavalioti and Master Dhanil from Voskopojë left two polyglot dictionaries, while Bishop Grigor Argjirokastriti of the island of Eubea supervised the translation of the Gospels into Albanian. This translation was published in Korfu in 1827.[8]

In the late eighteenth century Russian agents began stirring up the Orthodox subjects of the Ottoman Empire against the Sublime Porte. In the Russo-Turkish wars of 1768–74 and 1787–91, Orthodox Albanians rose up against the Turks. In the course of the second revolt the "New Academy" in Voskopojë was destroyed (1789), and at the end of the second Russo-Turkish war more than a thousand Orthodox fled to Russia on Russian warships.[9] As a result of these revolts, the Porte now applied force to Islamicize the Albanian population, adding economic incentives to provide positive stimulus. In the face of these pressures some Kosovar Albanians adopted a stratagem known as "crypto-Christianity," which means that they adopted Muslim names and performed Islamic rites in public, but observed the Christian faith in private.

Throughout the period of Ottoman rule, the Ecumenical Patriarchate (at Constantinople) opposed the creation of Albanian-language schools for the Orthodox, fearing that this would diminish its cultural influence and possibly even lead to the emergence of an autocephalous Albanian church. After disturbances in 1878–80, the Porte relaxed its prohibition on use of the Albanian language for education and periodicals. Very soon a number of Albanian-language schools sprang up in villages near Korçë and in the district of Kolonjë. Albanian-language books, newspapers, and periodicals also made an appearance. Up until then, only Catholic schools had been conducted in Albanian; Muslim schools used Turkish as the language of instruction, while Orthodox schools taught in Greek and figured, thereby, as vehicles of Hellenization. In 1892 Philaretos, archbishop of Kastoria, anathematized all who associated themselves with the new Albanian-language Orthodox schools, declaring that the Albanian language "does not exist" and that the true aim of these schools was to spread "freemasonry and Protestantism" among Albanian Christians.

Under pressure from the Ecumenical Patriarchate, the Porte reimposed the ban on Albanian publications and shut down the Orthodox schools teaching in Albanian.[10]

Not surprisingly, under these circumstances the Greek idea had considerable influence on the thinking of Albanian Orthodox. Bilingual in Albanian and Greek, some educated Orthodox Albanians in the latter years of the nineteenth century desired union with independent Greece, and two émigré Orthodox patriots in Egypt, Thimi Mitko and Spiro Dine, argued for the creation of a Greco-Albanian dual monarchy, on the Austro-Hungarian model.

Meanwhile, Bulgarian nationalists sought to enlarge ethnic "Macedonia," which they viewed as "western Bulgaria," by establishing Bulgarian-language schools and seminaries in ethnic Albania. In 1894 a group of three hundred Albanians addressed a letter to the Ottoman sultan, objecting to the permission granted the Bulgarian and Serbian churches (the latter, by then, in Prizren) to extend their influence, and demanded authorization to open Albanian-language schools. The appeal complained that Bulgarian schools were being established in Dibër and Tetovo, "where not a word of Bulgarian is spoken," and charged the Bulgarian church with aiming to Bulgarianize the local Albanian population. Albanian nationalists began to promote the idea of an autocephalous Albanian Orthodox church as a necessary bulwark against denationalization. Opposition to the Hellenizing and Bulgarianizing thrust of local Orthodox hierarchs also encouraged the conversion of a small number of Orthodox Albanians to the Uniate church; they hoped that Habsburg protection would safeguard their Albanian heritage, but under strong pressure from Russia the Uniate movement in Albania petered out by 1907.[11] The Albanian Uniate movement continued in emigration, among Albanians in Italy.

The nationalist cause was given impetus in 1905 when Albanian priest and poet Popa Kristo Negovani was killed by Greek chauvinists after he had introduced the Albanian language in Orthodox liturgy for the first time.[12] Yet the first Albanian church was to be the creation of émigrés. In the course of the nineteenth century groups of Albanian Orthodox believers had settled in Romania, Bulgaria, and the United States. The Romanian and American communities came to play a role in the establishment of an Albanian church, a central goal of Albanian nationalists from about 1880. On May 27, 1900, the Albanian Orthodox in Romania promulgated a program demanding autocephaly and liturgy in the Albanian language; two vain attempts to erect an Albanian church in Bucharest were subsequently undertaken.

It was thus not until 1908 that the Albanian Orthodox church was born—its first incarnation being among Albanian émigrés in Boston. Its founder and first bishop, the Harvard-educated Fan Noli, who later translated Shakespeare, Ibsen, and other playwrights into Albanian, was actually ordained a priest only on March 8, 1908. His formal ordination as a bishop occurred only in 1919, but he was unable to secure recognition from the Ecumenical Patriarchate.[13]

Independent Albania came into being in 1912, on the eve of World War I. The "Great War" turned neutral Albania into a battlefield as Greek, Serbian, Italian, and even French armies took up positions on its territory.[14] But by 1920 the last troops (the Italian) departed from Albania, which regained its independence and entered the nascent League of Nations.

One of the central issues facing the new Albanian government was land reform—an issue that divided the population, to some extent, along religious lines, in that most of the large landowners, especially in the south, were Muslims, whose estates were worked generally by Orthodox Christians. Predictably, the Muslim landowners favored preservation of the status quo, while the Orthodox generally urged land reform. Rival political parties sprang up advocating these rival interests: the Progressive party, opposed to land reform, was led by Shevket Verlazi, the largest landowner in the country; the Popular party, which favored land reform, was led by Ahmed Zog and Bishop Fan Noli. The latter had in fact been elected to the National Assembly as a representative of the American Albanian community.[15]

Zog and Noli cooperated at first but split in 1922 over policy toward Kosovo, which Zog was willing to write off, despite its large Albanian population. Meanwhile, Noli had campaigned for an independent ecclesiastical organization *within* Albania already in 1921, and in September 1922 the Albanian government under Prime Minister Zog convened a congress at Berat to address this issue. Predictably, the congress declared the church autocephalous, proclaimed that the liturgy should be conducted in Albanian, and set up a council under Vassili Marco to appoint bishops to an Albanian church synod and to oversee church activity. At that time there were some 200,000 Orthodox believers in Albania.

The Congress of Berat issued a church constitution for the "Albanian Autocephalous Orthodox church," and in token of its endorsement of church autocephaly the government entered the church constitution in its official gazette on October 26, 1922. The ecumenical patriarch responded cautiously and sent two bishops of Albanian origin as his representatives: Ierotheos, bishop of Militopoli, and Kristofor Kissi, bishop of Synada. They recommended to the ecumenical patriarch that he accord the church autonomy but not autocephaly. Subsequently, Bishops Ierotheos and Kristofor, by then elevated to the rank of metropolitans, consecrated Fan Noli a bishop, in St. George's Cathedral in Korçë, in what may well have been Noli's third episcopal consecration.

Noli was deeply involved in both ecclesiastical politics and national politics. In January 1924 a national synod of the Albanian church convened at Korçë. In attendance were Bishops Ierotheos, Kristofor Kissi, and Fan Noli.[16] That same month Zog's parliamentary faction went down to defeat in national elections, and Noli's faction was able to put together a coalition government. But Noli's government lasted only five months when Zog returned from Yugoslavia with a force of two thousand troops and seized power. By 1928 Zog had crowned himself, thus turning Albania into a kingdom.

Zog, like Noli, wanted ecclesiastical autocephaly. But in the absence of a local hierarchy, the decisions of the Congress of Berat had not been carried out even by the end of 1928. Hence, King Zog convened a meeting in his villa in February 1929 with Greek-educated Bishop Vissarion and Serbian Bishop Viktor, naming them to a five-man synod and persuading them to consecrate three uneducated priests for the remaining three seats. The Ecumenical Patriarchate excommunicated four of the five members of this synod, all but the Serb, hoping in vain that the patriarch of Belgrade would, on his own part, chastise Bishop Viktor. In reply, the Albanian government expelled the first patriarchal representative, Ierotheos, and imprisoned the second, Kristofor Kissi, in a monastery. Understandably, under these circumstances the rank and file of Orthodox believers remained suspicious of the new synod.[17]

The Albanian Orthodox church thus created had an archbishop ("of Durrës, Tirana, Elbasan, and all Albania") and three metropolitans. Its jurisdiction was divided among the following dioceses: (1) the archbishopric of Tirana-Durrës, headed by the archbishop and subdivided into districts of Tirana, Durrës, Shkodër, Kavaga, and Elbasan; (2) the bishopric of Berat, subdivided into districts of Berat, Vlorë, Fieri, and Lushnja; (3) the bishopric of Gjirokastër, subdivided into districts of Gjirokastër, Pogoni, Delvina, Saranda, Himarë, and Përmeti; and (4) the bishopric of Korçë, subdivided into districts of Korce, Kolonya, Leskoviku, and Pogradeci.[18] The Albanian church replaced Greek liturgy with liturgy in the Albanian language in many parishes, allowing Greek to continue to be used where desired.

The Greek Orthodox church, the Church of Cyprus, the patriarchate of Alexandria, and the Moscow patriarchate joined the Ecumenical Patriarchate in condemning Albanian autocephaly. On the other hand, other

Orthodox churches, such as the Serbian, Romanian, and Polish churches, and the patriarchate of Antioch, maintained a discreet silence, which, at least in the Serbian case, reflected acceptance.[19]

Searching for a way out of the impasse, the government finally proposed the candidacy of Kristofor Kissi to head the church. This move came in October 1933. The Ecumenical Patriarchate seemed at first to reject this olive branch, however, and proposed Eulogio Kurila, a priest of Albanian origin. Either way, Primate Vissarion Xhuvani had become an obstacle to settlement, and by May 1936 the Albanian synod reached the decision that Bishop Vissarion had to be retired. Rumors now emerged, conveniently, that Bishop Vissarion was leading a loose and scandalous life, and eventually an agreement was reached whereby Kristofor Kissi would be named primate of the church, which would in turn be recognized by Constantinople.[20]

Early in 1937, therefore, King Zog relieved Vissarion of his post and appointed Kristofor Kissi to succeed him. The Holy Synod of Constantinople accordingly convened in an extraordinary session on March 15, 1937, to consider the proposed accord and approved it unanimously a month later, issuing an official "Tomos" ceding autocephaly to the Albanian ecclesiastical organization.[21]

Albanian Orthodoxy since the Communist Takeover

Many Orthodox clergymen had supported Enver Hoxha's partisans during World War II.[22] They therefore hoped to be allowed to continue their religious activity in Hoxha's communist republic unobstructed. Indeed, the constitution of 1946 guaranteed freedom of religion and conscience to all citizens.

Yet already in August 1945 the new communist regime passed a land reform law nationalizing church lands, and in December of that year set up a Union of Orthodox Priests, to divide the lower clergy from their bishops.[23] The years 1945 to 1950 proved to be years of assault on the church's position. Church revenues were curtailed. Religious instruction was forbidden. All religious publications and communications, including sermons, pastoral letters, and even public memoranda, had to be approved by the government before dissemination. The church was banned from operating charitable institutions. And the state asserted control and veto over the election and appointment of candidates to ecclesiastical posts. In the first five years of communist rule, most Orthodox hierarchs were either killed or imprisoned or sent to labor camps, including Archbishop Vissarion Xhuvani of Elbasan; Bishop Irine of Apollonia; Bishop Agathangjel Cance of Berat; Bishop Irine, deputy metropolitan of Korçë and Gjirokastër; and Papas Josif Papmihaili, an advocate of Uniatism.

At that time Albania's regime wanted to place the Albanian Orthodox church under the care and authority of the Moscow patriarchate, but this met with resistance from the clergy. Finally, in January 1948, a small group of Albanian clergy visited Moscow, Kiev, and Leningrad, and consulted with Russian Orthodox hierarchs. At the end of this visit a statement was issued:

> Whereas all the other Churches, and especially the Vatican, wanted to put an end to the existence of the Albanian Church, the Russian Orthodox Church is its great defender.
>
> The Russian Orthodox Church is national and patriotic. The emancipated Albanian nation is moving rapidly along the path of progress and wishes its Orthodox Church to be likewise national and patriotic. In this connection the experience of the Russian Church provides a valuable lesson.
>
> In the common struggle against Fascism, the Albanian nation has come [to feel] close to the Russian people and wishes to be in close relationship with its Church.[24]

Later that year a Russian bishop visited Tirana, and Moscow played host to the 1948 Orthodox church conference. Archbishop Kristofor Kissi's absence from these meetings is a sign that he was opposed to the direction in which the church was being forced. His refusal to cooperate led to his early removal. Deposed on August 28, 1949, for "plotting to detach the Church from the Eastern Orthodox faith and surrender it to the Vatican,"[25] Kissi was imprisoned and replaced by Archbishop Paisi Vodica, who was distinctly sympathetic to the communists.

On January 26, 1949, the Albanian regime issued a general decree (No. 743) on religious organizations and required that each of the four religious organizations (Sunni Muslim, Bektashi Muslim, Orthodox, and Roman Catholic) draw up statutes within three months to present to the Council of Ministers. None of them complied,[26] and so the state issued statutes on their behalf. The Orthodox statute (Decree No. 1065) was issued on May 4, 1950. In a key clause, the statute declared: "The Autocephalous Orthodox Church of Albania will report connections or cooperation with the Orthodox sister-churches who practise the high principles of the Gospel with regard to peace and true brotherhood, and every activity and attempt to destroy peace, love and brotherhood among the nations of the whole world."[27] Though vague, this clause evidently codified the church's responsibility to report its activities to the state and subordinated it to the

Moscow patriarchate, especially insofar as it could easily be argued that Orthodox churches in countries other than Stalin's "socialist camp" were not "sister-churches who practise the high principles of the Gospel with regard to peace."

According to a religious census conducted in 1938, Albania's population was 72.8 percent Muslim, 17.1 percent Orthodox, and 10.1 percent Catholic.[28] The party introduced antireligious propaganda in the schools at an early date, and in April 1955 a party plenum resolved that religious beliefs were obstructing "the spread of . . . socialist culture among the masses."[29] Yet it was another twelve years before the Albanian Communist party made its decisive move to eliminate all forms of religion in Albania, Orthodoxy included.

In a speech to the party Central Committee on February 6, 1967, Enver Hoxha announced the inception of a new policy toward religion, as part of the party's Cultural Revolution. Hoxha returned to this theme in his address to the Fifth Party Congress in June 1967:

To be a revolutionary means not only to have no religious faith but also to struggle continuously against religious beliefs, which are an expression of feudal and bourgeois reactionary ideology; it means not only to condemn with words and on principle the backward habit of despising and enslaving woman or other backward habits which stem from the remnants of feudal and bourgeois relationships in life and in the family, but it also means to struggle concretely and courageously for the liquidation of these reactionary habits and for the creation of new, socialist and communist, habits.[30]

Teams of young agitators were dispatched throughout the country with the assignment to persuade or force people to abandon their religious practices, and ultimately their religious beliefs as well.

On November 13, 1967, the Albanian People's Assembly approved a decree annulling the religious statutes governing the Islamic, Orthodox, and Catholic communities and rescinded the guarantee of freedom of worship. By the end of 1967 all 2,169 churches, mosques, and monasteries of the three faiths had been closed and confiscated. For the Orthodox church this meant the loss of 608 churches and monasteries (including those at Ardenica, Narta, Vlorë, and Voskopojë) and its only seminary.[31] Archbishop Damian, who had inherited the primacy in 1966, died in prison in November 1973, and as of 1975 the entire surviving hierarchy of the Albanian Orthodox church, as well as most of its priests, were all being held in prison.[32] Illegal since 1967, religious organizations became also unconstitutional under the new constitution adopted in 1976. Article 54 of this document declares: "The creation of any type of organization of a fascist, anti-democratic, religious, or anti-socialist character is prohibited."[33]

In the mythology of the Albanian Party of Labor, the suppression of religion—which was carried out with speed and vigor—is portrayed as having enjoyed broad popular support. An account in *Studime Historike*, which clearly reflects the regime's outlook, held that "the struggle against religious dogmas, rites, and beliefs was carried out in conformity with the line of the masses. It was the people themselves who rose up and condemned the religious ideology. This job was done through discourse and reasoned polemics. Peruasion, the elevation and activation of public opinion—these were the decisive factors that assured success in this struggle."[34]

In its desire to expunge all traces of religious heritage the regime began advising parents as to which names were or were not appropriate for their children. Official lists of "Illyrian" names were published, but people ignored them, until finally, on September 23, 1975, the government issued a decree (No. 5339) requiring everyone to assume a nonreligious name.[35]

The antireligious campaign was portrayed as a reflection of authentic Albanian nationalism, and all three religions were described as foreign penetrations.[36] Repeated appeals from both Albanian Orthodox ecclesiastical organizations in the United States have had no impact on Tirana's policy, and there has been no relaxation of the tough policy. Still, repeated complaints in party forums of the survival of religious practices and of the inadequacy of party activities in this area are sufficient to lead one to conclude that religion is scarcely dead in the self-proclaimed "first atheist state." In 1975 a Yugoslav observer noted that Orthodox believers in the south, some of them Greeks, *always* observed religious holidays and refused to work at Easter.[37] In the summer of 1980 an Albanian sociologist revealed that during the previous ten years only 3 percent of rural marriages and only 5 percent of urban marriages involved people of different religious backgrounds—itself a measure of the tenacity of religious consciousness, while a Tirana publication conceded the following year that religious marriages and rituals continued to be practiced.[38]

The Albanian communist regime has tried to popularize the notion that the Albanian people have never been religious and that Catholicism, Orthodoxy, and Islam alike are *foreign* religions, opposed to the natural atheism of the people. This claim has been disputed in the West, and certainly, if there was a certain amount of opportunism in religious conversions historically, it should be emphasized that many conversions were the result of coercion.[39] It does appear, however, that the religious *institutions* were too weak to put up an effective resistance to Enver Hoxha's repression.

The Albanian Orthodox church, less than fifty years old at the time, was institutionally the weakest of the three faiths, and, in consequence, it is the faith of which the least has been heard since then.

FACT SHEET

The Albanian Orthodox Church

Year of autocephaly
  Proclaimed: 1922
  De facto: 1929
  Recognized by Ecumenical Patriarchate: 1937

Strength of the church
  250,000 believers (1937)
  160,000 believers (1977)

Number of churches and church facilities in operation
  608 churches and monasteries in 1966; 0 in 1987
  2 seminaries in 1937; 1 seminary in 1966; 0 in 1987

Archbishops of Tirana since 1929
  Vissarion Xhuvani, 1929–37
  Kristofor Kissi, 1937–49
  Paisi (Pashko) Vodica, 1949–66
  Damian Kokonesi, 1966–73

9

The Bulgarian Orthodox Church

Spas T. Raikin

The Bulgarian Orthodox church has always been a nationalist church, and nationalism has always been the single most important factor affecting its relations with the Bulgarian state. Nationalism led to its reestablishment in the 1870s and accounts today for its co-opted status under the communist regime. To understand the Bulgarian Orthodox church's behavior toward the sundry governments with which it has had to coexist, it is necessary to understand that the church sees itself as the protector of the Bulgarian nation and the defender of its territorial claims.

Church-state relations in Bulgarian history were determined at the time of the conversion to Christianity under Prince Boris I, in 865. He perceived the function of the church as essentially political and proceeded to make it a vehicle for his political goals. Above all, he was concerned not to allow it to fall under foreign control and demanded from Patriarch Photius of Constantinople and Pope Nicholas I of Rome permission to have a Bulgarian patriarch. He was turned down by both of them. But he preferred to join the Eastern church, because, among other things, he saw that his chances and opportunities for an independent church there were greater than with Rome. His son, Simeon (892–927), disregarding canon law, unilaterally elevated the Bulgarian church to the status of patriarchate.[1] He repudiated the use of Greek in the liturgy and introduced the Old Bulgarian version of the Slavic language, with its newly created system of writing, in religious services, in literature, and for official purposes.[2]

The Bulgarian Orthodox church became an ethnic church. Reading through medieval manuscripts, which span centuries, one will discover in religious services and in the lives of saints a deeply embedded spirit of Bulgarian nationalism.[3] In 1872 a local church council in Constantinople excommunicated the Bulgarians and pronounced them schismatics for having embraced the doctrine of *philetism*, i.e., nationalism. While the Greeks condemned Bulgarian philetism, they used their ostensible ecumenism as a cover for promoting ecclesiastical Hellenism. This was the incunabula of the contest between the Bulgarian and Greek hierarchies in the Balkans.

The Greek-Bulgarian church quarrel of the nineteenth century, initiated and carried on by intellectuals as well as by members of the middle and lower middle classes, was a contest for the use of the national language, for a nationally indigenous hierarchy, for Bulgarian national identity, and for secular concerns—not for religious principles.[4] As this struggle progressed, it turned into a struggle for national territory, for ethnically organized dioceses, and ultimately it determined the parameters of what came to be called Bulgarian national ideals. The territories that in one form or another were recognized as a diocese of the Bulgarian exarchate, established in 1870, became the ideal of Bulgarian nationalists for the establishment of a Greater Bulgaria. Whenever the church has acquired prominence in Bulgarian history, it is invariably as contributor to the national cause and sustainer of national culture; historical accounts ignore the church's purely religious activities and, indeed, often hold them in scorn. The Bulgarian church is either blamed for its "Byzantinism" or deplored for not having joined the Roman Catholic church, through which, it is sometimes argued, it would have associated Bulgaria with the progress and civilization of the West.[5] Yet the role of the church in national affairs has always been strictly defined. It has always been expected that it follow policies paralleling those of the state. Failing in this, the church would lose its raison d'être.

The Constitutional Framework of
Church-State Relations

With such an understanding of the role the church had played, and should play in the future, the framers of the Turnovo Constitution of 1879, Bulgaria's first constitution, defined its legal status (in Article 39) as follows:

The principality of Bulgaria as, from an ecclesiastical point of view, forming an inseparable part of the jurisdiction of the Bulgarian church, is subject to the Holy Synod, which is the highest spiritual authority in the Bulgarian church, wherever that may exist. Through the same authority the principality remains united with the ecumenical Eastern church in matters regarding dogma and faith.[6]

This article of the Turnovo Constitution emerged as the Pandora's box of church-state relations in Bulgaria for over half a century. The leaders of the church read it as a charter of church sovereignty over the state. The state, on the other hand, read it as a license to rule over the church. This constitutional definition made an implicit distinction between spiritual and material affairs of the church. The church leaders interpreted everything of concern to them as comprising their spiritual responsibilities, while the state tended to expand its domain and impose its controls over the Holy Synod. These conflicting claims over jurisdiction between church and state in Bulgaria were never resolved to the full satisfaction of all parties. In the course of the struggles it generated, both sides developed their views and defended their positions to the bitter end.

Almost immediately after the adoption of the Turnovo Constitution, the government moved to enact a set of "Provisional Rules" for the government of the church. The bishops interpreted this as an intrusion in church affairs, and in consequence they formulated the doctrine of "prior consent." Exarch Iosif wrote to Prime Minister Dragan Tsankov from Constantinople:

> Because you neither informed us in advance, nor have you received the consent and the approval of our Holy Synod of the government's draft law respecting the church in the principality, and, as we hear, you are preparing to introduce in the National Assembly the said draft law, we consider it our duty to forewarn you that it will be rejected if it does not have the prior consent of the Holy Synod, and consequently you have to implement it by force.[7]

The exarch accused the government of attempting to subordinate the church to the state, by transforming each diocese into a separate governmental department and dealing directly with every metropolitan as an individual government official, thus ignoring the synod as a body governing the church. He argued that "the Ministry of Foreign Affairs and Confessions does not have the right to issue rules for the government of the Holy Church without the knowledge and the consent of her governing body, the Holy Synod; that the ministry does not have the right to order the revered prelates to execute decisions on matters concerning the church without the knowledge of the exarch, who is the executive authority of the Holy Synod."[8] He threatened the prime minister that he would refuse to issue orders for compliance with the rules if they were issued without the prior consent and the approval of the synod, even though they might be voted by the National Assembly. He instructed the metropolitans in the principality to refrain from carrying them out, despite Tsankov's orders. Exarch Iosif also developed a doctrine of the absolute sovereignty of the church and its independence from the state and argued forcefully for the synod's right to refuse any draft law on religious affairs passed by the National Assembly.[9]

Though Tsankov insisted that the state had the right to legislate unilaterally with regard to the church's secular activity, he failed to silence the synod, and the bishops continued to defend their autonomy under his successors. They effectively blocked Stefan Stambolov from doing the same. After his fall in 1894, when Ferdinand sought reconciliation and recognition from Russia, during the regime of Konstantin Stoilov, they prepared their own draft bylaws. The government promulgated the new statutes on January 13, 1895, and they remained in effect until 1950, when a new set of bylaws, worked out under the supervision of the communist regime, was enacted. The statutes of 1895 definitely and unequivocally established the Holy Synod as the supreme and sole authority in the church, excluding altogether the participation of lower clergy and laymen in the high church councils. The articles of the old exarchate's bylaws of 1871, stipulating quadrennial church national councils, were dropped, and Article 180,[10] legislating the "prior consent" doctrine of the Holy Synod, was added, thus depriving the state of arbitrary intervention in church affairs. During the following decades the church most vigorously defended these statutes as its sacred charter and fought bitterly every attempt to take away its privileges accorded by Article 180. In 1914 the government of Vasil Radoslavov threatened to revise the law of 1895 and cancel Article 180. The prelates reluctantly surrendered to his demands that the church remain silent on his foreign policies, leading Bulgaria to an alliance with Germany against Russia, and Radoslavov withdrew his draft.[11] In 1920 the government of Alexander Stamboliysky, in contravention to Article 180, passed a law ordering the synod to call a church national council. The synod strongly resisted and, though finally conceding under enormous pressure, effectively manipulated the crisis and the council and eventually defeated the intents of the government. The new draft, prepared by the council, was never promulgated, and church-state relations remained unchanged until 1950.

Under the provisions of the Turnovo Constitution and the statutes of 1895, church-state relations in Bulgaria could go two ways. They could flourish in an atmosphere of mutual understanding and cooperation, or they could freeze in conditions of strife and conflicting claims. As history was to unfold, between 1879 and 1950 they froze in bitter antagonisms. The leaders of the church plunged into national politics, and for as long as they could play this game, they firmly stood their ground in defense of church autonomy.

Cassocks and Politics in the Late Nineteenth Century

As Bulgaria emerged from the Turkish yoke, the church was already deeply involved in national politics. First, former exarch Antim had been deposed under Turkish pressure in April 1877, at the outset of the Russo-Turkish War, by a group of anti-Russian and pro-Turkish clergy and laity. He returned to Bulgaria to preside over the Constituent Assembly in Turnovo. Metropolitan Simeon of Varna served as its vice-president. On the opposite side of the barricades was Metropolitan Grigoriy of Rousse, whom Antim despised. Grigoriy had betrayed the revolutionary committee in his diocese to the Turks in 1876, and for this betrayal had been awarded one of the highest medals by the Ottoman Empire. In addition, he had issued a special proclamation calling on the Bulgarians to fight the Russians and defend the Turkish sultan. On the other side was Metropolitan Meletiy of Sofia, who had supported the revolutionary movement in Bulgaria. Having been denounced to the Turks, he had been saved by Grigoriy of Rousse, but recalled to reside in Constantinople. He escaped and joined the victorious Russian armies in the war for the liberation of Bulgaria. The church authorities in Constantinople, acting under pressure from the Ottoman government, had defrocked him, but it was left in abeyance after the liberation. A few years later partisan and political intrigues led to his arrest by government authorities, utter humiliation, downfall, and death in self-exile in Egypt. But in the meantime he became a firebrand in the Constituent Assembly. His center-stage performance in the constitutional debate in favor of a conservative government structure led to a physical confrontation between him and the leader of the liberal party, Dragan Tsankov. The most political of all, however, was the metropolitan of Turnovo, Kliment, a former member of Rakovski's *Legia* in Belgrade and a leading Bulgarian writer. He was urged by some metropolitans and lay leaders to don the cassock in order to serve his nation better. He followed this advice and was destined to become the Bulgarian Thomas à Beckett—minus a martyr's death. Like most of the metropolitans of the Bulgarian church, he plunged into the thick of politics.

At one time or another all these men were to surface in the bitter political struggles that erupted in the first years after the liberation. Grigoriy of Rousse, having joined the conservatives, prodded the prince to suppress the constitution. Having tried to rule without it, and having failed, Alexander Battenberg appointed a commission to review it. Grigoriy of Rousse, Simeon of Varna, and Kliment of Turnovo were members of this commission. Soon Kliment turned against the Battenberg prince and plotted for his dethronement. He became prime minister of the government proclaimed by the plotters, but quit when Stefan Stambolov, president of the National Assembly and leader of the counterplot, threatened to shoot him. Though he had been designated metropolitan of Turnovo, he continued to reside in Sofia, as representative of Exarch Iosif. His office became a center of political intrigues against the Stambolov regime. Kliment went so far as to conspire with Radoslavov for Stambolov's overthrow. This politicization of the Bulgarian Orthodox church was seen by one of its contemporaries, not sympathetic to the political orientation of the church, as self-destructive. This admirer and biographer of Stambolov wrote: "The bishops . . . took an active part in our political squabbles and this reflected fatally upon the spiritual and religious disposition of the people, causing the decline of piety among lower clergy and the masses."[12]

But the conflict between church and state in Bulgaria had deeper roots. It was not merely a question of colorful personalities with adventurous proclivities concealed under priestly cassocks. Beneath the surface of the repeated clashes between individual church leaders and political factions there was a bigger issue. It was the issue of Bulgarian foreign policy, the issue of the orientation of Bulgaria in European politics, which pitted church against state. In the second half of the nineteenth century, and indeed up to 1918, the Balkans were a bone of contention between Austria-Hungary and Russia. In a larger context it was a conflict between Russia and the West, which, in many ways, continues to this day. In Bulgarian politics this conflict took the form of a relentless struggle between Russophiles and Russophobes. Where the church was concerned, this conflict took the form of a struggle between the Bulgarian church hierarchy and the German princes, whether Battenbergs or Coburgs. The Battenberg era was only a dress rehearsal for the more dramatic struggles of the Coburg reign, which began with the arrival of Prince Ferdinand in the country. This struggle between church and monarchy reflected the continuing uncertainty as to whether Bulgaria would lie within the Russian sphere of influence or would come under German influence. The Bulgarian Orthodox church clearly favored Russia.

The Russophilia of the Bulgarian Orthodox church should be taken for granted. The common Slavic origins, the common Orthodox faith, the common cultural traditions, the common political cause between Russians and Bulgarians in the nineteenth century, the memories of Ignatievs and of San Stefano suffice to explain this dogma of Bulgarian orientation in international affairs. Bulgarian church leaders had been educated in Russian theological seminaries and academies. All religious service books in Bulgarian churches and monasteries had been printed in Russia, since Bulgaria long lacked printing facilities of its own, even after liberation in 1878. These books included litanies for the Russian tsars, tsarinas, princes, and princesses, and were recited daily by Bulgarian priests, bishops, and monks.

Ferdinand of Coburg vs. Kliment of Turnovo

Church-state relations in Bulgaria reached a breaking point at the beginning of the reign of Prince Ferdinand of Coburg-Gotha. The Bulgarian Orthodox church did not participate in the selection of the new prince in 1887. No churchman was designated to the search committee, and the Bulgarian church was not consulted regarding the future prince of Bulgaria. Exarch Iosif was not invited to Turnovo for the swearing in of Ferdinand; nor was the metropolitan of Turnovo in his capital for the occasion. The swearing in was administered by the former exarch, Antim.

This represented a confrontation between church and state in Bulgaria, a head-on collision between the Russian and Austro-Hungarian influence in Bulgaria, and between the Bulgarian church and the Bulgarian dynasty. When Ferdinand stepped on Bulgarian territory at Vidin on August 13, 1877, Metropolitan Kliment was celebrating a Te Deum in Sofia and delivering a long political speech. He publicly advised Ferdinand to find the way toward reconciliation with "Liberating Russia."[13] When Ferdinand finally arrived in Sofia and came to the cathedral, the indomitable metropolitan greeted him with these words:

> Welcome, Royal Prince! The Bulgarian people thank you for your courage in coming here at this critical moment. The Bulgarians will be grateful, and you may count on their devotion and attachment in fulfilling the heavy task which you have undertaken. This same people is grateful to Russia, who made immense sacrifices for our deliverance, and to whom we owe our liberty and independence. Do not forget those sacrifices, and use your best efforts to reestablish relations between Russia and Bulgaria, to reconcile the liberator and the liberated.[14]

The showdown between the Russophile church hierarchy and the Germanophile monarchy came in December 1888. Prime Minister Stambolov (1887–94) had asked the synod to meet and prepare a plan for securing the parish priesthood and to pay their salaries. Instead, the synod, presided over by Simeon of Varna, opened discussions on the legality of Ferdinand's rule and the suitability of mentioning his name during church services. Predictably, the decision was negative, and Stambolov was informed that the synod had found that "the prince of Coburg, having been chosen against the will and without the approval of Russia, is illegal, and consequently, his name should be removed from the church litanies and the divine liturgy." Shortly thereafter, on the Sunday before Christmas, the synod dramatically forced the issue to a crisis. Konstantin of Vratsa, replacing the temporary metropolitan of Sofia, Bishop Kiril, at the last minute at the altar to celebrate the Divine Liturgy, omitted Ferdinand's name during the grand entrance procession. Nor did the other celebrants mention the prince's name. This was a formal declaration of war on Ferdinand by the church. Indeed, this was how an earlier Bulgarian metropolitan had proclaimed the secession of the Bulgarian church from the patriarchate of Constantinople on April 3, 1860—by not mentioning the patriarch's name.

Stambolov tried to get the exarch in Constantinople to intervene on behalf of the prince, but the exarch declined and refused to respond to his repeated messages. Stambolov therefore sent the police to force the metropolitans out of their offices and escort them out of Sofia. They were put on the trains and sent to their respective sees of Turnovo, Vratsa, and Varna. But the prelates did not cease their opposition and instructed the priests of their jurisdictions to stop mentioning the name of the prince in the liturgical services. Kliment became even more aggressive and openly assailed "the Catholic prince," warning the people to keep their Orthodox faith. On one occasion he came very close to being seized by a mob and being lynched. Metropolitan Simeon of Varna was physically forced out of his cathedral and sent to Rousse. The orders of Konstantin of Vratsa to the priests not to mention Ferdinand's name in the course of the liturgy caused a split between church and civil authorities. Stambolov sternly ordered the metropolitans to discontinue their travels in the dioceses and stay home. The crisis was defused briefly in 1890 after the prime minister had obtained some important concessions from the Turkish government for the exarch in Macedonia. The reconciliation between synod and government was sealed when the metropolitans had an audience with Ferdinand at the palace and were granted a state subsidy of 800,000 leva for priests' salaries.[15]

These clashes between church and state were to flare up again and again. When Ferdinand married Marie-Louise of Bourbon-Parma, the crisis peaked. The duke of Parma had posed as a conditio sine qua non that Article 38 of the Bulgarian constitution, stipulating that the heirs to the throne be baptized in the Orthodox church, be changed. A special Great National Assembly was convened and the offending article was changed. The marriage was arranged by Ferdinand's mother, Princess Clementine, Austrian Emperor Franz Josef, and the Austrian foreign minister, Count Gustav Kalnoky. Princess Radziwill wrote: "The Catholic will not let the Orthodox sleep in peace." Count Agenor Maria Adam Goluchowski, the future foreign minister of Austria-Hungary, told a German diplomat: "Sooner or later, Constantinople will fall to the Bulgarians. . . . [It] could not fall into better hands than those of the now firmly established Coburg dynasty . . . which maintains its Catholic character."[16] This is also how the marriage was seen by the Bulgarian Orthodox church. Metropolitan Kliment of Turnovo commented, "These are days of temptation. They want to force a Catholic cap on the Bulgarian head." When the mayor of Turnovo invited him to celebrate a Te Deum on the occasion of the betrothal (February 14, 1893), he delivered a blistering attack on those who were betraying the Bulgarian Orthodox church. Stambolov ordered him arrested and put on trial. At the end of his trial Kliment was sentenced and imprisoned in the Glozhene Monastery, where he stayed until the fall of Stambolov in 1894.

Certainly this led to a broad change of policies, in the first place to a reconciliation with Russia, where the heir to the throne, Prince Boris, was confirmed into the Orthodox church. But the damage to church-state relations was done. For the rest of Ferdinand's reign, that is, until he was forced to abdicate in 1918 by the Allies, church and state remained cool toward one another, and the church was pushed to the periphery of national life. Ferdinand never won the affection of the Bulgarian people. He complained to the French ambassador, Michael Paleologue, "They have always detested me. They will always detest me."[17]

In one respect, however, the church was found useful by the prince of Bulgaria: it promulgated Bulgarian nationalist propaganda in Macedonia. The Bulgarian governments and the Bulgarian church leaders, notwithstanding their bitter political conflicts, never wavered in their determination to continue their cooperation in this field and to support each other, even when church-state relations were at their coolest. The result of this cooperation was that by 1912 the Bulgarian exarchate maintained seven metropolitans, 1,331 churches, 275 monasteris, 1,373 schools, 2,266 teachers, and 78,854 students in Turkish-occupied Macedonia.

King Boris III and the Muzzling of the Church

The agrarian regime of Alexander Stamboliyski (1920–23) was only an interlude in the Coburg domination of Bulgaria. But the Coburgs had suffered an ignominious defeat in 1918. Their pro-German policies and pro-German Bulgarian nationalism had led to a national catastrophe. The church had not fared any better, as Russia had gone Bolshevik and the bishops had no stomach for bolshevism. Moreover, the church was expelled from Macedonia and Thrace and had thus lost the key to its leverage with the government. The departure of Ferdinand might have been a blessing under other circumstances, but he was succeeded by King Boris III, who was not much different. The Bulgarian monarchy had never established close ties with the Bulgarian church, for, unlike the Serbian royal houses, which were native and Orthodox, the Bulgarian kings were foreigners and remained outsiders to Bulgaria. They remained Germans to the very end. At least Ferdinand was honest about it and made no bones about his desire to promote Catholicism. But Boris was a different man. He was apathetic toward the church but very tactful in his dealings with it. Outwardly religious and attentive to it, he did not go beyond the formal observance of Orthodox rituals at public functions. He never showed any affection or special interest in its affairs. Instead, he had fallen under the spell of an occult society headed by a Petar Dunov, whose "apostle," Lubomir Lulchev, was his closest adviser. Boris consulted with Lulchev and Dunov on important state matters instead of with the leading political figures in the country during the war, least of all with representatives of the church. The indifference of King Boris and his court toward the Bulgarian Orthodox church further contributed to the alienation of the nationalist intelligentsia and the state bureaucracy from its influence, so much so that in 1942, prodded by the synod, the government issued orders making church attendance mandatory for all state and other public officials.[18]

Much has been said by Bulgarian church leaders in the communist era to the effect that King Boris had prevented the church from organizing itself into an exarchate or even a patriarchate. The standard explanation offered was that the Bulgarian church could not properly be an exarchate or a patriarchate before all Bulgarian lands were united in one state.[19] But even when this happened in 1941, under German tutelage and under the crown of King Boris "the Unifier," the church was not allowed to take this decisive step. The true explanation is probably that Boris could not brook the challenge to his national leadership that might have been presented by a patriarch or an exarch. He methodically destroyed every strong personality who threatened to overshadow him. He had Stamboliyski murdered.

He had Alexander Tsankov maneuvered out of power. He had the leading generals of the army checkmating each other. And he had every articulate political leader removed from the stage. He selected all his ministers from the faceless and submissive bureaucracy and diplomatic corps. The Bulgarian bishops and metropolitans, socially tied to the lowest classes of Bulgaria, being themselves sons of poor peasants, had no access and no ties to the court.

Under King Boris church-state relations may be characterized as a variation of the model established by Peter the Great in eighteenth-century Russia, continuing until 1917. The church was not allowed to elect a successor to Exarch Iosif after his death in 1915 and became a de facto synodal institution, governing itself according to the bylaws of 1895, but dependent on the state for its maintenance. Boris would not share the limelight of national leadership with an exarch or a patriarch whom he could not control, especially an exarch or patriarch with a powerful personality like that of Metropolitan Stefan of Sofia, who undoubtedly would have been elected to that position. Stefan was removed even from the presidency of the Holy Synod in 1934 and replaced by the phlegmatic Metropolitan Neofit of Vidin. The governments of King Boris repeatedly tried to influence the elections of new metropolitans of Turnovo, Vratsa, and Varna, but failed in their attempts to take direct control of the church. Eventually they dispatched their candidate to the United States to spare themselves the embarrassment of failure.

At the same time the regime leaned heavily on the church for the ideological underpinning of the system. Philosophically, ideologically, and socially the church was a conservative force and in the absence of any other commonly accepted ideology to oppose the rampant communist agitation in the country, religion appeared to be the only available response to the challenge, even if this response was used deceptively, to distract attention from the economic and social problems that were undermining the stability of the political order in Bulgaria. Indeed, the church was in the forefront of the fight against communism. Bulgarian communists, for their part, focused much of their venom on the church, which they viewed as part of the establishment they sought to overthrow.

The Communist Takeover

By the time the Coburg regime in Bulgaria collapsed on September 9, 1944, the church had become an adjunct to the regime—effectively deprived of any opportunity to rise to a respectable position of national spiritual leadership, thus reduced to a servant of the state in small ways and economically dependent on state subsidies. In 1944 it had to face a new political order as an ideological and political enemy of the communist regime. Its predicament was made worse by the fact that it had become alienated from the people. By the time communism came to Bulgaria, virtually every social class had abandoned the Bulgarian Orthodox church. The Bulgarians had become the least religious people in Europe.[20] The priest saw most of his parishioners only at baptism, at weddings, and at funerals. The adversary relations between the church and the communists in the past now came to haunt the church. The time for settling of accounts was at hand.

The new constitution of December 4, 1947, which replaced the Turnovo Constitution, ruled out any privileges based on religion, proscribed preaching of religious hatred, and guaranteed to all Bulgarian citizens "freedom of conscience and religion and of the performance of religious rites." It decreed the separation of church and state and prohibited the formation of political parties along religious lines.[21] The 1971 constitution, which replaced that of 1947, made little change where religious matters were concerned, except to add a guarantee of the rights to "religious rites and the conduct of anti-religious propaganda."[22] These constitutional provisions were further supplemented by the Law of Confessions, promulgated on February 24, 1949. This law recognized the Bulgarian Orthodox church to be "the traditional Church of the Bulgarian people . . . inseparable from their history," and allowed that it might become "in form, substance, and spirit, a People's democratic Church."[23]

But while these documents were being drawn up, numerous village priests were being murdered. Others were dragged before people's courts. Two of the leading metropolitans—Kiril of Plovdiv, the future patriarch, and Paisi of Vratsa—were jailed and tortured, in anticipation of a trial of war criminals, and then freed. Three second-rank clergy, Archimandrites Paladi of Vidin, Iriney of Sofia, and Nahum of Rousse were murdered without a trial, while three others were dragged before a people's court for having participated in the Nazi-sponsored international investigation of the Katyn Forest massacres, one of them the present metropolitan of the Bulgarian Synodal church in New York. There followed a stream of arrests and imprisonment of hundreds of priests in concentration camps, labor brigades, and political reeducation camps. At the same time the church was constantly threatened with suspension of the state subsidy, which was done on several occasions, thus contributing to its insecurity. With every suspension the government extracted more and more concessions from the Holy Synod, until the time came when there was nothing more left for the church to concede. Gradually, the church was transformed into an obedient and useful tool in the hands of the government. In exchange, it was allowed to register some ostensibly important but in practice hollow gains, among them the restoration of the patriarchate in 1953.

The taming of the church in the late 1940s involved expropriation and desecration of church buildings, intimidation of worshippers at church doors, and proliferation of fear. Step by step, the church was stripped of its privileges and freedoms and completely deprived of carrying out activities of educational and missionary work outside of church buildings; it was limited to performance of religious rituals only. Prayers and religious instruction in schools were discontinued at once and replaced by classes in atheism. Church marriages, church funerals, divorces, and baptisms, previously mandatory by law, were now left to the discretion of the individuals concerned. Fearing to compromise their career opportunities, the young preferred, in general, to stay away from church.

The first step taken by the church in accommodating itself to the new conditions was to change its leadership. Metropolitan Neofit of Vidin, vicar-president of the Holy Synod, was a liability and was replaced by Metropolitan Stefan of Sofia, whose credentials were acceptable to the new regime. He had been close to the political forces allied with the communists in the Fatherland Front government, and his sympathies for the Allies, in opposition to the pro-German orientation of the previous government, were a matter of public record. In January 1945 Stefan was elevated to the position of exarch and presided over the liquidation of the schism with the ecumenical see in Constantinople.

Stefan's rise to power had the inadvertent effect of consolidating the position of the Holy Synod as the indisputable authority in the church. This authority came under challenge from the Priests' Union, led by a procommunist clergyman, Georgi Georgiev. Together with two other clergymen—Bogomil Bosev and Athanas Gashtev—Georgiev, backed by the Communist party, formed a Committee to Reform the Church. The committee proved evanescent, but Georgiev, as head of the Priests' Union, pressed for the reorganization of the church along the lines of Renovationism in postrevolutionary Russia, under which the priests and laity could wrest control of the church from the Holy Synod. Stefan's prestige and dominance of the scene dwarfed their influence and strengthened the synod, but in the course of a critical confrontation between church and state in 1948 he mysteriously resigned and was deposed as metropolitan of Sofia by his colleagues, apparently on orders from the government. He was sent into exile and died there in 1957. His fall has never been adequately explained, but circumstantial evidence suggests that he was removed from the leadership of the church for political reasons.[24] In this crisis in church-state relations the Priests' Union stood with the government against the Holy Synod. Bit by bit, the regime eroded the autonomy of the church, bullied it into partnership, forced the theological schools to revamp their programs to meet specific political criteria, and exercised a veto over hierarchical appointments.

The Law of Faiths (February 1949) placed the church under state control and restricted it to the performance of rituals. It also required the religious denominations to submit to the Ministry for Foreign Affairs "their budgets [and] all circular letters, epistles, and publications of a public character published by them." If they were found to be contrary to "the law, public order, and to public morality," their circulation could be prohibited. The churches were ordered to register with the ministry and submit the names of the members of their executive bodies for review. The churches were forbidden to engage in educational activities among the youth or to operate youth organizations. Likewise, the churches were forbidden to engage in political activities based on religious principles. The churches were further forbidden to open hospitals, orphanages, or similar institutions. They were allowed to have relations with their central headquarters abroad, where applicable, and to receive material support and donations, but only with the permission of the Ministry for Foreign Affairs. Religious organizations owning property abroad were to be represented by that ministry in any transactions involving that property, and the Ministry for Foreign Affairs was empowered to defend the religious rights of Bulgarian citizens abroad. Finally, the churches were ordered to submit to the ministry their statutes within three months for approval. Failure to do so, or refusal to comply with suggestions for revision, would result in denial of official recognition.

The church was now constrained to draw up new bylaws. These held advantages for both church and state. The Priests' Union was happy with the provision for the participation of lower clergy and laity in the government; the hierarchy was pleased to have been given the last word on administrative and judicial matters within their respective dioceses, while the church's national council, composed of bishops, lower clergy, and laity, was vested with legislative power, albeit still under the presidency of the synod. But the composition of the synod was made dependent on the lower clergy and the laity, placing the synod, thus, at the mercy of forces that heretofore had been excluded from the high councils of the church and that were now subject to control from outside the church. Under this threat the synodal prelates, in order to retain their position of power in the church, had no other choice but to try to ingratiate themselves with the government. By 1955 the regime was satisfied that it had successfully co-opted the church, and the Priests' Union was dissolved.[25]

Reactions to the new bylaws varied. The progovernment forces in the black clergy (the monks) hailed it. Bishop Jonah saw in it a "return to ancient church democracy," with the inclusion of laymen in the governing bodies of the church.[26] Bishop Pimen, praising the democratic character of the bylaws, declared that this "blessed and happy" event could not have happened under the previous regimes in the country and that the church should be grateful to the People's Republic and the Communist party.[27] The union representatives were not so happy. Some of them, pointing to the retention of the right of the bishops to punish the priests for infractions of church discipline, called it "reactionary and conservative."[28] The larger issue, of course, was that the bylaws left the power of the bishops intact.

The new bylaws provided for the election of parish councils, whose representatives would elect district delegates, who in turn would choose the diocesan electoral college (composed of three clergymen and laymen). The diocesan electoral colleges were to choose the diocesan metropolitans when vacancies occurred, and the patriarchal electoral college when the patriarchate became vacant (with three clergymen and three laymen from each diocese involved). The democratic character of these bylaws—the inclusion of parish clergy and laymen in the high councils of the church— could be defeated by the apathy of the congregations at the parish level or abused by forces seeking to control the church from outside. The second round of the elections, where representatives of the parish councils were to pick district representatives, showed that the union could control the church. Even before the enactment of the bylaws union leaders were writing in *Naroden pastir* that only individuals "with clear and positive attitudes toward the present people's government" should be elected, "only the most worthy and most capable . . . and finally, sincerely accepting the people's government, good loyal citizens of the republic, should be elected."[29] The synod apparently tried to stave off a victory of the union, but its effort was so inept that it gave it up. The elections were a landslide victory for the union. It was a victory for the government too. Thus, though the bylaws still left the episcopate in charge, it was the union (and behind the union the state) that were to dictate the destiny of the church.

The defeat of the synod at this time was turned into a resounding victory in a few years by the metropolitan of Plovdiv, Kiril. Prisoner of the communists in 1944–45, he started toeing their line in 1946. On August 28 he delivered a speech at the Bachkovo monastery to some twenty thousand worshippers in celebration of an icon of the Madonna to which the church attributed miraculous powers. The next day the party press gave a distorted report of his sermon, claiming that the prelate had attacked the monarchy and spoken in favor of the republic. Although this was a misrepresentation of his speech, Kiril avoided overt opposition to the regime and cultivated friendship with more moderate sections in the Priests' Union. He also traveled to the Soviet Union several times and wrote books and articles supporting the new regime in Bulgaria. Eventually Kiril was appointed vicar president of the Holy Synod, and subsequently proved to be the first choice of synod, union, and party alike for the position of patriarch (in 1953).

The last act in the drama between synod and union was played out on July 8, 1955. During the previous months some leading personalities of the union had started a vicious campaign against the synod in their press and in their speeches. They apparently raised questions on the governance of the church, challenging the supremacy of the bishops. The synod dissolved the union and took over its assets and newspaper. The same day Kiril paid a visit to Prime Minister Vulko Chervenkov to seek the government's approval for the synod's drastic action. The government surprisingly acquiesced in the ecclesiastical coup d'état. At the same time the synod fired its general secretary, former seminary teacher Bishop Jonah, a progovernment prelate forced on the church in 1949, and dispatched him to serve as abbot of the Backhovo monastery, where he died a few years later. Archimandrite Maksim, vicar of the Bulgarian church at the patriarchate of Moscow, was summoned to take his place. That the government did not interfere in these changes indicates that the synod now enjoyed its complete confidence.

Only ten years after the communist takeover the synod had recovered the same position in the church that it had held under the old regime: full, absolute, unlimited power in internal church affairs. The provisions of the bylaws for the participation of lower clergy and laity in the governing bodies of the church had been implemented, but these bodies had been quickly transformed into obedient tools of the synod and lost all their meaning. The position of the Holy Synod in the church was not different from that of the Politburo in the Communist party. Just as the party would not permit the formation of opposition factions in its Central Committee or the reestablishment of alternative political parties in the country, so the synod would not allow dissent in the ranks of the church. Such a contingency would have been atypical for any organization in a socialist-communist country anyway. There had been much more dissent and strife in the halls of the church before 1923. In 1907 the synod had dissolved the then budding Priests' Union under similar, if milder, circumstances.

But, all things considered, the position of the synod was not enviable. Unchallenged as its authority was, it had under its power a mutilated church, in the chains of the Law of Faiths.

The Fiscal Dependence of the Church

The most sensitive aspect of church-state relations in Bulgaria has always been the financial dependence of the church on the state. Whenever the church found itself in any kind of conflict with the governing party it was always subject to financial pressure to change its policies. The state subsidy always proved the most effective lever to move the bishops to obedience. Sometimes used as a bribe, and sometimes figuring in the guise of a threat of withdrawal or temporary suspension, the subsidy has always worked for the benefit of the state. Always vulnerable on this score, the church seems to have been ever ready for concessions and accommodation when the question of money would be brought up. The Bulgarian Orthodox church has not been self-supporting for more than a century, and in fact has been dependent on the state subsidy ever since the liberation in 1878. Such lands as the church owned were never sufficient to assure the church of fiscal independence. In 1920, for example, the church, together with its monasteries, possessed only 47,256 acres of land, out of which only 7,851 acres were arable.[30] Neither did the church have any large real estate holdings in the cities from which to derive tangible income. The Bulgarian church was poor prior to the communist takeover, and remained poor thereafter.

Once the separation of church from state was an accomplished fact, the government requested that the church submit a plan for its future self-financing. The synod appointed a commission, chaired by Metropolitan Kiril. Kiril prepared a plan providing for a church bank, which was to have pulled together all church resources—monasterial lands, real estate, and monetary funds. In addition to collection of fees for private religious services and Sunday collections, the plan provided for special stamps to be sold freely to the citizenry. As soon as the plan was submitted, the government vetoed it.[31] First, the clause relating to land and real estate clashed with the government system of a state-controlled economy and the collectivization of land, which was not yet in a mature stage. Second, the stamp tax might be abused by forces outside the church, perhaps to build up an opposition center to the government. The state then promised to continue the subsidy until the church could organize its finances.[32] It soon became very clear that the only autonomous source of church income would be the sale of candles.

The fiscal catastrophe of the church was admitted on March 25, 1955, when the synod addressed the believers in Bulgaria with a special message that the church was in a difficult material position and that it could not depend for its existence on the sale of candles. There were many adjustments to be made, of course, as the overall budget was small. In 1974 a synodal publication revealed that the state's subsidy constituted some 13 percent of the church's annual budget.[33]

Uneven Partners

This is not the first time that the Bulgarian Orthodox church has found itself in such a predicament. In the eleventh century the country had fallen under Byzantine control and had lost its national hierarchy for two hundred years to the Greeks. It suffered the same fate from the fourteenth to the nineteenth century under the Turks. But the fall to communism in 1944 put the church to a different test. The new regime left its institutional structure and its upper hierarchy intact, but at the same time it challenged the validity of its message, the scope of its functions, and the relevance of its existence. Its message was subjected to an all-out attack, its functions were restricted by a series of legal enactments prescribing the parameters of its interests, and its activities were reduced to an absolute minimum. Translated into practical policies, all this amounted to muzzling the church and forcing it to play the politics of its own ultimate demise.

The lower clergy, the foot soldiers of the church, were the most vulnerable segment of the church hierarchy. The government sought to encourage desertions and to discourage ordinants. Attrition, intimidation, and financial insolvency in the course of the decades after 1944 have taken a heavy toll among the parish clergy. In 1938 the church was served by no less than 2,486 priests. In 1948 the number still stood at 2,446, but thereafter, the number gradually declined. In 1951 it was reported to be 2,263. In 1977 Patriarch Maksim gave it as "over 1,700," while Metropolitan Pimen, addressing a Mexican audience, spoke of 1,500. It is quite reasonable to assume that by 1986 this number may have fallen to below 1,200. The one theological seminary, at the Cherepish Monastery, and the Theological Academy in Sofia are reported to have a total of 250 students. They could hardly graduate fifty seminarians a year—half of them already ordained clergy—which is far from enough to fill all the vacancies.[34] Synodal bishops in the United States have complained that after graduating from the theological schools lay students are drafted in the armed forces, where they are turned against the church, and never opt for ordination. Those who return to the church usually occupy civilian positions in its administration and prove accommodating vis-à-vis the government.[35] Very often the hierarchy resorts to ordaining untrained and unqualified individuals, without theological education, just to perform liturgical services and keep the churches open. But the upper hierarchy of the church has remained the same as in prewar times. It would not be an exaggeration to say that they belong to the class of the privileged few in Bulgarian society who are free to travel abroad on church business. They are continually paraded at international peace conferences and in visiting Bulgarian communities in the West, as a testimony to the church's acceptance of the status quo.

Short of outlawing religion, which would have created more problems for the regime than it would have solved, the state, by allowing a minimal existence for the church, under government control and supervision, has discovered how to exploit the church for its own purposes. The church has proven to be a most useful and effective tool of propaganda abroad. The Bulgarian bishops, led by Patriarch Maksim, play a leading part in the world peace movement.[36] Likewise it appears that the church has been assigned the exclusive task of being the regime's principal agent for winning the support of the Bulgarians living in the West by organizing them into church parishes under the spiritual jurisdiction of the Holy Synod. Bishops and priests are generously subsidized to visit émigré communities and preach patriotism and loyalty to the homeland. In 1978 the patriarch paid such a visit to the Bulgarians in the United States and Canada.[37] Similarly, for the promotion of Bulgarian patriotism and loyalty to the regime in Sofia, the government publishes a monthly, *Rodolyubie* (*Patriotism*, formerly *Slavyani*), exclusively circulated abroad, where the church is featured prominently. While the national press in Bulgaria would hardly ever mention any church activities, *Rodolyubie* is replete with pictures of monasteries, icons, churches, religious celebrations, bishops, and priests. Bulgarian heroica, if one trusts *Rodolyubie*, is a pantheon of church leaders, from the ninth century to the twentieth, including Patriarch Maksim.[38] Maksim is described in glowing terms: "We see him often, the noble, snow-white prelate, in his severe vestments or in his white veil . . . among state leaders. Foreigners attending national celebrations always ask who he is. And they are told: 'The Bulgarian Patriarch Maksim!'"[39] The Bulgarian émigrés are told of the extraordinary services which the patriarch has performed for the People's Republic of Bulgaria. They are also told how much the patriarch has done for them, for their organization in the church parishes in Europe, America, and Australia, so that they can still maintain their ties to the motherland. He is then placed in the same company of Bulgarian national heroes as Patriarch Eftimiy, Paisii Khilendarski, Exarch Iosif, and Patriarch Kiril.

It would be untrue to charge that the church in Bulgaria is subjected to crude persecution, but it is nonetheless a fact that aside from performing its rituals, the church is in no position to defend itself against the erosion of its social presence or the restrictions on its activities. It cannot even develop a theology of socialism, along the lines of the so-called liberation theology, popular in the Third World. Tendencies in that direction—apparent in the works of the leading Bulgarian theologians in the postwar period, Radko Poptodorov, Metropolitan Pimen, Boris Marinov, Dimitar Penov, and Ivan D. Panchovsky—are viewed as modernistic attempts at ingratiation with the ideology and the policies of the ruling communist party, which, in the final analysis, are said to be only a fraudulent representation of the scientific, moral, and social issues of the day. Such tendencies, "even the most daring modernistic theological attempts," are seen as "only new, in a greater or lesser degree, specious, finely veiled tricks of the perpetual struggle of religion against progress, and, as such, because of their deceptive appearance, to be much more harmful than the open struggle waged by 'crude' religion." [40] The authority of Lenin is invoked in support of this assessment of the attempts of the Bulgarian theologians to adapt to the new order of things. If such a theology of socialism, as a means of accommodation to the system, is viewed in negative terms, it is unthinkable that the church could openly oppose the Marxist precepts of society, morality, religion, and culture. Such a reaction to the system would clearly be considered a departure from the "sphere of serving the religious needs of the believers." The apologists of the system argue that "any activity outside these limits goes beyond the proper function of the church and violates the freedom of conscience in socialist Bulgaria, and is forbidden by the laws of the country." [41] This would be an involvement of the church in politics, and such politics, even in defense of fundamental church rights, is not permitted. Politics in service to the state is, on the other hand, a permissible sphere of church activity.

Conclusion

The Bulgarian Orthodox church has preserved its nationalism, but, lacking broad popular support and independent means of self-support, it has settled for a precarious existence. In the mid-1980s, it functions as a propaganda tool for the regime, which is actively working to extinguish all traces of religion at some point in the future. Because its doctrines retain content incompatible with Marxism-Leninism, the church is still able to attract those seeking some means of registering their opposition to communism. But this is an empty opposition, since the church serves the communist government with more zeal and more obedience than it had displayed toward any of the prewar princes.

Thus the uneven partnership of church and state—the state enjoying unrestricted power over the church and the latter with no other choice but to submit—resolved itself in a set of practical politics, where the point of contact between the two institutions was reduced to an absolute minimum, and where their divergent views were clearly recognized as unbridgeable. They further recognized that the politics of tolerance for each other was mutually beneficial to both parties. It is in this set of circumstances that the church, accommodating itself to political reality, makes its bid for legitimacy, relevance, and survival. In its quest for legitimacy the church has chosen history as its single most potent and irrefutable witness to justify its case before the Bulgarian people. When General Secretary Todor Zhivkov failed to give credit to the church in his speech at the solemn celebration of the 1300th anniversary of the Bulgarian state in 1981,[42] *Tsurkoven vestnik* responded with a series of quotes from the patriarch, Georgi Dimitrov, and both Soviet and French academicians, arguing that, "the Bulgarian patriarchate, as far back as in the tenth century, has thrown a solid spiritual bridge across the precipices of the times to unite three epochs of the uneven historical path of the centuries-old Bulgarian state" and claiming that "the history of the Bulgarian Orthodox church is the history of Bulgarian culture."[43] All of this appeared in 16-point bold, Old Bulgarian script.

But the historical record of the services the Bulgarian Orthodox church has rendered to the Bulgarian nation is so overwhelming that, notwithstanding the unceasing efforts of militant atheists to negate it, it has found much recognition from leading party officials and prominent communist scholars. The statement of Georgi Dimitrov, the celebrated leader of the Bulgarian Communist party in the 1920s and 1930s and prime minister in the late 1940s, is worth quoting here:

It is to the credit of the Bulgarian Orthodox Church that throughout its history it has preserved Bulgarian national sentiments and consciousness. In the struggle for the liberation of our people, the Bulgarian Church has acted as a preserver and protector of the national spirit of the Bulgarian people during centuries of severe trial. . . . It can be said without fear of contradiction that the new democratic Bulgaria of the Fatherland Front would not be in existence if, during the grim, black period of the foreign yoke there had been no pastors to preserve the nation. . . . We, the Fatherland Front, and in particular, we communists, express our gratitude and thanks to these patriots, the servants of the Bulgarian national Church. I would frankly stress that as a Bulgarian, I am proud of the Bulgarian Church.[44]

Likewise, Simeon Damyanov, editor of *Istoricheski pregled*, published by the Bulgarian Academy of Sciences, prefaced his critical observations on the role of the church in the nineteenth-century struggles for liberation with the following words of praise: "It is well known that one will find the names of a host of church leaders inscribed in the pantheon of immortal sons of our people who have given their lives in the revolutionary struggles for liberation from the five hundred years' yoke. The cassock did not impede these men from serving the revolutionary cause with all their soul, and to die with guns in their hands for national freedom."[45]

In its quest for relevance and survival the church plays up its role in the world peace movement, in service to the objectives of Soviet and Bulgarian foreign policy, always placing its activities in the framework of the Christian message. Lacking the wherewithal to pursue its quest for the philosophical validity of its message in active engagement with society, the church retreats into the darkest corner of its mysticism and medieval scholasticism, where no ray of light from the contemporary world can penetrate its flight from reality. The communist state in Bulgaria has reduced the Orthodox church to a state of absolute impotence. While this is more or less the case for all churches in Eastern Europe, in Bulgaria this policy has been carried to the point of the total annihilation of religious freedom.

FACT SHEET

The Bulgarian Orthodox Church

Patriarchate
  Of Preslav-Drustur: Proclaimed in 917. Recognized by Constantinople in 927.
  Of Ochrid: Transferred from Preslav-Drustur in 972. Suppressed in 1767.
  Of Turnovo: Established in 1235. Recognized by Constantinople. Suppressed in 1393.
  Of Sofia: Reestablished in 1953.

Current strength of the church
  8 million believers (nominal)
  3 million believers (casual or regular churchgoers)
  1,700 priests (1977)

400 monks (1977)
11 metropolitans, 11 bishops, 12 archimandrites

Chief news organs
Tsurkoven vestnik (2,000 copies)
Dukhovna kultura (2,000 copies)

Number of churches and church facilities in operation
1,500 churches (1980) (estimated)
1 theological seminary, at Cherepish Monastery
1 theological academy
120 monasteries (1980) (mostly inactive)

Patriarchs since 1953
Kiril (Markov), 1953–71
Maksim (Marin Naidenov Minkov), 1971 to the present

10

The Orthodox Church of Greece

Theofanis G. Stavrou

The presence of Archbishop Seraphim at the inauguration ceremony of President Sartzetakis, in March 1985, directed the attention of millions of television viewers and several political analysts to the persistent close relationship, however troublesome at times, between church and state in Greece. It was also a reminder that in the Orthodox world of the twentieth century only the church of Greece enjoys official recognition as the state religion. Finally, it reinforced the impressions shared by many visitors to Greece that despite increasing secularization the presence of the Orthodox church is real, at times even lending that small Mediterranean country a "theocratic" aura. Assessing the extent to which appearances correspond with reality is a difficult matter, although political legislation and the church's response to it makes an attempt at such assessment a reasonable exercise. In any event, the whole phenomenon of church and state in Greece strikes one as being rather anomalous, almost anachronistic, especially when considered in the context of the fate of Orthodoxy at large in the twentieth century. The destruction, as a result of the First World War, of the three multinational empires (Russian, Ottoman, and Habsburg) where Orthodoxy thrived and the growing secularism of the age following or accompanying political and social revolutions forced Christianity in general and Orthodoxy in particular into a great retreat characterized by agonizing experiences and readjustments. Central to these changes has been the nature of church-state relations and their impact on the evolution of the Orthodox churches. The purpose of this essay is to examine this process by concentrating on the case of Greece in the twentieth century.[1]

The nature of church-state relations in contemporary Greece has its basis in a rich heritage, established first through a thousand years of Byzantine theory and practice, expanded upon by four centuries of coexistence with Ottoman authorities, and continued under the modern Greek state during the last 150 years of its existence. What made the presence of Archbishop Seraphim at the recent presidential inauguration symbolically significant and problematic at the same time was the fact that the inauguration reflected the ultimate victory of the Socialist party, PASOK, or more precisely of its leader Prime Minister Andreas Papandreou, whose social policy threatens to affect the status of the Greek Orthodox church more profoundly than any other policy or development in its modern history. President Sartzetakis was visibly solemn as befitting the occasion, but careful not to kiss the hand of the prelate, limiting their contact to a handshake,[2] whereas Papandreou unreservedly and smilingly embraced the archbishop. For a while it looked as if nothing had changed in the long and colorful tradition of church-state relations. The state called in the church to provide pomp and badly needed cohesion at a moment of national importance and the church responded eagerly in its customary role. The casual observer, conversant with Orthodox matters, could have mused that the "Byzantine symphonia" between church and state had reemerged. It looked strikingly similar to earlier political ceremonies, especially inaugurations, and reminiscent of former president Constantine Karamanlis's statement made in 1981 that "the nation (*ethnos*) and Orthodoxy . . . have become in the Greek conscience virtually synonymous concepts, which together constitute our Helleno-Christian civilization."[3] Or, for that matter, the familiar slogan of the Colonels pounded during the seven-year military dictatorship (1967–73) when they spoke of "Greece of Christian [Orthodox] Greeks." I remember how impressed I was by a huge canvas, prominently displayed in Athens's Constitution Square in the summer of 1969, portraying the three ingredients which at that time were put forth as representing the essence of Greek civilization and culture: the Acropolis dominated by the Parthenon and a procession heading toward it led by black-robed hierarchs followed by military officers. The whole picture was reminiscent of "socialist realism" at its best or worst, depending on one's artistic or political point of view. The canvas clearly demonstrated the attempt of the military leaders to politicize the Greek church that claimed as its members 95 to 97 percent of the country's 10 million population[4] and thus strengthen the regime's claim to legitimacy.

The above three examples of attitude toward the church by the Greek political leadership, ranging from the extreme right of the Colonels to the socialist PASOK of Papandreou, underscore their recognition of the centrality of the Orthodox church in social and political matters. Politicians are not the only ones perceptive enough to appreciate the significance of the Orthodox presence in their midst. Writers, social critics, theologians, and artists have been doing it all along. They are definitely sensitive to the spirit and fate of Orthodoxy, and since the main objective of this essay is to trace the impact of church-state relations on the church both as a political and social institution in the twentieth century, it might be a good idea to acquaint ourselves with some basic perceptions that the Greeks have of themselves in relationship to their church and state in the modern world.

At the beginning of the twentieth century, as Greek society was becoming increasingly aware of its transition, however gradual, from tradition to modernity with all the adjustments that such a process usually entails, the leading prose writer and newspaper columnist Alexander Papadiamantis (1851–1911) articulated epigrammatically a situation that may still be true for the Greek people in our days: "The Greek nation . . . has and will always have need of religion." Papadiamantis is known as a religious writer whose life and work have been permeated with the Orthodox ethos.[5] He has been compared to Dostoyevsky in his ability to capture the essence of Orthodoxy and articulate concerns about the intrusion of European institutions and ideas into the Orthodox realm. He became critical of the manifestations of modernism in politics, economics, and above all, culture. For Papadiamantis, modernism became synonymous with westernism, a cultural orientation toward which the Greek state and society were inevitably drifting. Against this development, he juxtaposed his worldview, heavily religious and laden with a nostalgia for Orthodoxy and its Byzantine associations. Though decidedly a religious writer in word and deed (he has been called the saint of modern Greek letters), he recorded a world and registered a concern corresponding to the sentiments of the majority of the Greek people at the time. His continuing popularity as a writer in Greece attests to that. In some respects his durability may be viewed as a "cultural mystery," for as the Nobel Prize winner Odysseus Elytis has pointed out, the pillars on which Papadiamantis built his edifice have already been demolished by industrialization and secularism, and one would have thought that he too would have been lost and forgotten.[6] Yet he is very much with us. Perhaps Elytis should have added that Papadiamantis's durability is in reality a testimony to the durability of Orthodoxy despite the assault of a secular age.

Half a century later, another significant man of letters and above all a social critic, George Theotokas (1905–66), belonging to the current of cultural modernity of which Papadiamantis was quite critical, also registered a warm endorsement for the significance of Orthodoxy for the modern Greeks. Writing in 1960, he reminded his readers that

> Orthodoxy, as the Greek people see it today, is a national religion, indissolubly woven with the customs and character of these people, the climate and fragrance of the country . . . its family life and the passing of the seasons. Its organization is democratic, its language warm, its ethical stance humane, consistent with the Greek mentality, its symbols familiar and irreplaceable in the popular conscience. Its great holidays . . . amount to the great days of Greece, the days when the nation as a whole feels, more than at any other time, its unity, its reinforcement, the mutual love of its membership.
>
> This sense of comfort, these warm spiritual waves, transmitted uninterruptedly throughout Greece from the Orthodox churches and their Byzantine liturgies, constitute an essential element . . . of Greek life. For this reason *it is impossible to conceive separation of church and state in Greece*, neither has there developed here a political anticlerical movement as has taken place elsewhere. We criticize the church frequently—sometimes very sharply—but we do so from within, as its members who expect from it to become better. We do not fight it as if it were an alien body from which we want to separate.

But then Theotokas hastened to add that "new historical conditions of the century demand of the church a reappraisal and readjustment."[7] As will be discussed later in this chapter, the 1960s in Greece witnessed a great debate about the social relevance of the church and the need for reforms. With characteristic optimism, Theotokas envisaged the Greek church as capable of responding to the challenge of the times and playing a major role in revitalizing and guiding modern Greek society.

Yet a little over two decades after Theotokas's exposition, a young Greek scholar-theologian, reflecting on some of the same issues, expressed grave concern about the fate of the church during the period under consideration. "What are the factors," he asked, "that have transformed the Church of Greece to a socially impotent and politically neutral 'religious supplement' to human existence?" He charged that "the administration of the church seems totally satisfied with the decorative role imposed upon it . . . satisfied with its accommodating mission as a state agency servicing the religious needs of the people. In exchange for this convenient *aphasia* [the church] enjoys the economic support and typical customary honors provided by the state."[8]

Clearly, the above representative views speak of continuity and promise, but also of problems inherent in the Orthodox experience of twentieth-century Greece. Some of these problems may be unique to the Greeks, others may be shared by other Orthodox churches, but central to all these developments is the nature of church-state relations.

The nature of church-state relations in modern Greece was partly determined by the fact that the latter's political independence from the Ottoman Turks (1829) was followed by ecclesiastical independence, four years later, from the Ecumenical Patriarchate of Constantinople, under whose jurisdiction the church of Greece had been since the eighth century. Provisions in Islamic law and Ottoman statecraft had made it possible for the Orthodox churches of the Near Eastern patriarchates to operate as a state within the Ottoman structure, enjoying considerable privileges in exchange for important services. It was a remarkable, almost paradoxical arrangement by which the members of the Greek "millet" or nation, as the Orthodox were generally identified, with the ecumenical patriarch serving as their ethnarch, emerged as "junior partners" of the Ottoman Empire and the church as a major political, social, and cultural institution.[9] Among other things, this arrangement helped preserve Orthodox and more specifically Greek identity, while simultaneously providing for it a broader context or world view, a sense of ecumenicity. The arrangement was paradoxical in another sense: it basically championed preservation and continuation of the political and religious status quo on which so much else depended; yet consciously and unconsciously, it fostered nationalist aspirations that ultimately contributed toward the dissolution of the Ottoman Empire and the undermining of religion itself as the main point of reference. The Greek Revolution (1821–29) led to the establishment of the first independent state, with secular pretensions, carved out of the Ottoman Empire. Thus the Ottoman sultan lost a political and the Greek patriarch an ecclesiastical province. Both of them accepted their loss grudgingly and only after they realized that they had to yield to an inevitable sociopolitical process—the emergence of national states with secularistic tendencies.

The question of an independent Greek church was debated heatedly by politicians, theologians, and intellectuals who argued for or against it.[10] But it was finally decided by politicians with the support of "separatist hierarchs." Political leadership, beginning with the first Greek president, Ioannis Capodistrias, supported church autonomy that would remove any remnants of subservience to the Turks through the ecumenical patriarch residing in Constantinople. There were international dimensions to the problem as well, complicated by varying attitudes of the three protecting powers—England, France, and Russia—that influenced Greek politics after independence.[11] But it was the "Bavarian Monarchy," ushered into Greece by the European powers, after the assassination of Capodistrias in 1831, that introduced a solution to the problem, the repercussions of which were many and far-reaching. By and large, the "Bavarian Monarchy," beginning with the reign of King Otho, a Catholic with an Evangelical wife, and his regents (Otho was a minor when he went to Greece), were indifferent to the cultural sensibility of their Greek subjects, but they were astute and determined to exploit the religious crisis and inaugurate a policy of church-state relations, which on the whole survives to these days despite some modifications imposed upon it at historical intervals.[12]

A formal government declaration on July 23, 1833, established the church of Greece as "autocephalous." This decision, embodied in the church constitution of the same year, was taken without the patriarch's consent and it marked the beginning of the disintegration of a "religious commonwealth," overseen up to that time by the patriarch. It was the first official disruptive consequence, for the Orthodox church, of the Greek Revolution, for whose success the church had made considerable sacrifices, including the lives of many of its leaders.[13] For two decades the patriarch refused to have any contacts with the new administrative body of the autocephalous Greek church, the Holy Synod. The latter had been set up on the model of the Russian synod, and in the mind of the Bavarian Monarchy it constituted a department of state. A special government official or procurator was to attend the synodal meetings and no decision taken in his absence or without the approval of the government was valid. More crucially, the bishops forming the governing body of the synod were always appointed by the government. It was not until 1850 that the ecumenical patriarch recognized the new situation by issuing a special synodal *Tome*, through which he also attempted to reassert some of the authority enjoyed earlier by the mother church. The *Tome* stipulated that the church of Greece should be ruled by a permanent synod presided over by the metropolitan of Athens, but that in important matters it should consult with the patriarchate.[14] This was an awkward move, attempting to deal with a reality that for all practical purposes had slipped out of patriarchal control. From then on, the administration of the Greek church was basically determined by the 1833 arrangement that is in force even today despite several modifications incorporated in subsequent legislation.

The 1833 arrangement providing autonomy for the Greek church, allegedly to safeguard the political autonomy of the Greek state as well as the health of the church, also set in motion the process of separation of church and state. Strange as it may seem, this process has not received the attention it deserves, by historians, political scientists, sociologists, or even legal historians. References to the phenomenon are usually general, pointing to the fact that legislation tried to limit the church's activity to purely religious functions. Education was to be primarily the province of the state, even though the church was not prevented from participating in public education. The church, to be sure, maintained its control over matters of marriage and divorce, but they lost a good deal of their direct economic base as a result of the state's confiscating church properties resulting chiefly from the closing of monasteries. Interestingly enough, the government's suppression of monasteries was done through the Holy Synod. Proceeds from the sale of monastic lands were put into an ecclesiastical fund to support the church and public school system. It could, of course, be argued that monastic and other church lands if distributed to landless citizens could ease some economic pressure. As could be expected, the latter did not happen and the ruthless closure of 412 monasteries in 1833–34 (leaving only 148 monasteries, with a total of two thousand monks, and three convents for nuns for the whole country) caused great resentment and frustration in a society with a profound respect for the monastic tradition and accustomed to viewing monasteries as a natural extension of the country's landscape. The confiscation of church properties and attempts by the government to reduce the number of bishops to ten, in order to correspond to the number of new political divisions of the country, symbolized the government's determination to expand civil authority in as many areas of Greek life as possible.

The state's religious policy, supported in part by some political and religious leaders, co-opted by the government, was part of the latter's overall policy of modeling the Greek state along European lines in matters of administration, education, and cultural tastes, and of course, church-state relations. In a way the church was helpless, rendered more so by the fact that communication between itself and the ecumenical patriarch was nonexistent until the issuing of the 1850 *Tome*. The church's one consolation during the early phase of its autocephalous status came as a result of the 1843 bloodless revolution when King Otho was forced to grant a constitution in which it was stipulated that his successor to the Greek throne should belong to the Orthodox faith.[15] For the remainder of Otho's reign (he was ousted in October 1862), the civil authorities maintained the upper hand in their dealings with the church. The new constitution made discussion of religious issues before a general assembly an easier matter, but when in 1852 the patriarchal *Tome* of 1850 was discussed, only those parts of it not directly challenging civil dominance were accepted. At this time the government, however, consented to the increase of the number of episcopal sees to twenty. Still, it is important to keep in mind that encroachments by the state were synonymous with separation of church and state more in the mind of state officials than in the mind of the church leaders. From the beginning the hierarchs appreciated sufficiently the benefits accrued from the official status accorded the church by the state. Neither should it be assumed that the Greek church, headed by the archbishop of Athens, accepted passively the state's encroachment in its domain. Even in the early stages of this relationship when the church's finances and personnel were depleted, it had a sense of confidence about the political influence it could exercise at propitious moments. It was a matter of assessing realistically the new political situation and then acting accordingly through strong representation and careful negotiations, frequently utilizing the art of compromise. In fact, with the passing of time, the Greek hierarchy identified itself more and more with the state's policy objectives both on domestic and foreign issues.

As far as foreign policy is concerned, it is understandable that for ideological and practical reasons the church supported the *Megali Idea* (Great Idea) whose main objective was to expand the frontiers of the modern Greek state to incorporate unredeemed Greeks in the north and on the islands and if possible re-create the old Byzantine Empire. Ironically enough, this policy, which enraged the sultan at whose expense this political dream could have been realized, also displeased the patriarch, who anticipated that any political changes would inevitably affect the size of his ecclesiastical jurisdiction. Nevertheless, the expansion, which the Greeks described as a policy of irredentism although their critics spoke of it as an act of imperialism, was already in the making.

It began with the political incorporations of the Ionian Islands into the Greek state in 1864. The British had ruled the islands for most of the nineteenth century, even though ecclesiastically they were under the jurisdiction of the Constantinople patriarch. They decided to return the islands to the Greeks as a gesture of goodwill and in order to strengthen the position of the new monarch, Prince George, whom the British supported and who assumed the throne following Otho's ousting in 1862. The islanders as well as the patriarch at first resisted this double incorporation, political and ecclesiastical, by the Athens regime, but in the end the patriarch consented to the transfer. From then on, the administrative radius of the Greek church was largely determined by the expansion of the geographic frontiers of the Greek state as a result of either wars or diplomacy or both. Thus, for example, Thessaly and part of Epirus were annexed in 1881, Macedonia and Crete in 1912 (with special provisions), and the Dodecanese in 1945.[16] These new lands, or "Neai Khorai" as they came to be known, added to the number of dioceses under the jurisdiction of the patriarch while enjoying limited local autonomy, and Mount Athos, the center of Orthodox monasticism, on the Chalcidice Peninsula, has its own form of government: the "Holy Community" representing the twenty active monasteries on its territory. The latter is in fact an autonomous republic with a civil governor appointed by the Greek state and residing along with the "Holy Community" at Karyes. These three ecclesiastical jurisdictions (Crete, the Dodecanese, and Mount Athos), autonomous though they may be, are becoming increasingly part and parcel of the Greek state, their fate determined partly by the precarious status of the patriarchate of Constantinople.[17]

Thus the present administrative arrangement of the Greek church consists of the archbishop of Athens and of all Greece as its head, assisted by an elected twelve-member permanent Holy Synod residing in Athens. The synod manages the executive church business, with the help of various commissions which function within the synod. Members of the synod are equally divided between those representing the new territories in the north and those representing the original territory of modern Greece. In all, presently the church of Greece consists of ninety dioceses, with 8,548 parishes, served by 9,682 priests and deacons. The number of dioceses fluctuates depending on jurisdictional rearrangements determined by the Holy Synod. The bishops to the permanent synod are elected by a larger body, the hierarchial synod, made up of all the active metropolitans in the country and whose main responsibility is to pass ecclesiastical legislation. This administrative arrangement provides a certain pyramidal structure which may lend itself to either centralization or decentralization depending on the "reigning" archbishop and the political climate in which he has to operate. For in the final analysis church leaders have to work in close association with the Ministry of Education and Religious Affairs, the department through which the state maintains its formal association with and control over the church. Through this ministry, for example, the state disperses funds to the church as well as watches over areas of concern involving both church and state.[18]

A constant irritant in church-state relations from 1833 to the present has been the government's tendency to interfere in the election of the archbishop by manipulating the voting bishops. Needless to say, this process had the effect of sharpening the political acumen of the church and taught its officials to anticipate political crises and prepare for appropriate responses. Unfortunately, this relationship consumed too many of the resources of the church which otherwise might have been used for improving the church's conditions in fields such as education of the clergy and other general religious concerns. In view of the fact that in the Orthodox world politics have always been closely connected with the question of survival, and improvement is senseless without the latter, the church has no choice in the matter but to find itself constantly involved in politics. In general, the history of this relationship between church and state may be divided into four periods: 1833–52, characterized by the efforts to establish the autocephalous church of Greece; 1852–1923, when the church struggled to emancipate itself from some of the excessive types of state control, especially those exercised by the government procurator; 1923–38, dedicated to the struggle for reforms; and the era of the Second World War and its aftermath, when the church's volatile position became even more so by the archbishop's acting temporarily as head of state and by the demands made upon it by the Civil War in the 1940s and the military dictatorship in the 1960s. The return of democracy in Greece in 1974 and the adoption of a new constitution the following year may be viewed as the beginning of a new era for the church, even though the present archbishop is a carryover from the era of the Colonels.

Perhaps because of these conditions, no consistent ecclesiastical policy emerged during the century and a half under consideration. There were a few visionaries who tried to imagine the role and future of the church in long-range terms, but by and large the response to these developments was one of improvization, which at times could be interpreted as timely, perhaps, but also opportunistic. The best example to illustrate this tendency is to recall the turn of church-state relations during the turbulent years of 1910 to 1922 that witnessed the Balkan Wars, the First World War, and what the Greeks refer to as the Anatolian disaster. During this period the dominant personality in Greek politics was the Cretan Eleftherios Venizelos. A liberal, reformist, and expansionist at the same time, Venizelos did not ignore ecclesiastical matters, and his first political acts included sponsoring legislation to upgrade the salaries of the clergy and to define more responsibly the duties of parish priests and other church officers. In broader national politics Venizelos and his liberal policies, especially his criticism of King Constantine over Greek participation in World War I, led to the Great Schism between his followers known as the Venizelists and those of the king known as the Royalists. The Great Schism profoundly affected Greek political life at home and abroad, and no understanding of later Greek history is possible without a proper understanding of it. The church was divided too. But by and large the synod of the Greek church supported the king and even anathematized the prime minister, when the latter, in October 1916, created a rival, provisional government in Thessaloniki. The Royalist church paid the consequences for this act when Venizelos came to Athens in June 1917 following the abdication of King Constantine and had the archbishop and most of the synod ousted. After a five-month vacancy the archbishopric was filled with a resourceful and progressive individual, Meletios Metaxakis, who unfortunately stayed in office for only two years. As could be expected, when Venizelos was defeated in the 1920 elections and the Royalists returned to power, the Royalist archbishop was reinstated. But these were difficult years for church and state, complicated by the Greek military disaster in Anatolia in 1922, followed by a new political revolution in Athens with Colonel Nicholas Plastiras assuming power. King Constantine had again abdicated. The Royalist Archbishop Theoklitos was dismissed, the Holy Synod dissolved, and a new assembly of bishops was called by a special committee to set the house of the church in order.[19]

What emerges from the above brief account is that by 1922 the role of the archbishop of Athens was looming large in the Orthodox world, obscuring that of the ecumenical patriarch, the latter weakened pathetically because of political developments in Turkey. In fact, in 1922 he was given the title of exarch of all Greece and in 1923 was changed to that of archbishop of Athens and of all Greece. During the last fifty years the archbishops became progressively more visible in Greek national life, either because of their personality or because political circumstances demanded it. They also became more assertive either because they were convinced of the significance of their missions of service to both church and state, or because of personal ambitions. This new breed of archbishops, some of them from Asia Minor background, began with the well-known professor of church history Chrysostomos Papadopoulos (1868–1938), who managed the affairs of the church during the interwar years beginning in 1923 until his death in 1938. He was followed by Archbishop Chrysanthos (1881–1949), who stayed in office until his refusal to cooperate with the pro-Nazi government in Athens led to his deposition in 1941.[20] His successor was the well-known hierarch Archbishop Damaskinos (1890–1949), whose controversial office tenure is associated with the bitterest years in recent Greek history: the Nazi occupation and the Civil War that followed liberation. Damaskinos, whom at one point Churchill had described as "a pestilent priest, a remnant from the Middle Ages," played a crucial role in the political as well as ecclesiastical affairs of the Greek state, especially in 1944–46 when he served as regent during the king's absence. In fact, it was the first time in the history of the modern Greek state that the religious leader of the country enjoyed such political visibility at home and abroad, obscuring, temporarily at least, political figures. Throughout the war years and after, Damaskinos dealt with the Occupation Powers and the British and with all the Greek political factions ranging from the extreme right to the extreme left. And, of course, he participated in the arrangements that determined the political outcome of postwar Greece. For his policies and personal ambitions he has been criticized by some and praised by others, and this should be expected, since this was a time when Greeks met the invaders and each other in a pitiless combat. His role as a political or even ecclesiastical figure during this period has not been properly assessed as yet, but there is a consensus that no other individual combined the qualities and prestige of Damaskinos to see the Greek state and society through their incredible ordeal. Even Churchill became impressed by Damaskinos's activities and became his strong supporter and admirer. Certainly no one doubted his patriotism and his opposition to the Axis Powers. Damaskinos left his mark especially in the area of philanthropic activity. In defiance of the Germans, he set up an impressive network of relief organizations to support the families of those executed by the Germans. He also worked indefatigably to protect Jewish families from their Nazi persecutors. In short, through Damaskinos the church had a golden opportunity to be an agent of social reconstruction and on the whole it executed its task admirably. Finally, Damaskinos sought to improve the position of the Greek clergy by putting them on the public payroll, increasing educational opportunities, and most importantly by strengthening the independence of the church from the vexatious interference of the state. On the whole, during the war and reconstruction years, the role of the church was an efficacious one, especially if one keeps in mind that it, too, had been ravaged by the war and its aftermath.[21] After Damaskinos's death in 1949 the church continued to participate in the rebuilding of the country under two old hierarchs: Spyridon Vlachos of Yannina, 1949–56, and Archbishop Chrysostomos Hadjistavrou. The latter directed the church from 1962 until the military takeover on April 21, 1967, when he was forced to resign. The person who officiated during most of the junta period was the energetic Archbishop Ieronymos Kotsonis, who remained in office from 1967 until the first part of 1974, when the present archbishop, Seraphim, was elected.[22]

Among the above, those who did not die in office were forced to resign, a sign perhaps that the hierarchs were not as docile as generally assumed. What is even more significant is that each one of these church leaders can be identified with some important attempt at reform or improving the position of the church vis-à-vis the state, regardless of other unpleasant circumstances surrounding their tenure of office. Thus, Archbishop Chrysostomos, soon after his election in 1923, put rigid demands to the government of General Plastiras asking for greater freedom for the church, less dependence on the state, and more importantly, less interference by government representatives in synodal matters. Their demands were incorporated in the 1923 church constitution, favored by General Plastiras. Unfortunately, the constitution was suspended two years later during the dictatorship of General Pangalos, with whom Archbishop Chrysostomos was constantly at odds. This reverted all details of church administration and its relation to the state back to its pre-1923 pattern, which meant the 1833–52 pattern. But the question of a new constitution did not die, and after considerable debate a new one was published in 1931 that provided among other things that a general synod consisting of the bishops of Greece would be the ultimate base of authority and it would meet every three years to execute its duties. A permanent holy synod consisting of eight rotating members plus the archbishop of Athens would administer church affairs between sessions of the general synod of bishops. Specific references to the government procurator present at synod meetings reduced his role considerably: he could present or defend his position on issues but he had no voting power. In fact, his presence was not essential for a vote to be taken. Such church constitutions were usually favored by liberal or democratic governments, and the one of 1931 was made possible because Venizelos had returned to power in 1930. With the beginning of the Metaxas dictatorship on August 4, 1936, the state tightened its control over the synod, which was more cooperative than usual in an effort to provide national unity and an anticommunist front. The decade of the forties was one of survival for church and state, and constitutional questions over church administration receded in the background, although Damaskinos had a constitution approved in 1943 which along with that of 1931 served as the base for church government into the 1960s. During the 1950s and 1960s church and state embarked upon a policy of reconstruction made possible by the attainment of political stability and economic improvement. The church also tried to strengthen its position by dealing rather harshly with deviant or what they described as heretical groups.[23] Above all, it watched the drift of Greek politics from the Karamanlis era of the late fifties and early sixties, to the overthrow of the democratic government by the Colonels in 1967, and the restoration of democracy in 1974. During this period the church concerned itself with some important issues, such as the question of the transfer of bishops and education of the clergy, to which we shall return later. But they also were mindful of problems in church administration. Capitalizing on the goodwill of Prime Minister Papadopoulos, whom the church supported against a counter-coup by young King Constantine in December 1967, Archbishop Ieronymos managed to procure for the church a new constitution, which was supposed to give the church greater freedom to manage its administrative, educational, and financial affairs, but could also give the archbishop greater central control in his effort to bring about what he viewed as badly needed reforms.[24]

The pattern that emerges from this brief examination of church-state relations from 1923 to 1969, and for that matter to the present, is that the church could stand to gain a great deal more by assuring those in authority of its loyalty than by any other method. Still, it should not be presumed that the leaders of the church sacrificed principles indiscriminately for the sake of political accommodation. Occasionally church and state were at odds. But when all is said and done, church and state have on the whole supported each other as long as they both gained from the alliance. But an alliance or a pact of that sort is dangerously anachronistic if it offends public conscience, even the conscience of an Orthodox society with a great capacity to tolerate or accept fatalistically the behavior of its venerable institutions. It becomes even more so when society, either through education, affluence, or exposure to outside influences, is becoming more critical of its own traditional values and institutions. Something like that must have happened during the two postwar decades in Greece, the period of the so-called Greek economic miracle. The 1967–73 military dictatorship, despite the unpleasantness it heaped on the nation, also forced many Greeks into a healthy introspection.[25] In the process they found the church's collaboration with the Colonels exceedingly offensive, even though Archbishop Ieronymos demonstrated on occasion that he could outwit the dictators while attempting to reinvigorate the church through reforms. All this brought to the surface the need to reexamine a more fundamental question stemming to be sure from the general consideration of church-state relations, but also from an even broader one, namely, the place or relevance of the Orthodox church in modern society.

The return of democracy to Greece in the summer of 1974, under the leadership of Constantine Karamanlis, provided new opportunities to reconsider several political and social questions. Deliberations for a new democratic constitution approved by Parliament on June 7, 1975, generated extensive discussions about the nature of church-state relations. During the deliberations, the church leaders suddenly realized that the question of the separation of church and state had taken on a new dimension which could conceivably be reflected in the forthcoming constitution. Even though the latter would affirm Orthodoxy as the "dominant" religion, it was suggested that certain references, such as the invocation to the Trinity at the opening of the constitution, could be omitted. More important, there was to be no requirement that the head of the state, the president, hold membership in the Orthodox faith. In short, the general tone of the deliberations was that freedom of religious conscience is inviolable and that enjoyment of individual and civil rights should not depend on the religious convictions of the individual. Consequently, there was no need to include a proscription in the constitution specifically against proselytizing Orthodox church members. These deliberations alarmed church leaders, who were by no means ready to abandon the special privileges historically guaranteed to the church by the constitution. Neither did they want to jeopardize the financial support which the state provided for the maintenance of the churches, the salaries of the clergy and the teachers of religion in the school system, and the endowment of the seminaries. The church further insisted that this violated "harmony" between church and state and that the church was not prepared to take "such a momentous step." In short, the church suddenly found itself on the defensive on issues it had come to take for granted for 150 years. It therefore emphasized the need for a "proper relationship" between church and state since they constitute a single "Christian body." But church leaders also emphasized the fact that while "cooperating closely with the state, the church is not to be dominated by it, but must preserve its independence."[26]

The ratified constitution emerged as a compromise, including some of the church's demands while ignoring others. The Orthodox church would still be the dominant religion in Greece, but there was no mention that the president need be a member of the Orthodox church. The constitution affirms that the church "is autocephalous and governed by the Holy Synod consisting of the bishops actually functioning and by the permanent synod which derives from the above and which is compared, as the Constitutional charter of the church specifies, in accordance with the provision of the patriarchal *Tome* of June 29, 1850, and the synodal act of September 4, 1928."[27] This was the first time that references to the 1850 *Tome* and to the 1928 synodal act were included in the constitution and it was viewed as a great victory for the church. But the church lost out on the question of proscribing proselytizing. The latter should apply to all "recognized religions," not just the Orthodox. Finally, there was no reference to the former constitutions' provision on education that it should be "based on principles of Greek-Christian civilization."

The church of Greece has displayed remarkable resilience, as evidenced by its capacity to survive as a political institution. To be sure, it did not experience any of the persecutions of the kind and on the scale that befell the Orthodox churches in the Soviet Union and Eastern Europe. But it had its own set of problems and obstacles to overcome. Some of them were of the church's own making, but most had been introduced either by the state or by political, social, and economic changes in the land. Still, at this point in the mid-eighties, despite some setbacks, the church as a "political" or bureaucratic institution is enjoying good status under the new constitution. If, however, survival is to be viewed as the capacity of the survivor to live with stress and tension and do so creatively, it is important to inquire how the church has been faring as a social institution and what are the prospects for the future. Issues confronting the church in this regard have become more complex because of the social transformation of Greece during the postwar era. As has been repeatedly pointed out, the village, or rural Greece, has lost out to the big city, a trend that began at the turn of the century. Nearly half of the population of Greece lives in the Athens metropolitan area. The rest of it is claimed mainly by other cities, chief among them being Thessaloniki, Patras, Yannina. Its needs as well as tastes have changed. It is indeed a society in great transition, making it difficult for the church to sustain any meaningful leadership.

The gravity of the dilemma facing the church may be illustrated by considering three issues that the church cannot afford to ignore much longer: the question of education, especially the education of the parish clergy; the question of dissent; and finally the recent legislation concerning marriage and divorce. An imaginative response to these questions by the Orthodox hierarchy may make the difference as to whether the church will emerge as a creative or stifling force as it is moving toward the twenty-first century.

Probably the most serious issue facing the church today is that of educating the parish clergy. It has always been a basic problem, but neither church nor state did much about it. It is even maintained that this may have been the most serious mistake made by both church and state in recent Greek history. Several ecclesiastical schools were established but somehow they missed the mark. The Theological Academy of Athens (1837) and that of Thessaloniki (1942), founded more than a century apart, aimed primarily at educating scholars and theologians. Their theological and political differences aside, these two institutions did a creditable job in producing several distinguished theologians and church historians who in addition to establishing a scholarly tradition[28] established and maintained a dialogue with their counterparts outside Greece, thus mitigating the sense of isolation experienced by national churches under close state supervision. Many of them also attended international meetings of the World Council of Churches after 1949 when the Orthodox church joined that body. But the clergy was left to its own ignorance and illiteracy. Beginning in 1844 a special school, the *Rizarios*, was established with the expressed purpose of educating those who wanted to become priests. But it trained a very small number of priests, as did several other similar schools that were established throughout Greece by 1914. Pressed by the need for a more effective program, the church historian and later archbishop Chrysostomos Papadopoulos, along with the theologian Amilkas Alivizatos, opted for a temporary solution through the establishment of *ierodidaskaleia* (schools for priests), which met with some success. Unfortunately, however, few graduates from these schools reached their parishes, because upon graduation many became teachers instead, waiting until they reached age thirty when they could be ordained. Papadopoulos supplemented his program with the opening of special schools, the Higher Church "Frontistiria," which aimed at training priests who happened to have had a gymnasium education. According to some, this yielded spectacular results, but unfortunately they became confused with the "Lower Frontistiria" of 1946 whose quality of instruction was not commendable. If one takes into consideration the number of priests killed during the Second World War and the Greek Civil War one can surmise the bad condition of the parishes during the fifties and sixties. Peter Hammond, a contemporary observer, offered this depressing picture of the Greek church during this period:

> During the years of [German] occupation it was possible for the Greek people as a whole to maintain some semblance of normal life. . . . During 1945 and 1946 violent disturbances of the peace were, on the whole, on a smaller scale. . . . Early in the following year, however, the full violence of the armed sedition, which had slowly been gathering in energies since its temporary set-back of December, 1944, was let loose upon the country dioceses. It was from this point onwards that there began to occur the flight of whole villages from their lands and homes, which soon resulted in the complete abandonment of large areas of northern and central Greece to the roving bands of *andartes* [rebels, insurgents] and in the collapse of the whole parochial organization in many of the mountain dioceses. . . .
>
> Many of the parish clergy were killed before they could make their escape from the undefended villages. No single category of the population (unless it be the gendarmerie) has sustained heavier casualties in the slaughter of these years than the village *papades*, the Greek country parsons. . . .
>
> It is now becoming possible to gain some idea of the extent of the material damage which the Church has sustained since 1940. . . . In countless parishes, the church has been wholly destroyed. . . .
>
> It has also to be borne in mind that even in villages where the fabric of the church has survived, there is often a desperate need of liturgical books, vestments, and other accessories of worship.[29]

The problem, then, was both quantitative and qualitative. The Greek Orthodox church needed churches, books, and vestments, as well as spiritual leaders. Assuming that education contributes toward better spiritual
leadership, one is not heartened by the fact that the 1919 circumstance,
wherein only 1 percent of the clergy (that is, forty-three out of a total
of 4,433) had a university degree had not improved dramatically for the
rest of the twentieth century. During the 1960s education offered by both
church and state affected only 5 percent of the parish clergy. And in 1975,
out of 7,413 clergy, 589, approximately 8 percent, could claim university
education. The figure improved slightly during the last decade. Neither
is the picture more encouraging when one realizes that the majority of
the parish clergy, many of whom minister to a growing urban flock,
are of traditional peasant background, a background that is not substantially modified through any educational process or experience afforded the
priests. In short, then, neither state nor church even though constantly
discussing this issue has given it the priority it deserves or allocated sufficient funds for the purpose. In 1960 it was estimated that it would require
10 percent of the state budget in order to meet the needs of the church,
including education, and that such funds simply could not be expected
from church properties. The state, through the Ministry of Education and
Religious Affairs, was expected to increase its contribution.[30] It was also an
admission that the general ecclesiastical fund established in 1910 to handle
proceeds resulting from the expropriation of lands by the state up to that
time and during the 1920s was barely meeting the needs of the church.
The picture did not improve much with the creation of the Organization
for the Management of Church Property (ODEP). The inflation resulting
from the Second World War complicated matters further, and it was only
in 1962 that a social security fund for the Greek clergy known as TAKE
was initiated.[31] Education, better salaries, and better pension provisions
are all linked together and need to be coordinated if a general upgrading
of the Greek clergy in general and the parish clergy in particular is to be
expected.

Such provisions may make it easier to reverse the declining trend of
men going into the priesthood. It should also be pointed out that many
Greeks interested in ecclesiastical service choose to serve by becoming lay
theologians. As such, they avoid the onerous tasks of the parish clergy,
enjoy a university education, and, because of the latter and the places
where they serve—usually in big cities—they also enjoy greater prestige.
Important as this "disproportionate" number of lay theologians may be,
it will never replace the parish clergy, and without improved parish clergy
the future of the Greek church looks bleak.

To be sure, the church has been carrying on an enlightenment policy of its own, most effectively through the *Apostoliki Diakonia* headquartered at Moni Petraki in Athens. This coordinating agency run by a council headed by the archbishop himself has developed a nationwide activity through its departments dealing with questions of religious enlightenment in general, preaching, and catechetical schools and through an active publishing and broadcasting ministry.[32] This sort of activity helps allay some of the depressing feeling resulting from the generally unsatisfactory condition of the clergy, as does the work of several brotherhoods. The brotherhoods, the most important of which is the *Zoe* brotherhood founded by Eusebius Matthopoulos in 1911, constitute one of the most interesting features of religion in modern Greece. As it has been pointed out, they amount to "missionary movements directed toward an internal apostolate in the Greek Church itself."[33] *Zoe* has claimed among its members some of the best-known activists in twentieth-century Greek religious history, including the previous archbishop of Greece Ieronymos. *Zoe*, as well as one of its dissenting offshoots, *Sotir*, were very active, and even though their reputation was somewhat tarnished because they were identified with the political right, they provided a badly needed spark in the Greek church's firmament. Their contribution should be even more appreciated when viewed in the context of declining monasticism in Greece. For it is equally difficult, maybe more so, to attract people to the monastic life as it is to the priestly life and for some of the same reasons. With the exception of the remarkable revival on Mount Athos during the last twenty years, the monasteries in Greece have been declining precipitously. There has, however, been a growth in the number of convents for nuns.

It is obvious from the above that the education of the clergy should be a constant concern of the church, and it is a burden that in the future may have to be carried with reduced assistance from the state. New expropriations of church properties by the Papandreou government will make the church's task even more difficult. Regardless of cost, it has to be done because through it the church as a whole will be able to conduct itself more efficiently in a society which is fast becoming more complex and unpredictable. As long as the church meets most of the needs of the larger section of society, it will be a force to be reckoned with by the state. When the church loses its spiritual and social significance, no legislation can prevent it from falling into decline and becoming an object of criticism and ridicule.

Better education may also enable the church to respond more creatively to dissenting elements, religious and social. Like every other official church, the Orthodox Church of Greece defended its position as

interpreter and guardian of religious belief and practice. But challenges
to this monopoly of "ecclesiastical jurisdiction" appeared simultaneously
with the establishment of the modern Greek state and continue to this
day. Some of these dissenting voices came from within the ranks of the
church, some from without. Among the former, reference should be made
to two monks, Flamiatos and Panayotopoulos (affectionately referred to
as Papoulakos), who, during the first half of the nineteenth century,
led a resistance faction, especially in the Peloponnese, against the non-
Orthodox King Otho.[34] The church's position on the Papoulakos movement was ambivalent, since it was aimed primarily against Otho. But it
was decidedly hostile toward the best-known of these dissenting movements led by the theologian Apostolos Makrakis (1831–1905). The latter,
a fiery preacher and prolific writer castigated the hierarchy for neglecting
its religious duties and from drifting away from true Orthodox Christianity by submitting to the state and to Western influences. Makrakis
enjoyed a great following and literally shook the church of Greece with
his energetic outburst of criticism. He was declared a heretic and therefore
excommunicated, but his following continues both in Greece and in the
diaspora.[35]

The church of Greece was equally hostile to the *demotic* movement,
a linguistic controversy with ideological and political overtones. The demotic movement began in the 1880s as part of a larger liberal movement
in the land. It sought to give respectability to the popular spoken language
by making it the language of literature, the press, and of course public
instruction. Adamantly opposed to this movement were the purists who
clung to the use of an artificial language, *katharevousa*, and who dominated
the government, educational establishments, and the press. For nearly a
century this explosive controversy between the purists and the demoti-
cists served as a barometer of Greek politics and educational reforms—
conservative regimes supporting the purist tradition and liberal regimes
favoring the demotic.[36] Paradoxically, but understandably, the church supported the purists and consequently opposed vigorously the translation
of the New Testament into the demotic in 1901. The incident came to
be known as the *Evangeliaka* or gospel riots, which caused the deaths
of eight people and the resignation of the government. The incident is
symbolically important because it characterized the church as culturally
conservative and reactionary, a view reinforced by the excommunication
of writers such as E. Roidis (1835–1904) and A. Laskaratos (1811–1901)
who satirized the clergy in what have become classics of anticlericalism.
It is also interesting to note that even though several other attempts were
made to present the Scriptures in the demotic, a complete edition of the

New Testament in the demotic did not appear until the spring of 1985. It had been preceded by an important translation (1967) known as that of the "four" professors from the theological school of the University of Athens. The 1967 edition, however, was in what could be described as "simple Katharevousa." The demotic was finally recognized as the official language of instruction by the constitution of 1975, and the political and social implications of the appearance of the New Testament in demotic Greek will have a direct bearing on the status of the church and its claims to spiritual interpretations. The 1985 edition known as that of the "six" professors from the University of Athens and Thessaloniki has in fact generated appreciable controversy and is viewed critically by spokesmen of the church. The point is that the church's attitude toward "dissenters" earned it much bad feeling, as did its attitude toward the Old Calendarists or *Palaioimerologites* who refused to go along with the church when the latter adopted a new calendar to correspond with the Western one in 1924. The Old Calendarists, who number approximately one million, reside mostly around Athens and Thessaloniki.[37] The official church was not that vehemently criticized when dealing harshly with missionaries and other "heretical groups," because until 1975 it was protected by the constitution and also because such groups could be presented as constituting a national as well as religious threat. That can no longer be the case, and the church will have to adjust its attitude accordingly; otherwise it runs the risk of being viewed as a most unprogressive and reactionary institution at a time when all political and social trends go the opposite direction.

In the summer of 1976, while doing research in Athens, I engaged in a discussion with a colleague, a political scientist from the University of London.[38] Our discussion centered on the so-called changing nature of Greek society. At that time we seemed to reach a consensus that Greek society, with all the changes it was undergoing, was still basically a conservative society. We based our consensus on the fact that the two most important institutions in the land, the church and the family, were remarkably intact. We acknowledged that the 1975 constitution in a subtle way began to threaten the position of the church and its role in society but felt that as long as it maintained its influence over society through the family, the so-called social revolution could be moderately controlled. The church exercised that type of influence, since its establishment in 1833, by ministering to the sacramental needs of its people, and especially by being the arbiter on the question of marriage and divorce and other moral issues such as sexual freedom and abortion. Needless to say, Greek society experienced a sexual revolution too, and abortion, without the approval of the church, was not an uncommon occurrence. The church did not have to condone it, but it did not have to fight it.[39] It could afford to ignore some of these issues because the law both civil and ecclesiastic was on its side. But that is changing fast and dramatically, beginning with the 1983 legislation introducing civil marriages and divorces in Greece. In the opinion of this writer, the 1983 legislation opens a new era for church and state, indeed for the whole of Greek society.[40]

While this chapter was in press, a new round of controversy between church and state occurred in March 1987, which will have lasting repercussions in the relations between the two and a strong impact on Greek society. The controversy centered on the state's attempt to introduce a new law enabling it to take over certain church properties allegedly for purposes of distributing such properties among needy Greek villagers. The whole issue was heatedly debated in the press and on television by representatives of both church and state. Regardless of its outcome, the debate over the future of church properties attests to the inevitable and growing tension between church and state despite their attempts to accommodate each other.

Historical circumstances have given the Orthodox Church of Greece a unique opportunity to preserve and perpetuate a tradition that had been threatened in all the other states where Orthodoxy had come under hostile political leadership. Besides the Orthodox churches of the diaspora, the only other case where for a while it seemed that Orthodoxy reigned supreme was on Cyprus, and that was chiefly due to the personality of Archbishop Makarios (1913–77), who in addition to being head of the autocephalous Church of Cyprus was also president of the Cyprus Republic.[41] That picture changed decidedly in July 1974 with the Athens-engineered coup against Makarios, followed by the Turkish invasion of the northern part of Cyprus. That crippled the wings of the last "Byzantine Eagle," as Makarios was sometimes called, and during the last three years of his life his role as ethnarch was limited to marking time. The role of his successor, Archbishop Chrysostomos, is even more severely limited by the political crisis on the island. Any solution to the Cyprus problem will, at best, confine his influence to the Greek community that constitutes 80 percent of the island's population. That still leaves the Orthodox church of Greece in a category all by itself, and its ability to survive well is important not only for its own sake but for the sake of the rest of Orthodoxy. The question is whether the Greek church has the resources to live up to its task as beacon of Orthodoxy. Despite the encroachments by the socialist government, and one can expect more, the church is by no means a discarded institution. Even the anticlerical book published in 1976 by George Karanikolas, *Robed Men: A National Pestilence,* is more interesting for the attention it directs to the centrality of that institution to modern Greek life than its criticism of the clergy and the church as a whole.[42] It may be a sleeping giant, as some have suggested, but a giant institution it still is. Which brings us to some of the opening premises of this essay. Papadiamantis stated in 1905 that the Greek people will always need their religion. In 1985, 95 percent of the Greek population was registered as Orthodox, participating in the basic sacraments of the church. From birth to death their existence is colored by some aspect of ecclesiastical presence or intervention. Church attendance on Sundays may be low (between 20 and 30 percent) but it is impressively high during important religious holidays, especially at Easter, Christmas, and the Fifteenth of August. Even the few hundred declared atheists participate in some of the essentially social functions of the church. This is also true of members of the Greek Communist party and of Greek Marxists in general.[43]

As for the claim of people like Theotokas and Karamanlis that the separation of church and state among the Greeks is inconceivable, it may very well be a perceptive commentary on a continuing social as well as a political reality. The latter has been reaffirmed by the 1975 constitution and the willingness of Papandreou to woo the church when needed and to oppose it when viewed as obstructive. And unpleasant as it may be for non-Greeks who are attracted to and even converted to Orthodoxy and like to see the latter as an "autonomous" religious realm, it cannot be taken out of its historical context without serious damage to its profile. It is easier to be Orthodox and non-Greek outside Greece. As one young theologian reminded us soon after Theotokas made this statement, "We are not just Christian Orthodox, but we are also Greek."[44]

In the final analysis, of course, a lot depends on the quality and nature of the Orthodox hierarchy, especially its top leadership. If the latter accommodate themselves passively and comfortably to the political leadership of the day, they will invoke the wrath of the educated elite and of society at large as reflected in the statement of one such critic in the beginning pages of this chapter. On the other hand, they could rise to the occasion, and meet the challenge of both state and society.

FACT SHEET

The Greek Orthodox Church

Year of autocephaly: 1833

Current strength of the church (1986)
  9.7 million faithful

9,682 priests and deacons

3,500 monks (of which 1,555 at Mount Athos)

2,000 nuns

200–250 seminarians (estimate)

90 bishops (of which 78 of the Autocephalous Church of Greece, 8 of
Crete, and 4 of the Dodecanese Islands)

Number of churches and church facilities

8,548 parish churches

20,000 chapels

2,000 cemetery churches

2 theological schools

27 other middle and higher ecclesiastical schools

230 convents

200 monasteries (of which 20 at Mount Athos), hospitals, schools

Chief news organs

Theologia (quarterly)

Ekklisia (biweekly)

Efimerios (biweekly)

Ekklisiastiki Alithia (biweekly)

Orthodoxia (earlier monthly, now quarterly); chief organ of the Ecumenical Patriarchate at Constantinople

Archbishops of Athens since 1900

Prokopios Oikonomidis, 1896–1901

Theoklitos Minopoulos, 1902–17, 1920–22

Meletios Metaxakis, 1918–20

Chrysostomos Papadopoulos, 1923–38

Chrysanthos Philippidis, 1938–41

Damaskinos Papandreou, 1941–49

Spyridon Vlachos, 1949–56

Dorotheos Kottaras, 1956–57

Theoklitos Panagiotopoulos, 1957–62

Iakovos Vavanatsos, 1962

Chrysostomos Hadjistavrou, 1962–67

Ieronymos Kotsonis, 1967–73

Seraphim Tikas, 1974–present

Patriarchs of Constantinople since 1900

Konstantinos V, 1897–1901

Joachim III, 1901–12
Germanos V, 1913–18
Meletios IV, 1921–23
Gregorios VI, 1923–24
Konstantinos VI, 1924–25
Vasilios III, 1925–29
Photios II, 1929–35
Veniamin, 1936–46
Maximos V, 1946–48
Athenagoras, 1948–66
Dimitrios V, 1966–present

11

The Romanian Orthodox Church

Alan Scarfe

The Romanian Orthodox church is one of the most flourishing examples of Eastern Orthodoxy in the twentieth century.[1] It has achieved this position in spite of dubious political connections in the early part of the century and difficult circumstances in the later period. In effect, the church in the twentieth century has had to weather two major efforts to take it over and make it serve a secular cause. Some would say that the second of these attempts is still under way and proving successful, but this would be a premature judgment. The Romanian Orthodox church has been able to maintain its identity and as such has earned the respect of the religious community throughout the world, especially in the World Council of Churches where it has provided executive council representatives since becoming a member in 1961.[2]

One folkloric explanation of the Romanian Orthodox church's stability was proferred by one of its bishops: "The waters flow, but the stones remain. We are the stones."[3] This chapter examines the strength and direction of the "stream's current" and assesses the shape and weight of the "stones." For, to be true to the metaphor, while the stones remain, the current does play a part in reshaping the stones as it flows around and above them. We shall see that this is true for the Romanian Orthodox church. We shall look at the roots of the historical and political identities of the church, its relations with other churches, its relation to very different governments of the early and late twentieth century, and the church's role in a socialist Romania.

Among the various themes that are connected with the history of the Romanian Orthodox church, none is as pervasive as nationalism. The concept "to be Romanian is to be Orthodox"[4] has endured with time, though it has been frequently questioned by religious pluralism in the Romanian community, particularly in the years after World War I. Romania's acquisition of Transylvania in 1918 strongly challenged the fundamental notion of what constitutes a Romanian's religious identity, both from Protestant and more strongly Catholic quarters. It could be claimed that the prominence of the Romanian Orthodox church in Romania today has been at the expense of the Catholic communities. Protestant congregations, particularly Baptists, have always suffered discrimination at the instigation of the Orthodox authorities, and during the years of the Second World War under the fascist government they were actually outlawed.[5] Their fate under the communist regime can be characterized as less overtly harsh, but nevertheless as one of oppression by government and Orthodox church officials alike. The battle between Orthodoxy and evangelicals is strictly religious. Baptist recruitment has come mainly from the Orthodox ranks. Orthodoxy and evangelicalism see each other as ecclesio-antagonists. Baptists wish to call Orthodox believers to a rejection of liturgical life for a more personal piety, while the Orthodox have a great deal of difficulty viewing the Baptists as anything other than an historical sectarian group with no religious rule of life and cut off from the historical tradition of the Catholic church.[6] These differences are not readily reconciled, though it is to the credit of the communist government of Romania that the legal framework of the Law of Cults has provided a buffer between the two churches; and in the modern political climate, where Baptists have become as equally useful in Romanian foreign policy as the Orthodox,[7] rapprochements have been created to allow Billy Graham to visit Romania and use Orthodox churches and monasteries as his preaching posts.[8] There is, as we can see, no blanket categorization that can be made on the contemporary religious scene in Romania.

The relations between Catholic and Orthodox communities, however, contain a history of fiercer mutual distrust and hostility. At stake in the past in the encounter between Catholic and Orthodox have been more than theological differences but issues of political power and national dominance. The Orthodox have consistently shown great insecurity in relating to the Greek and Roman Catholic communities, an insecurity that is a legacy of the Byzantine experience as well as a fear of the modern power of the Vatican. It was also an insecurity intensified by the lack of political decisiveness on the part of the Romanian secular politicians in the first half of the century.[9] The Orthodox experience in Transylvania before 1918, where the Orthodox religious community was treated as a class of noncitizens for many centuries, added greatly to this phenomenon.

Orthodoxy lays legitimate claim to be the original expression of Christianity among the Romanian people. While Latin-rooted words form the basic[10] theological vocabulary of the faith (indicating the ancient nature of Christianity in Romania dating from the days of the Roman army), Slavic influence is evinced in the vocabulary used for ecclesiastical structures and ceremony. This combination of Latinized Orthodoxy is the unique character of the Romanian church, mirroring the distinctiveness of Romanian people as the "Latin isle in the sea of Slavs."[11] Ancient Latinity, however, is not to be confused with modern Roman Catholicity in the minds of the Orthodox. Roman Catholicism, in fact, was brought to the Romanian communities in Transylvania with the rise of the Habsburgs and as such is seen as having been of foreign import. A visitor to the monasteries of Moldavia today can see the contempt of Habsburg soldiers for Romanian Orthodoxy in the "historical graffiti" on the ancient walls and murals. Apart from a short-lived Catholic diocese in Milcov (Moldavia) in the thirteen and fourteenth centuries,[12] Orthodoxy has predominated in the northeast and south of the country. What, therefore, was the nature of the insecurity, if the national tradition tied the people so clearly with Orthodoxy?

The issue is a modern one because the possibility for Orthodox political prominence has been realistic only since 1877 when Romania gained its independence from the Turks. Orthodoxy had been able to develop the culture of the Romanian people under the Ottoman Empire but was politically a vehicle of Romanian subservience under the Greeks of the Phanariot families. With independence it became clear that moral hegemony alone did not ensure political respect as the religion of the people. The Orthodox authorities were constantly afraid that other denominations, especially the Catholics, were being afforded more support in their development than themselves. Catholic influence within the royal family was seen as truly threatening. The Orthodox church, therefore, in the first decades after independence can be said to have had the task of establishing in concrete form its leadership within the nation. It had to do this while providing for its own ecclesiastical independence and church organization. The years from 1877 to 1925, thus, were formative in a number of different areas.[13] Along with its struggle for political visibility and its formation of an ecclesiastical structure, the church emphasized improved educational standards for clergy, spiritual renewal in the monasteries, social action, and the creation of new publishing organs.

In a certain respect the improvements in education of the clergy and the renewal of Orthodox publications were prompted by the state's interest in a closely controlled church. From 1877 to 1908 the government passed four laws designed to promote Orthodoxy's dominant position in society but also to bring the church under regular supervision. In 1872 the Law for the Selection of Metropolitans and Diocesan Bishops and the Composition of the Holy Synod of the Romanian Orthodox Church united the historic metropolitanates of Wallachia and Moldavia in a single church under the governance of the Holy Synod. The synod included the two metropolitans, six diocesan bishops, and eight arch-hierarchs. Appointments to the synod were made by an electoral council that was predominantly lay and therefore open to political appointments. This possible abuse of the electoral system did not go unprotested, especially since monastic and clerical participation in such elections was excluded. Nevertheless, the price of possible political control was the cost for the provision of an organizational unity that was able in subsequent years to pass extensive statutes dealing with urgent church affairs.

The second law in 1893 was the Law Governing Clergy and Seminaries. Again, leadership in the education of the clergy was placed within the Ministry of Religion and Public Instruction, but the law established seminaries in Iaşi and Bucharest, requiring five years of study for a high degree, and lower seminaries in Roman, Rimnic, and Curtea de Arges, requiring three years of preparation. Eventually the goal of each diocese with its own seminary for preliminary three-year preparation was to be achieved. Bishops could be elected only from those who had completed earned degrees. The law of 1902 established a center for the control of ecclesiastical property, administration of a national budget, and the handling of all personnel matters. Alongside it, as a further unifying measure, in 1909 a Superior Church Consistory was designed with a majority of lay participants who received authority over areas that had hitherto been the sole possession of the Holy Synod. Both these laws received great criticism, the chief of which was that it opened the door to too much politicking, especially among the lay members, and it overrode the canonical central authority of the bishops. By 1921 the center was closed, and the Superior Church Consistory was replaced in 1925 by the new law and statutes of the Romanian Orthodox church as it was elevated to the rank of patriarchate. The Holy Synod maintained control of the essentials of the faith, and the consistory was replaced by the National Church Congress. Laity made up two-thirds of the latter assembly.[14]

The price, therefore, of acquiring a unified organization recognized in law was the vulnerability of the church to interference by political factions. There were, however, many benefits for the church as it developed alongside the state patronage. Independence from the Ecumenical Patriarchate in Constantinople was the major benefit, which itself resulted from the increased emphasis on education among the hierarchs and clergy. Specifically, it was the excellent research of canon law by Melchizedek of Rome that persuaded the patriarchate to issue the Tomos of autocephaly on April 13, 1885.[15] Since Carol I's visit to Constantinople in 1866 the Romanian state had pressured for such independence, and with the emergence of a united Romania in 1877 it was only a matter of time before the Phanar would yield to the request. They were, however, able to stall any decisionmaking well into the next decade and prompted Romanian Primate, Calinic, to undertake his own ceremony of the blessing of oils in 1882, which had previously been blessed only in Constantinople and then brought to Romania for church use. This ancient expression of spiritual authority became a symbol of independence and self-assertion for the Romanians. Though Calinic was denounced by the ecumenical patriarch, his seriousness was heeded.

The life of the Orthodox church during the first two decades of the twentieth century contains all the signs that have been recognized as typical of the church in more recent years. The church was clearly a church of the people, involved in medical work, and assisting in the war effort by blessing the armies and by turning monasteries into hospitals. The events of 1907 among the peasants saw the members of the priesthood fighting alongside the rebels. In the literature of the church after the revolt there was an indication that many churchmen were pondering their role in supporting all the people of Romanian descent and not just the upper classes. There was a popular, social consciousness evident among the clergy.

This development, however, parallels the politicization of appointments at higher levels within the church. For example, the metropolitan primate proved to be a difficult position to maintain for very long. In 1893 Metropolitan Iosif Gheorghian was forced to resign by Take Ionescu for his opposition to the 1893 Law concerning Clergy and Seminaries. Three years later he was back in office after the removal of his successor, Ghenadie Petrescu, who supported the 1893 bill.[16] In turn, Petrescu found himself in opposition to the proposed Catholic baptism of the future King Carol II. Petrescu's resignation was the price paid for an agreement by the royal family to baptize Carol in the Orthodox church. Eleven years later Gheorgian was succeeded by Athanasie Mironescu, who himself lasted only three years because of his opposition to the government-proposed synodal changes of 1910. Konon Avramescu-Donici, his successor, proved even more controversial for the church as well as the state. Konon was overly lenient in his sympathies with the Germans during their occupation of Bucharest, agreeing to appoint at German request a Uniate, Theodorian, as director of the metropolitanate. The Germans curried Konon's influence in seeking a reduction of Romanian participation in the war; Theodorian hoped to convince the primate to sign over the church to acknowledge the primacy of the see of Rome. Theodorian's efforts were stymied by the official responsible for the ecclesiastical discipline for the metropolitanate, who ousted the director and encouraged his primate to remain strong in resisting German attempts to undermine him.

After the war Konon was replaced by Miron Cristea, who was to become the first patriarch of the Romanian Orthodox church. Cristea was able to maintain his position until his death in 1938. He further established the organization of the patriarchate and encouraged education among the clergy. He showed concern for the social work of the church, especially in the areas of alcoholism, orphans, and the urban poor. Under his patriarchate relations with the Anglican church became closer than those between any two churches of the Orthodox and Anglican traditions,[17] and he oversaw the expansion of a number of dioceses as the territories of Greater Romania were incorporated under the unified Romanian Orthodox church. He was unable, however, to bridge the political gap between the upper classes of the Orthodox and the popular Orthodox masses. While he remained a close supporter of the royal family, many of his clergy and faithful alike were being persuaded that the Christian cause of Romanianism was to be identified in the rising fascist force of the Iron Guardists.[18]

Cristea's ineffectiveness in the political realm was clear when he was made prime minister in 1938 during King Carol II's attempt to subvert the Iron Guard. Cristea was not the first Orthodox patriarch or primate to hold such an office. Nifon had been president of the Romanian Senate from December 1864 to June 1868; and Calinic from June 9, 1875, to March 25, 1879. Orthodox hierarchs had sat in the Romanian Parliament since 1864. Originally they shared this honor with no other clergy, but by 1926 the Orthodox hierarchs were joined by four Greek Catholic bishops and leaders of the Roman Catholic, Lutheran, Reformed, and Unitarian churches.[19] The Orthodox presence in the Romanian Parliament was also unable to stem Orthodoxy's most feared tide, the increasing political and spiritual influence of Catholicism.

The growing political influence of Catholicism and the increase in fascination with the new messianism of the Iron Guard were the two principal issues facing the Romanian Orthodox church as it entered into the early years of its new patriarchate. The concern over Catholicism, as we have seen, was not new. Before Cristea's time there had been frequent complaints that the state was permitting an unequal contest between the Orthodox and Roman Catholic and Uniate churches in the area of education.

Many Catholic teachers from abroad staffed schools that drew a majority of Orthodox children into them. Now, in the 1920s, the competition was heightened as the Catholics gained political power through the Uniate presence in Greater Romania and through some prominent Catholic converts among politicians. The proposal of a concordat between Romania and the Vatican in 1927 met with outspoken Orthodox criticism.[20]

The concordat effectively gave a privileged position to the Catholic community in Romania, according to Orthodox spokesmen. Metropolitan Nicolae Balan of Ardeal was the leading critic of the bill as it reached the Romanian Senate for ratification. He opposed the concordat as primarily anticonstitutional, denying the equality of minority religious as written in the Law of Cults.[21] In contrasting the numbers of bishops allowed within the concordat for the Greek and Roman Catholic churches, Balan pointed out that if the Orthodox were to have hierarchs and other clergy in the same proportion as the Catholics, then the number of diocese and higher church officials would need to be greatly increased. It seemed clear to him that the Catholic churches were being given an expanded organizational structure by which they could increase their membership and influence throughout the country. Balan doubted that the state could afford to pay the salary bill on such an overload of top church officials for a minority religion.

The metropolitan of Ardeal was referring to the provision within the concordat for establishing new dioceses in Maramures (Uniate) and Oradea (Roman). The Catholic bishops had only to swear allegiance to the Romanian king and to the pope; they could then directly communicate on church matters to the Vatican without having to use any Romanian state intermediary. Catholic institutions, such as orphanages, schools, and hospitals, were removed from government control. In short, it was feared that the Catholics were being allowed to set up a state within a state. The school system in Transylvania was viewed suspiciously as a breeding ground for Magyarization.[22] (It is interesting that today under Ceaușescu, Romanianization of the Hungarians is under way, with the state according equal prominence to the Orthodox church—sometimes out of proportion to its congregational size.)

The concordat was the creation of a decade of discussion. Catholic influence at the Treaty of Versailles had drawn a commitment from the Romanian government to equalize the status of the Catholic communities within Greater Romania. Its timing also coincided with the new policy of the governing National Peasant party to throw open Romania to attract foreign capitalist investments. The leader of the Peasant party, Iulio Maniu, was himself a Uniate native of Blaj, the Uniate cultural center.

The contest between Orthodoxy and Catholicism also reflected a deeper concern in Romanian philosophy. The issue was one of national identity. The past belonged clearly to the Orthodox, but did that mean that the Orthodox should determine the future? As the relative value for progress of an Eastern- or Latin-oriented civilization was discussed, comparative studies of the influence of Catholicism on the development of the Western civilizations were made. Uniatism certainly had equal right to claim its role in the history of developing Romanianism. The Transylvania school provided the basis of the modern Romanian theory of origins.[23] Only through exposure to Latin peoples and culture could the Uniate scholars, Gheorghe Sincai, Petru Maior, and Innochentie Clain, have come to their illuminating understanding of the links of Romanian people with Latins. Romanianism is therefore Uniatism as much as it is Orthodoxy, and on this basis a new possibility of future alliances and direction could be considered.

The Orthodox hierarchy concentrated great efforts on withstanding the encroaching influence of the Catholics. But the hierarchs were less able to see the implications of another advancing movement that was to become even more successful in shaping Romanian self-identity throughout the 1930s. While Metropolitan Balan hotly debated the ratification of the concordat in 1929, Corneliu Codreanu was organizing his own brand of Orthodoxy in the guise of the Iron Guard.

Though Codreanu represented the most extreme form of right-wing terrorism, other groups revealed the Orthodox difficulty in remaining detached if not opposed to the political movements of the time. We have already seen Patriarch Miron's participation in Carol II's government, which was known as the Front of National Rebirth. The king had in fact used the Iron Guard indirectly to break the democratic forces within the country and was himself interested in his own brand of fascist dictatorship. Similarly, Octavian Goga, who wrote a glowing account of an Orthodox prayer service led by pietist priest, Tudor Popescu,[24] nevertheless saw no contradiction between his "spiritual interests" and his leadership of the notoriously anti-Semitic National Christian party.

Eventually, as the Iron Guard grew in strength and political prominence, it could be seen that its mission was imbued with religious overtones and that many believers and clergy alike found in it a compatible political vehicle. In the trials of Legionnaires under Antonescu, hundreds of priests were found among the guilty. "Two hundred eighteen Orthodox priests are under judicial investigation because they had participated in the rebellion, forsaking the cross and altar of peace in order to fight with criminals at arms and terror against their flocks. Many from among these even had active functions in the Legionary movement incompatible with their quality and mission."[25] In 1933 four Orthodox priests were seated in the Legionnaire Senate. Priests and teachers provided good heads of section in local Legionnaire cells or "nests."[26]

Guardism was rooted in a "fundamentalist Orthodox populism."[27] The very adoption of the name "The Legion of the Archangel Michael," the warrior angel, indicates this debt. The Legion was purposed to save Romania from foreign ideologies and the ultimate enemies, the Jews. Anti-Semitism, which was traditional in Romania from the early nineteenth century, gained new life within a new ideology. The Jews were joined in their persecution by Russian Bolshevik sympathizers, some of whom were simply socially conscious peasants.

The Orthodox hierarchy condemned the terrorism of the Legionnaires but could not gainsay their Christian mission. That Christian mission was itself co-opted by the obsession of Romanian Orthodox nationalism. The same fuel, namely an overwhelming concern for Romanian identity to be seen as an Orthodox one that drove church leaders to combat the concordat, now mellowed their prophetic judgment in facing the ferocity of Romanian society. The concern for Catholicism and intrigue with the various fascist movements of the 1930s were common compulsions. These same compulsions explain the unique ability of the church to later adapt to a new life under an opposite regime and provide the link for our under-standing of modern socialist Romanian Orthodoxy. It is the principle of double fidelity, to use the phrase of Professor Fischer-Galati, or of double attachment: belief in the Romanian people and in God.[28] It is not far from the ancient Byzantine dream of the new Byzantium.[29]

For all its tragedy, the years between the wars also witnessed favor-able developments within the Orthodox church, matched perhaps only by the Ceauşescu years of the 1970s and 1980s. Miron Cristea ruled as primate from 1919 to 1925 and as patriarch from 1925 to 1939. He saw the fulfillment of the vision of the great Transylvanian bishop, Andrei Şaguna, in establishing dioceses in Cluj, Oradea, Timişoara, and Mara-mures, along with Alba Iulia and the metropolitanate of Transylvania (Ardeal) in Sibiu.[30] The great provinces of Ardeal, Wallachia, and Moldova were united within the one church.

In the social arena new charitable organizations continued to spring up. Professors and graduate students traveled abroad for advanced edu-cation, providing a stronger faculty for the theological institutes, which was to bear fruit in later years. There were many publications, with a range of philosophies from the evangelical and pietist to the intellectual and philosophical. *Gindirea* was the most famous in the latter category.[31]

Right–wing in orientation, it was an effort to search for Romanian solu-tions to Romanian problems. Its contributors showed differing degrees of harmony with the nationalism of the day. The most idealistic and progres-sive thinking Guardists, writing in *Gindirea*, included Nichifor Crainic, Mircea Eliade, and its editor, Nae Ionescu. Philosopher-poet Lucian Blaga debated on Romanian spirituality with theologian Dumitru Staniloae,[32] a proponent of the Romanianism-is-Orthodoxy philosophy but perhaps also its most orthodox and spiritually mystical interpreter. There are no hints of militarism in Staniloae's expositions. Staniloae was joined in *Gindirea* by other Orthodox voices, notably Vasile Voiculescu's. Staniloae's study of *Ortodoxie şi Natiune*[33] addressed the spiritual and nationalist implications of the concordat, being a theological critique of the spirit of Catholicism and comparing it with the traditional Romanian spirituality provided by Orthodoxy.

There were numerous attempts by the Orthodox to at least match the rising popularity of the new Protestant movements coming in from Transylvania and the Ukraine. Greater Romania increased the tendency to religious pluralism. The Orthodox were the main targets of the new evangelists. Many pamphlets were produced attacking the new church movements. Baptists, Adventists, and Pentecostals were the chief protago-nists. One constructive response among the Orthodox was to experiment with their own brand of "born-again" Christianity within Orthodox con-fines. This meant a call for personal faith among the believers and greater emphasis on Bible reading and evangelical preaching. In the 1920s in Bucharest Fr. Tudor Popescu, influenced by an Orthodox deacon, Dumitru Cornilescu, introduced such practices in his parish church. Hymn singing increased as people began to flock to hear his preaching. Cornilescu also preached, his notoriety being established by his translation of the Bible into Romanian. Popescu and Cornilescu were expelled from the church, and Popescu's followers helped him set up a new church that later became known as the Evangelical Christians (Crestini dupa Evanghelie), an official neo-Protestant denomination to this day.[34]

A second movement of a similar nature in Transylvania did not enjoy such a final transition from movement to denomination. This was partly because it was more deeply rooted within Orthodoxy and partly because it did not manage to remain aloof from the violent politics of the times. The Oastea Domnului,[35] the Lord's Army, was started by Fr. Josif Trifa in Sibiu in 1923 under the initial auspices of the metropolitan. Inspired at first by the goals of the Oxford Moral Rearmament Movement, Trifa aimed to improve the morality of the Orthodox faithful. Alcoholism was a particular target. Trifa gradually came to believe in the need for spiritual rebirth as an additional experience to participation in the sacraments of the church. Baptism needed to become a living experience for the adult believer, and personal devotion became a prime emphasis in his spiritual scheme of things. Lay leaders proliferated in the movement, though hundreds of clergy were also involved. The Lord's Army held mass rallies of tens of thousands in the open air, but its success without ecclesiastical accountability led to a split between the movement and the hierarchs of the church. The Lord's Army continued as a lay-led organization attracting many adherents, including clergy, but not forming a separate denomination. The movement produced many popular hymns and poems. Its chief poets were Traian Dors and Nicolae Moldovan.[36] Its publications also fed into the spiritual life of the neo-Protestants, and in some sense, therefore, the Lord's Army represented a bridge between two traditions. Such a concept was not acceptable to the communist regime when it came to regularize the religious of the country, or to the Orthodox leaders who disowned its leaders. Consequently, the movement was disbanded in 1947 and its leaders imprisoned.

Imprisonment was not confined to disowned splinter groups in the late 1940s. The coming to power of the communist regime announced retribution for hundreds and thousands of Orthodox who had been implicated in one way or another with the identification of Romanian Orthodox messianism and fascism. A large number of young people, caught up in the youth organization of the Iron Guard, were lost to the prisons, producing a gap of leadership within the church that has only recently been closed. Theologian Staniloae was imprisoned for his part in Gindirea, as were hierarchs and clergy.

Ironically, the price of restoring the church to the favor of the Communist party included the church's participation in the demise of the Greek Catholic church, which was abolished by decree in 1948.[37] Officially, the church was reintegrated with the Orthodox—tantamount to organizational annihilation. Ultimately, the entire Uniate hierarchy died in prison, and four hundred priests were executed with another two hundred imprisoned.[38] Communism also answered the insecurity of the Orthodox in the face of the concordat with the Roman Catholics by abrogating the concordat and outlawing the Catholic church's connections with Rome.[39] The Roman Catholic church has been tolerated under the communist government, but only in recent years have ties with the Vatican been reestablished. In some sense therefore the concerns of the Communist party and those of the Orthodox can be seen to have coincided at the very outset. After Ceauşescu, those concerns would shift to the second area of Orthodox sensitivity, namely, the question of Romanian national identity.

The move to abolish the Uniates, masterminded by the Soviets, was carefully orchestrated between church and party. The Soviets relied heavily
on the Russian Orthodox church to provide a political model to other
Orthodox churches.[40] Abolition of the Uniates was one expression of this
enforced emulation, imitating events in the Ukraine in 1946. Orthodox
historians in Romania justified their actions on the basis of allegations that
the Uniate church had been a contrivance of the Jesuits and that Greek
Catholic Romanians were "really" frustrated and manipulated Orthodox.

The Greek Catholics have continued to preserve their separate identity
from the Orthodox in various ways. Some parishes "converted" only in
name but continued practice as Greek Catholic. Clandestinely consecrated
bishops are today well known to the Romanian secret police and somewhat tolerated. Several efforts have been made to petition the government
for restoration of the Uniates, but none has met with success. More and
more the Orthodox assume the rights to the historical contributions of
the Greek Catholic church and feel that there is no place for two churches
representing the Romanian people. In 1977 an enterprising appeal was
sent to President Ceauşescu requesting that he reevaluate the Uniate's position.[41] Ceauşescu was reminded that only Slavophiles would be capable
of hatching such a plot as the destruction of a community that had been
so vital in the development of Romanian national consciousness. Indeed,
according to the petitioners, the decision to abolish the Uniate church
was handed down from the Pan-Orthodox conference in Moscow. They
appealed to Ceauşescu's love (and use) of the history of Romanian independence to permit the Greek Catholic church its rightful place alongside
the Orthodox church in promoting Romania.

In the 1980s the Romanian Orthodox church stands head and shoul-
ders above the other legally permitted denominations in the country. Its
supremacy is not only in numbers (17 million of a 21 million population
are baptized Orthodox) or in physical presence (there are 240 churches in
Bucharest alone, though a number of the more historical buildings have
recently been removed or demolished in modernization plans in the city),[42]
but also in the theological preparedness of its clergy and in the proliferation of theological publications. These publications are in small circulation, but they highlight the finest minds of the church.[43] The necessity
for doctoral students to publish their research in diocesan or national
journals during their second and third years of study also broadens this
phenomenon. The church has been said to be top-heavy in this respect; it
has also been criticized for falling behind smaller denominations in such
parish activities as catechism and other adult teaching, though there has
been improvement in this area in recent years. The hierarchy has still to

be completely involved in the decisions of the secular authority, and so the historical division of hierarchy and populace persists. Publications are on sale in various church shops, but in spotty supply. It is much easier to obtain theological works from Romania if one resides abroad.

The present relations between the Romanian Orthodox church and the communist government have been designated by the term "the Romanian solution." This "solution" entails a mutual agreement on spheres of influence between the religious and secular parties. Considerable license is granted to the church to develop its life, in exchange for noninterference in domains of the party and in exchange for promotion of Romanian national prestige, especially abroad. As we have seen, the church's entire history has emphasized the mutual interdependence of Romanianism and Orthodoxy. In one sense, therefore, the church has genuinely found its role within the socialist setting, though with its political wings severely clipped. Its chief political participation is in the United Socialist Front, where the hierarchs have a seat.[44]

The Romanian solution is symbolized by the close physical proximity of the Patriarchal Cathedral and the Grand National Assembly, which stand literally feet apart.[45] In recent modernization of the capital city, however, this architectural symbolism has been challenged by the party architects. Several historical churches have been removed to make room for roads and buildings that are designed to portray socialist Romania on its own. There is a conscious effort to break down this traditional symbolism, an action that has not gone unnoticed by the church.

Nevertheless, it is arguable that the state will ever be able to relegate the church to a secondary or marginal position. Respect for the church and its theological and philosophical preparedness lurks in high places of state. Many members of the Communist party are baptized Orthodox or have had their children baptized. In smaller towns it is not impossible to find that a church council member is also a member of the local communist cell. This could be viewed as subversion, but it is unclear who is subverting whom. The funerals of President Ceauşescu's father and mother were handled as major events on television and in the newspapers, with Ceauşescu present while Orthodox ceremonies were administered.

There is precedent for this in post-World War II times. The first president of the People's Republic of Romania, Petru Groza, was the son of a priest and an Orthodox sympathizer. He was also known to be tolerant of evangelicals. Similarly, Patriarch Justinian rose to prominence through his personal relationship with Gheorghiu–Dej, the first general secretary of the party after the war. Justinian had hidden Gheorghiu–Dej following his escape from prison under Antonescu. That relationship assisted the patriarch in directing his church through the turbulent period immediately after the war.

Justinian Marina succeeded Nicodim Munteanu as patriarch in 1948. Munteanu had been patriarch from 1939 to 1947. There is little information about his patriarchate; the official church history of the theological institute presents him as a wise old man who became patriarch at seventy-four and died at eighty-three.[46] His major claim to fame was that he attended the 1917 congress of the restoration of the Russian Orthodox patriarchate and was the first "builder of the new relations between the Russian Orthodox church and the Romanian Orthodox church after August 23, 1944." Nicodim introduced Justinian to the Russians in 1946. By popular accounts, Nicodim was seen as a scholarly man of respected personal spirituality. Rumors circulated on the exact nature of his death. Unfortunately, the official accounts devote only a single page to the nine years of his patriarchate.

Patriarch Justinian will be seen historically as the right man in the right place at the right time.[47] His twenty-nine years as patriarch helped him guide his church through the harsh days of the Stalinist period and to a place where, by a quirk of history, the church could regain a national role. Personally, he brought to the church a concern and understanding of the social dimensions of the new regime and was able to mold the church accordingly. He was predisposed to the social emphasis of communism. He saw sense in making the monasteries self-supporting collectives. In this he drew on the historical roots of monastic life. The flourishing of the monasteries today testifies to his expediency.

Justinian stressed theological education as a key to a thriving religious community, and when it became possible he encouraged the best students to study abroad. At first this meant using facilities in the Soviet Union, but increasingly as Romania moved into its maverick foreign policy of the 1960s and 1970s Orthodox students were being sent to France, Germany, the Middle East, Ethiopia, England, Rome, and the United States. The student exchange has been a two-way street, with the Romanian Orthodox church using its resources to provide scholarships to foreign students for study in Romania.[48] Through diplomatic channels, studies could be carried out in the state archives as well as the church's theological libraries. Resources range from the collections of the libraries in Bucharest and Sibiu to the libraries brought to the capital from the closed theological institutes of Cernauti and Chisinau. Other collections of books and papers are found in the patriarchate archives and individual archives of dioceses, parishes, patriarchal administrative offices, and monasteries such as Neamtz, Putna, and Sihastria. Many works related to the Orthodox church found their way into the academy library, and researchers must enter into the labyrinth of modern Byzantium to acquire the necessary permits from the patriarchate, the Ministry of Education, and the Department of Cults to get access to them. This exercise in itself is a reminder that perhaps not too much has changed.

The strength of educational training within the Romanian Orthodox church should not be underestimated. Bucharest and Sibiu institutes for higher theological learning handle the flood of seminarians from the seven diocesan seminaries throughout the country. Three thousand seminary students contend for the 1,100 to 1,200 positions in the two institutes. Parish priests are mostly seminary students from the more rural parishes, but the more prominent positions in the church are reserved for those with the highest academic training (including the possibility of having studied abroad).

The uniting of Transylvania with the Romanian principalities produced an influx of new blood into the church. The effect of persecution and dispossession created a strong identity among the Orthodox in Transylvania. Many of today's outstanding theologians come from Transylvania. This is also testimony to the struggle of men like Bishop Andrei Şaguna, who established the independent bishopric of Sibiu as the metropolitanate of Ardeal in the nineteenth century.[49]

In Moldavia the monasteries are the centers for theological learning and spiritual vitality.[50] The administrative center of the metropolitanate is Iaşi, which was geographically more central when Romania also contained the communities of Cernauti and Chisineu as cultural places. When these cities were annexed by the Soviets, the Romanian Orthodox church lost both two theological institutes and contact with a vibrant religious center. From Moldavia has come the revival in monastic prayer, known as the hesychast revival, which focused on the life and teaching of Paissie Velichkovschi.[51] Claimed as a son of Russia and Romania, he was a significant figure in the history of both Orthodox churches. The monasteries of Putna, Sihastria, Agapia, and Neamtz, without being overcome by being the star attractions of tourist routes throughout Romania, still maintain their atmosphere of spirituality. The more elaborate painted monasteries of Suceavita, Moldovita, Humor, and Voronetz have been less successful in maintaining their original function. All the existing monastic communities today have survived efforts in the mid-1950s to decimate them.[52] For a brief period in 1956 Patriarch Justinian found himself under house arrest as he wrestled with the question of signing the government's legislation for reducing the number of nuns and monks. Many of the younger religious were thrown out of their communities and forced to enter secular life. The monastic buildings, on the whole, were preserved as historical monuments or, as one cynic put it, as potential hotels for party vacationers. The communities, however, have grown again in number, and an unofficial system of giving spiritual direction has developed. Young people once more are found among the religious.

Publications have been another form of education in Justinian's time. Each diocese boasts its own journal, and the national printing house of the patriarchate has been able to publish doctoral dissertations, Bibles, and liturgical books as well as, more recently, translations of the church fathers, editions of the Filokalia, a series on dogmatics, and another on church history.[53] Without doubt the Romanian Orthodox theologians have preserved high standards in their scholarship. Among their more notable number are men like Dumitru Staniloae (systematic and dogmatic theology), Alexandru Elian (Byzantologist), the late Ioan Coman (patristics), and Antonoie Plamadeala and Ion Bria who have written in the areas of ethics and ecumenism.[54] In addition, the programs of the theological schools in Sibiu and Bucharest are supplemented by visiting theology professors of world renown. Thus, students can experience limited exposure to scholars such as Oscar Cullman, Jürgen Moltmann, and A. M. Allchin.

This exposure to scholars of foreign and non-Orthodox persuasion exhibits another element of Justinian's policy, namely, the importance of ecumenical relations.[55] After the mid-1960s this policy, which it would seem was carried out in concert with the Soviets as both Orthodox churches entered the World Council of Churches at the same time in 1961, nevertheless became a platform for greater contacts abroad as Ceauşescu began his push for a more independent foreign policy. The church was in a good position to represent the nation, and participation in international conferences flourished. The Romanian Orthodox church has confidence in being able to silence its most outspoken foreign critics by offering a single invitation to its homeland. For example, the Rev. Michael Bourdeaux of Keston College, the most important center for the study of religion in communist lands in the English–speaking world, went to Romania as the patriarch's guest, even while under a ban from entering the Soviet Union because of his work as director of the College. Poland was issuing similar bans on Keston staff at the time.

This reputation for hospitality has made the Romanian Orthodox church the topic of media intrigue in the West. Not only does the church provide access to a lively popular Orthodoxy, second to none in the Western world, but it does this within the context of an ideological contradiction between the nation's government and the people. The Soviet Union is less secure in allowing outsiders to see its religious makeup, and this comparison gives us a glimpse of the difference in religious policies between the two nations. An excellent BBC television program was made on Romania with full state cooperation.[56] It included an in-depth conversation with Bishop Justinian of Maramures, on the one hand, and an interview with a church vestry member, on the other. The latter saw no contradiction between his party membership and his role in the church. No doubt there are many like the bishop with his obvious spirituality and single-mindedness and the vestry member with his faith and pragmatism.

The legacy of Patriarch Justinian, therefore, who died shortly after the Bucharest earthquake in 1977, is rooted in his concern with preserving the closeness between the Orthodox church and the Romanian people, especially as the people entered into the unfamiliar territory of becoming a People's Republic. He achieved this at the expense of the Uniates and Romanian Latin-rite Catholics, and with much personal suffering among his own clergy and religious in the fifties. He preserved the physical presence of the Church intact and was able to play a more vigorous role as Ceauşescu turned his interests toward creating a Romanian national communism. Without this turn of events it would seem inevitable that the Romanian Orthodox church would have suffered the ignominy of its counterparts in Bulgaria and the Soviet Union.

Legally, Justinian supervised the establishment of new statutes for the church that placed greater power in the hands of the patriarch himself.[57] The patriarch could intervene in diocesan matters with or without the bishop's permission. Centralization made control by the state more readily accessible, but it seems that within limits Justinian could safeguard his church from overt interference. According to the Law of Cults, decreed on August 4, 1948, the Orthodox church was upheld as autonomous and unified in its organization and was given the distinction of being singled out for a separate mention within the law, although no reference was made to its being dominant.

The concentration of authority in the hands of the patriarch made the election of Justin of Moldova as Justinian's successor crucially important. Lacking Justinian's popularity or connections, which allowed for a certain sympathy for the church, Justin was criticized as being less able to stand against the wishes of the party.[58] The demolition of a number of distinguished churches in Bucharest for the sake of party promotion of socialist architecture led some observers to second-guess what Justinian in his prime might have done. Justin also had to handle the fury over the dismissal and imprisonment of priests whose situation attracted the attention of world media and members of Western governments who trade with Romania. Justin appeared as a remote man, lacking the popular sympathy of his predecessor. He was better-known abroad for his activities as head of the church's foreign relations department. However, he initiated a number of publishing projects and oversaw the erection of a new ecumenical center on the outskirts of Bucharest. (This, of course, may have been an attempt by the government to remove the physical presence of the church from the center of Bucharest in accord with the new city planners' design for a socialist capital city.)

Justin died in late July 1986, leaving a legacy of impressive theological tracts published during his patriarchate. Metropolitan Antonoie Plamadeala of Transylvania, a man known for his loyalty to the state, was considered a possible successor.[59] But after several months of deliberation, the bishops finally elected Metropolitan Teoctist Arapasu of Moldavia as patriarch on November 9. His investiture was conducted on November 13, and he was received by President Ceauşescu the following day. On the latter occasion, according to an Agerpres news release, "the patriarch voiced the resolve of the Romanian Orthodox Church, of the clergy to make all efforts to support the people's work for progress and welfare, for the building of a new, independent and sovereign Romania, to back and promote, under any circumstance[s], the policy of peace, understanding and cooperation pursued by the Romanian state." The release added that

> the hierarchs, the clergy and the believers, like all the sons of the homeland, are highly appreciative of President Nicolae Ceauşescu's creative capacity, activity [as] genuine builder of a new life in Romania, and daring thought put in the service of Romania's continuous progress, of the entire people's happiness. The [patriarch] also expressed thanks and deep gratitude for the conditions of full religious freedom in which the Romanian Orthodox Church, [and] the other denominations in Romania carry on their activity.[60]

However much the hierarchs may sing Ceauşescu's praises, Justin's earlier snub of Elena Ceauşescu was said to have prompted a series of reprisals against monasteries, including forbidding children to visit the monasteries and limiting the issuance of permits for novitiates to the monasteries and convents. In July 1978 it was reported that monasteries could not hold services, except in their side chapels, thus preventing outsiders from attending. (Often these kinds of reprisals are of a temporary nature and are then forgotten.)

The state has been hard-pressed to restrict the church's influence and prove the tenets of its atheist teaching on the withering away of religion in the communist state. Schoolchildren are as prominent as ever in the huge Easter congregations. Even groups such as the Lord's Army that were outlawed and thought to be extinct are attracting new generations of priests, theological students, and young lay people. Where the Orthodox church is unable to keep the children, they are being attracted to the more independent circles of the evangelicals.

Nevertheless, the state has not given up on its exclusive right to develop the education of the young in matters of philosophy and spiritual and cultural awareness. Some administrative measures have been issued to limit access of young people who are either openly religious, and avoid the Communist party, or are the children of clergy, to the university faculties such as law, philosophy, history, and psychology. New congregations too are scarcely permitted in the sprawling new regions of the major cities such as Bucharest's Balta Alba. Prominent Orthodox churches do appear however in predominantly Hungarian and German areas of Transylvania. The idea of the party is to play for time, waiting for a shift of emphasis from the religious and mystical to the secular and material.

The policy has not gone unchallenged by dissenters in parishes and among clergy. The movement in Eastern Europe for human rights, which reached a peak in the late 1970s, especially from 1977 onward, encouraged similar though more sporadic outbursts in Romania.[61] Some Orthodox "dissenters" were clearly influenced by contact with Baptist dissenters who had begun speaking out on their conditions from 1973 onward. A new question was posed to party and church alike regarding the nature of the identity of the church with its people when protests began to arise over the divisiveness and oppression generated by the party against the people, namely, how far does identity go within the present arrangement between church and state?

The circulation of protest appeals to various forums in the West under the inspiration and protection of international understandings about freedom of religion and individual human rights is a relatively recent phenomenon. The Helsinki Accord, the UN Convention on Religious Freedom, and the increased diplomatic activity between Eastern Europe and the Western democracies have spawned human rights watchdogs in the West, centers for the study of religion and communism, and the need in governmental and ecclesiastical administrations for appropriate offices to handle complaints and inquiries about religion and human freedom. Romania has been spotlighted within this forum a number of times in the 1970s and 1980s. Little had been reported on the problems between church and state prior to 1970. It is as though the new direction given Romania by Ceauşescu, with the general amnesty to political and religious prisoners in 1964, has been seen as the valid new starting point for assessing church-state issues in the country. In this sense, therefore, much

from the early period remains hidden. Some actions, such as the abolition
of the Uniates, are diplomatically forgotten and one presumes forgiven.
Nevertheless, in 1974 the first document of the modern samizdat type was
sent out of Romania from an Orthodox priest.[62]

The document was a letter from a priest in Oltenia, Fr. Stefan Gavrila.
He recounted the difficulties of being a local parish priest in dealing with
party officials. He criticized the lack of defense, even by his own hierarchy,
for a priest who ran afoul of local state officials. It was as though he had
broken a secret code of self-restraint in relating to the true governors
of the church. He protested at using church time on Sundays to gather
the people for patriotic field work rather than celebrating the liturgy.
Overall, he believed that the church hierarchy used clergy gatherings to
impose their policy of reconciliation with the state at any cost. The parish
network was a kind of unofficial blanket of nonconfrontation to squelch
any independent-mindedness by people and clergy alike.

Fr. Gavrila sent out other protests after he had been dismissed and later
reinstated because of his outspokenness. Yet other parishes followed his
lead in their own way. Fr. Costica Maftei, now a resident of Chicago,
was prevented from building a new church in one of the suburban areas
of Bucharest. His parishoners wrote favorably on his behalf. Maftei felt
impelled to apply for emigration as he felt that his ministry could not be
fulfilled in Romania.

Leonid Pop, a young priest from Sinaia, provided evidence of arbitrary
discrimination by the authorities against the church in the restoration
period after the 1977 earthquake. Village churches were being left unre-
paired, while more visible buildings were being restored. He also opened
up the story of the resurgence of the Lord's Army among the Orthodox
and told of the sufferings and fines imposed on them. Direct contact with
the Lord's Army further confirmed this report.[63] Travelers to Romania
were beginning to take notice of Romanian Orthodox clergy and religious
and found an increasing number ready to speak of their problems. Much
control lay behind the posturing of the state in its easy relation with
the church. An intimate insight into this posturing came in 1978 when
a Romanian priest was arrested and sentenced to ten years for alleged
"neofascism."[64] Such an accusation was a throwback to the early days of
the communist regime. Why in the 1970s was the Romanian government
risking its reputation in imprisoning a well-known Orthodox priest under
such circumstances?

The sentenced priest was Fr. Gheorghe Calciu. He had already been in
prison as a teenager immediately after the war, allegedly implicated in the
activities of the Young Legionnaires. His age alone indicated the implausi-

ble nature of the initial accusation for which he served sixteen years in the
Pitesti prison. Calciu was permitted to enter the seminary and trained for
the priesthood. He characterizes his decision to become a priest as an act of
gratitude for God's helping him in prison. In 1973 he became a professor
in the seminary in Bucharest. He was a fine preacher and admired by the
students. In 1978 he was asked to preach a Lenten series in the seminary
chapel.[65]

He chose to use the occasion for a series of sermons addressing the confrontation between Christian belief and the atheistic materialism taught
in the schools.[66] He called atheism a philosophy of despair and took the
opportunity to denounce two particular actions of the government to which
he took special exception. He saw the struggle between atheistic teaching
and the church typified in the demolition of churches in Bucharest and
Focsani, which had been undertaken on pretext of the buildings being in-
secure after the earthquake.[67] In fact, Enea Church in Bucharest was the
first of the Bucharest churches to be cleared under the modernization program of the city center, which has since removed a number of churches.

To link preaching to such concrete actions was an unforgivable breach
of the code of conduct for an Orthodox priest. Fr. Calciu was barred from
continuing his series. Students were physically prevented from attending the sermons, and yet the series was completed and reached almost
fever-pitch excitement.[68] Calciu was becoming a new model for the young
seminarians. He was quickly dispatched from his teaching post and given
an administration appointment under the eye of the patriarchate. His
reputation spread, however, and he became the center of a number of differing dissident factions. From the government's point of view his most
outrageous act was to house the meetings of the newly formed Free Trade
Union, a movement influenced by the Solidarity Trade Union in Poland.
Other religious problems were becoming openly debated in an increasing number of samizdat: the Lord's Army, the Greek Catholic church,
discrimination against religious minorities among Hungarians.[69] The government decided to move with a heavy hand. Fr. Calciu was arrested,
together with founding members of the Free Trade Union, and was secretly tried. He was never told the exact nature of the accusations against
him. His treatment in prison was brutal at times, giving rise to a number
of rumors about his condition.[70] Newspaper articles began to appear denouncing the alleged neofascism, spurred on by Western sources, that was
arising in society. It was clear that Calciu had created panic and was being
set up as an example.[71]

The imprisonment of a priest after so many years of relative quiet only increased attention on Romanian church-state relations. Calciu cast a long shadow over the claims of the Romanian solution to the church in a socialist society. Unfortunately, the church hierarchy recorded its opinion of Calciu in a way that displayed the lack of freedom and independence it actually enjoyed. A letter was circulated by church officials denouncing Calciu in similar terms to those used in newspaper articles and the speeches of Ceauşescu.[72] Not all, however, shared the view of Calciu as a neofascist. There were many protests at his imprisonment from parishes, groups of young clergy, and the seminarians to whom he had preached. The protests indicated that thousands of priests are in basic disagreement with the direction that their hierarchy had taken them and that the faithful look out for such priests and ignore the leadership. The real division in the church is not between church and people but between hierarchy and people. As we have seen, this has been true of the church in its political activities both before and after the coming of the communist regime.

The case of Fr. Calciu serves to underline the inherent tension within the Romanian Orthodox church: that there is still a two-tier system of identity within the church. Justinian, in his own person, and individual hierarchs, on their own merits, have sought to break down that division, but it remains. Fr. Calciu and the young priests who have begun to protest the effectiveness of current church–state relations are focusing on this issue of unity and division. They see social involvement as more than ecumenically participating in the buildup of international prestige for Romania, preserving Romanian Orthodoxy against Catholicism, or protecting the rights of minorities or evangelicals. Social involvement—the church for the people—means defense against injustice, against atheism, against inappropriate state control. In a fifteen-point memorandum, signed by five priests from the archdiocese of Timisoara, they state: "Ritual without spirit is magic, sterility, materialism and hypocrisy." They ask therefore for the following:

1. Opportunity for the church to grow up with the times and enter into renewal at all levels. (This entails growing with the cities.)
2. The creation of an official department to propagate the faith and counter atheism.
3. The gaining of access to the media by the church.
4. The recognition of the disbanded Lord's Army as a potential force for spiritual renewal.
5. The creation of Christian societies for charitable works.
6. Legalized holidays for Christmas and Easter.

7. True practice of the social apostolate.
8. Reform of the theological education system to include a more scientific approach toward theology.
9. The release of Fr. Calciu from prison.
10. The ability to organize catechism classes for young Orthodox and to promote Orthodox education among Romanian intellectuals.
11. The reestablishing of annual pilgrimages to holy places.
12. A broadening of the selection of students studying abroad from the seminaries, and an increasing accessibility to theological education at home.
13. The regeneration of Romanian monasticism as the focus of the national and cultural heritage.
14. Restoration of the Greek Catholic church as historical partners in the spiritual life of the Romanian people.
15. Promotion of a more genuine ecumenical gathering at local levels rather than the orchestrated meetings of the present.[73]

Such a statement would never have been made ten years ago. The five priests will have to see these issues taken up by others in the future as they were all removed from active duty and permitted to emigrate to the United States. They did, however, see one issue resolved. Fr. Calciu was released in August 1984. He too lives in the United States.

The issues will not go away. They reveal a maturity of spirit that needs to be dealt with in a similar way. The governments of East Germany and Poland, for example, have shown that alternative methods of relating between church and party can be adopted. The central focus of the appeal is that the church be truly the church of the people and break out of its tendency for submitting to Caesaropapism. For it can be seen that the so-called model of the Romanian solution is precisely an adaptation of the traditional Caesaropapist state of Byzantium. Perhaps this is why the two institutions sit so readily in tension with one another. It is a tension that has its comforts. For it is the first time that a Romanian patriarch and a Romanian prince have been able to rule side by side in a manner appropriate to a Byzantine emperor and bishop.[74]

FACT SHEET

The Romanian Orthodox Church

Year of autocephaly
    Metropolitan autocephaly established:

Transylvania, 1864
Bucharest, 1885
Patriarchate autocephaly established:
Bucharest, 1925

Current strength of the church
15–17 million faithful (1983)
9,200 priests (1980)
1,500 nuns (1975)
700 monks (1975)
1,500 institute students
1,500 seminary students

Chief news organs
Biserica Ortodoxa Romana (5,000 in 1983)
Ortodoxie (10,000)
Studii Teologice (5,000)
Romanian Orthodox Church News (in English for distribution abroad)
(1,000–2,000)
Telegraful Roman (Biweekly newspaper, Sibiu)
Five metropolitanate journals (1,000–2,000 each)

Number of churches in operation (1983)
11,000 places of worship
8,100 parishes
122 monasteries and convents
2 institutes of higher theological education
7 seminaries and cantor schools (secondary school level)

Patriarchs since 1925
Miron (Cristea), 1925–39
Nicodim, 1939–48
Justinian (Marina), 1948–77
Justin (Moisescu), 1977–86
Teoctist (Arapasu), 1986–present

12

The Serbian Orthodox Church

Pedro Ramet

It is more or less routine for the communist press in Yugoslavia periodically to assail the Serbian Orthodox church for chauvinism, Greater Serbian nationalism, and reactionary attitudes. The sensitivity with which that church has often reacted to such attacks betrays a psychological vulnerability fostered by the vicissitudes in the church's fortunes during the twentieth century and by the erosion of its power on several fronts, and expressed in the hierarchy's self-image as a *suffering* church, even of a church marked out for *especial* suffering. Having lost a fourth of its clergy and many of its churches during World War II, the Serbian church had to endure the postwar harassment of its priests and the continued obstruction of church construction. Having lived to see the extinction of the artificially created Croatian Orthodox church, the Belgrade patriarchate has had to deal with two further schisms, resulting in the loss of effective jurisdiction over part of the American and Australian congregations as well as the Macedonian dioceses. And while most of the Serbian clergy resisted the Nazis and their allies tenaciously, they find themselves strangely isolated, derided, chastened today. The Serbian church remains defiant, but there is a sense of pessimism or perhaps of impotence to that defiance.

It was not always this way. In the early part of the century the Serbian church took its numerous privileges for granted and identified the purposes of the Serbian kingdom so totally with its own purposes as to be incapable of comprehending differences of interest, except as misinterpretations of their common interest. Yet it should be stressed that the comparatively weak position of the Serbian church today is not the result merely of the decimation of World War II, let alone of communist rule, but has its roots deep in the past.

The second suppression of the Serbian patriarchate of Peć in 1766 no doubt undermined the institutional power of the church. Thus, at the opening of the twentieth century, the Serbian Orthodox church was organized differently in the different political systems in which it had dioceses and lacked a centralized authoritative head. In the Kingdom of Serbia, for instance, the leading church figure was the metropolitan of Belgrade, assisted by a synod, and the clergy received state salaries. In Montenegro, the government set up a synod, in 1903, as the highest church authority in Montenegro, including in its membership all Montenegrin bishops, two archimandrites, three protopriests, and a secretary. In Hungary, Orthodox church affairs were regulated autonomously by a national church council presided over by the metropolitan of Karlovci. And in Bosnia-Herzegovina, the Orthodox clergy again regulated its internal life independently, although the Austrian emperor appointed its bishops.[1]

More significant for the vitiation which began in the late nineteenth century were the ideas of materialism, positivism, and progressive secularism, which infected even some of the clergy (e.g., Jovan Jovanović, rector of the Orthodox Theological Seminary in Belgrade), and the persistent encroachments by the state on ecclesiastical turf. Repeated intellectual attacks on the Serbian church eventually resulted in a sapping of religiosity among the Serbs. Meantime, infused with notions of social activism, many of the clergy became involved in Serbian political parties, which encouraged the state to interfere ever more and more in ecclesiastical affairs. By 1881, with the dismissal of Belgrade Metropolitan Mihailo and the passage of a new law, whereby the government was able to pack the church synod with its own lay delegates, the state had effectively taken over the church, reducing it to something akin to a state agency; even the reinstatement of Mihailo in 1889 did not invigorate the church's power.[2] The very organization of the Serbian Orthodox church was eventually regulated by a law on church districts passed by the state with the consent of the church.

Yet there were benefits for the church in the old Kingdom of Serbia too. For one thing, under the Serbian constitution of 1903, Orthodoxy was recognized as the official state religion and all state and national holidays were celebrated with church ritual. Religious instruction was mandatory throughout Serbia. And all bishops, Serbian church officials, religion instructors, and army chaplains received state salaries. Moreover, after the establishment of a unified Yugoslavia at the end of 1918, and the revival of the patriarchate, the Serbian patriarch would sit on the Royal

Council, while several Orthodox clergymen had seats in the National Assembly as deputies of various political parties.

Given the disunity in church organizations that existed in the first two decades of this century, it was inevitable that the Serbian church viewed the unification of the South Slavs as *also* a unification of the Serbian Orthodox church, and thus perhaps even as a great turning point. Within six months of the establishment of the interwar Kingdom of Serbs, Croats, and Slovenes (as Yugoslavia was initially called), the Serbian bishops convened in Belgrade and proclaimed the unification of all the Serbian Orthodox provincial churches into a single unified ecclesiastical structure. The following year, on September 12, 1920, the bishops completed the process by solemnly proclaiming the reestablishment of the Serbian patriarchate, in the presence of the highest dignitaries of both church and state. These moves were fully canonical, undertaken with the concurrence and blessing of the Ecumenical Patriarchate.

The state's interest in this was clear from the outset. Even before the unification conference, a governmental delegate, Dr. Vojislav Janić—later to become the minister of faiths—revealed that it was "the wish of the government that the reestablishment of the patriarchate be accomplished as soon as the church is unified."[3] Furthermore, once the patriarch had been elected, the government lost little time in drafting a law that would have imposed greater legislative and judicial unity on the church and thus made it simpler to regulate and control. Because this draft bill provoked immediate protests from all sides, but especially in the metropolitanate of Karlovac and in Bosnia-Herzegovina, where the local clergy dreaded the diminution of their autonomy, it was withdrawn and a different bill was submitted to the assembly the end of 1923. This draft also failed to be passed, and two further drafts were likewise defeated before the government finally succeeded, in 1929, in passing a law drafted by the minister of justice, Milan Srškić. The prolonged controversy over this law revealed the existence of considerable differences of opinion between church and state regarding state jurisdiction over the church, and also considerable division within the Serbian church itself.

In the meantime the Serbian church and the government signed an agreement in 1926 (between the Episcopal Synod and the Ministry of Faiths) which was the equivalent of a concordat, arranging many questions pertaining to their mutual relations. The state now discovered that instead of simplifying its control over the church the reestablishment of the patriarchate gave the church new resources; and in the course of the 1920s, as a result both of the passage of a new church constitution (in

1924) and of the fluidity produced by the drawn-out controversy over the church law—as well as the financial strength derived in part from state subventions to the church—the Serbian Orthodox church improved its position vis-à-vis the state and showed itself willing to confront the state over matters of importance. The church became, at the same time, a unified structure, as differences between provincial churches disappeared.

Under Yugoslavia's King Alexander (1921–34), "not only was the dynasty Serbian, but all the important ministries were monopolized by Serbs, the bureaucracy was predominantly Serbian, the police were controlled by Serbs, [and] the high ranks of the military were occupied by Serbs."[4] The monarchy gave the Serbian Orthodox church generous subsidies. As a result of these, the Serbian church was able to establish a metropolitanate in Zagreb and to construct three churches in Catholic Slovenia.[5] There was even talk, in the early 1920s, that the Serbian Orthodox church might open a theological faculty in Zagreb.[6] During the 1920s non-Orthodox believers repeatedly complained that the Serbian church was manipulating the state to serve its own confessional objectives, and reports that the Royal Dictatorship (established 1929) was persecuting Catholic schools only deepened the alienation of the Catholic sector of the population.[7]

Although it enjoyed, thus, in some ways, a privileged position in the interwar kingdom, or perhaps precisely *because* it did, the Serbian church was deeply troubled by the Roman Catholic church's quest for a concordat, which, it feared, would greatly strengthen the position of the Catholic church throughout Yugoslavia. Catholic Archbishops Bauer and Stepinac were very much in favor of the concordat, and Vlatko Maček, chairman of the Croatian Peasant party, lent his endorsement to the Holy See's efforts to secure it. The concordat was finally signed on July 25, 1935, shortly after Milan Stojadinović became prime minister, though its contents were not published by the state. The Serbian Orthodox church, however, published what purported to be a complete draft of the concordat, together with a point-by-point critique.[8]

The Serbian patriarchate claimed that the concordat was designed to give the Catholic church exclusive privileges in Yugoslavia. These privileges were said to include: the guarantee that Catholic bishops, clergy, and believers would enjoy complete freedom of direct contact with the Vatican, whereas in the case of the Serbian church, only the patriarch was guaranteed such access to fellow Orthodox clergy abroad; an extension to Catholic clergy of the same state protection enjoyed by state employees and the protection of the privacy of the confessional; the right to retain buildings and property even in hypothetical cases in which the local congregation should convert en masse to another faith; privileged exemption from the payment of telegraph tax; the assurance that Catholic bishops would enjoy unlimited rights to inspect religious instruction, whereas the Serbian church could conduct such inspections only once a year, and the Islamic community only twice a year; the guarantee that Catholic schoolchildren not be obliged or even invited to attend religious instruction of any non-Catholic denomination, and that the school program be arranged so as not to obstruct Catholic students from carrying out their religious obligations; and the exemption of Catholic priests and monks, but not Orthodox clergy, from military conscription, except in case of general mobilization.[9] The Serbian church also objected to Article 8 of the proposed concordat, because it would have banned *all* clergymen in *all* churches from participation in political parties, even though the Serbian Orthodox church had not been consulted in this regard.[10] Finally, the patriarchate claimed that in the broad sense the guarantee in Article 1, that the Catholic church might carry out its "mission," could embrace a right of proselytization "which is contrary to Article 16 of the state constitution and which can disturb the interconfessional balance."[11]

The Serbian Orthodox church created a huge uproar over the bill. The Serbian church even allied itself with opposition Serbian parties in efforts to bring down the pro-concordat administration. The government offered to guarantee the Serbian church the same privileges, but the uproar did not die down; under fire from various quarters, Stojadinović eventually decided not to present the document to the senate for approval, and on October 27, 1937, informed the Catholic episcopate that the concordat was decidedly dead. This constituted a major victory for the Serbian Orthodox church, which had been fighting the concordat for more than twelve years.[12] Thus, on the eve of World War II the Serbian church could congratulate itself on two major victories—in the controversy over the church law and in the struggle over the concordat.

The Great Catastrophe

The systematic destruction of hundreds of monasteries and church buildings, the liquidation of hundreds of Serbian Orthodox clergy, and the wartime deaths of at least six of the church's top hierarchs[13] (three murdered by the *Ustaše*) had a traumatic effect on the Serbian clergy, and even today they live with a complex of bitterness rooted in the wartime debilitation. The Serbian church had shared in the Serbian nationalist enthusiasm to see Croatia as a zone for Serbian political, economic, and cultural expansion, and viewed Catholicism as a degenerate form of the true faith: this orientation made it all the more painful for the Serbian church to bear the fruit of wartime Croatia's program of eliminating all traces of Serbdom and Orthodoxy from Croatia. Soon after the proclamation of the Independent State of Croatia (*Nezavisna Država Hrvatska* or NDH), the Croatian paper *Novi list* wrote (May 29, 1941): "In the independent State of Croatia, the Catholic and Islamic faiths will enjoy protection and will have the possibility of free development, in harmony with the basic interests of the Croatian nation, which, protecting themselves, freely defend the interests of Catholicism and Islam from their bitterest and most dangerous foe—Orthodoxy."[14] The fact that the program of forced exile and liquidation was supplemented by the coercive conversion to Catholicism of part of the Orthodox population in the NDH, in order to "Croatize" them, deepened both the identification of Serbdom and Orthodoxy in the consciousness of the Serbian church and the sense of threat from the *Ustaše* party of the NDH. Moreover, the Catholic church by and large seemed to welcome the conversions, even if it sometimes distanced itself from the coercion employed; and though the Muslims of Banja Luka very early began to protest the assault on the Orthodox population, a Serbian Orthodox source charges that the Catholic population at first remained quiescent.[15] Mile Budak, NDH *Doglavnik* (second-in-command to Ante Pavelić), told an assemblage of representatives of the Catholic action organization on June 8, 1941: "The Orthodox came to these districts as guests. And they should now leave these parts once and for all. Of course, many will not be able to leave, but in that case they will want to convert to our faith."[16]

In April 1941 there had been 577 Serbian Orthodox clergymen in the territory of the NDH. By the end of 1941 all of them had been removed from the scene: three were in prison, five had died of natural causes, 217 had been killed by the *Ustaše*, 334 had been deported to Serbia, and eighteen had fled to Serbia earlier.[17] Serbian clergy were treated in a similar fashion in parts occupied by other powers. In Vojvodina, there was pressure on Orthodox believers. In Bulgarian-occupied Macedonia the Bulgarian Orthodox church asserted its jurisdiction (in the conviction that Macedonians are Bulgarians rather than Serbs, as the Serbian church has always insisted), expelled or arrested those clergy who considered themselves Serbs, and sent in about 280 of its own clergy to administer the faith in Macedonia.[18] In the Italian-occupied littoral Orthodox clergy were imprisoned and executed, and numerous church edifices were destroyed.[19]

The losses suffered by the Serbian church during the war were colossal both in real terms and in psychological terms. Of the more than 4,200 churches and chapels and 220 monasteries owned by the Serbian church in

Europe prior to the war,[20] almost 25 percent had been completely destroyed
and 50 percent of those in Yugoslavia were seriously damaged. As much
as a fifth of the clergy in Yugoslavia as a whole had been killed (perhaps
as many as seven hundred), and another three hundred had died of natural
causes during the war. Of a total of 8.5 million believers before the war,
Slijepčević claims that 1.2 million had lost their lives.[21] The government
claims that 1.7 million Yugoslavs lost their lives in the war. At war's end,
without any assured income and with an estimated wartime damage of
2.4 billion dinars, the Serbian church still had 2,100 parish priests, 537
lay employees, and about 1,000 retired priests (on pension).[22] Under these
circumstances, the Serbian church was faced with a difficult challenge.
The church wanted to rebuild its world as it had been before, but the
preconditions for that world no longer existed.

The Communist Assault and the Effort to Rebuild

Understandably, the Serbian clergy had taken an active part in the resistance against the occupation, and some of its clergy, including Patriarch
Gavrilo and Bishop Nikolaj Velimirović, had been incarcerated in German concentration camps. But the Serbian church had naturally viewed
the resistance in quite different terms from the Communist party. For the
church the resistance was a nationalist cause of the Serbian people against
traitorous Croats and imperialist Nazis. For the communists, on the other
hand, the war—henceforth known in Yugoslav writings as the national
liberation struggle (*narodnooslobodilačka borba*)—was at the same time a
social revolution whereby the different peoples of Yugoslavia would subordinate their divisive ethnic interests to joint class interests and through
which exploitative "vestiges of the past," such as the Serbian Orthodox
church, would be pushed into an inferior position, in which they could
subsequently be snuffed out. Serbian nationalism, which has always been
close to the heart of the Serbian church, was now described not merely as
an archenemy of the new Yugoslavia but even as an enemy of the Serbian
people itself.

The aims of the Communist Party of Yugoslavia (CPY) diverged from
those of the patriarchate in a number of ways. The CPY wanted, first
of all, to legitimize its federation and most especially its reconquest of
Macedonia in every possible way. Hence, if there were Orthodox clergy
in Macedonia eager to set up an autonomous or autocephalous church,
so much the better, as this would reinforce the image of a distinctive
Macedonian ethnicity. The patriarchate, which was an expression of a

union achieved only with some difficulty in 1920, was hostile to any assault on its unity.

Second, the CPY wanted a tame and cooperative church which would eschew anything smacking of opposition but be available to support CPY policies when such support was desired. To this end, the government revived the priests' associations (which actually traced a tradition back to 1889), hoping, with some cause, to use these associations to control the church. The patriarchate was prepared to cooperate with the new regime but not to be its tame and obedient tool. Thus, while there were those on each side who desired to reach an accommodation, there was much less agreement as to the form that accommodation should take.

Third, the CPY, then still in its Stalinist phase, wanted to uproot religion and to resocialize the population according to the precepts of atheistic dialectical materialism. That is, it was willing to tolerate churches as institutions, but not as teachers and leaders of the people. The regime therefore initiated a policy of obstructing religious education, confiscating church buildings, and fining the clergy on various pretexts. Orthodox clergy were, in the early postwar years, harassed, beaten up, and imprisoned on trumped-up charges. And, in the hope of compromising the prestige of the church elders, the regime began a practice—which has continued to this day—of accusing various Serbian hierarchs of wartime collaboration with the Nazis, such as Bishops Irinej Djordjević and Nikolaj Velimirović, though in fact both of these bishops had been interned by the Axis and were as antifascist as they were anticommunist.[23] But therein lay another problem, for the communist regime was strongly opposed to an anticommunist clergy. Velimirović was, moreover, an outspoken Serbian nationalist.

There were, at the same time, two respects in which the Serbian church could be useful to the communist regime. First, insofar as the patriarch of the Serbs would be seen to be on decent terms with the regime, this would tend to give the lie to accusations that the regime was anti-Serb; this was especially important in the early period, when the regime was preparing to put Chetnik leader Draža Mihailović on trial. Second, the Serbian church could be useful as a vehicle for maintaining contacts with other communist countries in which there were prominent Orthodox churches, i.e., the Soviet Union, Romania, and Bulgaria.

There was thus an ambivalence in the communist attitude toward the Serbian church—an ambivalence not shared by the patriarchate, though it must be emphasized that many lower clergy felt disposed to strive for accommodation with the regime and at least a part of the membership of the priests' associations seems to have felt this way. Reformist lower clergy met as early as November 1942, in Bosnia, to revive the Orthodox priests' association, and at war's end, priests' associations were set up, with government backing, along federated lines, corresponding to the federal units erected by the regime. According to Stella Alexander, these Orthodox priests' associations were, in the beginning, "completely under government control."[24] By mid-1952 *Borba* would claim that some 80 percent of the remaining active clergy (approximately 1,700) were members of priests' associations.[25] It was these associations which were now authorized to publish the newspaper *Vesnik*, which began publication on March 1, 1949. *Vesnik*, supposedly a church paper, immediately published attacks on the Serbian church synod and on Bishops Irinej of Dalmatia and Nikolaj of Žiča (both in emigration) and, in other ways, showed itself to be a pliable tool for the regime. Understandably, the synod repeatedly turned down the association's application for official recognition and the patriarchate remains formally opposed to the associations, though this opposition is tempered by some forms of accommodation, and a number of bishops have been elected from the ranks of the association.[26]

The years 1945 to 1955 were the most difficult for the Serbian church of the entire postwar period. During these years Belgrade gave a strict interpretation to clauses of laws curtailing the activity of churches, imposing heavy penalties on clergymen for any infractions but light punishment, at the most, on those infringing the rights of religious groups.[27] In a striking illustration of the mood of this period, Bishop Nektarije of Tuzla was roughed up by a mob after he pointed out that the Law on the Legal Status of Religious Communities (1953) expressly permitted the holding of religious services.[28] Under the Law on Agrarian Reform and Colonization (May 27, 1945), the state seized 173,367 hectares of land belonging to the religious organizations (85 percent of their total); 70,000 hectares of what was seized had belonged to the Serbian Orthodox church. The Serbian church had had considerable investments in apartments, affording it tangible rental income, but by 1958 the regime completed the nationalization of apartments, depriving the Serbian church of 1,180 buildings, worth 8 billion dinars.[29] The church's two printing presses were also expropriated after the war, without compensation,[30] and various difficulties were encountered in the reopening of religious seminaries and in their maintenance, due to bureaucratic pressure.

Yet despite all this, the Serbian church was able to rebuild. Between 1945 and 1970 the church built 181 churches and restored 841, built 115 chapels and restored 126, and built eight monasteries and restored forty-eight. Even in the Zagreb Eparchy twenty churches were restored and two new chapels built.[31] By 1949 a makeshift seminary was operating in the Rakovica monastery near Belgrade, and shortly thereafter the church was able to reopen its seminary in Prizren. Subsequently, in 1964, Orthodox seminaries were also opened in Sremski Karlovci and at Krka, in the Dalmatian hinterland. Meantime, the Theological Faculty in Belgrade had, by 1966, developed a permanent staff of eight professors and lecturers and had about 120 students.[32] Today there are about 100 to 110 students in each of the four seminaries, which is close to the capacity of 120, and there are about seventy students studying at the Theological Faculty in Belgrade. While the number of male clergy has held almost steady at about two thousand for the past two decades, the number of Orthodox nuns has inched upward from 468 in 1965 to 519 in 1966 to about 700 in 1980.[33]

Although the Serbian church had had a lively and plentiful press in the interwar period, with numerous church magazines, newspapers, and journals, established in the 1920s and 1930s,[34] its publishing activity had to be rebuilt essentially from scratch after World War II. Initially this activity was limited to a single official organ. *Glasnik*, the Serbian church's oldest journal, was being published in 2,100 copies in 1955 and, beginning in 1965, in 3,000 copies. The church established the quarterly educational magazine *Pravoslavni misionar* in 1958, and by 1968 it was being printed in 50,000 copies. The patriarchate brought out its first popular newspaper, *Pravoslavlje*, on April 15, 1967, which, as of summer 1987, was being printed in 23,000 copies (of which 1,500 go to foreign subscribers). A monthly children's magazine, *Svetosavsko zvonce*, was added in 1968 and had a circulation of 15,000 in 1982. The wartime deaths of a number of leading theologians complicated the task of the resumption of theological publication, and *Bogoslovlje*, the scholarly journal of the Theological Faculty, which had ceased publication during the war, did not resume until 1957, although three special collections of articles (*Zbornik radova*) were issued in 1950, 1953, and 1954. A decade later the archbishopric of Belgrade-Karlovac created its own theological journal, *Teološki pogledi*. In addition to these theological periodicals, there is also *Pravoslavna misao*, a magazine for church questions, which, in 1970, had a circulation of 2,000.[35] Book publication resumed slowly, after hesitation, in 1951, but by 1982 the patriarchate was literally boasting of its fine editions, scholarly tomes, ample publication, and so forth.

Whittling the Church Down

To understand the Serbian Orthodox church is to comprehend it as an institution that has been repeatedly whittled down—sometimes unsuccessfully, sometimes successfully. The first twentieth-century challenge to the Serbian patriarchate in this sense was the establishment of the Croatian Orthodox church in April 1942. Although no Serbian hierarch would accept office in this artificial church (so that two Russian émigré clergymen had to be contracted to head the dioceses of Zagreb and Sarajevo), a number of Serbian Orthodox clergy did in fact cooperate with that structure and a number of Serbs joined it in the vain hope of saving themselves and their parishioners thereby. The attempt of the Bulgarian Orthodox church to "annex" the faithful in Macedonia likewise met ultimate defeat.

On the other hand, the Serbian patriarchate lost its jurisdiction over its Czechoslovak dioceses between 1945 and 1948, and in 1951 these became the Czechoslovak Orthodox church. Some Serbian parishes lying within Romania's borders were similarly transferred to the Romanian Orthodox church in 1969, though the Diocese of Timisoara is still administered by the Serbian church. The Serbian church suffered a formal schism in 1963, when Bishop Dionisije Milivojević of the American-Canadian diocese summoned an assembly to declare that diocese an autonomous church. And finally, on July 17, 1967, the Macedonian clergy, in open defiance of the Serbian patriarchate to which it had taken oaths of loyalty, unilaterally declared itself an autocephalous Macedonian Orthodox church, electing a Smederevo native, Dositej, as Archbishop of Ohrid. It is natural, then, that the Serbian patriarchate has been anxious whenever the regime has given encouragement to ecclesiastical separatism in Montenegro, as it did in the early postwar years,[36] and in this context, Patriarch German's comment, in 1970, that Montenegrins are simply Serbs by another name becomes readily intelligible.[37]

Although the Serbian church remained apprehensive of a regime-backed Montenegrin schism at least into the early 1970s, it is the Macedonian schism which has caused the church the most grief. And despite its inability to do anything to change the situation, the Serbian Orthodox church has refused to recognize the schismatic Macedonian church.

The collaboration of the Macedonian clergy with the communists stretches back to the war. At the end of 1943 the Partisan high command appointed a Macedonian, Rev. Veljo Mančevski, to take charge of religious affairs in liberated areas. Shortly after the occupation forces were driven out of Belgrade, three Macedonian clergymen (Metodije Gogov, Nikola Apostolov, and Kiril Stojanov) presented themselves to the Serbian synod as representatives of the Orthodox church in Macedonia and members of the Organizing Committee for the Founding of an Independent Church in Macedonia. A premature declaration of autocephaly at this point in time was stymied, but relations between the Serbian patriarchate and the

CPY remained tense as long as the patriarchate refused to compromise. The Orthodox priests' association, often inclined to take a stance at odds with the patriarch, supported Macedonian autocephaly all along, despite the misgivings among some Serbian members. Finally, in 1958, after the Macedonian clergy declared themselves an "autonomous" church on their own initiative, the new Serbian patriarch accepted the fait accompli, though he underlined that it should go no further than autonomy. Directly as a result of the patriarch's acceptance of Macedonian ecclesiastical autonomy, the Serbian church's relations with the government improved markedly, and by 1961 the regime's encouragement of separatism among Montenegrin clergy and its encouragement of intraecclestiastical divisions generally seemed to have died down.[38] The interest of the government in the Macedonian church was shown in its hints of a subvention of sixty million dinars to the Serbian church if it came to terms with the Macedonian clergy.[39]

The Communist party was, at this time, seriously divided between advocates of "organic Yugoslavism," led by Slovenian party ideologue Edvard Kardelj, who wanted to knit the country together by making generous allowances to the cultural and national distinctiveness of its component peoples, and advocates of "integral Yugoslavism," led by Vice-President Aleksandar Ranković, who wanted to encourage the development of a Yugoslav consciousness in the ethnic sense and who tended to view non-Serbs as "less reliable" than Serbs. The former group thus favored decentralization to the federal units, while the latter favored political and administrative centralism. Ranković, whose Serbian nationalism was never much below the surface, was known for having promoted discriminatory practices against non-Serbs in Croatia, Bosnia, Vojvodina, and Kosovo.[40] The fall of Ranković in July 1966 proved instrumental in fostering a change of regime policy vis-à-vis the Serbian church, as Ranković had wanted to prevent the erosion of the Serbian position in any sphere, including the ecclesiastical. He dealt with the church roughly, and used threats to obtain ecclesiastical compliance.[41] But as long as he was in office the Macedonians held back from declaring autocephaly.

After Ranković's fall, at a joint meeting of the Serbian and Macedonian synods on November 18, 1966, the Macedonian clergy demanded full autocephaly. The demand was renewed on December 3, with the attendant threat of unilateral action if the Belgrade patriarchate did not concur; since the patriarchate refused to accept this, the Macedonians declared autocephaly on their own authority at an ecclesiastical assembly in Ohrid in summer 1967. Although the government has, since then, repeatedly encouraged the two churches to resolve their differences, and has advised the Serbian patriarchate that its failure to recognize this latest fait accompli has a negative impact on the political climate, more particularly on Serb-Macedonian relations, and in the Party's ongoing dispute with Bulgaria over the ethnicity of Macedonians, the patriarchate unbudgingly insists that Macedonians are Serbs and that the Macedonian Orthodox church has no canonical raison d'être, basing the latter position on the fact that the Macedonian church was not established on the basis of pan-Orthodox agreement, as prescribed by ecclesiastical tradition.[42]

Church-State Relations, 1970–86

It is a remarkable fact that communist regimes, which always talk about wanting the complete separation of church and state, have consistently been the most eager to assert state control or influence over church policies and appointments. In Yugoslavia, the communists hoped that their backing of the priests' associations would lead not merely to the co-optation of those associations, but to the co-optation of the churches themselves, i.e., to the revival of the situation in old Serbia, when the Serbian Orthodox church functioned in effect as a bureaucratic department of the state.

Instead, however, the Serbian patriarchate's relations with the associations have remained complex, and the continued activity of the latter has provided yet another element of internal opposition within the Serbian church. The regime has repeatedly praised the cooperation it has received from the Orthodox association,[43] and has occasionally presented awards to its members,[44] but the patriarchate itself remains cool and distrustful toward the priests' association.[45] Indeed, this distrust has occasionally provoked outbursts of frustration from convinced members of the association. In 1978, for example, Archpriest Ratko Jelić, a representative of the Croatian wing of the Orthodox association, told members of a committee of the Socialist Alliance of Working People of Yugoslavia, which is concerned with religious matters, and a group of his colleagues from other republican priests' associations, that the patriarchate (presumably through its organ, *Pravoslavlje*) was presenting a distorted picture of the work of the association, and proposed to increase the circulation of the association's organ, *Vesnik*, as a foil to *Pravoslavlje*. He continued:

> We have been publishing our *Vesnik* for the past 30 years. True, the number of copies printed per issue is small, a mere 3,000 copies, but I believe that there is no more positive periodical among all of those published by the church press in this country, especially among those put out by the Serbian Orthodox Church. But this periodical

is, unfortunately, not accessible to the public at large. For this reason, I believe that the situation would be entirely different if we were able to inform the members of our faith as to the true nature of our association. As things now stand, it is directly and falsely suggested to them that we are some kind of communist association which wants to destroy the church and so on and so forth. Thus, people know nothing at all about the work that is being done by our association.[46]

On the same occasion Archpriest Milutin Petrović, president of the Central Union of Orthodox Priests of Yugoslavia, complained that some clergy had declined to join the association because they feared reprisals from the hierarchy (although 83 percent of all Orthodox priests in Yugoslavia were, in 1978, members of the association), while Veselin Čukvaš, president of the Montenegrin wing of the Orthodox association, accused the hierarchy of frustrating and ignoring the work of the associations.[47]

But even in 1889 the priests' association was conceived in the spirit of opposition to the hierarchy; over the years the association has felt free to arrive at conclusions that diverged from the policy of the patriarchate. Hence, it should come as no surprise that the patriarchate views the Orthodox association as an internal opposition, even as a Trojan horse.

Another species of internal opposition was highlighted by *Vesnik* in 1971. *Vesnik* charged that there was no practical ecclesiastical unity in policy matters and painted the patriarchate as a kind of bodyless head, "presiding" over a collection of eparchies that operate according to the discretion and wishes of the local archpriests. According to *Vesnik*, the episcopal council was failing to reconcile these divergent views and functioned as no more than a sounding board for adamantly held positions.[48]

With only half the clergy it had before the war and a tangibly diminished income, the Serbian church has been conscious of its weakness. Despite this, it has never allowed itself to be co-opted by the communist regime and assumes an oppositional posture from time to time. In this respect, one must speak of two realms: the assertion of church interests and the demand for policy change, even if church interests appear to be in opposition to the regime's; and actual opposition by the church in matters pertaining to the Serbian nation and its culture. That is to say, the Serbian church is an opposition force insofar as it is a nationalist institution.

Although the Catholic church and the Islamic community experience little difficulty in obtaining official approval for the construction of places of worship, and although the Macedonian Orthodox church too has done well in this area, the Serbian Orthodox church continues to complain of difficulties in obtaining building permits, especially in the cities.[49] Styling itself as a "patient" church, it nonetheless spoke out in May 1977 in a petition addressed by the Holy Synod to the presidency of the Republic of Serbia and signed by Patriarch German and two other bishops. The letter asked, inter alia, for (1) routinization of permission to build new churches; (2) extension of the state social insurance to the teaching staff and students at theological faculties and seminaries; (3) an end to discrimination against children enrolled in Orthodox religious education; (4) an end to state interference in church matters; (5) an end to the practice of libeling and slandering clergymen, both living and deceased, in the media; (6) unhindered celebration of funeral rites according to the wishes of the bereaved; (7) the return of confiscated church property.[50]

Since then the church has chalked up some progress. In 1984 Serbian authorities granted permission to complete the construction of the monumental Church of St. Sava (started 1935–41 but, thus far, never finished).[51] The following year, the Republic of Croatia returned various icons, books, manuscripts, and sacred objects from the thirteenth to nineteenth centuries to the church; they had been confiscated at the end of World War II and kept in state museums for four decades.[52] And in 1986 permission was granted for reconstruction of the historic monastery of Gradac in central Serbia.[53] In an even more striking move, the ideological commission of the Serbian Socialist Youth Federation declared subsequently that young believers can enjoy full equality in the youth organization, even serving in leadership positions, and proposed to support an initiative to create a postgraduate program in religious studies at the University of Belgrade.[54]

Patriarch German has a reputation, both at home and abroad, for being cautious and circumspect in his dealings with the government. That this reputation is both deserved and open to diverse interpretation was suggested by the sending of an impassioned letter to the patriarch, on February 26, 1982, on the part of Orthodox priests from the Raška-Prizren diocese in Kosovo. Their letter touched on matters concerning Kosovo in particular, such as the harassment of Orthodox clergymen and believers by local Albanians, and issues affecting the church's life in other parts, such as their allegation that officials in the Šabac-Valjevo diocese were interrogating and harassing families that attempted to send their children to Orthodox catechism classes. They pointed out that the Roman Catholic church was faring tangibly better in this regard, and expressed their dismay that *Pravoslavlje* had ignored these problems and had limited itself to bland announcements that church representatives and state authorities were conferring about matters of "mutual interest." Their letter was not published in the Orthodox religious press, but appeared in print abroad.[55] Perhaps partly in response to this critical letter, the patriarchate's news organ, *Pravoslavlje*, published a long critique of the regime's policy in Kosovo in its May 15 edition, appealing for the protection of the Serbian population and Orthodox shrines in Kosovo.[56]

The Serbian church's clashes with the regime over the Macedonian Orthodox church and over regime policy in Kosovo both stem from the church's self-appointed guardianship over the Serbian people—a guardianship which the regime wants to deny but which both the church and the state label as "nationalist." The Serbian nationalism of the Serbian church, expressed in numerous ways over the decades, confronts the regime as a challenge both to its nationality policy and to its claim to be the *exclusive* representative of the political interests of the population. As a nationalist institution, thus, the Serbian church is, de facto, in opposition, even if in *loyal* opposition.[57]

Conclusion

What I have tried to produce here was not an exhaustive history of the Serbian Orthodox church in this century, but rather an interpretation of the meaning of that history. To understand the Serbian Orthodox church today is to understand its mind set, its set of working assumptions about the world that are the product of the problems, privileges, conflicts, advantages, and setbacks experienced by the church over the years.

The central experience of this century that colors the entire outlook of the Serbian Orthodox church today is the savage assault suffered in World War II. This assault, which was experienced as trauma, has both stiffened the resolve and defiance of the church and, reinforced by the communist takeover, deepened its pessimism. The Serbian church views itself as identical with the Serbian nation since, for itself, religion is the foundation of nationality.[58] The hierarchs of the Serbian church deny that Macedonians are anything but "south Serbs." For the Serbian patriarchate, then, the Macedonian Orthodox church is, in essence, a reincarnation of the spirit of the Croatian Orthodox church since, in the view of the patriarchate, the one, like the other, represents an endeavor to reduce the Serbian nation by transforming the religious affiliation of a part of its number. The Serbian church might well repeat the words of the poet Tanasije Mladenović, who, in a controversial poem, asked,

> Serbia, poor and wretched . . .
> will you be able,
> as in time past,
> to renew your strength with a sudden crack?

Or will you,
discouraged and feeble,
disappear among the mountains and nations . . .
torn to pieces by apocalyptic forces?[59]

FACT SHEET

The Serbian Orthodox Church

Year of autocephaly
  Archdiocese of Žiča
    autocephalous 1219
    elevated to Patriarchate of Skopje 1346
    abolished 1459
    reestablished 1557 as Patriarchate of Peć
    extinguished 1766
  Patriarchate of Belgrade
    established 1920

Current strength of the church
  10 million faithful (1987)
  2,100 priests and monks (1982)
  563 nuns and 49 novices (1987)
  455 seminarians (1978)

Chief news organs (circulation figures for 1987)
  Pravoslavlje (23,000 copies, biweekly)
  Vesnik (2,500 copies, monthly)
  Glasnik, official gazette (3,000 copies, monthly)

Number of churches and church facilities in operation (1987)
  3,000 churches (estimated)
  4 theological seminaries
  1 theological faculty
  155 monasteries and convents

Patriarchs since 1900
  Dimitrija (Pavlović), 1920–30
  Varnava (Rosić), 1930–37
  Gavrilo (Dožić), 1938–50
  Vikentije (Prodanov), 1950–58
  German (Djorić), 1958–present

IV
OTHER CHALCEDONIAN-ORTHODOX CHURCHES

13

The Czechoslovak Orthodox Church

Ludvík Němec

The notion of autocephaly is central to the development and structure of Orthodox churches. *Autocephali*[1]—a term derived from the Greek *avtos* (self) and *kefale* (head), and thus meaning self-governing—was introduced by Greek canonists to distinguish independent metropolitans or exarchs from patriarchs. Historically, it denoted an ecclesiastical independence within the framework of church organization, a juridical exemption from subordination to another authority on a *praeter legem* basis. Some autocephalous Orthodox churches have existed entirely within the boundaries of a single state and nation (the concept of ethnarchy), while others have worked within political frameworks embracing various nationalities. Occasionally, the term *autocephalous* also came to be applied to members of the clergy who dissented from patriarchal or metropolitan jurisdiction.[2] At any rate, the link between political sovereignty and ecclesiastical autocephaly has historical roots.

Although the Czechoslovak Republic has existed since 1918, formed as a result of the political reconstruction of Europe after World War I,[3] the Czechoslovak Orthodox church did not come into being until 1951.

The Orthodox in Czechoslovakia, 1918–45

The Czechoslovak constitution of February 29, 1920, guaranteed freedom of conscience and proclaimed religious toleration. More specifically, it provided for freedom of creed and worship, freedom of religious expression, and equality among the faiths. The constitution also guaranteed that no one should be compelled to take part in any religious ceremony.

In the framework of these laws no drastic changes occurred except within the context of the proselytizing activities of rival church organizations, especially between the Uniates (Greek-Rite Catholics) and the Orthodox in Slovakia. Between the two world wars the Orthodox church had an ethnically mixed composition, like Czechoslovakia itself. Under the provisions of the minorities treaty, signed on September 10, 1919, at St. Germain, the Czechoslovak government had willingly promised to constitute Subcarpathian Ruthenia, where most of Czechoslovakia's Orthodox population lived, "as an autonomous unit within the Czechoslovak state and accord to it the fullest degree of self-government compatible with the unity of the Czechoslovak state."[4] This included protection of religion as well.

In Ruthenia the religious issue was intertwined with the national question. Many of the Ruthenian Catholic clergy became victims or instruments of Magyarizing endeavors in the course of the nineteenth century, and the endless struggle to maintain the Old Slavonic liturgy against the encroachment by the Hungarians was a tense period in the history of the Ruthenian church. It caused division even among the faithful, some of whom defended Magyarization and some of whom became Russophiles. The situation was exploited by the Orthodox church. A dissident movement, slowly emerging from concealment as time progressed, was organized as a reaction against the Magyarization and Latinization of Subcarpathian Ruthenia. The majority of the Ruthenian priests were able to distinguish between the national and religious issues and put up resistance to both the Magyarophile and Russophile tendencies. In the twentieth century, however, they felt constrained to join the Orthodox church to defend their national and religious heritage, because of the unscrupulous Magyarization policy, which forced Latinization upon Catholics rather than supporting the church's traditional policies of preserving Uniate privileges.[5] To forestall the loss of their ethnic identity, some looked to the Russian Orthodox church for help. Not surprisingly, Orthodox propaganda proved very successful there after 1918, so that by 1930 about 112,000 in this region had left the Catholic church.

Another influx of Orthodox in Czechoslovak lands came from the radical wing of the Czech *Jednota*, the avant-garde of clerical progressivism and unionism,[6] from which the National Czechoslovak church emerged on January 8, 1920, and to whose first congress in 1921 all schismatic churches sent their delegates. The Orthodox church was represented there by Father Grovanin, the Russian Orthodox church by Professor Jastrebox. The telegram of the Serbian Bishop Dositej was read, containing his answer to the suggestion that the two churches (National Czechoslovak and

Orthodox) be amalgamated. With a view to this eventuality the assembly of the Serbian Orthodox church, upon the recommendation of Bishop Dositej, had decided in September 1921 to confer episcopal rank on Father Matthias Pavlík (1879–1942), then administrator of the Moravian-Silesian diocese of the National Czechoslovak church. On September 25, 1921, Father Pavlík, taking the name Gorazd,[7] was consecrated a bishop by Patriarch Dimitrii, according to the rite of the Serbian Orthodox church, at Sremski Karlovci. Participation of all government authorities in this event was taken to indicate the magnitude of political prestige which the Yugoslav government hoped to derive. The subsequent election of Father Karel Farský as bishop of the diocese of West Bohemia, and, ex officio, patriarch of the entire Czechoslovak church, created a great deal of tumult, for Dr. Farský was accused by some of being unfit to be a leader of the church. The situation was aggravated by the appearance of a new Czechoslovak catechism,[8] which contained some very liberal, modernizing doctrinal tenets that seemed entirely incompatible with those of the Orthodox church and killed all hope for any kind of unification of the two churches. In fact, the Serbian bishop, Dositej, condemned the catechism for "theological absurdity," showing the intensity of feeling generated by this publication.[9] The result was that the nascent church split into its two components: the liberals of the National Czechoslovak church and the Orthodox. The exodus of Bishop Gorazd and his Orthodox followers was imminent, especially after the progressives gave a complete mandate to Dr. Farský. Meanwhile, several members of the Orthodox group made their exit, preferring to affiliate with the Orthodox community in Prague.

Almost immediately after the split, the question of property ownership arose. The Moravian diocesan assembly met at Brno on August 25, 1924, and voted to affiliate with the National Czechoslovak church. Nevertheless, the Orthodox were able to set up fourteen parishes: eleven in Moravia, with an enrollment of 6,116 members, and three in Bohemia (Prague, Tabor, and Svinov), with a total of 3,300 members.[10] As the only validly consecrated non-Catholic bishop in the country, Bishop Gorazd had hoped for some rapprochement and, for this reason, had remained officially in the National Czechoslovak church as long as he thought feasible. When he saw that his hopes would not be fulfilled, he pulled out, and the exodus of the Orthodox followed on August 10, 1924. After their departure the National Czechoslovak church adopted a new constitution at its first church council (August 29–30, 1924), declaring itself anti-Roman, anti-Orthodox, and pro-Unitarian.

Following the final solution of this religious crisis, Bishop Gorazd was confronted with the difficult task of introducing the newly adapted "Oriental" liturgy (as it was called), to make Orthodoxy more acceptable to the people and to put the reorganization of the Orthodox church on solid legal footing. He was surprised to encounter difficulty in this. The Czechoslovak Orthodox Bishop Sabbatios (Sawatij), previously appointed by the ecumenical patriarch, informed Gorazd in September that he could not appoint him to the administration of the Orthodox church in Moravia unless he presented his dismission papers from the Serbian Orthodox church. This evidently reflected a jurisdictional struggle between the two rival patriarchates of Belgrade and Constantinople. Gorazd then had to document that the Serbian Orthodox bishop of Zadar had enjoyed jurisdiction in the Czech Crown lands during Habsburg rule, while Slovakia and Subcarpathian Ruthenia had been ecclesiastically subordinate to the Serbian metropole of Sremski Karlovci.[11] This ecclesiastical status was never really changed, because the first law of the Czechoslovak Republic (of October 28, 1918) accepted as valid all laws and ordinances of the Austrian Empire.

On the recommendation of the Serbian synod of May 16, 1925, the formal reconstruction of the Czechoslovak Orthodox community in Prague was ordered, with official approval of the Czechoslovak authorities. A general assembly was called for this purpose on November 22, 1925, in the city of Česká Třebová, where Bishop Gorazd was unanimously elected as the spiritual administrator. The assembly also set up a central council to assist him. The previous March the synod of the Ecumenical Patriarchate in Constantinople had issued a decree creating an archbishopric in Prague, on the assumption that there were already three bishoprics in Czechoslovakia—in Prague, Moravia, and Subcarpathian Ruthenia—"which would be augmented according to the pastoral needs,"[12] although in reality not a single bishopric had as yet been organized in Czechoslovakia.

The patriarch of Constantinople appointed Bishop Sabbatios archbishop in 1925, authorizing him to supervise the expansion of the Orthodox church. The patriarch even protested against the interferences of government authorities in church affairs, although these greatly helped Bishop Gorazd's efforts, but the Supreme Court rejected his complaint in 1931, as immaterial. The Czechoslovak government was interfering in church affairs at every turn. Bishop Gorazd meanwhile continued with the church's reorganization wherever he thought it was needed and moved his residence from Olomouc to Prague.

The stabilization of the Orthodox church was greatly helped by the state's financial assistance, which had been sought above all by Catholic deputies, led by the minister of the People's party, Dr. Josef Nosek, but was welcomed by all other churches, including the Orthodox. On March 12, 1929, the Czechoslovak Ministry of Education approved the constitution of the eparchy in the Czech lands and in Moravia-Silesia, observing that "this Czech eparchy will constitute an integral part of the independent [autocephalous] Orthodox church in the Czechoslovak Republic."[13] On December 12, 1929, another Orthodox eparchy was formed in the territory of Subcarpathian Ruthenia, which was divided into four protopresbyteriates: Mukachev, Chust, Terebishov, and Terešov, to facilitate its administration. Bishop Damaskin was appointed administrator of this eparchy.

As the church developed its administrative apparatus, membership climbed steadily. In 1921 there were some 7,292 Orthodox believers in Bohemia, and only 1,929 in Moravia-Silesia; by 1930 the number of Orthodox in Bohemia had doubled—reaching 14,878—while the number in Moravia-Silesia now came to 9,695. In all Czechoslovakia there were some 145,583 Orthodox believers in 1930.[14]

The Orthodox church's growth elicited wide attention and yielded additional state subsidies. In 1930 Bishop Gorazd succeeded in obtaining 40,000 crowns for administrative purposes; in 1931 he received 70,000 crowns, and in 1934 he received a permanent state subsidy to defray all expenses for the eparchy, which otherwise could not have been covered. This development makes clear the degree of support the Orthodox church enjoyed from the Czechoslovak Republic.

To increase the interest of the faithful in the liturgy and church life, the Orthodox church published a collection of prayers and liturgical songs in 1934, a liturgical handbook for church schools also in 1934, and a Czech Orthodox catechism in 1940.

The Czechoslovak Orthodox church felt allied with the fate of the Czechoslovak Republic. Hence, when Sudetenland was ceded to Nazi Germany in September 1938, Bishop Gorazd reacted passionately.[15] Meanwhile, changes were occurring in the internal life of the Czechoslovak Republic. On October 6, 1938, Slovakia's political parties met in Zilina, demanded autonomy for Slovakia, and set up a regional government. Shortly thereafter, Ruthenia finally secured its autonomy within the republic. A constitutional law of November 22, 1938, provided for a three-member cabinet and for a regional parliament, elections for which were held on February 2, 1939. On January 1 the cabinet officially changed Ruthenia's name to Carpatho-Ukraine. But this arrangement was short-lived. Hungary, which had already annexed a portion of the region, including its capital, Užhorod, under the terms of the Vienna Award of November 2, 1938, started preparations to annex all of Ruthenia. Hitler, however, found it expedient to make the Budapest government wait temporarily. Meanwhile, there were stirrings in favor of Ruthenian independence. On March

14, 1939, as Nazi troops marched into Prague, the Slovak parliament declared Slovakia's independence. Bohemia and Moravia were annexed by
Germany as a Reichs-protectorate, and now, the Hungarian army—this
time with Hitler's approval—invaded Ruthenia and quickly subdued it.
From March 1939 until the entry of Soviet troops in 1944, Ruthenia was
administered as part of Hungary.

Bishop Gorazd, sensing approaching danger for his clergy, wrote a personal letter in May 1941 to the Orthodox Archbishop Serafim in Berlin,
asking for advice. He never received an answer. Suddenly, in October
1941, Bishop Gorazd received a telegram from Berlin, announcing that
Archbishop Serafim would arrive in Prague. In the wake of Serafim's visit
Gorazd learned that the Orthodox eparchy of Bohemia and Moravia was to
be annexed to the Orthodox episcopate in Berlin.[16] Gorazd was surprised
and angered by this fait accompli. He protested, but in vain; the Reich
ministry set a deadline of November 21, 1941, for compliance with this
decision.

The situation became acute as a result of an unusual turn of events on
May 27, 1942, when Reich Protector Reinhard Heydrich was assassinated
by a group of Czechoslovak parachutists. Afterward Jan Sonnevend, an
Orthodox believer, and Rev. Dr. Vladimír Petřek, an Orthodox priest, hid
the parachutists in the crypt of the Orthodox Church of Saints Cyril and
Methodius in Prague. Bishop Gorazd was unaware of this at first, but when
informed by Sonnevend, he urged the parachutists to hide elsewhere, lest
discovery by the Nazis bring reprisals against the church. Unfortunately,
before anything could be done one of the parachutists turned informer, and
on June 18 the Gestapo raided the church. Bishop Gorazd, in a melodra-
matic attempt to save his church, wrote a letter to the minister of schools,
Emanuel Moravec, and to the office of the Reich protector, declaring: "I
am giving my person to the disposal of all pertinent organs and I am willing to submit myself to any punishment, including death!"[17] On June 22
Sonnevend was arrested. Two days later Gorazd was arrested and taken to
the Petchek Palace in Prague for interrogation. A military court tried the
four persons concerned—Sonnevend, Gorazd, Petřek, and Rev. Wences-
laus Čikl, pastor of the church—in September 1942 and convicted them
of helping the parachutists. They, like the parachutists themselves, were
executed forthwith.

In addition, all the parachutists' relatives, as well as another 253 persons
of Czech nationality convicted of having somehow helped the parachutists
were taken first to the concentration camp at Terezín and later deported to
the infamous camp at Mauthousen, where on October 24, 1942, all were
liquidated. The Reich protector, in a script of September 1, 1942, curtly

noted: "The Czech Orthodox communities [churches] of the Serbian and Constantinople jurisdiction in the Protectorate of Bohemia and Moravia are hereby dissolved."[18] The Gestapo took over all properties, and by September 27, 1942, all Orthodox churches and houses of prayer were closed. Orthodox priests were taken to Germany for forced labor, and the Orthodox believers were left without spiritual leadership.

The Postwar Period

It is a matter of historical fact that, according to the plan of President Eduard Beneš and his chief adviser, Dr. Hubert Ripka, the orientation of the Czechoslovak government-in-exile in London was going to be toward the Soviet Union. The signing of the Soviet-Czechoslovak Agreement on December 12, 1943, in Moscow, was one token of this.

During the years 1945 to 1947 communists were busy consolidating their power and influence, and manipulating people's feelings. They also exploited the sense of relief and joy of all who believed that peace had at long last arrived. Some of the non-Catholic churches decided to co-operate with the communists. This is astonishing, given the well-known hostility of communism toward all religions. Thus, the Church of the Czech Brethren took a special stand. Bohdan Chudoba critically analyzed the "stages in the Czech Protestant tragedy," in which the leading role was played by F. L. Hromádka, dean of the Hus Faculty in Prague. Hromadka brought his church ideologically into a cooperative stance with the communist regime,[19] and the National Czechoslovak church followed the example set by Hromádka and the Czech Brethren, as did the Unitarians and some other denominations in Prague. The Orthodox church was under Moscow's influence and not only cooperated with the communists but even played the role of a Trojan horse by dispersing the Uniate church, in Ruthenia, Slovakia, Moravia, and Bohemia. The regime favored the Orthodox church, probably because the Soviet regime had had great success in pushing the Russian Orthodox church into a position of obedience and servility.

As a result, Orthodox Bishop Nestor's successor, Archbishop Makarij of Lviv and Ternopil, cooperated in the liquidation of the Uniates. On March 20, 1947, the Orthodox church seized the Catholic monastery of the Basilian Fathers in Mukačevo, and on October 27, 1947, Uniate Bishop Theodore Romža was run over by a military truck and died of his injuries a few days later. On February 22, 1948, the Greek-Catholic cathedral in Užhorod was seized and presented to the Orthodox. Officially, the liquidation of the Greek Catholic church was accomplished on August 28,

1949, when Archbishop Makarij met with his clergy and decided on the move. They passed a resolution to send a telegram to Patriarch Aleksii and to Exarch Ivan of the Ukraine.[20] Yet no synod had been convoked in Ruthenia, as had been done in Lviv in 1946 and as would be done in Prešov in Slovakia. This in itself reveals the forceful nature of the liquidation of Greek Catholics in Ruthenia, more so in that it was done against the will of the Uniate priests, of whom only one, Father Irenej Kondratović, is known to have switched before August 28. The dissolution of the Greek Catholic church was seen by the communists as a necessary first step to weaken Catholicism, shake the faith of the people, and thus more easily exterminate all religions.

The Uniates were also subjected to persecution in postwar Czechoslovakia, although it took a somewhat moderate course when compared with their treatment in Soviet-occupied Ruthenia.

The Orthodox church was affected most because of the territorial changes created by the Soviets' annexation of Ruthenia, which had been officially sealed by an agreement with the Czechoslovak president on June 29, 1945. After this annexation, only about twenty thousand Orthodox believers were left in Czechoslovakia. Of this number, about nine thousand were former Uniates in eastern Slovakia, who had joined the Orthodox church previously, under the leadership of their priests, with the remainder consisting of Russian émigrés and converts to Orthodoxy. There were about twenty Orthodox priests. Now these Orthodox communities broke away from the patriarch of Constantinople and the Serbian metropolitan, under whose jurisdiction they had been placed until 1942, and accepted the jurisdiction of the patriarch of Moscow. In May 1945 Aleksii, patriarch of Moscow, sent the Russian bishop Yelevferij (Eleutherius) to Czechoslovakia, to the vacant seat of Orthodox Archbishop Sabbatios, giving him the title of metropolitan of Prague and all Czechoslovakia. He assumed office on August 11, 1946, and the Orthodox church in Czechoslovakia was made an exarchate of the patriarchate of Moscow, disregarding the claims of the ecumenical and Serbian patriarchs. After the coup d'état of the communists in February 1948 the Orthodox metropolitan Eleutherius became a more important personality in public life. He appeared at all state functions and celebrations and was frequently mentioned in the communist press.

At that time there were about thirty thousand Orthodox in Czechoslovakia, of whom some ten thousand were Czechs who had converted to the Orthodox church in the last century.

Under the personal direction of Eleutherius, the Orthodox church initiated a system of propaganda that reached as far as eastern Slovakia.

The public authorities everywhere deferred to Eleutherius. Orthodoxy was considered the religion of "the great Russian nation, which has brought us freedom," while the Uniates were stigmatized as "allies of the Western powers and enemies of the nation." The Orthodox offensive was felt especially among Ruthenian Uniates of northern Zemplin and Sariš. There Orthodoxy posed as the symbol of Russian culture, which many Ruthenes considered their own, while Catholicism was presented as the mark of Westernness.

More than once Uniate Bishop Gojdič of Prešov was molested and interrogated, on charges that he had received aid from Rome, that he had sent several priests to the Ukraine during the war, and that after the war he had given shelter to Ukrainian priests and laymen who had fled to the West before the advancing Soviet army. The Orthodox church, meanwhile, was hailed as a "people's church"—an appellation simultaneously being applied to the Bulgarian Orthodox church—while the Greek Catholic church was maligned as the enemy of the people.

After the communist coup of February 1948, attacks on the Uniates were intensified. Two new Orthodox bishops were appointed in 1949: Čestmír Kračmár for Olomouc and Aleksis Dechterev for Prešov. The latter was a Russian, who had recently returned to Russia from Egypt. A special delegation was sent from Russia to attend the consecration of the two bishops: at its head was Nicholas, metropolitan of Krutice and Kolomna. The two new bishops were consecrated in February 1950. Meanwhile, the communist regime allocated public funds for the construction of an Orthodox church ("of Alexander Nevsky") in Prešov.

After his consecration, Bishop Aleksis immediately began preparations for the liquidation of the Uniate church in Slovakia. His chief collaborator in this enterprise was the Ukrainian National Council, the representative of the Ukrainians and Ruthenes in northern Slovakia. In March 1950 representatives of the Orthodox church and the Ukrainian National Council met government agents in a secret session in Ruzbachy near Podolinec. Plans were laid for the liquidation. A central committee for the "return to Orthodoxy" was set up. Its members were, besides Orthodox clergymen: P. Babej and V. Kapišovsky of the Slovak National Council, and A. M. Rudlovčak, vice-president of the Ukrainian National Council. Their task was to assist local and district committees in their efforts to make it possible for the entire Greek Catholic population to transfer "voluntarily" to the Orthodox faith.[21] Local communist agents, accompanied by gendarmes, mobilized the Uniate inhabitants for an alleged peace rally in Prešov. In some places they forced people into the buses along the roads. Once in Prešov they took the Uniates to the main dining room of the

Čierny Orol (Black Eagle) Hotel. The front wall of the room was adorned
with a large Orthodox cross and portraits of Moscow Patriarch Aleksii and
Prague Metropolitan Eleutherius; on the rear wall there were portraits of
Josef Stalin and Klement Gottwald, the general secretary of the Czechoslovak Communist party. The entire room was festooned with communist
and anti-Catholic slogans and banners, such as "Slavs, fear Rome!" According to the communist press, this "historic synod" was attended by
820 delegates of the Committee for the Return to Orthodoxy and about
four thousand other participants, including one hundred priests. However,
only twelve Greek Catholic priests are mentioned by name, and, of these,
only six spoke at the conclave.

The session was opened by the chairman of the Central Committee for
the Return to Orthodoxy, the educational adviser of the Regional National Committee in Prešov, Benický. The delegates of the Committee for
the Return to Orthodoxy approved the decision of the synod, abolishing
the union with Rome, and issued a manifesto to the Uniate clergy and their
adherents. Specifically, they resolved to abrogate the Užhorod union of
1646, and to seek affiliation with the Orthodox church, under the ecclesiastical jurisdiction of the patriarch of Moscow.[22] After the program the synod
closed with the Czechoslovak national anthem and dispatched a certain
number of participants to the Greek Catholic cathedral in Prešov. Finding
it locked, a delegation entered the bishop's residence and demanded the
keys from Uniate Bishop Paul Gojdič, who refused to surrender them.
The neo-Orthodox therefore seized the cathedral by force.

A delegation now invited Bishop Aleksis to come to the cathedral. On
arrival, Aleksis announced that "by coincidence" Exarch Eleutherius himself was in Prešov. A delegation set out to invite him likewise to the
cathedral. There he was greeted with thunderous cries of "Is polla eti
despota."[23]

Patriarch Aleksii responded with a telegram dated May 3, 1950, saying:
"I received your telegram about the reunion of the Greek Catholics with
the Orthodox church. I rejoice with you and impart the blessing of God
on the new children of our Holy Orthodox church."[24] The Czechoslovak
government also endorsed the move, in a letter dated May 27, 1950:

Esteemed Exarch:
    The State Office for Ecclesiastical Affairs has noted the contents
    of your letter, in which you submit the resolutions adopted by the
    synod of the Greek Catholic clergy and laity held on April 28, 1950
    in Prešov.
    Respecting the manifestly expressed will of the faithful, the State

Office for Ecclesiastical Affairs considers the resolution of the synod of April 28, 1950, about the liquidation of the Union and the return of the former Uniates to Orthodoxy completely valid. By it, the Union and the so-called Greek Catholic church have been dissolved in this Republic. By it, the priests and faithful of the former Greek Catholic church have returned to the Orthodox church, and by it, the Orthodox church has [assumed] all rights to the property and possessions of the former Greek Catholic church.

From now on, therefore, in all matters concerning the former Greek Catholic priests, whether there is question of their person, their salary, or their residence, all civic and state agencies shall have recourse to the bishops of the Orthodox church.

I ask you at this time, esteemed Exarch, to convey our greetings and best wishes to Aleksii, patriarch of Moscow and all Russia, for health and success in this work of reorganization. To you personally and also to the entire Orthodox church in our land, we express our thanks for the patriotic attitude of the Orthodox church in Czechoslovakia and our best wishes for complete success in your work.

> For the State Office of Ecclesiastical Affairs
> (signed) Zdeněk Fierlinger
> Vice-President of the State, and Minister-
> Commissar for Ecclesiastical Affairs [25]

This document, even more than the synod itself, was a violent blow to the Uniate church in Czechoslovakia. The synodal resolution would not have produced any notable results since three quarters of the clergy and many of the laity certainly did not favor it. But by a governmental document, the Uniate church was officially dissolved and all its facilities were handed over to the Orthodox church.

The Uniate bishop of Prešov, Paul Gojdič, and his auxiliary, Basil Hopko, were imprisoned and later sentenced to terms of life and fifteen years, respectively. After the removal of these bishops the Orthodox were free to seize the episcopal residence in Prešov, the seminary, and the other institutions of that diocese. They could not yet take over all the parishes, because they did not have enough Orthodox priests to staff them. In many places the people kept the keys of the church and, even when bereft of priests, gathered in the churches on Sundays, singing and praying together. This state of affairs did not last long, however. The Orthodox arranged courses over a period of several months and in a short time scores of Orthodox priests were ordained to fill the vacancies in former

Greek Catholic parishes. It is possible that some of these new priests were secret police. Be that as it may, on July 26, 1950, finally, the government issued a permit for the establishment of an Orthodox seminary in Prešov, with a faculty of Orthodox theology. It was opened on October 15, 1950. The school of theology was in the former Greek Catholic seminary and the seminarians resided in the former diocesan orphanage.

In an attempt to get the people to Zemplin the Orthodox grasped the opportunity of Cyril and Methodius Day, so popular with the Slovak Uniates. The July 9, 1950, celebration, publicized also as a "peace rally," was attended by Archbishop Eleutherius, Bishop Aleksis, and the district government representative. Some 25,000 people attended. Archbishop Eleutherius addressed the crowds in Russian; then the former Greek Catholic priest, Ján Kokincak, gave a Slovak address in the Zemplin dialect.

They soon came forward with the proposal to create a Slovak Orthodox diocese in Michalovce, with its seat in the former Redemptorist monastery. This was approved in July 1950. A general vicariate was also established in Košice.

After 1946 the Orthodox church in Czechoslovakia was under the jurisdiction of the Russian Orthodox church, with status as an exarchate of the Moscow patriarchate. After the dissolution of the Union of Užhorod and the confiscation of Greek Catholic parishes in eastern Slovakia, the Prešov Orthodox eparchy claimed some 259 registered parishes and 1,022 missions. The total number of Orthodox Christians in Czechoslovakia (counting in the former Greek Catholics) now came to nearly 400,000. In view of this, the Russian Orthodox church bestowed autocephaly on the Czechoslovak Orthodox church in December 1951, and Archbishop Eleutherius was "unanimously elected" first metropolitan of the new church. The installation ceremonies were attended by delegates from the Russian, Georgian, Romanian, Bulgarian, and Albanian Orthodox churches.

With the aged bishop of Michalovce, Alexander Michalič, unable to accomplish much for the aggrandizement of Orthodoxy in Zemplin, Michael Milly, likewise a lapsed Greek Catholic priest, was appointed his auxiliary. At his consecration on February 15, 1953, he received the name of Methodius and the title of bishop of Trebišov. In October 1954 a third lapsed Uniate clergyman, Nicholas Kelly, was consecrated bishop of the Orthodox diocese of Olomouc-Brno, with the name of Clement, to succeed in the see vacated by Bishop Čestmír Kračmár. Some of these conversions, at the least, were motivated by opportunism.

Having put the Czechoslovak Orthodox church on what they hoped was solid footing, Metropolitan Eleutherius and Bishop Aleksis returned to the USSR in 1955. Eleutherius was now appointed metropolitan of Leningrad, and Aleksis became archbishop of Vilna. Since then, the organizational and legal structure of the church has been essentially unchanged. It is worth noting here that the autocephalous state of the Czechoslovak Orthodox church, which had been granted by the Moscow patriarchate, was recognized belatedly, in 1960, by the ecumenical patriarch of Constantinople.[26]

After 1948 the Czechoslovak Orthodox church was busy with proselytization of other churches' adherents. To accomplish this missionary work, the church needed more priests. Candidates for the priesthood were given two-year courses in Carlsbad and Prague, where the seminarians were well taken care of materially. After 1950 the school of theology in Prešov became vital to the growth of Czechoslovak Orthodoxy. It published a theological review and had a Slavonic press for printing liturgical books, largely for export to Russia, where, interestingly enough, the church has no printing facilities of its own.

In May 1950 an Orthodox monthly in the Slovak language, *Svetló pravoslavia*, began publication, its name being changed in June 1952 to *Hlas pravoslavia*. But since the word *Orthodoxy* ("pravoslavia") seemed forbidding to the former Greek Catholics, the title was changed again in May 1955 to *Odkaz Sv. Cyrila a Metoda*—its present name. At the same time a Russian-language edition began publication, intended for Ruthenian readership. This publication was discontinued in 1955, after five years, for lack of readers. It was revived in 1958 under the title *Zapovit Sv. Kyrila i Metodija*, but is now written chiefly in Ukrainian, with only occasional articles in Russian. Publication of a Russian theological quarterly entitled *Mysl pravoslaviya* (Orthodox Thought) began in 1956 and continued for four years. In addition, since 1950 there has been an annual church calendar, with almanacs published in Czech and in Russian. And in 1951 *Věstník Pravoslavného Exarchátu Moskovského Patriarchatu v Československu*, a monthly, began publication. It is still being published.

The fact that the Orthodox church in Czechoslovakia enjoyed such benevolent understanding from the authorities, even while the Catholic church was being subjected to severe persecution, is indicative of the different attitude that the authorities bore toward the former. The new Orthodox faithful were given various privileges. In 1950, for example, several recreational tours were sponsored for Orthodox youth from eastern Slovakia to the well-known spa of Marianské Lázně. Various ecclesiastical/political rallies, frequently sponsored by the communist regime, were designed to popularize Orthodoxy. No doubt the authorities were encouraged by the history of Orthodox church subordination to state authority in Russia[27] and in the Balkans.

The Greek Catholic church suffered from a further debility in communist eyes, that is, its association with the concept of Ruthenian nationality. The Soviets did not recognize a Ruthenian nationality, as the annexation of Subcarpathian Ruthenia had been justified on the grounds that Ruthenes are Ukrainians. Historically the identification of Greek Catholic faith with Ruthenian national identity was strong, although there were of course also Slovak Uniates in the region.[28]

The national animosity—between Slovaks and Ruthenes—inspired the authorities to promote greater use of the vernacular in liturgical worship, stirring up resentment and conflict in places where the Old Slavonic liturgy had kept peace for ages. The liturgical fragmentation was designed to contribute to the undermining of church unity.

Recent popes have tried to ease relations between the Orthodox church and the suppressed Uniate church in Eastern Europe. Thus, Pius XII[29] and John XXIII[30] have defended the Greek Catholics, while John Paul II has attempted in various ways to improve the lot of the Uniates in the Soviet Ukraine and Eastern Europe.[31]

The Uniates remained illegal until the "Prague Spring" of 1968, when a governmental decree of June 13 reestablished the Greek Catholic eparchy of Prešov and allowed parishes to vote on whether to remain with the Orthodox church or to rejoin the Greek Catholic church. The result was that out of 246 parishes, 204 returned to the Catholic church. Father Jan Kirka was appointed ordinarious of the diocese, by the government, and was concomitantly recognized by the Vatican, which granted him the title of monsignor. Auxiliary Bishop Basil Hopko was also rehabilitated by the government and was allowed to function as an auxiliary bishop in Prešov to perform all episcopal rites in the cathedral, which was returned to the Greek Catholic church too.[32] This arrangement was made to accommodate the circumstance that Monsignor Jan Kirka was never consecrated bishop, although he was the de facto administrator of the diocese. Auxiliary Bishop Basil Hopko lived in Prešov until his death in July 1976. The Greek Catholics continue to be tolerated by the present regime, and the situation of the eparchy remains the same.

In conformity with the Kremlin's general practice in the bloc, the patriarch of Moscow has kept a close control of the Orthodox church in Czechoslovakia. And as was shown previously, the national element inherent in the basic structure of the Orthodox church has predisposed the church to cooperate and even collaborate with the state.

Since the Moscow patriarchate's recognition of Czechoslovak Orthodox autocephaly in 1951, the relationship between these two churches has always been friendly. The Moscow patriarch has exercised his influence in the election of Czechoslovak bishops and has maintained his control of that church's policies. It is interesting to note that leaders of the Catholic union of priests, "Pacem in Terris," also coordinated their relationship with the Moscow patriarch, especially since the papal ban on priests' membership in pro-regime organizations such as Pacem in Terris (issued March 8, 1982).[33] Perhaps more significant was the visit, March 14–17, 1984, of a delegation of Catholic clergy, led by Bishop Josef Feranec of Banská Bystrica and accompanied by professors of the two Catholic theological faculties (at Litoměřice and Bratislava) to the Soviet Union, for meetings with Patriarch Pimen of Moscow.[34]

According to some Western reports,[35] Vasil Bilak is supposed to have made a proposal, at a secret mountain-top meeting of Pacem in Terris somewhere in Slovakia, for the creation of a national Catholic church in communion with the Moscow patriarchate. Reportedly, there was such outrage that even some regime-loyal priests stormed out of the conference hall. Czechoslovak sources have not mentioned the presence of Bilak or any other government official at the event, but admit that a theological seminar was held in Dolní Smokovec in the Tatra Mountains in June 1985, during which a "rich and deeply inspiring discussion" on questions of peace and faith took place.[36] It is also a fact that closer ties with the Russian Orthodox church are being openly encouraged and that a high-level Pacem in Terris delegation visited the Soviet Union in March 1985 for that purpose. Bilak may not have been the official spokesman, and a proposal may not have been formally made, but the question of relations with the Russian Orthodox church was certainly discussed. Other accounts report, however, that Bilak proposed that Patriarch Pimen be invited, rather than the pope, to the impending celebrations of the 1100th anniversary of St. Methodius's death. Bilak also once again advocated the separation of Czech and Slovak Catholics from Rome, in a formula that would transform the Catholic church in Czechoslovakia into a "sister church" of the Czechoslovak Orthodox church. Whether or not either the party or the Orthodox church entertains notions of absorbing the Catholic church entirely into the Czechoslovak Orthodox church, over the long term, is impossible to say on the basis of what evidence is available.

Yet it was at the instigation of the Czechoslovak Orthodox church and the patriarch of Moscow that attempts to restore the enfeebled Pacem in Terris were made. For this purpose, the head of the Federal Bureau for Church Affairs, Vladimír Janků, invited all Czechoslovak ordinaries to Vicar's Restaurant, in Prague, to endorse the organization. František Cardinal Tomášek, Catholic archbishop of Prague, showed up at the beginning, and announced that there was nothing to be negotiated, because it was already resolved in Rome, and left.

Obviously, the entire celebration of St. Methodius (807–85) was resented by the communists, who, with the help of historian Josef Poulík, tried to perpetrate the interpretation that this jubilee was a purely "cultural" one, which was being abused by the Vatican. They even organized a seminar in Brno to discuss "how to interpret this anniversary of St. Methodius in the spirit of atheistic propaganda."[37]

These and all other events were possible only with the support of the Moscow patriarch, who not only favored them but exploited a widespread tension in Czechoslovakia to induce all churches into a passive posture, urging them to follow the example of the Russian Orthodox church in collaborating with the communist regime.

FACT SHEET

The Czechoslovak Orthodox Church

Year of autocephaly
    1929: recognized by the patriarch of Constantinople
    1951: recognized by the patriarch of Moscow

Current strength of the church
    20,000–30,000 faithful (1984)
    124 priests (1982)
    3 bishops (1982)

Chief news organ
    Hlas pravoslavia (circulation not available but probably less than
        1,000)

Number of churches and church facilities in operation (1987)
    143 parishes
    1 theological faculty (at Prešov)
    0 convents
    0 monasteries

Metropolitans since 1951
    Eleutherius, 1951–55
    Jan Kuchtin, 1955–present

14

The Finnish Orthodox Church

Metropolitan John of Helsinki

The Orthodox Church of Finland is one of two national churches in the Republic of Finland.[1] The Lutheran church, which commands the loyalty of the vast majority of the population, was for several centuries the only established church in the country, during the period of its inclusion as one of the provinces of the Kingdom of Sweden. But Orthodoxy spread in the beginning of the second millennium to the areas inhabited by the Finnish tribe of Karelians in the neighborhood of Lake Ladoga and to some extent north and northwest of Lake Ladoga. Later on, the influence of the Orthodox church was extended northwards until it reached the shore of the Arctic Ocean, where a monastery was founded in the sixteenth century. In the older Orthodox area near Lake Ladoga, the spiritual life was centered in the monasteries, which had been originally founded in the twelfth century. The most significant among these was the great historical monastery of Valamo (Valaam), situated on a group of islands in Lake Ladoga. Its founder was the Greek monk St. Sergius. It should be stressed that the spread of Orthodoxy among the Finnish Karelians was largely due to monastic missionary activity.

Another fact that should be made clear in this connection is that all these regions remained, for a long time, outside the control of the Kingdom of Sweden. It was only in the sixteenth century that the first areas of Orthodox Karelia were conquered by Sweden and annexed to the kingdom, and thus united with the Swedish province of Finland. Sweden was originally a Roman Catholic country, but in the early sixteenth century the Lutheran reformation extended its influence. As a result, Sweden established a Lutheran state church as the only legal religion of the country at a time when the first Orthodox parishes were being absorbed into the kingdom.

This led to confrontations and complications of various kinds. During the following centuries there were several wars between Lutheran Sweden and Orthodox Russia. But although there were many changes of the frontier, some Orthodox parishes and a certain number of Orthodox always remained west of the frontier and thus politically united with the other Finns. In 1809 the whole situation changed radically, when Russia conquered the entire Finnish part of the Swedish Kingdom, and Lutheran Finland, with its small Orthodox minority, came under the tsars of Russia, not as a fully integrated province, but as an autonomous grand duchy, governed according to Swedish law but with the Orthodox Russian tsar as its grand duke. The Lutheran church retained its position as the state church, but it was only natural in this new situation that the Orthodox parishes, now assigned to the diocese of St. Petersburg, gained new rights and became more secure.

Orthodoxy and Russian Aims in Finland (1900–1917)

In the beginning of the twentieth century the imperial government in St. Petersburg showed a keen interest in the situation of Orthodoxy in Finland. A few years earlier the country had received a diocese of its own, and thus the Orthodox parishes in Finland were now under the archbishop of Viborg, a historical town in the eastern part of the country. The interest of the authorities had two very different sources, and it served, therefore, two very different aims. First, the Russian authorities no doubt earnestly and sincerely wanted to strengthen the position of the Orthodox minority church in the grand duchy and to improve, in various ways, the conditions of the Orthodox believers. The new governor general, N. I. Bobrikov, who came to the country just before the turn of the century, actively promoted the consolidation of Orthodoxy in Finland. Second, the imperial government also wanted to use the Orthodox church as a means for a gradual Russification of Finland, and the new governor general fully and strongly supported these endeavors. He acted in cooperation with Archbishop Nicholas, who had been appointed to Finland in 1899. Thus in the beginning of the twentieth century so-called Russification schools were founded in the Orthodox parishes in order to promote, in principle, both Orthodoxy and Russian language, in villages with Finnish-speaking Karelian Orthodox populations. Finnish-language schools already existed all over Karelia; the new Russian schools were not needed for the elementary education of the Karelians. Moreover, Orthodox religious instruction was also already available in the regular public schools instructing in Finnish. Hence, there was no religious deficit to be corrected either. Rather, the main purpose of these Russian-language schools was to Russify the Orthodox Karelians. In many cases certain material benefits were offered to those enrolling in the Russian-language schools.

Although the Orthodox church schools had taught in Finnish, some of them offered Russian as one of their subjects. By the turn of the century Russian-language instruction was offered in all Orthodox church schools, and the position of Russian as a second language was strengthened. In 1903 Finnish schools were instructed to give preference in the hiring of new teachers for the church schools to those fluent in Russian: this was in direct violation of provincial law. In addition, there were special plans for radical changes at the teachers' training college, which served the needs of the Karelian regular schools, since the college was thought to be an anti-Russian institution. But before these plans could be brought to fruition, the governor was murdered (in 1904), and his supporter, Archbishop Nicholas, was transferred from Finland a year later.

In 1905 the Finnish diocese received a new head when Sergiei was appointed archbishop. At first he favored instruction in Finnish because he understood the importance this had for the consolidation of Orthodoxy and the knowledge of the Orthodox faith in its competition with Lutheranism, as well as in its struggle against sects and dissidence within the Orthodox flock. After a few years, however, Sergiei—later to become the metropolitan of St. Petersburg—reversed himself and became a strong supporter of the Russificatory measures being advanced by F. A. Seyn, governor general after 1909. The number of Russian-language "ministerial" schools increased to seventy. They were largely maintained with funds granted by the imperial authorities. Meanwhile, the church founded a religious organization, the Karelian Brotherhood, in 1907. This organization spread its activities throughout Finnish Karelia and served in various ways to advance the Russification policy of the tsarist authorities, e.g., through the libraries and schools maintained by the Brotherhood, and through the literature it published. A corresponding Finnish-Orthodox organization, established in 1885, was not able to compete with the Karelian Brotherhood and its work was nearly paralyzed until the end of Russian rule in Finland.

The Russian Revolution of 1917 created a new situation for the Orthodox church, both in Russia proper and in the Grand Duchy of Finland, which, in December 1917, declared its political independence. The Orthodox diocese of Finland, with its Russian leadership and largely Russian clergy, and with memories of close cooperation with the imperial authorities as with the Russification program, was suddenly on its own in a predominantly Lutheran, independent state. Canonically and in principle, the diocese was still part of the Russian church, but in practice the links were almost totally severed. This meant also that the church missed every possibility to receive economic support from St. Petersburg. But above all, it was no longer necessary to equate Orthodox Christianity with Russian culture—and this, on the other hand, created a new opportunity for the Finnish Orthodox church.

The Orthodox Church in Independent Finland (1917–18)

The political changes in Russia took place gradually, with the abdication of the tsar in March 1917, then a period of uncertainty under the so-called Provisional Government between March and November 1917, and finally the Bolshevik coup in November of that year. These events had immediate consequences for Finland, not least for the Orthodox diocese. Already after the March revolution some of the Russian-language schools were closed and some of the Russian clergy were harassed. It was clear that the Karelian Orthodox population felt quite differently from the Russian or Russophile leadership of the church when it came to Russia.

National (Russophobe) elements convened a meeting in April 1917 in order to take up the circumstances of the Orthodox diocese in Finland. This meeting highlighted the incompatibility between Finnish provincial law and the laws governing the Orthodox church. The meeting proposed to the senate (which was the government of the autonomous Grand Duchy) that a special committee be appointed to investigate the problems of the Orthodox church in the country. (Another committee was to deal with matters concerning schools and education in Karelia.) When the senate agreed to this and established the suggested committee, it appointed only national-minded members and did not accept those who had been proposed by the leadership of the church. The national-minded elements were thus ready to make use of the state authorities, in the new political situation, at the expense of the canonical order of the church.

After Finland became independent, the struggle between the Russian leadership and some active groups in the Karelian Orthodox community intensified. The state authorities became more involved than ever in this struggle. The government took an active interest in the affairs of the Orthodox church, obviously mainly for political and practical reasons, although it is also true that the national character of the Karelian Orthodox was both recognized and appreciated. The state authorities wanted to see the former "Russian institution in Finland"—as the Orthodox church was typically described in some governmental documents of the time—become a truly national (i.e., Finnish) Orthodox church. It was understood that a positive and successful solution would again make the Orthodox Karelian population an integral element in the Finnish nation, diminish its isolation, and through all this also strengthen the newly independent young state. The government also wanted to cut off any close, administrative ties linking the Orthodox population in the eastern part of the country with the Russian church on the other side of the border. The government preferred "nationalization" of the Orthodox church in order to assure itself of the loyalty and reliability of the Orthodox population. Thus it is fairly obvious that the policy of the Finnish government toward the Orthodox church was determined in large part by considerations of internal security. It must also be borne in mind that alongside the Karelian (Finnish) Orthodox population, in the eastern part of the country, there were some Russians, particularly in the south, though there were also Russians in the Orthodox parishes in the western regions of Finland. At the time of independence there were approximately 63,000 Orthodox believers in Finland, of whom some 15,000 were Russians. The Russian element thus constituted a significant proportion of the Orthodox component.[2]

After the fall of the tsar, the special committee appointed by the Finnish government presented a plan for ecclesiastical autonomy, although the Finnish diocese would still have been canonically dependent on the church of Russia. This plan, which won considerable support among the clergy and laity of the diocese, was remitted to the so-called All-Russian Church Assembly of Moscow, convened in 1917, but the assembly was dissolved before it could take up this proposal, due to the growing political chaos in Russia at the time. Instead, the synod of the Russian church took certain parts of the proposal under consideration and authorized them after a considerable revision. The real power concerning ecclesiastical development in Finland was, however, no longer in the hands of the Russian synod: the decisions would now be made in Finland.

Although it was possible to say in early 1917 that the Finnish senate remained in the background where the affairs of the Orthodox diocese were concerned, there was clearly a new attitude as early as 1918. In the activity of the senate two goals could be discerned. First, the internal order and administration of the diocese were to receive a Finnish national character. Second, the canonical conditions and situation of the Orthodox diocese were to be altered in the manner necessitated by the changed political circumstances, even if this was not solely in the hands of the political leadership of the country.

After the loss of Russian subsidies, the Finnish Orthodox church found itself in difficult economic straits. In August 1918 the senate decided to grant economic assistance to the Orthodox church for the maintenance of its schools and also for salaries for the clergy. The Karelian Brotherhood had already been dissolved by the senate in July 1918, and its property was later turned over to the Finnish Orthodox church.

The senate took other measures as well, such as expelling several members of the Russian clergy in early 1917. Since it had become impossible to receive new priests from the seminaries in Russia, the church quickly found itself short of clergy, which did not help to deal with the various practical problems created by changed circumstances. Hence the senate came to the church's rescue and established a seminary for the church, undertaking to finance it as a state institution. This was done in such haste that the seminary was able to begin its work in September 1918. Administratively, it was directly under the senate, while the church was in control of religious education and theological instruction. The role of the state authorities was by no means formal: they intervened actively, either openly or behind the scenes, in order to guarantee the national spirit of the seminary. It was expressly forbidden to make any use of Russian in the seminary, in spite of the fact that initially there were no Finnish textbooks available.

Even more important for the Orthodox population in Finland was the detailed and extensive government edict issued on November 26, 1918. This event was regarded, particularly by the Finnish national-minded majority in the church, as a declaration of ecclesiastical independence and as the foundation day of the Orthodox church in Finland. It is ironic that Orthodoxy acquired legal status on a par with the Lutheran church not during the rule of the Orthodox tsars, but at the hands of the non-Orthodox senate of the politically independent new state of Finland.

The main points of the edict of 1918 merit attention. First, it was in principle an act *by* the state authorities *for* the church. Second, although the representatives of the church, including the archbishop, had had the opportunity to express their opinions on the preparatory propositions and even to participate more concretely in the preparation of the edict, the final version was issued on the authorization of the senate, without remission to the church authorities. Third, although certain observers have denied it,[3] every comparison with the church law of the Lutheran church of Finland indicates that several elements in the edict were more or less directly taken over from the Lutheran church law, and thus were not necessarily in harmony with the canonical Orthodox tradition as regards the life and the administration of the church. Fourth, the edict states expressly that the government of the country is the highest administrative authority of the church, although the concrete significance of this is not expounded in any way.[4] As regards the real and formal independence of the church of the state authorities, the points mentioned did not in any way mean a greater dependence than that existing for centuries in Orthodox Russia. The basic difference was that this arrangement had been settled in an essentially non-Orthodox state.[5] It was hardly surprising, thus, that Archbishop Seraphim of Viborg, head of the Orthodox church in Finland, displayed a negative attitude toward the new edict. He was particularly critical of the sections concerning the election and status of the bishops and the ecclesiastical courts. Even a slight comparison with the canons of the church fully explains the dissatisfaction of the archbishop. However, the Finnish government had its way, supported by the broad majority of the Finnish Orthodox, for whom the canonical tradition seemed a comparatively remote thing and in no case a living reality.

The Canonical Status of the Church

The legal status of the Finnish Orthodox church was but one of two central problems concerning Orthodoxy which confronted the government. The question regarding the canonical status of the Orthodox remained open. Because of the difficulties connected with this matter, the whole question was deliberately omitted from the edict of 1918. From the canonical point of view the Orthodox church in Finland, in spite of the edict of 1918, was still a diocese of the Russian church and thus formally under the canonical jurisdiction and authority of the Russian synod, however unrealistic this was under the circumstances and however contrary to the new edict. Archbishop Seraphim made all this quite clear to his congregation and stressed that, in his view, the edict was of temporary duration, pending the approval of the patriarch and the Holy Synod of the Russian Orthodox church. He was firmly convinced that in the event the patriarch of Moscow demanded it, the edict would have to be revised. After a strong protest from the government, however, the archbishop had to modify his public position.

The representatives of the church were divided among themselves regarding the form of the canonical status of the church in Finland. A small minority pleaded for autocephaly, i.e., complete ecclesiastical independence—an idea definitely rejected by the archbishop and also by many others, who thought, in general, that autonomy or self-government should be the immediate goal for the Finnish church. In practice this lack of unity produced the disposition to leave the whole matter to the government. For its own part the government, in the prevailing conditions, was interested

in promoting the evolution of the Finnish Orthodox church into an autocephalous institution, fully independent of Moscow. In the beginning it
seems to have been fairly unclear how this goal could best be achieved or
whether it would prove possible at all.

It was not long before the government adopted a more active attitude
in these matters. In May 1918 the government turned to the parliament
and asked for special powers to settle the religious circumstances in the
country. In the beginning this seemed to pertain only to the conditions of
the Roman Catholic church, which wanted to become disentangled from
the administrative structure in Russia. When the matter was discussed in
the parliament it became clear that the real cause for the request for the
powers in question was to be found in the affairs of the Orthodox church.
It is characteristic of the general attitude of the parliament, in distinction
from the government, that there was very little interest in settling the
affairs of the Orthodox church. The economic aspect of the matter was
nearly the only aspect that was discussed when the question came, after
a considerable delay, before the parliament. During the parliamentary
debate the government maintained that a special new law was needed, not
merely for the Roman Catholic church, but also for the Orthodox church.
The government frankly admitted its ambition to see the Orthodox church
made autocephalous, i.e., independent of any authority outside Finland.
It is undoubtedly obvious that the government had a very clear line and a
very definite policy as to the Orthodox church. It is equally clear that the
government was prepared to intervene in the affairs of the church in order
to fulfill its aims.

The attitude of the government became openly clear at the general assembly of the church held in June 1919, according to the stipulations of the
edict of 1918. One of the matters of the agenda deserves special attention:
the assembly had to express its opinion on the relationship between the
church in Finland and the church in Russia. This was remarkable in itself
in that, though the edict presupposed that the assembly had powers to
make necessary decisions concerning the canonical position of the church,
it was now required to state its opinion on a quite different, though vital,
question. What this meant, in effect, was that the government reserved to
itself the right to make the final decision concerning the canonical position
of the Orthodox church in Finland. During the work of the assembly the
government exerted strong pressure on some and made its position clear
to all. Obviously a majority of the delegates shared the standpoint of the
government and wanted to sever all ties with Moscow, but the matter was
very strange, from the canonical point of view, regardless of the merits

or drawbacks of the government's preferred outcome. Here the national elements of the church were making use of the political, non-Orthodox leadership of the country in open and conscious opposition to the legal and canonical leadership of the church. To say this does not mean that the standpoint of the ruling archbishop should be seen as a positive thing in itself. It only implies that, in the light of the canonical tradition of the church, the attitude of the government and the activity of the national elements among the members of the assembly expressed an obvious lack of understanding—to use a neutral expression—as to the requirements of normal canonicity. In perfect harmony with this manner of dealing with the matter at issue, the assembly was given to understand that the church hardly could expect any economic assistance from the government if it persisted in acknowledging subordination to a patriarch or synod outside the country. The reason given was quite interesting and revealing. It was asserted that in such a case it would not be possible to trust that the church would work in a national spirit for the benefit of "common great moral principles." In comparison with these harsh realities it hardly mattered that the government's principal spokesman also emphasized that it was the right of the church to settle its own canonical relations.

The general assembly came to the conclusion that because the limited resources and circumstances of the Finnish church did not seem to impel autocephaly, it could perhaps be achieved in another way: the Karelian Orthodox parishes in Russian Karelia (in the diocese of Archangel) and the Estonian Orthodox parishes (in the then diocese of Riga) could, together with the Finnish Orthodox church, constitute an ecclesiastical unit large enough to become autocephalous. Without going into any details in connection with the later fate of this suggestion, it is sufficient to say that it could never be made a concrete reality, because it was in practical terms impossible, in the light of political realities. It is worth mentioning, however, that the initial attitude of the Finnish government toward this proposal was positive.

The Government's Campaign Against Archbishop Seraphim

Before dealing with the further development of the canonical status of the Orthodox church in Finland, we have to draw attention to another question regarding which the government played an active role. The Finnish-national elements of the church wanted to diminish the significance and influence of Archbishop Seraphim as much as possible, since he was viewed as the main obstacle to the transformation of the church into an openly

Finnish and national institution and to the reform of its traditional structures of administration. These elements decided that a suffragan bishop could be useful to this end.

The government again openly sided with the national elements, although this implied at the same time a negative attitude to the leading hierarch's opinion concerning various aspects of the matter. With the active support of the government, this question was put on the agenda of the extraordinary general assembly of the church that was convened in 1919. Characteristically, the government's spokesman stated that the government was ready to approve of the election of the suffragan, provided that a specific candidate be approved. The candidate in question in fact received the majority of votes, but the archbishop, who did not participate in the election process, declared that the role of the government constituted interference.[6]

In various ways the Finnish government promoted the national elements in the ecclesiastical administration. Thanks to the government's persistence, the Moscow patriarchate approved of the government edict of 1918 and also granted autonomy to the Finnish church. Actually, political developments had already rendered all contacts impossible between the Finnish and Russian church administrations. The Finnish government played an active role in creating new opportunities for the Finnish church, turning its attention first to Greece and then to the patriarch of Constantinople. Here the Finnish government made fruitful use of the diplomatic services of the Swedish Embassy in Turkey.

The government had already made it clear that it was desirable to elect a new suffragan bishop. A new candidate, a widowed parish priest named Herman Aav, had been found in Estonia. His election, facilitated by certain governmental measures, took place at the first regular general assembly of the Finnish church in 1922. The assembly itself took a very outspoken stand on the situation in the Soviet Union, expressing its disapproval and regret as to the persecution of the Russian church and its leaders. But while the government welcomed the bishop's election, the archbishop did not accept the result and stated that he would not take any action to get the election canonically confirmed. In this situation the government found it ever more urgent to continue its discussions in Constantinople.

As matters proceeded, the attitude of the government toward Archbishop Seraphim became more openly negative. This could clearly be seen in certain developments that took place in September 1922. Professor E. N. Setälä, who had previously represented the government on various occasions in its contacts with the Orthodox church, suggested to the government that the following two steps be taken to promote the development of the church: first, Archbishop Seraphim ought to be removed from his office, either with his consent or not; and second, the government should turn to the central administrative board of the Finnish Orthodox church in order to get its proposal and opinion as to the autocephaly of the church. These goals were eventually reached, but where the latter is concerned, the original suggestions never led to the original goal. From the perspective of this chapter's focus, it is interesting that the deepest motives of the government once more were made clear: according to the standpoint of the Finnish government, it was important for the state that the Orthodox church in the country would achieve a complete independence and thus become definitely free from foreign influence. This was thought to be necessary for both political and national reasons.

Toward the end of September 1922 the government asked the central administrative board of the church to draft a proposal regarding the nature of the highest canonical authority in the church and an application to the ecumenical patriarch for autocephaly for the Finnish church. In addition, the government still sought confirmation of the election of Herman Aav and his consecration by Constantinople as a suffragan bishop. The government gave Archbishop Seraphim a last chance to cooperate, at least formally, but at the same time the situation was made extremely difficult for him, particularly with his canonical loyalty to the Russian church in view.

Archbishop Seraphim unequivocally refused to support any endeavor to turn to Constantinople for help. This meant he was sure to be set aside and to lose all chance of exerting further influence on these matters. As developments unfolded, the church administrative board came to play a central role, without the consent of the archbishop but with the approval and active support of the government of the country. Thus, the documents required by the government were prepared and handed over in October 1922. According to the proposals of the church, a special delegation was to be sent to Constantinople to give the documents in turn to the Ecumenical Patriarchate. The government thought that it would be sufficient to forward the documents through diplomatic channels, together with the statement that the government fully supported it. It was decided, furthermore, that the Rev. Herman Aav, the bishop-elect, should travel to Constantinople at the expense of the state for the canonical confirmation of his election and for the necessary consecration.[7]

In March 1923 Ecumenical Patriarch Meletios sent an unofficial message to Finland. In this message the Finnish church was asked to join the Ecumenical Patriarchate as an autonomous church. The patriarch was of the opinion that the offer was a good one and that the canonical conditions required were very limited. This was not, however, in harmony with the attitude of the Finnish government and thus led nowhere. The government wanted some kind of positive assurance regarding the possibility of autocephaly, before there were any discussions in Constantinople. But when inquiries about these matters were made in June 1923, through the Swedish envoy in Constantinople, the patriarch declared, after having first been somewhat reticent, that he was willing to receive a Finnish delegation in order to settle the matter in the best possible way. The patriarch was not willing to be any more definite than this regarding the question of autocephaly. Interestingly enough, and quite correctly from the canonical point of view, he underlined that the delegation had to have the authorization of Archbishop Seraphim to participate in the intended negotiations.

In early 1923 the government hurriedly conferred Finnish citizenship on the bishop-elect in a way highly divergent from the normal procedure. The government justified this action by observing that he could not assume his duties in Finland unless he was a Finnish citizen and that it was vital to promote the ecclesiastical independence and nationalization of the Finnish church. In March of the same year the president of the republic appointed the Rev. Herman Aav suffragan bishop in the Finnish Orthodox church. In spite of this, the new bishop remained in his native Estonia, as the question of his consecration had not yet been resolved. The government even relaxed the language requirement in his case: only after a period of two years would he have to present a certificate of perfect knowledge of Finnish.

The same law concerning knowledge of Finnish was used against Archbishop Seraphim quite differently; in his case the government opted for a rigid enforcement of the requirement. The position of the archbishop was discussed by the government on various occasions, particularly in the spring of 1923, as it was feared that his remaining in office might create difficulties for the government's plans for the affairs of the church. Even earlier there had been various expressions of the desire to force the archbishop to step down. Professor E. N. Setälä was perhaps the leading advocate of the position that the hierarch should simply be removed "administratively," without any legal procedure. Seraphim had vehement opponents also among the members of his own central administrative board. Now it was decided that the requirements for the language certificate could be used to settle the whole matter in a "decent" way. The government gave the archbishop thirty days to produce the certificate in question, fully aware of his lack of knowledge of Finnish. At the end of the thirty days he was of course unable to prove competence in Finnish. Even so, the government did not dismiss him immediately, since that would have left the Finnish church without any bishop at all, since the suffragan bishop had yet to be confirmed.

Negotiations with Constantinople

When it became clear that the delegation from Constantinople would visit only Poland, and would not come to Finland, the government decided to send a three-man delegation to the Ecumenical Patriarchate, consisting of Herman Aav and Setälä, representing the government, and the Rev. Sergei Solntsev, representing the central administrative board of the church. Of these, only the first two had their expenses covered by the government, even though it was the government that had appointed Solntsev to the delegation. In this connection it became quite clear how weak the church's finances were, in that the church had to obtain a loan from the monastery of Valamo (free of interest), supplemented by a regular bank loan, to pay for Solntsev's expenses.

The Finnish delegation arrived in Constantinople in early July 1923, at a fateful moment in the history of the Ecumenical Throne. The Turkish government had issued an order according to which Patriarch Meletios had to leave the country two days after the scheduled arrival of the delegation. Without the active and effective assistance of the Swedish legation in Constantinople, it would have been impossible for the delegation to have carried out its task. Thanks to Swedish efforts, the patriarch's departure was delayed by several days, and thus the situation was saved for the Finnish delegation. All the same, it is obvious that the atmosphere in the Phanar, the patriarchal center in Constantinople, was greatly troubled during this period.

The patriarch proved unsympathetic to the proposal that the Finnish church become autocephalous, and the contact, which had been established with such difficulty, would have broken down practically in the beginning if the Finnish delegation had not retreated from this proposal. The patriarchate was simply unwilling to grant this demand, not only because the essential presuppositions[8] were lacking, although this had not been understood by all circles in Finland, but also for a very different reason. The representatives of the patriarchate explained in the discussions that there was in the Christian world a clear trend toward unity, which would reunite the different churches, and that it would thus be out of place to create new autocephalous churches. The patriarchate also pointed out that the small size of the Finnish Orthodox congregation did not seem to warrant the grant of autocephaly.

The patriarchate made it clear that a very extensive autonomy under

Constantinople could be granted to the Finnish church, in harmony with the proposal made earlier to Archbishop Seraphim. It is interesting that according to the preserved documents it was in the first place Setälä who argued against the attitude of the Phanar and found it impossible to accept the principle that the bishops should have a general right of appeal to Constantinople. He underlined that, from the point of view of the Finnish government, there were, however, two requirements that were not "dangerous": the commemoration of the name of the patriarch in certain liturgical prayers and the obligation to receive holy myrrh from the Phanar. It is not known to what extent the ecclesiastical members of the delegation fully shared the attitude of the representative of the government. The Finnish delegation was willing to accept the conditions of the autonomy offered by the Phanar, and Setälä explained in the official session of the Holy Synod of Constantinople on July 5, 1923, that a decision could be taken, with a reservation for later approval by the Finnish government. It became exceedingly clear that for him—and for his government—the whole issue was a matter between the Finnish government and the Ecumenical Patriarchate, while it was, for the Phanar, basically a matter of ecclesiastical concern. The text of the agreement was approved by the Holy Synod on July 6, 1923, and communicated to the Finnish delegation the next day. The document is known in Finland as the Tomos of 1923 and regarded as the basic charter of the status of the church. It was ratified by the Finnish government on August 31, 1923.

The Tomos is expressly mentioned in the revised governmental edict of 1925, concerning the Orthodox church. It is a commonly accepted interpretation that the Tomos can be seen as the equivalent of a concordat between the government of the Republic of Finland and the Ecumenical Patriarchate of Constantinople. At first, there was a legal weakness, in that the Tomos was covered in an edict, which could be changed by an administrative decision, not in a law. This was changed in 1969 when a new law concerning the Orthodox church was passed, incorporating elements from previous edicts.[9] As to the character of the Tomos as such, the fact remains that it was not signed by two parties, but by Patriarch Meletios and the other members of the Holy Synod: it was their decision, taken at the request of the Finnish church. In other words, there is no reference to the Finnish government in the text of the Tomos. This suggests that for the Phanar the role of the Finnish government in these matters was that of an intermediary, although of a very involved and deeply interested one.

The canonical status of the Finnish church was not the only matter dealt with in Constantinople. The problems of the consecration of Herman Aav and the calendar question were still open. As to the former, after a canonical election by the members of the Holy Synod, the bishop-elect was nominated the bishop of Karelia to serve as the suffragan bishop of the archbishop of Finland. The solemn consecration took place in the patriarchal cathedral in the Phanar of Constantinople, on Sunday, July 8, 1923. It was the patriarch's last Sunday liturgy in the Phanar before he had to leave the country. As to the calendar, the Finns were asked to follow the decision, made on these matters by the pan-Orthodox congress in Constantinople in June, before the arrival of the Finnish delegation. The congress had approved the so-called Meletian calendar, which differed very little from the Gregorian calendar, the official calendar of Finland. Later on it became clear, however, that the question of the date of Easter remained a problem in that the other Orthodox continued celebrating it according to the Julian calendar.

When the Tomos was ratified in August 1923 the government appointed a committee whose task it was to prepare a proposal to the revision of the governmental edict of 1918. One of the reasons was the need to bring it into harmony with the principle of the Tomos. The constitution of the committee again indicated how actively interested the government was in the affairs of the church: two members represented the government and only one the church, and the latter too was chosen by the government. Setälä presided over the committee, which turned in its proposal in November, urging that the church should be divided into two dioceses.

When the second diocese was established in December 1923 the offices of the bishop and the suffragan bishop were combined, and the suffragan was transferred to the new diocese of Karelia to be its bishop. The edict made no reference to Archbishop Seraphim, who was now placed on the superannuation list, nominally because of his lack of the required language certificate, and confined to a monastery. At the second ordinary general assembly of the Finnish church in June 1925, Bishop Herman was elected archbishop of the church, and owing to the lack of competent candidates, the diocese of Karelia remained vacant. Herman remained the only Finnish Orthodox bishop until 1935 when a second bishop was elected.[10]

The outbreak of the Russo-Finnish War in the winter of 1939 showed to what extent the Finnish Orthodox church had become an integral part of the Finnish nation, in that hierarchy and clergy were uniformly affected by the anti-Soviet nationalism generated by the Soviet invasion. Even the small Russophile currents in the church, in that they were at the same time anti-Soviet, displayed unmistakable Finnish nationalism. Among the Finnish Orthodox there also existed the idea that if the Soviet state were defeated, some sections of Soviet-controlled Karelia might be turned over to Finland, thus enlarging the jurisdiction of the church.

After World War II the Finnish Orthodox church was in a very difficult position. The majority of its members had lived in the eastern province of Karelia, the main part of which had been ceded to the Soviet Union at the close of the Russo-Finnish War (confirmed at the end of World War II). Some 90 percent of the Finnish Orthodox church's property had been located in those parts of Finnish Karelia which were ceded to the USSR, and there were large numbers of Finnish Orthodox believers too, though most of them left their homes at the end of the war and moved to Finland. The Finnish Orthodox church thus had to make a fresh start and to rebuild.

In December 1949 eighteen evacuated parishes (in Soviet-annexed Karelia) were dissolved, and fourteen new parishes were established by government edict. On December 21, 1949, the government passed a law concerning church reconstruction, and the next day issued an edict concerning the property of the dissolved parishes.

The new division of parishes took effect on January 1, 1950. The years 1950 to 1960 were years of energetic reconstruction, with many new churches, chapels, parish houses, and cemeteries created with state funds. A special construction program for chapels was confirmed by the government in June 1953, and in October 1954, after some delay, the first new church was consecrated. Despite the encouragement given to church reconstruction, including the provision of necessary funding, it became obvious in the course of 1959 that the reconstruction program could not be completed within the original schedule. The program was thus extended through the end of 1960, though even then not all the work was completed. Altogether, the state allocated some 862.5 million Finnish marks under the church reconstruction program; in addition, the government turned over 53 million marks to the church's central fund, and gave the church yet another 43 million marks from the funds of the dissolved parishes. The record shows that thirteen new churches, forty-four chapels, nineteen parish houses, and twenty cemeteries were built in all under the ten-year reconstruction program.

Recent Developments in the Finnish Church

A new, greatly revised governmental edict concerning the church was issued in 1953. Subsequently, the church received its first law in 1969, and in 1970 the government issued a new edict relative to that law. With respect to this legislation, a few points should be made. First, it still needs the ratification of the state to become valid, by the parliament and the president in the case of laws, by the government and the president in the case of edicts; but the legislation largely and basically takes place after a proposal by the church assembly, although the government is not absolutely bound by its proposals. Second, certain decisions by church authorities need the approval or the ratification of the government, which means that there is a certain dependence, in principle. In recent years, the government has made it clear, however, that the legislation of the two national churches—the Lutheran and the Orthodox—should be divided into two separate categories: one of them should contain the matters still in need of state confirmation; another one should constitute some kind of ecclesiastical rule, which would be the prerogative of the church alone. The work in this reform has only begun.[11]

The accession of Archbishop Paul in 1960 ushered in a new phase in church-state relations in Finland. The current archbishop has, in particular, engaged the state authorities in discussions and contacts in a more active way than did his predecessor, and especially since the beginning of the 1970s these contacts have often had concrete significance. Since the 1960s the government has shown a benevolent interest in the Karelian cultural tradition, in which the Finnish Orthodox church has played an important part. The growing ecumenical role of the Russian Orthodox church in pan-Orthodox affairs has also, indirectly, stimulated the Helsinki government in this respect.

The church press of the Finnish Orthodox church is relatively uncontroversial and, as a rule, devotes its attention largely to local matters. *Aamun Koitto*, published in Joesuu and edited by Irja Laine, publishes a variety of materials but focuses primarily on events of a local character. This organ has tried to maintain a balanced attitude in matters of church policy and to avoid extremes. Lack of economic resources has imposed certain limitations, though the organ receives an annual subsidy through the general budget of the church, and circulation is limited to 5,500–5,800 copies. *Uskon Viesti*, published in the Helsinki diocese, has a circulation of 11,000 copies.

As to the history of the Orthodox church, a couple of recent events may illustrate my conclusion that the state has not entirely relinquished its active interest in the affairs of the Orthodox church. In May 1945 Patriarch Aleksii of the Russian Orthodox church, in a letter to Archbishop Herman, expressed the opinion that the Finnish Orthodox church ought to return to the jurisdiction of Moscow. To the disappointment of most Finnish Orthodox believers, the government in Helsinki, obviously motivated by political considerations, urged that this request be accepted. The bishops were even urged to sign a declaration to this effect.[12]

The decision was postponed, however, and over the years it became more certain that the Finnish church wanted to remain under the jurisdiction of Constantinople. The Phanar encouraged the Finns in this respect and strengthened their confidence. Although Moscow even offered autocephaly, this did not influence the attitude of the majority, which indicates an interesting development. After various phases, the matter suggested by Patriarch Aleksii was finally put on the agenda of the general church assembly in 1955, and the result was that the assembly pronounced itself clearly in favor of retaining autonomous status under the Ecumenical Patriarchate in Constantinople. This time the government made no move to change this decision. The Moscow patriarchate accepted this result in 1957 and restored its interrupted relations with the Finnish church.

Around 1980, when some circles in the Finnish Orthodox church once again showed an interest in the idea of autocephaly, although without any result, the government once more played its "traditional" role. As the attempt to promote autocephaly presupposed certain additional factors and structures in the administration of the church, above all more bishops, the government acted in 1978, before the official organs of the church had expressed any opinion, and offered to give the church a suffragan, and later on, a new diocese with a third diocesan bishop, while retaining the office of the suffragan, which was now given a permanent status by the state, even though the church had not formally requested it.[13] But the canonical status of the church has remained stable since 1923.

Conclusion

When thinking of the various phases and developments in the relations between the Finnish government and the Orthodox church in Finland, it seems fair to assert that before the national independence of Finland, the tsarist government to a certain extent tried to use the church for political purposes, particularly to further the Russification of the Orthodox population. In independent Finland the state has made strong efforts to nationalize the church, for reasons of national security, among other things. The attitude of the state in the 1940s obviously had its political basis, although clearly misjudged, in a double sense. Regardless of the unclear developments at the outset of the 1980s, it must be strongly underlined that the main interest of the government, in recent years, has been to promote the cultural values of the Orthodox tradition and to strengthen the church's possibilities of surviving as a small minority church in a predominantly Lutheran republic. Orthodoxy and the values represented by it are ever more seen as a positive and enriching element in the entire national life of Finland and thus deserving the support of the state. It remains to be seen whether the newest developments will lead to a more traditionally canonical state of affairs in the structure and life of the church.

The Finnish Orthodox Church

Year of autonomy
  1918: granted by the Moscow patriarchate
  1923: granted by the Ecumenical Patriarchate in Constantinople

Current strength of the church (1983)
  57,607 believers
  50 priests
  4 monks
  5 nuns

Chief news organs
  Uskon Viesti (11,000 copies)
  Aamun Koitto (5,800 copies)

Number of churches and church facilities in operation (1984)
  42 churches
  74 chapels
  1 theological seminary; 1 convent; 1 monastery

Archbishops since 1900
  Archbishop Nicholas, 1898–1905
  Archbishop Sergius, 1906–17
  Archbishop Seraphim, 1918–24
  Archbishop Herman, 1925–60
  Archbishop Paul, 1960–present

15

The Georgian Orthodox Church

C. J. Peters

There are innumerable problems associated with the study of church life in the Soviet Union. There are, for instance, no reliable published statistics on the number of believers, working churches, monks, baptisms, and so on, and Western observers are reduced to less than perfect methods of measurement in their estimates. Official church information is heavily censored, and church leaders are not only prevented from saying what they want, but are forced to say things they do not want.[1] Many of the state's laws relating to religion remain unpublished and parishioners' concern for their jobs, and other social pressures, means that much of church life remains invisible to the outsider.

Given such handicaps, Western students of Soviet church life are forced to draw conclusions from imperfect data. Thus the assumption that there is a link between the strength of belief and the number of baptisms in a country, or between belief and the desire to preserve Christian monuments or wear a cross, are often made. This would not do in the West, but in the study of the Soviet Union two allowances must be made: first, for the lack of precise data; and second, at least in the case of baptisms or church marriages, the recognition that these are acts which oppose official state ideology and may incur punishment (since the 1960s baptisms have officially required the permission of both parents). This and the need in some cases to make a special effort because of inadequate church facilities gives such behavior a different significance than it has in the West. One agrees with Alexander Pyatigorsky that "the only valid measure of religiosity in modern Russia is whether or not an individual considers himself to be religious," but that still leaves us with the problem of measurement.[2]

In the case of the Georgian church (full title—the Georgian Orthodox Apostolic church), we suffer from a further problem. Unlike the Russian Orthodox and Armenian Gregorian churches, it has no large organized diaspora or overseas religious press that can analyze events in the "home church." It remains much more isolated than other Orthodox churches in the USSR.

That is not to say we are devoid of data. Since the 1970s there has been a flood of Georgian samizdat concerning the church, and useful data can be extracted from official sources and church publications. A number of Georgian church calendars have reached the West, and since 1978 a biannual church journal has been regularly published. The ecumenical activities of the present patriarch, Ilia II, have also improved our knowledge of the Georgian church.

A Brief History

Georgians see their church as an important national symbol. In a country with a history of national disunity and constant invasion by Muslim neighbors, the Georgian church is seen as having played a key role in the preservation of Georgian national consciousness and identity. The history of the Georgian church is inseparable from Georgian political history. Historically, the defense of the Georgian nation and the Christian religion went hand in hand. Even under the Christian Russian Empire, religious and national forces combined to reestablish autocephaly (removed by the Russian tsar in 1811), and the church's opposition to Russification policies in both this and the last century are seen as a vital part of the Georgians' fight for national self-expression. This historical identification of the church with the nation, though not as strong as in neighboring Armenia, is an important part of Georgian national consciousness today.

The establishment of Christianity in Georgia is attributed to St. Nino of Cappadocia around A.D. 330. Over the next six centuries, the church of Iberia (the old Eastern Kingdom of Georgia) secured increasing autonomy from the patriarch of Antioch and in 1057 achieved full autocephaly, over five hundred years before the Russian church. The church occupied a powerful position in the Georgian kingdom, but its preoccupation with secular matters and the constant invasions of Muslim armies led to a gradual decline in spiritual life. When its autocephaly was abolished by Alexander I in 1811, there was little opposition among Georgians.[3] The Georgian church was reorganized into an exarchate, and all exarchs except the first were Russian.[4]

The introduction of Russian services and clerics, the replacement of

Georgian feast days with Russian ones, and the low level of the "imported" Russian clergy led R. A. Fadeev to write at the close of the nineteenth century: "People have stopped going to church [in Georgia] even on feast days; they pay nothing to their priests and claim they are strange to them, that they cannot read or speak well in Georgian."[5] A petition by the Georgian nobility to the viceroy of the Caucasus in 1905 blamed the "empty churches" and "extreme misery" of the Georgian clergy on the lack of their own patriarch[6] and urged the restoration of autocephaly. The question was assigned to a commission of the Russian Holy Synod, but was effectively quashed.

Agitation for autocephaly by the Georgian clergy continued intermittently throughout the nineteenth century. It intensified after 1905 and in May 1908 Exarch Nikon was assassinated (it was never discovered by whom) and the most outspoken Georgian clerics were conveniently exiled.[7] Continuing calls by seminary students for teaching in Georgian were firmly rejected by the Holy Synod.

The Restoration of Autocephaly

With the fall of tsarism in 1917 the authority of the Russian Orthodox church among the empire's non-Russian nationalities was seriously undermined. On March 12 (old style) a meeting of Georgian bishops, clergy, and laity announced the abolition of the exarchate and the reestablishment of autocephaly. Metropolitan Leonide was elected locum tenens, and an executive committee was formed to administer church affairs until the election of a new catholicos-patriarch.[8] This was achieved in September 1917 at the first full council of the Georgian church. According to one Georgian observer there was serious rivalry between the supporters of the two candidates, Leonide and Kirioni. Whether the differences were on questions of policy or personality he does not say, but when Kirioni died in September 1918, it led to accusations of murder against the supporters of Leonide.[9]

Kirioni was formally installed as the 133rd catholicos-patriarch in October 1917. He declared triumphantly that "the Georgian church after one hundred years of slavery . . . has regained its independence."[10] The Russian Orthodox church, facing problems of its own, was initially silent,[11] but in December 1917 Tikhon, the new patriarch of Moscow and all Russia (elected November 1917), wrote to the Georgian church leaders condemning their action. He made three points. First, the declaration of autocephaly broke the unity of the Russian church; second, the question of autocephaly raised by the Georgian clergy in 1905 was still in the hands of a Holy Synod commission; and third, over the last one hundred years the Georgian church had not protested its status. Patriarch Leonide, who succeeded Kirioni in 1918, rejected Tikhon's arguments and attacked the chauvinist record of the Russian church in Georgia. Citing canon passed by the various ecumenical councils (Nicaea, Constantinople, and Chalcedon), he declared that the removal of autocephaly in 1811 was illegal, that the commission of the Holy Synod never took Georgia's autocephaly seriously, and that opposition among the Georgian clergy to Russian exarchs and their policies was always evident.[12] After this altercation there was no further dialogue between the two churches until 1943.[13]

In 1917 the Georgian clergy also faced opposition from the Provisional Government, which passed two laws concerning the Georgian church. The first, on March 27, recognized Georgian autocephaly on a national basis but declared that the Russian exarchate should remain intact until a final decision was made by the Constituent Assembly.[14] The Georgian clergy protested that the organizational principle of the Orthodox church was territorial, not national, and that a second ecclesiastical authority on Georgian territory, such as the Russian exarchate, was uncanonical. The protest was ignored, and in July the Russian Orthodox church established a metropolitan see in Tbilisi. The second law of July 25 tried to clarify the position but refused to recognize the Georgian church on a territorial basis. The Georgian church leaders interpreted this and the hostile attitude of Provisional Government representatives such as Professor V. N. Beneshevich (adviser on Georgian affairs in Petrograd) as a continuation of state support for the privileged position of the Russian church.

Before the Storm: 1918–21

The revolution in the Transcaucasus, after an initial experiment in federalism, led to the establishment of three independent states. The Georgian Democratic Republic declared its independence in May 1918.[15] The new government was socialist and Menshevik. Although it was ideologically hostile to religion, it rarely interfered in church affairs, and there was none of the systematic repression that took place in Bolshevik Russia. The Georgian Mensheviks did not see as their task the creation of an antibourgeois dictatorship or the imposition of a proletarian ideology. Rather they strove for national conciliation. Very little government legislation was directed specifically at the church. A project for the separation of church and state was drafted but never passed. In contrast to Bolshevik legislation, the project did not envisage nationalization of church property or disenfranchisement of the clergy, although it did propose as a means of state control that all religious organizations should submit an annual financial report to the Ministry of Internal Affairs. Also, should a religious organization act against the government, its churches could be closed.[16] Only in February 1921, when the country was in the throes of a Soviet invasion, was a law on separation of church and state passed as part of the constitution (Chapter 16, Articles 142–44). The constitution also declared that there could be no restrictions on a person's "political or civil rights for reason of his religion" and that everyone had the right "to profess his own religion . . . or not to have any religious creed."[17]

In practical terms the Georgian church received material support from the Menshevik government. Although seminaries were requisitioned and church lands above a certain norm confiscated as part of the land reform, the government continued to subsidize the church. In February 1920, at the church's prompting, it formally abolished the Russian exarchate in Georgia, and when there were protests in December 1919 after the Georgian church expelled some Russian priests from Sukhumi in West Georgia, the government lent its support and claimed they were being removed for antigovernment activity.[18] Toward the end of 1920 relations deteriorated when it was discovered that church treasures from Gelati monastery in west Georgia were being sold by the clergy to replenish church funds. The government promptly put all the monastery's treasures into state care. The church protested, and sharp words were exchanged at a meeting between President Zhordania and Patriarch Leonide on December 6. However, the pressing concerns of national defense against the Red Army in February 1921 united church and government, and church leaders took a strong patriotic line.

What was the strength of the Georgian church on the eve of Soviet power? In 1913 the exarchate in Georgia, with approximately 1.25 million parishioners, comprised 2,055 parishes, twenty-seven monasteries with 1,098 monks, and seven convents with 281 nuns. There were two seminaries (Tiflis—the old name for Georgia's capital Tbilisi—and Kutaisi) with just under four hundred students between them. In addition there were six diocesan and 380 parochial schools under the exarch's control. There were four dioceses with (in 1900) six bishops, sixty-two archpriests, 1,647 priests, and 231 deacons.[19] In 1917 the Georgian church established four sees, three with metropolitans, one with an archbishop; there were also two bishops in Gori and Alaverdi (both in east Georgia).

There are no statistics for the 1917–21 period. One suspects there was a decline in the number of church schools, as the Georgian government dramatically expanded state education at all levels, and the new Georgian university no doubt took many of the seminary students.

The Church under Soviet Power, 1921–41

With the establishment of Soviet power in Georgia in February 1921, all Soviet religious legislation passed before 1921 was rapidly introduced into Georgia. Henceforth, instructions on religious policy and legislation came from Moscow.

The union-republic relationship that emerged in the 1920s has not changed significantly since. The Georgian Soviet Republic has extremely limited legal powers to formulate an independent legislative policy in the religious or any other field. The laws of the Supreme Soviet of the USSR are binding throughout the Soviet Union and prevail in case of discrepancy over republican laws. In addition, the centralized party organization that effectively controls the formulation and administration of law ensures that the policies of the Georgian government, religious or otherwise, conform with those of the center.

One of the first legislative acts of the new Georgian government (a revolutionary committee) was a decree on the separation of church and state similar to the one introduced in the RSFSR in January 1918. The Georgian version, passed in April 1921, remained the basic guideline for religious policy in Georgia in the twenties.[20] Compared to subsequent religious laws, it was quite liberal. It made religion "the private business of each citizen" and all had the right "to profess, or not to profess, religious belief." Paragraph four declared that any laws and decrees limiting this right were null and void. On the other hand, all church property was nationalized (the church could lease back the property it needed for religious observance), religion could not be taught in state or public schools, the church was not granted a legal personality, and it could not collect "obligatory dues" from its members. The freedom to practice one's belief "only in so far as it does not encroach on the rights of citizens of the Soviet Republic" was guaranteed by paragraph six (paragraph five in the RSFSR decree). Although on the face of it this was a reasonable stipulation, it was used both in Georgia and Russia to restrict the public expression of religious belief.

The Georgian constitutions of 1922 and 1926 and the 1922 constitution of the Transcaucasian SFSR (a federated republic of which Georgia was a part until 1936) all recognized the freedom of religious and antireligious propaganda,[21] but following the RSFSR example, the Georgian constitutions disenfranchised "monks and spiritual servants of the church and religious cults."[22]

The Georgian criminal code of 1926, based on that of the RSFSR, emphasized the protection of political order and introduced the concept of the "socially dangerous act" and the "counterrevolutionary" crime. These could be applied to any "act or omission directed against the Soviet state" (Art. 5) or to "the spreading of propaganda or preservation of literature" that called for the weakening of the Soviet state (Art. 58), and were used against religious organizations.

Chapter four of the code was devoted to violations of the law on the separation of church and state. It was a crime to use "religious prejudices" to deceive the masses into opposing Soviet law, to teach religion in private and state schools, and for religious organizations to fulfill "administrative, judicial, or other public functions."[23] A Georgian government decree in July 1923 laid down further rules for religious societies. They had to register with their local soviet and give full details of their organization, membership, and aims. If they did this, they were entitled to a church and other property necessary for religious observance.

Such laws crippled the Georgian church both economically and judicially. The laws were imprecise enough to allow a wide degree of interpretation. A plenum of the Georgian party central committee in October 1924 warned against misapplication of the law: "In the sphere of antireligious propaganda . . . the party organizations must be ordered to stop closing churches. . . . In those regions . . . where a certain part of the peasantry demands the opening of a church, they (the party organizations) must allow and facilitate this."[24] A month later at a further plenum, members were told that "talk of the peasant not wanting churches and willing to see their closure is self-deceit."[25]

There was a spate of warnings against overzealous measures after an attempted rising by a Menshevik-led underground Independence Committee in Georgia in August 1924, although there was no direct church involvement in the revolt. Before the uprising, the regime had been more militant in its approach, in particular using the services of the Georgian Komsomol (Young Communist League). It had produced its own antireligious journal (*rhvtis tsinaarmdeg*) (Against God) on the lines of E. M. Yaroslavsky's Moscow journal *Bezbozhnik* (The Atheist), and V. Lominadze, a secretary of the Georgian party central committee, had proudly boasted in 1923 that in a few months in west Georgia local party organizations had closed 1,500 churches.[26]

In July 1921 Patriarch Leonide died. He was succeeded in September by Patriarch Ambrosi, who adopted a firm anti-Soviet position. In February 1922 he sent a daring appeal to the Inter-Allied Conference in Genoa, due to meet in April. It was fiercely patriotic and anti-Russian. It talked of the 117 years of "cruel despotism" suffered by Georgia under "Russian bureaucratism" and accused Russians of always oppressing small nations. He

declared that the "occupying forces" were desecrating Georgia's language
and culture and that the church, "which for centuries constituted the main
strength of the grandeur and power of the national Georgian State, is
today deprived of all its rights to such an extent that it is no longer able to
procure the permanent means for its very existence."[27]

The publication of the appeal led to an orchestrated press campaign
against the church, and in February 1923 Patriarch Ambrosi and the nine
members of his church council were arrested. They were accused, like
Patriarch Tikhon and his followers in Russia, of refusing to comply with
the February 1922 decree (issued in the RSFSR, although a Georgian version
followed in November 1923) which demanded that church treasures not
needed for religious use be given to the state for famine relief. Ambrosi
was found guilty and sentenced to eight years' imprisonment, and four
of the church council received between two and five years. The rest were
acquitted, although one of the defendants, Archbishop Nazari, was shot
while "trying to escape."[28] The trial and imprisonment of Ambrosi, which
caused considerable public indignation in Georgia, was a serious blow to
the church. He was released shortly before his death in March 1927.

After the trial the Georgian authorities, in line with the policy adopted
at the twelfth congress of the Russian Communist Party (Bolshevik) in
April 1923, tried to halt what they called "administrative measures"
(forcible closures of churches and intimidation of believers) and concentrate on "scientific propaganda." They were unable to exploit any schisms
within the Georgian church like their counterparts in Russia and neighboring Armenia,[29] although there are indications that Ambrosi's successor,
Patriarch Kristopore II, sympathized with the Russian reformist "Living
Church" movement. More important for the Georgian authorities was Patriarch Kristopore's public statement of loyalty to the Soviet regime in
1927 following the example of Metropolitan Sergii in Russia. Kristopore
repudiated the Genoa appeal of Ambrosi and denounced the anti-Soviet
activities of Georgian émigrés.[30]

Kristopore's move produced little in return. By 1928 the Georgian
church had little influence and could not teach in schools or take part in
charitable work. Nor did it have many intellectual resources, and there
was a shortage of new blood. Kalistrate Tsintsadze, who became patriarch
in 1932, noted that in 1923 the Tiflis seminary received only four pupils.[31]

The shift toward rapid industrialization and collectivization in 1928
was accompanied by a new All-Union Society antireligious campaign. A
plenum of the Georgian party central committee in June 1928 called for
"the strengthening in every possible way of work on the antireligious

front by organizing the necessary propaganda and agitation, by the formation of circles around the paper *Atheist* . . . and by antireligious education in the schools."[32]

In 1929 a new decree on religious associations was introduced in the RSFSR and other republics that gave the state enormous powers of control over church life. Religious societies (which required a minimum of twenty persons) could not establish libraries, make group excursions, meet in private buildings (other than in a church or specially adapted building), or hold conferences without permission, and they were liable to instant liquidation if they broke their own rules. Representatives of the local authorities responsible for supervision of religious organizations could attend any meeting and could refuse to register a society if its "methods and forms of authority are contrary to the laws in effect, or threaten public order and safety," (Art. 46 of the RSFSR decree.) As the teaching of religious faith in "state, social, and private" educational institutions was now banned (Art. 18 of the RSFSR decree), the right of religious propaganda was, logically, removed from the constitution.[33]

The collectivization campaign met with serious resistance, and a temporary halt was called by Stalin in March 1930. A central committee resolution of the same month ordered party committees to stop closing churches, as this had also antagonized the peasantry. Although the antireligious campaign continued, there was a slight improvement for believers until 1937.

Patriarch Kristopore died in the spring of 1932. He was succeeded by Patriarch Kalistrate, who reigned for the next twenty years. Until the war, when church-state relations dramatically improved, the Georgian church was reduced to a shell-like existence. Throughout the thirties, antireligious propaganda continued, and unlike anywhere else in the Soviet Union, the League of Militant Godless maintained high membership levels in Georgia. According to Walter Kolarz, the league had 101,586 members in Georgia in 1931, and by 1938 it had climbed to 145,413, or 4 percent of the republic's total population.[34] They had as many atheist lecturers as the province of Moscow, and between 1930 and 1941 they produced four atheist journals.[35]

There is some disagreement among Western scholars as to the scale of religious persecution in Georgia in the 1930s. Elia Melia argues it was less harsh than elsewhere because of the lack of believers and priests, whereas Kolarz, citing the strength of the Georgian atheist organizations, believes it was worse.[36] Whatever the degree of persecution, the result was the almost complete elimination of the Georgian Orthodox church. One Georgian émigré recalls that in Upper Imereti, west Georgia, in the

1930s there was only one priest and no working churches.[37] In 1937, in recognition of the contracting church organization, the Georgian Holy Synod introduced a rule permitting "one-man administration" by the patriarch.[38]

Nevertheless, the state failed to eradicate all religious observance. From the evidence of conversations with Georgian émigrés, secret baptisms continued in particular. This is confirmed by Valerian Sangulia, son of a Georgian priest, in a testimony to a U.S. Congress select committee in 1954.[39] There is also evidence that with the suppression of the Christian faith, there was a resurgence of old Georgian pagan beliefs, particularly in the mountain areas.[40]

The War and After: Interlude, 1941–59

The war years brought significant changes to the Georgian church. In common with other major religious organizations in the USSR, it received official recognition of its canonical status and was awarded limited judicial rights, including the right to rent and acquire church buildings. For the Georgian church, however, reconciliation with the Russian Orthodox church in 1943 was perhaps more important, as it meant an end to its religious isolation within the USSR.

The state's change in attitude was due to a recognition of the link between the church and nationalism. During the war the Georgian church, like its Russian and Armenian counterparts, set up a war fund and urged defense of the state. In 1942, on the twenty-fifth anniversary of Soviet power, Patriarch Kalistrate sent a telegram to Stalin and congratulated him on "this important day," wishing him the strength to "break the spine of the enemy" and expel them from "the sacred borders of our great homeland."[41] Kalistrate's loyalty was rewarded when in October 1943 the Russian Orthodox church, probably on Stalin's instructions, recognized Georgian autocephaly.[42]

The Russian church justified its change of heart, which ended years of "mutual recriminations, suspicion, and sad misunderstandings," on the basis of Georgia's independent territorial unity within the USSR.[43] No mention was made of the Georgian church's canonical rights to autocephaly. Patriarch Sergii ordered all Russian and Armenian parishes in Georgia to submit to Georgian church authority. Archbishop Anton, who traveled to Tbilisi to formalize the new agreement, declared that recognition implied the cessation of Georgian church relations with dissident Russian Orthodox groups.[44]

Recognition of Georgian autocephaly and other concessions exacted a price. Henceforth public proclamations of loyalty to the Soviet regime were de rigeur, particularly in the field of foreign affairs. After the war Kalistrate joined the Soviet campaign against the "opponents of peace." He participated in various "Conferences of the Defenders of Peace" and in August 1950 signed a joint appeal for peace with the Russian and Armenian patriarchs addressed to "all the Christians of the world."[45] He also condemned British and American involvement in Korea.

Although such collaboration continued throughout the fifties, the anti-religious struggle was not halted completely. Decrees were passed by the CPSU Central Committee in 1944, 1948, and 1954 calling for greater effort in antireligious work; a new All-Union Society for the Dissemination of Political and Scientific Knowledge was set up in 1947, and in 1949 Georgian First Party Secretary K. N. Charkviani reported the expulsion of forty-nine people from the Georgian Communist party for "observing religious rites."[46]

Nor was there any significant revival of the Georgian church after the war, as in Russia. The Georgian church did not produce a journal (like the Armenian and Russian churches), and Kalistrate failed in his attempts to reestablish a seminary. In 1956 there were only seven students training as priests, and the 1980 edition of the Georgian church calendar noted that during this period "there were so few Georgian clerics that the service in the native language was rarely taken."[47]

In April 1952 a new patriarch, Melkisdek III, was elected following the death of Kalistrate earlier that year. He continued the policy of public support for the Soviet government, and within a month of his election he attended a peace conference in Moscow. Very little is known about Melkisdek, and he presided over a period of extreme quiescence in the Georgian church.

Khrushchev's Antireligious Campaign, 1959–64

In 1959 Khrushchev, alarmed at the growth of the church since the war and keen to demonstrate his "orthodoxy" despite his de-Stalinization measures, launched a new attack against religion. The Georgian party, led by First Party Secretary V. P. Mzhavanadze, a Khrushchev appointee, launched its own campaign as early as spring 1959, when a number of anti-religious articles began to appear in *Zaria Vostoka*.[48] At the end of April there was a conference of local atheist propagandists, and in May a conference of the propaganda and agitation department of the Georgian central committee. Both emphasized the need for improved atheist propaganda, and the latter boasted a recent "great increase in work." It announced the establishment of scientific-atheistic circles in thirty-eight Tbilisi schools and claimed that 1,600 lectures on atheist themes were read in 1958.[49] At the twentieth congress of the Georgian party in January 1960 Mzhavanadze urged "more offensive" antireligious propaganda.[50] The campaign led to the establishment in Tbilisi of seven "atheist universities," fifteen lectureships in scientific atheism, and the preparation of over one hundred atheist propagandists (the latter in 1963 alone).[51] However, in January 1964 Mzhavanadze was still insisting on "serious improvements" to counter "church-going or sectarianism which has recently increased."[52]

During the Khrushchev period the Georgian church experienced growing state interference in its affairs. The two councils set up by Stalin during the war that were attached to the All-Union Council of Ministers and designed to serve as a liaison between church and state were transformed in the early sixties into powerful supervisory organizations of church life.[53] They were given wide administrative and legislative powers and had to be consulted on any draft of legislation involving religion. They had extensive rights of observation and could refuse to register a religious society or nullify an existing one. In their surveillance of religious societies they were aided by the local militia, special departments in local soviets, Party commissions, and the KGB. The councils (which amalgamated in 1966 to form the Council for Religious Affairs) were centralized organizations and they appointed representatives to the regions. The representative attached to the Georgian council of ministers has always been Georgian. At present there are also representatives in Batumi and Sukhumi in west Georgia. It is difficult to judge the degree of flexibility permitted in the application of policies decided in Moscow, but because of the separate Georgian church organization some allowance is probably made.[54]

In December 1960 the Georgian Supreme Soviet published a new Georgian criminal code. It was an improvement on the one operating under Stalin, and the principles of guilt by association and crime by analogy were dropped. Two new chapters on personal rights were introduced. The chapter on the political and labor rights of citizens included the articles previously listed under crimes against the separation of church and state (Articles 148 and 149 in the 1960 Georgian code). However, Article 233, which expanded Article 58 of the old Georgian code, made it a crime to direct a group "whose activity, although carried on with the appearance of preaching religious beliefs and performing religious ceremonies . . . causes harm to the health of citizens or with any other infringements of the person or rights of citizens."[55] Such a vague formulation, which was repeated in other republican codes, gave the authorities a great deal of scope. Also, Article 71 on anti-Soviet agitation and propaganda differed little from provisions on counterrevolutionary agitation applicable in ear-

lier Soviet codes. It covered mere possession of literature which defamed
the Soviet political or social system.

The Georgian church suffered from Khrushchev's measures, but because
of its long stagnation, not to the same extent as the Russian Orthodox
church, which lost approximately half of its churches. Perhaps one minor
indication of the impact of antireligious measures in Georgia was in the
1960 Georgian church calendar, which, compared to the previous year,
was much shorter and contained many omissions.[56] On the other hand,
in 1963 Patriarch Eprem II (elected in February 1960) published a New
Testament and a Prayer Book (263 pages) and opened a two-year religious training school (officially recognized as a seminary in 1970). These
concessions may have been in recognition of Eprem's loyalty, or could
have been connected with the Georgian church's application to the World
Council of Churches in 1962. The Soviet government might have felt it
advantageous to have as many seats as possible on the World Council's
central committee, a possibly useful propaganda platform.

When the latter met in August 1962, Eprem personally traveled to Paris
to put his church's case. He informed the World Council in his application
that the Georgian church had seven bishops, 105 priests, eighty parishes,
two monasteries, two convents, and a publishing house (compare this with
the 2,055 parishes and 1,700 clergy at the beginning of the century).[57]
After admission of his church, Eprem in a speech of thanks claimed that
there were 4 million Christian inhabitants in Georgia, 1 million of whom
were not believers.[58]

When Eprem died in April 1972 there were only two metropolitans and
three bishops, with ten of the fifteen dioceses unoccupied. Only forty-
four churches were working. Toward the end of the sixties there was
a revival of religious interest in Georgia due in part to the relaxation
of the antireligious campaign under the post-Khrushchev leadership, but
Eprem's continued subservience to the regime began to provoke opposition among believers. In 1965, at a ceremony in Svetiskhoveli Cathedral,
Eprem allegedly declared: "You present have read and no doubt know
the 1961 [party] program. This program is wonderful. After two decades
people will live well, as Jesus Christ predicted in his time, but it needs
more work from us. Idlers and loafers will not find paradise in the other
world."[59] Zviad Gamsakhurdia, a Georgian human rights activist who
campaigned against church corruption in the 1970s, claimed Eprem in his
later years was intimidated by the authorities. He refused to lend books to
lay members of the church or open a library for them and allegedly told
Gamsakhurdia that "when Moscow plays the piano, we must dance to its
tune."[60] Gamsakhurdia also accused Eprem of simony and of permitting

abuses by the Georgian clergy.[61] Under Eprem, there were indications of
strained relations with the Russian church. In 1961 the Georgian church
had no representative at the Pan-Orthodox Conference in Rhodes. The
authorities blamed "visa problems," but Elia Melia believes the exclusion
of a Georgian representative was with the connivance of Patriarch Aleksii
of Moscow, who stipulated as one of the conditions of the Russian church's
participation that the ecumenical patriarch communicate with the Georgian church only through Moscow.[62] In 1962, during Eprem's visit to Paris,
conflict with the Russian church representatives led to his early departure
on the same day he was invited to attend a Russian church service. However, with the gradual acceptance of the Georgian church's autocephalous
status in the international Orthodox community, the Russian church no
longer challenged its canonical rights.

The Georgian Church since Khrushchev, 1964–84

With the fall of Khrushchev in 1964, crude antireligious propaganda and
excessive coercive measures were dropped. Such measures, it was claimed,
had only driven religion underground and encouraged the formation of
"unofficial" sects.

The religious policies (as distinct from policy on dissent) under L. I.
Brezhnev, Y. V. Andropov, and K. U. Chernenko continued the pattern adopted since 1945. This entails preferential treatment for the established churches (as opposed to the unofficial sects) combined with an
extension of the administrative and legal controls over religious communities. In March 1966 the presidium of the RSFSR Supreme Soviet passed
two resolutions and a decree that expanded existing legislation on religious
cults (the Georgian Supreme Soviet Presidium followed suit in October
1966), and in 1975 (March 1977 in Georgia) a new law on religious
associations was passed that gave the Council for Religious Affairs wide
discretionary powers and, for the first time, juridical status.[63]

Khrushchev's religious policies had provoked serious opposition among
some members of the established churches, which in the first half of
the sixties had spilled over into active dissent. Religious protest became
closely intertwined with national and civil rights movements. Until the
late seventies political constraints prevented a major crackdown, but with
the cooling of East-West relations, the invasion of Afghanistan, and partial boycott of the Moscow Olympics, such constraints were removed and
most leading dissenters, religious or otherwise, were arrested. This did not
affect the "official" churches, as long as they remained within the narrow
framework of Soviet religious law.

Antireligious propaganda in Georgia from 1964 until the fall in disgrace in September 1972 of V. Mzhavanadze, the Georgian party first secretary, took on a desultory character. At the twenty-third congress of the Georgian Communist party in March 1966, Mzhavanadze made no mention of religion in his attack on "survivals of the past." There was some attempt to replace religious festivals with secular ones (a recurring theme in Georgian antireligious campaigns) and excessive Georgian funeral feasts (kelekhebi) were singled out by *Izvestiia* as "a harmful tradition."[64] However, overall there is little evidence in the Georgian press of any systematic antireligious activity during this period.

The new ideological enemy in the sixties—as Mzhavanadze indicated in a speech in 1966—was nationalism.[65] The relaxation of economic and political controls from Moscow under Khrushchev and his successors led to the consolidation of power by the Georgian political elite. It pursued pro-Georgian policies that discriminated against other national minorities within the republic and allowed the development of economic and political "localism." There was also a growing national awareness among Georgians that the weakening of ideological controls over art and literature under Khrushchev allowed them to express themselves more openly. This growing national pride may in part have been due to Khrushchev's campaign against nationalism and his denigration of Stalin. The church benefited from the new mood among Georgians, as Mzhavanadze indicated in 1964, but at the same time it suffered from the spread of corruption among the republic's political and economic institutions. The moral decay of the church and its manipulation by the authorities came into the open in the 1970s.

In April 1972 Eprem died. In a highly controversial election in July the church council chose Metropolitan David of Urbnisi as his successor. According to an unpublished report by David Koridze, an assistant procurator in Tbilisi, the election "took place in illegal circumstances." He alleged Eprem's will was falsified in favor of Metropolitan David, that key church leaders who should have been invited to the Holy Synod to approve the new patriarch's candidacy were not, and that David V, as he became, did not fulfill the Georgian canon law requirement that the patriarch have higher education.[66] Koridze declared that the Georgian church, particularly since the accession of David V, was on "the path of complete degeneration." He accused Bishop Gaioz (Bidzina Keratishvili), who was secretary to Eprem II, of stealing church property, and David V of restoring to church employment "persons who had previously been expelled from the clergy for corruption, immorality, drunkenness, and other criminal activities."[67] He claimed that the local representative of the Council for Religious Affairs, D. Shalutashvili, was involved in illegal activities in the church, as were KGB representatives and the wife of the party first secretary, Victoria Mzhavanadze. Koridze insinuated that between them they extracted large amounts of money and valuables from the church. The report, which was circulated in the Georgian party central committee in 1973, produced no action. This was surprising, given that the new party first secretary, E. A. Shevardnadze (appointed September 1972), was leading a fierce anticorruption campaign in the republic. The inaction gives some credence to dissident Zviad Gamsakhurdia's assertion that important officials outside Georgia were involved in the scandal, or that the Mzhavanadzes still exercised considerable power within government circles in 1973. In October 1974, after a translation of his report had reached the West, Koridze was summoned to the KGB, and despite his thirty years' party membership was accused of being anti-Soviet and a believer. The following year he was compulsorily retired.[68]

The situation in the church highlighted by Koridze was based on oppositional reports of certain parishioners, in particular Valentina Pailodze, Teimuraz Djvarsheishvili, and Zviad Gamsakhurdia, who all petitioned the government for action. Gamsakhurdia took the case to Shevardnadze, but nothing was done until May 1978, when Bishop Gaioz was arrested for selling church precious stones.[69] His trial in the summer of 1979 confirmed Koridze's accusations. He was sentenced to fifteen years after over 288,000 rubles' worth of valuables was found in his flat.[70]

Throughout the 1970s Georgian religious samizdat proliferated. Much of it dealt with the corrupt church leadership.[71] An attempt was made by Djvarsheishvili and others to set up a "Christian court" in January 1974, to investigate accusations against the church hierarchy, but KGB intimidation prevented its taking place.[72] Soon afterward Djvarsheishvili was arrested and sentenced in August 1975 to four years' corrective labor for alleged rape.[73] Valentina Pailodze was tried in June 1974 for writing anonymous letters that "insulted the Soviet social system and people," and for systematically conducting "religious propaganda." She was sentenced to one and a half years' imprisonment.[74]

Gamsakhurdia, the most active campaigner against corruption in the Georgian church, was finally arrested in April 1977. A member of the church since the mid-sixties, he provided a link between the civil rights and dissident religious movements in Georgia. Along with Merab Kostava, Victor Rtskhiladze, and others, he founded the Initiative Group for the Defense of Human Rights in Georgia (1974) and the Georgian Group to Assist the Implementation of Helsinki Agreements (1977).[75] He produced two Georgian samizdat journals in the mid-seventies, the *Georgian Mes-*

senger and the *Golden Fleece*, which contained a large number of articles on the church. He was active in the church's defense against Russification, and identified the Georgian church with the general struggle for national self-expression. Gamsakhurdia was sentenced to three years' imprisonment and two years' internal exile for "anti-Soviet propaganda." His removal seriously weakened the opposition movement within the Georgian church.

David V took part in the campaign against Gamsakhurdia. The 1976 Georgian church calendar published a speech by Archbishop Gabriel made in 1882, which was a thinly veiled attack on Gamsakhurdia. Gabriel condemned "secret, anonymous . . . letters" and betrayals of the church to the government.[76] Six days before Gamsakhurdia's arrest, an article entitled "No Slander" appeared in *Literaturuli Sakartvelo* signed by David V, Metropolitan Gaioz, and two other bishops. It accused Gamsakhurdia without any apparent foundation of being an "incorrigible hooligan" and condemned the "sectarianism" that with "Satan's help has established itself in some Georgian church circles."[77]

The struggle in the church highlighted the extent of government interference in ecclesiastical administration. From Koridze's report and other samizdat materials, it was clear that the KGB was closely involved in securing the election of David V. According to Gamsakhurdia he was informed in 1972 by R. Metreveli, a member of the Georgian central committee: "I have been told to choose the candidate for the patriarchate, and I am asking the opinion of the intelligentsia representatives."[78]

Every church council is attended by the local representative of the Council for Religious Affairs, and in an open letter to Brezhnev in March 1982, Gamsakhurdia complained that the present incumbent in Georgia, Givi Maisuradze, "interferes not only in the placing of priests and especially bishops, but in various minor matters of church life."[79]

David V's record as patriarch was poor. He made no attempt to fill the ten vacant eparchies or improve the quality of services and the priesthood, and refused funding for restoration work. According to Koridze, teaching at the seminary went into serious decline under David V.

The Georgian Church Today: Rejuvenation?

David V died on November 9, 1977. On December 23 the present patriarch, Ilia Shiolashvili (Ilia II) was elected at the age of forty-four. Under Ilia, who had graduated both from the Moscow Theological Seminary and its academy, the fortunes of the Georgian church—at least on the surface—improved. Within his first year a record number of seven diocesan bishops were appointed, and by 1980 all fifteen eparchies were reestablished and filled. Churches were reopened and a new stone church built in Batumi. A restoration program was inaugurated and a corresponding architecture and building department set up in the patriarchate. Ilia, who was an active ecumenist before his election, also established a foreign relations department. In 1979 he was made one of the six presidents of the World Council of Churches, and the Georgian church also joined the Conference of European Churches.[80] A whole series of improvements were introduced to the seminary, including grants, better teachers, and uniforms. Besides the church calendar, which is of high quality, a new biannual church journal, *jvari vazisa*, started to come out in 1978. A publication entitled *Theological Studies* is also regularly produced. A modern Georgian translation of the New and Old Testaments has begun, and a number of extracts have been published in the church calendars. In an interview in February 1980 Ilia claimed there were two hundred working churches in Georgia, 150 more than under Eprem II.[81] However, despite his popularity, Ilia has his critics. Gamsakhurdia accuses him of "opportunism, " and more recently he has been charged by a number of the Georgian higher clergy with nepotism (Ilia's brother, who has no theological training, is secretary to the patriarchate), self-aggrandizement, arrogance, and neglect of moral standards among the priesthood. Ilia's two severest critics are Metropolitan Shio of Batumi and Shemokmedi and Bishop Ambrosi of Nikortsminda. In an open letter to Ilia they complained of widespread homosexuality and depravity among Georgian clergy and of misuse of church funds. They accused Ilia of turning a blind eye to such abuses and of failing in his patriarchal duty to cleanse the church.[82]

Ilia, like every patriarch since 1921, has to operate within very narrow confines. If he is to achieve concessions from the state (the opening of new churches, increase in seminary students, money for restoration), he must profess public loyalty for the regime and its policies. This he has done. He has condemned the right-wing Christian militia in Lebanon, the Chinese invasion of Vietnam, the neutron bomb, and praised the peace program of the Soviet Union.

On the other hand, Ilia has not proved totally subservient to state demands, and in 1980 he signed a statement by the World Council of Churches that condemned the invasion of Afghanistan.[83]

In the 1970s and 1980s the state has continued its ideological battle against the church. In Georgia antireligious propaganda has been part of a much broader assault on ideological "backsliding." In March 1972, in a prelude to the removal of Mzhavanadze later that year, *Pravda* printed a CPSU Central Committee decree condemning the party organization in Tbilisi for, among other things, "inadequately tackling ideological work."[84] The installation of Shevardnadze as Georgian first party secretary led to an all-out attack on corruption in Georgian life. Within two years 25,000 people were arrested, 9,500 of them party members, although many seemed to have been released without trial.[85] Antireligious propaganda concentrated on religious festivals, church marriages, baptisms, and other "harmful traditions." Evidence from government and church officials is that such work has had little impact.

In November 1975 the Georgian central committee signaled a new stage in the campaign against religion when it passed a decree calling for the strengthening of the struggle against "harmful traditions." Two new organizations were created, the Republican Commission on Propaganda and the Introduction of New Traditions and Rituals and the Center for the Scientific Coordination of Problems of Social and Cultural Traditions, to direct "antireligious propaganda and propaganda for new socialist traditions."[86] The number of people's universities was increased from 350 in 1972 to 520 in 1977, and a new Center of Festivities was formed in 1978 to introduce new festivals and improve secular marriage services.

Such measures have not brought the desired result, and all the agencies concerned with antireligious work have been criticized by the party. One year after the 1975 decree, T. Panjikidze, writing in *Zaria Vostoka*, noted that "very little" had been achieved, and blamed it on the "inertia" of the organs responsible.[87] In March of the following year, the same author declared that a significant part of the population still observed "customs characterized by religious forms."[88] At conferences of "Ideological Workers" held in 1976 and 1978, soviets, party committees, and people's universities came under attack for poor results. Finally in 1981 at the Georgian twenty-sixth party congress, Shevardnadze sharply criticized "Tsodna," the Georgian Society for the Dissemination of Political and Scientific Knowledge, for "formalism" in its propaganda and agitation.

The attempt to introduce secular festivals has had mixed success. *Zaria Vostoka* admitted in 1979 that religious festivals "continue to attract many of our youth," and in another article in 1980 confessed that the new festivals and civil wedding ceremony were "unsatisfactory for many."[89]

Although the official policy is to fight religion by "democratic means," coercion is also used. Georgian samizdat have recorded a number of occasions when religious festivals have been forcibly prevented.[90] Those attending Easter services are frequently detained as they leave the church, and there are numerous cases of people being dismissed from their jobs or the party for religious sympathies.[91]

The government has shown particular concern at the growing influence of religion on Georgian youth. At the twenty-fifth Georgian party congress in 1976 Shevardnadze referred to "a certain reorientation in the convictions of a part of our population, particularly the youth,"[92] and in 1982 I. Orjonikidze, first secretary of the Georgian komsomol, condemned the increasing number of young men applying to the seminary, and the "not insignificant" proportion of couples who choose a church wedding.[93] In one of his latest articles T. Panjikidze admitted that the number of people attending church had increased over the last decade. He went on: "It is the young people in church who capture one's attention. . . . They are for the most part well-dressed . . . with intelligent faces. You cannot say of any of them that they have come to church out of ignorance or lack of education."[94]

One recent statistical survey of 1,500 young Georgians (eighteen to thirty-three years) showed that only 46 percent considered religion a "negative phenomenon" (there was no breakdown of the percentage who disagreed with this view, possibly for ideologically unpalatable reasons). V. Lordkipinadze, the new Georgian komsomol first secretary, reported to the Georgian party central committee in July 1983 that ten thousand baptisms and one thousand church weddings occurred every year.[95] Another concern of the Georgian party, which Lordkipinadze also highlighted in his report, was the growing fusion of nationalist and religious dissent among Georgians.

In this century, despite assimilationist pressures, Georgians have continued to consolidate their ethnic separateness. In the last fifteen years Georgian national pride, combined with a fear of growing Russification, has resulted in an increasingly assertive nationalism. This has been particularly evident since 1978, when a demonstration of at least five thousand people protested at an attempt to remove the clause confirming Georgian as the state language of the republic from the new Georgian constitution. Since then, there have been frequent nationalist outbursts going beyond the small circle of dissidents, generally concerned with the decline of the Georgian language but often touching on the rights of the Georgian church.[96]

Georgian dissident nationalists view a free Georgian church as a vital part of their national struggle. Gamsakhurdia, in an open letter to a local newspaper, declared: "The struggle against the Georgian church is a struggle against the Georgian language and culture . . . surely it must be clear that atheist propaganda today . . . fights the very idea of Georgia."[97] In February 1978 leaflets were distributed calling for the defense of Georgian "historical monuments, language, and the Georgian church," which represented the "nation's spiritual buttress," and in 1981 approximately five hundred demonstrators gathered in a religious building, Svetiskhoveli Cathedral, to commemorate the 1978 language demonstration.[98]

The church itself takes a more cautious, but strongly patriotic line. It celebrates the great Georgian heroes of the past, publishes articles in defense of Georgian language and culture, and assigns the church a vital role in the historical development and preservation of Georgian national consciousness. For instance, Ilia II in his Christmas message of 1980 declared that "without Christianity we would not be a distinctive nation, we would die," and went on to praise the Georgian language, warning his listeners that "where language declines, so the nation falls."[99] The 1976 calendar edited by Bishop Gaioz was even more explicit in its defense of the Georgian language. It contained an article by Archbishop Gabriel (written in the 1870s) that rejected the idea of a single language in a multinational state. Gabriel wrote: "The union of a small people with a large one . . . is possible—in spirit, heart, and mind . . . but the destruction of its language is not possible, and its preservation will not harm or hinder such unity."[100]

Conclusion

The Georgian church today is probably at its strongest this century as an organization. Ilia II has achieved important improvements while keeping the Georgian government content with his professions of political loyalty. Under Ilia II, as *sakartvelos kommunisti*, the Georgian party theoretical journal, has had to admit, the "churches have come to life."[101] The church's influence among the population is not as great as that of its Armenian counterpart, but it is incomparably greater than it was twenty years ago. However, the church still faces serious internal problems which put its support among the population in jeopardy. Ilia does not seem to have overcome the problem of corruption in church ranks.

The growth of the Georgian church has alarmed the Georgian government, but given the volatile nature of Georgian society, especially its youth, overt repressive measures could be counterproductive, possibly dangerous. The party continues its propaganda campaign and probably reasons that by a combination of social pressure (demotion or removal of practicing believers at work) and tight administrative control of church activities, it can keep the religious resurgence within limits. It continues to repress, however, all religious dissidence.

The growth of religious belief in Georgia is symptomatic of a much broader ideological disaffection. The problem is that Marxist ideology in the Soviet Union has become nothing more than a rationalization of the status quo and can no longer provide inspiration for young educated

Georgians who feel an intense attachment to their language and culture. The Georgian church, particularly under its new patriarch, Ilia II, provides an alternative avenue for national pride and expression.

Ilia II has practiced the "art of the possible" more successfully than any other Georgian patriarch this century. He summed up his policy, which has brought some stability to Georgian church-state relations, as follows: "The state and church . . . are separated, we must always remember this. At the same time the church has its own mission and its own tasks, which must be achieved within the requirements of present conditions."[102] This policy, for which there is little alternative in Soviet conditions, has produced some good results. However, the church remains firmly under state control, and is at the mercy of any future change in Soviet religious policy.

FACT SHEET

The Georgian Orthodox Church

Year of autocephaly
 Patriarchate of all Georgia
  established 1057*
  abolished 1811
  reestablished 1917
 Catholicos-patriarchate of west Georgia
  established 1390
  abolished 1795

Current strength of the church
 5 million members (1979); number of believers unkown
 180 priests
 40 monks
 15 nuns

Chief news organs
 sakartvelos eklesiis kalendari (4,500 printed in 1982)
 jvari vazisa (1,000 printed in 1984)

---

*There is some dispute as to when full autocephaly was established. The Georgian church dates autocephaly from when the first catholicos (Peter) was sent from Constantinople to Georgia in 471, although it is not clear whether he or his successors were fully independent of the patriarch of Antioch before the eleventh century. Other evidence points to the achievement of autocephaly in the middle of the eighth century.

Number of churches and church facilities in operation
    200 churches (estimated)
    1 theological seminary (10 students per year maximum allowed)
    3 convents (1984)
    4 monasteries (1984)

Patriarchs since 1900
    Kirioni II (Sadzaglishvili), 1917–18
    Leonide (Okropiridze), 1918–21
    Ambrosi (Khelaia), 1921–27
    Kristopore II (Tsitskishvili), 1927–32
    Kalistrate (Tsintsadze), 1932–52
    Melkisdek III (Pkhaladze), 1952–60
    Eprem II (Sidamonidze), 1960–72
    David V (Devdariani), 1972–77
    Ilia II (Shiolashvili), 1977–present

16

The Ukrainian Autocephalous Orthodox Church

Bohdan R. Bociurkiw

The post-1917 history of the Ukraine offers an example of a modernizing religious organization that attempted to restructure the Orthodox church and reinterpret its doctrine in such a way as to bridge the gulf separating it from the contemporary Ukrainian national and social aspirations. This ecclesiastical organization, known officially as the Ukrainian Autocephalous Orthodox church (UAOC),[1] forms the focus of this study. Without delving into the continuing polemics concerning the "canonicity" of this church, this chapter will attempt to reconstruct briefly the genesis and evolution of the UAOC and analyze the changing Soviet policy toward it through the church's forcible "self-dissolution" in 1930. The chapter will also deal with the limited reconstitution of this church in the same year, under a changed name and statute, as the "Ukrainian Orthodox church" and its gradual liquidation during the 1930s, and conclude with a brief account of the revival of the UAOC in German-occupied Ukraine 1941–44.

The Russian revolutions of 1917—in their political, social, and nationalist dimensions—led to the rapid disruption of the symbiotic relationship of tsarist autocracy and Orthodoxy. This process culminated in a revolutionary disestablishment of the Russian Orthodox church effected by the Bolshevik separation decree of February 5, 1918.

The secularization and expansion of the new revolutionary polity[2] involved a total secularization of education, law, and public life, a nationalization of the entire ecclesiastical property, and the imposition upon the church—now deprived even of a corporate status—of the far-reaching polity dominance. The Soviet regime undertook a complete transvaluation of political culture with religion condemned to eventual extinction, to be replaced with a secular "political religion" officially designated as "Marxism-Leninism."

In the Ukraine the secularizing impact of Bolshevik rule was delayed by two years, by the emergence of at first autonomous and then independent Ukrainian statehood. Until 1919 the Orthodox church in the Ukraine was threatened not by the loss of its established status but by the rise of the Ukrainian national church movement. From the perspective of this movement's leaders—a small group of the "nationally conscious" urban priests, military chaplains, and lay intellectuals—the Russian Orthodox church appeared to represent a major obstacle to the national and social emancipation of the Ukrainian people; the church's past role as a legitimizer of autocracy, imperial unity, and the old social order, its hostility to "Ukrainian separatism," its contempt for the Ukrainian language, its employment of religious sanctions against "rebels" (e.g., Hetman Ivan Mazepa [1639–1709]) and, in recent memory, its close collaboration with the reactionary Union of the Russian People—all these features of the old religio-political system have contributed to the alienation of the large majority of the Ukrainian intelligentsia from the established church prior to World War I. The Ukrainian church movement, which combined the renovationist objectives of the church's post-1905 "liberals" with Ukrainian national and social aspirations, was determined to wrest the control of the church away from its conservative Russian episcopate and infuse it with the Ukrainian values, culture, and language through the democratization of its structure. Hence the movement's three guiding principles of "autocephaly," "Ukrainianization," and "conciliarism" (*sobornopravnist*). Perhaps more basic was the movement's desire to bring the church into the mainstream of the Ukrainian revolution as a legitimizing, integrating, and nation-building force that would bolster the fragile structure of the Ukrainian state.

The Ukrainian church movement failed to realize its objectives during the short-lived Ukrainian statehood.[3] Opposed by the Russian episcopate and the conservative majority of the clergy, it was unsuccessful in its attempts to secure a timely and forceful intervention on its behalf either from the socialist-dominated Central *Rada* or from the conservative Hetman regime. When finally the Directorate decreed in January 1919 the autocephaly of the Orthodox church in the Ukraine,[4] it was too late. Before it could effectively "Ukrainianize" the church, the Ukrainian state was engulfed by the successive waves of the invading Bolshevik and White armies.

Paradoxically, it was only after the Soviet takeover of the Ukraine that the autocephalist movement, centered on the All-Ukrainian Orthodox

Church Council (Rada) in Kiev, could successfully challenge the Russian control over the church through an ecclesiastical "revolution from below." Having "recognized" the Soviet separation decree[5] (at the time when the Moscow patriarchate continued its confrontation with Lenin's regime), the Ukrainian autocephalists took advantage of the new legislation by promptly "registering" a number of Ukrainianized parishes under the All-Ukrainian Orthodox Church Council; by early 1920 the government formally recognized the Union of Ukrainian Orthodox Parishes as a separate ecclesiastical organization in the Ukraine under the All-Ukrainian Rada. Soon afterward the Russian episcopate suspended all clergy of the Ukrainianized parishes to which the Rada responded, in May 1920, with a formal proclamation of autocephaly for the Ukrainian Orthodox church.[6]

The three-year-old struggle for control of the church between Russian nationalism entrenched in the hierarchy and the upper clergy and Ukrainian nationalism of the lower clergy and lay church intelligentsia thus culminated in a split of the Orthodox church in the Ukraine into two hostile entities: the Russian (patriarchal) church headed by a Moscow-appointed exarch, which derived its strength from its control of the entire hierarchy in an episcopate-centered church, as well as from its canonical continuity and habitual allegiance of the conservative majority of believers; and a minority Ukrainian Autocephalous church centered on the lay-dominated councils (*rady*) that embraced the nationally conscious believers attracted by the national language and rites of the church and its message of national independence, ecclesiastical democratization, and social radicalism.

Having severed its links with the Russian episcopate, the All-Ukrainian Church Rada was able at first to secure archpastoral leadership for the Ukrainian Autocephalous Orthodox church in the person of a retired Ukrainian archbishop, Parfenii Levytskyi of Poltava. However, when the Russian episcopate decided in February 1921 to unfrock all the autocephalist clergy and ordered, under threat of anathema, an immediate dissolution of the UAOC, Archbishop Parfenii broke off his connections with the latter.[7] With no bishop now willing to assume the canonical leadership of the Ukrainian Autocephalous church or to ordain its episcopate,[8] the First All-Ukrainian Sobor of the UAOC, which met on October 14–30, 1921, took a fateful decision to create its own episcopate by resorting to what it claimed to be the practice of the ancient Alexandrian church.[9] On October 23 Archpriest Vasyl Lypkivskyi, the spiritual leader of the Ukrainian church movement and one of the organizers of the All-Ukrainian Church Rada (in 1919 he celebrated in Kiev the first liturgy in the living Ukrainian language), was ordained metropolitan of Kiev and all Ukraine through the laying on of hands by the clerical and lay members of the sobor;[10] then jointly with the sobor members, Metropolitan Lypkivskyi consecrated Archpriest Nestor Sharaivskyi as another bishop, and late in October the two hierarchs ordained four other priests as bishops for several Ukrainian dioceses. This departure from the established Orthodox procedures as well as a series of canonical reforms adopted by the 1921 sobor not only alienated some clerical supporters of the Ukrainian church movement but also resulted in a virtual isolation of the UAOC from other Orthodox churches, which refused to recognize the canonic validity of its episcopate.

Nevertheless, despite a determined opposition on the part of the Russian church, the UAOC rapidly expanded its following among the Ukrainian peasantry and intelligentsia. By early 1924 it embraced thirty bishops and approximately 1,500 priests and deacons, serving nearly 1,100 parishes in the Ukrainian SSR.[11] At the peak of its influence, the Autocephalous church might have had as many as three to six million followers.[12] The UAOC seriously weakened the hold of the Russian church over the Ukrainian peasantry, especially in the provinces of Kiev, Podill'ia, Chernihiv, and Poltava, and it virtually deprived it of any following among the Ukrainian intelligentsia. During the 1920s the influence of the UAOC spread beyond the Ukraine into Ukrainian settlements in Central Asia, among émigrés in Western Europe, and in particular to the Ukrainians in the United States and Canada, where a separate diocese was formed (with some 148 parishes by 1927) under Archbishop Ioan Teodorovych.[13]

After 1922, regardless of the autocephalist protestations of loyalty to the Soviet system, Soviet authorities began to impose increasingly severe restrictions upon the Ukrainian Autocephalous church, which they accused of nationalistic tendencies. Having failed to force a merger between the UAOC and the regime-supported "Living Church" in 1922–23,[14] the authorities attempted during the next three years (1923–26) to split the former by manipulating internal cleavages within its leadership, offering their support to "progressive" factions within its ranks—in particular, the so-called Active Christian church.[15] When the Active Christian church failed to seize control of the church, the Soviet police resorted to direct administrative repressions in the summer of 1926, suppressing the activities of the All-Ukrainian Church Rada and arresting the primate of the church, Metropolitan Lypkivskyi. The government made it clear now that the church would be allowed to function only if it would adopt a more "acceptable" policy, under such new leadership as would have the confidence of the authorities. By playing on the growing anxiety in the Autocephalist ranks about the future of the UAOC and by encouraging hopes that submission to the government's pressure might assure the church of some of its long-denied rights, the authorities succeeded in bringing about a change in the leadership and orientation of the UAOC. There was a striking analogy between the line taken by the regime in the Ukraine and the tactics used to break down the remaining opposition in the Russian Orthodox church.[16]

In return for its confession of political error and the purge of Metropolitan Lypkivskyi and some other Autocephalist leaders unacceptable to the regime, as well as the church's adoption of a more loyalist posture vis-à-vis the regime including its submission to stricter governmental control, the Soviet Ukrainian government allowed the UAOC to resume its activities and to hold its second sobor in 1927. This sobor now elected Metropolitan Mykolai Boretskyi to replace the purged Lypkivskyi.[17]

Despite the fact that some new concessions were now offered to the church, including the dissolution of the Active Christian church, the UAOC had to pay an additional price for its survival in terms of the growing alienation of its grassroots following, who grew suspicious of the new Autocephalist leadership. Indeed, some laymen openly accused the new All-Ukrainian Rada of having sold out to the atheist state. Perhaps this deepening division between leaders and followers was one of the principal expectations motivating the shift in the regime's tactics toward the UAOC.

By mid-1928 the Soviet authorities began to withdraw their recent concessions to the reformed UAOC. Its publications were suppressed and more and more of its churches and clergy were deprived of the official registration. By the summer of 1929 the Soviet secret police (OGPU) began mass arrests of Autocephalist leaders and clergy, without sparing even those who had faithfully collaborated with the regime in purging the old church leadership. In November of that year the OGPU announced the alleged discovery of a "counterrevolutionary" League for the Liberation of the Ukraine and accused the UAOC of having served as a branch of this organization[18]—an accusation that amounted to a death verdict for the Autocephalous church.

The end was not long in coming. Terrorized remnants of the Autocephalist episcopate and clergy were assembled at the so-called Extraordinary Sobor in Kiev in January 1930 and compelled to dissolve the UAOC and to admit to all charges addressed against it by the authorities. The resolution of this sobor—undoubtedly drafted with the participation of OGPU[19]—sheds some light on the motives underlying the Soviet decision to liquidate the Ukrainian Autocephalous Orthodox church. According to this resolution,

After liberating itself from political-monarchic oppression, the UAOC was not destined to become a true Christian church, free and removed from the peculiar nationalistic, chauvinistic politics (*politykanstvo*). This is a fact, because the UAOC was reborn during the political struggle and it was revived and later led by people who had suffered defeat on the open political front and who, having joined the church, intended to, and actually did, exploit it as an instrument for further struggle against the Soviet regime and hence also against the justice of the social revolution.

It was natural that the leading organs of the UAOC . . . revealed themselves through clearly non-ecclesiastical actions of a nationalist-political, anti-Soviet, counterrevolutionary nature. The same can also be said of the clergy of all ranks, beginning with Metropolitan Lypkivskyi. . . .

All this, accordingly, made the UAOC a synonym of counterrevolution in the Ukraine. . . . Under the circumstances, *it was completely logical that autocephaly should become a symbol of Petliurite independence, that Ukrainianization should be exploited as a means of inciting national enmity, and that conciliarism should transform itself into a demagogical means of political influence in order to reach the appointed end.*[20]

At the Kharkiv show trial of the so-called League for the Liberation of the Ukraine, held March 9–April 19, 1930, the Ukrainian Autocephalous church was cast in the role of an essential link between the accused prominent Ukrainian scholars and writers and the popular masses.[21] While the UAOC was represented at the Kharkiv trial by only three persons, they included the chief lay ideologist of the church—Volodymyr Chekhivskyi—who was presented as the evil spirit of the UAOC, through whom the League had allegedly directed every move of the church.[22] Chekhivskyi and other defendants were given lengthy terms in the Gulag. Metropolitan Mykhail Boretskyi and many bishops and clergy of the UAOC were imprisoned or exiled without even the benefit of a show trial. Most of them were never to be seen alive again.

Not long thereafter the Soviet authorities apparently developed doubts about the wisdom of having abolished all the central and regional organs of the UAOC, as the church retained a significant following in the Ukraine. Hence, less than two months after the trial of the league, an All-Ukrainian Provisional Organizational Church Committee was organized in Kharkiv, under the leadership of Archbishop Ivan Pavlovskyi.[23] Obviously with official blessing, the committee addressed a circular letter to some three hundred surviving Ukrainian parishes on June 9, 1930, inviting them to unite in a single church organization,[24] provided that they would sign a declaration pledging unconditional loyalty to the regime and renouncing all political activity.[25]

The Second Extraordinary Sobor of the UAOC, which met in Kiev December 9–12, 1930, once again condemned the past activities and leadership of the UAOC and confirmed its dissolution. Having done that, it then declared itself the sobor of a "Ukrainian Orthodox church," pointedly dropping the politically suspect term *Autocephalous* from the name of the church.[26] The sobor also reviewed the canons approved at the 1921 all-Ukrainian sobor, and removed those provisions that had been assailed by the regime as politically unacceptable. The conciliar principle (*sobornopravnist*) became one of the principal victims of this apparently officially inspired revision. Accordingly, the new organizational scheme adopted by the December sobor removed laymen from direct participation in the ecclesiastical government, which was now centered in the episcopate. At the head of the church now stood the metropolitan of Kharkiv and all Ukraine, Ivan Pavlovskyi, who also headed the "new" all-Ukrainian church Rada, with its membership, however, limited to three priests.[27] The surviving Ukrainian parishes were now gathered together in seven dioceses, each to be governed by a bishop assisted by two priests; together, they formed the diocesan rada.[28] The sobor warned all members of the church, however, that "should anyone express in [his] ecclesiastical activities views hostile to the Soviet regime, he would harm the cause of the church and shall be subjected to ecclesiastical punishment."[29]

The tactical nature of the Soviet concessions to the "new" Ukrainian Orthodox church soon became apparent. The short lease on life granted to it by the Soviet regime proved to be only a prolongation of the church's agony. The surviving Ukrainian parishes were burdened with extremely high taxes, which impoverished and demoralized the faithful.[30] With more and more parishes finding it impossible to meet this exorbitant taxation, the total number of Ukrainian parishes fell to two hundred by 1933.[31] Not long after the Second Extraordinary Sobor, the police resumed their arrests of Ukrainian bishops and clergy, driving some of them to repudiate the priesthood and even religion.

By August 1934, only two Ukrainian parishes were still functioning in Kiev,[32] and in the fall of that year only one remained intact, served by Metropolitan Pavlovskyi, who moved to Kiev following the transfer of the Soviet Ukrainian capital there.[33] In the spring of 1936 even this single parish was closed by the authorities.[34] The last Ukrainian parish was apparently liquidated sometime in 1936,[35] although as late as April 1939 the

Ukrainian Godless claimed that some isolated or disguised autocephalist parishes still existed in the Ukraine.[36]

In February 1938 the secret police (redesignated the NKVD) arrested Metropolitan Vasyl Lypkivskyi, who had been living in forced retirement since 1927.[37] Taken to Kiev, he was either shot in prison or deported from the Ukraine, meeting his death in exile, as he was never heard from again.[38]

By the end of the 1930s nearly all of the churches, Orthodox (of all orientations) and non-Orthodox, were wiped out in the Ukraine. Not a single active bishop remained in the republic within its pre-1939 borders. Of no more than a dozen churches still open, the majority evidently recognized the authority of the patriarchal locum tenens, Sergii, and one or two remained in Renovationist hands.

Soviet occupation of the western Ukraine in September 1939 brought under the Kremlin's rule the populous Orthodox diocese of Volyn with its lively national church movement. During the interwar period, when this eparchy had been part of the Autocephalous Orthodox church of Poland, this movement had succeeded in Ukrainianizing a significant part of Volyn's 689 parishes and in having one of its ecclesiastical spokesmen, Polikarp Sikorskyi, ordained in 1932 as Bishop of Lutsk, vicar of the Volyn diocese.[39] The immediate effect of the Soviet occupation was the disappearance of the Ukrainian language from church services and the regime-supported efforts by the moribund Moscow patriarchate to extend its jurisdiction over the Volyn diocese. In the spring of 1940 the patriarchate dispatched its exarch, Archbishop Nikolai Iarushevich, to Volyn; he was able to persuade the diocesan archbishop, Oleksii Hromadskyi, as well as one of his vicars, to formally accept the supremacy of the Moscow patriarchate, which Bishop Polikarp (and, in the adjoining Polissia diocese, Archbishop Aleksandr Inozemtsev of Pinsk) refused to do.[40]

As the Germans invaded the USSR in June 1941, a spontaneous religious revival began in German-occupied Ukraine, with believers reopening or reconstructing churches and searching out the surviving clergy to minister in these churches. The episcopal leadership in this spontaneous resurgence of Orthodoxy in the Ukraine came from the Volyn and Polissia hierarchy, which—in the manner resembling interwar church history—split by early 1942 into the majority Autonomous church, recognizing the canonical authority of the Moscow patriarchate, and the minority Ukrainian Autocephalous Orthodox church. However, in contrast to its interwar predecessor, the UAOC reestablished in the winter of 1941–42 was headed by canonically ordained bishops with Archbishop Polikarp Sikorskyi as administrator of the UAOC, under the spiritual authority of Metropolitan Dionisii Valedinskii of Warsaw.[41] The latter's support of the revived UAOC, as well as the vital assistance rendered to this church by Archbishop Alexander Inozemtsev of Pinsk, were not without historical irony: both senior hierarchs were Russian. It is also significant that the wartime Ukrainian Autocephalous Orthodox church broke with its predecessor's "revolutionary" approach to Orthodox canons. But as it expanded into central and eastern Ukraine, the new UAOC found it necessary to admit into its ranks, without reordination, over two hundred surviving Autocephalist priests of the old UAOC—an act that earned it a lasting condemnation by its Russian critics.[42] Its only hierarchical link with the interwar church in the Soviet Ukraine was supplied by Metropolitan Feofil Buldovskyi of Kharkiv, one of the early pioneers of Ukrainianization in 1917, who had left the ranks of the patriarchal episcopate in 1925 to establish, together with four other canonically ordained bishops, a canonical alternative to the Ukrainian Autocephalous Orthodox church of Metropolitan Lypkivskyi.[43] In 1942 Buldovskyi joined the new UAOC, bringing into its ranks several hundred parishes in left-bank Ukraine. Eventually, the Ukrainian Autocephalous Orthodox church in the German-occupied Ukraine expanded to fifteen bishops and some 1,500 clergy,[44] attracting into its ranks the more nationally conscious strata of the Ukrainian Orthodox, who welcomed the reintroduction of the Ukrainian language in liturgy and the revival of native religious traditions of the church.

To heal the widening ecclesiastical rift, leaders of the Autocephalous and Autonomous churches met in Pochaiv in the fall of 1942 and reached a tentative agreement to unite the two groups into a single Ukrainian Autocephalous Orthodox church. The union failed to materialize, however, in the face of strong opposition on the part of the Russian-oriented majority of the Autonomous bishops and, in particular, due to the intervention of the German occupation authorities, who clearly preferred a continued ecclesiastical conflict.[45]

With the German retreat from the Ukraine in 1943–44, all the Autocephalist bishops except Metropolitan Buldovskyi, and part of the clergy, sought exile in the West. In the territories reoccupied by the Soviet army, representatives of the Moscow patriarchate incorporated those Autonomous bishops who remained in the Ukraine, and the Autonomous clergy, into the Russian Orthodox church. The remaining Autocephalist parishes were also absorbed into the patriarchate's jurisdiction, while Metropolitan Buldovskyi and some clergymen were stripped of their sacerdotal functions. An unknown number of Autocephalist priests and lay activists were subjected to police and administrative repression. Since World War II the Ukrainian Autocephalous Orthodox church has existed only in the West.[46]

The Ukrainian Autocephalous Orthodox church was a religious manifestation of a great surge of Ukrainian national consciousness that had begun with the nineteenth-century cultural revival and that reached its political culmination in the revolution of 1917 and the subsequent struggle for an independent state. The revolutionary energies released by the events of 1917–19, although frustrated politically, were channeled into the cultural and spiritual renaissance of the 1920s, until the latter was abruptly and brutally stopped by the massive terror applied against the Ukrainian cultural elite after 1929.

Throughout the 1920s the Ukrainian Autocephalous Orthodox church was perhaps the most important organized expression of the new urge of the Ukrainian people to reaffirm their own identity, to emancipate themselves from the forced status of a spiritual and cultural colony of Moscow, and to follow their own unique path of national development freely. This should not be taken to mean, however, that the UAOC was a predominantly secular phenomenon, alien to true religiosity. Although strongly affected by the national and social ideals of the Ukrainian Revolution, the Autocephalous church was above all an outgrowth of, and the answer to, the genuine religious needs of a large and important segment of the Ukrainian people. Although it lacked the canonical status enjoyed by the Russian Orthodox church, the Ukrainian Autocephalous Orthodox church probably came closer to the Orthodox ideal of the Christianization of popular life. To its faithful, it offered a profound religious experience intensified by the use of a familiar language, of national rites, and of the symbolism that was a part of folk tradition. It was a popular church, free of rigid distinctions between the priesthood and the laity and drawing the latter into almost every phase of ecclesiastical functions and activities. The servants of this church knew apostolic poverty and encountered ridicule, calumnies, and persecution from both the atheist regime and the former established church. In common with other religious communities in the USSR, the Ukrainian Autocephalous church had its share of weaklings and defectors, but it nevertheless contributed a disproportionately large number of martyrs during the years of antireligious terror.

As a religious body, the UAOC was subjected to the same legal and administrative limitations and repressions as the other churches in the Soviet Union, but, unlike the others, it was completely destroyed by the regime, which never again, even with the arrival of the wartime "religious NEP," allowed the restoration of the Ukrainian Autocephalous church. The reason evidently lies in the other facet of the UAOC—the fact that it was also a national institution embodying Ukrainian aspirations toward ecclesiastical and spiritual independence from Moscow.

Religious nationalism has not been the exclusive preserve of the Ukrainian church. An integral feature of national Orthodox churches, such nationalism has been an important element for centuries in Russian Orthodoxy, especially in its attitude toward the Russian state and the minority nationalities of the empire. Indeed, the passionate identification of the Moscow church with the Russian national interest was not only accepted but came to be explicitly praised by the Soviet leadership after the late 1930s. In the final analysis, it was primarily Russian nationalism that provided the common ground for the paradoxical alliance between the Russian Orthodox church and the Soviet state during and after World War II. Thus, what was condemned as the chief vice of the Ukrainian church became, in the eyes of the Kremlin, the principal virtue of the Russian church—a dual standard that became characteristic of Soviet nationality and religious policy in the Ukraine.

FACT SHEET

The Ukrainian Autocephalous Orthodox Church

Year of autocephaly
  1919: declared by Directorate
  1920: proclaimed by the All-Ukrainian Rada

Strength of church (1924)
  30 bishops
  1,500 priests and deacons
  1,199 parishes
  3–6 million believers
  No monasteries or seminaries

Metropolitans
  Of Kiev
    Vasyl Lypkivskyi, 1921–27
    Mykolai Boretskyi, 1927–30
  Of Kharkiv
    Ivan Pavlovskyi, 1930–36
  Archbishop
    Polikarp Sikorskyi, 1941–44 (declared metropolitan in 1942;
    1945–53, metropolitan of the Ukrainian
    Autocephalus Orthodox Church abroad.)

17

Minor Orthodox Churches of Eastern Europe

Suzanne Gwen Hruby, Leslie Laszlo, and Stephan K. Pavlowitch

Among the more neglected churches of the Orthodox community are the Polish Autocephalous Orthodox church, the Macedonian Orthodox church, and the Orthodox congregations in Hungary. In large part these are the religious organizations of ethnic minorities: of Ukrainians and Belorussians in Poland, of Serbs, Romanians, and Bulgarians in Hungary, and of Macedonians in Yugoslavia. As such, these churches play a peripheral role in the politics of their respective countries, and their demeanor tends to be docile and uncontroversial. Both the Polish and Macedonian churches are creations of the twentieth century, with the latter established, with the regime's blessing, in 1967 as part of Belgrade's effort to authenticate its claim that the Macedonian people has a culture and identity of its own, that is, distinct from the Bulgarian.

The Polish Autocephalous Orthodox Church

As a religious community of national minorities—chiefly Ukrainians, Belorussians, and Russians, but also encompassing Lemkians,[1] Greeks, Czechs, and some Poles—the Orthodox church in Poland was caught between the competing interests of the Polish crown and the Russian. Because the Orthodox were extended patronage by an expansionist neighboring power that was also Eastern Slav and Orthodox, their very existence assumed a political character. Within Polish popular culture, Orthodoxy came to symbolize an alien force tied to Poland's traditionally most repressive and culturally aggressive enemy, Russia, and Poland's Orthodox faithful were deemed unreliable citizens.

There can be no doubt that the tsarist program of Russifying those parts of Poland it had seized in the late eighteenth century profoundly influenced Polish attitudes about nationality and religion and that those attitudes have affected relations between Poland's Catholic and Orthodox communities throughout this century. The Russian authorities' persecution of Catholics strengthened the Poles' identification of their own culture and ethnic identity with Catholicism, since the Roman Catholic church served as the primary vehicle of continuity in Polish culture when the Polish state had ceased to exist. Simultaneously, collective feelings about Orthodoxy were colored by the Polish sense of humiliation inspired by the partitions and Russian control. Orthodoxy acquired a negative connotation, symbolizing a foreign enemy's aggressive policy for subverting the Poles' national identity and religion of choice. For many Poles the Orthodox church became associated with Russian cultural and political imperialism, and they thereby overlooked its separate Ruthenian historical legacy.

After Poland's statehood was restored following World War I, the country's Orthodox community, estimated at four to five million, confronted the staggering task of rebuilding and unifying the church after more than a century under Russian domination.

At the beginning of the First Republic, the Orthodox remained under the Russian church's jurisdiction. However, the bishop of Warsaw, Jerzy Jaroszewski, and his supporters in the hierarchy soon began to advocate full independence for the church. Not surprisingly, the new Warsaw government, with an eye toward increasing its own influence by removing the Orthodox from a foreign ecclesiastical authority, urged the church to separate from the Moscow patriarchate through autocephaly. But autocephaly was resisted by a Russophile faction within the church leadership,[2] which contended that the church was bound by unbreakable historical ties to the Russian mother church and warned that autonomy would make the Orthodox in Poland more vulnerable to enforced union with the Roman Catholic church.

Despite the clergy's division on the issue, a general episcopal synod proclaimed autocephaly in 1922, citing canon law and Orthodox tradition.[3] Patriarch Tikhon of Moscow agreed to give Poland's Orthodox a certain measure of autonomy and raised Bishop Jerzy to the rank of provincial metropolitan. But insisting on Moscow's supremacy over the Orthodox population in Poland, the Moscow patriarch refused to grant complete self-government.

The mounting controversy over autocephaly took a violent turn in 1923 when a Russian monk, Smaragd, assassinated Metropolitan Jerzy to protest the church leader's policy. Yet Jerzy's death did not deter the movement for a self-governing Polish church. Rebuffed by Patriarch Tikhon, the Polish hierarchy turned to the patriarch of Constantinople, who used the historical argument that the 1685 transfer of the Kiev metropolis to Moscow was a simonical act in order to grant complete independence under Metropolitan Dionizy Waledynski, Jerzy's successor, on November 13, 1924. The Russian church was virtually the only Orthodox church that refused to acknowledge this act of autocephaly.

Within Poland's Orthodox community a small number of Russian adherents did not accept the church's new canonical status, on the grounds that independence could not be realized without the Russian church's approval. They created an "Old Church" parish in Wilno that continued to recognize the Moscow patriarch as their spiritual leader.[4] Several of the bishops who had opposed autocephaly were either confined to monasteries or encouraged, and sometimes pressured, to emigrate.[5]

The church was governed by a holy synod, which included the metropolitan (patriarch of Warsaw, Volhynia, and all Poland), and four bishops, who had to be approved by the civil authorities. Each of the church's five dioceses—Warsaw-Chelm, Volhynia-Krzemienic, Wilno-Lida, Grodno-Nowogrodek, and Poliesia-Pinskia—was governed by its own bishop and synod. Two seminaries in Wilno and Krzemienic, as well as a faculty of theology attached to the University of Warsaw, provided religious training for approximately five hundred clerical and lay students. In addition to an official review, the church published two religious weeklies—one each in Russian and Ukrainian.

Normalization of relations between the Orthodox church and the state remained a major stumbling block throughout the period between the wars and caused the Orthodox considerable frustration and anxiety. Among their grievances against the government, the Orthodox were especially sensitive to the fact that the constitutions of 1921 and 1935, while formalizing the principle of religious liberty, also accorded the Roman Catholic church a preeminent position among Poland's religious denominations and that the government granted the Catholics special privileges. (For example, with some minor exceptions, the government agreed to pay Catholic priests' salaries and made Catholic religious instruction on public school premises mandatory.)[6]

It was not until the end of 1938 that the state formally defined the church's legal status. According to the government decree issued on November 18, the church was to enjoy complete freedom of action within the scope of state legislation. The document declared the episcopal synod, consisting of bishops and clerical and lay representatives, as the organ of church authority. The metropolitan was to be elected by an electoral synod composed of clergy and lay representatives from each diocese. Candidates for the office of metropolitan had to receive approval from higher government authorities. Polish was designated as the church's official language, except that other languages could be used when individuals or other institutions addressed the church in a language other than Polish. The church was made responsible for praying for the welfare of the Polish Republic and its president. In exchange, the government assured legal protection of the Orthodox church's institutions equal to that extended to other religious denominations. The Orthodox secular and regular clergy were to enjoy the same rights as the clergy of all other churches recognized by the state. Pending a special law concerning the ownership of church real estate held by Orthodox corporations, the decree left all property in their possession, with the proviso that any future claim by any third party would have to be considered.

An even more fundamental source of the Polish Orthodox church's weakness and instability from 1918 to 1939 was internal dissension that erupted into conflict among the clergy and between the hierarchy and the laity. Poland's four to five million Orthodox represented not one ethnic group but several, including the country's largest and third-largest minority nationalities, the Ukrainians and Belorussians. Given the explosion of nationalist feeling in Central Europe during the 1920s and 1930s, it was almost inevitable that attempts to revitalize the Polish Orthodox church took on political and nationalist overtones. Competing Ukrainian, Belorussian, Russian, and Polish national interests among the Orthodox members were reflected in controversies over ecclesiastical appointments and practices, particularly the choice of language to be used in church services and administration.

Almost exclusively of Russian origin, the higher church dignitaries were accustomed to the bureaucratic synodal-consistorial rule that had been imposed by the Russian church during the partitions. They resisted efforts to reorganize the Polish church along lines that would take local prepartition traditions into account. Their conservative policy came increasingly under attack from the younger clergy, mostly of Ukrainian and Belorussian background, who sought to derussify the church and reintroduce Ruthenian patterns of ecclesiastical administration that had traditionally encouraged lay participation.

Growing ethnic awareness and assertiveness among Poland's ethnic minorities also spilled over into church politics. The Orthodox community's larger nationality groups started to demand greater representation in the church's administration and a larger role in determining church policies. Influenced both by the Ukrainian revival in Poland and by the activity of the Ukrainian Autocephalous church in the Soviet Ukraine, the Ukrainian Orthodox campaigned vigorously for the use of their language in the pulpit and of Ukrainian Church Slavonic in the liturgy, as well as the appointment of more Ukrainian bishops, the creation of a separate archbishopric in Volhynia, and the observance of local church traditions and customs.[7] Advocating independence from Moscow, they sometimes openly expressed hostility to the Russian church and opposition to the Soviet regime, attitudes influenced by reports of forced collectivization and mass starvation among Ukrainian peasants living under Soviet rule.

Belorussian nationalism in Poland's Orthodox church was less pronounced and less effectively organized. The smaller Belorussian community also demanded a larger voice in local ecclesiastical activities. Their modest program included the use of Belorussian in the pulpit and in exchanges between priest and parishioner, as well as the introduction of Belorussian catechisms for children of Belorussian origin and the appointment of Belorussian clergy to predominantly Belorussian parishes.[8]

The church hierarchy, dominated by Russians, tended to reject the Ukrainians' and Belorussians' proposals and tried to suppress their attempts to organize. In turn, the non-Russian nationalities accused the higher Orthodox officials of being "alien" to the "Ukrainian and White-Ruthenian [Belorussian] nations" and "altogether devoted to the government."[9] Yet church officials could boast that they permitted the use of Ukrainian, Belorussian, Polish, and Czech in worship services and religious instruction. But, according to critics within the church, conservative priests often set up practical obstacles to block the introduction of non-Russian languages into church life.[10]

Aside from the friction between the higher authorities and the non-Russian clergy, and the tension between the leadership and representatives of the Belorussian and Ukrainian Orthodox, the Polish Orthodox church was strained by conflicts at the highest levels of the church leadership. An adamantly pro-Russian element within the hierarchy criticized Metropolitan Dionizy for what it perceived as a gradual, but unmistakable, drift toward polonization.[11] It accused the metropolitan and his supporters of effacing the external differences between the Orthodox and Catholic churches by adopting the Gregorian calendar and introducing Polish as the church's official language.

At the same time that the Orthodox were preoccupied with internal dissension, the church was subjected to mounting pressure from a society that was increasingly divided over its nationalities question. Poland's national minorities were becoming more and more alienated from the state as the Poles failed to reconcile their Ukrainian and Belorussian populations to life within the existing political framework. By the mid-1930s many Poles began to look on the Orthodox church as a breeding ground for Ukrainian and Belorussian nationalist agitation and incipient irredentism.

The Polish government adopted a complicated strategy of favoritism and discrimination vis-à-vis its ethnic and religious minorities, often entrusting the actual formation of policy to local military commanders, especially in northern Poland, where a high percentage of the ethnic minorities resided. In general, it favored Ukrainian and Belorussian Catholics and neo-Uniates over Orthodox Belorussians and Ukrainians, who were subjected to a combination of economic pressure and psychological intimidation. Under the initiative of local army commanders, attempts were made to convert the Orthodox population in Volhynia and the Chelm region to Catholicism. In the Lemko region, however, the political authorities targeted the Galician Uniates and Ukrainian Catholics for discrimination and granted the Orthodox preferential treatment, encouraging the Lemkians to leave the Uniate church and join the Orthodox.

In the 1930s the bitter confrontation between the Orthodox and Catholics and between the minorities and Poles became most dramatically focused on the issue of church property, a legacy of Poland's dismemberment during the period of the partitions.[12] For nearly two decades the Catholic episcopate had tried to obtain the return of over six hundred church buildings that, it claimed, had belonged to the Roman Catholics and Uniates before Poland was partitioned. The Catholic church now demanded the return of property illegally confiscated by the Russians and handed over to the Orthodox.

The Polish government refused to act decisively on the emotionally charged issue either through legal or through administrative channels. Instead, without consulting the Orthodox community, it concluded a separate agreement with the Vatican in June 1938. Warsaw and Rome determined that the disputed churches not in current use were to become state property or be turned over to the Catholic church—a decision that could hardly satisfy the Orthodox.

Fanned by ethnic antagonisms and religious rivalry, the conflict over church real estate reached crisis proportions as local parishes and army commanders began to take matters into their own hands. In the eastern districts of Lublin province, Catholics, apparently with the support of local clergy and military, seized one to two hundred churches and chapels claimed by both congregations. In what they viewed as justifiable self-defense against Catholic provocation, some Orthodox attempted to regain possession of vacant churches. According to one Polish historian, in the struggle to gain control over the places of worship, approximately 120 were destroyed, mostly (according to government claims) chapels no longer in use.[13]

During World War II the German General-Government under Hans Frank applied the classic strategy of *divide et impera* to drive wedges within the occupied population and thwart the formation of a unified resistance. The Nazis favored many ethnic and religious groups that they perceived as antagonistic to or different from the Poles, including Ukrainians, Lemkians, Goralens, and Cassubians, and attempted to exploit any self-serving ambitions evident among religious or national leaders. Their policy of preferential treatment for minorities met with a fair degree of success, fanning the resentment and enmity of the largely Catholic Polish population. Thus, during the occupation, the Polish Orthodox church was generally favored.

In 1945 the church emerged from the war with a drastically reduced membership, an acute shortage of adequately trained clergy, the loss of almost all their intellectuals, and substantial material setbacks. A few vital statistics illustrate the devastating impact of the war and accompanying redrawing of Poland's frontiers.[14] Approximately 350,000 Orthodox remained in Poland, concentrated primarily in the Bialystok region. In other words, the church was reduced to less than one-tenth of its 1938 size. Of the five interwar dioceses, only the Warsaw diocese remained. The Orthodox were left with only three of their former ten bishops and one of their former eighteen monasteries and convents. Only a few priests and one theologian with an advanced degree remained to begin the task of rebuilding the church in postwar Poland.

Aleksii, the patriarch of Moscow, was eager to take advantage of postwar Soviet dominance in Eastern Europe to extend his own ecclesiastical influence in the region. The result was pressure on Polish Metropolitan Dionizy to renounce the autocephaly of the Polish Orthodox church. In 1948 the recalcitrant Dionizy was placed under house arrest, and in April he was deposed, on grounds of alleged wartime collaboration with the Nazis.[15] The following month the Polish government ordered the church to submit to the authority of the Moscow patriarchate.[16] Archbishop Timoteusz Szretter of Bialystok, a Russian prelate known for his subservience to Patriarch Aleksii, now succeeded to the Polish metropolitanate, and Moscow recognized the Polish church's autocephaly.

Throughout Poland's often turbulent postwar history the Orthodox church has adhered consistently to a policy of loyal cooperation vis-à-vis the secular authorities. It has rejected, and explicitly criticized, the role adopted by the Roman Catholic church, which has fluctuated between confrontation and occasional cooperation with the ruling party. Unlike the Catholics, the Orthodox leaders have not seen themselves as critics of the regime or spokesmen for society at large, based on a concept of the church's fundamental opposition to the communist system. Nor has it adopted the institutional model of the "servant Church," which Hungarian Protestants have followed, stressing service to society as the church's essential task.

In exchange for limited government tolerance, which includes state subsidies for Orthodox educational institutions, clergy salaries, and church renovations, the Orthodox church has put up with bureaucratic restrictions on the construction of churches, religious instruction for children and youth, supplies of liturgical materials, and church publications. Church officials have suspended public criticism of the regime's treatment of religion. According to Metropolitan Bazyli Doroszkiewicz, the church's current spiritual leader since 1970, no "contentious" issues exist between the church and the state.[17] Moreover, the church has committed itself to positive support for state policies at home and abroad. Besides regularly expressing gratitude for the freedom of religion and equal status of religious communities guaranteed in the constitution, the Orthodox hierarchy has endorsed the Polish United Workers' party's social and political strategies, as well as its periodic campaigns to promote higher productivity, or to combat alcoholism, or to encourage support for the international peace movement.

During the 1950s the Orthodox church joined the Polish Ecumenical Council, a consortium of otherwise Protestant churches, officially founded in 1946 to promote cooperation among non-Roman Catholic denominations. Since 1960 the church's activities have expanded into international ecumenical contacts and organizations, especially those devoted to the government-sponsored peace offensive. In 1961 it joined the World Council of Churches and became active in the Christian Peace Conference, the Prague-based organization formed in 1959 to allow close cooperation between the East European churches and the Soviet regime in pursuing common international objectives. By their own admission, church officials have not been very active in the intra-Orthodox ecumenical movement, although they claim to be preparing for the one thousandth anniversary celebrations of Russian Orthodoxy in 1988.[18]

Ecumenical contacts with the Polish Catholic church have been far more problematical. Deep-seated theological and attitudinal differences, as well as mistrust and recrimination engendered by a long history of Orthodox–Catholic/Uniate conflict in Poland, have stood in the way of strong ecumenical ties between the two religious communities. Although many Orthodox and Catholic intellectuals have cooperated on joint academic ventures and some Orthodox and Catholic parishes have developed a cooperative relationship and share sanctuaries, continued tension and suspicion still appear to be the rule rather than the exception.

In a recent interview with a Polish journalist, Metropolitan Bazyli described the current state of Orthodox-Catholic relations as "neither hot nor cold."[19] Orthodox representatives do not disguise their displeasure that Polish Catholics tend to treat the Orthodox as a cultural artifact alien to Polish society or as a holdover from the despised tsarist partition of the country, thereby ignoring Orthodox contributions to Polish culture. Neither do they hide their fear about any developments that suggest increased Roman Catholic influence on Poland's cultural and public policy reminiscent of the interwar period.

Despite persistent hostility, small, tentative signs of gradual improvement have surfaced in recent years, especially since Jozef Archbishop Glemp succeeded Stefan Cardinal Wyszyński as Polish primate in 1981. In April of that year the first Orthodox-Catholic Subcommission for Theological Dialogue convened. In January 1982 Archbishop Glemp delivered a sermon at St. Mary Magdalene's Orthodox Church in Warsaw at a service marking the Week of Prayer for Christian Unity. The occasion marked the first time that a high-ranking Catholic had addressed an Orthodox congregation. During the 1983 Week of Prayer for Christian Unity, Metropolitan Bazyli delivered a sermon at a Roman Catholic church.

During the 1970s the most significant Polish Orthodox development was the church's growing involvement with activities geared to children and young adults. A group of young theologians inspired a movement of Orthodox youth that emphasizes religious education and liturgical life.[20] Similar to the Oasis/Light-Life movement of religious renewal for Poland's Catholic youth, which first appeared in 1972, the Orthodox youth movement holds annual retreats at the convent of Grabarka and regional meetings in Gdansk and Warsaw. Young people are supervised in constructing new churches and rehabilitating old ones.

Neither the Polish Orthodox church nor the Polish government keeps official statistics on the church's membership. Until recently church officials, using parish statistics, have estimated membership at about 500,000 faithful. In private, their estimates have run as high as more than 800,000 practicing Orthodox out of one million baptized. Since 1983 both the church press and the official government media have used the higher figure of 852,000 Orthodox believers with no explanation for the sudden jump in the estimate from preceding years. It remains unclear why the published figures have climbed so dramatically, but it seems likely that this reflects a policy to use the Orthodox as a foil against the increasingly powerful

Catholic church and to undermine the Uniates, who have many grievances against the regime.

In the absence of reliable data it is impossible to determine whether the church's growing numbers have kept apace with population growth or outdistanced the rate of population increase. However, it is clear that the Orthodox have not suffered the heavy losses of membership that have affected some of Poland's Protestant denominations.

Most Orthodox live in eastern Poland, where Orthodoxy in Poland has its roots, especially in the Bialystok region. According to Metropolitan Bazyli, about 350,000 Orthodox, many of whom were transferred from eastern Poland after the Second World War, now reside in western and northern Poland. The metropolitan describes the country's Orthodox as primarily polonized Ukrainians and Belorussians, with approximately 250,000 Poles and much smaller numbers of Russians, Lemkians, and Greeks. His use of the ambiguous term "polonized" needs to be taken with a grain of salt because it bears upon the extremely delicate question of assimilation of Poland's minority nationalities, especially the Ukrainians.

The clergy conduct services in Old Church Slavonic and often deliver sermons—at least in theory—in the language of the congregation's choice. In some parishes, however, the priest may not be familiar with the language preferred by the parishioners. In 1974 church services were conducted in Polish in only one or two churches in Warsaw. At present, according to Metropolitan Bazyli, Polish is used in several cities.

Aside from church calendars, catechisms, prayer books, liturgical books, and publications on theology and Orthodox history, the Polish Orthodox church's publishing activities are limited to two major journals.

The Polish crisis of the 1980s—the birth of the independent trade union Solidarity, General Wojciech Jaruzelski's declaration of martial law in December 1981, and the current political stalemate between the political authorities and Polish society—has made the Orthodox church's role a little more visible to the outside world and afforded a revealing glimpse into developments within the Orthodox community. The political turmoil of recent years has not appreciably changed the church's policies and attitudes about relations between church and state. Church officials have not rallied to the support of Solidarity and its goals; nor have they suspended their expressions of loyalty to the state. Before Solidarity was banned, the hierarchy issued public statements implicitly criticizing the trade union and its supporters for sowing "seeds of discord" and urged Orthodox parishioners to refrain from activities that would disrupt society.[21] Interviews with Metropolitan Bazyli and other Polish Orthodox have suggested how heavily the past history of Orthodox-Catholic conflict weighs on the collective consciousness of the older generation of Orthodox. Their comments underline their resentment and fear of the nationalistic and religious overtones that surfaced in the Solidarity movement, which, they felt, were resonant of a still-present Polish Catholic exclusivism that continues to threaten the Polish Orthodox church.

Like the Catholic church, which has traditionally benefited from increased government concessions during periods of social and economic instability or the turnover of political leadership, the Polish Orthodox church has made limited, highly publicized gains during the 1980s. Because of Solidarity's demands that churches be allowed access to public broadcasting, which initially applied only to Roman Catholic masses, the Orthodox, along with other members of the Polish Ecumenical Council, Adventists, and Jews, have won the right to broadcast their church services on Polish radio.[22] Since January 1982, even under martial law, thirty to forty minutes of airtime, three to four times a year, have been made available to the Polish Orthodox church for religious broadcasting.[23]

Finally, the state has granted significantly more building permits for new churches—an issue that has always created difficulties for the country's religious organizations. Twelve new churches are now under construction—as of this writing—which represents slightly more than a third of all the churches built since the war. The Orthodox have also been permitted to establish their first new diocese since 1951, in Przemysl-Nowosadek, a formerly Ukrainian ethnic border area known as the spiritual center of the Uniates.

Orthodoxy in Hungary

During the parliamentary debate over the bill that legalized the 1864 division of the Orthodox church in Hungary into the Serbian and Romanian autocephalous metropolitanates (enacted as Act IX of 1868), the leaders of three Orthodox parishes (Pest, Szentes, and Kecskemét) presented a memorandum to the House in which they protested in the name of the *Greek* Orthodox communities against the tendency to equate all the Orthodox in Hungary with either Serbs or Romanians. They demanded separate autonomy for those who, though descended from Greek ancestors and remaining faithful to their Orthodox religion, had become "true Hungarians," as they put it, often not knowing any language other than Magyar.[24] In response to the petition, the original text of the bill was amended by a clause specifying that "those members of the Eastern Orthodox religion whose tongue is neither Serb nor Romanian shall preserve forthwith all their rights which they had exercised until now in the autonomous direction of their parish and school affairs, as well as in the management of their parish properties and endowments."[25] Thus, the Hungarian Orthodox were officially defined as those who are "neither Serb nor Romanian." To call them Greek, besides sounding tautological,[26] was not possible after having protested their "Hungarianness" so vigorously in the memorandum. To call them "Magyar," on the other hand, would have been quite inconceivable for the legislators, since, for the Hungarians as a whole, an Orthodox Hungarian was anything but normal and seemed even somewhat of a cultural freak.[27] To tell the truth, the Hungarian Orthodox were not so sure about themselves either; otherwise they would have demanded the use of their native tongue in the liturgy—an elementary right for every nation in Eastern Christianity. But they did not insist, and so the abnormal situation continued whereby the "neither Serb nor Romanian" Orthodox parishes conducted all their business, including the writing of the official register of births, marriages, and deaths in Hungarian, while performing their religious services in Greek, Old Church Slavonic, or even Romanian, all of them languages incomprehensible to most of the congregation.

The state of Orthodoxy in Hungary was most radically altered by the drastic territorial adjustments in the wake of the country's defeat in the First World War.[28] The Treaty of Trianon detached all the non-Magyar-inhabited territories and more. In consequence, Eastern Orthodoxy, which before the war was numerically the second largest religious denomination in the country, with some 3 million adherents constituting 14.3 percent of the total population of 20 million inhabitants, shrank to an insignificant 0.6 percent.[29] According to the 1920 census, there remained only 50,990 Eastern Orthodox within the new boundaries. Of these, 35.7 percent were Romanians, 31.2 percent Serbs, 26.8 percent Hungarians, 0.4 percent Slovaks, 0.3 percent Germans, 0.1 percent Ruthenes, and 5.2 percent of other nationality groups.[30] Since only the Serbian bishop of Buda had his seat within the Trianon borders, he now claimed ecclesiastical jurisdiction over all of this diverse flock. He in turn paid homage to the patriarch of Belgrade in Yugoslavia and was accepted as a member of the Holy Synod of the Serbian church.[31] It was probably because of the small numbers involved that the Horthy regime did not attach much importance to the issue and, in fact, tacitly accepted this strange situation whereby thousands of Hungarian citizens, two-thirds of them not Serbian, were subordinated in church matters to a Serbian prelate, who was in turn subordinated to the leading ecclesiastical prelate in an unfriendly neighboring state.[32]

In the meantime the evolution of the Hungarian Orthodox church continued.[33] The "neither Serb nor Romanian" Orthodox parishes, originally founded by Greek settlers, declared themselves in 1931 to be the "Hungarian Orthodox parishes of Greek origins." They contacted the ecumenical patriarch of Constantinople, who was ready to take them under his jurisdiction. This provoked the protests of the Serbian Bishop of Buda, György Zubkovics, who in 1932 presented a memorandum to the Hungarian government. In this memorandum he reaffirmed his claims of jurisdiction over all Orthodox but offered to establish a separate deanery for the "neither Serb nor Romanian" parishes. At the same time he reiterated his strenuous objection to the introduction of Hungarian into the liturgy, a practice that was gaining momentum in those very communities. In fact, during the thirties two new purely Hungarian Orthodox parishes were established, to which a third was added in 1944. Moreover, in the spring of 1940 several Romanian parishes, situated on the eastern border areas, declared their intention of joining a Hungarian Orthodox church organization as soon as such an entity was formed.[34]

With the territorial changes that occurred in 1938–41[35] those of the Eastern Orthodox faith became again a substantial component of the enlarged country's population.[36] The Serbian and Romanian Orthodox had, of course, their well-developed ecclesiastical organizations in the newly acquired territories and these continued to function during the war.[37] The greatly increased Ruthene and the by then strongly nationalist Hungarian Orthodox lacked such organs and had no desire to be placed again under the jurisdiction of the Serbian or Romanian hierarchy. Groping for a solution, the Hungarian government invited the exarch of the patriarch of Constantinople, Metropolitan Sawatij of Prague, asking him to transfer his see to Hungary and to take the Ruthenian and Hungarian Orthodox under his jurisdiction. Responding to the invitation, the metropolitan paid a visit to Budapest in 1941, then toured the northeast areas (Subcarpathian Ruthenia), where he ordained several priests, thus provoking the wrath of Bishop Zubkovics of Buda. Before his return to Prague, Metropolitan Sawatij, acting on the request of the Hungarian government, named as his vicar Archpriest Michael Popoff, a Russian émigré, with the mandate to give the Ruthenian and Hungarian Orthodox a solid church structure. Thereupon Popoff was named by Regent Horthy to serve as administrator of the Ruthene Eastern Orthodox and Hungarian Eastern Orthodox church districts. These "church districts" encompassed the Ruthene Orthodox parishes in Subcarpathian Ruthenia, the parishes of Greek origin, the Magyarized Romanian Orthodox parishes, and the Hungarian Orthodox parishes of the Székely region in Transylvania, as well as three more recently founded purely Hungarian parishes. This structure had a somewhat dubious canonicity, given the rather tenuous link, through Prague, with Constantinople.

The newly created church organization was soon rocked by the news that its administrator, Archpriest Popoff, was being stripped of his priestly status by the Synod of Karlovci, the official body of the Russian émigré bishops. What little authority the unpopular Popoff possessed was now lost. Most of the parishes placed under his administration were reluctant to accept the directives of a defrocked priest. To escape from this embarrassing situation the government appointed two vice-administrators, one for the Ruthenian Orthodox, the other for the Hungarians, both being the preferred choice of the respective clergy, while Popoff was relieved of his title and office.

At this point it seems worthwhile to relate that in the spring of 1942 an Eastern Orthodox theological academy opened its doors in Budapest. It was established and maintained by the government for the formation of the Orthodox clergy in Hungary, regardless of nationality. Incredible as it may sound, Serbs, Hungarians, Ruthenes, Romanians, all studied and taught there in brotherly harmony while around them a savagely fratricidal war was raging. The academy was suppressed in June 1944 in the wake of the German occupation of the country. By then, three school terms had been completed and a number of fine works had been published by the faculty.[38]

After the Second World War Hungary was once again reduced to its Trianon borders. The juridical situation of its Orthodox population reverted to the status quo ante. This meant that in accordance with Orthodox canon law, there was again only one duly constituted ecclesiastical authority, namely, the Serbian bishopric of Buda.[39] The latter's continuity was personified by Bishop György Zubkovics, who administered his diocese without interruption for nearly forty years, from 1913 until his death in 1951.

The Romanian parishes, which in 1940 had declared their Hungarian character, reversed their decision in 1946 and placed themselves under the jurisdiction of the Romanian bishops across the border.[40] The status of the Hungarian parishes of Greek origin, and of the three new Hungarian parishes, remained unresolved.[41] These last two groups cooperated in their common endeavor to obtain the canonical recognition of their separate existence and the legalization of their use of Hungarian in the sacred liturgy. There seemed to be three possible roads for them to proceed toward these goals: by way of the Ecumenical Patriarchate of Constantinople, through the bishopric of Buda, and through the patriarchate of Moscow.

The contact with Constantinople was established soon after the war's end on the initiative of the Budapest parish of Greek origin through the services of their priest, Archimandrite Hilarion Vezdekas. The negotiations dragged on until June 1950. They did not bear fruit since the ecumenical patriarch refused to accept the Hungarian character of the formerly Greek Orthodox parishes, totally ignored the newer Hungarian parishes, and strictly forbade the use of Hungarian in church services.

Parallel negotiations were conducted between 1945 and 1947 with the Serbian bishop of Buda, aiming at a more realistic and at the same time global solution to the jurisdictional problem of all the Orthodox in Hungary. The plan elaborated by representatives of the Hungarian Orthodox proposed the union of all Orthodox parishes under the jurisdiction of the bishop of Buda, whose diocese would have three vicariates, a Serbian, a Hungarian, and a Romanian, each of which would use its own language in the liturgy. It was apparently too much to ask of Bishop Zubkovics to agree to such a transformation of his hitherto exclusively Serbian bishopric, even if this would have meant a considerable growth in the number of his flock. In his answer to the petition of the parishes of Greek origin, which incorporated the above proposals, he reiterated the gist of his 1932 memorandum, in which he defended the jurisdictional status quo and forbade the use of Hungarian in the liturgy. True, his letter again offered the prospect of a separate deanery for the Greek parishes, but then continued in a cautionary tone:

> I must note, however, that I have to delay the implementation of this decision regarding those parishes which claim, or wish to claim, to be of Hungarian character (especially by means of their willful and unconstitutional introduction of the Hungarian liturgical language) since precisely on the basis of alleged petitions of certain of these parishes, it is His Holiness the Patriarch of Moscow and of All Russia who wishes to take them under his jurisdiction. Until such time as the Serbian and Romanian patriarchates do agree with the Patriarchate of Moscow as to where these parishes of Hungarian character should belong, I have to suspend my jurisdiction provisionally in their regard.[42]

The reference to Moscow in this letter, dated July 26, 1947, shows Bishop Zubkovics's awareness of the fact that a new powerful actor, to whom all others had to bow, had entered the picture. Indeed, the patriarchate of Moscow, which had never before played a role in the life of Hungarian Orthodoxy, sent an observer to Hungary already in August 1946, in the person of Nestor, bishop of Munkačevo. This was followed by diplomatic negotiations between the Hungarian government and the Moscow patriarchate. In the summer of 1948, Nestor, by that time bishop of Kursk, was sent to Hungary the second time. It was also reported in June 1948 that both the patriarch of Belgrade and the patriarch of Bucharest paid a visit to the patriarch of Moscow, who advised them to agree to have the bishop of Buda alone exercise jurisdiction over all the Orthodox in Hungary. Thereupon, Bishop Zubkovics petitioned the Ministry of Religion and Public Education in Budapest, once again, for recognition of his jurisdiction over the Greek parishes, conceding his tacit toleration of the use of Hungarian where it was already being used, and leaving the question of the originally Hungarian parishes open for later settlement.

What happened next was an unprecedented, though in view of the postwar geopolitical situation not totally unexpected, development: by virtue of a synodal decision of the Moscow patriarchate, dated November 11, 1949, His Holiness Aleksii, patriarch of Moscow and of all Russia, accepted the Hungarian Orthodox parishes into his jurisdiction, including both those of Greek origin and those of Hungarian origin. Though it is said that this was done according to the wishes of the Hungarian government and at the express invitation of the parish communities involved,[43] one cannot escape the suspicion that political considerations, extraneous to purely church interest, must have played a certain role. It is difficult to believe that the Russian patriarch would have so suddenly trespassed onto the jurisdictional territory claimed so tenaciously by the Serbian bishop of Buda and would so easily have given his blessing to the use of a non-Slavic language in the liturgy, had it not been for the Soviet-Yugoslav rift and the resultant poisoning of the atmosphere between the two Orthodox Slavic nations. This explains also the absence of any protest on the part of Bishop Zubkovics. At a time when the Hungarian communist regime of Mátyás Rákosi was breaking all relations with Yugoslavia, denouncing Tito as the "running dog of imperialism," and unleashing a veritable persecution of the small Serbian minority within Hungary, the only wise course for the Serbian prelate was to lie low and pray for the storm to pass.

We would not want to suggest that what happened to the Hungarian Orthodox church was some kind of Muscovite imperial expansion, a conquest by force. After all, it was by default on the part of the Serbian church and of the Ecumenical Patriarchate that the Hungarian Orthodox were left in limbo for such a long time. When the Moscow patriarchate stepped in to fill the void, it expressly specified that it would take under its jurisdiction only the Greek and Hungarian parishes whose canonical status was uncertain, not touching those which paid allegiances to a properly constituted hierarchy, such as the Serb, Romanian, and Bulgarian Orthodox in Hungary. Notwithstanding this admirable restraint, it remains a fact that from all of the autocephalous churches in Orthodoxy, it was Moscow, at the end, that took the tiny orphan communities of the Hungarian Orthodox under its wings, and that this was unmistakably the consequence of the postwar geopolitical situation. There is no exaggeration in saying that before 1945 no Hungarian Orthodox could have imagined, in his wildest dreams, that eventually Moscow would become his mother church.

The formal establishment of the Hungarian Orthodox church proceeded under the guidance of Archpriest Ivan Kopolovics, who was sent to Hungary by Patriarch Aleksii to serve as dean-administrator of the "Provisional Governing Board of the Hungarian Eastern Orthodox Parishes of Hungary." Paragraph seven of the organizational charter of this new body, which was approved by Patriarch Aleksii on November 15, 1949, specified that "all divine worship and ceremonies are to be performed in the Hungarian language."[44] The Hungarian liturgical texts, hitherto available in most cases only in typescript, were now printed with the canonical permission of the Moscow patriarchate. A last step in this evolution was the replacement of Kopolovics in 1954 by a Hungarian Orthodox theology professor, Archpriest Feriz Berki, as dean-administrator, and the renaming of the "Provisional Governing Board" as "Hungarian Orthodox Administration." To crown all this, the deanery of the Hungarian Orthodox became, in 1962, a member of the Ecumenical Council of the Hungarian Churches, achieving thereby a status which enabled it to play an active role on the national and international scene.

Orthodoxy in Hungary is, at present, composed of six nationalities under four ecclesiastical jurisdictions:

1. The Serb diocese of Buda, with the episcopal see actually at Szentendre, governed by an episcopal vicar, with the aid of a diocesan consistory. It has seventeen parishes. Its jurisdiction extends also to all Serbian Orthodox in Hungary. Its supreme ecclesiastical authority is the patriarch of Belgrade, resident in Yugoslavia.

2. The Romanian diocese of Gyula, governed by an episcopal vicar, assisted by a diocesan consistory. It has eighteen parishes. Its jurisdiction extends to all Romanian Orthodox in Hungary. Its supreme ecclesiastical authority is the patriarch of Bucharest, resident in Romania.

3. The Hungarian deanery of Budapest, headed by a dean-administrator. It has nine parishes.[45] Its jurisdiction extends to all Hungarian, Greek, and Russian Orthodox in Hungary. Its supreme ecclesiastical authority is

the patriarch of Moscow and of all Russia, resident in the Soviet Union.

4. Two Bulgarian parishes headed by the rector of the Budapest parish whose jurisdiction extends to all Bulgarians in Hungary. Its supreme ecclesiastical authority is the patriarch of Sofia, resident in Bulgaria.

This fourfold fractured structure provides spiritual home to about forty thousand Orthodox Christians altogether, of whom less than ten thousand consider themselves Hungarian by mother tongue.

It is well known, on the one hand, that the Soviet regime is the foremost propagator of Marxist-Leninist atheism and that it combats religion in any form, and, on the other, that it uses the church, more precisely the Moscow patriarchate, in the furtherance of its goals, especially in its propaganda for foreign consumption. One should only think of the role played by the Russian Orthodox church and of the other sister churches living in the Soviet bloc within the World Council of Churches and within the Christian Peace Conference, established in 1958 in Prague. At the meetings of these international bodies as well as in other international forums, ecclesiastical representatives from the Soviet bloc countries routinely engage in one-sided condemnations of the West, while having nothing but praise for the policies of the Soviet Union. The sorry state of human rights and the lack of religious freedom in their homelands are passed over in silence, and, if they are challenged on such issues, they deny the very existence of such problems under communism.

How does Hungarian Orthodoxy fit into this picture? First of all, one should bear in mind that the Orthodox churches in Hungary are far from being free agents. Like all other religious organizations, they are subjected to the strict control of the State Office of Church Affairs, established at the height of Stalinism in 1951. In addition, in the case of the Hungarian Orthodox deanery, as we have seen above, direct ecclesiastical control is in the hands of the Moscow patriarchate. Under these circumstances, it should not be a surprise that the Hungarian Orthodox church faithfully echoes Moscow's stand in all its publications and public manifestations. Whether this reflects the true inner feelings of the Hungarian Orthodox clergy and of the faithful is open, of course, to question.

One would get a distorted picture, however, attributing undue significance to such behavior. Its very small size prevents Hungarian Orthodoxy from playing a real role of any kind, be it pro-regime or contra-regime. It is in the ranks of the predominant Roman Catholic church and of the major Protestant churches that the regime finds its honey-tongued supporters, just as it is within those churches that we hear of dissidence and outright opposition. Similarly, Hungarian representation on the World Council of

Churches and at the Prague Christian Peace Conference is composed of prominent clergymen from the powerful Calvinist and Lutheran churches, while only minor roles are assigned on occasion to the smaller Protestant sects or to the Orthodox.

The Macedonian Orthodox Church

If the Kingdom of France was ever *la fille aînée de l'Eglise*, the Macedonian Orthodox church must be the favored religious child of the Yugoslav socialist state. The reason for this is not a question of religion, but one of politics, insofar as support for Macedonian national consciousness is seen by the regime as a vital stabilizing strategy in a region where both frontiers and identities are often hotly contested.

Macedonia is the territory over which the Bulgarian and Serbian medieval monarchies had expanded at the expense of Byzantium. It has always been the center of the Balkans, for the control of which neighboring states, and foreign powers interested in the peninsula, have vied with one another. In modern times it was the region that remained longest in Turkish hands. Over it, the aspirations of Serbs, Bulgarians, and Greeks mingled through the mass of the mostly undifferentiated Slavophone population. Out of this rivalry—at once nationalistic, cultural, and ecclesiastical, as always in the Balkans—a separate Macedonian consciousness slowly began to emerge, recognized by none of the three contending nation-states who were busy Serbianizing, Bulgarianizing, and Hellenizing their outlying Macedonian territories.

At first the authorities of the autonomous Principality of Serbia sympathized with Bulgarian aspirations, but they became increasingly frightened after 1870 when, according to the statute granted to it, the autonomous Bulgarian Orthodox church began to expand. By 1878 the Bulgarian Orthodox church enjoyed *ecclesiastical* jurisdiction in areas that were passing under the *political* control of Serbia. Serbia responded, in the 1880s, with a proselytizing campaign of its own.

Constant warfare between 1912 and 1918, following on years of terrorism and anarchy, left Macedonia devastated and underpopulated. The policy of the government of the newly created "Kingdom of Serbs, Croats, and Slovenes" in the interwar period was one of assimilation reinforced by colonization. All Macedonian Slavs were considered to be Serbs. At the same time the availability of fertile land attracted Orthodox Serbs from the poorer regions of the Adriatic hinterland to the new territories of Kosovo and Macedonia. Anxious to help the integration of these contested and coveted lands, the government provided financial incentives. Likewise the ecclesiastical assimilation of the local clergy was assisted by the seminaries in Prizren and Bitola, and by the addition of clergy from other regions.

The reactions to this policy were mixed. It was in the Yugoslav part that the real Macedonian problem was concentrated. It was heading toward a solution in the Greek part (about half the total area of Macedonia) through population exchanges with Bulgaria and the resettlement of refugees from Asia Minor. By far the smallest part was the Bulgarian part (about 10 percent of the total area of Macedonia), and this population was eventually mostly Bulgarianized, because it was small and because assimilation had been an ongoing process since the 1870s. The large number of Bulgarianized Macedonians settled in Bulgaria pined, however, for the annexation of Greek and Yugoslav Macedonia, and provided militants for the Internal Macedonian Revolutionary Organization (IMRO). In fact, IMRO was torn between loyalty to Bulgaria, which supported it, and separatism. Macedonian separatism was backed by the Bulgarian government in an effort to revise the territorial settlement, but it was also courted by other organizations that did not like the South Slav state, from the fascist-inspired Croatian *Ustaša* movement to the Communist Party of Yugoslavia (CPY). While the continuous agitation of IMRO fed the Macedonians' distrust of the Yugoslav state, even their hatred of Serbs, it also generated weariness with terrorism and something approaching a passive acceptance of Yugoslav rule.[46]

Such mixed feelings toward Yugoslavia made it relatively easy for the Bulgarians to secure an initial acceptance of their occupation of Yugoslav Macedonia in 1941. Gradual disillusionment nevertheless crept in when the nationalistic policy of the new authorities made it evident to the Macedonians that they had been freed from Serbianization only to be subjected to intense Bulgarianization. The area taken over embraced the three Serbian dioceses of Skopje, Zletovo-Strumica, and Ohrid-Bitola, whose bishops were immediately expelled. The Bulgarian exarchate extended its jurisdiction to the new territories, and sent away a certain number of Serbian-oriented clerics to join their hierarchs in the German-occupied rump of Serbia. Generally speaking, there was no persecution,[47] but owing to the insufficient number of clergy, priests were sent for short periods from their own parishes in Bulgaria, which could have little effect on the Bulgarianization of local clergy and faithful.

The disappointment with Bulgarian rule after its initial acceptance— indeed, the Macedonian section of the CPY had at first decided to merge into the Bulgarian Communist party—gave the Yugoslav communist leadership the chance to woo the Macedonians back to Yugoslavia by all-out support for local feeling. It had decided in 1943 that Yugoslavia should be reorganized on a federal basis as a community of nations, one of which would be the Macedonian. Some local priests had actively cooperated with the new Bulgarian administration of the diocese, but others sympathized with the Yugoslav communists when their partisans emerged in the latter half of the war. The first fruits of this collaboration appeared in western Macedonia after Italy's withdrawl from the area that had been joined to Albania, when, under the auspices of the partisan command for Macedonia, deaneries were reorganized in the liberated territory.

The CPY took the view that the Serbian Orthodox church was the chief advocate of the Greater Serbian idea, and that the removal of its influence over the population in Macedonia would accelerate the new strategy of cultivating a Macedonian consciousness. This would not only consolidate Yugoslav communist control of the region, but provide a pivot around which Bulgarian and Greek Macedonia could also eventually be unified. An open attack on the Orthodox church was not in the interest of the authorities. But a move against the authority of the Serbian patriarchate in Macedonia would introduce disunity into the church, and weaken its resistance to communism. The new authorities may well have been aware of the part played by the Bulgarian exarchate in spreading Bulgarian influence in the past. Now that both the obviously pro-Serbian and the obviously pro-Bulgarian priests had left, the local leadership had passed to that group who had cooperated actively with the Yugoslav partisans from the autumn of 1943 and who enjoyed communist support.

To begin with, the bishops and priests expelled by the Bulgarian authorities were not allowed to return. Then, in January 1945, Christmas greetings were sent to the Holy Synod in Belgrade, "on behalf of the Orthodox church in Macedonia," by the local clerics, who described themselves as the "Organizing Committee for the Establishment of an Independent Macedonian Orthodox Church and the Restoration of the Historic Archbishopric of Ohrid." The response to the warning from the Belgrade patriarchate not to act against the canons was a gathering, in liberated Skopje in March, where three hundred delegates of clergy and laity, under the rubric of a "Council of the Church and People," adopted a resolution claiming the Macedonian nation's right to its own church.

The Macedonian demands were then toned down. In May 1946 a purely clerical gathering in Skopje resolved that the People's Republic of Macedonia should have its own bishops, chosen by the laity and the clergy, but that the Macedonian church should be integrated into a reorganized "Orthodox Church of Yugoslavia," whose federal structure would replicate that of the political system. At the same time the organizing committee was renewed under Archdeacon Nestor Popovski. In their desire to cut off the Serbian heritage or to destroy the authority of the hierarchy, the local associations of clergy, supported by the authorities, or the local communist leadership, might well have gone further than the central authorities had intended.[48]

When Patriarch Gavrilo died in 1950, the Council of Bishops made a conciliatory gesture by inviting the Skopje committee to attend the election of his successor. This was Vikentije Prodanov, one of the bishops from Macedonia, who was anxious to settle the differences. The committee then called on the synod in November 1951 and acknowledged the jurisdiction of the patriarchate "insofar as it respects the national sovereignty of the Macedonian people." It set forth formal demands for exclusively local clergy and for the use of the Macedonian language, and nominated two candidates for then vacant sees: Bishop Dositej Stojković and priest Tomo Dimevski.

Born in Smederevo (in Serbia) of parents who had moved there from Macedonia, Dositej Stojković had been a monk since 1924. He had just been raised to the episcopacy in order to be appointed one of the new patriarch's auxiliaries (alongside the future patriarch, German). According to one authority,[49] the intention was indeed to send him to Skopje, but the government at the time was not prepared to allow a "Serbian" bishop to be appointed there. Since the Macedonian clergy were ready enough to receive him, this would appear to be an instance in which the political authorities were more "Macedonian" than the leaders of the local clergy. The organizing committee then submitted a new and fuller list of candidates, which retained Dimevski but omitted Dositej.

In 1957 use of the Macedonian language in diocesan administration in Macedonia was sanctioned, and Serbian Patriarch Vikentije ordained a number of Macedonian priests—the first ordinations for the region since the war.

Renewed Bulgarian claims on Macedonia, in 1958, induced the Belgrade government to expedite the settlement of the status of the Macedonian church. Within this context, the leaders of the Macedonian clergy summoned a new sobor. A breach was also made in the episcopate: Dositej, after seven years as an auxiliary, was ripe for persuasion. He was received by the secretary of the Macedonian central committee and turned up at the meeting of delegates of clergy and laity held at Ohrid in October 1951, without the knowledge of his fellow bishops. The delegates proclaimed the restoration of the see of Ohrid (originally established in 1019), adopted a statute for the Macedonian Orthodox church, decided that the church be governed by a synod of bishops under a metropolitan but with the patriarch of Belgrade as its nominal head, and elected its bishops. Dositej was elected metropolitan of Skopje and archbishop of Ohrid and was immediately installed.

While the new patriarch, German Djorić, would not have opposed the election to Skopje of his one-time colleague, Dositej, he could not approve of the irregular manner in which the election had been carried out. The Macedonian bishops had been elected not by their peers but by an ad hoc assembly of delegates which included not one hierarch. Dositej himself was bound by his oath to the established (Serbian) church. He would need to find another bishop to help him consecrate two new bishops, Kliment and Naum. In short, the foundations of the Macedonian Orthodox church had been laid in circumstances contrary to the canons and the practice of the Eastern church. The government used a blend of political pressure and financial incentive to get the Serbian episcopate to accept the fait accompli. Anxious to save what could still be saved, the hierarchy accepted it by recording it without approving it at its July 1959 session.

Patriarch German went himself to consecrate and install Macedonian bishop-elect Kliment in his see at Bitola. By this gesture of trust German gave the Macedonian church the power to consecrate further bishops in the apostolic succession. Dositej and Kliment then consecrated Protosynkellus Naum, so that the new bishops of Macedonia, if irregularly elected, were consecrated in a regular fashion. For all practical purposes the three dioceses now formed an autonomous metropolitanate dependent on the patriarchate in Belgrade, and it was as such that the Serbian church referred to them in official documents, even though the Macedonian metropolitanate preferred to describe itself as "independent" (*samostojna*)—an adjective with no ecclesiastical meaning. It adopted many of the trappings of a fully constituted church, in imitation of the Serbian church, and made the most of historical antecedents. At the same time the church was clearly emphasizing *national* qualification in its training of clergy. And thus, since 1961, all newly ordained priests have been tested for their knowledge of the Macedonian language and have been required to take an examination in Macedonian national and church history.

During 1966 the Macedonian Orthodox church braced itself for formal separation. It had acquired a fourth hierarch with the historical name and title of Metodij, titular bishop of Velika, who was in fact an auxiliary to Metropolitan Dositej.

Macedonian sources say that the church's request to the patriarch of Belgrade "to present the Macedonian Orthodox church to the sister Orthodox churches" had been turned down before it decided to demand autocephaly. There were meetings with Macedonian government leaders. The Macedonian bishops collectively went to Belgrade in November for talks with the

Serbian synod and, on their return home, sent a formal application. At the same time they threatened to act unilaterally, if necessary, through a synod of their own, in order to resolve matters to their satisfaction.[50]

The church was but the prime factor in the conspicuous nation-building of Macedonia by the Titoist regime in 1967. The problem of Yugoslavia's nationalities was again causing concern, and the resurgence of tension with Bulgaria gave the Belgrade government reason to want to strengthen the loyalty of a republic where not more than 71 percent of the population was registered as Macedonian. Culture and church were traditional attributes of nationhood in the Balkans, and both provided ways of giving the party leadership in Skopje full satisfaction, as well as of making the Macedonian beacon shine even more brightly toward Bulgaria and Greece. Government intervention was blatant.

One can think of other, secondary, reasons. The genuine, if fragile and transient, blossoming of ecumenism in the late 1960s, which made it more difficult to exploit the ancient mistrust between the Eastern and the Western church for political ends, might have added to the wish to create a breach within the Orthodox church itself. Moreover, if Aleksandar Ranković lent his weight to the resistance put up by the Serbian episcopate, his overthrow in July 1966 removed that brake.[51] Macedonian clerics were increasingly irritated by the difference between their own interpretation of the "personal union" between two sister churches and that of the Serbian hierarchy of an "autonomous part" of the Serbian church. Last, but not least, 1967 was a convenient date, for it would be the bicentenary of the abolition of the original archbishopric of Ohrid.

In April of that year Metropolitan Dositej journeyed again to Belgrade, with his auxiliary Metodij and the perennial Fr. Popovski, now settled in his role of éminence grise as chair of the Macedonian Priests' Association. They held talks with government leaders and with Patriarch German on the eve of the annual session of the Council of Bishops, and presented a formal request for ecclesiastical autocephaly. On May 24 the Council of Bishops considered this request, and rejected it, arguing that the church in Macedonia did not possess full qualifications for autocephaly, that its organization was too slender, and that it had too few bishops. Moreover, those bishops that it did have had transgressed the canons. The civil authorities had been involved in a question of internal ecclesiastical organization. The Macedonians were also warned that if they went ahead nevertheless, they would be setting themselves up as a schismatic religious organization.

The Macedonian synod hurriedly elected another titular bishop (Kiril of Tiveriopol) as second auxiliary to the metropolitan. The Metropolitan

Council, which met from July 17 to 19, 1967, could thus boast five bishops out of a total clergy of forty-four. The sobor started by reorganizing the dioceses, which were increased to five (to match the number of bishops, permitting all of them to maintain diocesan seats). This was done by setting up part of the diocese of Prespa and Bitola as a separate diocese of Velika (with its seat at Ohrid) and by uniting the six overseas parishes into a diocese of America-Canada-Australia (with its seat at Skopje). The two auxiliary bishops were elevated to the new sees—Metodij to Velika and Kiril to the émigré community—while Kliment of Prespa-Bitola was raised to the dignity of a metropolitan. Only after this window dressing was the Macedonian Orthodox church proclaimed autocephalous under a primate restyled archbishop of Ohrid and Macedonia.

The arguments put forward were historical continuity, de facto separation, indirect recognition by the Serbian patriarchate, political and ethnic rights. The historical claim was that the newly autocephalous church was the successor to the archbishopric of Ohrid. The Ottoman sultan had had no right to abolish it, and the Ecumenical Patriarchate had had no right to interfere in its internal affairs, even less to hand Macedonian sees over to the Serbian patriarchate. The historic claim went further, however, linking the continuity of the Macedonian church to a continuity of Macedonian history over the last one thousand years, and to the struggle of the Macedonian people for their national freedom.

The Serbian bishops convened in mid-September and deplored the "schismatic" action by the Macedonian clergy. The Serbian hierarchy likewise rejected the historic and political arguments advanced by the Macedonian clergy in support of their autocephaly. The Macedonian synod in turn rejected the resolution of the Serbian bishops, and since then, the two hierarchies have remained at odds.

In October 1983 the Macedonian Orthodox church celebrated the fortieth anniversary of that first meeting of clerics under partisan auspices in 1943. Presiding over the celebrations were the late primate, Archbishop Angelarij Krstevski (successor to Dositej, who had died in 1981) and the long-lasting Archpriest Popovski (still chair of the priests' association, now renamed the Society of the United Orthodox Clergy of Macedonia). When Angelarij died in a car accident in June 1986, Gavril Miloševski, a graduate of Belgrade University, was elected to succeed him.

How much had been achieved since 1967? With full cooperation from the authorities, the Macedonian church had applied itself to establish its position. It had obtained permission to build a new and imposing archbishop's residence (combining neo-Byzantine with late Stalinist architectural styles) in the center of Skopje, and had opened a new seminary, the

St. Clement of Ohrid Faculty of Theology. Its official bimonthly journal, *Vesnik*, launched in 1958, had a circulation of about one thousand in
1967—a figure that has since risen to about three thousand. In general,
however, church statistics have been difficult to obtain. Whereas in 1967,
on direct application to the church authorities in Skopje, I had been provided with relevant figures, in 1982 no answer was forthcoming on the
numbers of faithful and clergy in Macedonia.[52]

The Macedonian Orthodox church has spared no effort to establish
communications with other Orthodox churches by sending out seasonal
greetings and by sending its dignitaries on visits (notably to Constantinople, Romania, Russia, and Bulgaria). It has now established a tradition
of having high-ranking delegations go to Rome every year in May, to
pray at the tomb of St. Cyril in the basilica of St. Clement. None of this
has resulted in formal recognition. The mother church of Constantinople
has, in modern times, always rejected nationalism as an argument valid
in itself for the establishment of an autocephalous church and has insisted
on the unity of Orthodox jurisdiction within the territory of a sovereign
state. In the case of Yugoslavia, from the 1920s to the present day, it has
stressed the territorial and jurisdictional unity of the church to the point
of addressing the patriarch by a title of its own invention, which avoids
the ethnic adjective "Serbian" and covers the whole territory of the state.[53]
The splendid visit of Patriarch Athenagoras to Patriarch German in 1967
was meant, among other things, to encourage the Serbian episcopate in its
stand over a unified patriarchal jurisdiction.

All the same, what is the position now? In spite of periodic outbursts
of official impatience from the political authorities, the Serbian Orthodox
church maintains a dignified silence, and publicly ignores the Macedonian
church. The Serbian patriarchate has issued no anathema, has not severed
relations with the faithful of Macedonia, and has not pursued the matter
of canonical procedure against the bishops. Indeed, there have even been
discreet and intermittent talks between the two hierarchies since 1978 (albeit at the prodding of the political authorities). Their only result so far is
that the Serbian patriarchate has expressed the view that the matter could
be solved by a future ecumenical council that would decide on conditions
for the granting of autocephaly.[54]

The Macedonian schism in Yugoslavia is the dividing line between two
conceptions of the church as well as between two nations. The statute of
the Macedonian church requires its primate to take an oath of loyalty "to
the people's authorities." The church celebrates thanksgiving services on
state occasions, while bishops turn up at official inaugurations and festivities, almost as in those last remaining Roman Catholic countries where

the church is still under a concordat regime. Congratulatory messages and addresses to federal and local state and party dignitaries are real eulogies rather than mere formalities. In return, these officials and the press are full of praise for the Macedonian Orthodox church, which they set up as a model of behavior for religious denominations. Established in all but name, the Macedonian church promotes, as an auxiliary to the political authority, what it considers to be the interests of the Macedonian nation. It belongs to a nineteenth-century tradition, where the church was hardly more than a government department, a factor in the service of state nationalism, along with education or history, or culture in the widest sense of the word.

The Serbian church, on the other hand—an established church in all but name under the Kingdom of Yugoslavia—promotes what it perceives as the interests of the Serbian nation, but it does so nowadays in spite of the state, and increasingly to the distaste of the government. In practice, therefore, it is impossible to imagine it renouncing its Serbianism for the sake of church unity—at least in the foreseeable future. It fits into another tradition, that of the pre-1766 patriarchate of Peć.

Of the two conceptions, which one can win? Both are looking backward to past models. Both are being used by secular forces. Both are guilty of ethnophiletism (nationalism)—the one keeping on the right side of ecclesiastical legality, the other straying beyond it.

Conclusion

The minor Orthodox churches of Eastern Europe cannot afford to play for big stakes. Realism dictates a policy tailored to promote survival and a modicum of comfort. Their profile has thus been distinctly low-key. To the extent that they do speak out, it is to lend support to the state. The Orthodox tradition has long emphasized transcendental contemplation and personal, familial piety over social action. Lacking institutionalized doctrines of religious activism and evangelism, the Orthodox hierarchy has perceived its primary mission as continuing to offer the "mysteries of salvation" to the faithful, convinced that God will not allow the church to perish. With a highly developed sense of the temporary nature of all sociopolitical orders, the Orthodox hierarchy in these states has shown itself inclined to favor flexible strategies to ensure the church's survival. And thus the Orthodox church has defined its role as that of a spiritual institution concerned with religious and moral values rather than with political affairs. In a typical remark concerning the church's mission in communist society, Polish Metropolitan Stefan Rudyk noted in 1966, "The Orthodox church does not consider it the task of a church to engage in political discussions. We observe most strictly the separation between secular power and the competence of the church."[55]

In return, the regimes have frequently praised the Orthodox leaderships' cooperation, particularly their contributions in "easing social tensions" and "consolidating public order in the country" during periods of economic and social instability. And on major national anniversaries, politically loyal hierarchs have been rewarded with awards and sashes, in recognition of their support for government policies.[56]

FACT SHEET

Minor Orthodox Churches

Polish Autocephalous Orthodox Church

Year of autocephaly
1924: granted by the Ecumenical Patriarch
1948: recognized by the Patriarch of Moscow

Current strength of the church (1984)
855,000 faithful
246 priests
14 monks
14 nuns
60 seminarians

Chief news organs
Tserkovnyi vestnik (in Russian)
Wiadomosci polskiego autokefalicznego kosciola prewoslawnego (in Polish)

Number of churches and church facilities in operation (1984)
310 churches
1 seminary
1 convent
1 monastery

Metropolitans since 1924
Dionizy Waledynski, 1924–48
Makarii (Makarios) Oksiiuk, 1951–59

Timoteusz (Timotheus) Szretter, 1960–62
Stefan Rudyk, 1965–69
Bazyli Doroszkiewicz, 1970–present

Orthodoxy in Hungary

Jurisdictions
  Serbian diocese of Buda, under the Patriarchate of Belgrade: 17
    parishes
  Romanian diocese of Gyula, under the Patriarchate of Bucharest: 18
    parishes
  Hungarian deanery of Budapest, under the Patriarchate of Moscow: 9
    parishes
  Jurisdiction of the Patriarchate of Sofia: 2 parishes

Current strength of the church (1984)
  40,000 believers
  40 priests
  0 nuns
  2 seminarians (in Leningrad)

Chief news organ
  Egyhazi Kronika, since 1952 (circulation: 700 copies)

Number of churches and church facilities in operation
  52 churches
  0 seminaries
  0 convents
  0 monasteries

Macedonian Orthodox Church

Year of autocephaly: 1967

Current strength of the church (1983)
  600,000–1 million believers
  250 priests
  15 monks

Chief news organ
  Vesnik na Makedonskata pravoslavna crkva (3,000 copies circulation
    in 1983)

Number of churches and church facilities in operation (1983)
- 225 parishes
- 500 churches
- 1 theological seminary
- 1 theological faculty
- 102 monasteries (Since there are only 15 monks, this figure must refer to monastic buildings rather than to active monastic communities.)

Archbishops since 1958
- Dositej (Stojković), 1958–81
- Angelarij (Krstevski), 1981–86
- Gavril (Miloševski), 1986–present

V

NON-CHALCEDONIAN CHURCHES

18

The Armenian Apostolic Church

Claire Seda Mouradian

For many Armenians and foreign observers, the Armenian Apostolic church in the USSR seems to enjoy a privileged status and seems to have succeeded in accomplishing its pastoral mission, particularly since the Second World War. A closer analysis indicates, however, that the history of this national institution during the Soviet era passes through the same phases and was subjected to the same crises as the other churches of the Soviet Union. To the extent that it has had some particularity, this consists in its role as a Vatican for an Armenian diaspora that followed the genocide of 1915. The diaspora represents more than one-third of the nation.

Although constituted on only a portion of the ancestral land—and not the portion where the majority of the diaspora has its roots—and although endowed with a regime that has been imposed by force, the Soviet Republic of Armenia has attempted to present itself as the motherland of all Armenians, as the only place where Armenian renaissance and survival can take place, the only land where prosperity and development of the nation are secure under the necessary protection of the Russian "nucleus."

Benefiting from the increasingly conciliatory attitude of the state, the Armenian church, through the catholicos of Echmiadzin, has maintained energetic contact with the diaspora; by its rediscovered opulence, it has testified to the benefits of the regime and has made itself an authorized mouthpiece for national claims. In so doing, is the church pursuing its own goals and those of the nation, or is it merely a cog in the machine directed by the state? To answer this question, it is useful to introduce an analysis of the contemporary status of the religious institution, not only in the Soviet context in general but also in the context of the nation's distant past that has best determined the specificity of the Armenian church.

The Armenian Church,
Sanctuary of National Identity

Throughout its tormented history the church has been the symbol and refuge of national personality.[1] By detaching itself from the universal church, following the Council of Chalcedon (A.D. 451), more for political considerations (the struggle against Byzantine influence) than for theological reasons ("Armenian monophysism"), by adopting the title of "Apostolic," and by securing the recognition of the Sasanid kings, it established itself very quickly as the national church, fully autocephalous.

Deeply involved in most initiatives appealing for crusade by European monarchs for the liberation of the country, the church even went as far as participating in armed struggle. In 1826–27 the bishop of Tiflis and future catholicos, Nerses Ashtaraketsi, headed the Armenian volunteers who fought on the side of the Russian army for the conquest of Erevan against the Persians. In the second half of the nineteenth century Patriarch Khrimian made undisguised appeals in favor of a war of liberation in western Armenia. Even after the progressive secularization of the Armenian movement and the emergence of revolutionary parties, socialist or Marxist, the ties of all leading intellectual and political personalities in Armenia with the Armenian church remained strong. From Simon Vratsian, prime minister of the independent Republic of Armenia (1918–20) and a major figure in the Dashnaktsutiun,[2] to Aghasi Khandjian, first secretary of the Communist party of Armenia (1930–36), or the illustrious Anastas Mikoyan, longtime member of the Politburo and eventual ceremonial president of the USSR, most national leaders were nurtured in the Armenian culture and taught in parochial schools or in the major seminaries, such as the Kevorkian of Echmiadzin and the Nersesian of Tiflis, before moving toward very different ideological horizons.

The Juridical Status of the Armenian Church

The Armenian Apostolic church is managed by two catholicosates, independent and equal in rights: that of Echmiadzin in Soviet Armenia, and the Great House of Cilicia, transferred to Antilias, near Beirut, from Sis, in 1930. In effect, the seat of the catholicosate has followed the movements of political power during many invasions and foreign occupations of Armenia. Vagharshapat, Echmiadzin, Dvin, Ani, Dzamentav (Tormarza),

Ramgla, Akhtamar, and then beginning in 1293, Sis, capital of the Cilician
Armenian kingdom, have been successively the centers of the Armenian
church. The conquest of Sis by the Mamluks of Egypt in 1375 brought
in its wake a period of troubles and intrigues (assassinations of six successive catholicoses), while the increasing influence of Roman Catholicism
stimulated fears of a union with Rome. This resulted in the initiative (in
1441) of the clergy in the eastern Armenian monasteries to transfer the
catholicosate to Echmiadzin, the original site of the national church. The
clergy of Cilicia, however, refused to recognize the move. The controversy
over the respective legitimacy of these rival sees was not settled until
1652, when an agreement between the two primates ended the dispute by
dividing ecclesiastical jurisdiction between them. Tacitly, the duality was
also taken as a guarantee of the continuity of the Armenian church in the
event that one of the sees should be suppressed by the Muslim forces of
either the Ottoman or the Persian empires.

The conquest of eastern Armenia by tsarist Russia in the nineteenth
century opened a new era of crisis. Rivalries between the Ottoman and
Russian empires had repercussions on the relations between the two
catholicosal sees. The *Pologenye* (Regulation) of 1836 recognized the
Armenian Apostolic church as a national institution but also placed it
under the strict control of Russian authorities and reduced the traditional
role of the laity in the administration of church affairs. The choice of
bishops and the catholicos himself was henceforth made, ultimately, by
the tsar.

In the Ottoman Empire, beginning in 1461, an Armenian patriarchate
in Istanbul was created by Sultan Mehmet II as the official representative
for the *millet* (community) of Armenians. The patriarchate's temporal
powers were redefined and institutionalized by the Armenian national
constitution of 1863. But during the 1860s there were already attempts
by the Sublime Porte to reevaluate the spiritual and political power of the
catholicos of Sis, most probably to counterbalance the role of Echmiadzin,
which was suspected of entertaining pro-Russian feelings.

In addition to the opposition of the patriarch in Constantinople, who
saw in Ottoman policy an abrogation of its prerogatives, this attempt
revived the quarrel between the two catholicosal sees. At the height of
the Russo-Turkish tension, the authoritarian catholicos of Echmiadzin,
Kevork IV (1866–82), proclaimed the see of Sis heretical and secessionist,
and proscribed the bishops of the Great House of Cilicia from officiating
in the diocese of Echmiadzin unless Sis paid allegiance to Echmiadzin. The
relations between the two sees were normalized only with the election
of Khrimian Hairig to the see of Echmiadzin (1890–1907) and of Sahag

Khabayan at Sis, the friendship between the two men being parallel to their concern with the increasing perils to Armenians in both empires.

The two sees have equal rights from the spiritual and administrative points of view. Both sees have the power to ordain bishops and archbishops, to send legates, to call national councils, to bless the holy oil, to modify canonical rules, to dissolve marriages, and so forth. But the catholicos of Echmiadzin enjoys an honorary primacy over the catholicos of the Great House of Cilicia, whose authority extends only to the diocese of his own province. The full title of the catholicos of Echmiadzin reads: "Servant of Jesus Christ and, by the Will of God, Supreme Archbishop and Catholicos of All Armenians, Supreme Patriarch of the Very Eminent See of the Apostolic Mother Church of Ararat at the Saint Cathedral of Echmiadzin."

Between 1915 and 1920, with the genocide and dispersion of western Armenians on the one hand and the sovietization of eastern Armenia on the other, the situation turned upside down. In 1921 the seat of the catholicosate of Sis was transferred to Aleppo and in 1930 to Antilias near Beirut. The catholicos of Cilicia continued to exercise his authority over the churches and communities of Lebanon, Syria, and Cyprus. The patriarch of Constantinople was left with nothing but the spiritual direction of a few tens of thousands of surviving Armenians in the new Republic of Turkey. The role of the patriarch of Jerusalem, guardian of the traditional privileges of the Armenian church in the holy sites, was now limited more and more to that of a head of a monastic congregation within the walls of the convent of St. James; at the same time the old Armenian colonies of Palestine and Jordan and the bishoprics of Haifa, Jaffa, and Amman declined. By contrast, the jurisdiction of the catholicos of Echmiadzin, now lying within Soviet frontiers, has expanded its jurisdiction and doubled in importance. It not only extends over the five dioceses situated within the USSR but also exercises authority over thirty dioceses, prelacies, and vicariates on five continents. Thus, Echmiadzin has become the religious center and focus of loyalty for dispersed Armenians, invested with a moral and national authority that makes it a natural mediator between Soviet Armenia and the diaspora. It is this latter character that gives importance to the debate about its actual autonomy in relation to the Soviet state.

The Armenian Church during Stalin's Rule

Under the Bolsheviks, all properties of the church were nationalized; churches were confiscated or simply demolished. The seminary of Echmiadzin was closed. Catechism was proscribed. The printing press and library of the catholicosate were seized, and the most precious treasures were sent to Moscow. Priests were hunted down and high clergy limited to the walls of the monastery. The clergy was cut off from its flock.

With the start of the New Economic Policy (NEP), the repression diminished. In order to rally the support of a population that had proven its ability to revolt and in order not to alienate a diaspora whose financial support was needed and which had started to organize, some concessions were made: restitution of the treasury and the vineyards of Echmiadzin, the reopening of some churches, and reestablishment of relations with the dioceses.

The old catholicos, Kevork V, refused allegiance to the new regime. He was isolated but lived in relative peace until his death in 1930. Nonetheless, the church gradually lost its power. The respected hierarchy was still cut off from the population. Processions, pastoral visits, diocesan inspections, sermons, patriarchal bulls were all proscribed. The ecclesiastical institution was represented soon by no more than a few parish priests, the *kahanas* (noncelibate priests) who, in contrast to the *vartabeds* (archimandrites) and high clergy, were hardly literate, lived more and more miserably, and inspired little deference.

Following the model of the Living Church of Russian Orthodoxy, an Armenian "Free Church" made its appearance in 1922, under the guise of a purification movement. Its aim was no less than to undermine the authority of the traditional church.[3] Founded in the 1920s, the Armenian section of the League of Militant Godless organized antireligious parades and indoctrination classes for children, while its organ, *Anastvatz* (Atheist), ridiculed religion and believers. Schools, of course, became the place where the atheistic and materialistic education of the youth was imparted most effectively.

In the spring of 1929 Moscow decreed a new law governing religious activity, emphasizing the state's control of the parishes. An amendment to the constitution made it illegal to proselytize, just a few months before the "second revolution" (collectivization campaign) proceeded to liquidate the church altogether.

The attitude toward the hierarchy was more ambiguous. The monks at Echmiadzin could not wear their ecclesiastical garments outside the monastery and had to request police authorization to leave the walls of the monastery. By the beginning of the 1930s, only twenty monks remained there. Nonetheless, after the death of Catholicos Kevork V, the state did not hesitate to authorize the reunion of the council to designate a successor. The state undoubtedly found it useful that Echmiadzin continued to assure the selection of the heads of the Armenian dioceses throughout the world, rather than leaving it to the catholicos of Antilias to assume this prerogative.

In November 1932, during a tolerant interlude of the antireligious campaign, the locum tenens, Khoren I Muradbegian, archbishop of Erevan, an energetic man with a high sense of spiritual and moral integrity, was elected catholicos by a council of seventy-three members, of whom fifty-three were laymen and seven were delegates from foreign countries, whose degree of sympathy for the regime had been tested before they were granted visas.

This period of relative tolerance, during which the selection of the catholicos took place, was aimed mainly at the diaspora. The question was the legitimation, in the eyes of the diaspora, of the idea that the regime had a benevolent attitude toward the church as a national institution, at a time when the first repatriation was being organized to bring diasporic Armenians "back" to Soviet Armenia. In this context, some priests and bishops, who had been deported to Siberia, were now released; the monks of Echmiadzin were once again allowed to teach; and the movement of the "Free Church" was scuttled. But soon the great purges of 1936–38 signaled a resumption of a determined offensive against churches throughout the Soviet Union. Relations with the diaspora were practically ended and general repression against the clergy did not spare even the catholicos himself. On April 6, 1938, he died—most likely by strangulation at the hands of the secret police, to whom he had refused to turn over the keys of the treasures of Echmiadzin.[4] The monastic clergy were decimated. In 1945 only four monks could participate in the congress to elect a new catholicos.

The Great Patriotic War

Following the example of the Russian metropolitan, Sergii, who, since June 21, 1941, had denounced the foreign aggressor and appealed for a divine benediction for the defenders of the fatherland—in contrast to Stalin's initial silence—the Armenian church prayed for the salvation of the Soviet soldiers and for victory. Faced with the necessity to mobilize all the living forces of the country, the state abolished the antireligious periodicals and dissolved the League of Militant Godless. The press recognized the contribution of the church to the war effort. The church, in fact, multiplied its patriotic declarations and the appeals for contributions to the defense of the country among others for the financing of the armored divisions that were baptized "Dimitri Donskoi" in Russia, and "David of Sasun" in Armenia, in reference to the national epics.

The result was a general thaw in church-state relations. The Armenian church was allowed to reopen a seminary, to resume publication of the catholicosal review, *Echmiadzin*, and to convene a congress to elect a new catholicos. A council for the religious affairs of the Armenian church was set up as well.

In June 1945 an election council was convened at Echmiadzin, in the most solemn circumstances, in the presence of the patriarchs of Constantinople and Jerusalem and the catholicos of Cilicia. The council sealed the reconciliation between church and state and named the locum tenens, Kevork VI Chorekjian, to the catholicosal seat that had been vacant for seven years.

Under the supervision of the federal representative of the Council of Religious Affairs and his Armenian counterpart, 113 delegates convened as an Armenian representative assembly, representing Armenian parishes both in the Soviet Union and in diaspora, though representatives for the latter were of course carefully screened and thus included, for example, the editors of communist or pro-Soviet journals, members of the Armenian General Benevolent Union (AGBU,[5] or pro-Soviet "national fronts," created to support Soviet Armenia and the Armenian cause during World War II. Of the twenty-seven clergymen present, only those representing the external dioceses belonged to the hierarchy, while Soviet dioceses were represented exclusively by lower clergy or laymen, except for the diocese of Shirag-Leninagan, which was represented by an archimandrite. Despite the official separation of church and state, the congress participated in the cult of the personality and proletarian internationalism, paying homage to Grand Marshal Stalin, the Great Russian people, and the regime itself.

Especially important was the catholicos's inaugural speech, which announced the postwar campaign of repatriation en masse and raised the problem of Armenian territories lying within Turkish boundaries. Within the context of the Soviet-Turkish tension following the war, the catholicos, the moral representative of the Armenian people, made himself the spokesman for national irredentism, which had a very strong impact on the diaspora.

Like the Russian Orthodox church, the Armenian Apostolic church had to pay for its survival as an institution, beginning in 1943, with unquestioning loyalty. The church has had to sanction both the internal and external policies of the USSR. Thus, both the Armenian catholicos and the Moscow patriarch signed the Stockholm appeal when NATO was created, citing the Christian values of peace, love, and fraternity. The catholicos also condemned "American imperialist aggression" in Korea later, as did the other religious leaders in the USSR.[6] In his messages to the Armenian

believers overseas and in the ecclesiastical review *Echmiadzin*, he anathematized the activities of the Anglo-American alliance, "the makers of war
and their accomplices, enemies of the Armenian people, of the fatherland,
and of the Armenian church" in diaspora (i.e., the Dashnaktsutiun).[7]

Parallel to these declarations, celebrations of the mass in certain Armenian dioceses overseas, particularly in the Balkans, Iraq, Iran, and India,
began to commemorate the sovietization of Armenia as its liberation. In
Iran, however, this led to the expulsion of Bishop Vahan Kostanian of
Isfahan, in 1951, who was suspected of being an agent of the Soviet secret
police.[8]

And finally, upon the death of the catholicos of Cilicia in June 1952,
Echmiadzin, citing its "preeminence" and the necessity to "unite the
Armenian church," challenged the independence of the see of Antilias and
proposed its own candidate. This led to protests from the Dashnaktsutiun.[9]
All the same, Kevork VI of Echmiadzin (1945–54) must be credited with
the reopening of some churches and monasteries and the consecration of
ten bishops, six of whom were destined for the diaspora.

From Hostage Catholicoses to Co-Opted Catholicoses

In May 1954 Kevork VI, the last survivor of the old generation of Armenian hierarchy formed before the revolution and a witness to great up-
heavals in the life of his people, died at the age of eighty-five. In contrast
to the silence of the preceding period on religious events—except on the
occasion of the congress of 1945—the republican and federal Soviet press
(*Pravda*, *Izvestiia*, and Tass included) announced the death of the Armenian catholicos. Kevork VI was paid homage as the "champion of peace,"
who had "rendered great service during the war by organizing patriotic
activities."[10] Kevork VI was given a solemn funeral, presided over by
Khat Adjapahian, the locum tenens of the see of Cilicia and the candidate favored by Echmiadzin, in the presence of representatives of most of
the Armenian dioceses, of various foreign churches, and presidents of the
councils for religious affairs of the USSR and the Armenian SSR. Radio
Erevan devoted a number of programs to the death of the catholicos.

By contrast, the Dashnaktsutiun denounced the "Machiavellian character of the Soviet propaganda [which hoped] to play upon the religious
feeling of the Armenian people with the purpose of extending its influence to the Armenians of the diaspora."[11] Commenting on the personality
of the deceased catholicos, the Dashnaks endeavored to demonstrate his
total dependence on the state, but also welcomed his efforts for the survival of the catholicosal see, while their adversaries, the Ramkavars and

Hunchaks,[12] insisted on the constructive character of his work and his independence.[13]

The former bishop of Isfahan, now Archbishop Vahan Kostanian, was soon named locum tenens and president of the Spiritual Council, but there were no signs of preparations for the succession. It was only after it was announced in June 1955 that a council would convene in October 14 of the same year to designate—finally, after a three-year delay—the successor to the throne of Cilicia that in August 1955 a date was fixed (September 30) for convening the electoral congress to elect the catholicos of Echmiadzin. New passions were unleashed in the diasporic communities, where the anti-Soviet groups protested against the conditions for the convocation of the Congress of Echmiadzin. They considered the latter an attempt to interfere in the succession of the Cilician see and appealed to their clergy to boycott the Echmiadzin congress.

Of the eighteen bishops of the Armenian Apostolic church, only nine, three of whom were from the Soviet republic, were present in Echmiadzin for the elections. The patriarch of Constantinople, the locum tenens of Jerusalem and Antilias, did not participate. The dioceses of Teheran, Tabriz, Athens, Aleppo, Lebanon, and Cyprus, communities where the Dashnak party was well implanted, refused to send delegates. Finally, of the 170 delegates predicted to participate in the congress, only 137 did so. Of this total, 108 came from Soviet dioceses.

This congress, the first and only one since the death of Stalin, deserves some attention. The report presented at the opening of the congress, read by the locum tenens on September 29, focused on the strengthening of the congregation of Echmiadzin in its relations with the Soviet state, the overseas dioceses, and other Christian churches, and analyzed the financial situation of the holy see of Echmiadzin by soliciting the assistance of believers and in particular the "wealthy Armenians of the diaspora." This first session ended with the unanimous vote on a proposition of a Cilician bishop, Derenik Poladian, "to thank the government of Armenia which had brought to completion the restoration of the Cathedral of Echmiadzin."[14] The following day, by a vote of 126 out of 137, the young bishop of Romania, Vazken Baljian, was elected catholicos. Ordained late in life (having been a teacher until 1943), he had been practically unknown until then. On October 2 he was consecrated with the name Vazken I.

The main question of this session was supposed to be the examination of the constitution of the Armenian church, which had already been placed on the agenda during the council of 1945 and then shelved due to "lack of time." However, it was postponed again to a subsequent date in order to allow the Spiritual Council to conduct a serious study.

In the final tally the congress dealt only with the elections of the catholicos and of the Spiritual Council of Echmiadzin, the results of which seemed to have been decided in advance by the regime. No other important question, particularly the status of the church, was really discussed or resolved. As with the Soviet representative assemblies, the National Council of the Armenian Apostolic church came to play the role of a rubber stamp. Yet, as in the case of the Supreme Soviet, no effort was spared to ensure the appropriate externalities of official consideration. The ceremony of the consecration of Vazken I was described in detail in the catholicosal review as well as in the organs of the party and the government, *Kommunist* and *Sovietagan Hayastan*. In addition, it was broadcast in Erevan.

Despite the opulence of Vazken I's consecration, the status of the Armenian Apostolic church was not so radiant at the time. Bishop Derenik Poladian, one of the two dignitaries of the Cilician clergy to have participated in the election of 1955 and guest professor of theology at Echmiadzin (1953–54), made the following comment in a travelogue published later: "Monasteries are abandoned and in ruin everywhere, hardly inhabited by one or two isolated monks. Churches serve more often as depots for harvests or as clubs. Priests have disappeared and youth have lost all contact with those who a generation before constituted the soul and identity of the Armenian people." [15]

Neither the catholicosate nor the Soviet regime has ever furnished precise numbers on the state of the faith and the church in Soviet Armenia. A few sparse pieces of information may provide an idea nonetheless. Of the 1,500 Armenian parishes before 1917,[16] there seem to have been fewer than one hundred remaining in 1954.[17] In Erevan there are only three churches open for worship. Of two thousand clergymen before 1914, there are only 150 left.[18] During the election congress of 1945 the Armenian parishes of the USSR could delegate no more than six priests and one *vartabed*, while the Echmiadzin monastery itself seemed to have been reduced to four monks. In 1955 the situation was slightly improved. According to the report presented to the election congress, the Echmiadzin monastery had seventeen members, including one archbishop and two bishops. Immediately following the consecration of Vazken I, this number increased to thirty members. The report provides no indication of the number of priests. The Academy of Theology, reopened in 1954, had thirty-four students in 1954–55, of whom many were Armenians from the diaspora. The teaching staff was composed entirely of laymen.[19] To the few churches open for worship, one should add five monasteries: Echmiadzin, St. Hripsime, Keghart, St. Shokhagat, and St. Gayaneh (the restoration of which is being planned with help from the diaspora). The income of Echmiadzin, which possesses no endowment, comes from the sale of candles and offerings of the believers and especially of donations from the diaspora, to which appeals are constantly made.

The catechismal activities of the church are just about nonexistent. It seems that there had been no printing of the Bible until after the death of Kevork VI. In addition to an annual calendar, the catholicosal see publishes the review *Echmiadzin*, the editorial board of which is in the hands of lay persons. More Armenological than theological, and allotting much space to the church's political message (letters to the diaspora and to the Soviet government, declarations in favor of peace and against the Vatican, etc.), *Echmiadzin* does not escape either the censorship or the style of official periodicals. Finally, the president of the Council for Religious Affairs, who assures the contact between the ecclesiastical institution and the government, supervises the relations with the believers and the management of the church. He is often, if not always, recruited from among the cadres of the party, predisposed to ideological control. This was the case especially with Hrachia Krikorian, council president from 1948 to 1957; previously he had been president of the Armenian Writers' Union (1938–39 and 1946), editor of *Kommunist* (1939–44), Armenian correspondent for *Pravda* (1948–49), and editor of the monthly *Sovietagan Hayastan*, destined for the diaspora (1959–63). More recently, Karlen N. Tallakian, a former member of the Executive of the Komsomol and later chief of Agitprop (1971–75), served as president of the Armenian Council, 1963–70.

The Cilician Elections of 1956

Despite the immensity of the domestic tasks required to give life to the Armenian church in the Soviet Union, following the ordination of some new bishops and monks, the first act of the catholicos of Echmiadzin was to rush to Beirut in February 1956 to assist in the election of the catholicos of the Great House of Cilicia and to attempt to impose his own candidate. The see had been vacant since the death of Karekin I in June 1952. But, although the elections ought to have taken place at the very most within six months, the candidate favored by Echmiadzin, namely, the locum tenens, Archbishop Khat Adjapahian, postponed them on a number of occasions. Once he was accused of systematic obstructions. Accusations forced him to resign at the end of 1955. He was replaced by Bishop Khoren Paroyan, president of the diocese of Lebanon, said to have been a Dashnak, who fixed the elections for February 14, 1956.

From the beginning the Ramkavar/Hunchak bloc tried to invalidate these arrangements and to prevent the election of an "anti-Echmiadzin" candidate, going so far as to demand that the Syrian authorities, by then pro-Soviet, should dissolve the national and ecclesiastical organs of the diocese of Aleppo. This maneuver was intended to eliminate Bishop Zareh, president of the diocese of Aleppo and an energetic supporter of the independence of the Great House of Cilicia, as a contender. The passions were so intense that there were clashes between the rival political factions, some of which took place in the Cathedral of Aleppo itself.

It was in this charged atmosphere that Vazken I, ten days before the election, informed Bishop Khoren that "having in mind the defense and consolidation of the interests of the Armenian church," he had decided to assist personally in the election and consecration of the catholicos of Cilicia. This decision was without precedent and had the effect of a bomb.

On February 12, following a stopover in Paris, Vazken I was welcomed in Beirut by a gigantic crowd and various Lebanese personalities, representatives of other religious denominations (Orthodox, Maronite, Catholic), and, of course, all the Armenian clergy as well as the Soviet ambassador and consul. In his welcoming speech Bishop Khoren, while recognizing Echmiadzin as the spiritual center of all Armenians, insisted on the independence of the Cilician see. Vazken I avoided the subject, being content with his affirmation that he had come to "reinforce the ties of friendship and unity which exist between the holy see of Echmiadzin and the other holy sees of the Armenian church," implicitly putting the catholicosate of Cilicia on the same level with the Armenian patriarchates of Constantinople and Jerusalem.

On February 14 Vazken I opened the Assembly of Dioceses and Delegates of Cilicia and demanded to close it immediately and postpone it. The assembly quickly became polarized. The minority, led by the lay Soviet delegate and member of the Spiritual Council, Professor A. Arakelian, felt that it was necessary to follow the advice of the catholicos and leave immediately. The majority agreed to delay the election a week. Twelve discontented delegates, of whom two were Soviets, left the session. During the following days the polemics in the Armenian press indicate the political games involved in the elections. The Dashnak organ, *Atzak,* denounced the Soviet maneuvers to dominate the diaspora community:

> It is now evident that the delegation presided over by the Catholicos
> of All Armenians came to Beirut with a particular mission, that is
> to sabotage at all costs the election of the Catholicos of the Great
> House of Cilicia, so that this See is left vacant and the Catholicosate
> becomes a simple diocese. We have understood very quickly what

dangers were threatening the Holy See of Cilicia since the masks have been taken off and, behind the Armenian delegation coming from Echmiadzin, one could hear the orders from Moscow.[20]

However, the Ramkavar newspaper, *Zartonk*, took issue with *Aztak*, accusing the Dashnak leaders of wanting "to prove to their foreign masters that they are ready always and everywhere to oppose the 'Soviet' Echmiadzin."[21] For *Zartonk*, Vazken I was the symbol of "unity and fraternity among the Armenian people."[22]

Following the failure of some appeals for reconciliation by deleting the candidacies of Bishops Khoren and Zareh, Vazken I left Lebanon on February 20. On the same day Bishop Zareh was elected catholicos of Cilicia.

The mission to reinforce the unity of the Armenian church ended thus in a grave crisis. On the day following the election of Zareh I the Antilias congregation was divided in two, reproducing the division between the rival parties in the community—some contesting the legality of the election of a catholicos "imposed from abroad," and the others insisting on the legitimacy of Zareh's election but still denying Echmiadzin the right to meddle in the affairs of the see of Cilicia, which was not subordinate to it. Vazken I did not leave the conflict aside either. He took the question of relations between the two sees to a council of bishops that he convened in Cairo on March 5, 1956. This assembly, whose legality is contested,[23] was dominated by the partisans of Echmiadzin. It decided to consider the elections at Antilias as "irregular and unacceptable," unless Zareh I accepted the terms of an agreement addressed to him, a veritable ultimatum subordinating the see of Cilicia to that of Echmiadzin and reducing it to the rank of a patriarchate, even a diocese, without any economic or administrative independence.[24] Refusing to accept this, Zareh I was finally consecrated on October 2, following a final appeal by Vazken I to the Lebanese government to proscribe the consecration.

This situation produced a schism within the Armenian church and aggravated the political tensions within the diaspora, going as far as provoking armed confrontations. Allegiance toward Antilias or Echmiadzin became eventually a form of denial or acceptance of the Soviet reality and the fiction of an Armenia preserving its autonomy within the USSR. The Antilias congregation and the communities subordinate to the Cilician see were divided into two rival blocs. Iran, Greece, and parts of the North and South American dioceses declared themselves outside the jurisdiction of Echmiadzin and accepted the jurisdiction of Antilias. Within the United States particularly, churches multiplied, even in small communities.

Atheist Propaganda and the Rebirth of the Church

The crisis of the Antilias elections brought harm to the prestige of Vazken I. He was purely and simply accused of being an agent of the KGB, associated with the Soviets after having collaborated with the Nazis in Romania.[25] Perhaps in order to erase the bad feelings stirred up by these accusations, Vazken announced, in July 1956, that he anticipated receiving permission later in the year to reopen some twenty churches and four monasteries in Soviet dioceses. In May 1957 the Tass news agency mentioned that Vazken I had undertaken a series of diocesan visits to Leninakan and Nor Nakhichevan, where he was received with full honors by the executive committees of the cities. There he celebrated mass, attracting thousands of believers.[26] The press presented this as evidence of the tolerance and even benevolence of the Soviet state vis-à-vis the Armenian church. Nonetheless, the attitude of the state toward the believers and the faith, although watered down by détente, did not really seem in essence to differ from the preceding period.

On July 24, 1954, an editorial in *Pravda* dedicated to the necessity of energetic measures to eradicate "religious prejudices" let it be known that a new atheistic campaign might be on the way. Indeed, the press was mobilized throughout the country and ridiculed the persistence of religious practices which supposedly were leading to the abandonment of work, destroying professional and social conscience, and encouraging alcoholism since ceremonies and religious feasts habitually involved drink. On September 17, 1954, Radio Erevan recalled that Lenin had compared religion to vodka.[27] Nonetheless, on November 11, a resolution of the Central Committee of the CPSU called a temporary halt to the antireligious propaganda. The Central Committee urged patient persuasion on the basis of "scientific facts." Indeed, since 1947, the League of Militant Atheists had been replaced with the more respectable-sounding Society for the Diffusion of Political and Scientific Facts, which publishes a monthly review, *Nauka i zhizn*, with special editions for all the republics. The Armenian edition is known as *Kidelik* and has been edited, since its establishment in 1947, by Professor Victor Hamparsoumian, an astrophysicist by training. *Kidelik* claims to have multiplied the number of its members many times over (from 175 in 1947, to more than 14,000 in 1973), including forty-six members of the Academy of Sciences, fifty-one corresponding members of the academy, 287 professors, and 1,536 candidates of science. It has also organized more than 100,000 lectures.[28]

In November 1956 *Partiagan Giank* (Party Life), relying on a new resolution of the CPSU Central Committee, stated: "Religion darkens the

conscience of man, makes it passive toward the forces of nature and en-
traps its creative activity and initiative." The article repeated the necessity of developing an "atheistic, scientific propaganda," since "religion has
always been and continues to be the enemy of science, of culture, and
of progress." The newspaper also criticized the laxness of the Armenian
Communist party and youth section in the face of the persistence of religious manifestations.[29]

In 1959 the state began a new antireligious campaign throughout the
USSR. The *Znanie* Society was endowed with a new periodical—*Nauka i
religiya*—and all media were mobilized to demonstrate the incompatibility
between science and religion, between communist reality and religious
morality. Administrative measures (application of decrees forbidding a
priest to serve a number of parishes, increases in taxation, the closing of
churches situated too near schools on the grounds of contaminating the
public or even of causing traffic congestion) soon diminished the number
of churches open to prayer to a third, and also affected the monasteries.
At the same time steps were taken in Armenia to diminish the role of
parishioners in the administration of religious affairs, and, at the same
time, to strengthen the control of the authorities.

After a short period of calm following the fall of Nikita Khrushchev in
autumn 1964 and during the period of international détente (1964–75), the
assault against religion began anew. In June 1975 an article on *Leninian
Ughiov* (On Lenin's Path) complained of the diffusion of "bourgeois propaganda" through all the various religious broadcasts of foreign radios and
contacts with tourists. The article refuted the idea that "religiosity is the
principal guarantee of the survival of Armenian ethnicity and the symbol
of national differences," and criticized the Pedagogical Institute of Erevan,
the Organization of Komsomols, Armenian radio and television, and even
Kidelik for lack of vigilance in this regard. The article prescribed as a solution: (1) a better appreciation of the cultural, spiritual, and psychological
needs of the youth; (2) the protection of children against the influence
of religious communities; (3) actions against pious women; (4) the creation of socialist holidays to provide substitute rites. The article expressed
concern about the persistence of pilgrimages, of the reconversion of old
chapels to prayer halls, the expansion of private religious meetings, and
the appearance of itinerant priests.[30] A few months later, in September
1975, the editor of *Kidelik* disclosed plans to develop a chair of the history
and theory of atheism at the University of Erevan, and to establish a house
of scientific atheism in that city. In spite of all of this, some 90 percent of
Armenian infants were being baptized as of the late 1970s,[31] and weddings
and particularly funerals were frequently blessed, often at home.

All those who have had an opportunity to visit Armenia have been able to observe that during major church holidays, such as Easter and the Assumption, pilgrimages to holy sites of the Armenian church attract large crowds. Pilgrims often cannot enter the holy places due to the size of the crowds, and they listen to the mass in the monastery gardens, much in the atmosphere of a family picnic. Nor is it rare to encounter people in the streets who are carrying crosses. Moreover, according to various observers, including Father Oppenheim,[32] Soviet Armenia—thanks to the modus vivendi achieved by Vazken I—enjoys greater leeway in religious practice than the other republics of the USSR. The evidence for this is that during three years of residence in the USSR, it was only in Armenia that he was able to find Bibles freely and legally on sale, only in Armenia that one could find a portrait of the local hierarch (in this case, Vazken I) on sale in many public places. There was also the fact that liturgical music is continually broadcast in memory of the genocide or on the occasion of cultural jubilees, such as the feast of the medieval mystical poet Nerses Shnorhali.

The repression of the believers, the persecution of nonofficial sects such as Baptists and Pentecostals, and the failure of the Armenian Catholic patriarch's attempts to ensure a spiritual service to his believers all indicate that the conciliatory attitude of the state in religious affairs in Armenia concerns not the "opium of the people," rival to the "scientific" ideology of Marxism-Leninism, but a policy specific to the established religious institution and especially its leader.[33]

Slowly, a subtle cult has been created around the person of Vazken I. An official biography and a collection of speeches were published on the occasion of his fiftieth anniversary, and there has been a great deal of publicity surrounding his travels and messages. His portrait has, as already mentioned, been diffused freely, and he regularly welcomes foreign visitors. All of this tends to present the catholicos as the "uncontested" patriarch of the Armenian nation and its spokesperson both within and outside the USSR. However, despite the emphasis placed on the prestige of his function, the results of his domestic activities remain modest.

In 1972, during a relatively relaxed period, he revealed some data on the Armenian church in the USSR. Of the thirty-eight Armenian bishops, there were only six inside the Soviet Union, of whom three were in Armenia. To these one should add eight monks, about thirty archimandrites, and 120 priests. This small complement must cater to some 3.5 million Soviet Armenians.[34] In 1979 the membership in the Echmiadzin monastery increased to forty-nine, of whom twenty-one were archimandrites, eight were novices, nineteen deacons, and three bishops. This represents an increase of about twenty members since 1954. The theological academy has about forty seminarians today, mostly from the Middle East. At least twenty-seven of the twenty-eight archbishops were also born in the Middle East, as well as fourteen of the twenty-one archimandrites, three of the eight novices, and thirteen of the nineteen deacons. Among the seminarians born in Armenia, many came from families that returned in the 1940s. The annual calendar of Echmiadzin that provides these data on the hierarchy remains curiously discrete on the number of priests: there are supposed to be around thirty at the present time.[35] Indeed, the Gospels and the New Testament have been reedited, in 1969 and 1975. But the editions were limited (ten thousand for the Gospels, twenty thousand for the New Testament as a whole), and most of these were intended for export. Hence, they were soon out of print. At the Bible black market, however, older or foreign editions are preferred anyway, since they are less suspect of having been censored. *Echmiadzin*, which is sold at the catholicosate, is a good review but reads more like an ecclesiastical monitor, filled with the news of the religious world (official meetings, messages for peace, and the commemoration of important religious and civilian holidays) than a theological journal. One looks in vain for essays about christology, ecclesiology, or Christian morality. Problems of dogma, rites, and liturgy are dealt with only from a national and secular point of view, in the context of the quest for the historical patrimony.

The catechistic activities of the church are almost nonexistent. It is true that in the tradition of oriental Christianity it is religious practice that provides the basis for learning the liturgy, ritual, and dogma, rather than preaching. There are also very few churches open for prayer: still only three in Erevan with a population of one million, and only fifty for all of Armenia, according to an article in *France URSS*, which was euphoric about religious prerogatives in this republic.[36] The *Soviet Armenian Encyclopedia*, silent on the total number of churches that are now in service, indicates nonetheless that, in addition to Echmiadzin, there are six monasteries presently accessible, kept up, and open to pilgrims and tourists alike—which means two more than in 1955. These monasteries do not have monastic communities. Of the six abbots, five are noncelibate priests. On the whole, though, chapels, churches, and monasteries are in ruin, despite the notable effort of the Committee for the Preservation of Historic Monuments, created in 1966 by some nationalist intellectuals. In addition to the damage over time—some of it in the course of ancient invasions—many buildings have suffered from the zeal of militant atheists in early Bolshevik days and have still not been rebuilt.

It is difficult to distinguish the personal action and loyalty of the catholi-

cos from that of the patriotic intelligentsia in the realization of an atmosphere of relative tolerance in regard to the external signs of religious life
in Armenia. In contrast, if there is one success of which Vazken I can be
proud, it is the transformation of his image outside the country since the
grave crisis of 1956, and the elaboration of a strong national personality
within Soviet Armenia. Cultivated, multilingual, more of an administrator than a theologican, the catholicos of Echmiadzin has proven to possess
exceptional qualities of diplomacy, useful in recovering lost ground. It is
possible, in fact, to consider that his complex relations with Soviet power,
based on compromises and reciprocal concessions, have not always been
one-way, but are based on diplomatic give and take. It is also from this
diplomatic aspect that his external actions should be understood.

Vazken I, Ambassador of All Armenians

In the context of the periods of relaxation in the mid-1950s and latter
1960s, the Russian Orthodox church abandoned its centralizing ambitions,
came to an agreement on the Orthodox ecumenical see, stopped vituper-
ating the Vatican, and took a deep interest in the Christian ecumenical
movement. The patriarch of Moscow came to take an active part in the
World Council of Churches, espousing the Kremlin's foreign policy line
and assailing Western "imperialism." The dignitaries of the Muslim clergy
have also opened up to the outside world, through official exchanges, to
demonstrate to the Arab world and to the various developing Islamic countries that the USSR is also a country of Islam, where all the rights of
Muslims are preserved and that it can serve as a model for other countries.

It was during this same era that Echmiadzin undertook its slow-moving
diplomacy of opening up and laying claim to the confidence of the dia-
poric communities. In order to prevent the defection of other dioceses,
following the defections of Iran and Greece (which attached themselves
to Antilias), the catholicos undertook a series of pastoral visits in 1960 to
overseas dioceses, including the United States, Latin America, Portugal,
France, and then, in June 1961, Istanbul and Vienna. In October 1963 he
made a pilgrimage to the holy places and visited the non-Chalcedonean
churches of Egypt and India. In 1965, the year of the fiftieth anniversary of the genocide of the Armenians, he participated in a conference
of heads of Oriental, non-Chalcedonean churches in Addis Ababa, before
visiting Cairo, Paris, and London. In 1970 he visited France and the Vatican, and in 1975 made a tour of Romania, Great Britain, Paris, Amman,
and Jerusalem. Three years later he participated in the conference of the

World Council of Churches in Geneva, and visited Paris. There were also visits to diasporic communities in 1979, 1982, and 1984.

Along with the Russian patriarch and other heads of Christian churches recognized in the USSR, the Armenian catholicos actively supports the Christian Peace Movement created in Prague in June 1958. He is involved in the ecumenical movement and had the Armenian Apostolic church admitted to the World Council of Churches in 1962, following the example of the Russian Orthodox church. He has also participated in the overtures made to the non-Chalcedonean churches in Malabar and Ethiopia. Nonetheless, his essential work is directed toward the diaspora and the see of Antilias.

Following the death of Zareh I in February 1963, a détente evolved between the two sees. In October 1963 a summit meeting took place between Vazken I and the new catholicos of Cilicia, Khoren Paroyan, at the patriarchate in Jerusalem. In a joint message to the Armenian nation the two catholicoses made an appeal to "eliminate all elements of discord and establish a new fraternal life in the interest of all Armenians."[37] Some tensions remain, however.[38]

Freer in his actions, Khoren I was one of the first chiefs of the Armenian Apostolic church to send observers to the Second Vatican Council and was warmly received by Pope Paul VI in May 1967, well before Vazken I. Then, in 1969, came the boycott by Antilias of the episcopal conference in Echmiadzin, where important matters were to be discussed, such as the reform of the liturgy and of monastic discipline, unification of the date of Easter, the translation of the Bible into the two Armenian dialects—the Occidental and the Oriental[39]—and the unity of the church.[40]

Nonetheless, in the spring of 1977 the delegation of the two representatives of Echmiadzin to the election and enthronement of a coadjutor catholicos, with the right of succession in Cilicia, Karekin II Sarkissian, was a clear sign of détente. As bishop, Karekin II had never taken a position against Vazken I and has promised a tacit accord on one of the two points of dispute, that is, Antilias's arrogation to itself of the right to establish new parishes within territories traditionally placed under Echmiadzin's jurisdiction, as a consequence of Armenian migrations from Lebanon and Syria (this being especially true for the United States). Recognizing the persistence of "misunderstandings and divergences" of an essentially jurisdictional nature that dialogue could dispel, Karekin II insisted, in his enthronement speech, on the internal unity of the church. At the same time, as the Lebanese crisis unfolded, there seemed to be an unmistakable tacit understanding between pro-Soviet and anti-Soviet

Armenians in order to protect the community as a whole. Finally, on October 12, 1979, the Communiqué of Five Points by the synod of Echmiadzin reaffirmed the "vocation of the universal pastor of the Armenian Apostolic church, his vocation as catholicos of all Armenians," and restated the principle of returning to the administrative situation preceding 1956.[41] Thus, in twenty-five years, Vazken I has been able to ease tensions somewhat, neutralize anti-Soviet reflexes, and create a consensus around his person. Nonetheless, if he has been more convincing, the catholicos still echoes the official line, albeit in a less ideological tone. With constant references to the fraternity of peoples and the achievements of the regime, borrowing from the Bible the notion of the "promised land," he affirms Soviet Armenia as the only possible homeland of all Armenians.

In the name of unity, a concept particularly charged with meaning for a nation divided, Vazken I has condemned the emigration of Soviet Armenians, advised their political organizations to forget their differences and to unite around Soviet Armenia. He has often chosen symbolic dates, tied to Armenian national history, to deliver messages with frankly ambivalent thrusts, in order to rally all political factions. Thus, on May 27, 1979, commemorating the Battle of Sardarabad, which, in 1918 had halted the advance of the Turks near Erevan and allowed the birth of an independent Republic of Armenia, he justified the attachment of the province of Erevan to Christian Russia in 1828 as preferable to the annihilation at the hands of the Islamic-Turkish offensive. But he did not hesitate to affirm that the great dates of history from 1828 to November 29, 1920 (the date of Soviet annexation of Armenia), all belong to the nation and thus should not be made the subject of political controversies.[42]

His repeated transparent allusions to the Armenian question, seen from a territorial and anti-Turkish point of view, coincide with the notions proposed by workers of culture, patriotic intelligentsia, and even some of the political leaders.[43]

Conclusion

The Armenian Apostolic church, whether in the diaspora or in Soviet Armenia, perpetuates the idea that, facing the Turkish danger and considering their weakness, the Armenians are incapable of governing themselves and that their attachment to the Soviet Union has therefore been "generally positive," if not indispensable. Echmiadzin often considers the overseas communities annexes of the motherland and demands their unquestioning devotion to the Armenian state, to which all Armenians are supposed to move some day. During his most recent trip to Paris, in

June 1984, Vazken I expounded on the latter point, observing that it is necessary, in his view, to be "realistic" and to consider life in the diaspora a permanent phenomenon. But he gave directives for the development of dioceses and educational organizations under the aegis of the AGBU, whose Soviet Armenian patriotism is as well known as its assets.

Still more recently, on November 9, 1984, a few months after his June interview with Karekin II, which had been trumpeted as "cordial and fraternal," Vazken I seemed to be rekindling the old rivalry between the two sees, as he called on Antilias, in the name of Echmiadzin's claim to be "the only legal see, anchored in the Holy Land of the fatherland," to accept status as a "patriarchal see."[44]

By remaining silent on the political dimensions of the national question and especially by subordinating independence to security, democracy to national unity, Echmiadzin contributes to colonialization of the spirit in the Armenian world. By its traditional prestige and the obvious privileges of the primate, it gives legitimacy to a regime that is itself opposed to Christian morality. Constantly playing on the nostalgia for unity and the theme of "legitimate aspirations" (i.e., Armenian irredentism), Echmiadzin participates, whether consciously or unconsciously, in the manipulation of an increasingly demoralized diaspora, in support of the perpetuation of the domesticated status of Soviet Armenia and the myths attached to the "motherland." Is this collaboration with the Soviet state a premeditated strategy to "annex" the diaspora or is it, rather, a last-ditch effort to save the church while waiting for better days? Most Armenians in the diaspora are inclined to the latter view.

FACT SHEET

The Armenian Apostolic Church

Date of autocephaly
  Catholicosate of Echmiadzin
    established in 302
    transferred to Dvin in 484
    reestablished in Echmiadzin in 1441
  Catholicosate of Sis (Cilicia)
    established in 1293
    transferred to Antilias (Lebanon) 1930
  Patriarchate of Constantinople
    established in 1461
  Patriarchate of Jerusalem
    established in 638

Current strength of the church
    6 million faithful (of which, 4 million in the USSR)
    50–100 priests in the USSR; 200 priests in diaspora
    38 bishops (3 in Soviet Armenia; 3 elsewhere in the USSR; 32 in
        diaspora)
    0 nuns in the USSR; 0 nuns in diaspora
    40 seminarians at Echmiadzin, 50 at Jerusalem, 50 at Antilias, 25 at
        Istanbul

Chief organs
    Echmiadzin (in Soviet Armenia)
    Hask (Antilias)
    Shoghakat (Istanbul)
    Sion (Jerusalem)

Number of churches and church facilities in operation (in the USSR)
    20–30 churches (estimate)
    1 theological seminary
    1 theological institute
    6 monasteries

Catholicoses since 1900
    Of Echmiadzin
        Meguerditch I Khrimian, 1892–1907
        Matteos II Izmirlian, 1908–10
        Kevork V Surenian, 1911–30
        Khoren I Muradbegian, 1932–38
        Kevork VI Chorekjian, 1945–54
        Vazken I Baljian, 1955–present
    Of Sis (Cilicia)
        (The see was vacant 1894–1902)
        Sahak II Khabayan, 1902–39
        Betros I Sarajian, 1940
        Karekin I Hovespian, 1943–52
        Zareh I Payaslian, 1956–63
        Khoren I Paroyan, 1963–83
        Karekin II Sarkissian, 1983–present

19

The Ethiopian Orthodox Church

Haile Mariam Larebo

Unlike the Greco-Roman world, where Christianity spread from the lower classes to the ruling elite, Christianity in Ethiopia made its inroads without a mass base. It came as a court religion and then was imposed by imperial fiat on the lower classes, about whose reaction no historical data exist. From its start as an official religion until the fall of the monarchy in 1974, the throne remained the central force behind the expansion and consolidation of Christianity. It encouraged the advent and settlement of Christian missionaries when the need for preachers was closely felt. Christianization intensified toward the end of the fifth century with the arrival of the Nine Saints and certain missionary monks, apparently Syrian, fleeing from anti-Monophysite persecution in the Byzantine Empire.[1] The monarchy bolstered the prestige and economic status of the clerical profession with extensive material benefits and privileges of all kinds, which no doubt attracted many individuals to it. New arrivals were allocated fresh lands, churches were built, monasteries and their schools were provided with generous endowments and protection from local anti-Christian groups.

The missionaries were invariably monastic leaders. The secular clergy entertained little enthusiasm for missionary work, and in any case had serious weaknesses in its leadership. Until recently, the nominal head of the Ethiopian Orthodox church was always an Egyptian monk appointed by the patriarch of Alexandria. As a foreigner to his own constituency, ignorant of its language and customs, bereft of any connections or relationships that could bolster his authority, and unfamiliar with the forces and issues that dominated political life, the religious life of the metropolitan (*abun* in Amharic) was normally limited, with some exceptions, to the consecration of the Holy Ark (*Tabot*) of the local churches and the ordination of deacons and priests. Politically, he was a person of considerable importance through his weapon of excommunication, which, in this deeply religious society, was as useful as the king's own armies in suppressing rebellions.[2] The inevitable consequences of his limited religious role for the official church were a lack of proper organization and a chronic shortage of trained clergy.

Consequently, the major burden of evangelization fell upon the leaders of the monastic institutions, but they have never been conspicuous for methodical activity. Since their foundation, monasteries were not only renowned for their ascetic life, as centers of learning, but also well known for their political role, especially in the late medieval period. Religiously, the monasteries formed a counterbalance to an established church. With their austerity, their withdrawal from society into the desert, they fulfilled a prophetic and eschatological ministry in the life of the Ethiopian church. Intellectually, whatever literary and artistic achievements the Ethiopian church and state could claim were entirely to the credit of the monasteries. Secular clergy, church scholars known as *dabtara* (literally, scribes), princes and emperors, as well as ordinary men, were trained in monastic schools, which by the end of the fifteenth century had become centers for a literary renaissance. These were mainly of an ecclesiastical character that found expression in numerous Ge'ez works, as well as translations from Coptic and Arabic literature.

It has to be borne in mind that, except in a few cases, these institutions normally flourished under imperial favor, which remained not only the initial inspiration and guiding force behind their development and revival, but also the dispenser of considerable economic resources. It was not surprising, then, that with the waning of imperial interest and the decline of its power both at home and abroad, they relapsed into isolationism, conservatism, and immobility, in the same way as the secular clergy. Nevertheless, until their golden age, which is said to have lasted until the Muslim onslaught, came to a close and their missionary zeal was overtaken by a combined struggle for political ascendancy in the imperial court and factional theological disputes that sapped most of the kingdom's material and spiritual resources, the monasteries played an outstanding role in the expansion and consolidation of the Abyssinian Empire. What was, in fact, unique to these institutions from the beginning was that their leaders were explorers and colonialists at the same time. A first generation of monks in search of a solitary life established themselves in the wilderness in the frontier zones, pushing forward the boundaries of Abyssinian "civilization" and reducing the forest to cultivated land.

These explorer monks were not only colonists but missionaries too. As they penetrated farther into the interior, they often successfully converted the surrounding tribes, thus bringing them under the influence of the Christian community. Intrinsic to their success was the fact that conversion brought neither dramatic experience into the adherents' belief system nor a disruption of their social customs. Rather, Christian ideas were superimposed onto the old beliefs and practices. In this process the Ethiopian Orthodox church enriched itself with diverse strands of religious beliefs and practices, merging them in a remarkable syncretism that until today has formed the idiosyncratic version of Ethiopian Christianity. Politically, the state's territory was increased and new groups were brought under its control. But the alliance of such state-monastic orders had many far-reaching and disastrous consequences: the state became impregnated with monastic observances, foreign to its nature and disastrous to its healthy development. As a result, the whole nation submitted itself to the external rigors of monastic life, fasting for more than half the days of the year and duly observing the numerous feasts of the saints. Extensive land property was accorded to the monasteries, free of tax, in order to allow them to pursue their educational and charitable activities, which they controlled virtually as an *imperium in imperio*, without any government interference, thereby impoverishing the state treasury.[3]

Yet the church's utility in Abyssinian territorial expansion is only one aspect of Church-state relations that must be balanced with the equally important role the state played as an agent of religious diffusion among its conquered people, and with its program of military resettlement, under which Christian soldiers and colonists were stationed in the conquered territories as part of the program of evangelization. Through intermarriage and prolonged interaction, often combined with inducements and indirect pressure, the local people were absorbed into the Ethiopian church.

The harmonious cooperation that characterized church-state relations culminated in the early period of the Solomonic dynasty, between the end of the thirteenth and the middle of the fifteenth century, in an almost total fusion of the two institutions. Events of this period universally attest to the fact that not only had the church become entrenched as the personification of the religion of Abyssinian society, developing into its strongest integrative force, but it had also assumed a prominent political role, which it has maintained with undiminished zeal ever since.

In the ensuing struggles between the Zague and Solomonic dynasties, which took place at the beginning of this active development period, the church emerged as the principal supporter of the new dynasty, claiming partial credit for the "restoration" of the Solomonic line, described as

Abyssinia's "rightful" rulers, thus becoming in the process the author of a
national ideology. This included the cardinal tenets of Ethiopian national
ethos that formed a collective consciousness as symbolized by religion and
institutionalized in the Ethiopian Orthodox church. A close examination
of this ideology reveals nothing new apart from its being the inevitable
crystallization of an already existing process in church-state relations,
embellished with biblical myth. But its importance cannot be underrated
in the universal bearing it has had on the minds of average Abyssinians,
and for the legacy of its ideals, which shaped church-state relations in
every aspect of the country's life, and in every phase of its subsequent
history. The result has been a unique pattern of church-state relations in
Ethiopia. Any attempt to minimize the relevance of this national ideology
to twentieth-century Orthodoxy and politics would lead to superficial and
distorted conclusions.

The central themes of this ideology are developed in the book of Kebra
Nagast (*The Glory of Kings*),[4] a work compiled, it is thought, around the
fourteenth century. In it, the Abyssinian nation is presented as a polity
entirely Christian in its principles of government and daily life. Church
and state are conceived as one organism, with no rigid separation between
the religious and the secular. The relationship is not simply one of Caesaropapism, of subordinating the church to the state, but of a symphony
in which neither element exercised absolute control over the other. Such a
symphony, unlike that of Byzantine Orthodoxy, has been attributed historical roots that transcend its Christian origin. Through the fable of King
Solomon and the queen of Sheba (a legend of ancient origin and with wide
currency in the Middle East), the Jewish origin of the Ethiopian state and
people was affirmed. The ancient city of Axum, where the Abyssinian
tribal settlements were established, is presented as the repository of the
Ark of the Covenant, said to have been brought back by Menelik I after
a visit to his father, Solomon. It became *Seyon*, a term used in much the
same way as the biblical Mount Zion, to symbolize the special identity
of Christian Ethiopia: a fortress besieged by a hostile Muslim and pagan world in northeast Africa. Menelik came back with the sons of noble
Israelite families, among whom was Azaras, the son of Zadoch.

The political implications of such an idealization are clear, and Kebra
Nagast's book does not hesitate to make this its central message: the
Ethiopian nation is endowed with a noble and ancient past, and its people
were construed as the immediate heirs of the Jews as the elect of God,
His chosen people with a national mission to promote the true faith as
expressed in the Ethiopian Orthodox church. It is interesting to note that
Kebra Nagast, ignoring the pagan conditions from which Ethiopians had

been converted to Christianity, claims that they worshipped the true God of the Old Testament before espousing Christianity. It does not stop there. With the Jewish rejection of Christ, a true *translatio imperii*, from Israel to Ethiopia, took place, as the light of God "flew to the country of Ethiopia and it shines there with exceeding great brightness, for it willed to dwell there." The claims of divine election of the Ethiopian nation to pursue a mission assigned to it by God, no doubt, amounts to identification of national expansionism with divine sanction.

Consequently, Christianity has been identified with Ethiopia, becoming in the process "the most profound expression of the national existence of its people," namely, the Abyssinian ethnic group.[5] The corollary to this is that any group confessing an alien creed cannot be Ethiopian; nor can any Ethiopian adhere to any other creed, since the cardinal criterion of "Ethiopianness" is an acceptance of Christianity. Thus, in popular usage, the very terms "Ethiopian" and "Christian" became synonymous and even interchangeable.[6]

This confusion has led the church to serve the ends of national politics, interpreting its pathetic jingoism as an evangelical enterprise. It does not, in fact, seem mistaken to assert that nationalism has been the bane of Ethiopian Orthodoxy since its inception. Church documents have invariably depicted the wars of national conquest and the continuing southward expansion of the Ethiopian kingdom as a struggle between good and evil, light and darkness, attributing its victories to the might of God, while describing the enemy as being guided by Satan.[7]

The major agent in the process is the monarchy, which Kebra Nagast, through a genealogical link with Solomon, brings into a blood relationship with the House of David, and ultimately with Christ Himself. Underlying this assumption is that the rule of the Solomonic dynasty over the Ethiopian nation is divinely ordained, and its legitimacy is put on a footing which is beyond human challenge. The multiplicity of titles, for example—"The Lion of Judah," "God's Appointee," "King of Kings of Ethiopia," borne by the emperors—stands to substantiate this point.[8]

The symbiotic church-state relationship which developed is self-evident in the coronation ceremony when the emperor swears to maintain and defend the Orthodox religion, and in return receives the blessing of his emblem of authority and the submission of the metropolitan in the name of the whole Ethiopian church/nation.[9] The king's leadership was tempered by the ethos of dynastic tradition and by the legal dictates of Fetha Nagast, the Laws of the Kings, the only authoritative traditional law book that was more ecclesiastical than secular, both in content and origin.[10] Whenever the emperor's actions seriously threatened the dominant position of the Orthodox church, the ecclesiastical hierarchy mobilized its adherents in opposition to the regime's course of action. Fetha Nagast explicitly states that when such intervention is called for, "the king, if he becomes a heretic, from that moment . . . is no longer a king, but a rebel." Accordingly, there are ample historical examples of kings charged with apostasy or heresy, who forfeited the allegiance of their subjects, and as a result, their right to rule the nation. In 1916, for example, a charge of alleged apostasy proved instrumental in the overthrow of Lij Iyasu. And as recently as twenty years ago, when the clergy referred to the 1960 insurgents as agents of the Devil, Patriarch Basilios excommunicated them as criminals and traitors.[11]

Military conquest at the beginning of the twentieth century doubled the domains of the Solomonic kingdom and radically altered its social composition. As a result, the Christian Abyssinians of the north found themselves becoming a minority, although militarily dominant, among a large number of peoples of diverse origin, culture, and religion. The state no longer had the resources or the energy to assimilate them. The church, as the integrating force and custodian of Ethiopian culture, was neither sufficiently organized for the task (as it had been in the past), nor suited—given the meager religious training of its clergy—for this challenge. Of course, churches appeared wherever northern conquerors congregated, staffed by northern clergy, but their essential function was merely to cater for the routine religious needs of the military garrisons or civilian settlers from the north. In the absence of an evangelization program, the state once again proved to be the major agent of conversion. Wherever possible, mass conversions were dictated by imperial fiat, or promoted through persuasion and inducements. Thus, for example, offers of titles, offices, or land convinced a few chiefs to accept Christianity and to enforce it, in turn, on their people.[12] Hence, just as in the past, in new areas church membership was secured through the activities of the state and economic and political stimuli. But gains tended to be negligible, leaving the state in a dilemma. Even though Christianity was the state religion, contemporary political considerations, combined with past experience, dictated that the state use moderation and restraint in its proselytizing policy, rather than military muscle.

Patterns of Church Organization and Their Political Significance

The metropolitan's temporal power extended as far as the extension of his own *gult*, i.e., his land traditionally assigned to him as a fief. From here he drew his annuity and, in the same manner as the secular nobility, exercised administrative, judicial, and military power over the peasantry cultivating his fief. His spiritual jurisdiction included all the empire, in theory, but in practice this was often exercised as a mandatory of the crown. Moreover, his viceroy, the high priest (*Liqa Kahnat*), one residing in each of the empire's provinces, never exercised more than nominal control over the xenophobic clergy of the rural churches, the lowest unit of the three existing forms of ecclesiastical organization. Where he did, it was invariably with the help of the crown. Being more or less a government appointee, it was not uncommon for the high priest to behave ostentatiously against the metropolitan. What often determined his nomination were more political and economic considerations than his ability to cater to the religious needs of the community. His office was often sought as a means of rewarding deserving and loyal clergymen. Even though he was a monk, his behavior normally fitted that of a nobleman in clergyman's clothing, for his role as intelligence gatherer kept his master well informed about the actions and movements of the local people and their rulers, who, aware of his political importance, treated him with marked respect, and invited him to all important events as an adviser. He had no fixed jurisdiction, as the size of his territory shifted according to his importance. His economic life depended on the revenue provided from the rural churches under his jurisdiction and, as a result, he was careful not to antagonize them. These kept him at bay, denying him any opportunity to interfere in their internal affairs. In view of this, they tried to resolve their problems in their own homes, and court cases were only rarely brought to him, and even then, only with mutual consensus between the parties involved.[13]

The rural churches were self-sufficient and self-regulating, with their economic life revolving around land, and needed nothing from the hierarchy except consecration of their ark and ordination of their clergy, actions normally performed without any serious test. The continuous flow of religious services was ensured not only by social prestige that any kind of land ownership entailed, but, even more important, by a set of advantages entrenched in church land, such as its relatively high productivity, better tenure security, partial or total exemption from taxation, as well as military service that made its possession more attractive than the rest.[14] As is often the case when privileges are involved, it was not long before this became a source of gross abuse by both sides, laity and clergy alike, with the ecclesiastical authority powerless to intervene.

This situation was further compounded by the rules intrinsic to such land use. Since the burden of the obligation to arrange church services fell on the land and not on the person, it was immaterial who worked on it or what rights he had over it, insofar as the beneficiary did not fail to fulfill them. Thus people made their own arrangements whereby a layman using the land hired a clergyman, through payment or a share of the land, or sent his son to be a clergyman. Upon his death, he passed his land on to his son, thereby preserving the land in the family. This process led ultimately to a kind of "secularization" of church land, whereby "laymen not only worked most of the land over which the church claimed rights, but many holders of such rights became themselves laymen."[15] Through intermarriage with members of the local community, the secular clergy could gain extra land by manipulating the existing system of kinship relations. Thus the clergy frequently acquired a dynastic influence in the village and established a hereditary monopoly of ecclesiastical offices.

From all of this, it appears that the church leadership lacked an organizational link to its base and its rural clergy. It lacked the means to influence either the allocation of resources or the choice of clergy and their education. The impotence of the church hierarchy over its outposts and its profoundly Erastian character becomes even clearer in regard to the abbeys and monasteries, the two most important categories of church institutions. These were exempt from interference by the high priests; nor did the metropolitan have any influence over them. The metropolitan's power was limited to pronouncements on judicial matters and expression of opinions on questions of dogma. Even then he acted not as a competent and independent authority, but as the emperor's chief adviser. The only hierarchical approach to these institutions was through the *ecage* (the abbot of Dabre Libanos), regarded by many as the supreme head of these institutions. But the ecage, despite his considerable prestige in the imperial court, to which he owed his position as the successor of Takla Haymanot, the universally acclaimed apostle and mastermind of the "restoration" of the Solomonic dynasty, remained in practice primus inter pares. His prestige had been more of an obstacle than a benefit to the organization of the church, as he always remained a powerful rival to the metropolitan, who, because of him, could not exercise all the authority of his office.

Both the abbey and the monastery received special treatment from the emperor and owed their loyalty to him. This was true in recent times, during the reign of Emperor Haile Selassie, as much as in the past. Each foundation was normally granted large landholdings, often consisting of vast districts worked by peasant farmers who came under the institutions' judicial, administrative, and military control. At the time of their creation the emperor regulated their secular administration, allocating fiefs, fixing the number of beneficiaries; he nominated their leaderships, often assigning particular insignia with or without a title; and he set up or approved the rules. In addition, the abbey and the monastery alike were important centers of learning, though in the case of the latter, imperial influence over the nomination of the spiritual leadership was limited, often consisting only in the confirmation of those elected by the unanimous consensus of the monastic assembly. Moreover, while the abbeys were normally situated around or at the imperial court or royal capitals, the monasteries tended to be located in remote and inaccessible areas far from the towns and villages.

These institutions, as an arm of the secular authority (being used sometimes, for example, in surveillance), provided their support enthusiastically and in the process reinforced each other's authority. Nevertheless, occasional conflicts sometimes arose with the monasteries particularly, when the secular authority attempted to interfere in their entrenched privileges. Most of the time these attempts were unsuccessful.[16] Overall, the monasteries proved to be the most imposing and decisive power in the land, politically as well as religiously. Their moral force derived mainly from the fact that every important ecclesiastical office was filled from among their ranks. They commanded great respect from the general population, who, less than edified by the conduct of the secular clergy and often tormented by incessant harassment from secular authorities, particularly feudal lords, looked to the monks as protectors and messengers of peace and justice, accredited with holiness in their opinions and utterances. Well aware of their political weight, successive emperors endowed the monasteries with extensive land grants and often gifts, to the extent that some of them controlled entire districts.

By asserting control over the church's finances and highest offices, the state secured its hold on the church and ensured economic dependency. Ecclesiastical institutions, founded under religious palliative, had been made to serve the political interests of rival forces, for they were effective tools with which to subdue the rebellious masses and to check the ambitions of unruly chiefs. These latter regarded them as valuable elements in their opposition to the entrenchment of central authority. One vital result of this process was the continuous proliferation of institutions that were already superfluous to existing pastoral needs, resulting in an army of unproductive clergy that grew fat in idleness on the labor of the working class.

At the same time the complete disorganization of the church was quite obvious. Each of the three institutions was self-sufficient and self-governing, running its own affairs without any meaningful influence or supervision from the ecclesiastical hierarchy. Thus the church constituted a corporate group in theory only. In practice, it had no integrated organizational structure that linked its leadership to the base. There was no central treasury or central administration. The outcome of such a legacy was quite predictable: lack of discipline and low cultural attainment characterized its clergy, who roamed the countryside and urban centers, taking up residence wherever they wished, engaging in all forms of employment, in government departments, as retainers of nobility or confessors in the houses of ladies, or involving themselves in all kinds of trades from traditional witchcraft and magic to modern, highly profitable economic enterprises.[17] The church was thereby weakened and further undermined by the advance of state modernization and the strengthening of central political authority. This was particularly true in the field of education, where the inroads of Western education broke the church's traditional monopoly.

In the face of these developments, the main thrust of the state since the opening of the twentieth century had focused on the attempt to reverse the weakening of the church through a program of centralization and modernization of its organization. Underlying this drive was the belief that an effective central organization would equip the church with structures adequate for its internal administration to enforce its authority over its peripheral institutions and to control its human and economic resources. As a result, the church, with renewed energy and coordinated resources, would reestablish itself, as in the past, as an effective unifying force in the program of cultural integration and nation-building. Politically, the reforms followed a definite pattern. New institutions were created. However, they were designed in such a way as to make government control over them paramount, thus providing the monarch with levers that his predecessor lacked.

In 1926 the church was given a constitution that established a holy synod, a head office, and various committees designed to relieve the metropolitan of certain administrative tasks. With the 1931 regulations the income of the top church echelons was defined. A modern system of administration was imposed on the abbeys and monasteries in and around Addis Ababa, on top of the traditional ones, accompanied, as usual, by land grants and the bestowal of titles. These piecemeal changes were limited in scope, occurring in a few churches of the capital and its immediate surroundings, where there was greater receptivity to reform and where implementation was easier, but they were cut short by the Italian invasion. Serious reforms began only after the restoration of independence in 1941.

Church and Nationalism during the Italian Occupation

Despite their officially declared policy of "absolute respect for all religions insofar as these did not conflict with the public order and general principles of civilization,"[18] the Italians initially resorted to measures aimed at weakening and controlling the church. In their view the church was a stronghold of Ethiopian nationalism and the nerve center of its resistance. Thus terrorist tactics and repressive measures against the church and its property, including even the killing of clergy, were combined with programs of active promotion of other religions, such as Islam. The church's prestigious status was abolished. Symptomatic of their resolve to strike Ethiopian nationalism at its deepest roots was the wholesale butchery of "all 297 monks and 129 deacons of Dabre Libanos monastery on the grounds of its alleged complicity in the attempt upon the life of Marshal Graziani, the viceroy of Italian East Africa."[19] But none of these harsh measures had so strong an impact on the clergy and laity during the war and in subsequent generations as the execution of Metropolitan Petros, one of the four Ethiopian bishops consecrated on May 30, 1929. After independence, he was immortalized in a magnificent statue as the personification of the "martyrdom of an Ethiopian patriot."

Despite all these measures, resistance continued unabated, and the Italians realized that to make the church an irreconcilable enemy was a costly affair; they decided, therefore, to try to use its great influence wherever possible to induce the country to accommodate itself to their rule. Accordingly, a policy of conciliation was adopted side by side with terroristic measures. No efforts were spared, or means excluded, for increasing the church's dependence on the government and bringing it into a collaborative relationship. With the hope of stirring up the nascent Ethiopian religious nationalism against Alexandrine domination and at the same time detaching it from Egypt and Jerusalem (places where British influence was strong and where a number of Ethiopian refugees were gathered), a unilateral declaration of independence was made from the patriarchate of Alexandria. For the first time in its history Ethiopian Orthodoxy had its own countryman as head of the church. Soon after his installation the new patriarch took up the task of pacifying his people, anathematizing them under threat of a denial of sacred burial to all rebels and their supporters. However, his pastoral letter was no more successful in stopping the insurgency than the might of Italian arms had been. The deadline for surrender issued by the patriarch passed completely unheeded. Nevertheless, despite their abysmal failure to achieve the popularity they had initially envisaged through policies that bore all the traces of a great show of religious devotion, the Italians were able to maintain their hold on an important segment of the church. But it is difficult to assess the sincerity of the church's policy of compliance with the conquerors' wishes; the refusal of many largely unsubdued clergy of Gojjam province to attend the synod for patriarchal election at Addis Ababa seems to suggest that it was far from compliant. All in all, the period of Italian colonialism left the church bitterly divided and weak.

Independence, Autocephaly, and Nationalism

With the restoration of political independence Haile Selassie took advantage of the general disarray that prevailed in the church after the interregnum and, strengthened further by British military presence, promoted his scheme for the total reorganization of the church largely unopposed. Even though he did not accept the situation of the Italians' making, his program began where the Italians had left off. His activities focused on the issues of autocephaly and internal reform, which were his concern even before the occupation.

The Ethiopian Orthodox church had been founded through missions from Egypt and Syria, and through the ages it remained linked to the see of Alexandria, from which it always received its metropolitan, and to which it owed its creed, liturgy, and monastic spirituality, as well as most of its external contacts. Even though autonomy from Alexandria had been a long-standing question, it was never pursued with determination until after the mid-1920s.

With the death of the controversial Metropolitan Mathewos in 1926, the whole issue had become more acute, with Egypt strongly resisting Ethiopian demands. Later, a compromise was reached whereby the Ethiopians accepted the consecration of four bishops among their own nationals for the first time in the church's recorded history. However, the whole issue resurfaced again after the restoration of independence with greater vigor. By that time, Alexandria was in a weaker position in many respects than it had been before the war, because of its allegedly reprehensible conduct, pastoral as well as political, during the occupation. But more importantly, Metropolitan Qerlos's easy submission to the Italians and his readiness to collaborate with them angered many, further increasing Ethiopian distrust of foreign bishops.

Qerlos's abrupt and inexplicable departure strengthened the Ethiopian view that a foreign bishop could be quite unreliable in times of crisis. Consequently, attitudes toward Alexandria were hardened, while they softened toward clergy who collaborated with Italy and whom Egypt had excommunicated.[20]

The controversy had its own extremists, who sought an immediate and unconditional declaration of an independent church in an independent state. These nationalists deprecated the part the Egyptian prelates had played in the Ethiopian Orthodox church's history, seeing them as the cause of moral laxity and intellectual debasement among the Ethiopian clergy.[21] A series of articles that undoubtedly reflected the attitudes of most educated groups and that of a considerable section of the capital's inhabitants appeared in the official newspaper. They dealt with the issue in such unsympathetic terms that the Egyptian guardianship was dubbed the "intolerable regime of servitude" and the "alien yoke."[22]

While the government accepted back the aged Egyptian primate, Metropolitan Qerlos, it at once began negotiations to ensure that future primates would be Ethiopian. The government's interest in this was clear from the outset. Ecclesiastical independence was eventually achieved on July 13, 1948, when it was agreed that the next primate would be an Ethiopian. So when Qerlos died in October 1950, Bishop Basilios, prior of Dabre Libanos, and already an acting archbishop, was elected in his place and solemnly installed in Cairo, in January, as metropolitan-primate of Ethiopia.

Church-State Relations after Autocephaly

With ecclesiastical independence the church was cut off from the only remaining external source of legitimacy that was beyond the emperor's control. As a result, the significance of church autonomy was eroded and its role remained tied more closely than ever to the service and support of the crown. This development gained its most resounding expression in the revised constitution of 1955, which made appointments to key posts in the church hierarchy subject to imperial approval. In addition, the emperor was empowered to promulgate all church regulations other than purely spiritual and monastic ones.

Despite the state's official grant that "religion is personal," the government used its machinery to foster Christian practices and assimilate the people of outlying areas into the national religion. Christian laws were imposed as state laws, and most state holidays were church holidays and were celebrated with church rituals. The state supported all church activities by public funds, and paid salaries to its officials. Under the cover of moral education, churchmen taught Orthodoxy in all state schools.

All these measures aimed at easing the expansion of Christian culture remained within the framework of past Abyssinian tradition with no significant modification.

Thus, as in the past, the state assumed that Christianity, as long as it maintained social and economic advantages and political dominance, would gradually prevail over all other religions. With the constitutions of 1931 and 1955, the state attempted to ensure that power, the essential prerequisite for success in this process, remained preserved in the hands of Christian Amhara and the Solomonic dynasty. As in the past, it leaned heavily on the church as an ideological underpinning of its rule. Accordingly, church officials invariably and monotonously repeated a long litany of the monarchy's achievements and its divine kingship. The vast priestly corps, from the capital to the last village in the countryside, performed an invaluable service, constantly hailing almost ad nauseam, God and the emperor equally.

Administrative Reforms—Challenge and Response

On November 30, 1942, the first regulation dealing with church administration was issued. The decree defined the different sorts of church lands and made them liable to taxation, it created a unified financial structure with a central church treasury, and it abolished the temporal jurisdiction of the church courts over both ordained and lay members, thus limiting the church's temporal and independent power base. The selection and appointment of the highest officers in the monasteries, abbeys, and rural churches was vested in the Ecclesiastical Council upon the approval of the emperor.

The significance of this law was that it gave legality to church land that was formerly governed by customary rules. With the introduction of taxation, the semiautonomous power of the church institutions was reduced. As a result, their independent economic position was undermined and they were made agents in the collection of revenues under the central church treasury. The law also limited the number of clergy that could be maintained at any given church institution.

It should be emphasized, however, that these provisions never fully succeeded in affecting the traditional autonomy of the individual institutions. The imposition of taxes on traditionally tax-free lands was naturally not a popular move, and as such it met with almost universal opposition in most of the traditional Christian areas.[23] In regions like Gojjam, where provincialism had its strongest base and where communications were poor, the institutions joined forces with the peasantry and local gentry, both of whom were equally threatened by the government's new gospel of centralization. This led, in 1968, to a serious provincial uprising in the face of which the government (even with the use of the prestigious ecclesiastical hierarchy of Gojjam) remained impotent. The government had no option but to retreat. Consequently, Gojjam and most of the northern churches remained outside the control of the Ecclesiastical Council; nor did the patriarchate have any accurate knowledge of the lands over which most of its three institutions and clergy claimed rights, and from which they collected tributes.

The government was also in disarray as a result of the strong reaction of the clergy against its attempt to substitute cash payment for corvée labor. As a result, in most of the northern, traditionally Christian areas, the clergy maintained all its traditional privileges of land tenure almost intact. Its fiscal system remained untouched by the changes brought about by the forces of modernization. The outcome of this situation was that while all government-imposed taxes were paid only in cash, the church continued to extract a variety of dues in kind and services from its peasants in the form of tribute.

The taxes raised on church lands were squeezed out of the peasant population and the rural clergy by the patriarchate and transferred to the church treasury. From there it was invested in buildings, light industry, and so forth. In areas where such transition consisted of more than one-third of the total taxes, modern education is said to have suffered considerably as the education tax went to enrich the coffers of the church, which normally looked on modern education with considerable disdain. But a more serious outcome was the widening cleavage that was developing between the higher and lower clergy as a result. Outside sources close to the church from as early as late 1960 continually warned about the need of the church to use its wealth more wisely so that it could "benefit its congregation rather than the church's hierarchy alone."[24] But no action was taken by the authorities responsible. One result was that in 1974, when the whole national social fabric was coming apart, about a thousand clergymen closed ranks with the revolutionary forces.

The Policy of Imperial Reforms and Their Legacy

Despite all the reform measures undertaken by the emperor, the church organization remained quite amorphous in nature, and the quality of its leadership remained poor, and its clergy, as in the past, devoid of any missionary zeal. The monarchy had been the greatest force behind the reforms, but its policies had also been instrumental in limiting them. In the appointments or approval of key officials, the cardinal criterion was personal loyalty to the throne rather than ability. As a result, the emperor often balanced personalities or overlooked individuals of great caliber and talent, thus stifling creative change and independent initiative. Those he promoted were, in a sense, patrimonial retainers, whose essence was personal and unconditional dependence on the ruler, with little capacity for independent action. The holder of the post had no greater influence than that which he gained from personal qualities and imperial favor. This becomes explicit from a close look at the succession of the patriarchate leadership and the forces it had to contend with.

The scribe Lessanu, during his tenure as administrative director of the patriarchate, took direct orders only from the emperor on the grounds that Patriarch Basilios, incapacitated by ill health, could not play any meaningful role in the administration. Archaic in his attitude, he lacked both the capacity and the inclination to make a positive contribution. He staffed the patriarchate's high offices with untrained and incompetent men. Until his retirement in 1965, the institution of the patriarchate functioned purely on personal contacts, characterized by immobilism and inefficiency. There was hardly any diffusion of authority and little differentiation between departments. Then, after a power vacuum of three years, a rapid changeover of personalities took place, with the inevitable result that the incumbent was deprived of the opportunity of becoming thoroughly acquainted with his job. In 1968 Demetros Gorfu, the éminence grise of Eritrean politics, was recalled from Axum. Demetros was made general manager, with the rank of minister, and given a deputy minister as his assistant. Demetros was a leading and powerful Eritrean churchman, but anachronistic. As one who, in cooperation with Asfaha Wolde Michael, chief executive of Federal Eritrea, maneuvered Eritrea into its restive union with Ethiopia, his appointment was made as a suitable means of rewarding him with a greater and more honorable position than that conferred on him in his previous post as prelate (*nebura ed*) of Axum. In this post he was the center of criticism for having occupied an office traditionally reserved for those who were of local origin. During his leadership Demetros made no valuable contribution and spent most of his time promoting his own private projects, leaving the job largely to his deputy, Makonnen Zewde. In 1972, a year after the election of Metropolitan Tewofilos as patriarch, Demetros was removed as a result of personal antagonism and rivalry.

The task of general manager, without any secular title, passed to a less weighty and more amenable man, Ermias Kebede, another prelate of

Axum, a position in which he had made himself unpopular. In the process of encouraging and organizing tourism and some other innovations, he offended the sensitivities of the local establishment, whose elders also resented his youth, given the prestige of his position. Ermias successfully reorganized the patriarchate's administrative structure, but in the process he created more problems by engaging in favoritism and nepotism. This caused deep resentment between the hierarchy and the lower clergy, which burst into open conflict during the first wave of the revolution, forcing Ermias's demotion. His successor, Makonnen Zewde, was given the task of introducing the changes called for by the revolutionaries. However, his public denial of the urgency of reform of the church immediately brought about his replacement by another man, this time a bishop.

To this continuous shift of leadership must be added the traditional techniques inimical to reforms employed by the emperor at the same time as his centralization policy. These were measures intended to prevent the patriarchate from becoming a source of independent authority while providing the emperor with freedom to kill policies that he disliked in their formative stage. In line with this, semiautonomous institutions were created which acted in competition with, and even against, the patriarchate, as well as separate channels of communication with powerful local church establishments. Thus, in line with the tradition of the court clerics, certain abbeys and monasteries were made to function independently of the patriarchate, under the benevolent protection of the emperor, as is the case with the Holy Trinity Church under its dean, Habte Mariam.

As the first ranking court cleric, Dean Habte Mariam was the emperor's church troubleshooter. The role of his office was to furnish the emperor with a source of information independent from the established administrative channels, and to act as a watchdog over the church officials, primarily in the patriarchate. As a result, he fulfilled, in imperial orders, a critical function. With the emperor's financial backing—his office received about 20 percent of the imperial budget coming out of the church's own income—he embarked on an ambitious program of development and reform of the church. He established institutions with a modern outlook and orientation, such as schools, religious associations, missionary organizations, radio programs, and the publication of magazines.[25] He invested in buildings and local handicraft industries to make these institutions self-supporting. Subsequently, his headquarters became the center of wide-ranging developmental activities run independently of, and even in competition with, those of the patriarchate. Not surprisingly, Patriarch Tewofilos saw the institution as a threat to his own policy of strengthening the patriarchate. However, he did not dare to challenge it or undertake any coordinated efforts against it. He simply planned to neutralize it and avoid continued unhealthy competition, which resulted in constant friction between his office and that of his imperially backed rival. Yet his plan to consecrate the latter as bishop and relegate him to a distant southern diocese was foiled by the emperor's personal intervention, when the candidate appealed directly to him.

Dean Habte Mariam is a prime example of what a modern, educated, and dynamic clergyman, enjoying full imperial trust, could achieve when working within the context of the government's program of modernization of the church. But men of his caliber were few and far between: among these few, some were absorbed as technocrats in the lethargic patriarchate bureaucracy, patterned along the lines of its secular equivalent, where they accommodated themselves to work within the bounds of a prescribed code of behavior. A handful of others, who happened to occupy responsible positions, were forced to resign themselves to inaction, since any move that smacked of a new initiative or independent thinking was subject to interpretation as being a stratagem to build up personal power. But as a general rule, the church refused to absorb men with modern education. The reasons were as much lack of sufficient funds to employ them as fear of a threat that this new group presented against the maintenance of the status quo.

The main issue that led the emperor to open a theological college in 1944 was that it could serve as an agency for religious reformation and give "birth to an educated and enlightened clergy in place of an ill-trained and reactionary priesthood,"[26] for whose degrading intellectual situation at the time of the autocephaly dispute the Alexandrian see was blamed. With the inauguration of the Haile Selassie I University in 1960, the college was elevated to one of the university's branches and came under the university's administration. However, following the church's unsuccessful attempt to control the selection of students, the curriculum, and the administration, the church leadership ignored its existence. As statistics of 1971 indicate, of twenty-five graduates of 1971 and those of the preceding years, none was working directly within the Ethiopian Orthodox church. Three of them became lecturers at the college. Two were employed as librarians at the Haile Selassie I University. Two worked with private agencies, while the rest served as teachers under the Ministry of Education.[27] The exposure of this situation to the public led to a bitter conflict between the university and the church authorities, culminating in the closure of the institute in 1973 on the grounds that it was not fulfilling its purpose.

Church and People

On the eve of the revolution the church was still a strong force in the old heartland of the kingdom. Despite its low cultural attainment—which was scarcely higher than that of the ordinary peasant—and its conspicuously worldly ways, its clergy commanded immense influence. Life revolved around religious events and rituals. Most of the rural settlements had no other names than those of their churches. In the southern regions, however, people saw Orthodoxy as the enemy religion and clung to other faiths.

The nationalist intelligentsia was alienated by the church's stagnant and rigid posture. A growing number of them, including the university students, criticized the church for blocking land reform policies that would have benefited large sections of the peasantry.[28]

Church and State under the Marxist Military Regime of the Derg

The revolution caught the Ethiopian Orthodox church by surprise. It was unprepared to adjust to such a vast change of fortune. It had flourished under imperial favor without any significant degree of independence from the control of the state. Its economic position had rested on land and a large state subsidy. Even though it was a state church, it was a minority religion. The large non-Christian majority had been more or less reduced to second-class citizenship. Thus, rather than being a viable unifying force, Christianity had become a source of ethnic, confessional, and class antagonisms. A succession of uncoordinated events during the early period of the revolution stood to show that there was a determined national consensus to overthrow the church from its power base. A large group of fifteen thousand Muslims, organized jointly with Christians (mostly students), marched through the streets of Addis Ababa. It showed at once the strength of Islam, which had for centuries been stifled by the Orthodox church, and made plain that Muslim grievances were shared by some Christians too. They requested "the secularization and democratization of the state" whereby Muslims could enjoy equal treatment and identical rights with the Christians.[29] The Church hierarchy's attempt to vindicate itself with a counterdemonstration was not successful; even the lower clergy boycotted it.

The Marxist Derg's revolutionary socialism is by no means different from that of most of the radical ideologies being implemented in various other developing countries. It is first and foremost a "nationalist" one. The revolutionary leaders' main concern has been to maintain the integrity of the national borders, already seriously undermined by both internal secession and external aggression and further exacerbated by economic crisis, and ethnic and confessional differences. Their socialism is a strategy for survival, entailing the mobilization of mass support by defusing ethnic and religious conflict through emphasis on unity rather than contradictions among people hitherto divided. For them, socialism offers the prospect of integrating within the nation people living on the periphery of the country.[30] Its system of mass organizations promised to give the population a sense of participation and to provide a system of strict control that Christianity could not match. As a first step, the Derg decided to disestablish the church.

The draft constitution presented in early August 1974 announced the separation of church and state and stressed equality of all religions, thus putting the church on a level with the other creeds. With this move the revolution ended the church's monopoly and struck at the very roots of Amhara power. The church reacted vigorously.[31] A memorandum sent by Metropolitan Tewofilos with the backing of the Ecclesiastical Council made no impact on the drafters of the constitution, despite its threat of strong measures should the church's proposals be rejected. The revolutionary council knew full well that the church itself was shaken by recent events. In the Derg's view the March 12, 1974, demonstration by one thousand lower clergy—in which the demonstrators made serious allegations against the hierarchy and demanded the removal of all bishops and archbishops including the patriarch—showed that the higher clergy could not claim to speak on behalf of the entire church. Indeed, the hierarchy itself could not speak with one voice, and was internally divided.[32] For the revolutionaries the division within the church made their task much easier, and the prospect of concerted ecclesiastical resistance to their reforms quite remote. As a result, Patriarch Tewofilios's protest passed unheeded, and none of his demands were answered.

According to the provision of January 17, 1985, religious holidays were redefined and public holidays were reduced to only thirteen. These include three Muslim holidays. For the first time in Ethiopian history, the birthday of the Prophet Muhammed is celebrated—under the motto, "Ethiopia First" (*Ethiopia tiqdem*).

Nationalization of rural land with the proclamation of March 4, 1975, deprived the church of its economic base, where its alliance with the ancien régime was conspicuous. The proclamation abolished the status of the church as a landowner without any compensation and freed the peasants from all their traditional obligations toward the church, giving them pos-

sessory rights over the land under their cultivation. Thus the church, like
the rest of the traditional elite, was completely neutralized, first by taking
away the source of its supremacy, then by going over its head to make
the rural communities themselves responsible for carrying out reforms
through their duly formed peasant associations. As expected, the church
authorities made strong protests, but to no avail. However, it must be
emphasized that nationalization of the land eliminated only the church's
position as a landlord, while its traditional status among rural communities remained largely undisturbed. This was the case almost everywhere
in the north, where the leading figures in each parish were often found
as leaders of the peasant associations. In Tigre, for example, one-fifth of
the chairmen were clergymen, and the situation in Begamdir and Gojjam
was similar. With the Ownership of Urban Lands Proclamation of July 26,
1975, which nationalized all buildings for rent and urban landholdings, the
revolution severely hit the economic resources of many church institutions.[33] Later, the already badly attended moral classes were banned from
state schools, and the ill-trained teachers, who were often derided and
mocked by their students for incompetence, were removed. Compulsory
Marxism classes with Marxist teachers took their place.

On the other hand, the government, faced with an ever greater threat
of secession in the north and east, was forced to look around to salvage
structures of national survival, even very traditional ones. It soon became
clear that the Ethiopian Orthodox church could still be among the more
helpful. With the assistance of a handful of educated clergymen and laymen, mostly trained in the Eastern church's theological establishments,
links were reestablished, and under the patronage of Atnafu Abate, the
vice chairman of the Derg, an ad hoc committee was set up.[34] Following
the outcome of its investigations and studies on the church's human and
economic resources, as well as its various activities, a real purge began: un-
desirable elements were demoted or temporarily imprisoned, and favored
groups were promoted to occupy high offices. In the process the controversial Patriarch Tewofilos was deposed rather ignominiously, along with
three other bishops, upon a number of serious allegations that included
corruption and secret contact with restorationist elements.[35] Tewofilos was
succeeded by a monk, Abba Malaku Wolde Mikael, who took the name
of Takla Haymanot. Cheered by the government's controlled mass media
as "The Man of the People," he was contrasted in many ways with his
predecessors: his "democratically" carried out election by laity and clergy
was without government interference and his distinguished background
as a philanthropist and ascetic monk stood out against the government-
appointed and corrupt leadership of the past, who respected more "the

laws of the powerful than those of the Almighty." Undoubtedly, the new
leader possesses some unusual qualities that his predecessors lacked, and
in this he seems to embody the new ideals congruent with the spirit of
the times: apolitical, submissive, partly illiterate, poorly dressed, shoeless,
but with a remarkable life spent in the promotion of social welfare of the
underprivileged. Thus he is a man of little political weight, and certainly
no personal ambition.

Soon after his election, he had to contend with a most hostile synod,
albeit eroded by factional infighting. A few advocates of close cooperation
with the state, supported by revolutionary enthusiasts, were confronted
by a large number of opposing bishops. Takla Haymanot's attempt to get
out of the situation by dismissing most of the opposing groups, desperately denouncing them as supporters of the ancien régime, rather than
improving the situation, actually gave a new dimension to the tension.

With the consecration of thirteen bishops in March 1979, and the
replacement of the general manager, Mikre Sellassie Gabre Amanuel, with
qes Salomon, an enthusiastic supporter of the revolutionary regime, the
conflict subsided and the church set forth on a new course of cooperation
charted mainly by men in contact with the Moscow patriarchate, which
had lived so long in a comparable situation, and had had close links with
the Ethiopian patriarchate even before the revolution. A flamboyant and
outspoken young clergyman, qes Salomon emerged as an articulate and
strong exponent of the new trend. In his view there was not only ideological compatibility between socialism and Christianity, but their message
was identical. Subsequently, he attempted to make the church a vehicle
of the regime's Marxist ideology, and as a symbolic gesture of his conviction he gave his cross to the socialist motherland, an act still vividly
remembered in religious circles.

The pattern of church-state relations established by qes Salomon is in
many ways reminiscent of that prevailing prior to the Derg's takeover. A
number of features make this clear. As in the past, the church's foreign
relations department is constantly and actively promoted. Church delegates have appeared at every important international religious conference,
and in its darkest moment, when the government was isolated from most
of the international community for its rampant violation of human rights
in the wave of brutal and bloody massacres of both high and low during the
"Red Terror," the church authorities staunchly defended the government's
policy and its actions. In internal politics it unfailingly upheld national
unity and its frontiers as its sacrosanct duty against the secessionists, and
acted as a rallying point during the Somali invasion.

The church received an annual subsidy of $2 million for the 1,729 patriarchate workers, and a monthly allowance of $11,000 as salary for its higher officials, a figure roughly corresponding to the church's own prerevolutionary revenues earned from land taxes and some other sources. But the church's 19,770 parishes were told to feed their own clergymen. Even with the issue of land, the government has been rather conciliatory. Although under law all land belongs "to the broad masses," in practice the government has, in a number of cases, granted land to rural clergy and monasteries, provided that they work it themselves to produce more food and thus make the country's green revolution a success.[36] These gains were never called into question even after the disbanding of the ad hoc committee that followed the fall of its patron, Colonel Atnafu Abate.

But the support for the modus vivendi between church and state was not universal. Some individual clergymen did not fail to criticize it publicly, including the government's own policies. But their number was so insignificant and their action so disorganized as to make no visible impact on the general public. The government was able to get rid of them quite easily by imprisoning some and passing the others on to revolutionary justice. Only the group known as Bahtawi (literally, hermits) were capable of raising their voices high and with considerable effect on people's emotions. Some five hundred Bahtawi were sent to a rehabilitation camp at Lake Zaway, 160 kilometers west of Addis Ababa, on a site built with the Inter-church Aid financial assistance fund as a clergy training center at the beginning of 1970, before the revolution.

The government's harsh measures against foreign missionaries, combined with a leak of an "official" document revealing its plan to destroy religion, led many leaders to interpret these moves as "a prelude to a systematic persecution of [all] religions in Ethiopia."[37] But the government's own policy of cooperation with ecclesiastical authorities, the World Council of Churches' investigation team results, and the regime's own persistent denial of the authenticity of the document as well as the unanimous denials by the church leaders inside the country, make the allegation of "systematic persecution" dubious. The views that came in its support from some Ethiopian circles seem to be politically motivated rather than reflecting the real situation. There is no denial that within the government machinery there exist elements who would like to see the church disappear and who work toward that end. The document may be the work of these few individuals and not a government policy document. Equally, one may attribute certain incidents of harassment of the churches to these fanatics. Conflicts existing between the state and the established missionary churches, such as Makane Iyasus, Catholics, and Anglicans, can be interpreted as reflecting the tension between the political center and the periphery, where the activities of these churches are focused—rather than being a concerted effort to eradicate religion as such. But all evidence stands to give little support to the view that there is an integrated philosophy within the government directed against religion.

The revolution did not directly attack the Ethiopian Orthodox church, because the church itself did not attack the revolution, nor challenge its new authority. As a rule, the state has had no definite policy toward the church, partly because its entire energy has been absorbed in the more pressing problem of survival. It has followed a defined pattern of action that can roughly be described as a blend of control and transformation, but hardly of repression.

With the installation of a patriarch of its own choice and a careful elimination of potentially critical elements on the grounds of their association with the ancien régime, the state has undoubtedly secured a total grip on the church's central organization, but its political inability to control the northern provinces has resulted in most of the churches in these areas being outside the state's influence. At the same time the state's policy of social transformation has suffered considerable setbacks. Marxist-Leninist political education has replaced religious teachings in the schools. Mass organizations have been formed aimed at replacing the traditional voluntary associations that had the church as their focus. There are political and economic incentives that make membership in state associations more attractive. But a number of factors indicate that rather than weakening the position of the church, this policy has tended to have the opposite effect. Churches are filled to capacity, and there is a growing interest in the Bible. Increasing disenchantment with the government's inability to deliver the goods it promised seems to have resulted in the discrediting of socialism and all that it stood for, despite the charm of its appeals to people's deep emotions.

FACT SHEET

The Ethiopian Orthodox Church

Year of autocephaly
    1951: metropolitanate
    1959: establishment of patriarchate

Current strength of the church
    18,000,000 faithful (1984 estimate)
    73,563 priests (1982)

52,552 deacons (1982)
39,040 dabtara (1982)
12,078 monks (1972)
Figures for numbers of nuns and seminarians not available

Chief news organs
Zena beta-Kristiyan (circulation 4,000–7,000 estimated)
Demsa Tawahedo (circulation figure not available)

Number of churches and church facilities in operation (1972)
12,589 churches (11,364 rural; 1,225 abbey)
795 monasteries
1 theological seminary
3 paraseminaries
7 clergy training centers

Patriarchs since 1900
Mathewos, 1889–1926
Qerlos, 1929–50
Basilios, 1950–70
Tewofilos, 1971–76
Takla Haymanot, 1976–present

Notes

1 Introduction

I am indebted to Olga Hruby for permission to quote from her translation of Furov's report, the complete text of which was published in *Religion in Communist-Dominated Areas*, and to Dimitry Pospielovsky for his extensive comments on an earlier draft of this chapter.

1. Georges Florovsky, *Christianity and Culture* (Belmont, Mass.: Nordland, 1974), p. 132.

2. R. W. Southern, *Western Society and the Church in the Middle Ages* (Harmondsworth: Penguin Books, 1970), pp. 61–65, 73.

3. Ibid., pp. 55–56.

4. John Lawrence, *A History of Russia*, 6th ed. (New York: Meridian Books, 1978), pp. 33–34.

5. Timothy Ware, *The Orthodox Church*, rev. ed. (Harmondsworth: Penguin Books, 1980), pp. 139–45. The Christian communities of the Middle East are discussed in detail in Robert Brenton Betts, *Christians in the Arab East*, rev. ed. (Atlanta: John Knox Press, 1978).

6. Ware, *The Orthodox Church*, p. 151; and Donald Attwater, *The Christian Churches of the East* (Milwaukee: Bruce Publishing, 1947), Vol. 2, pp. 116–17.

7. Dimitry Pospielovsky, "Some Remarks on the Contemporary Russian Nationalism and Religious Revival," *Canadian Review of Studies in Nationalism*, 11, No. 1 (Spring 1984), p. 73.

8. For a more thorough treatment of this theme, in the Soviet/East European context, see Pedro Ramet (ed.), *Religion and Nationalism in Soviet and East European Politics* (Durham, N.C.: Duke University Press, 1984).

9. Christel Lane, *Christian Religion in the Soviet Union* (London: George Allen & Unwin, 1978), pp. 31, 49; and "Impegno nella Chiesa (Una communità di giovani ortodossi russi)," *Russia Cristiana*, 3, No. 3 (May–June 1978), p. 9.

10. Pospielovsky, "Some Remarks," p. 79.

11. Attwater, *The Christian Churches*, p. 129.

12. Werner Völker, "Aus der Bulgarisch-Orthodoxen Kirche," *Kirche im Osten*, 23 (1980), p. 127.

13. Bertold Spuler, *Gegenwartslage der Ostkirchen*, 2nd ed. (Frankfurt: Metopen Verlag, 1968), p. 161.

14. For details, see Pedro Ramet, "Religion and Nationalism in Yugoslavia," in Ramet (ed.), *Religion and Nationalism*.

15. J. D. Pennington, "The Copts in Modern Egypt," *Middle Eastern Studies*, 18, No. 2 (April 1982), pp. 163, 177.

16. Quoted in Mark Popovsky, "Protopop Avvakum XX veka," *Russkaia mysl*, No. 3375 (August 27, 1981), p. 12, as cited in Pospielovsky, "Some Remarks," p. 73.

17. Adrian Hastings, *A History of African Christianity, 1950–1975* (Cambridge: Cambridge University Press, 1979), p. 36.

18. Ibid., p. 37.

19. Peter R. Prifti, *Socialist Albania since 1944: Domestic and Foreign Developments* (Cambridge, Mass.: MIT Press, 1978), pp. 158–59; and Bernd Jürgen Fischer, *King Zog and the Struggle for Stability in Albania* (Boulder, Colo.: East European Monographs, 1984), pp. 170–71.

20. See Ludvík Němec, "Czechoslovakia: Situation of the Catholic and Orthodox Churches," in *Religion in Communist-Dominated Areas*, Vol. 25, No. 2 (Spring 1986), pp. 62–66; and Ludvik Němec, *Church and State in Czechoslovakia* (New York: Vantage Press, 1955), pp. 124–27.

21. Friedrich Heiler, *Die Ostkirchen* (Munich: Ernst Reinhardt Verlag, 1971), p. 86. Altogether, between 1922 and 1939, some eight hundred Orthodox churches in Poland were destroyed, closed, or confiscated.

22. Spuler, *Gegenwartslage*, pp. 196–97.

23. Xavier Jacob, "An Autocephalous Turkish Orthodox Church," *Eastern Churches Review*, 3, No. 1 (Spring 1970), pp. 59–61, 64, 69, 71; and Stephen P. Ladas, *The Exchange of Minorities: Bulgaria, Greece, and Turkey* (New York: Macmillan, 1932), pp. 1–23, 335–52.

24. V. Furov, "Cadres of the Church and Legal Measures to Curtail Their Activities," smuggled to the West and originally published in *Vestnik R. Kh. D.* (Paris); this translation by Olga S. Hruby, in *Religion in Communist-Dominated Areas*, 19 (1980), Nos. 9–11, pp. 149–50.

25. Dimitry Pospielovsky, *The Russian Church under the Soviet Regime, 1917–1982* (Crestwood, N.Y.: St. Vladimir's Seminary Press, 1984), Vol. 2, p. 400n.

26. Most of the information in this paragraph is drawn from Pospielovsky, *The Russian Church*, Vol. 2, pp. 400–401, 407, 411, 415, 440. See also Otto Luchterhandt, "Geknebelt, und dennoch lebensfähig: Die Russisch-Orthodoxe Kirche in der Ära Breschnew," *Herder Korrespondenz*, 36, No. 5 (May 1982), pp. 333–35.

27. Lane, *Christian Religion*, pp. 35–36; *Frankfurter Allgemeine*, May 11, 1982, p. 4; and William C. Fletcher, *Religion and Soviet Foreign Policy, 1945–1970* (London: Oxford University Press, 1973), pp. 117–39.

28. Philip Walters, "The Russian Orthodox Church, 1945–1959," *Religion in Communist Lands*, 8, No. 3 (Autumn 1980), p. 220.

29. Trevor Beeson, *Discretion and Valour: Religious Conditions in Russia and Eastern Europe*, Rev. ed. (Philadelphia: Fortress Press, 1982), p. 343.

30. Werner Völker, "Aus der Bulgarisch-Orthodoxen Kirche," *Kirche im Osten*, 24 (1981), pp. 154–55.

31. *Corriere della Sera*, May 12, 1984, p. 4.

32. *Keston News Service*, No. 187 (November 17, 1983), p. 7.

33. Quoted in Radu Constantin Miron, "Aus der Rumänisch-Orthodoxen Kirche," *Kirche im Osten*, 25 (1982), pp. 148–49.

34. Charles A. Frazee, *The Orthodox Church and Independent Greece, 1821–1852* (Cambridge: Cambridge University Press, 1969), pp. 73–74, 105–7, 109, 111–14; and Attwater, *The Christian Churches*, pp. 120–21.

35. Haile Larebo, "The Religious Situation in Ethiopia," public lecture presented at the *Cross and Commissar* public forum, University of Washington, Seattle, January 19, 1985.

36. Ernest W. Luther, *Ethiopia Today* (Stanford, Calif.: Stanford University Press, 1958), p. 35.

37. Paul H. Brietzke, *Law, Development, and the Ethiopian Revolution* (Lewisburg, Pa.: Bucknell University Press, 1982), pp. 101–4, 154, 167–68.

38. Michail Meerson-Aksenov, "La Chiesa ortodossa nello Stato ateo," *Russia Cristiana*, 4, No. 6 (November–December 1979), p. 18.

39. *The Orthodox Church* (July 1984), p. 1.

40. Branko A. Cisarž, "Crkvena štampa izmedju dva svetska rata," in *Srpska Pravoslavna Crkva, 1920–1970: Spomenica o 50-godišnjici vaspostavljanja Srpske Patrijaršije* (Belgrade: Kosmos, 1971), pp. 154–55.

41. For details, see Ramet, "Religion and Nationalism in Yugoslavia," pp. 159–63.

42. Pennington, "The Copts," p. 168.

43. Ibid., pp. 171–72.

44. *Monday Morning* (Beirut), November 16–22, 1981, pp. 56–58.

45. *Al-'Amal* (Beirut), September 8, 1981, p. 10, trans. in JPRS, *Near East/South Asia Report*, No. 79509 (November 24, 1981), pp. 107–8.

46. *Al Sha'b* (Cairo), January 15, 1980, p. 4, trans. in JPRS, *Near East/North Africa Report*, No. 75286 (March 12, 1980), p. 39; and *Al-Nahar al-'Arabi Wa al-Duwali* (Paris, in Arabic), May 23–29, 1983, pp. 22–23, trans. in JPRS, *Near East/South Asia Report*, No. 83891 (July 14, 1983), p. 6.

47. *Al-Mujtama'* (Kuwait), February 21, 1984, pp. 32–33, trans. in JPRS, *Near East/South Asia Report*, No. NEA-84-066 (April 23, 1984), p. 18.

48. Marin Pundeff, "Church-State Relations in Bulgaria under Communism," in Bohdan R. Bociurkiw and John W. Strong (eds.), *Religion and Atheism in the USSR and Eastern Europe* (London: Macmillan, 1975), pp. 329–30.

49. Lawrence, *A History*, p. 262.

50. Pospielovsky, *The Russian Church*, Vol. 1, p. 52.

51. Ibid., p. 62.

52. Ibid., p. 84.

53. M. S. F., "La situazione della Chiesa ortodossa e le prospettive di rinascità (L'ultima conferenza di padre Jakunin)," *Russia Cristiana*, 5, No. 1 (January–February 1980), pp. 3–5; Michail Meerson-Aksenov, "Die Russische Orthodoxe Kirche heute," *Kirche in Not*, 28 (1980), p. 46; and Gernot Seide, "Die Russiche-Orthodoxe Kirche in der Gegenwart," *Osteuropa*, 33, Nos. 11–12 (November–December 1983), p. 867.

54. "The 'Lord's Army' Movement in the Romanian Orthodox Church," *Religion in Communist Lands*, 8, No. 4 (Winter 1980), pp. 314–15. See also Alan Scarfe, "The Evangelical Wing of the Orthodox Church in Romania," *Religion in Communist Lands*, 3, No. 6 (November–December 1975), pp. 15–17.

2   The Doctrinal Foundation of Orthodoxy

1. See Aileen Guilding, *The Fourth Gospel and Jewish Worship* (Oxford: Oxford University Press, 1960).

2. Henry Volokhonsky, "Opyt liturgicheskogo istolkovania knigi otkrovenia Ioanna Bogoslova" (Essay on the liturgical interpretation of the Book of Revelation of St. John), in *Vestnik Russkogo Khristianskogo Dvizheniia* (Paris), Vol. 134, pp. 32–49.

3. Pavel Florensky, "Iz Bogoslovskogo Naslediia" (From the Theological Heritage), in *Bogoslovskye trudy* (Moscow), No. 17 (1977), pp. 87–248.

4. Quoted in Timothy Ware, *The Orthodox Church*, rev. ed. (Harmondsworth: Penguin Books, 1980), p. 271.

5. Leonid Ouspensky, *Theology of the Icon* (Crestwood, N.Y.: St. Vladimir's Seminary Press, 1978), pp. 23–24. See the "Office at the Consecration of a Church," especially the following prayer: "O God, without beginning and eternal . . . , who didst give a law and pattern unto Moses, and didst inspire Bezaleel with the spirit of wisdom, and didst enable them to complete the perfect building of the Tabernacle of thy Covenant, wherein ordinances of divine worship were instituted, which were the images and types of the true; who didst bestow upon Solomon breadth and greatness of heart, and thereby didst rear of old the Temple; and upon thy holy . . . Apostles didst renew the service in the Spirit, and the grace of the true Tabernacle, and through the same . . . didst plant thy churches and thine altars in all the earth . . . ," in *Service Book of the Holy-Orthodox-Catholic Apostolic Church*, trans. by Isabel Florence Hapgood (Englewood, N.J.: Antiochian Orthodox Diocese, 1975), p. 496.

6. See Fr. Alexander Schmeman, *Introduction to Liturgical Theology* (London: Faith Press, 1966).

7. Ware, *Orthodox Church*, pp. 219–21.

8. The priest's prayer in the Cherubic Hymn of the Divine Liturgy.

9. Paul Evdokimov, *L'Orthodoxie* (Paris: Delachaux et Niestle, 1959), p. 208.

10. Fr. Sergius Bulgakov, "Eucharistic Sacrifice" (manuscript), quoted in Leo Zander, *Bog i Mir* (Paris: YMCA Press, 1948), Vol. 1, p. 150.

11. See Fr. Sergius Bulgakov, "Evcharistichesky Dogmat" (Eucharistic Dogma), in *Put* (Paris), No. 20 (June 1930), pp. 3–40; and No. 21 (September 1930), pp. 16–21 and ff.

12. Ibid., No. 20, p. 25.

13. Fr. Sergius Bulgakov, *Agnets Bogii* (The Lamb of God) (Paris: YMCA Press, 1933), p. 433.

14. Fr. Sergius Bulgakov, *The Orthodox Church* (London: Centenary Press, 1935), p. 141.

15. See Fr. Sergius Bulgakov, *Ikona i Ikonopochitanie* (On the Veneration of Icons) (Paris: YMCA Press, 1931).

16. Ware, *Orthodox Church*, pp. 277–78.

17. Ibid., p. 206.

18. Bulgakov, *Orthodox Church*, p. 42.

19. Fr. Sergius Bulgakov, *Nevesta Agntsa* (The Bride of the Lamb) (Paris: YMCA Press, 1945), p. 297.

20. Ibid., p. 296.

21. This idea was fully explored by the Russian theologian, Fr. Pavel Florensky, in his early work, *Stolb i utverjdenie istiny* (The Pillar and Foundation of Truth) (Moscow: Put, 1912).

22. See Bulgakov, *Orthodox Church*, pp. 12ff.

23. Bulgakov, *Nevesta Agntsa*, p. 298.

24. At the Council of Florence and at the First Vatican Council.

25. Bulgakov, *Nevesta Agntsa*, p. 300.

26. Zander, *Bog i Mir*, Vol. 2, p. 303.

27. Bulgakov, *Nevesta Agntsa*, p. 304.

28. Zander, *Bog i Mir*, Vol. 2, p. 303.

29. Sergius Bulgakov, "One Holy, Catholic and Apostolic Church," in *Journal of the Fellowship* (Oxford), 12 (June 1931), p. 25.

30. Zander, *Bog i Mir*, Vol. 2, p. 290.

31. John Meyendorff, *The Orthodox Church* (Crestwood, N.Y.: St. Vladimir's Seminary Press, 1981), p. 212.

32. At the Orthodox office of the consecration of a bishop-elect, bishops assembled for the ordination invoke the name of Jesus Christ with the following words: "Do thou, the same Lord of all, who also graciously enabled this chosen person to come under the yoke of the Gospel and the dignity of a bishop through the laying-on [of] hands of us, his fellow bishops here present, strengthen him by the inspiration and power and grace of thy Holy Spirit, as thou did strengthen thy holy Apostles and Prophets; as thou has consecrated bishops and make his bishopric to be blameless; that he may be worthy to ask those things which are for the salvation of the people, and that thou mayest give ear unto him." "The Order of Consecrating a Bishop," in *Service Book*, pp. 329–30.

33. See chapter 6 in this volume.

34. See Bulgakov, *Orthodox Church*, pp. 48–103.

35. Ware, *Orthodox Church*, p. 250.

36. Bulgakov, *Orthodox Church*, p. 108.

37. Meyendorff, *Orthodox Church*, p. 144.

38. Ibid.

39. Ibid., p. 145.

40. Bulgakov, *Orthodox Church*, p. 187.

41. Ibid., p. 189.

3   The Historical Tradition of Church-State Relations under Orthodoxy

1. Dimitri Obolensky, "Russia's Byzantine Heritage," *Oxford Slavonic Papers*, 1 (1950), pp. 39–40; Dimitri Stremooukhoff, "Moscow the Third Rome: Sources of the Doctrine," *Speculum*, 28 (1953), pp. 84–101.

2. The sincerity of Constantine's conversion has frequently been questioned. That it was not a calculated political move is now generally, if not universally, recognized. See the authoritative verdict of A. H. M. Jones, *Constantine and the Conversion of Europe* (New York: Collier Books, 1962); idem, "The Social Background of the Struggle between Paganism and Christianity," in A. Momigliano, (ed.), *The Conflict between Paganism and Christianity in the Fourth Century* (Oxford: Clarendon Press, 1963), pp. 17–37.

3. See especially the thorough treatment of the evidence by Joseph Vogt, *The Decline of Rome: The Metamorphosis of Ancient Civilization* (New York and Washington, D.C.: Praeger, 1969), pp. 87–176.

4. I. A. Heikel (ed.), *Eusebius Werke*, (Leipzig: J. C. Hinrich Buchhandlung, 1902), Die griechischen christlichen Schriftsteller, Vol. 7, Part I, p. 201. In reality the idea was not so new as it might seem. Earlier Christian historiography had expressed similar ideas. See

especially R. A. Marcus, "The Roman Empire in Early Christian Historiography," *Downside Review*, 81 (1963), p. 343. Cf. A W. Ziegler, "Die byzantinische Religionspolitik und der sog. Caesaropapismus," in E. Koschmieder and A. Schmaus (eds.), *Münchener Beiträge zur Slavenkunden: Festgabe für Paul Diels* (Munich: Isar Verlag, 1953), pp. 88, 89–90. For an analysis of Eusebius's *De Laudibus Constantinii*, see Timothy D. Barnes, *Constantine and Eusebius* (Cambridge, Mass.: Harvard University Press, 1981), pp. 253–55.

5. Cf. the remarks of patriarch Anthony IV addressed to Basil of Moscow in 1397, in F. Miklosich and J. Müller (eds.), *Acta et diplomata graeca medii aevi sacra et profana* (Vienna: Carolus Gerold, 1862), Vol. 2, p. 191: "It is not possible for Christians to have the Church and not to have the Empire; for Church and Empire form a great unity and community, and it is not possible for them to be separated from one another."

6. Johannes A. Straub, *Von Herrscherideal in der Spätantike* (Stuttgart: W. Kohlhammer Verlag, 1964), p. 113.

7. Francis Dvornik, *Early Christian and Byzantine Political Philosophy* (Washington, D.C.: Dumbarton Oaks Center for Byzantine Studies, 1966), Vol. 2, p. 720.

8. For some of the details that follow, see Alexander Schmemann, *Church, World, Mission: Reflections on Orthodoxy in the West* (Crestwood, N.Y.: St. Vladimir's Seminary Press, 1979), pp. 33–34; and Vogt, *The Decline of Rome*, pp. 87–88.

9. R. Schoell (ed.), *Corpus juris civilis* (Berlin: Wiedmann's, 1928), Vol. 3, pp. 35–36; translation in Deno J. Geanakoplos, *Byzantium: Church, Society, and Civilization Seen through Contemporary Eyes* (Chicago: University of Chicago Press, 1984), p. 136.

10. The *Epanagoge* was probably penned by Patriarch Photius. For an English translation, see E. Barker (ed.), *Social and Political Thought in Byzantium* (Oxford: Clarendon Press, 1961), pp. 89–93.

11. John Meyendorff, *Byzantine Theology: Historical Trends and Doctrinal Themes* (New York: Fordham University Press, 1974), p. 213.

12. See especially A. J. Toynbee, *Civilization on Trial* (Oxford: Oxford University Press, 1948), pp. 164; and the hostile essay, with its unconcealed Roman Catholic bias, of Cyril Toumanoff, "Caesaropapism in Byzantium and Russia," *Theological Studies*, 7 (1946), pp. 213–243.

13. The case is scrupulously argued by two leading contemporary Byzantinists: Hélène Ahrweiler, *L'idéologie politique de l'Empire byzantin* (Paris: Presses universitaires de France, 1975), pp. 130–32; and Alexander Kazhdan and Giles Constable, *People and Power in Byzantium* (Washington, D.C.: Dumbarton Oaks Center for Byzantine Studies, 1982), pp. 145–49. See also Herbert Hunger (ed.), *Das byzantinische Herrscherbild* (Darmstadt: Wissenschaftliche Buchgessellschaft, 1975), p. 6. This last work contains a valuable bibliography.

14. Maximus the Confessor, *Acta*, in J. P. Migne, *Patrologia Cursus Completus: Series Graeca* (Paris, 1857–1866), Vol. 90, col. 117A.

15. *Leoni sacellario* (Letter 129), in Migne, *Patrologia Graeca*, Vol. 99, col. 1417 C.

16. Kazhdan and Constable, *People and Power in Byzantium*, p. 148.

17. Cf. Ronald D. Ware, "Caesaropapism," in Joseph Dunner (ed.), *Handbook of World History* (New York: Philosophical Library, 1967), pp. 136–37.

18. Georges Florovsky, "Antinomies of Christian History: Empire and Desert," in Georges Florovsky, *Christianity and Culture* (Belmont, Mass.: Nordland, 1974), Vol. 2, pp. 97–98.

19. Friedrich Giese, "Die geschichtliche Grundlagen für die Stellung des christlichen Untertanen im osmanischen Recht," *Islam*, 19 (1931), p. 264.

20. Aristeides Papadakis, "Gennadius II and Mehmet the Conqueror," *Byzantion*, 42 (1972), pp. 88–91.

21. E. H. Palmer (trans.), *The Koran (Qur'an)* (Oxford: Oxford University Press, 1928), p. 7.

22. Peter F. Sugar, *Southeastern Europe under Ottoman Rule, 1354–1804* (Seattle: University of Washington Press, 1977), p. 5; and Halil Inalcik, *The Ottoman Empire: The Classical Age, 1300–1600* (New York: Praeger, 1973), pp. 7–8.

23. The system, it should be emphasized, was adopted slowly over the years and was to a degree ad hoc in nature. See especially, Benjamin Braude, "Foundation Myths of the Millet System," in Benjamin Braude and Bernard Lewis (eds.), *Christians and Jews in the Ottoman Empire: The Functioning of a Plural Society* (New York and London: Holmes and Meier, 1982), Vol. 1, pp. 69–89, and p. 12 (introduction).

24. Richard Clogg (ed.), *The Movement for Greek Independence, 1770–1821: A Collection of Documents* (London: Macmillan, 1976), p. 29. For a discussion of the authorship of this text, see Theodore H. Papadopoulos, *Studies and Documents Relating to the History of the Greek Church and Its People under Turkish Domination* (Brussels: 1952), p. 146, n. 2.

25. L. S. Stavrianos, *The Balkans since 1453* (New York: Holt, Rinehart and Winston, 1961), p. 105.

26. V. Laurent, "Les premiers patriarches de Constantinople sous domination turque," *Revue des études byzantines*, 26 (1968), p. 233.

27. Cf. the useful and detailed discussion by Richard Clogg, "The Greek Millet in the Ottoman Empire," in Braude and Lewis, *Christians and Jews*, Vol. 2, pp. 187–88.

28. An exception to this general rule was the attempt of the Greek-controlled patriarchate in the eighteenth century to impose Greek bishops and to replace Church Slavonic with Greek as the liturgical language for the Serbs and Bulgarians. This Greek hegemony, however, was by no means characteristic of the entire Turkish period. Besides, this centralization and uniformity was necessary and inevitable given the church's struggle to retain its unity and integrity. See the remarks of Sugar, *Southeastern Europe*, p. 253.

29. Cf. B. H. Sumner, *A Short History of Russia* (New York: Harcourt, Brace, 1949), p. 175.

30. Philip Sherrard, "Church, State, and the Greek War of Independence," in Richard Clogg (ed.), *The Struggle for Greek Independence* (Hamden, Conn.: Archon Books, 1973), pp. 184, 198.

31. Charles A. Frazee, *The Orthodox Church and Independent Greece, 1821–1852* (Cambridge: Cambridge University Press, 1969), p. 196.

32. Ibid., pp. 106, 115.

33. Alexander Schmemann, *The Historical Road of Eastern Orthodoxy* (Chicago: Henry Regnery, 1963), p. 291.

34. Cited in Stremooukhoff, "Moscow the Third Rome," p. 91.

35. John Meyendorff, *The Orthodox Church* (London: Darton, Longman and Todd, 1962), p. 108.

36. Cf. William K. Medlin, *Moscow and East Rome: A Political Study of the Relations of Church and State in Muscovite Russia* (Geneva: Librairie E. Droz, 1952), pp. 228–29.

37. F. Dvornik, "Byzantium, Muscovite Autocracy, and the Church," in A. H. Armstrong (ed.), *Re-discovering Eastern Christendom* (London: Darton, Longman and Todd, 1963), p. 117.

38. William Palmer, *The Patriarch and the Tsar* (London: 1876), Vol. 3, p. 250.

39. Cf. Reinhard Wittram, "Peters des grossen Verhältnis zur Religion und den Kirchen," *Historische Zeitschrift*, 173 (1952), pp. 261; and the detailed treatment by James Cracraft, *The Church Reform of Peter the Great* (Stanford, Calif.: Stanford University Press, 1971).

40. Medlin, *Moscow and East Rome*, p. 222.

41. A. V. Muller (trans.), *The Spiritual Regulation of Peter the Great* (Seattle and London: University of Washington Press, 1972), p. 10.

42. Cf. Marc Szeftel, "Church and State in Imperial Russia," in Robert L. Nichols and Theophanis George Stavrou (eds.), *Russian Orthodoxy under the Old Regime* (Minneapolis: University of Minnesota Press, 1978), p. 137.

43. Cf. the cutting characterization of Prokopovich by Georges Florovsky, *Ways of Russian Theology* (Belmont, Mass.: Nordland, 1979), pp. 122–30.

44. John Meyendorff, "Russian Bishops and Church Reform in 1905," in Nichols and Stavrou, *Russian Orthodoxy*, p. 171.

45. Cited in John Shelton Curtiss, *Church and State in Russia: The Last Years of the Empire, 1900–1917* (New York: Octagon Books, 1972), pp. 25, 73–74.

46. Alexander Solzhenitsyn, *A Lenten Letter to Pimen Patriarch of All Russia* (Minneapolis: University of Minnesota Press, 1972), p. 6.

47. See the evidence cited in Meyendorff, *The Orthodox Church*, pp. 114–20; and Timothy Ware, *The Orthodox Church* (Baltimore: Penguin Books, 1963), pp. 128–37.

48. Cf. Demetrios J. Constantelos, *Byzantine Philanthropy and Social Welfare* (New Brunswick, N.J.: Rutgers University Press, 1968).

49. Schmemann, *Church, World, Mission*, p. 65.

4   The Russian Orthodox Church

1. See Robert F. Byrnes, *Pobedonostsev: His Life and Thought* (Bloomington: Indiana University Press, 1969).

2. See Gerhard Simon, *Church, State, and Opposition in the USSR* (London: C. Hurst, 1974), pp. 130–33; Walter Kolarz, *Religion in the Soviet Union* (London: Macmillan, 1961), pp. 128–49.

3. The most comprehensive and authoritative account in English of the Slavophiles and their heritage is Andrzej Walicki, *The Slavophile Controversy: History of a Conservative Utopia in Nineteenth-Century Russian Thought* (Oxford: Oxford University Press, 1975). See also Peter K. Christoff, *An Introduction to Nineteenth-Century Russian Slavophilism*, 2 vols. (The Hague: Mouton, 1961 and 1972); S. V. Utechin, *Russian Political Thought: A Concise History* (London: J. M. Dent, 1963), pp. 78–127.

4. See Dimitry Pospielovsky, "The Neo-Slavophile Trend and Its Relation to the Contemporary Religious Revival in the USSR," in Pedro Ramet, ed., *Religion and Nationalism in Soviet and East European Politics* (Durham, N.C.: Duke University Press, 1984).

5. See Utechin, *Russian Political Thought*, pp. 71–75.

6. For an analysis of why both Slavophiles and westernizers in the nineteenth century rejected this official ideology, see Dimitry Pospielovsky, "The Resurgence of Russian Nationalism in *Samizdat*," *Survey*, 86 (1973), pp. 57–58.

7. For the general religious revival and the political and social debate at the time, see Nicolas Zernov, *The Russian Religious Renaissance of the Twentieth Century* (London: Darton, Longman and Todd, 1963); George F. Putnam, *Russian Alternatives to Marxism: Christian Socialism and Idealistic Liberalism in Twentieth-Century Russia* (Knoxville: University of Tennessee Press, 1977); Gerhard Simon, "Between Reform and Reaction: Church, State

and Society on the Eve of the Russian Revolution," in his *Church, State and Opposition in the USSR*, pp. 1–40; idem, "Antoni (Vadkovsky), Metropolitan of St. Petersburg," ibid., pp. 41–63; Christopher Read, *Religion, Revolution, and the Russian Intelligentsia, 1900–1912: The "Vekhi" Debate and Its Intellectual Background* (London: Macmillan, 1979).

8. For a detailed study of the preparations for the council in 1905–1906, see James W. Cunningham, *A Vanquished Hope: The Movement for Church Renewal in Russia, 1905–1906* (Crestwood, N.Y.: St. Vladimir's Seminary Press, 1981).

9. Simon, *Church, State, and Opposition in the USSR*, p. 28.

10. See Nicolas Zernov, "The 1917 Council of the Russian Orthodox Church," *Religion in Communist Lands*, 6, No. 1 (Spring 1978), pp. 12–25.

11. Dimitry Pospielovsky, *The Russian Church under the Soviet Regime, 1917–1982* (New York: St. Vladimir's Seminary Press, 1984), Vol. 1, pp. 33–38.

12. The most comprehensive if unstructured account of the Living Church movement is A. Levitin and V. Shavrov, *Ocherki po istorii russkoi tserkovnoi smuty* (Kusnacht, Switz.: Glaube in der 2 Welt, 1977). Levitin was personally involved in the movement and knew all the leading personalities. See also Pospielovsky, *The Russian Church*, pp. 43–92; A. Krasnov-Levitin, *Likhie gody, 1925–1941* (Paris: YMCA Press, 1977); Philip Walters, "The Living Church 1922–1946," *Religion in Communist Lands* 6, No. 4 (Winter 1976), pp. 235–43.

13. Boris V. Titlinov, *Novaya tserkov* (Petrograd: Byloe, 1923), pp. 41–50.

14. See Sergei N. Bulgakov, *Dva grada* (Moscow: Put, 1911), especially "Khristianstvo i sotsialnyi vopros," in Vol. 1, pp. 206–33.

15. Pospielovsky, *The Russian Church*, p. 54.

16. Ibid., p. 84. Pospielovsky offers a very interesting diagnosis of the Renovationist ideology in terms of Hegelianism, Nietzscheanism, and traditional Orthodox "Christian socialism." He shows convincingly how for a time, in the climate of the New Economic Policy of the early 1920s, it was in fact possible for a Christian movement to combine socialist aspirations with support for the "nationalist" regime into which Bolshevism was (wrongly) perceived to be evolving; but he also shows how the coherence of this movement inevitably collapsed after the abandonment of NEP and the consolidation of Stalinist socialism. Ibid., pp. 85–92.

17. Before the 1971 council of the Orthodox church took place, some Orthodox dissenters attempted to open a discussion of purely theological issues within the church. Four members criticized theological innovations which they claimed Metropolitan Nikodim had introduced into his pronouncements on peace at international gatherings. Fr. N. Gainov, F. Karelin, L. Regelson, V. Kapitanchuk, "Obrashchenie k Pomestnomu Soboru Russkoi Pravoslavnoi Tserkvi," April 26, 1971. Photocopy of most of the typewritten text in archive of Keston College.

18. For an assessment of Sergi see Pospielovsky, *The Russian Church*, pp. 183–91.

19. The gender of the pronoun in the original Russian text makes it clear that Sergi was declaring loyalty not to the Soviet system as a political system, but to the Russian motherland. The meaning is that while the Soviet Union is recognized as the motherland, it is the joys and successes of the latter which are said to be those of the church. This distinction had no practical consequences, however, and no bearing on the subsequent action of the state.

20. Levitin and Shavrov, *Ocherki po istorii russkoi tserkovnoi smuty*, pt. 1, p. 129; Lev Regelson, *Tragediya russkoi tserkvi, 1917–1945* (Paris: YMCA Press 1977), pp. 117–8. See also B. V. Talantov, "Sergievshchina ili prisposoblenchestvo k ateizmu," August 1967, Arkhiv Samizdata No. 745.

21. See William C. Fletcher, *A Study in Survival: The Church in Russia, 1927–1943*

(London: SPCK, 1965). The subject of the underground church is too complex to be treated here. The best book on the subject is William C. Fletcher, *The Russian Orthodox Church Underground, 1917–1970* (New York, Toronto, London: Oxford University Press, 1971). See also Pospielovsky, *The Russian Church*, pp. 179–83, 365–86.

22. See Wassilij Alexeev and Theofanis G. Stavrou, *The Great Revival: The Russian Church under German Occupation* (Minneapolis, Minn.: Burgess, 1976); Wassilij Alexeev and Keith Armes, "German Intelligence: Religious Revival in Soviet Territory," *Religion in Communist Lands*, 5, No. 1 (Spring 1977), pp. 27–37 and 5, No. 2 (1977), pp. 109–16.

23. It seems that the number of churches reopened rose to a maximum of half the prerevolutionary total. For a discussion of the divergent figures given by different authorities, see Philip Walters, "The Russian Orthodox Church 1945–59," *Religion in Communist Lands*, 8, No. 3 (Autumn 1980), p. 219 and n. 9.

24. For a description of the courses offered, see Rev. A. Shmemann, "Bogoslovskaya shkola v SSSR," *Vestnik* (Munich: Institute for the Study of the USSR), 1 (1957), p. 99.

25. See William C. Fletcher, *Nikolai: Portrait of a Dilemma* (New York and London: Macmillan, 1968).

26. Levitin has characterized the postwar arrangement as that of "a conservative Church in a conservative State." A. E. Levitin-Krasnov, *Ruk tvoikh zhar (1941–1956)* (Tel Aviv: Krug, 1979), pp. 196–97.

27. The subjects discussed and conclusions reached at the conference, including attacks on Protestantism, the Vatican, and the ecumenical movement in the Western churches, too obviously reflected Soviet political preoccupations. The close link which existed at this time between the state's foreign policies and the activities of the church can be seen in the development of the patriarchate's relations with the Serbian Orthodox church. The latter accepted Moscow's leadership in 1945, but the Moscow patriarchate severed links in 1948 when President Tito broke politically with Moscow, and restored them only in 1957 when Khrushchev was reconciled with Tito.

28. Michael Binyon, "Peace Issue Marks Church Revival," *The Times*, May 10, 1982, p. 6.

29. *Zhurnal Moskovskoi Patriarkhii*, 2 (1978), p. 4.

30. Fletcher divides Soviet foreign policy into several fields of endeavor, and identifies the realm of influencing world public opinion about Soviet intentions and realities as the specific area in which religious organizations can contribute. William C. Fletcher, *Religion and Soviet Foreign Policy, 1945–1970* (London: Oxford University Press, 1973), p. 3.

31. For assessments of the achievements and personality of Metropolitan Nikodim, see Fletcher, *Religion and Soviet Foreign Policy, 1945–1970*, pp. 123–24; Pospielovsky, *The Russian Church*, pp. 359–63; Dimitry Pospielovsky, John Lawrence, and Paul Oestreicher, "Metropolitan Nikodim Remembered," *Religion in Communist Lands*, 6, No. 4 (Winter 1978), pp. 227–34.

32. See Michael Aksenov Meerson, "The Russian Orthodox Church 1965–1980," *Religion in Communist Lands*, 9, Nos. 3–4 (Autumn 1981), pp. 107–9.

33. For an attempt to define four stages in antireligious activity in the late 1940s and 1950s, see Nikita Struve, *Christians in Contemporary Russia* (London: Harvill Press, 1967), pp. 93–94. See also D. Konstantinov, "Tserkovnaya politika Moskovskoi Patriarkhii," *Russkaya Pravoslavnaya Tserkov v SSSR* (New York: Vseslavianskoe izdatel'stvo, 1967), pp. 211ff.; William B. Stroyen, *Communist Russia and the Russian Orthodox Church, 1943–1962* (Washington D.C.: Catholic University of America Press, 1967), pp. 90ff.

34. See Pospielovsky, *The Russian Church*, pp. 350–59; Struve, *Christians in Contem-*

porary Russia, pp. 292–93. On the campaign as a whole, see Michael Bourdeaux, *Patriarch and Prophets: Persecution of the Russian Orthodox Church Today* (Oxford and London: Mowbrays, 1970); idem, "The Black Quinquennium: The Russian Orthodox Church, 1959–1964," *Religion in Communist Lands*, 9, Nos. 1–2 (Spring 1981), pp. 18–23; Donald A. Lowrie and William C. Fletcher, "Khrushchev's Religious Policy, 1959–64," in Richard H. Marshall (ed.), *Aspects of Religion in the Soviet Union, 1917–1967* (Chicago and London: University of Chicago Press, 1971), pp. 131–55.

35. Indeed, the antireligious campaign was justified in terms of a return to "Leninist legality" after Stalin had allegedly departed from this norm in awarding concessions to the church.

36. For substantiation of the claim that the synod was uncanonical, see Bourdeaux, *Patriarch and Prophets*, reference "Regulations, Orthodox Church (1961)" in the index. For a description of the synod, see the anonymous samizdat document *Opisanie arkhiereiskogo sobora 1961 g.*, mid-1960s, Arkhiv Samizdata No. 701, excerpts translated in *Religion in Communist Lands*, 9, Nos. 1–2 (Spring 1981), pp. 24–27.

37. N. Eshliman and G. Yakunin, *Letter* to Patriarch Aleksi, November 21, 1965; *Letter* to N. V. Podgorny, December 15, 1965. These and other documents from the whole debate are to be found in abridged translation in Bourdeaux, *Patriarch and Prophets*, pp. 189–254.

38. The Council for Religious Affairs, set up in 1965, combined the functions of the Council for the Affairs of the Russian Orthodox Church, set up in 1943, and the council for all other confessions together, set up in 1944.

39. A. I. Solzhenitsyn, *Letter* to Patriarch Pimen, Lent 1972. English translation in Simon, *Church, State, and Opposition in the USSR*, pp. 202–5.

40. Fr. Gleb Yakunin, "Doklad . . . o sovremennom polozhenii Russkoi Pravoslavnoi Tserkvi i o perspektivakh religioznogo vozrozhdeniya Rossii," August 15, 1979, in Russian, in *Documents of the Christian Committee for the Defense of Believers' Rights in the USSR* (San Francisco: Washington Research Center, 1982), Vol. 11, pp. 1128–68.

41. Shmemann, "Bogoslovskaya shkola v SSSR," pp. 82ff.

42. Konstantinov, "Tserkovnaya politika Moskovskoi Patriarkhii," pp. 160–65.

43. Pospielovsky, *The Russian Church*, p. 440.

44. A photocopy of the report is in the archives of Keston College. Parts of it have been published in *Vestnik RkhD* (Paris), No. 130 (1979), pp. 275–344; No. 131 (1980), pp. 362–72; and No. 132 (1980), pp. 197–205. Translation of extracts in English appear in *The Orthodox Monitor*, Nos. 9–10 (July–December 1980), pp. 58–80. Extracts from the 1974 report have appeared as *Rapport Secret au Comité Centrale sur l'Etat de l'Eglise en URSS* (Paris: Seuil, 1980).

45. See David Kelly, "Nairobi: A Door Opened," *Religion in Communist Lands*, 4, No. 1 (Spring 1976), pp. 4–17; Helene Posdeeff, "Geneva: The Defence of Believers' Rights," *Religion in Communist Lands*, 4, No. 4 (Winter 1976), pp. 4–15.

46. See Jane Ellis, "The Christian Committee for the Defence of Believers' Rights in the USSR," *Religion in Communist Lands*, 8, No. 4 (Winter 1980), pp. 279–98.

47. See John Dunlop, "The Eleventh Hour," *Frontier*, 18, No. 2, pp. 71–82. For the whole spectrum of Russian nationalist thought in Soviet Russia, see John Dunlop, *The Faces of Contemporary Russian Nationalism* (Princeton, N.J.: Princeton University Press, 1983).

48. See John Dunlop (ed.), *VSKhSON* (Paris: YMCA Press, 1975) (in Russian); idem, *The New Russian Revolutionaries* (Belmont, Mass.: Nordland, 1976).

49. See Philip Walters, "Vladimir Osipov: Loyal Opposition?" *Religion in Communist Lands*, 5, No. 4 (Winter 1977), pp. 229–34.

50. See Jane Ellis, "USSR: The Christian Seminar," with appended documents, *Religion in Communist Lands*, 8, No. 2 (Summer 1980), pp. 92–112; Philip Walters, "The Ideas of the Christian Seminar," with appended documents, *Religion in Communist Lands*, 9, Nos. 3–4 (Autumn 1981), pp. 111–26.

51. The authors of *Iz-pod glyb* were liberal Orthodox Christians and were consciously imitating the example of those new converts from Marxism to Orthodoxy who had collaborated on the symposia *Vekhi* (1909) and *Iz glubiny* (1918). M. S. Agursky, E. V. Barabanov, V. M. Borisov, A.B., F. Korsakov, A. I. Solzhenitsyn, I. R. Shafarevich, *Iz-pod glyb* (Paris: YMCA Press, 1974). Published in English as *From Under the Rubble* (London: Collins and Harvill, 1975).

52. *Slovo natsii*, 1970, Arkhiv Samizdata No. 590. Translated as "A Word to the Nation," in *Survey*, No. 80 (1971), pp. 191–99.

53. Gennadi M. Shimanov, *Idealnoe gosudarstvo*, May 29, 1975. In archive of Keston College.

54. National Bolshevism was a product of the period of the New Economic Policy of the 1920s when it seemed that the Bolshevik dictatorship might be preparing to abandon Marxist-Leninist orthodoxy for a more pragmatic and nationalist ideology. See Utechin, *Russian Political Thought*, pp. 253–56. John Dunlop distinguishes two main trends in contemporary Russian nationalism: the *vozrozhdentsy* (representatives of the religious renaissance), and the modern proponents of National Bolshevism (who are essentially chauvinist neopagans). Dunlop, *The Faces*, pp. 242–73.

55. Alexander Yanov, in his book *The Russian New Right: Right Wing Ideologies in the Contemporary USSR* (Berkeley: Institute of International Studies, University of California, 1978), argues that a future Soviet regime could find it natural to make an alliance with right-wing nationalist movements; but he indiscriminately criticizes *all* Slavophile tendencies within the Orthodox dissent movement for their alleged contribution toward creating a climate in which this might happen. Yanov's thesis is challenged by Darrell P. Hammer in his article "Russian Nationalism and the Yanov Thesis," in *Religion in Communist Lands*, 10, No. 3 (Winter 1982), pp. 310–16. Dunlop names the following Politburo members as having shown sympathy toward Russian nationalism: Polyansky, Shelepin, Solomentsev, Kapitonov. See Dunlop, *The Faces*, pp. 38, 269.

56. See Walter Sawatsky, "The New Soviet Law on Religion," *Religion in Communist Lands*, 4, No. 2 (Summer 1976), pp. 4–10; idem, "Secret Soviet Lawbook on Religion," *Religion in Communist Lands*, 4, No. 4 (Winter 1976), pp. 24–34.

57. David E. Powell, *Anti-Religious Propaganda in the Soviet Union* (Cambridge, Mass., and London: MIT Press, 1975).

58. The most recent, most comprehensive, and most authoritative study of the Russian Orthodox church over the last twenty years is Jane Ellis, *The Russian Orthodox Church: A Contemporary History* (London and Sydney: Croom Helm, 1986; and Bloomington: Indiana University Press, 1986).

5   Publications of the Russian Orthodox Church in the USSR

This chapter is adapted from the author's *The Russian Orthodox Church: A Contemporary History*, published in London by Croom Helm and in Bloomington by Indiana University Press.

1. Paul Masson, "La Religion en Union sovietique," *La Libre Belgique* (Belgium) October 9, 10, 11, 12, 13–14, 15, 16, 1979; the quote, October 11. Although it is doubtful that the archbishop would have used the phrase "servants of the cult," this is the translation given in the source quoted.

2. John Paxton (ed.), *The Statesman's Year Book, 1980–1981* (London: Macmillan, 1980), pp. 1224, 1226. Complaints about the shortage of paper figure frequently in the USSR. However, it appears to be generally accepted that this is due not so much to an absolute shortage of paper as to the ordering of priorities over what is published.

3. Fr. Gleb Yakunin, "Report of Father Gleb Yakunin to the Christian Committee for the Defense of Believers' Rights in the USSR on the Current Situation of the Russian Orthodox Church and the Prospects for Religious Renascence in Russia" (August 15, 1979) ArKhiv Samizdata (AS) No. 3751, *Documents of the Christian Committee for the Defense of Believers' Rights*, Vol. 11, pp. 1128–68; partial but extensive translation into English in the same volume, pp. xvi–xxx (San Francisco: Washington Research Center, 1979).

4. Typewritten texts of Deacon Rusak's works are in the possession of Glaube in der 2 Welt (Zurich) and Les Editeurs Réunis (Paris). A section of this work entitled "The Problem of Printing" (*Tipograficheskaya problema*), from which all references in the present essay are taken, is available in photocopied form from Keston College (Kent, England). Rusak's appeal to the Vancouver Assembly is available in English translation from Keston College.

5. In the samizdat form in which the CRA reports have reached the West, they are prefaced by the title "Extracts from informational reports of the Council for Religious Affairs under the Council of Ministers of the USSR to the Central Committee of the CPSU." A photocopy of the reports is in the Keston College archives. Parts of it have been published in *Vestnik RkhD*, Paris: the extracts from the 1974 report in No. 130 (1979), pp. 275–344; from the 1970 report in No. 131 (1980), pp. 362–72; and from the 1968 report in No. 132 (1980), pp. 197–205. A translation into English has been published in *Religion in Communist-Dominated Areas* (New York). The extracts from the 1974 report have been published in French as a book, *Rapport Secret au Comité Centrale sur l'Etat de l'Eglise en URSS*, introduction by Nikita Struve (Paris: Seuil, 1980).

6. Archbishop Pitirim of Volokolamsk (ed.) *The Moscow Patriarchate, 1917–1977* (Moscow: Patriarchate, 1978), p. 26.

7. Walter Sawatsky, "Bibles in Eastern Europe since 1945," *Religion in Communist Lands*, 3, No. 6 (November–December 1975), p. 9; Rusak, "*Tipograficheskaya problema*," p. 20.

8. Sawatsky, "*Bibles in Eastern Europe*," p. 13, n. 8, which provides further details; Rusak, "*Tipograficheskaya problema*," p. 20.

9. Philippe Sabant, "Religion in Russia Today," *The Tablet*, January 19, 1980, p. 56; Rusak, "*Tipograficheskaya problema*," p. 21.

10. *UBS* [United Bible Societies] *World Report*, No. 164, December 1983.

11. Vladimir Pozner, " 'Unexpected' Reason for Ban on Bible Imports," Radio Moscow in English for North America (January 21, 1978), in *Summary of World Broadcasts* (January 26, 1978) SU/5723/A1/6.

12. *Ecumenical Press Service*, No. 16 (June 8, 1978), p. 7.

13. *One World*, 38 (July–August 1978), p. 6; *Journal of the Moscow Patriarchate* (JMP), (1978), No. 6, p. 3.

14. Pozner, Radio Moscow.

15. *One Church*, (1979), 3, pp. 111–12; *UBS World Report*, No. 141 (January 1982).

16. *The Moscow Patriarchate, 1917–1977*, pp. 26–27, and issues of *JMP* list the publica-

tions but not the numbers printed; some of these are given in the 1974 CRA report (*Vestnik RKhD*, No. 130, p. 328) and *Episkepsis*, No. 252 (May 20, 1981), p. 6.

17. Rusak, "*Tipograficheskaya problema*," p. 22.

18. *Vestnik RKhD*, No. 130, p. 328.

19. Masson, "La Religion en Union sovietique," October 11, 1979.

20. The overseas dioceses are the exarchate of Argentina and South America, the exarchate of Berlin and Central Europe, and the six dioceses of Baden-Baden and Bavaria; Brussels and Belgium; The Hague and the Netherlands; Sourozh (London, England); Vienna and Austria; and Zurich. Estimates of the sizes of their memberships are not available.

21. Rusak, "*Tipograficheskaya problema*," pp. 22, 23.

22. *The Moscow Patriarchate, 1917–1977*, p. 27; *Vestnik RKhD*, No. 130, p. 32.

23. *Vestnik RKhD*, No. 130, p. 32.

24. CRA report for 1970, p. 18; this gives the dates for publication of *JMP* in the thirties, but states erroneously that it recommenced in 1941. The fortieth anniversary of the journal was celebrated by its staff on September 22, 1983. *JMP*, 10 (1983), p. 5.

25. *Vestnik RkhD*, No. 130, p. 327.

26. Ibid., p. 328; CRA report for 1970, p. 18.

27. The Yakunin Report, p. 34; Masson, "*La Religion en Union sovietique*," October 11, 1979.

28. Rusak, "*Tipograficheskaya problema*," pp. 21, 22.

29. *Vestnik RKhD*, No. 130, p. 329.

30. Rusak, "*Tipograficheskaya problema*," pp. 21, 22.

31. *Vestnik RKhD*, No. 130, p. 328.

32. Yakunin Report, pp. 34, 35. The only other religious publication in the USSR to have an English edition is *Muslims of the Soviet East*, which appears in several foreign languages.

33. CRA report for 1970, p. 18.

34. *Vestnik RKhD*, No. 130, p. 330.

35. Ibid.

36. Ibid., p. 331.

37. Ibid., pp. 329–30.

38. Ibid., p. 332.

39. Ibid., p. 333.

40. Ibid., p. 337.

41. In the period in question, it would have been the Council for Russian Orthodox Church Affairs (CROCA).

42. Popular acronym for the *Glavnoye upravleniye po delam literatury i izdatel'stva* (Chief Administration for Literature and Publishing), responsible for censoring all published matter in the USSR.

43. A. Levitin-Krasnov, "Censorship and Freedom of Speech," *Radio Liberty Research* (May 25, 1979), reprinted in *The Orthodox Monitor*, Nos. 9–10 (July–December 1980), pp. 31–33.

44. *Klir* derives from the Greek and has been used since New Testament times to refer, variously at different times, to the clergy or sections of the clergy. In Russia, as elsewhere in Eastern Christendom, the word came to designate all clergy including and above deacons, with the exception of bishops. (In Western Christendom, the term included bishops.) *Pricht* in Russian Orthodox usage customarily meant the body of clergy serving in a particular church building. Neither word, however, is customarily used by church people today, since *dukhoventstvo* is perfectly adequate and no other term has been found needful. The point of

the censorship seems to be to distort a natural usage in order to avoid repetition of a word with "spirit" (*dukh*) as its root.

45. Rusak, "*Tipograficheskaya problema*," pp. 6–12.

46. *Vestnik RkhD*, No. 130, p. 329.

47. Rusak, "*Tipograficheskaya problema*," pp. 24–28.

48. "Soviet Archbishop at Media Festival," *The Orthodox Church*, September 1979, p. 7.

49. Letter to the publisher *Zhizn s Bogom* (La Vie avec Dieu), from "a priest" (Moscow, October 1979), in *Religiya i ateizm v SSSR* (April 1980), p. 13.

50. Reports of the searches and arrests are given in *Vestnik RkhD*, No. 136 (1982), pp. 277–78; *USSR News Brief*, 10, (1982); *KNS*, No. 151 (June 17, 1982), p. 6; Analysis in *KNS*, No. 180 (August 11, 1983), p. 10.

51. *KNS*, No. 155 (August 12, 1982), p. 2, and 158 (September 23, 1982), pp. 12–13; also samizdat appeals and reports by Krakhmalnikova's husband, Felix Svetov, and others in Keston College archive. Sentence, *KNS*, No. 171 (April 7, 1983), p. 2.

52. Rusak, "*Tipograficheskaya problema*," p. 18.

53. Michael Binyon, "Moscow Opens Lavish Bible Centre" *The Times*, September 23, 1981, p. 6; correction, October 6, 1981, p. 8; *JMP* (1982), No. 1, p. 21.

54. Rusak, "*Tipograficheskaya problema*," p. 19.

55. Statement at a press conference in Rome; quoted in the *Catholic Herald* (November 19, 1980).

56. Interview with Pitirim in the NBC documentary film "The Church of the Russians," screened in the United States in July 1983. In this interview Pitirim said that the publishing department had had twenty-two employees at its inception.

6 The Orthodox Church in America

1. Pavel Vasil'evich Shkurkin, "Pervye Russkie na Aliaske," in *Yubileyny sbornik v pamiat' 150-letia Russkoi Pravoslavnoi Tserkvi v Severnoi Amerike* (New York: Ed. Yubileynoi Komissii Russkoi Pravoslavnoi Tserkvi v Severnoi Amerike, 1944), Vol. 1, p. 25; and Barbara Smith, *Orthodoxy and Native Americans: The Alaska Mission* (Crestwood, N.Y.: St. Vladimir's Seminary Press, 1980), pp. 7–9.

2. Bishop Gregory, "Tserkov' na Alaske posle dvukhsot let," in *Ezhegodnik Pravoslavnoi Tserkvi v Amerike* (New York: OCA Press, 1976), p. 26.

3. *Orthodox America, 1794–1976* (New York: OCA Press, 1975), p. 15.

4. "Zhizn' valaamskogo monakha Germana," in *Yubileyny sbornik*, Vol. 1, pp. 48–51.

5. A detailed biography of St. Innocent can be found in Paul Garrett, *St. Innocent, Apostle to America* (Crestwood, N.Y.: St. Vladimir's Seminary Press, 1979).

6. Dmitry Grigorieff, "Materialy k biografii mitropolita Innokentiya Veniaminova," in *Ezhegodnik Pravoslavnoi Tserkvi v Amerike* (New York: OCA Press, 1977), p. 43.

7. Ibid., pp. 44–45.

8. *Orthodox America*, pp. 33–34.

9. Ibid., pp. 40–41.

10. Alexander Padlo, *Clergy and Laity in OCA* (Master of divinity thesis, St. Vladimir's Seminary, 1970), p. 13.

11. Ibid.

12. See Anton Kartashov, *Ocherki po istorii Russkoi Tserkvi* (Paris: YMCA Press, 1959), Vol. 2, pp. 448–51 and 453–64.

13. Padlo, *Clergy and Laity*, pp. 9–14.

14. Antiminsion is a square piece of silk or linen cloth containing relics and bearing the signature of a ruling bishop. In the Orthodox church, priests are their bishop's delegates and the signed antiminsion certifies that a community and its priest are canonical. Therefore, no liturgical celebration is possible without an antiminsion.

15. John Matusiak, *Orthodox Church in America following the Russian Revolution, 1917–1922* (Master of divinity thesis, St. Vladimir's Seminary, 1975), pp. 29–32.

16. Uniate churches are former Orthodox churches which accepted the authority and doctrine of the Vatican but retained their respective languages, rites, and customs, such as the married clergy.

17. "The 'Unia' and the Return to Orthodoxy," in *Orthodox America*, pp. 43–46.

18. Padlo, *Clergy and Laity*, pp. 13–19.

19. Matusiak, *Orthodox Church*, p. 93.

20. See *Orthodox America*, pp. 127–28, 133–34.

21. Sergei Troubetskoi, "Iz istorii Pravoslavnoi Tserkvi v Amerike," in *Ezhegodnik Pravoslavnoi Tserkvi v Amerike* (1977), pp. 83–85.

22. See Constantin Pobedonostsev, *Reflections of a Russian Statesman*, Trans. Robert Crozier Long (Ann Arbor: University of Michigan Press, 1965), pp. 254, 27–28, 32–58.

23. For Theophan the Recluse, the most popular Russian spiritual writer of the second part of the nineteenth century, all political philosophy begins with the tsar, who is appointed by God and represents the head of the whole body of society. Every member of the society must be related to the tsar, "to show him silent obedience in everything, because he pronounces the will of God, to cling to him with thankful love." All governmental institutions and persons are "the arms, the legs, and the eyes of the Czar." See Theophan the Recluse, *Put' ko Spaseniu: (Nachertania christianskogo nravouchenia)*, 2d ed. (Moscow: Efimov, 1895), pp. 514–18.

24. Dimitry Pospielovsky, *The Russian Church under the Soviet Regime, 1917–1982* (Crestwood, N.Y.: St. Vladimir's Seminary Press, 1984), Vol. 1, pp. 25–31.

25. *Yubileyny Sbornik*, p. 285.

26. For a detailed account of the Renovationist movement, see Anatoly Levitin and Vadim Shavrov, *Ocherki po istorii tserkovnoi smuty* (Kusnacht, Switz.: Glaube in der 2. Welt, 1978); and Pospielovsky, *The Russian Church*, Vol. 1, pp. 43–92.

27. Dmitry Grigorieff, *Russian Orthodox Church in America* (Master of divinity thesis, St. Vladimir's Seminary, 1958), pp. 21–25.

28. Ibid., p. 26.

29. Alexander Schmemann, *Tserkov' i tserkovnoe ustroystvo* (Paris: Izdanie "Tserkovnogo Vestnika," 1949), p. 13.

30. Ibid., p. 18.

31. Alexander Schmemann, "Znamenatelnaya burya," *Vestnik russkogo zapadnoevropeyskogo exarchata*, 75–76 (1971), p. 196.

32. For a history of ethnic jurisdictions in the United States, see Matusiak, *Orthodox Church*; and *Orthodox America*, pp. 182–95.

33. See Pospielovsky, *The Russian Church*, Vol. 1, pp. 113–33; and Protopresbyter Gr. Lomako, *Tserkovno-kononicheskoe polozhenie russkogo rasseiania* (New York: Ed. Mitropolii Russkoi Pravoslavnoi Tserkvi v Severnoi Amerike, 1950).

34. Matthew Spinka, *The Church in Soviet Russia* (New York: Oxford University Press, 1956), p. 26.

35. Pospielovsky, *The Russian Church*, Vol. 1, p. 135.

36. For details, see ibid., Vol. 1, pp. 93–112.

37. Grigorieff, *Russian Orthodox Church*, pp. 40–42.

38. Ibid., pp. 47ff.

39. Ibid., pp. 60–74.

40. Pospielovsky, *The Russian Church*, Vol. 2, pp. 257–79.

41. See Schmemann, *Tserkov'*, p. 18.

42. George Maloney, *A History of Orthodox Theology since 1453* (Belmont, Mass.: Nordland, 1976), p. 77.

43. See Nikolai Afanasiev, *Trapeza Gospodnia* (Paris: YMCA Press, 1952); and "La Doctrine de la primauté a la lumiere de l'ecclesiologie," *Istina* (1957) No. 4, pp. 401–20.

44. See Alexander Bogolepov, *Toward an American Orthodox Church: The Establishment of an Autocephalous Orthodox Church* (New York: Morehouse-Barlow, 1963).

45. See Schmemann, "Znamenatelnaya burya," p. 196.

46. Sarah Loft, *Converts Respond: A Report on a Survey of Converts* (Syosset, N.Y.: OCA Press, 1984), pp. 15–17.

47. *Yearbook and Church Directory of the OCA* (Syosset, N.Y.: OCA Press, 1985), p. 3.

7   The Russian Orthodox Church Abroad

1. In Russian: Russkaya Pravoslavnaya Tserkov Zagranitsei.

2. The Orthodox Church of America received in 1970 the autocephaly from the Moscow patriarchate.

3. The official name of the Paris Jurisdiction is the Autonomous Russian Archbishopric under the Jurisdiction of the Ecumenical Patriarch of Constantinople. Its headquarters are in Paris.

4. Despite its importance, the "Catacomb Church" will not be dealt with in this chapter. Discussion of this subject can be found in D. Konstantinow, "Die Russische Orthodoxe Kirche heute," *Ost-Probleme*, 18, No. 13 (July 1, 1966); "Impegno nella Chiesa (Una comunità di giovani ortodossi russi)," *Russia Cristiana*, 3, No. 3 (May–June 1978); Gernot Seide, "Die Russisch-Orthodoxe Kirche im Ausland (Wiesbaden: Otto Harrassowitz, 1983), p. 476; Gernot Seide, "Die Russisch-Orthodoxe Kirche in der Gegenwart," *Osteuropa*, 33, Nos. 11–12 (November–December 1983), pp. 866–68; William C. Fletcher, *The Russian Orthodox Church Underground, 1917–1970* (London: Oxford University Press, 1971).

5. The Russian Orthodox Church Abroad canonized John of Kronstadt in 1964; German of Alaska in 1970; Xenia of Petersburg in 1978; and, in 1981, "new martyrs," victims of the communist rule in Russia. Among the some 30,000 martyrs is also the last tsar of Russia, Nicholas II, and his family.

6. E.g., *Yearbook of the Orthodox Church* (Munich: Alex Proc, 1978), p. 22; and Gernot Seide, *Geschichte der Russischen Orthodoxen Kirche im Ausland* (Wiesbaden: Otto Harrassowitz, 1983), p. 476.

7. See, for example, *Religion and Atheism in the USSR* (Munich), 12, (December 1974), pp. 9–10.

8. *Zakon o religioznykh ob'edineniyakh RSFSR* (Moscow: Bezbozhnik, 1930), p. 7. This law was changed; *Journal of the Moscow Patriarchate* (1986), no. 1, p. 86, published the text under the rubric "Our legal advice." The text now says, "A religious society enjoys the rights of juridical persons."

9. In 1914 there were 51,105 parish priests in Russia, 54,174 Orthodox churches, about 1,200 monasteries and convents, 94,620 monks and nuns, four church academies, and fifty-

seven theological seminaries. In 1939 there were only a few hundred priests and churches, no monasteries, no academies, and no seminaries. Trevor Beeson, *Discretion and Valour: Religious Conditions in Russia and Eastern Europe*, rev. ed. (Philadelphia: Fortress Press, 1982), p. 58; and Albert Boiter, *Religion in the Soviet Union*, Washington Papers, Vol. 8, No. 78 (Beverly Hills: Sage, 1980), p. 16.

10. *Yearbook of the Orthodox Church*, p. 213.

11. Ibid.

12. See Seide, *Geschichte*, pp. 23–28.

13. V. Vinogradov, *O nekotorykh vazhneishikh momentakh poslednego perioda zhizni i deyalel'nosti patriarkha Tikhona (1923–25)* (1951–52; reprint, Munich: Orthodox Parish of St. Michail-Arkhangel, 1959), pp. 40–57.

14. Johannes Chrysostomus, *Kirchengeschichte der neuesten Zeit Russlands* (Munich: Anton Pustet, 1965), Vol. 1, pp. 374–78; and Seide, *Geschichte*, p. 46.

15. Archbishop Nikon (Rklitskii), *Zhisneopisanie blazhenneishego Antoniya, Metropolita Kievskogo i Galitskogo* (New York: All-Slavic Publishing House, 1961), Vol. 3, pp. 215–30.

16. Report of Diocesan Session of the German Orthodox Diocese in Munich on July 16–17, 1946 (manuscript).

17. *Russko-Amerikanskii Pravoslavnyi Tserkovnyi Vestnik* (No. 1, 1946); *Sovetskaya Rossiya*, November 8, 1945. (Both newspapers.)

18. Chrysostomus, *Kirchengeschichte*, Vol. 2, pp. 155–61.

19. William C. Fletcher, *Religion and Soviet Foreign Policy, 1945–1970* (London: Oxford University Press, 1973), pp. 30–34.

20. *Journal of the Moscow Patriarchate*, English edition (1974), No. 10, pp. 2, 3.

21. Seide, *Geschichte*, p. 342.

22. *Russkaya mysl'* (Paris), October 17, 1974, pp. 3–4.

23. *Vestnik Russkogo Khristianskogo Dvizheniya* (Paris), 1974, Nos. 2–3, pp. 99–116, and No. 4, pp. 89–120.

24. Seide, *Geschichte*, pp. 121–22.

25. *Russkaya mysl'* (Paris), December 6, 1979, p. 5.

26. *AP*, November 2, 1981.

27. *Sovetskaya Rossiya*, November 5, 1981, p. 3; *Nauka i religiya* (1975), Nos. 8–11; and *Molodoi kommunist* (July 1984), pp. 43–45.

28. See Beeson, *Discretion and Valour*.

29. *Sovetskaya Rossiya*, November 5, 1981, p. 3.

30. *Literaturnaya gazeta*, 44 (November 1981), p. 9.

8   The Albanian Orthodox Church

I am most grateful to Gjon Sinishta for sharing documentary material with me and for his comments on an earlier draft.

1. John Kolsti, "Albanianism: From the Humanists to Hoxha," in George Klein and Milan J. Reban (eds.), *The Politics of Ethnicity in Eastern Europe* (Boulder, Colo.: East European Monographs, 1981), p. 17.

2. Giuseppe Ferrari, "La Chiesa Ortodossa Albanese," *Oriente Cristiano*, 18, No. 4 (October–December 1978), pp. 12, 14.

3. Šukri Rahimi, "Verska podeljnost i razvoj nacionalne svesti kod Albanaca u drugoj polovini XIX veka," *Jugoslovenski Istorijski Časopis* (1978), Nos. 1–4, p. 299.

4. Ferrari, "La Chiesa Ortodossa," p. 16; J. Swire, *Albania: The Rise of a Kingdom* (London: Williams and Norgate, 1929), pp. 9, 39; and Peter Bartl, *Die Albanischen Muslime zur Zeit der Nationalen Unabhängigkeitsbewegung, 1878–1912* (Wiesbaden: Otto Harras-sowitz, 1968), p. 25.

5. Ferrari, "La Chiesa Ortodossa," p. 16.

6. Rahimi, "Verska podeljnost," p. 300.

7. Stavro Skendi, "Religion in Albania during the Ottoman Rule," *Südost-Forschungen*, 15 (1956), pp. 312, 316.

8. Stavro Skendi, *The Albanian National Awakening, 1878–1912* (Princeton, N.J.: Princeton University Press, 1967), pp. 17–18, 112.

9. Bartl, *Die Albanischen Muslime*, p. 24.

10. Constantine A. Chekrezi, *Albania Past and Present* (New York: Macmillan, 1919), p. 59; Charles and Barbara Jelavich, *The Establishment of the Balkan National States, 1804–1920* (Seattle: University of Washington Press, 1977), p. 226; Skendi, *The Albanian National Awakening*, pp. 133, 137–38; and Edith Pierpont Stickney, *Southern Albania or Northern Epirus in European International Affairs, 1912–1923* (Stanford, Calif.: Stanford University Press, 1926), p. 95.

11. Skendi, *The Albanian National Awakening*, pp. 296, 299–300, 303.

12. Bernhard Tönnes, "Religionen in Albanien," *Osteuropa*, 24, No. 9 (September 1974), p. 664.

13. Ferrari, "La Chiesa Ortodossa," p. 24.

14. For details, see Stefanaq Pollo and Asben Puro, *The History of Albania from Its Origins to the Present Day*, trans. Carol Wiseman and Ginnie Hole (London: Routledge and Kegan Paul, 1981), pp. 157–70.

15. L. S. Stavrianos, *The Balkans since 1453* (New York: Holt, Rinehart and Winston, 1958), p. 717.

16. Teodoro Minisci, "Come si giunse all'Autocefalia della Chiesa Ortodossa Albanese—Note di cronaca," *Oriente Cristiano*, 18, No. 4 (October–December 1978), p. 72.

17. Bernd Jürgen Fischer, *King Zog and the Struggle for Stability in Albania* (Boulder, Colo.: East European Monographs, 1984), pp. 170–72.

18. Friedrich Heiler, *Die Ostkirchen* (Munich: Ernst Reinhardt Verlag, 1971), p. 85; and Bernhard Tönnes, "Religious Persecution in Albania," *Religion in Communist Lands*, 10, No. 3 (Winter 1982), pp. 244, 246.

19. Minisci, "Come si giunse," p. 74.

20. Ibid., p. 76; Fischer, *King Zog*, p. 172.

21. Italian text in "Tomos di Autocefalia," *Oriente Cristiano*, 18, No. 4 (October–December 1978), pp. 83–86.

22. Anton Logoreci, *The Albanians* (London: Victor Gollancz, 1977), p. 73.

23. Bertold Spuler, *Gegenwartslage der Ostkirchen*, 2d ed. (Frankfurt: Metopen-Verlag, 1968), p. 140.

24. Quoted in Robert Tobias, *Communist-Christian Encounter in East Europe* (Indianapolis: School of Religion Press, 1956), p. 381.

25. Quoted in Peter J. Prifti, *Socialist Albania since 1944: Domestic and Foreign Developments* (Cambridge, Mass.: MIT Press, 1978), p. 152.

26. Tönnes, "Religious Persecution," p. 248.

27. Quoted in ibid., p. 249.

28. Prifti, *Socialist Albania*, p. 150.

29. Quoted in ibid., p. 154.

30. *Zeri i popullit* (June 27, 1967), trans. in Foreign Broadcast Information Service (FBIS), *Daily Report* (USSR and East Europe), Supplement—July 19, 1967, p. 17. See also Louis Zanga, "Enver Hoxhas Krieg gegen die Religion," *Osteuropa*, 30, No. 1 (January 1980), pp. 50–51.

31. Dilaver Sadikaj, "Revolutionary Movement against Religion in the Sixties," *Studime Historike* (1981), No. 4, trans. in *Albanian Catholic Bulletin*, 4 (1983), Nos. 1 and 2, p. 23.

32. Trevor Beeson, *Discretion and Valour: Religious Conditions in Russia and Eastern Europe*, Rev. ed. (Philadelphia: Fortress Press, 1982), p. 327. See also Bernhard Tönnes, "Religion und Kirche in Albanien," *Kirche in Not*, 24 (1976), pp. 101–9.

33. Quoted in Beeson, *Discretion*, p. 322.

34. Sadikaj, "Revolutionary Movement," p. 25.

35. Logoreci, *The Albanians*, p. 157.

36. ATA (Tirana), September 16, 1967, trans. in FBIS, *Daily Report* (USSR and East Europe), Supplement—October 17, 1967, p. 33. See also "Albanien: Götzen gegen Gott— 'Die Religion des Albaniens ist der Albanismus,'" *Osteuropa*, 24, No. 9 (September 1974).

37. Ramadan Marmullaku, *Albania and the Albanians*, trans. Margot and Boško Milosavljević (London: Archon Books, 1975), p. 77.

38. Tönnes, "Religious Persecution," pp. 254–55; and *Zeri i Rinise* (Tirana), March 25, 1981, trans. in Joint Publications Research Service, *East Europe Report*, No. 77958 (April 29, 1981), p. 2.

39. Review article, in *Albanian Catholic Bulletin*, 3 (1982), pp. 98–100.

9 The Bulgarian Orthodox Church

This study was partially subsidized by East Stroudsburg University, East Stroudsburg, Pennsylvania.

1. Ivan Snegarov, "Purvata bulgarska patriarshiya," *Godishnik na Sofiyskiya universitet, Bogoslovski fakultet*, 26 (1948–1949), pp. 14–15; Petar Stoyanov (ed.), *Churches and Religions in the People's Republic of Bulgaria* (Sofia: Synodal Publishing House, 1975), p. 20; Vasil Zlatarski, *Istoriya na bulgarskata durzhava prez srednite vekove* (1927; reprint, Sofia: Nauka i izkustvo, 1971), Vol. I/1, pp. 390–91; *Tsurkoven vestnik*, May 3, 1978.

2. Zlatarski, *Istoriya na Bulgarskata*, Vol. I/1, pp. 256–65.

3. See Yordan Ivanov, *Bulgarski starini iz Makedoniya* (Sofia: Durzhavna pechatnitsa, 1931), pp. 282–307, 312, 317, 442–46.

4. See Petar Nikov, *Vuzrazhdane na bulgarskiya narod: Tsurkovno-natsionalni borbi i postizheniya* (1930; reprint, Sofia: Nauka i izkustvo, 1971); Todor Subev, *Uchredyavane i diotsez na Bulgarskata ekzarkhiya do 1878* (Sofia: Sinodalno izdatelstvo, 1973); and Nikolai Genchev, *Bulgarsko Vuzrazhdane* (Sofia: Nauka i izkustvo, 1978), chap. 8, esp. pp. 127–37.

5. Dimitar Angelov, *Bogomilstvoto v Bulgariya* (Sofia: Nauka i izkustvo, 1969), pp. 86–105, 269–87; and Stefan Popov, *Bulgarskata ideya* (Munich: Author's edition, 1981), p. 94.

6. C. E. Black, *The Establishment of Constitutional Government in Bulgaria* (Princeton, N.J.: Princeton University Press, 1943), p. 294.

7. Khristo Vurgov, *Konstitutsiya na Bulgarskata pravoslavna tsurkva* (Sofia: Durzhavna pechatnitsa, 1920), pp. 51–52.

8. Ibid., p. 51.

9. Ibid.

10. Article 134 of the exarchate's bylaws reads: "After every fourth year, the Exarch, together with the Holy Synod, must convene, with the permission of the King's government, delegated representatives of each diocese and of the Constantinople Bulgarians to a general Council of the Exarchate, where they shall submit the Exarchate's accounts for review and approval. This Council will amend and supplement the by-laws, if experience indicates there is need to do so." In the version passed in 1895 this article was replaced by a new article (180): "No change whatsoever, or revocation of any of the by-laws, and no other ordinances regarding the Church government in the principality, will be undertaken without the prior mutual agreement between the Holy Synod and the Ministry of Confessions." Khristo Tanchev, *Ekzarkhiyskiy ustav s tulkuvaniyata i naredbite na Sv. Sinod, Ministerstvata, Vurkhovniy kasatsionen sud i suotvetnite zakonopolozheniya* (Sofia: Pechatnita "St. Atanasov," 1904), pp. 216–17.

11. Vurgov, *Konstitutsiyata na Bulgarskata pravoslavna tsurkva*, pp. 379–92.

12. D. Marinov, *Stefan Stambolov i noveishata ni istoriya* (Sofia: Pechatnitsa na T. Peev, 1909), p. 71.

13. *The Times* (London), August 15, 1887.

14. Ibid., August 24, 1887.

15. Vurgov, *Konstitutsiyata na Bulgarskata pravoslavna tsurkva*, p. 209; Marinov, *Stefan Stambolov*, pp. 569–79; Joachim von Königslow, *Ferdinand von Bulgarien* (Munich: R. Oldenbourg Verlag, 1970), pp. 106–7; and Richard J. Crampton, *Bulgaria, 1878–1918: A History* (New York: Columbia University Press, 1983), pp. 133–34.

16. Stephen Constant, *Foxy Ferdinand, Tsar of Bulgaria* (New York: Franklin Watts, 1980), pp. 140–42.

17. Hans Roger Madol, *Ferdinand de Bulgarie* (Paris: Librairie de Plon, 1933), p. 104.

18. Ilcho Dimitrov, "Suvetnikut na dvoretsa. Iz dnevnika na Lyubomir Lulchev. Komentari i belezhki," *Otechestvo*, Nos. 13–16 (1982); and Asparikh Avramov, "Bulgarskata pravoslavna tsurkva i antifashistkata borba prez godinite na vtorata svetovna voina," in Nikolai Mizov (ed.), *Pravoslavieto v Bulgariya, teoretiko-istorichesko osvetlenie* (Sofia: Izdatelstvo na Bulgarskata akademiya na naukite, 1974), p. 216.

19. *Naroden pastir* (1953), Nos. 16–18, pp. 32–34; *Tsurkoven vestnik*, July 1, 1980, p. 1; and Stoyanov, *Churches and Religions*, p. 92. See also Wolf Oschlies, "Kirche und Religion in Bulgarien," in Paul Lendvai (ed.), *Religionsfreiheit und Menschenrechte* (Graz: Verlag Styria, 1983), p. 185.

20. Königslow, *Ferdinand von Bulgarien*, p. 104.

21. Robert Tobias, *Communist-Christian Encounter in East Europe* (Indianapolis: School of Religion Press, 1956), p. 367.

22. William B. Simons (ed.), *The Constitutions of the Communist World* (Germantown, Md.: Sijthoff and Noordhoff, 1980), p. 49.

23. See the full text in Tobias, *Communist-Christian Encounter*, pp. 371–76.

24. See Spas T. Raikin, "The Communist and the Bulgarian Orthodox Church, 1944–48: The Rise and Fall of Exarch Stefan," *Religion in Communist Lands*, 12, No. 3 (Winter 1984), pp. 281–92.

25. D. Slijepčević, *Die Bulgarische Orthodoxe Kirche, 1944–1956* (Munich: R. Oldenbourg Verlag, 1957), p. 49.

26. *Tsurkoven vestnik* (1951), No. 18.

27. Ibid. (1951), No. 6/7.

28. *Naroden pastir* (1952), Nos. 7–9.

29. Ibid. (1951), No. 29/30; and *Tsurkoven vestnik* (1951), No. 19/20.

30. Yordan Nikolov, "Suyuzut na proletarskite svobodomislyashti (14. X. 1931-19. V. 1934 g.)," *Istoricheski pregled*, 21 (1965), No. 5, p. 5. See also Bogomir Bosev, "Pravoslavieto v usloviyata na kapitalizma v Bulgariya," in Mizov (ed.), *Pravoslavieto v Bulgariya*, p. 195.

31. The plan was openly discussed in church circles, but nothing ever appeared in print in reference to it.

32. In the course of 1948, the subsidy was suspended and restored three times.

33. Stoyanov (ed.), *Churches and Religions*, p. 62.

34. Trevor Beeson, *Discretion and Valour: Religious Conditions in Russia and Eastern Europe*, Rev. ed. (London: Colins Fount Paperbacks, 1982), p. 335; *Naroden pastir* (1952), No. 7; Marin Bonchev, "Intervyu na bulgarskiya Patriarkh Maxim pred spisanie *Slavyani*," *Slavyani* (Sofia), (September 1977), p. 32; *Tsurkoven vestnik*, April 21, 1978, p. 2; and Chavdar Popov, "Religiozniyat zhivot v Bulgariya," *Slavyani* (June 1980), p. 41.

35. Oral and written statements to that effect were made to the author by synodal clergymen in spring 1986.

36. Djeki Benadov, "Zhivot v mir i dobra volya: Intervyu s Negovo Sveteishestvo Bulgarskiya Patriarkh Maxim," in *Rodolyubie* (1983), no. 7, p. 1.

37. *Tsurkoven vestnik*, December 11, 1978, January 11, 1979, February 1, 1979, and February 12, 1979.

38. *Slavyani* (1980), No. 5, p. 17; *Rodolyubie* (1984), No. 7, p. 50, and (1985), No. 3, p. 36.

39. Lazar Petrov, "Bulgarskiyat Patriarkh Maxim," *Rodolyubie* (1985), No. 1, p. 32.

40. Petar Tsvetkov, "Modernizatsiya na pravoslavieto v Bulgariya," in Mizov (ed.), *Pravoslavieto v Bulgariya*, p. 265. See also Nikolai Mizov, "Problemata 'Religiya-ateism' v suvremenna Bulgariya," *Filosofska misul* (Sofia, 1974), No. 9, p. 77.

41. Nikolai Mizov, "Religiyata, tsurkvata i durzhavata," *Politicheska prosveta* (Sofia, 1975), No. 9, p. 53.

42. *Zemedelsko zname*, October 21, 1981, p. 2.

43. *Tsurkoven vestnik*, November 1, 1981, pp. 2–7.

44. Quoted in Tobias, *Communist-Christian Encounter*, pp. 365–66.

45. Simeon Damyanov, "Pravoslavnata tsurkva i bulgarskata natsionalna revolyutsiya," in Mizov (ed.), *Pravoslavieto v Bulgariya*, p. 153.

10 The Orthodox Church of Greece

1. The question of church-state relations in modern Greece, in its historical context, has generated extensive literature by modern Greek Orthodox scholars, which on the whole has not been sufficiently utilized by Western scholars. For example, see Christos Androutsos, *Ekklisia kai politeia ex apopseos orthodoxou* (Church and State from the Orthodox Point of View), originally serialized in *New Teaching* (1920) and later published as monograph (Thessaloniki: Vas. Rigopoulou, 1964); Pan. I. Panayotakos, *Ekklisia kai politeia ana tous aionas* (Church and State through the Centuries) (Athens: N.p., 1939), which traces the issue from the first Christian century to the twentieth; and Konstantinos Diovouniotis, *Sheseis ekklisias kai politeias en ti elelthera Elladi* (Church and State Relations in Independent Greece) (Athens: N.p., 1916).

2. It should be noted, however, that former Prime Minister and later President Constantine Karamanlis had introduced the idea of a simple handshake with prelates at official functions.

3. *Orthodoxos Typos* (Orthodox Press), 443 (February 9, 1981), quoted by Kallistos Ware, "The Church of Greece: A Time of Transition," in Richard Clogg (ed.), *Greece in the 1980s* (New York: St. Martin's Press, 1983), p. 208. Similar pronouncements are plentiful in the speeches of former president of Greece and scholar Constantine Tsatsos, conveniently published together in four volumes under the title *Omilies* (Speeches), with no date of publication but covering the years 1975–80. See especially his address to the Holy Synod of the Orthodox Church of Greece on February 24, 1980, in *Omilies*, Vol. 4, pp. 49–52. And, interestingly enough, President Sartzetakis, during his three-day visit to Mount Athos in August 1986 made several allusions to the close relations between church and state in Greece and was reported in the Greek press as stating that "Orthodoxy and Hellenism have for centuries been inseparable and it is impossible to imagine the Greek experience without Orthodoxy." *Ta Nea*, September 1, 1986, p. 2.

4. For statistical information on the Orthodox Church of Greece and indeed of other Orthodox churches, consult the very useful *Imerologhion tis Ekklisias tis Ellados* (Calendar of the Church of Greece), published annually in Athens by the Apostoliki Diakonia of the Church of Greece. The last volume (1986) consists of 781 pages and is dedicated to the Greeks in the diaspora.

5. On Papadiamantis and his Orthodox bent, see the recent essay by Theofanis G. Stavrou "A Greek Writer against the Current," in Louis Coutelle, Theofanis G. Stavrou, David R. Weinberg, *A Greek Diptych: Dionysios Solomos and Alexandros Papadiamantis* (Minneapolis: Nostos, 1986), pp. 63–97.

6. Odysseus Elytis, *I Mageia tou Papadiamanti* (The Magic of Papadiamantis) (Athens: Ermeias, 1984), p. 42ff, and T. G. Stavrou, "A Greek Writer," pp. 84–92.

7. Yorgos Theotokas, *Pnevmatiki Poreia* (Intellectual Journey) (Athens: G. Fexis, 1961), pp. 152, 154–55. Many of Theotokas's essays on the subject were published posthumously in: *I Orthodoxia ston Kairo mas* (Orthodoxy in Our Time) (Athens: Ekdoseis ton Philon, 1975).

8. Christos Yannaras, *I Neoelliniki tavtotita* (Modern Greek Identity) (Athens: Grigoris, 1978), p. 167.

9. In English, this well-known story is told eloquently by Sir Steven Runciman, *The Great Church in Captivity: A Study of the Patriarchate of Constantinople from the Eve of the Turkish Conquest to the Greek War of Independence* (Cambridge: Cambridge University Press, 1968). See also Steven Runciman's *The Orthodox Churches and the Secular State* (Auckland: Auckland University Press and Oxford: Oxford University Press, 1971), pp. 26–45 and ff.; and the classic study by Theodore H. Papadopoulos, *Studies and Documents Relating to the History of the Greek Church and People under Turkish Domination* (Brussels, 1952), which Runciman utilizes extensively.

10. The best study on the subject in English remains Charles A. Frazee, *The Orthodox Church and Independent Greece, 1821–1852* (Cambridge: Cambridge University Press, 1969), which also contains an extensive bibliography.

11. For a thorough discussion of the role of the Great Powers in Greek politics following independent statehood, see John Anthony Petropoulos, *Politics and Statecraft in the Kingdom of Greece, 1833–1843* (Princeton, N.J.: Princeton University Press, 1968).

12. Frazee, *Orthodox Church and Independent Greece*, pp. 89–124.

13. Despite the arguments that the Greek Orthodox hierarchy was on occasion skeptical, indeed critical, of a revolution against the Ottoman sultan and would have preferred the continuation of the status quo, when the revolt broke out the church overwhelmingly supported the struggle for independence. And as is known, the ecumenical patriarch Gregory V was

put to death by the Turkish authorities. The impact of the patriarch's death on Greek society has not lessened with the passing of time. According to Theodoros N. Zisis of the University of Thessaloniki, the incident has penetrated the conscience of the nation. See his monograph on the subject, *O Patriarhis Grigorios E' sti syneidhisi tou yenous* (Patriarch Gregory V in the Conscience of the Nation) (Thessaloniki: Kyriakidis Bros., 1986).

14. Varnavas D. Tzortzatos, *I Katastatiki nomothesia tis ekklisias tis Ellados apo tis systaseos tou ellinikou vasileiou* (The Constitutional Position of the Church of Greece from the Creation of the Greek Kingdom) (Athens: N.p., 1967), contains the relevant primary sources as well as commentary. For the first phase of this sensitive issue in church-state relations in Greece as well as the relationship with the patriarchate, see pp. 15–51.

15. Ibid., pp. 62–64; Frazee, *Orthodox Church and Independent Greece*, pp. 174–94.

16. For the territorial and political expansion of the modern Greek state, which affected the ecclesiastical jurisdictions as well, see Douglas Dakin, *The Unification of Greece, 1770–1923* (London: Ernest Benn, 1972), and Charles Frazee, "Church and State in Greece," in John T. Koumoulides (ed.), *Greece in Transition: Essays in the History of Modern Greece, 1821–1974* (London: Zeno, 1977), pp. 128–52.

17. The most detailed account of the history and present status of the "new lands" is Athanasios N. Angelopoulos, *Ekklisiastiki istoria: I ekklesia ton neon Khoron* (Church History: The Church of the New Lands) (Thessaloniki: Kyriakidis Bros., 1986). The deterioration of Greek-Turkish relations during the last decade rekindled the question of the fate of the patriarchate of Constantinople with some suggesting that it be transferred to Mount Athos.

18. *Imerologhion tis ekklisias tis ellados* (1985), pp. 381–772 provides a panoramic picture of the present state of the Greek church. See also the excellent article by K. Haralambides, "The Church of Greece," in *Thriskevtiki kai Ithiki Engyklopaideia* (Religious and Ethical Encyclopaedeia) (Athens: A. Martinos, 1964), Vol. 5, pp. 619–48.

19. *Thriskevtiki kai Ithiki Engyklopaedeia*, Vol. 6 (1965), pp. 240–41; and Chrysostomos Papadopoulos, *I Ekklisia Athinon* (The Church of Athens) (Athens: N.p., 1928), pp. 101–5.

20. *Thriskevtiki kai Ithiki Engyklopaideia*, Vol. 12 (1968), p. 399.

21. The following sources shed light on various activities of Damaskinos and the church during the period under consideration. *Thriskevtiki kai Ithiki Engyklopaideia*, Vol. 4 (1964), pp. 916–22; S. Kollias, *Archbishop-Regent Damaskinos* (Athens: N.p., 1962); Ilias Venezis, *Archbishop Damaskinos* (Athens: N.p., 1952); K. A. Vovolinis, *I Ekklisia eis ton agona tis eleftherias, 1453–1953* (The Church in the Struggle for Freedom 1453–1953) (Athens: Pan Kleisiounis, 1952), pp. 271–72, 367, 389, 408; Jean Tsatsos, *The Sword's Fierce Edge: A Journal of the Occupation of Greece, 1941–1944* (Nashville, Tenn.: Vanderbilt University Press, 1965), pp. 6, 21, 52–56; and the same author's *Ektelesthentes epi katohis* (Executed during the Occupation) (Athens: Ekdoseis ton Philon, 1976), which contains several reports by Greek hierarchs attesting to the church's humanitarian activities during the war.

22. Frazee, "Church and State in Greece," pp. 150–51. See also the rather hagiographic essay on Archbishop Serafim by I. M. Hadziphotis, *O Apo Artis kai Ioanninon Arkhiepiskopos Athinon kai Pasis Ellados Serafim* (Serafim from Arta and Ioannina, Archbishop of Athens and of All Greece) (Thessaloniki: N.p., 1984).

23. This controversial behavior of the Greek church, especially in view of the fact that the Greek constitution guaranteed tolerance of non-Orthodox groups, gave and continues to give the Greek church a bad press outside Greece.

24. As in the case of church-state relations in the Soviet Union, sometimes it is difficult to ascertain who exploits whom. It constitutes part of the politics of culture as analyzed

by Rodis Roufos, "Culture and the Military," in Richard Clogg and George Yannopoulos (eds.), *Greece under Military Rule* (New York: Basic Books, 1973), pp. 146–62. See also the same author's *Inside the Colonels' Greece* (London: Chatto and Windus, 1972), under the pseudonym "Athenian," translated by Richard Clogg.

25. This was characteristic of most Greeks who lived in Greece during this period but was articulated especially by those who lived abroad as political exiles.

26. Charles Freeze, "The Orthodox Church of Greece: The Last Fifteen Years," in John T. Koumoulides (ed.), *Hellenic Perspectives: Essays in the History of Greece* (Lanham, Md.: University Press of America, 1980), p. 156.

27. This is in article 3 of the constitution, devoted to "Relations between Church and State." The constitution was first published in the government newspaper (*Efimeris tis Kyverniseos*) June 9, 1975. It has also appeared in a separate volume, *To Syntagma tis ellados* (The Constitution of Greece) (Thessaloniki: V. Yannopoulos, 1984) with an introduction by Antonis Manitakis. Article 3 is on page 24 of this volume. A most useful compilation of laws affecting the church was done by I. M. Konidaris and S. N. Troianos, *Ekklisiastiki Nomothesia* (Athens: Ant. N. Sakkoula, 1984), which includes texts and commentaries.

28. Exemplary among them is Amilkas Alivizatos (1887–1969).

29. Peter Hammond, "The Present State of the Greek Church," *Eastern Churches Quarterly* (Summer 1950), pp. 366–68.

30. *Thriskevtiki kai Ithiki Engyklopaedia*, Vol. 9 (1966), pp. 1052–56.

31. Ibid., 5 (1964), pp. 631, 635.

32. Peter Hammond, *The Waters of Marah: The Present State of the Greek Church* (London: Rockliff, 1956), pp. 138–40, 149–50. With regard to the publishing accomplishments of the Greek Orthodox churches in general and the church of Greece in particular, see *Epetirida Ekklisiastikou Typou* (Annual of Church Press) (Athens: N.p., 1983), prepared by the press office of the Holy Synod of the Church of Greece in connection with an exhibit of church-related printed materials which took place June 15–24, 1983. It includes nine scholarly periodicals (pp. 33–36); three official publications (p. 36); ten calendars or yearbooks (pp. 37–38); eleven newspapers (pp. 39–41); eight newsletters (pp. 41–43); thirty-four periodicals by metropolitan centers, monasteries, etc. (pp. 43–50); six periodicals for young people (pp. 50–51); nine parish bulletins (pp. 51–52); and various other types.

33. John Meyendorff, *The Orthodox Church* (New York: Pantheon Books, 1963), p. 173.

34. *Thriskevtiki kai Ithiki Engyklopaedia*, Vol. 5 (1964), 643.

35. On Makrakis see the article by I. Karmiris in *Thriskevtiki kai Ethiki Engyklopaedia*, Vol. 8 (1966), 514–17; and *Apostolos Makrakis: An Evaluation of Half a Century*, ed. Constantine Andronis (Chicago: Orthodox Christian Educational Society, 1966).

36. The literature on the subject is vast. A good introduction in English is Peter Bien, *Kazantzakis and the Linguistic Revolution in Greek Literature* (Princeton, N.J.: Princeton University Press, 1972). For an extreme view on the church's position regarding the language question, see A. D. Delimbasis, *I glossa tis Orthodoxias* (The Language of Orthodoxy) (Athens: N.p., 1975). For a more analytical view, consult Christos Yannaras, "Theology in Present-day Greece," *St. Vladimir's Theological Quarterly*, 16, No. 4 (1972), 195–214. Yannaras maintains that the purist tradition was always evident among Greek intellectuals, including theologians influenced by the West (p. 206).

37. There is a dearth of scholarship on this little-known but important detail in recent Orthodox church history. In English there is Archimandrite Chrysostomos, *The Old Calendar Orthodox Church of Greece* (Etna, Calif.: St. Gregory Palamas Monastery, 1985), which though definitely confessional nevertheless is a good introduction to the subject of the Old

Calendarists. Consult also one of the Old Calendarists' newspapers, *Orthodoxos Christianikos Aghon* (Orthodox Christian Struggle) published in Athens and distributed free of charge.

38. I am referring to my discussion with Professor P. J. Vatikiotis, eminent political scientist and orientalist and author of *Greece: A Political Essay* (London: Sage, 1974).

39. In an interview with this writer, a forty-year old woman volunteered the information that she had had fifteen abortions.

40. The following recent publications reflect the growing interest in the impact of legislation on Greek society: Elizabeth-Besila-Makridi, *I Syntagmatiki katohyrosi tis arhis isotitas ton phylon* (The Constitutional Safeguard of the Principle of the Equality of the Sexes) (Athens: N.p., 1983), is the Ph.D. dissertation submitted to the Panteios School of Political Science in Athens; George A. Koumantos, *Paradoseis oikoyeneiakou dhikaiou* (Lectures on Family Law) (Athens; P. Sakkoula Bros., 1984, 3rd ed.); I. S. Spyridakis, *Encheiridion astikou dhikaiou 4: Oikoyeneiako dhikaio* (Handbook of Civil Law 4: Family Law) (Athens: Ant. N. Sakkoula, 1983). It should also be pointed out that these subjects are frequently discussed in the daily press.

41. Makarios was correctly referred to as "ethnarch," a title the archbishop of Cyprus enjoyed as a result of historical circumstances and privileges from the Byzantine and especially the Ottoman period.

42. There is a response to Karanikolas's book by Mel. Kalamaras, (*Eina oi rasophoroi symfora tou ethnous?*) (Are the Robed Men a National Pestilence?) (Athens: N.p., 1977).

43. Symbolic of this phenomenon was the funeral of Kostis Varnalis, the leading Marxist writer, in December 1974, which was conducted in all the pomp and circumstance of the Orthodox church. I attended the funeral and noticed that several Marxist poets and artists not only attended the funeral but served as pallbearers and partook in the religious aspects of the service. When the following day I tried to elicit some explanation for this seemingly contradictory behavior, Marxist poet Yannis Ritsos quite calmly and naturally informed me: "You must not forget that our personal as well as national experiences are invariably wrapped up with the course of Orthodoxy as well as Hellenism." These remarks anticipated those of President Sartzetakis by twelve years.

44. The statement was made by Elias Voulgarakis, assistant in the Theological faculty of the University of Athens, during an interview on July 28, 1966.

11   The Romanian Orthodox Church

1. Ernst Christopher Suttner, *Beiträge zur Kirchengeschichte der Rumänen* (Vienna: Harold Press, 1978); see also Keith Hitchens, "The Romanian Orthodox Church and the State," in Bohdan R. Bociurkiw and John W. Strong (eds.), *Religion and Atheism in the Soviet Union and Eastern Europe* (New York: Macmillan, 1975), pp. 314 ff.

2. Trevor Beeson, *Discretion and Valour*, Rev. ed. (Philadelphia: Fortress Press, 1983), pp. 360–61.

3. Ibid., p. 379.

4. The classic theological expression of this idea is in Dumitru Staniloae, *Ortodoxie si Romanism* (Sibiu: Tiparul Tipografiei Arhidiecezane, 1939), pp. 57–142.

5. J. H. Rushbrook, "The Baptist World Alliance," *Baptist Quarterly*, 9 (1938–39), pp. 76–78. Also see his report in *Sixth Baptist World Alliance Congress Official Report* (Atlanta: BWA, 1939), pp. 14–15, 46–48. On the Baptists in general, see Alan Scarfe, "A Call for Truth:

An appraisal of Rumanian Baptist Church-State Relationships," *Journal of Church and State,* 21, No. 3 (1979), pp. 431–49.

6. George Ursul, "From Political Freedom to Religious Independence: The Romanian Orthodox Church, 1877–1925," in Stephen Fischer-Galati, Radu Florescu, and George R. Ursul (eds.), *Romania between East and West: Historical Essays in Memory of Constantin C. Giurescu* (New York: Columbia University Press, 1982), pp. 217–31. See Grigore T. Marcu, "Regimul sectelor din Romania," *Revista Teologica* (Sibiu: June and July 1937).

7. *Continuous Most Favored Nation Tariff: Treatment of Imports from Romania, 1977,* Hearings before the U.S. Senate Sub-Committee on Finance (Washington D.C.: U.S. Government Printing Office, 1977). These hearings took place on June 27, 1977. They have been repeated on an annual basis, and each time the human rights record of Romania has come under review with a spate of lobbying by those advocating religious freedom and rights of minorities. The Romanian Missionary Society prepared such a report for April 1985 under the title *Religious Persecution in Romania* (Wheaton, Ill.: RMS, April 1977).

8. *Christianity Today,* September 20, 1985, p. 41; Keston News Service, September 19, 1985, pp. 3–4.

9. Hugh Seton-Watson, *Eastern Europe between the War Years, 1918–1941* (New York: Archon Books, 1962), pp. 198–216. See also Henry L. Roberts, *Rumania: Political Problems of an Agrarian State* (New Haven, Conn.: Yale University Press, 1951), pp. 3–222. Stephen Fischer-Galati, *Twentieth Century Rumania* (New York: Columbia University Press, 1970), pp. 50–54.

10. Hitchens, "The Romanian Orthodox Church," pp. 316–19; Ursul, "From Political Freedom to Religious Independence," pp. 228–31.

11. Ilie Georgescu, "A Latin Isle in a Sea of Slavs," in Erich Weingartner (ed.), *Church within Socialism* (Rome: IDOC Publications, 1976), pp. 108–9. See Aloise L. Tautu, "Crestinism oriental ori occidental," *Buna Vestire,* 14, No. 1 (January–March 1975), pp. 409 ff.; Nicolae Iorga, *Istoria Bisericii Ortodoxe Romane,* Vol. I (Bucharest: Editura Ministerului de Cultele, 1929), pp. 9–19; Gheorghe Moisescu, *Istoria Bisericii Romane* (Bucharest: N.p., 1957), Vol. 1, pp. 36–100; Mircea Pacurariu, "Marturi lingvistice pentru originea si vechimea crestinismului la Romani," in *Istoria Bisericii Ortodoxe Romane,* Vol. 1 (Bucharest: Editura Institutului Biblic si de Misiune al Bisericii Ortodoxe Romane, 1980), pp. 63–73.

12. Eric Tappe, "The Romanian Orthodox Church and the West," in D. Baker (ed.), *Studies in Church History, Vol. 13: The Orthodox Church and the West* (Oxford: Oxford University Press, 1976), p. 278.

13. Ursul, "From Political Freedom to Religious Independence," pp. 217–31. See Stephen Fischer-Galati, "Religion," in *East Central Europe under the Communists: Romania* (New York: Praeger, 1957), p. 135.

14. See Moisescu, *Istoria Bisericii Romane,* Vol. 2, pp. 601–7.

15. Ursul, "From Political Freedom to Religious Independence," pp. 224–26.

16. *Dare de Seama despre Judecata Rostita de Sf. Sinod asupra Fostului Metropolit Primat, Ghenadie Petrescu* (Bucharest: Institutul de Arte Grafice, 1896).

17. Conferinta romano-ortodoxa anglicana tinuta la Bucuresti, June 1–8, 1935.

18. Seton-Watson, *Eastern Europe,* p. 209.

19. *Parlamentul Romanesc,* Anul X, nr. 311/320 (December 31, 1939), pp. 119–21, 128–29.

20. Nicolae Balan, *Biserica impotriva Concordatului* (Sibiu: Tiparul Tipografieie Arhidiecezane, 1929).

21. Ibid., pp. 7–10.

22. Moisescu, *Istoria Bisericii Romanae*, Vol. 2, pp. 611 ff.; Onisfor Ghibu, *Catolicism hungaresc* (Cluj: N.p., 1924).

23. Keith Hitchens, *The Romanian Nationalist Movement in Transylvania, 1780–1849* (Cambridge, Mass.: Harvard University Press, 1969).

24. Octavian Goga, "Cuibul cu Barza," *Tara Noastra*, No. 2 (January 13, 1924). Published in translation in *Religion in Communist Lands*, 3, No. 6 (December 1975), pp. 18–19.

25. *Pe Marginea Prpastiei: 21–23 Januarie 1941* (Bucharest: Impremirea Centrala, 1942), Vol. 2, p. 102.

26. Ibid., pp. 102–6.

27. Stephen Fischer-Galati, "Autocracy, Orthodoxy, Nationality in the Twentieth Century: The Romanian Case," *East European Quarterly*, 18, No. 1 (March 1984), pp. 25–34.

28. Ibid., p. 33.

29. Nicolae Iorga, *Byzance après Byzance* (Bucharest: N.p., 1935).

30. Keith Hitchens, *Orthodoxy and Nationalism: Andreiu Şaguna and the Romanians of Transylvania, 1846–1873* (Cambridge, Mass.: Harvard University Press, 1977). See also Hitchens, "The Romanian Orthodox Church," pp. 317 ff.

31. *Gindirea* appeared from 1921 to 1944. Initially an instrument of expression for the literary and cultural society in Romania, it became increasingly politicized in the late 1920s and mid-1930s. See Dumitru Micu, *Gindirea si Gindirismul* (Bucharest: Editura Minerva, 1975).

32. See ibid., pp. 176–80; 183–85. For his most recent published work, see Dumitru Staniloae, *Teologia Dogmatica Ortodoxa*, in three volumes (Bucharest: Editura Institutului Biblic si de Misiune al Bisericii Ortodoxe Romane, 1978).

33. Dumitru Staniloae, "Ortodoxie si natiune," *Gindirea* (February 1935); "Crestinismul si natiune," *Gindirea* (1934), pp. 45–57.

34. See Alan Scarfe, "The Evangelical Wing of the Orthodox Church in Romania," *Religion in Communist Lands*, 3, No. 6 (November 1975), pp. 15–19.

35. Ibid.; see also "The 'Lord's Army' Movement in the Romanian Orthodox Church," *Religion in Communist Lands*, 8, No. 4 (Winter 1980), pp. 314–17.

36. Poems by Traian Dors have recently been published in *"Cintari Nemuritoare"* and included in *Cintarile Evangheliei*, compiled by Ieremie Hodoroaba (Paris: Glasul Indrumatorului Crestin, 1978).

37. See Dumitru Staniloae, "Problema Uniatismului in perspectiva ecumenica," *Mitropoilia Ardealului* (January–March 1969), pp. 23 ff.; see also Dumitru Staniloae, *Uniatism* (Sibiu: N.p., 1974); Nicolae Mladin, *Biserica Ortodoxa Romana: una si aceeasi in toate timpurile* (Sibiu: 1968); from a Uniate viewpoint, see Aloise L. Tautu, "Unirea cu Roma in cursul istorie romanesti," *Buna Vestire*, 14, No. 1 (January–March 1975), and Tautu, "Crestinismului."

38. Alexandru Ratiu, "Persecutia Bisericii Romane Unite," *Buna Vestire*, 13, Nos. 3–4 (October–December 1974), pp. 11–116. See also Alexandru Ratiu and William Virtue, *The Stolen Church: Martyrdom in Communist Romania* (Huntington, Ind.: Our Sunday Visitor, 1979).

39. Al. Cerna-Radulescu, *Spionaj si tradare in umbra crucii* (Bucharest: Tipografia Cartilor Bisericesti, 1948), with a short bibliography on p. 95.

40. William C. Fletcher, *Nikolai: Portrait of a Dilemma* (New York: Macmillan, 1968), pp. 54–84.

41. Appeal to President Ceauşescu from the Committee for the Restoration of the Roma-

nian Uniate Church, cited in *Religion in Communist Lands*, 6, No. 2 (Summer 1978), p. 136. English translation and copies of the original are available at Keston College, Keston, Kent, England.

42. Keston News Service, "Bucharest Redevelopment; Orthodox Heritage," June 13, 1985, p. 10.

43. Beeson, *Discretion and Valour*, pp. 359–60. See *De la Theologie Orthodoxe Romaine des origines a nos jours* (Bucharest: Editura Institutului Biblic si de Misiune al BOR, 1974). This splendid work in French, English, Romanian, and German is a bibliographical guide through the scholarship of the Romanian Orthodox Church Institutes. It introduces the leading church experts in their varied academic fields.

44. Beeson, *Discretion and Valour*, p. 372.

45. Ibid., p. 352.

46. Moisescu, *Istoria Bisericii Romanae*, pp. 617–18.

47. Hitchens, "The Romanian Orthodox Church," p. 322. See Justinian, *Apostolat Social*, Vols. 1–11 (Bucharest: Editura Institutului Biblic si de Misiune al BOR, 1948–77). See also Alan Scarfe, "Patriarch Justinian of Romania: His Early Social Thought," *Religion in Communist Lands*, 5, No. 3 (Autumn 1977), pp. 164–69. Dionisie Ghermani, "Kirchenverfolgung in Rumänien," page proofs of an article that was never published, pp. 172–77.

48. *Romanian Orthodox Church News*, September 1979, pp. 7–23; *Romanian Orthodox Church News*, December 1979, pp. 3–6.

49. Hitchens, *Orthodoxy and Nationalism*.

50. Sister Eileen Mary Slg, "Orthodox Monasticism in Romania Today," *Religion in Communist Lands*, 8, No. 1 (Spring 1980), pp. 22–27.

51. See *Blessed Paisius Velichkovsky* (Platina, Calif.: St. Herman of Alaska Brotherhood, 1976); Iorga, *Istoria Bisericii Ortodoxe*, Vol. II, pp. 176 ff.; Ghermani, "Kirchenverfolgung," p. 176; Beeson, *Discretion and Valour*, pp. 668–70.

52. Ghermani, "Kirchenverfolgung," p. 176; Beeson, *Discretion and Valour*, pp. 368, 370. See also Flaviu Popan, "Probleme de Biserica Ortodoxa Romana, 1945–1960," *Buna Vestire*, 15, Nos. 3 and 4 (1976); Earl Pope, "The Contemporary Religious Situation in Romania," a paper presented at Second World Congress for Soviet and East European Studies, Garmisch, West Germany (1980).

53. Beeson, *Discretion and Valour*, pp. 359–60.

54. Metropolitan Antonie, who studied for his doctorate at Oxford University, has published three major works in recent years: "Biserica Slujitoare," *Studii Teologice*, An XXIV, nr. 5–8 (May–October 1972), pp. 325–651; "Ca toti sa fie Una" (Bucharest: Editura Institutului Biblic si de Misiune al BOR, 1979); and *The Role of the Orthodox Clergy: Founders of the Romanian Language and Culture* (Bucharest: N.p., 1977).

55. Pope, "The Contemporary Religious Situation."

56. BBC-TV documentary entitled, "The Long Search"; the producers published a book under the same title edited by Ninian Smart.

57. Octavian Vuia, "Problems of the Relations between the State and the Churches in the Socialist Republic of Rumania," *Buna Vestire*, 12 (1973), pp. 41–87.

58. Ghermani, "Kirchenverfolgung," pp. 178–79; Beeson, *Discretion and Valour*, p. 379. See also *Romanian Orthodox Church News*, An. VII, Nos. 2–3, (April–September 1977), dedicated to the new patriarch, Justin Moisescu.

59. *Frankfurter Allgemeine*, August 22, 1986, p. 12.

60. Agerpres (Bucharest, November 14, 1986), in Foreign Broadcast Information Ser-

vice (FBIS), *Daily Report* (Eastern Europe), November 17, 1986, p. H4. See also Agerpress (November 13, 1986), in FBIS, *Daily Report* (Eastern Europe), November 14, 1986, pp. H7–H8.

61. Documents collected at Keston College cite numerous instances of persecution of Orthodox clergy and religious, including Gheorghe Samiznicu, Ioan Boboc, Stefan Gavrila, Ursu Zinica, Costica Maftei, Leonid Pop, Traian Dors, and a group of young priests from the archdiocese of Timisoara (Ambrus Cernat, Liviu Negoita, Ionel Vinchici, Cornel Avramescu, and Viorel Dumitrescu). Six of the last eight are now immigrants in the United States or Germany, indicating that emigration for the Orthodox, as with the Baptist churches, is becoming an open option for those who protest about existing conditions in Romania. Their documents are listed with a summary in issues of *Religion in Communist Lands* since 1975.

62. "Protest of Romanian Orthodox Priest," *Mennonite Brethren Herald*, September 5, 1975.

63. "The Lord's Army Movement." See also *Religious persecution in Romania*, p. 12.

64. See Alan Scarfe, "Dismantling of a Human Rights Movement: A Romanian Solution," *Religion in Communist Lands*, 7, No. 2 (Summer 1979), pp. 166–77. For government reaction, see *Le Monde*, April 12, 1979, p. 5.

65. Fr. Gheorghe Calciu-Dumitreasa, *Sapte Cuvinte catre Tineri* (Munich: N.p., 1979).

66. On the atheist campaign, see Dionisie Ghermani, "Zwangsatheisierung in Rumänien," *Kirche in Not*, 28 (1980), pp. 73–76.

67. Calciu, *Sapte Cuvinte catre Tineri*, p. 14.

68. *Memoriul unor elevi de la Seminarul Teologic Ortodox, Bucuresti*, addressed to Patriarch Justin, November 1978. (Document available at Keston College.)

69. See the report signed by Calciu and three others on the question of Hungarian minorities in Romania, dated 1979 (available at Keston College). Those involved with Calciu—Ioan Cana and Gheorghe Brasoveanu—were arrested with him for their founding of the Free Trade Union.

70. See his letter to friends in the West, "Concerning My Freedom," dated October 14, 1984. Fr. Calciu speaks of his conditions in prison, his spiritual state there, and the subsequent police surveillance after his release on August 20, 1984. This led him to seek emigration to the United States. He arrived in New York on August 9, 1985. His writings after prison are available at Keston College.

71. *Romania Libera*, September 10, 1979, p. 3; see also *Le Monde*, April 12, 1979, p. 5.

72. "Letter from Romanian Orthodox Priests," *Religion in Communist Lands*, 7, No. 3 (Autumn 1979), pp. 175–76.

73. Open Letter (dated November 2, 1981), broadcast on the "World of Religion" program of Radio Free Europe on November 8, 1981. See "Exiled Romanian Priests Protest Atheistic Control," *New York Tribune*, August 24, 1984, on Negoita and Dumitrescu.

74. See Trond Gilberg, "Religion and Nationalism in Romania," in Pedro Ramet (ed.), *Religion and Nationalism in Soviet and East European Politics* (Durham, N.C.: Duke University Press, 1984), pp. 170–86.

12 The Serbian Orthodox Church

The author is indebted to Stella Alexander, Stevan Pavlowitch and Radomir Rakić for comments on earlier drafts of this chapter.

1. Blagota Gardašević, "Organizaciono ustrojstvo i zakonodavstvo pravoslavne crkve izmedju dva svetska rata," in *Srpska Pravoslavna Crkva 1920–1970: Spomenica o 50-*

godišnjici vaspostavljanja Srpske Patrijaršije, hereafter *SPC 1920–1970* (Belgrade: Kosmos Publishers, 1971), pp. 37–39.

2. Miodrag B. Petrovich, "A Retreat from Power: The Serbian Orthodox Church and Its Opponents, 1868–1869," *Serbian Studies*, 1, No. 2 (Spring 1981), pp. 4–12.

3. Quoted in Gardašević, "Organizaciono ustrojstvo," p. 41.

4. James L. Sadkovich, "Il regime di Alessandro in Iugoslavia, 1929–1934: Un'interpretazione," *Storia Contemporanea*, 15, No. 1 (February 1984), p. 11.

5. Ibid., p. 25.

6. Bertold Spuler, *Gegenwartslage der Ostkirchen*, 2d ed. (Frankfurt: Metopen Verlag, 1968), p. 122.

7. Viktor Pospischil, *Der Patriarch in der Serbisch-Orthodoxen Kirche* (Vienna: Verlag Herder, 1966), p. 55; and Sadkovich, "Il regime," p. 25.

8. *Primedbe i prigovori na projekat Konkordata izmedju naše države i vatikana* (Sremski Karlovci: Patrijaršiska štamparija, 1936).

9. Ibid., pp. 9, 22, 34, 35, 41, 43, 50, 52–53, 56.

10. Ibid., p. 36.

11. Ibid., p. 33.

12. Ivan Lazić, "Pravni i činjenični položaj konfesionalnih zajednica u Jugoslaviji," in *Vjerske zajednice u Jugoslaviji* (Zagreb: NIP "Binoza," 1970), pp. 50–54; and Viktor Novak, *Velika optužba* (Sarajevo: Svjetlost, 1960), Vol. 2, pp. 131–36.

13. Bosnia's Metropolitan Petar Zimonjić, Banja Luka's Bishop Platon Jovanović, Gornji Karlovac's Bishop Sava Trlajić, Zagreb's Metropolitan Dositej, Bishop Nikolaj of Herzegovina, and Vicar-Bishop Valerijan Pribičević of Sremski Karlovci.

14. Quoted in Dušan Lj. Kašić, "Srpska crkva u tzv. Nezavisnoj Državi Hrvatskoj," in *SPC 1920–1970*, p. 185.

15. Ibid., p. 193.

16. *Katolički tjednik* (Sarajevo), June 26, 1941, as quoted in ibid., p. 184.

17. Ibid., p. 196.

18. Marko Dimitrijević, "Srpska crkva pod bugarskom okupacijom," in *SPC 1920–1970*, p. 213.

19. See Vaso Ivošević, "Srpska crkva pod italijanskom okupacijom," in *SPC 1920–1970*, pp. 217–20.

20. Milisav D. Protić, "Izgradnja crkava u poratnom periodu," in *SPC 1920–1970*, p. 253.

21. Djoko Slijepčević, *Istorija srpske pravoslavne crkve* (Munich: Iskra, 1966), Vol. 2, p. 687.

22. Risto Grdjić, "Opšta obnova crkvenog života i ustrojstva," in *SPC 1920–1970*, p. 243; and interview, Belgrade, July 1987.

23. Stella Alexander, *Church and State in Yugoslavia since 1945* (Cambridge: Cambridge University Press, 1979), pp. 164–73.

24. Ibid., p. 189.

25. *Borba*, July 3, 1952, cited in ibid.

26. Trevor Beeson, *Discretion and Valour*, Rev. ed. (Philadelphia: Fortress Press, 1982), p. 315; and letter to the author from Stella Alexander, October 17, 1983.

27. Alexander, *Church and State*, p. 224.

28. *Borba*, August 22, 1953, cited in ibid., pp. 200–201.

29. Ibid., pp. 213, 219. Also *Politika*, June 1, 1982, translated into German under the title "Die Serbisch-Orthodoxe Kirche und ihre Beziehungen zum jugoslawischen Staat," *Osteuropa*, 33, No. 1 (January 1983), pp. A53–A54.

30. Radomir Rakić, "Izdavačka delatnost crkve od 1945. do 1970. godine," in *SPC 1920–1970*, p. 291n; and interview, Belgrade, July 1982.

31. Protić, "Izgradnja crkava," pp. 254, 271–72.

32. Stevan K. Pavlowitch, "The Orthodox Church in Yugoslavia: Rebuilding the Fabric," *Eastern Churches Review*, 2, No. 2 (Autumn 1968), p. 171.

33. Rastko Vidić, *The Position of the Church in Yugoslavia* (Belgrade: Jugoslavija, 1962), p. 53; Pavlowitch, "The Orthodox Church," p. 170; *Europa Year Book 1972*, Vol. 1, pp. 1435–36, cited in Burton Paulu, *Radio and Television Broadcasting in Eastern Europe* (Minneapolis: University of Minnesota Press, 1974), p. 463; Beeson, *Discretion and Valour*, p. 291; and interview, Belgrade, July 1982.

34. For details, see Branko A. Cisarž, "Crkvena štampa izmedju dva svetska rata," in *SPC 1920–1970*, pp. 141–55.

35. Rakić, "Izdavačka delatnost," pp. 291–95 and passim; and interview, Belgrade, July 1982.

36. Alexander, *Church and State*, p. 169.

37. Fred Singleton, *Twentieth-Century Yugoslavia* (New York: Columbia University Press, 1976), p. 229.

38. Alexander, *Church and State*, pp. 270–71.

39. Ibid., p. 265.

40. For a fuller discussion of these political currents and of Ranković's role in the 1960s, see Pedro Ramet, *Nationalism and Federalism in Yugoslavia, 1963–1983* (Bloomington: Indiana University Press, 1984).

41. Interview, Belgrade, July 1987.

42. *Nova Makedonija*, Sabota supplement, October 10, 1981, p. 5, translated in Joint Publications Research Service, *East Europe Report* (Political, Sociological, and Military Affairs)—hereinafter JPRS/EE—(December 29, 1981); and interview, Belgrade, July 1982.

43. E.g., *Politika*, October 6, 1981, p. 6.

44. E.g., Tanjug (June 19, 1981), in Foreign Broadcast Information Service (FBIS), *Daily Report* (Eastern Europe), June 22, 1981.

45. Tanjug (February 25, 1982), translated in FBIS, *Daily Report* (Eastern Europe), February 26, 1982.

46. Quoted in *Vjesnik* (July 15, 1978), translated in JPRS/EE (October 17, 1978).

47. Ibid.

48. *Vesnik*, January 1–15, 1971, p. 1.

49. Interview with Patriarch German, *NIN*, No. 1637 (May 16, 1982), p. 18; and *Keston News Service*, No. 232 (August 22, 1985), p. 10.

50. "Informationsdienst," in *Glaube in der 2. Welt* (February 1978), p. 5, as summarized in "News in Brief," *Religion in Communist Lands*, 6, No. 4 (Winter 1978), pp. 272–73.

51. *Ilustrovana politika* (Belgrade), November 20, 1984, pp. 24–25.

52. *Keston News Service*, No. 229 (July 11, 1985), pp. 8–9.

53. Ibid., No. 244 (February 20, 1986), p. 11.

54. Ibid., No. 251 (May 29, 1986), p. 12.

55. Stella Alexander, "The Serbian Orthodox Church Speaks Out in Its Own Defence," *Religion in Communist Lands*, 10, No. 3 (Winter 1982), pp. 331–32.

56. *Pravoslavlje*, May 15, 1982, p. 1.

57. I have examined the nationalism of the Serbian Orthodox church in more detail in my chapter "Religion and Nationalism in Yugoslavia," in Pedro Ramet (ed.), *Religion and*

Nationalism in Soviet and East European Politics (Durham, N.C.: Duke University Press, 1984).

58. Manojlo Broćić, "The Position and Activities of the Religious Communities in Yugoslavia with Special Attention to the Serbian Orthodox Church," in Bohdan R. Bociurkiw and John W. Strong (eds.), *Religion and Atheism in the USSR and Eastern Europe* (London: Macmillan, 1975), p. 359.

59. Quoted in *Los Angeles Times*, December 18, 1980, Pt. I-B, p. 5.

13   The Czechoslovak Orthodox Church

1. See Ludvík Němec, "Autocephali," in *The New Catholic Encyclopedia* (Washington, D.C.: McGraw-Hill, 1966), Vol. 1, col. 1116–17.

2. Donald Attwater, *The Christian Churches of the East*, 2 vols. (Milwaukee: Bruce, 1946 and 1947); and John Meyendorff, *The Orthodox Church: Its Past, and Its Role in the World Today*, trans. John Chapin (New York: Pantheon Books, 1963).

3. J. Krajcar and M. Lacko, "Czechoslovakia," in *The New Catholic Encyclopedia*, Vol. 4, col. 593–98; Kurt Glaser, *Czecho-Slovakia: A Critical History* (Caldwell, Idaho: Caxton, 1961), pp. 11–30; Emil Valasek, "Veränderungen der Diozesangrenzen in der Tschechoslowakei seit 1918," in *Archiv für Kirchengeschichte von Böhmen-Mähres Schlesien* (Munich: Col. Carol, 1982), Vol. 6, pp. 289–96; Eduard Beneš, *Detruises l'Austriche-Hongrie* (Paris: V. Girard et E. Breire, 1916), chap. 1 and passim; Jan Opočenskj, *The Collapse of the Austro-Hungarian Monarchy and the Rise of the Czechoslovak State* (Prague: Orbis, 1928); and Dagmar Perman, *The Shaping of the Czechoslovak State: Diplomatic History of the Boundaries of Czechoslovakia, 1914–1920* (Leiden: E. J. Brill, 1962).

4. Victor S. Mamatey and Radomír Lůža, *A History of the Czechoslovak Republic, 1918–1968* (Princeton, N.J.: Princeton University Press, 1973), p. 41.

5. Basil Boysak, *The Fate of the Holy Union in Carpatho-Ukraine* (Toronto and New York: University of Toronto Press, 1963), pp. 210–26; and Michael Lacko, *Unio Uzhorodensis Ruthenorum Carpathicorum cum Ecclesia Catholica* (Rome: Gregorian University Press, 1955), passim.

6. Ludvík Němec, "The Czech Jednota, the Avant-Garde of Modern Clerical Progressivism and Unionism," *Proceedings of the American Philosophical Society*, 112 (1968), No. 1, pp. 74–100.

7. Jaroslav Šuvarský, *Biskup Gorazd, 1879–1975* (Prague: Orthodox Press, 1979), pp. 112–28 and passim.

8. Československý Katechism: Učebnice pro mládež a věřící Československé Církve (Příbram: Česky Zápas, 1922).

9. Orazio M. Premoli, *Contemporary Church History, 1900–1925* (London: Burns, Oates, and Washbourne, 1932), p. 242.

10. F. Cinek, *K náboženské Otázce v prvních letech naší samostatnosti* (Olomouc: C. M. Theological Faculty, 1926), pp. 233ff.

11. Vladimir Grigoric, *Pravoslavná Církev ve Státě Československém*, 2nd ed. (Prague: Ortend Press, 1928), p. 132.

12. Bishop Gorazd, *Pamětní spis o pravnim postaveni-církve pravoslavné v Republice Československe* (Prague: Orthodox Press, 1932), p. 9 and passim.

13. Šuvarský, *Biskup Gorazd*, pp. 188, 191.

Notes

14. Ibid., p. 197.
15. The text of October 1938 can be found in ibid., pp. 214–16.
16. Ibid., p. 221.
17. Quoted in ibid., p. 226.
18. Quoted in ibid., p. 228.
19. Joseph L. Hromadka, *Between East and West* (Prague: Huss Faculty, 1947), p. 151; and Joseph L. Hromadka, "The Modern Trends in European Protestant Theology," in *The University of Pennsylvania Bicentennial Conference: Religion and the Modern World* (Philadelphia: University of Pennsylvania Press, 1941), pp. 21–25.
20. *Zhurnal Moskovskoi Patriarkhii* (1949), No. 10, pp. 5–11.
21. *Svetlo pravoslavia*, June 1, 1950, p. 18.
22. Theodoric J. Zubek, *The Church of Silence in Slovakia* (Whiting, Md.: Jan Lach, 1956), pp. 223–24; and Lacko, *Unio Užhorodensis*, p. 169.
23. In the Russian church it is customary to sing this acclamation in Greek, meaning "Many more years!"
24. *Svetlo pravoslavia*, June 1, 1950, p. 25.
25. Ibid., p. 26.
26. Meyendorff, *The Orthodox Church*, p. 181.
27. Marc Szeftel, "Church and State in Imperial Russia," in Robert L. Nichols and Theofanis G. Stavrou (eds.), *Russian Orthodoxy under the Old Regime* (Minneapolis: University of Minnesota Press, 1978), pp. 127–53.
28. Of 321,000 Greek Catholics in Slovakia, about 25 percent were Ruthenian.
29. By encyclical letter, in *Orientales Ecclesias* (Rome, December 15, 1952).
30. By a decree on Eastern Catholic churches (November 21, 1964).
31. See, for instance, "Message of His Holiness Pope John Paul II to the Ukrainians," *Ukrainian Quarterly*, 35, No. 4 (Winter 1979), pp. 412–14.
32. For further details, see Michael Lacko, "Union of Užhorod," Ludvik Němec, "Czechoslovakia," and Thomas Bird, "The Orthodox Church of Czechoslovakia"—all in *Encyclopedic Dictionary of Religion* (Washington, D.C.: Corpus, 1978), respectively, Vol. 3, col. 3026–27, Vol. 1, col. 972–73, and Vol. 1, col. 974.
33. Two bishops, Josef Feranec of Banska Bystrica and Josef Vrana of Olomouc, were willing to continue patronizing this banned organization.
34. See *Journal of the Moscow Patriarchate* (1984), No. 4, pp. 58–63.
35. See numerous reports on this matter in *Die Welt* and *Die Presse*, during August 1984.
36. *Katolické Noviný* (Bratislava), August 29, 1984.
37. *Večerni pravda*, as quoted in *Nový Život* (Rome, 1985), Nos. 1–2, p. 26.

14 The Finnish Orthodox Church

1. The research for this chapter is based chiefly on the following sources: *Asetus Suomen kreikkalaisaskatolisesta kirkkokunnasta* (Government Edict on the Greek Catholic Church), November 26, 1918; *Asetus ortodoksisesta kirkkokunnasta* (Government Edict on the Orthodox Church), May 15, 1953; *Laki ortodoksisesta kirkkokunnasta* (Law on the Orthodox Church), August 8, 1969; *Asetus ortodoksisesta kirkkokunnasta* (Government Edict on the Orthodox Church), March 6, 1970; Fr. Ambrosius and Markku Haapio (eds.), *Ortodoksinin kirkko Suomessa* (The Orthodox Church in Finland) (Lieto, 1979); Heikki Koukkunen, *Tuiskua ja tyventä* (Whirlwind and Calm) (Pieksämäki, 1982); U. V. J. Setälä, *Kansallisen*

ortodoksisen kirkkokunnan perustamiskysymys Suomen politiikassa 1917–1925 (The Issue of the Foundation of the National Orthodox Church in the Finnish Politics of 1917–1925) (Helsinki, 1966); and N. Valmo (ed.), *Suomen ortodoksinen arkkipiispakunta* (The Orthodox Archdiocese of Finland) (Helsinki, 1935).

2. The number of Russians in Finland subsequently declined rapidly, as many left the country. By 1920 there were only 4,806 Russians remaining in Finland.

3. Some of the laymen, who had been actively involved in the preparation of the law of 1969 and the edict of 1970, based their work chiefly on the previous decrees and, as they were not aware of the serious canonical problems connected with these, were fairly convinced that they were founded on an Orthodox basis. This seemed safer since all these edicts reflected principles generally followed in local and state administration. The result was thus "acceptable" from the Finnish point of view. For these reasons the criticism of the canonicity of the said legislation was usually rejected by these people, no doubt often in good faith. A leading actor in this group was a lawyer named Simo Härkönen, who has rendered valuable services to the church in various responsible positions.

4. This is but one of the direct borrowings from the Lutheran church law.

5. Koukkunen, *Tuiska ja tyventä*, pp. 19–20.

6. The candidate, Rev. Mikael Kasanski, declared that he would accept the appointment only if sanctioned both canonically and by the government. But before the canonical consecration could take place, the candidate died.

7. Constantinople originally planned to send a special delegation to various European capitals to discuss the new ecclesiastical situation created by World War I and the Bolshevik Revolution with the national governments concerned. There were several jurisdictional questions to be solved. In addition, Constantinople also planned, at one point, to send a separate delegation to Estonia and Finland. But although the Finnish government welcomed this prospect, the visit never came about.

8. The view of the ecumenical patriarch was that the Finnish church was far too small to become autocephalous and that the independence of such a small church would only encourage the splintering of the church in general. This was made clear in the beginning of the discussions in the Phanar in July 1923. See Setälä, *Kansallisen ortodoksisen*, pp. 147–48.

9. *Laki ortodoksisesta kirkkokunnasta*, pp. 1045–56.

10. Valmo, *Suomen ortodoksinen*, p. 383; and *Asetus Suomen*, p. 70.

11. The Orthodox church appointed a special committee for this purpose in 1984 under the chairmanship of Metropolitan John of Helsinki. The Lutheran church, too, has a corresponding committee.

12. Ambrosius and Haapio, *Ortodoksinen kirkko*, pp. 145–46.

13. Koukkunen, *Tuiska ja tyventä*, p. 196.

15   The Georgian Orthodox Church

1. There are countless instances of this from the leaders of all officially recognized churches in the USSR. The present patriarch of Georgia, for instance, told a Portuguese journalist in 1978 that his church "does not suffer from discrimination," though this does not accord with the evidence (*jvari vazisa*, the journal of the Georgian patriarchate, 1978, No. 2, p. 42). His predecessors were forced into even more humiliating declarations. Kalistrate (patriarch from 1932 to 1952), in a telegram to Stalin on his seventieth birthday in 1949, praised his "evangelical" policies of "brotherhood, unity and freedom." *Zhurnal Moskovskoi*

Patriarkhii—henceforth *Zh.M.P.*—1950, No. 1, p. 5. All the Orthodox churches in the USSR have been used to promote Soviet foreign policy since World War II.

2. See his "Religion in the USSR: Current Trends," *Radio Liberty Research* (1975), No. 140.

3. With the support of the procurator of the Holy Synod, Prince A. N. Golitsyn, a tsarist investigation into Georgian church affairs in 1810 recommended the replacement of the Georgian patriarch with a metropolitan who would be responsible to the Russian Holy Synod. Tsar Alexander I approved the recommendation and abolished the Georgian patriarchate by imperial decree in July 1811.

4. The title exarch usually refers to bishops or metropolitans who have jurisdiction over a civil diocese. The Georgian exarch was responsible to the Russian Holy Synod for the three provinces that formerly made up the Georgian kingdom.

5. Professor A. A. Tsagereli, *Stat'i i zametki po gruzinskomu tserkovnomu voprosu k stoletiiu (1811–1911 gg.) vdovstva gruzinskoi tserkvi* (St. Petersburg, 1912), p. xx.

6. For the text of this petition see *MS Ward. C 19*, in the Wardrop Collection of the Bodleian Library, Oxford. A French translation of the text is in M. Taramati's *L'Église géorgienne des origines jusqu'à nos jours* (Rome: Société Typographico Editrice Romaine, 1910), pp. 393–95.

7. Notably Bishop Kirioni and Archimandrite Ambrosi, both of whom subsequently became patriarchs of the Georgian church (Kirioni from 1917 to 1918 and Ambrosi from 1921 to 1927). They both remained in exile until 1917.

8. The word "catholicos" was applied to the early Georgian primates. After the confirmation of Georgian autocephaly in 1057 at the Council of Antioch, the word *patriarch* was added.

9. R. Ingilo, *damoukidelebi sakartvelo* (Independent Georgia) (Paris, 1927), Nos. 17, 20, and 22.

10. *Wardr. MS C1* (Wardrop Collection), p. 157.

11. The new-found liberty of 1917 led the Orthodox churches of Poland, Finland, Lithuania, Latvia, and Estonia to demand autonomy from the Russian church.

12. For Leonide's reply see "The Epistle of His Holiness, the Catholicos-Patriarch of all Georgia Leonide to His Holiness Tikhon, Patriarch of Moscow and all Russia" (in Georgian). *samshoblo* (Paris, 1932), No. 11, pp. 36–56.

13. It is not clear what position the ecumenical patriarch took on this dispute. I have come across no evidence that his advice was sought by either the Georgian or Russian church leaders.

14. *Sbornik ukazov i postanovlenii Vremennogo Pravitel'stva. Vypusk 1. 27 fevralia—5 maia 1917g.* (Petrograd: Gosudarstvennaia tipografiia, 1917), p. 20.

15. On April 22 a Transcaucasian Federative Republic was proclaimed. A little over a month later the three countries making up the federation, Armenia, Azerbaidjan, and Georgia, declared themselves separate republics.

16. For highly partisan treatments of the project, see F. Makharadze, *Diktatura menshevistskoi partii v Gruzii* (Moscow: Gosizdat, 1921), pp. 90–91, and E. Drabkina, *Gruzinskaia kontrrevoliutsiia* (Leningrad: Izdatel'stvo Priboi, 1928), pp. 144–45.

17. For an English translation of the constitution, see Constantin Kandelaki, *The Georgian Question Before the Free World (Acts Documents Evidence)*. Translated from the French (Paris: American Council for Independent Georgia, 1953), pp. 192–209.

18. *Archives of the Delegation to the Conference of Peace and the Government in Exile.*

This Georgian archive contains state papers relating to the Republic of Georgia, and is deposited at the Houghton Library, Harvard. Box 22, Book 66, p. 105.

19. These figures are cited in E. Melia, "The Georgian Orthodox Church," in Richard H. Marshall, Jr. (ed.), *Aspects of Religion in the Soviet Union, 1917–67* (Chicago and London: University of Chicago Press, 1971), pp. 226–27.

20. The Georgian decree is in P. V. Gidulianov (ed.), *Otdelenie tserkvi ot gosudarstva v SSSR* (London: Gregg International, 1971), pp. 620–21.

21. The Georgian constitution of 1922 added the caveat (which is not in the RSFSR constitution) that religious propaganda was only allowed if it renounced "political or social aims." See *Istoriia sovetskoi konstitutsii v dekretakh i postanovleniiakh sovetskogo pravitel'stva 1917–1936* (Moscow: Izdatel'stvo Sovetskoe Zakonodatel'stvo, 1937), p. 206.

22. Article 120 in the 1922 constitution. See also Article 93 of the 1926 constitution. The 1926 constitution is in English in W. R. Batsell, *Soviet Rule in Russia* (New York: Macmillan, 1929), pp. 425–44.

23. For all references to the 1926 Georgian criminal code, see *Ugolovnye zakonodatel'stva SSSR i soiuznykh respublik* (Moscow: Gosizdat Iuridicheskoi Literatury, 1957).

24. *Kommunisticheskaia partiia Gruzii v rezoliutsiiakh i resheniiakh s"ezdov, konferentsii i plenumov TsK,Tom 1* (Tbilisi: Izdatel'stvo TSK KP Gruzii, 1976), p. 131.

25. Gidulianov, *Otdelenie tserkvi ot gosudarstva v SSSR*, p. 29.

26. Peter J. Barbis, *Silent Churches: Persecutions of Religions in the Soviet-Dominated Areas* (Illinois Research Publications, 1978), p. 256. Barbis goes on to say that 2,355 churches, twenty-seven monasteries, and seven convents were closed by 1923, but does not give his source. Ibid., p. 256.

27. C. Kandelaki, *The Georgian Question*, pp. 68–69.

28. For an account of the trial, see "Chronique des églises orthodoxes: IV, Eglise Géorgienne," *Echos d'Orient*, 22 (1923), No. 130, pp. 233–34. "The War against Religion in Georgia," *The Christian East*, 5 (1924), No. 2, pp. 72–74.

29. In Russia, the Soviet authorities promoted the schismatic "Living Church" movement. Its equivalent in Armenia was the "Free Church." Both wanted reforms.

30. Donald Attwater, *The Christian Churches of the East*. Vol. 2. *Churches Not in Communion with Rome* (London: Geoffrey Chapman, 1961), p. 117.

31. *sakartvelos eklesiis kalendari* (Tbilisi: Sakartvelos Sapatriarko, 1982), p. 152. Henceforth simply *S.E.K.*

32. *Kommunisticheskaia partiia Gruzii v rezoliutsiiakh*, p. 305.

33. As a Georgian version of the 1929 decree was unavailable, I have used the RSFSR decree for reference. One can be almost certain that the Georgian version differed little from that of the RSFSR.

34. Walter Kolarz, *Religion in the Soviet Union* (London: Macmillan, 1961), pp. 100–101.

35. These were *sakartvelos urhmerto* (The Georgian Atheist), Tbilisi, 1930; *Religiis tsinaarhmdeg* (Against Religion), Tbilisi, 1930–31; *Mebrdzole urhmerto* (Atheist Fighter), Tbilisi, 1932–34; *Mebrdzole ateisti* (The Fighting Atheist), Tbilisi, 1935–41. *Periodicheskaia pechat' SSSR 1917–49: Zhurnaly, trudy, biulletiny* (Periodical Literature in the USSR 1917–49: Journals, Works, Bulletins) (Moscow: Reprinted by Auxilibris, Montabaur, 1963), pp. 361–71. Despite the increase in the league membership in Georgia, between 1937 and 1938 the circulation of *Mebdrzole ateisti* declined from an already small six thousand to three thousand, and the number of pages from ninety-eight to forty-eight. *Letopis periodicheskikh*

izdanii SSSR (Moscow: Izdatel'stvo gosudarstvennoi tsentral'noi knizhnoi palaty, 1937 and 1938). One suspects the Georgian League's membership was exaggerated by its leaders. With a 145,000 membership, why did its journal have a circulation of only six thousand?

36. Elia (Ilia) Melia, "The Georgian Orthodox Church," pp. 230–31. Kolarz, *Religion in the Soviet Union*, pp. 100–101.

37. "Shurduli" (pseud.), "kartuli eklesiis rbeva," *mebrdzoli sakartvelo*, 10 (February 1953), pp. 22–24.

38. *S.E.K.*, 1976, p. 110.

39. He declared (under oath) that there were "numberless occasions when people . . . from surrounding villages . . . came secretly to my father and begged him to have their child baptized, or perform some other religious rite." *Communist Takeover and Occupation of Georgia. Special Report No. 6 of the Select Committee on Communist Aggression.* House of Representatives Eighty-Third Congress, Second Session. H.Res.346 and H.Res.438 (Washington, D.C.: U.S. Government Printing Office, 1955), p. 21.

40. Kolarz, *Religion in the Soviet Union*, pp. 102–3.

41. *Pravda*, November 7, 1942, p. 5.

42. Stalin received Russian Metropolitans Sergii, Aleksii, and Nikolai in September 1943. Recognition of Georgian autocephaly came seven weeks later.

43. Letters and documents relating to the recognition of Georgian autocephaly in 1943 are in *Zh.M.P.*, March 1944, No. 3, pp. 6–18. As Kolarz points out (*Religion in the Soviet Union*, pp. 103–4), recognition on the basis of territory—which was in accord with Orthodox canon law—should have led to the recognition of the autocephaly of all other Orthodox churches in the Soviet Union and Eastern Europe. The Russian church refused to accept this. Also, constitutionally Georgia had been a separate territorial unit and sovereign Soviet republic since 1922.

44. This may have been a reference to the previous flirtation of Patriarch Kristopore with the Living Church movement, or to contacts with members of the Truly Orthodox church living in Georgia. Data are insufficient on Russian schismatic movements in Georgia to make any confident hypothesis, and Kalistrate denied any such links.

45. *Zh.M.P.*, 1950, No. 8, p. 5–7. For his other pronouncements in support of Soviet policies, see *Zh.M.P.*, 1950, No. 1, p. 12, No. 11, p. 9, and 1951, No. 11, pp. 26–27.

46. *Zaria Vostoka*, organ of the Georgian Communist party, January 28, 1949, p. 4.

47. *S.E.K.*, 1980, p. 394.

48. On April 2, *Zaria Vostoka* criticized the poor work of the Georgian Society for the Dissemination of Political and Scientific Knowledge; on April 11 it published an article on antireligious work in Ajaria, and on April 28 there was an attack on Easter.

49. *Zaria Vostoka*, May 6, 1959, p. 2.

50. *Zaria Vostoka*, January 26, 1960, p. 5.

51. *Agitator*, journal of the CPSU Central Committee, November 21, 1964, pp. 45–47.

52. *Zaria Vostoka*, January 30, 1964, p. 4.

53. The two councils were the Council for the Affairs of the Russian Orthodox Church (established October 1943) and the Council for the Affairs of Religious Cults (formed in July 1944). The creation of two councils seemed to be an admission that in denominational matters, the Russian church was at least primus inter pares.

54. In 1974 a separate Council for Religious Affairs was set up in the Ukraine, and in the Baltic republics and Armenia there seems to be a wide degree of autonomy in local religious affairs.

55. *Ugolovnoe zakonodatel'stvo soiuza SSSR i soiuznykh respublik. V dvukh tomakh. Tom 1.* (Moscow: Gosizdat Iuridicheskoi literatury, 1963), p. 542.

56. For a systematic comparison of the 1959 and 1960 calendars, see Von, R. S., "Der Kalender der Georgischen Kirche—1977—und was er uns über die Georgische Kirche von heute sagt," *Glaube in der 2 Welt. Themaheft Georgien* (Zürich), October 1977, pp. 121–23.

57. For these figures see Michael Bourdeaux, Hans Hebly and Eugen Voss (eds.), *Religious Liberty in the Soviet Union: The World Council of Churches and the USSR: A Post-Nairobi Documentation* (Keston, England: Keston College, 1976), pp. 4–5. When recording the decline of the Georgian church in this century, we must remember that churches in the West have also experienced diminishing parishes and clergy. The equation between urbanization and religious decline is not a simple one, but the population shift from country to town in Georgia in this century contributed to the church's decline.

58. Nino Salia, "Le Catholicos-Patriarche de Géorgie au Congrès du Conseil Oecuménique des Eglises à Paris," *bedi kartlisa*, Vols. 13–14, p. 10. This seems to be a rather wild estimate.

59. D. Gegeshidze, "Pravoslavie v Gruzii," *Nauka i religiia*, 6 (1972), p. 44.

60. Cited by M. Bourdeaux in "The Georgian Orthodox Church," *Radio Liberty Script* 246, December 22, 1976.

61. Radio Liberty: *Arkhiv Samizdata*, Document No. 1821, pp. 2–3.

62. Elia Melia, "The Georgian Orthodox Church," pp. 232–33.

63. Other measures included the creation of public assistance commissions in November 1966, with the aim of helping local soviets in their task of religious control. Since 1969 local representatives of the Council for Religious Affairs have been responsible for collecting detailed material every year on all religious societies in their area.

64. *Izvestiia*, August 3, 1967, p. 6.

65. See *Zaria Vostoka*, March 3, 1966, p. 4.

66. Radio Liberty, *Archiv samizdata*, No. 1821a. The official report of David V's election paints quite a different picture of probity. See *samshoblo*, July 14, 1972.

67. *Archiv samizdata*, No. 1821a, p. 6. Bishop Gaioz had been sentenced for "hooliganism" in 1969 and had been expelled from Tbilisi University and the seminary. One year after taking holy orders in 1971 he was made a bishop. With the election of David V, he became rector of the seminary and metropolitan of Urbnisi at the age of thirty. For further biographical details of Bishop Gaioz and the official report of his subsequent trial for embezzlement of church property, see *Zaria Vostoka*, June 14, 1979, p. 4.

68. For an analysis of Koridze's report, see P. B. Reddaway, "The Georgian Orthodox Church: Corruption and Renewal," *Religion in Communist Lands*, 3 (1975), Nos. 4–5, pp. 14–23. See also his "The Georgian Church: A Controversy," *Religion in Communist Lands*, 3 (1975), No. 6, pp. 45–54), on the disagreements between him and Professor D. M. Lang on the condition of the Georgian church in the 1970s.

69. D. Shalutashvili, the representative of the Council for Religious Affairs in Georgia, was dismissed in October 1973. At Bishop Gaioz's trial in 1979, the Council for Religious Affairs was criticized for "turning a blind eye" to the situation in the church.

70. Only 100,045 rubles' worth of valuables was returned to the church; the rest was considered of "national and historical significance" and retained by the state. *Zaria Vostoka*, (June 14, 1979), p. 4.

71. See *Archiv samizdata*, Nos. 1821, 1821b, 1830, 1833, 1834, 1960, and 2581.

72. One "witness" for the court, Victor Shalamberidze, was killed in a car crash in February 1974. It is hard to say whether this was the work of the KGB.

73. Available documents strongly suggest that this was a KGB "setup." See the *Chronicle of Current Events*, 38 (1978), p. 130.

74. She was released in September 1975, rearrested in 1978, released again in 1980. In 1983 she was sentenced to a further eight years' corrective labor and three years' exile on bribery charges. For details of Pailodze's activities and trials, see "Delo Pailodze," in *Khronika tekushchikh sobytii* (New York: Khronika), 1974, No. 32, pp. 40–42. For the Soviet version, see *Zaria Vostoka*, June 2, 1983, p. 4.

75. In August 1975 the Soviet Union signed the Final Act of the Conference on Security and Cooperation in Europe (known as the Helsinki Agreements), which contained certain undertakings on human rights.

76. *S.E.K.*, 1976, pp. 37–39. The calendar was edited and compiled by Metropolitan Gaioz.

77. *literaturuli sakartvelo*, April 1, 1977, p. 4.

78. Radio Liberty, *Archiv Samizdata*, No. 2581, p. 9.

79. "Iz Gruzii soobshchaiut," *Russkaia Mysl'*, No. 3421 (July 15, 1982), p. 7. He also claimed Ilia's sermons were subject to censorship.

80. Despite the Georgian churches' improved status, in 1982 Ilia still found it necessary to request talks with the Russian church on autocephaly and to establish once and for all the "proper historical place" of the Georgian church. An article on the church's autocephaly was read at the meeting and sent to all Orthodox churches. There is still some resistance, notably from the Greek church, to acceptance of the church's autocephalous status. For an account of the meeting, see *jvari vazisa*, 1982, No. 1, pp. 19–20.

81. Brian Cooper, "Little Candles for the World," *The Church of England Newspaper*, February 15, 1980, p. B5.

82. *Archiv samizdata*, No. 5343. For other "open letters" addressed to Ilia, see *Archiv samizdata*, Nos. 5241 and 5272.

83. I have been told this, though there is no evidence that Ilia sought (and was granted) permission by Soviet authorities to sign this statement.

84. *Pravda*, March 6, 1972, pp. 1–2.

85. *Khronika tekushchikh sobytii*, No. 34, p. 69.

86. *Zaria Vostoka*, November 25, 1975, pp. 1–2.

87. Ibid., October 27, 1976, p. 4.

88. *Zaria Vostoka*, March 13, 1977, p. 2.

89. Ibid., September 14, 1979, p. 2, and November 27, 1979, p. 3.

90. Gamsakhurdia in his letter to Brezhnev (*Russkaia mysl'*) complained that the Shiioba festival at Shio-Mgvime monastery was stopped and the monastery was handed over to a local technical school (it has since been returned). Similarly, visitors trying to go to the St. Kvirike festival in Svaneti found militia guarding tree trunks that blocked the only road (*Archiv samizdata*, No. 2801).

91. See, for instance, *A Chronicle of Current Events*, 27 (March 1973), pp. 326–27, on the dismissal of a teacher for religious belief and *Zaria Vostoka*, February 21, 1978, p. 4, on dismissals from the party for participation in religious festivals.

92. *Zaria Vostoka*, January 24, 1976, p. 7.

93. Quoted in *Radio Free Europe Research* (1982), No. 188, p. 3.

94. Quoted in *Radio Liberty—Research* (1983), No. 453, p. 4.

95. This is an underestimation. Church marriages and baptisms are far more popular than Lordkipinadze suggests.

96. Such outbursts have taken the form of open demonstrations, petitions, and critical

speeches at the Georgian Union of Writers. In 1983 there were a number of arrests connected with opposition to the official celebration of the 1783 Georgievsk Treaty by which Georgia became a Russian protectorate.

97. This citation comes from an undated document by Gamsakhurdia entitled *The Fingerless Policeman and the Crazy Congregation*. The document is available at Keston College, Kent.

98. See *Chronicle of Current Events*, 48 (March 1978), p. 26, and *Keston News Service*, 132 (September 1981), p. 4.

99. *jvari vazisa*, 1980, No. 2, pp. 5–6.

100. *S.E.K.*, 1976, p. 32.

101. *Sakartvelos Kommunisti*, 1981, No. 4, p. 62.

102. *jvari vazisa*, 1981, No. 2, p. 13.

16   The Ukranian Autocephalous Orthodox Church

This chapter is based to a considerable extent on the author's earlier article, "The Ukrainian Autocephalous Orthodox Church, 1920–1930: A Case Study in Religious Modernization," which appeared in Dennis J. Dunn (ed.), *Religion and Modernization in the Soviet Union* (Boulder, Colo.: Westview Press, 1977), pp. 310–47.

1. The principal studies on the Orthodox church in Ukraine since 1917 are Vasyl Lypkivskyi, *Istoriia Ukrainskoi Pravoslavnoi Tserkvy, Rozdil VII: Vidrodzhennia Tserkvy v Ukraini* (History of the Ukrainian Orthodox Church, Chapter VII: Rebirth of the Church in Ukraine) (Winnipeg, J. Gryshuk, 1961); Friedrich Heyer, *Die Orthodoxe Kirche in der Ukraine von 1917 bis 1945* (Cologne-Braunsfeld: Rudolf Müller, 1953); Ivan Vlasovskyi, *Narys istorii Ukrainskoi Pravoslavnoi Tserkvy* (Outline History of the Ukrainian Orthodox Church), Vol. 4 (New York and Bound Brook, N.J.: Ukrainian Orthodox Church of the U.S.A., 1961); and Bohdan R. Bociurkiw, *Soviet Church Policy in the Ukraine, 1919–1939* (Ph.D. diss., University of Chicago, 1961). For Soviet accounts of the Ukrainian Autocephalous church, see Vasyl Ellan (Blakytnyi), *Ukrainska Avtokefalna Tserkva i ii poperednyky* (The Ukrainian Autocephalous Church and Its Forerunners) (Kharkiv, V-vo-Tsk-KSMU, 1923); Ivan Sukhopliuiev, *Ukrainski avtokefalisty* (Ukrainian Autocephalists) (Kharkiv, "Chervonyi Shliakh," 1925); and Iu. Samoilovich, *Tserkov ukrainskogo sotsialfashizma* (The Church of the Ukrainian Social-Fascism) (Moscow, Gosud. Ateist. Izd., 1932). For a Russian-émigré view of the UAOC, see K. V. Fotiev, *Popytki ukrainskoi tserkovnoi avtokefalii v XX veke* (Attempts at the Ukrainian Church Autocephaly in the Twentieth Century) (Munich: N.p., 1955).

2. A concept borrowed from Donald Eugene Smith, *Religion and Political Development* (Boston: Little, Brown, 1970).

3. The maximum offered by the Moscow patriarchate in response to Ukrainian demands was a limited autonomy approved by Patriarch Tikhon in September 1918. For details, see Dmytro Doroshenko, *Istoriia Ukrainy 1917–1923 rr.* (History of the Ukraine, 1917–1923), Vol. 2 (Uzhhorod: O. Tsiupka, 1932), pp. 328–30.

4. The Law on the Supreme Authority in the Ukrainian Autocephalous Orthodox church of January 1, 1919.

5. The Soviet Ukrainian Decree on the Separation of the Church from the State and the School from the Church (adopted on January 22, 1919) significantly omitted the provision of the Russian decree denying religious associations the rights of a juridical person (added only in 1921). See Iv. Sukhopliuiev, *Vidokremlennia tserkvy vid derzhavy: Zbirnyk*

zakonopolozhen (The Separation of the Church from the State: A Collection of Legislative Enactments) (Kharkiv, Iurydychne vydavnytstvo Narkomiustu USRR, 1929). Ukrainian Autocephalists were the first ecclesiastical organization to recognize this decree in Ukraine.

6. "Vid Vseukrainskoi Provoslavnoi Tserkovnoi Rady do ukrainskoho pravoslavnoho hromadianstva: Lyst pershyi" (From the All-Ukrainian Orthodox Church Council to the Ukrainian Orthodox Public: The First Letter), May 5, 1920, reproduced in *Tserkva i zhyttia*, No. 1 (1927), pp. 120–23.

7. See Ivan Shram, "Iak tvorylas Ukrainska Avtokefalna Tserkva" (How the Ukrainian Autocephalous Church Was Created), *Na varti* (Volodymyr Volynskyi), Nos. 7–8 (May 1925), pp. 2–5.

8. During the summer and early fall of 1921, the All-Ukrainian Rada desperately searched for sympathetic bishops to consecrate two of its candidates for episcopal offices in UAOC. Hopes that the newly autocephalous Georgian Orthodox church would assist UAOC in this respect proved vain, given Soviet-Georgian hostilities.

9. See Volodymyr Chekhivskyi, *Za Tserkvu, Khrystovo hromadu, proty tsarstva tmy* (For the Church, for the Christian Community, Against the Kingdom of Darkness) (Kharkiv: Vyd. Tserkovnoi Rady I-oi parafii Ukr. Pravosl. Tserkvy Mykolaivskoho Soboru, 1922).

10. For a description of the ceremony by a participant, see V. Chekhivskyi, "Osnovy vyzvolennia Ukrainskoi Avtokefalnoi Pravoslavnoi Tserky" (Foundations of the Liberation of the Ukrainian Autocephalous Orthodox Church), *Tserkva i zhyttia*, Nos. 2–3 (1927), p. 189.

11. See Vlasovskyi, *Narys istorii*, Vol. 4, pp. 359–62.

12. In 1925 Archbishop Iosif (Krechetovich) of the Renovationist church spoke of three million Autocephalists. The former secretary of the Renovationist synod in the Ukraine, Archbishop Serafim (Ladde), estimated the Autocephalist following in 1929 at some six million. See "Proiskhozhdenie i sushchnost samosviatstva lipkovtsev" (The Origin and the Essence of the Self-Consecration of the Lipkovtsy) (1925), as cited in A. Richynskyi, *Problemy ukrainskoi relihiinoi svidomosty* (The Problems of the Ukrainian Religious Consciousness) (Volodymyr Volynskyi: by the author, , 1933), p. 6; and Serafim Ladde, "Die Lage der Orthodoxen Kirche in der Ukraine," *Eiche*, 10 (1931), No. 1, pp. 11–40.

13. In December 1923 Archbishop Teodorovych was sent by the all-Ukrainian Rada to assume leadership of a combined American-Canadian diocese of the Ukrainian Orthodox church.

14. See *Zhivaia tserkov* (Moscow), No. 3 (1922), pp. 19–20; *Golos Pravoslavnoi Ukrainy* (Kharkiv), No. 4 (1925), p. 4; Heyer, *Die Orthodoxe Kirche*, p. 95; and Lypkivskyi, *Istoriia Ukrainskoi*, pp. 120–24.

15. See Sukhopliuiev, *Ukrainski avtokefalisty*, pp. 47–56; Lypkivskyi, *Istoriia Ukrainskoi*, pp. 124–37; *Kommunist* (Kharkiv), October 24, 1925; and V. Potiienko, "Tserkovna sprava na Ukraini" (The Church Cause in the Ukraine), *Dnipro*, August 1, 1925, p. 1.

16. Lypkivskyi, *Istoriia Ukrainskoi*, pp. 144–66; and Vlasovskyi, *Narys istorii*, pp. 198–207.

17. On Boretskyi, see Vlasovskyi, *Narys istorii*, pp. 142–43.

18. *Izvestiia*, November 22, 1929, *Proletarska pravda* (Kiev), December 22, 1929.

19. See Lypkivskyi, *Istoriia Ukrainskoi*, pp. 169–72.

20. Dmytro Ihnatiuk, *Ukrainska avtokefalna tserkva i Soiuz Vyzvolennia Ukrainy* (The Ukrainian Autocephalous Church and the League for the Liberation of the Ukraine) (Kharkiv-Kiev: D.V.U., 1930), pp. 23–31.

21. *Visti VUTsVK* (Kharkiv), March 2, 1930; and *Pravda*, March 11 and 19, 1930.

22. Ibid.

23. Samoilovich, *Tserkov ukrainskogo sotsial-fashizma*, p. 123.

24. *Dnipro*, August 1, 1930.

25. Ibid., June 15, 1931.

26. Samoilovich, *Tserkov ukrainskogo sotsial-fashizma*, p. 123.

27. Lypkivskyi, *Istoriia Ukrainskoi*, p. 174.

28. Ibid.

29. *Dnipro*, January 15, 1934.

30. Cf. Demyd Burko, "Z knyhy buttia Ukrainskoi Tserky," (From the Book of Existence of the Ukrainian Church), *Ridna Tserkva*, 5 (1956), No. 21, p. 5.

31. Metropolitan Lypkivskyi's letter to Rev. P. Maievsky of June 5, 1933, in *Lysty Mytropolyta Vasylia Lypkivskoho do O. Petra Maievskoho . . . vid 1933 do 1937* (Letters from Metropolitan Vasyl Lypkivskyi to Fr. Petro Maievskyi . . . from 1933 to 1936) (Los Angeles: Rev. P. Maievskyi, 1953).

32. Letter of August 28, 1934, in ibid., p. 20.

33. Letter of December 14, 1934, in ibid., p. 14.

34. Letter of June 15, 1936, in ibid., p. 30.

35. One of the last Ukrainian parishes to be closed was that in Kharkiv. On January 23, 1936, its priest, Mykyta Kokhno, was tried in Kharkiv together with three other Autocephalist leaders. All defendants were sentenced to long terms in exile. See M. Iavdas, *Ukrainian Autocephalous Orthodox Church* (Munich-Ingolstadt: Kraieva Rada U.A.P.TS., 1956), p. 9.

36. Speaking at the All-Union conference convoked by the central council of the League of the Militant Godless on April 22, 1939, the representative of the league's Ukrainian organization, G. Motuzko, declared that "the Autocephalous church nevertheless continues to exist up to the present time. We cannot say that this is a mass phenomenon, but the Ukrainian autocephalist priests do exist and there are not a few churches where mass is being celebrated largely in Ukrainian. Not a few Ukrainian churches, where masses were previously celebrated in the Ukrainian language, have now adopted [Church] Slavonic and joined the Synodical or the Tikhonite church; but this is only the external camouflage for the Petliurite clergy." G. Motuzko, "O religioznykh organizatsiiakh," *Antireligioznik*, No. 5 (1939), p. 21.

37. Until 1930, the metropolitan worked on a history of the Ukrainian Orthodox church, the manuscript of which was saved from the police by his sister. Only chapter 7 of the work, dealing with the Ukrainian autocephalist movement and the UAOC from 1917 to 1930, has reached Ukrainians abroad, and it was first published in 1959. Between 1933 and 1937 the metropolitan was engaged in correspondence with Father P. Maievskyi of the Ukrainian Orthodox church in Canada, to whom he had sent in 1934 a series of sermons that appeared (in mimeographed form) in Winnipeg, 1934–35, under the title, "Slovo Khrystove do Ukrainskoho Narodu: Propovidi na nedili i sviata tsiloho roku" (Christ's Word to the Ukrainian People: Sermons for Sundays and Feasts of the Entire Year).

38. *Materialy do Pateryka Ukrainskoi Avtokefalnoi Pravoslavnoi Tserkvy* (Materials on the Fathers of the Ukrainian Autocephalous Orthodox church) (Munich: N.p., 1951), pp. 22–23.

39. See Vlasovskyi, *Narys istorii*, Vol. 4, Pt. 2 (1966), pp. 120–21. On Metropolitan Polikarp Sikorsky, see his obituary in *Ukrainske Pravoslavne Slovo*, 3, No. 11 (November 1953), p. 2.

40. Vlasovskyi, *Narys istorii*, Vol. 4, Pt. 2, pp. 197–99.

41. Ibid., pp. 214–15.

42. Fotiev, *Popytki ukrainskoi*, p. 58.

43. See Bohdan R. Bociurkiw, "Ukrainianization Movements within the Russian Ortho-

dox Church, and the Ukrainian Autocephalous Orthodox Church," *Harvard Ukrainian Studies*, 2/4 (1979–80), pp. 101–10.

44. See Bohdan R. Bociurkiw, "The Orthodox Church in Ukraine since 1917," in V. Kubijovyc (ed.), *Ukraine: A Concise Encyclopaedia* (Toronto: University of Toronto Press, 1971), Vol. 2, p. 175.

45. Ibid., p. 176.

46. On the postwar church abroad, see Vlasovskyi, *Narys istorii*, Vol. 4, Pt. 2, pp. 271–375; and A. Zhukovskyi, "Ukrainska Pravoslavna Tserkva," in V. Kubijovyc (ed.), *Entsyklopediia Ukrainoznavstva, Slovnykova Chastyna* (Encyclopedic Dictionary of Ukrainian Studies), Vol. 19 (Munich: "Molode zhyttia," 1980), pp. 3381–83.

17 Minor Orthodox Churches of Eastern Europe

1. Also referred to as the Lemkos or the Lemko clan, the Lemkians are a predominantly peasant community who speak a Ukrainian dialect. Historically they inhabited the western fringes of ethnic Ukrainian territory, the remote Bieszczady mountain region. Before the mid-1800s they had little sense of a common identity. During the twentieth century some Lemkians have viewed themselves as a nationality separate from the Ukrainians. During the 1930s and again during the 1980s Polish officials have treated the Lemkians as a separate nationality in order to undermine the unity of the Ukrainian minority.

2. Among the most prominent opponents of autocephaly were Archbishop Eleutherius of Wilno (Vilnius) and Archbishop Panteleimon of Nowogrodek.

3. Friedrich Heyer, *Die Orthodoxe Kirche in der Ukraine von 1917 bis 1945* (Cologne-Braunsfeld: R. Müller, 1953), p. 137.

4. The Polish Research Centre, *The Orthodox Eastern Church in Poland: Past and Present* (London: Polish Research Centre, 1942), p. 34.

5. Aleksandr Svitich, *Pravoslavie v Pol'she* (Buenos Aires: N.p., 1957).

6. For a thorough examination of the legal dimension of church-state relations during the interwar period, see Jakub Sawicki, *Studia nad polozeniem mniejszosci religijnych w panstwie polskim* (Warsaw: Wydawnictwo Kasy im. Mianowskiego, 1937).

7. Polish Research Centre, *The Orthodox Eastern Church*, pp. 38–39.

8. Ibid., pp. 39–40.

9. *Natio/Pismo* (Warsaw, March/April 1927), p. 137.

10. Heyer, *Die Orthodoxe Kirche*, p. 161.

11. See Svitich, *Pravoslavie*, pp. 116–21, for a sustained criticism of Metropolitan Dionizy's and the Polish government's alleged attempts to polonize the Orthodox church.

12. For background information, see Edmund Przekop, "Die 'Neo-Union' in Polen in den Jahren, 1923–1939," *Ostkirchliche Studien*, 32, No. 1 (March 1983), pp. 3–20; "Chronicle of Events," *Eastern Churches Quarterly*, 3, No. 4 (October 1938), pp. 245–51; Federation des émigrés Ukrainiens en Europe, *L'Union des églises et les persecutions polonaises en Ukraine* (Brussels: N.p., 1939); Svitich, *Pravoslavie*, pp. 118–40; and Polish Research Centre, *The Orthodox Eastern Church*, pp. 43–46.

13. Wladyslaw Malinowski, *Najnowsza historiia polityczna Polski 1864–1945*, Rev. ed. (London: B. Swiderski, 1967), Vol. 2, pp. 827–29.

14. For postwar statistics on the church's losses, see Jan Anchimiuk, "Die polnische autokephale orthodoxe Kirche," in Jurgen Moltmann and Martin Stöhr (eds.), *Begegnung mit Polen: Evangelische Kirche und die Herausforderung durch Geschichte und Politik* (Munich:

Kaiser, 1974), pp. 112–13; and Marek Henzler, "Modlitwa zakleta w malowanym drewnie: Prawoslawie w Polsce," in *Polytika* (Warsaw), June 30, 1984, p. 4.

15. *New York Times*, June 11, 1948.

16. Ibid.

17. Metropolitan Bazyli, as quoted in *Przeglad Tygodniowy* (Warsaw), March 4, 1984, pp. 3–4.

18. Ibid.; and as quoted in *Episkepsis* (Geneva), 15, No. 321 (September 15, 1984), p. 3.

19. Metropolitan Bazyli, as quoted in *Przeglad Tygodniowy*, March 4, 1984, pp. 3–4.

20. For background information, see *Mensuel Service Orthodoxe de Presse* (Courveboie, France), 84 (January 1984), p. 5.

21. *Christian Social Association Information Bulletin*, No. 12 (December 1982), pp. 12, 17.

22. Ibid., No. 2 (February 1983), p. 14.

23. Ibid.

24. Feriz Berki, *Az orthodox Keresztenyseg* (Budapest: Magyar Orthodox Adminisztratura, 1975), p. 137. Two other recent publications that deal with the history of Eastern Christianity in Hungary are Imre Timko, *Keleti Keresztenyseg keleti egyhazak* (Budapest: Szent Istvan Tarsulat, 1971), and Istvan Pirigyi, *A gorogkatolikus magyarsag tortenete* (Nyiregyhaza: Gorogkatolikus Hittudomanyi Foiskola, 1982). The latter contains an extensive bibliography.

25. Paragraph 9 of Act IX of 1868, as quoted in Berki, *Az orthodox*, p. 138.

26. In Hungarian it would read "gorog gorogkeleti," i.e., Greek Greek-Oriental.

27. Berki, *Az orthodox*, p. 138.

28. The territory of Hungary before 1918 covered 325,411 square kilometers, while its population numbered 20,886,487. The Treaty of Trianon (1920) reduced these figures to 93,073 square kilometers and 7,990,202 people. One square kilometer equals 0.386 square miles.

29. See *Annuaire Statistique Hongrois*, Vol. 22 (Budapest, 1916), p. 20; and *Magyar Statisztikai Szemle*, Vol. 16, Pt. 1 (Budapest: N.p., 1938), p. 382.

30. Andor Csizmadia, *A Magyar allam es az egyhazak jogi kapcsolatainak kialakulasa es gyakorlata a Horthy-korszakban* (Budapest: Akademiai Kiado, 1966), p. 142.

31. With the integration of the Serbs of southern Hungary into the newly formed kingdom of Serbs, Croats, and Slovenes, later renamed Yugoslavia, the autocephaly of the metropolitanate of Karloca (Karlovci), under whose jurisdiction the bishopric of Buda belonged, was transferred to the Serbian national church, the patriarch of Belgrade assuming also the title of patriarch of Peć and metropolitan of Karlovci. The small town of Karlovci retained its significance for Orthodoxy only because it became the home of the synod of the Russian émigré bishops who claimed to be the true representatives of the Russian Orthodox church that had fallen under Bolshevik rule.

32. Actually, the Romanian parishes of Trianon Hungary continued to maintain their canonical ties with their former bishoprics, which were now across the border in Romania. See Berki, *Az orthodox*, pp. 141, 145.

33. Author's interview with Archpriest Feriz Berki, dean-administrator of the Hungarian Orthodox deanery, in Budapest, June 30, 1983.

34. Admittedly, in the case of the majority of these parishes the decision was made under political pressure; in others, that is, in communities thoroughly Magyarized where only a few understood Romanian, the desire was most likely genuine. See Berki, *Az orthodox*, pp. 145–46.

35. These included the territories ceded by Czechoslovakia in 1938 and Romania in 1940 in the First and Second Vienna Awards, as well as Ruthenia, a part of Czechoslovakia until 1939, and the Bacska-Baranya region to the south, held previously, as now, by Yugoslavia, which were occupied by military force and reannexed to Hungary in 1939 and 1941, respectively. The area of Hungary in 1941 covered 171,640 square kilometers, with a population of 14,683,323.

36. In round numbers there were 561,000 Orthodox, 3.8 percent of the population. See *Az 1941, evi Nepszamlalas* (Budapest: A Magyar Közpouti Statisztikai Hivatal, 1947), p. 20.

37. The new borders also created some problems for them. There was the case, for example, of the Serbian bishop of Bacs, Irinej Ćirić, who took his seat in the upper house of the Budapest parliament, as was his due. For this he was treated as a "collaborator with the enemy" in postwar Yugoslavia and put under house arrest in his residence in Novi Sad.

38. Berki, *Az orthodox*, pp. 148–49. Today the Hungarian Orthodox clergy receives its training at the Leningrad Theological Academy.

39. Since the episcopal residence in Buda was destroyed during the fierce fighting around it during the siege of Budapest, the diocese is administered today from Szentendre, a picturesque Serbian town north of Budapest, today the Mecca of Hungarian art and artists.

40. Outside intervention in the form of political pressure again played a role. See Berki, *Az orthodox*, pp. 149–50.

41. The vicar-administrator for the Hungarian Orthodox appointed by Regent Horthy in 1944, Dean Janos Olah, continued in his office until 1947, but then abdicated and returned to his previous post within the Romanian Orthodox community in Hungary.

42. Quoted in Berki, *Az orthodox*, p. 152.

43. This is the explanation found in Berki, *Az orthodox*, pp. 154–57, which can be regarded as the "official line." The hypothesis that follows is mine.

44. Berki, *Az orthodox*, p. 156. It is amusing to read in the documents how the Hungarian Orthodox in their long struggle for emancipation tried to buttress their desire to use the vernacular by pointing to the dangers of defections by their flock to the Uniates, who had conducted their services, in some places, in Hungarian, and to find that the same argument was used in the opposite direction by the Uniates in their own fight with Rome for the vernacular. The latter never tired of depicting the impending mass defections from Catholicism to Orthodoxy in the darkest colors, since, in their perception, the Orthodox were far ahead in Magyarizing their services. The truth is that in both cases the de facto use of Hungarian antedated by many years the official legalization. That was achieved in the case of the Orthodox, as we have seen, in 1949, while for the Uniates the long-sought relief came through the Second Vatican Council, 1962–65, with its blanket authorization of the vernacular everywhere in the Roman Catholic church, both in the Western and in the Eastern rite.

45. Two of these are "filiale," i.e., small communities without their own priests, affiliated to full parishes.

46. In 1927 the Committee of the Union of Macedonian Political Organizations addressed an open letter to Bishop Nikolaj Velimirović of Ohrid, demanding that he resign his see. See *La Macédoine*, organ of IMRO (Geneva), September 1, 1927, p. 5.

47. Due to the very conciliatory (in fact, pro-Yugoslav) feelings of Exarch Stefan himself. See Djoko Slijepčević, *Pitanje Makedonske pravoslavne crkve u Jugoslaviji* (Munich: Iskra, 1959), p. 26.

48. Stella Alexander, *Church and State in Yugoslavia since 1945* (Cambridge: Cambridge University Press, 1979), p. 186; Slijepčević, *Pitanje Makedonske*, pp. 243–44; and Evangelos

Kofos, *Nationalism and Communism in Macedonia* (Salonika: Institute for Balkan Studies, 1964), p. 137.

49. Alexander, *Church and State*, p. 261.

50. Done Ilievski, *The Macedonian Orthodox Church: The Road to Independence*, trans. James M. Leech (Skopje: Macedonian Review Editions, 1973), pp. 105–11.

51. As suggested by Alexander, *Church and State*, pp. 268, 281–82. The Macedonian leader Krste Crvenkovski certainly stated that the issue would have been settled a long time before had it not been for Ranković. See *Politika* (Belgrade), November 29, 1967, p. 5.

52. The latest available estimation of faithful seems to go back to 1970: 0.6 to 1 million, according to figures provided by the church. At that time the number of priests was given as 250 (versus 334 in 1967). There were 240 priests listed as of 1981, and 250 (along with fifteen monks) in 1983. Ivan Ceranić, "Konfesionalne zajednice u SPR Jugoslaviji," in Zlatko Frid (ed.), *Vierske zajednice u Jugoslaviji* (Zagreb: NIP "Binoza," 1970), pp. 7–44; *Intervju* (Belgrade), November 25, 1983, p. 5; and *Nova Makedonija*, August 22, 1981, p. 3.

53. "Patriarch of Belgrade and the whole Kingdom of the Serbs, Croats, and Slovenes" in the 1922 ratification of the unification procedure; "Patriarch of Belgrade and all Yugoslavia" in the late 1960s after the Macedonian schism. See Rajko Veselinov, "Ujedinjenje pokrajinskih crkava i vaspostavljanje srpske patrijarsije," in *Srpske Pravoslavna Crkva 1920–1970: Spomenica o 50-godišnjici vaspostavljanja Srpske Patrijaršije* (Belgrade: Kosmos, 1971), p. 32; and Stevan K. Pavlowitch, "The Orthodox Church in Yugoslavia, I: The Problem of the Macedonian Church," in *Eastern Churches Review*, 1, No. 4 (1967), p. 383.

54. *Nova Makedonija*, October 10, 1981, p. 5, and July 17, 1982, p. 5; and *NIN*, No. 1637 (May 16, 1982), pp. 17–19.

55. "Votum of the Metropolitan of the Autocephalous Orthodox Church in the Polish People's Republic," in *The Polish Ecumenical Review* (Warsaw), Nos. 1–2 (1966), p. 20.

56. For example, Polish Metropolitan Bazyli was awarded the Order of Chevalier of Poland's Renewal. See *Tserkovnyi vestnik*, (November 1979), p. 13.

18   The Armenian Apostolic Church

1. The principal sources for this chapter were "Hayastani Yekeghetsi," in *Soviet-Armenian Encyclopedia* (Erevan: RSSA Academy of Sciences), Vol. 6 (1980), pp. 153–54; Malachia Ormanian, *L'Eglise arménienne* (Antilias: Imprimerie du Catholicossat, 1954); Jean Mecerian, *Histoire et institutions de l'Eglise arménienne* (Beirut: Imprimerie catholique, 1965); Bedros Kassadijian (Pere), *L'Eglise apostolique arménienne et sa doctrine* (Paris: Vrin, 1943); Bishop Karekin Sarkissian, *The Armenian Church in Contemporary Times* (New York: Armenian Apostolic Church of America, 1970); Jirair Missakian, "The Church of Armenia," *Armenian Review*, 1, No. 2 (Summer 1953), pp. 65–69; James Tashjian, "Aspects of Armenian Church History," *Armenian Review*, 10, No. 6 (Winter 1957), pp. 28–40; Anahide Ter-Minassian, *Nation et Religion* (Milan: ICOM, 1980); Anahide Ter-Minassian, "L'Eglise arménienne," *Etudes* (June 1980), pp. 809–24; and *Notes et Etudes* [hereinafter, NED], No. 2239 (Paris: La Documentation Française, December 8, 1956).

2. The Dashnaks are the members of the Armenian Revolutionary Federation, created in Tiflis in 1890, with the goal of uniting all the Armenian parties in the liberation movement. This party first advocated the self-defense of the Armenian people by means of the organization of groups of guerrilla fighters. The Dashnaks were influenced by the Bulgarian haiduk model, the Garibaldi movement, Russian populism, and a type of Jauressian socialism. It became a member of the Second International in 1907 and was the moving

force behind the movement toward national emancipation. Because of its predominance, it naturally came to power after independence in 1918. See Anahide Ter-Minassian, "Le mouvement révolutionnaire arménienne," *Cahiers du monde Russe et Soviétique*, 14, No. 4 (October–December 1973), pp. 506–73; Louisa Nalbandian, *The Armenian Revolutionary Movement* (Berkeley and Los Angeles: University of California Press, 1963); and Richard Hovannisian, *Armenia on the Road to Independence* (Berkeley and Los Angeles: University of California Press, 1967), and *The Republic of Armenia*, Vols. 1–2 (Berkeley and Los Angeles: University of California Press, 1970, 1982).

3. The movement was begun by Bishop Benik Malian and some ecclesiastics, often unfrocked and even excommunicated. Thanks to the protection of the authorities, some bishops of the "Free Church" were named to dioceses of the diaspora, notably in Iraq and Greece. See George Agabekov, *OGPU* (New York: Brentano's, 1931).

4. See M. Herardian, "Interrelations of Echmiadzin and Cilician Patriarchal Sees," *Armenian Review*, 9, No. 2 (Summer 1956), pp. 16–32.

5. The Armenian General Benevolent Union, a philanthropic and cultural organization with roots in the Armenian liberal middle class, has considerable financial resources and is pro-Soviet. Its headquarters are in New York.

6. Gabriel Lazian, *Hayastane ev Hay Tad* (Armenia and the Armenian Cause) (Cairo: Husaper, 1957), pp. 382–84; and Nicolas Struve, *Les chrétiens en URSS* (Paris: Seuil, 1963), p. 90.

7. *Echmiadzin* (October–November 1948, and March–April 1949), cited in Lazian, *Hayastane*, pp. 380–81.

8. Reuben Darbinian, "Soviet Efforts to Control the Church Abroad," *Armenian Review*, 9, No. 2 (Summer 1956), pp. 3–15.

9. See the editorial in *Echmiadzin* (October 1953) and the protests of the Dashnak press. Translations of many of the latter can be found in NED, No. 2239, pp. 8–10.

10. *Izvestiya*, May 12, 1954, translated in *Current Digest of the Soviet Press* (CDSP), 6, No. 19 (June 23, 1954), p. 36.

11. *Aztak* (Beirut), June 1954, translated in NED, No. 2239.

12. The Ramkavar-azadakan (Constitutional-Liberal) party, established in Constantinople in 1908, had as its first goal the defense of the Armenian national constitution, controlling the Armenian millet of the Ottoman Empire. This upper-middle-class party, somewhat akin to the Russian Kadets, was in favor of liberalism and individual initiative; although not very large in numbers, it had considerable financial resources and often invested in philanthropic or cultural activities, such as the AGBU. It was close to the church and resigned itself to the loss of independence and made its sole aim the conservation of Armenian culture, leading it to defend Soviet Armenia.

The Hunchak party was founded in Geneva in 1887 by students close to Georgi Plekhanov and was an avowedly Marxist party, declaring its aim as the liberation of Turkish Armenia, independence, and socialism. It was weakened by successive internal divisions, and one of its branches became communist.

13. See the articles in the Armenian press, of different tendencies, translated in NED, No. 2239, p. 14.

14. NED, No. 2239, p. 20.

15. Bishop Dérénik Poladian, *Yerkir Haireni* (Fatherland) (Antilias: Imprimerie du Catholicossat, 1956), p. 64.

16. Some 1,600 according to Vahe Sarafian, "The Soviet and the Armenian Church,"

Armenian Review, 1, No. 3 (Summer 1955), pp. 83–107; 1,449 according to Struve, *Les chrétiens*, pp. 224–26; and 1,429 according to Ormanian, *L'Eglise arménienne*, pp. 187–89.

17. Fifty, according to Sarafian, "The Soviet," p. 99; eighty-nine according to Struve, *Les chrétiens*, p. 225; and about one hundred according to NED, No. 2239, p. 7.

18. Sarafian, "The Soviet," pp. 107–23.

19. NED, No. 2239.

20. *Aztak* (Beirut), February 17, 1956, trans in NED, No. 2239, p. 26.

21. *Zartonk* (Beirut), February 15, 1956, trans. in NED, No. 2239, pp. 26–27.

22. *Zartonk*, February 17, 1956, trans. in NED, No. 2239, pp. 26–27.

23. The Council of Bishops is an innovation brought in by Kevork VI, without the National Council of the Armenian Apostolic church having pronounced on this subject. On this point, see NED, No. 2239, p. 28; and A. Khonkarian, "The Legality of the Cairo Episcopal Assembly," *Armenian Review*, 10, No. 4 (Winter 1957), pp. 17–27.

24. Khonkarian, "The Legality," pp. 18–19; and NED, No. 2239, p. 29.

25. See Reuben Darbinian, "Political Sophistries of an Armenian Clergyman," *Armenian Review*, 9, No. 3 (Autumn 1956), pp. 27–33. This accusation should, of course, be placed in the context of the cold war and the crisis of the Armenian church but can be understood by examining some aspects of the unusually rapid career of Vazken I.

26. A. Aramian, "Visits of Vazken 1st, Catholicos of All Armenians to the 'Eparchies' of Leninakan and Rostov," in *Caucasian Review*, No. 5 (1957), pp. 133-35.

27. S. Kocharian, "Religion and Communism," *Caucasian Review*, No. 2 (1956), pp. 64–73.

28. See the article "Kidelik" in the *Soviet Armenian Encyclopedia* (Erevan, RSSA Academy of Sciences), Vol. 3 (1977), p. 80.

29. *Partiagan Giank* (Party Life), No. 11 (1956), quoted in "Chronicle of Events," *Caucasian Review*, No. 4 (1957), pp. 142–43.

30. See Vahakn N. Dadrian, "Nationalism in Soviet Armenia: A Case Study of Ethnocentrism," in George W. Simmonds (ed.), *Nationalism in the USSR and Eastern Europe in the Era of Brezhnev and Kosygin* (Detroit: University of Detroit Press, 1977), pp. 205–59.

31. Jean Fournier, "L'Eglise arménienne au hasard des rencontres," *France-URSS* (November 1978).

32. In his commentary on Eduard Oganessayan, "The Armenian Church in the USSR," *Religion in Communist Lands*, 7, No. 4 (Winter 1979), pp. 242–43.

33. On the problem of the Armenian Catholic church in the USSR, see Father I. H. Dalmais, "La longue marche des Arméniens," *Informations Catholiques Internationales*, No. 356 (March 15, 1970).

34. Gerard Stephanesco, "L'Eglise arménienne vivante: Un entretien exclusif avec S. S. Vazken Ier," *Revue des deux mondes* (March 1972), pp. 582–90.

35. Ter-Minassian, *Nation and Religion*, p. 7.

36. Fournier, "L'Eglise arménienne."

37. Dalmais, "La longue marche," p. 28.

38. When moving to the West, Armenian from the Middle East often refuse to change jurisdiction, even when they settle in communities subordinate to Echmiadzin, and thus create schismatic parishes tied to Antilias.

39. The Occidental dialect is used by Armenians from Turkey, i.e., by Armenians of the diaspora of 1915. The Oriental dialect is associated with the Armenians of the Caucasus and Iran.

40. On the question of languages, see Frédéric Feydit, "La langue," in Gerard Dedeyan (ed.), *Histoire des Arméniens* (Toulouse: Privat, 1982).

41. *Haratch* (Forward) Paris, October 20–21, 1979; and Ter-Minassian, "L'Eglise arménienne," p. 817.

42. *Hayastan* (Paris), May 1979), pp. 9–10.

43. See Claire Mouradian, "Problèmes linguistiques et culturels en Arménie depuis Staline: Résistance nationale ou intégration soviétique?" *Slovo*, No. 5 (1984), pp. 111–38.

44. *Haratch*, November 25–26, 1984.

19   The Ethiopian Orthodox Church

1. Taddesse Tamrat, *Church and State in Ethiopia* (Oxford: Clarendon Press, 1972), p. 23.

2. P. Gilkes, *The Dying Lion: Feudalism and Modernization in Ethiopia* (London: Julian Friedman, 1975), p. 57.

3. Jean Baptiste Coulbeaux, *Histoire politique et réligieuse de l'Abyssinie* (Paris: Geuthner, 1929), Vol. 1, pp. 72–73.

4. E. A. W. Budge, *The Queen of Sheba and Her Only Son Menelik I* (Oxford: Oxford University Press, 1932) is a translation of Kebra Nagast. According to its translator, the book is a compilation of Old Testament, rabbinical, Christian, and Arabic literature and legend. The Geez writer Yeshaq, *nebura ed* of Axum, from a text compiled much earlier (probably by an Egyptian priest), transformed it into a national saga of the highland kingdom.

5. E. Ullendorff, *The Ethiopians* (Oxford: Oxford University Press, 1973), p. 91.

6. Adrian Hastings, *A History of African Christianity, 1950–1975* (Cambridge: Cambridge University Press, 1979), p. 36.

7. J. Perruchon, "Histoire des guerres d'Amda Seyon, roi d'Ethiopie," *Journal Asiatique*, Ser. 8, Vol. 14 (1889), pp. 281, 287, 304; and *Corpus Scriptorum Christiannum Orientalium* (csco), Series Aethiopica, Vol. 3, p. 41.

8. M. Perham, *The Government of Ethiopia* (London: Faber and Faber, 1969), p. 70; and R. Greenfield, *Ethiopia: A New Political History* (London: Pall Mall Press, 1965), p. 168.

9. *Negarit Gazeta* (November 4, 1955), Article 21; Mahteme Sellassie Walde Meskel, *Zikre Nagar* (Addis Ababa: Freedom Press, 1942), pp. 525–27; and Asfa Yilma, *Haile Selassie, Emperor of Ethiopia* (London: Sampson, Law, Martson, 1935), p. 223.

10. Fetha Nagast is a free translation, with adaptation, of an Egyptian Coptic text into Geez around the fifteenth century. See "Fetha Nagast" (Law of Kings), trans. Paulos Tzadwa (Addis Ababa: Haile Selassie I University School of Law, mimeographed).

11. For the complete text, see Greenfield, *Ethiopia*, pp. 410–11.

12. Negaso Gidada and D. Crummey, "Introduction and Expansion of the Orthodox Church in Qalam Province, Western Wollega, 1886–1947," *Journal of Ethiopian Studies* (January 1972), p. 165; and A. Orent, *Lineage Structure and the Supernatural: The Kaffa of South West Ethiopia* (Ph.D. diss., Boston University, 1969), p. 192.

13. A. Pollera, *Lo stato Etiopico e la sua Chiesa* (Rome: SEAI, 1926), pp. 210–11.

14. Berhanou Abebe, *Evolution de la propriete fonciere au Choa (Ethiopie) du Regne de Menelik a la Constitution de 1931* (Paris: Librairie Orientaliste-Paul Beutthner, 1971), pp. 136, 140, 150.

15. G. Villari, "I 'Gulti' della regione di Axum," *Rassegna delle colonie*, 26, No. 9 (1938), pp. 1430–44; and J. Markakis, *Ethiopia: Anatomy of a Traditional Polity* (Oxford: Clarendon Press, 1974), p. 95.

16. Markakis, *Ethiopia*, p. 98. The most famous is that of the Emperor Tewodros (1855–68). See C. E. Shenk, *The Development of the Ethiopian Orthodox Church and Its Relationship with the Ethiopian Government from 1930 to 1970* (Ph.D. diss., New York University, 1972), pp. 45–48. For additional cases, see Pollera, *Lo stato Etiopico*, pp. 222–23.

17. Pollera, *Lo stato Etiopico*, pp. 189, 208; and Haile Gabriel Dagne, "The Gebezena Charter, 1894," *Journal of Ethiopian Studies* (1972), No. 2, p. 80.

18. Perham, *The Government*, p. 123. For a general view of this period, see Mikre Sellassie Gabre Ammanuel, *Church and Missions in Ethiopia in Relation to the Italian War and Occupation and the Second World War* (Ph.D. diss., University of Aberdeen, 1976).

19. A. F. Mathewos, "The Church of Ethiopia during the Italian Occupation" (mimeographed, 1943), p. 1; see also J. S. Trimingham, *The Christian Church and Missions in Ethiopia* (London: World Domination Press, 1950), p. 19.

20. See *Ethiopian Herald*, December 3, 1945.

21. On the whole controversy over autocephaly, see Adugna Amanu, *The Ethiopian Orthodox Church Becomes Autocephalous* (B.A. thesis, Haile Selassie I University, 1969); and Perham, *The Government*, pp. 126–30.

22. *Ethiopian Herald*, July 1, 1946.

23. G. Lipsky, *Ethiopia: Its People, Its Society, Its Culture* (New Haven, Conn.: Hraff Press, 1962), p. 108.

24. "Anglican Minister Urges Reforms for Orthodox Church," in *USA National Archives, Church and Religious Affairs—Ethiopia* (hereinafter, USA-CRAE), File No. 984.404 (June 6, 1967), p. 2; and "The EOC Looks Forward," in USA-CRAE (January 25, 1973), p. 4.

25. The radio program broadcast on the Radio Voice of the Gospel (operated by the Lutheran World Federation) was considered to be of high quality, and the magazine *Demsa-Tawahedo* included articles of great relevance to modern man, but its circulation, like all other publications with the exception of the police force publication, did not go beyond the city limits of Addis Ababa. There are two other publications, one irregular, *Tensae* (Revival), and the other annual, *Yasetoch Edgat* (Girls' Growth). These activities are all run by the Ethiopian Orthodox church mission established in 1963, whose patron was the emperor; Habte Mariam was chairman. For further details, see Shenk, *The Development*, pp. 282–85.

26. H. J. Schultz, "Reform and Reaction in the EOC," *The Christian Century*, 85, No. 5 (January 31, 1968), p. 143.

27. *Ethiopian Herald*, April 14–16, 1971.

28. Addis Hiwet, *Ethiopia: From Autocracy to Revolution*, (London: London Review of African Political Economy, 1975), Vol. 1, p. 69; and Fisseha Tekeste, *The Role of the Orthodox Church in the Political System of Ethiopia* (B.A. thesis, Haile Selassie I University, 1973), p. 59.

29. *Ethiopian Herald*, April 21, 1974.

30. Addressing the closing session of an eight-day seminar for Ethiopian Orthodox church leaders from Addis Ababa, Major Atnfu Abate, second vice-chairman of the Provisional Military Administrative Council, the Derg, made this point clear when he stated that "all Ethiopians must forget religious differences and work hard for the unity, independence, and progress of the country." He used the occasion to emphasize his conviction, reportedly basing it on the speeches of some speakers, that socialism is supported by both the Bible and the Koran, and strongly refuting the contrary view as reactionary and the product of either bigotry or fanaticism. See *Ethiopian Herald*, March 21, 1975.

31. The demands set forth in August were very moderate in both tone and expectation regarding the church's role in national affairs, compared to those of May 1974. In May the

church asked to be represented in almost all government departments and public institutions, saying that the top positions in these offices should be given to its adherents. The demands of August were limited essentially to a request that the draft constitution should include rules for the election of the patriarch and for assignment to the church of the administration and protection of the religious places, the rights to the coronation ceremony, and the maintenance of the church's status as the official religion. See *Ethiopian Herald*, August 18, 1974.

32. *Ethiopian Herald*, November 7 and 13, 1974; F. Göricke and F. Heyer, "The Orthodox Church of Ethiopia as a Social Institution," in *International Yearbook for Sociology of Knowledge and Religion* (1976), Vol. 10, pp. 186, 197; and for the earlier period, see Adugna Amanu, *The Ethiopian Orthodox Church*, pp. 57–58; and USA-CRAE, April 26 and June 4, 1971.

33. In Addis Ababa alone, fifteen church institutions owned rental buildings with a revenue of 976,322 birr a year. The highest top three earners were the patriarchate (318,768 birr), Trinity Cathedral (215,340 birr), and Ba'ata *gadam* (200,000 birr). *Ya-Zareytu Etiopia* (Maskaram 25, 1967), p. 7. With regard to land ownership in Addis Ababa, see *Addis Zaman* (Hamle 19, 1967), pp. 8–9; and R. Pankhurst, *State and Land in Ethiopian History* (Addis Ababa: Haile Selassie I University, 1966), p. 154.

34. The committee's declared objective was to eradicate corruption from the church and study the implications of nationalization on the church's life. As all links with the church had been severed, the creation of an "ad hoc" committee was a means of reestablishing such a link.

35. On the full report of these allegations, see *Ethiopian Herald*, February 19, 1976. Nobody knows his fate. Generally, he is assumed dead. See A. Horses, "La Chiesa Orthodossa d'Etiopia: A piedi scalzi," *Nigrizia*, 96, No. 1 (January 1, 1978), pp. 38–39.

36. *New Africa*, No. 143 (London, July 1979), p. 32.

37. Ibid.; *The Times* (London), November 15, 1984; and *The Observer* (London), November 18, 1984. This document is reprinted in *Religion in Communist-Dominated Areas*, 20 (1981), Nos. 7–9, pp. 108–11.

Index

Contributors

Oxana Antić is a researcher at the Russian Service, Radio Liberty, Munich, and vice-chair of the Association to Promote Independent Culture from the Soviet Union (GFUK). In addition to her regular contributions to *Radio Liberty Research*, her articles have appeared in *The Orthodox Monitor*, *Der Literat*, *Russia Cristiana*, and other journals.

Bohdan R. Bociurkiw is a professor of political science at Carleton University, Ottawa, Canada. He is the author of *Ukrainian Churches under Soviet Rule* (1984) and *Historische Perspektive der Sowjetischen Religionspolitik in der Ukraine* (1986) and coeditor (with John W. Strong) of *Religion and Atheism in the USSR and Eastern Europe* (1975). He has contributed chapters to *Lenin* (1967), *The Ukraine, 1917–1921* (1977), *Religion and Marxism in the USSR and Eastern Europe* (1975), and other books. His articles have appeared in *Kirche im Osten, Problems of Communism, Harvard Ukrainian Studies*, and other journals. He was president of the Canadian Association of Slavists 1962–63 and a Fellow of the Kennan Institute for Advanced Russian Studies, 1984–85.

Jane Ellis is a senior researcher at Keston College, Keston, England, and former editor (1981–86) of *Religion in Communist Lands*, to which she has contributed several articles. She is the author of *The Russian Orthodox Church: A Contemporary History* (1986) and editor of *Religious Minorities in the Soviet Union* (4th ed., 1984). She has also translated three books from Russian: *An Early Soviet Saint: The Life of Father Zachariah* (1976), *Letters from Moscow*, by Father Gleb Yakunin and Lev Regelson

(1978), and *Three Generations of Suffering*, by Georgi Vins (1979), and has contributed chapters to *Religious Liberty in the Soviet Union* (1976) and *Candle in the Wind* (forthcoming).

Suzanne Gwen Hruby is a research analyst for Foreign Broadcast Information Service, Washington D.C., and a member of the executive board of *Religion in Communist-Dominated Areas*.

Haile Mariam Larebo is completing his doctoral research on African history at the University of London. His articles have appeared in *Oriente Cristiano* and *Religion in Communist Lands*.

Leslie Laszlo is associate professor of political science at Concordia University. He is the author of *Resistance of the Spirit: The Churches in Hungary during the Second World War* (in Hungarian, 1980) and has contributed chapters to *Religion and Atheism in the USSR and Eastern Europe* (1975) and *Religion and Nationalism in Soviet and East European Politics* (1984). His articles have appeared in *East European Quarterly, Occasional Papers on Religion in Eastern Europe, Canadian Slavonic Papers*, and other journals.

Michael A. Meerson is rector of Christ the Savior Orthodox Church, New York, and a visiting professor of religion in the School of Sacred Arts, New York. In 1985 he was adjunct professor of Russian history, Hunter College. He has been a free-lance writer and broadcaster for Radio Liberty since 1976 and edits the Orthodox almanac *Puit* (in Russian). He is also the author of *Pravoslavie i Svoboda* (1986), editor of *Nikolai Berdiav* (Moscow, samizdat, 1970), *Two Covenants* (Moscow, samizdat, 1972), and *Georgii Fedotov: Rossia i Svoboda* (1981), and coeditor of *Political, Social and Religious Thought of Russian Samizdat* (1977). His articles have appeared in *Vestnik RChD, L'Etudes, Midstream*, and other journals.

Claire Seda Mouradian is chargée de recherche at the Centre National de la Recherche Scientifique, Paris. She is the author of *L'URSS depuis 1945* (1985) and *Sowjetarmenien nach dem Tode Stalins* (1985). She has contributed chapters to *Histoire des Armeniens* (1982), *Evolution des modeles familiaux en URSS et en Europe de l'est* (1986), and *Le politique et le religieux dans le monde contemporain* (1986). Her articles have appeared in *Cahiers du Monde Russe et Sovietique, Slovo, Esprit*, and other journals. She is a member of l'Association Internationale des Etudes Arméniennes and of the Society for Armenian Studies.

Ludvík Němec is professional instructor of church history at Chestnut Hill College and emeritus professor at Rosemont College. He is the author of *Church and State in Czechoslovakia* (1955), *Pope John Paul II* (1979), *Antonin Cyril Stojan* (1983), and other books, and editor of *Festschrift 80 Francis Dvornik* (1973). He has contributed articles to *The Catholic Encyclopedia* and *The Encyclopedia of Religion* and a chapter to *Proceedings of the Philadelphia Philosophical Society* (1968). His articles have appeared in *American Catholic Historical Review*, *Journal of Ecumenical Studies*, *East European Quarterly*, and other journals. In 1979 he was named a papal prelate by His Holiness, Pope John Paul II, with the title of reverend monsignor.

Aristeides Papadakis is professor of history at the University of Maryland and a former junior fellow at the Harvard University Center for Byzantine Studies, Dumbarton Oaks, Washington, D.C. He is the author of *Crisis in Byzantium: The Filioque Controversy in the Patriarchate of Gregory II of Cyprus, 1283–1289* (1983) and editorial consultant and contributor to the *Oxford Dictionary of Byzantium* (forthcoming). His articles have appeared in *Byzantion*, *Byzantinoslavica*, *Greek, Roman and Byzantine Studies*, and other journals.

Stevan K. Pavlowitch is professor of history at the University of Southampton, England. He is the author of *Anglo-Russian Rivalry in Serbia, 1837–39* (1961), *Yugoslavia* (1971), *Bijou d'Art* (1978), and *Unconventional Perceptions of Yugoslavia, 1940–1945* (1985). He has contributed chapters to *War and Society* (1975), *Balkan Society in the Age of Greek Independence* (1981), and *NATO and the Mediterranean* (1985). His articles have appeared in *Conflict Studies*, *Journal of Contemporary History*, *Survey*, and other journals.

C. J. Peters is a research fellow at the University of London. In 1984 he was named senior associate member of St. Antony's College, Oxford University. He has contributed an article to *Encyclopedia of the Russian Revolution* (forthcoming in 1988). His articles have appeared in *Slavonic and East European Review*, *Central Asian Survey*, and *Sbornik*.

Spas T. Raikin is associate professor of history at East Stroudsburg University. He is a graduate of the theological faculty of Sofia and current editor of *The Free Agrarian Banner*. He contributed a chapter to *Religion and Nationalism in Soviet and East European Politics* (1984). A recent article of his appeared in *Religion in Communist Lands*.

Pedro Ramet is assistant professor of international studies at the University of Washington. During the 1986–87 academic year he was a research scholar at the Kennan Institute for Advanced Russian Studies, Washington, D.C. He is the author of *Sadat and the Kremlin* (1980), *Nationalism and Federalism in Yugoslavia, 1963–1983* (1984), and *Cross and Commissar: The Politics of Religion in Eastern Europe and the USSR* (1987), and editor of *Religion and Nationalism in Soviet and East European Politics* (1984) and *Yugoslavia in the 1980s* (1985). He contributed chapters to *The Tito-Stalin Split in a Historic Perspective* (1982) and *Gorbachev and the Soviet Future* (forthcoming). His articles have appeared in *Political Science Quarterly*, *Slavic Review*, *World Politics*, and other journals.

Metropolitan John (Rinne) is metropolitan of Helsinki of the Orthodox Church of Finland, vice president of the Ecumenical Council of Finland, and a lecturer at the universities of Helsinki, Joensuu, and Abo. He was decorated with the Ecclesiastical Grand Cross of St. Lazarus of Jerusalem in 1974 and the Order of the Lion of Finland in 1978, and received an honorary doctorate from the University of Debrecen (Hungary) in 1972. He is the author of *The Kingdom of God in the Thought of William Temple* (1966) and *Skhesis enotetos kai homoiomorphias en te Ekklesia kata to pneuma ton Oikoumenikon* (1971). He has contributed chapters to *Luther et la reforme allemande dans une perspective oecumenique* (1983), *Kanon: Der Bischof und seine Eparchie VII* (1985), and *Theologia et cultura: Studia in honorem Gotthard Nygren* (1986), and other books. His articles have appeared in *Ortodoksia*, *Nakoala*, *Ortodoksinen kulttuuri*, and other journals. He is a member of the brotherhood of the Monastery of St. John the Theologian in Patmos, Greece.

Alan Scarfe is associate rector at St. Columba Episcopal Church, Camarillo, and former executive secretary and senior researcher, Keston College U.S.A. Between 1978 and 1982, he taught at Wheaton College Graduate School and at the Simon Greenleaf School of Law in Orange, California. He is the editor of *Christianity and Marxism* (1982) and *The CCDBR Documents*, Vol. 13 (1982), and contributed a chapter to *Religion and Nationalism in Soviet and East European Politics* (1984). His articles have appeared in *Journal of Church and State*, *Religion in Communist Lands*, *Fuller Seminary Journal*, and other journals.

Theofanis G. Stavrou is professor of history at the University of Minnesota where he has been instrumental in developing a graduate program in modern Greek studies and Greek-Slavic cultural relations in modern times. He teaches and publishes in both the Slavic and Greek fields. His publications include *Russian Interests in Palestine 1882–1914: A Study in Religious and Educational Enterprise* (1963); *Russian Orthodoxy under the Old Regime* (1978) with Robert L. Nichols; *Art and Culture in Nineteenth-Century Russia* (1983); *Kostis Palamas: A Portrait and an Appreciation* (1985); and *Russian Travelers to the Christian East from the Twelfth to the Twentieth Century* (1986) with Peter Weisensel. He has also contributed extensively to the *Religious and Ethical Encyclopedia* published in Greece, and he is the editor of the *Modern Greek Studies Yearbook*, which pays special attention to scholarly matters on Eastern Orthodoxy.

Philip Walters is research director at Keston College and a former research fellow (1976–79) at Cambridge University. Prior to coming to Keston, he scripted current affairs talks for the External Services of the BBC. He is coeditor (with Jane Balengarth) of *Light through the Curtain* (1985). His articles have appeared in *Religion in Communist Lands, Soviet Studies, Slavonic Review*, and other journals.